Quality
Management

KT-562-128

DISCARDED

DISCARDED

Loughborough College

LC036124

The McGraw-Hill/Irwin Series
Operations and Decision Sciences

Quality Management

Third Edition

Howard S. Gitlow
School of Business Administration
University of Miami

Alan J. Oppenheim
School of Business
Montclair State University

Rosa Oppenheim
Rutgers Business School—Newark
and New Brunswick
Rutgers The State University
of New Jersey

David M. Levine
Bernard M. Baruch College
Zicklin School of Business
The City University of New York

Mc
Graw
Hill

Boston   Burr Ridge, IL   Dubuque, IA   Madison, WI   New York   San Francisco   St. Louis
Bangkok   Bogotá   Caracas   Kuala Lumpur   Lisbon   London   Madrid   Mexico City
Milan   Montreal   New Delhi   Santiago   Seoul   Singapore   Sydney   Taipei   Toronto

The *McGraw-Hill* Companies

QUALITY MANAGEMENT
International Edition 2005

Exclusive rights by McGraw-Hill Education (Asia), for manufacture and export. This book cannot be re-exported from the country to which it is sold by McGraw-Hill. The International Edition is not available in North America.

Published by McGraw-Hill/Irwin, a business unit of The McGraw-Hill Companies, Inc., 1221 Avenue of the Americas, New York, NY 10020. Copyright © 2005, 1995, 1989 by The McGraw-Hill Companies, Inc. All rights reserved. No part of this publication may be reproduced or distributed in any form or by any means, or stored in a database or retrieval system, without the prior written consent of The McGraw-Hill Companies, Inc., including, but not limited to, in any network or other electronic storage or transmission, or broadcast for distance learning.
Some ancillaries, including electronic and print components, may not be available to customers outside the United States.

10 09 08 07 06 05 04 03 02 01
20 09 08 07 06 05 04
CTF SLP

Library of Congress Control Number: 2004049957

When ordering this title, use ISBN 007-112338-5

Printed in Singapore

www.mhhe.com

Loughborough
College

Dedicated to our families:

Shelly Gitlow
Ali Gitlow
Abraham Gitlow
Adam Oppenheim and Amy Sherman
David Oppenheim and Emily Boling
Sylvia Oppenheim
Esther Blitzer
Marilyn Levine
Sharyn Levine Rosenberg and Daniel Rosenberg

and to the memory of:

Beatrice Gitlow
Norman Oppenheim
Aaron Blitzer
Lee Levine
Reuben Levine

Preface

Continuous quality improvement is essential for any organization's survival in the twenty-first century. Leading corporations such as Motorola, General Electric, Allied Signal, Dupont, American Express, J.P. Morgan, and GE Capital have demonstrated that improved quality raises profits, reduces costs, and improves competitive position. Government agencies and other not-for-profit organizations have begun to reap the benefits of continuous improvement. The seemingly geometric growth in interest in quality bodes well for the future. Meaningful progress requires knowledge in many areas. We attempt here to present a unique and workable approach to the tools and methods necessary for real quality improvement.

Structure of the Book

This book is constructed in four parts. Part 1 describes the foundations of quality management. Part 2 presents the tools and methods for process improvement studies. Part 3 explains the administrative systems required for quality management. Finally, Part 4 showcases Six Sigma management, currently the most popular model for quality management.

Part 1: Foundations of Quality Management

Part 1 introduces the fundamental concepts that are necessary to understand and use quality management in an organization: a definition of quality and its relationship to costs and productivity, an appreciation of the theory underlying quality management, the fundamentals of statistical studies used in organizations employing quality management principles and practices, and a working knowledge of defining and documenting a process.

Part 2: Tools and Methods for Analytic Studies

Part 2 presents and discusses the tools and methods needed to conduct process improvement studies. These tools include graphical methods, descriptive statistics, control charts, brainstorming, cause-and-effect diagrams, check sheets, Pareto analysis, and design of experiments. These techniques form a powerful arsenal that can be used to pursue continuous, never-ending improvement.

Part 3: Administrative Systems for Quality Management

Top management, including the board of directors, must initiate and lead quality management efforts. One of the first tasks for top management is to learn about the various theories, models, and techniques in the field, and then formulate a quality management model suited to the nuances of the organization. Quality management models will differ from organization to organization. This part of the book presents one possible model, to stimulate the thinking of top managers. It represents an "ideal" for promoting quality management, which must be continuously pursued, and improved, by the leadership of an organization. The model presents a possible sequencing of activities that can be used to transform an organization.

Part 4: Current Thinking about Statistical Practice

Part 4 introduces Six Sigma management, developed at Motorola Corporation in the 1980s and popularized in large part by General Electric Corporation in the 1990s. Six Sigma management is the relentless and rigorous pursuit of the reduction of variation in all critical processes to achieve continuous and breakthrough improvements that impact the bottom line of the organization and increase customer satisfaction. Stated another way, it is an organizational initiative designed to create manufacturing, service and administrative processes that produce approximately 3.4 defects per million opportunities. The DMAIC (Define-Measure-Analyze-Improve-Control) model to improve processes is presented as a template for achieving the goals of Six Sigma management.

Educational Philosophy

This book endeavors to create a bridge between the theory and practice of quality management. All theories and practices are illustrated with detailed examples and/or actual case studies. The book ends by presenting the current best practices of quality management within the context of Six Sigma management. Consequently, the educational philosophy of this book is to present and illustrate best quality management practices in many different settings so that the reader can extend this to his or her own context.

Major New Additions in the Third Edition

The third edition of *Quality Management* has been dramatically modified and expanded, containing approximately twice as much material as the second edition.

- Part 1 now includes, in Chapter 1, discussions of Deming's well-known red bead experiment and Nelson's well-known funnel experiment. Both experiments highlight the destructive effects of treating common variation as special variation.
- Part 2 now includes the "seven new tools for management" in Chapter 10 and a presentation of factorial designs and fractional factorial designs in Chapter 12.
- Part 3 is entirely new and explains how to administer a quality management process in an organization "from soup to nuts." Chapter 14 explains how to initiate a quality management effort. Chapter 15 discusses the managerial issues in getting started. Chapter 16 discusses daily management. Chapter 17 discusses cross-functional management. Chapter 18 discusses policy management. Chapter 19 discusses the resources necessary for a quality management process.
- Part 4 is also entirely new. Chapter 20 presents Six Sigma management and the DMAIC model, along with a detailed case study.
- The third edition includes Minitab output for statistical analyses throughout the text. In addition, end-of-chapter Minitab appendices provide detailed yet easy-to-follow instructions (including screenshots of dialog boxes) for using Minitab 14, the latest version of Minitab. For a reasonable additional cost the student version of Minitab can be packaged with this text. To order this package, use ISBN 0-07-299692-7.

Continuing Features

- Chapter 1 of the second edition, "Fundamentals of Quality," is now covered in Chapters 1 and 2, "Fundamentals of Quality" and "W. Edwards Deming's Theory of Management."
- Chapter 2 of the second edition, "Fundamentals of Statistical Studies," is now covered in Chapter 3 under the same title.
- Chapter 3 of the second edition, "Defining and Documenting a Process," is now covered in Chapter 4 under the same title.
- Chapter 4 of the second edition, "Basic Probability and Statistics," is now covered in Chapter 5 under the same title.
- Chapter 5 of the second edition, "Stabilizing and Improving a Process with Control Charts," is now covered in Chapter 6 under the same title.
- Chapter 6 of the second edition, "Attribute Control Charts," is now covered in Chapter 7 under the same title.
- Chapter 7 of the second edition, "Variables Control Charts," is now covered in Chapter 8 under the same title.
- Chapter 8 of the second edition, "Out-of-Control Patterns," is now covered in Chapter 9 under the same title.
- Chapter 9 of the second edition, "Diagnosing a Process," is now covered in Chapter 10 under the same title.
- Chapter 10 of the second edition, "Specifications," is now covered in Chapter 11, "Process Capability and Improvement Studies."
- Chapter 11 of the second edition, "Process Capability and Improvement Studies," is now covered in Chapter 11 under the same title.
- Chapter 13 of the second edition, "Inspection Policy," is now covered in Chapter 13 under the same title.
- Chapter 14 of the second edition, "Deming's 14 Points and the Reduction of Variation," is now covered in Chapters 1 and 2, "Fundamentals of Quality" and "W. Edwards Deming's Theory of Management."

Structure for Alternative Courses

- Course 1: Tools and Methods of Quality Management
  section 1: Foundations of Quality Management (Chapters 1–4)
  section 2: Tools and Methods for Analytic Studies (Chapters 5–13)
  section 3: Current Thinking about Statistical Practice: Six Sigma management, focusing on quantitative tools and methods (Chapter 20)
  Prerequisite: None

- Course 2: Administrative Systems for Quality Management
  section 1: Foundations of Quality Management (Chapters 1–4)
  section 2: Administrative Systems for Quality Management (Chapters 14–19)
  Prerequisite: Course 1

Supplemental Packages

PowerPoint slides

Instructor's manual

CD-ROM containing datasets for Minitab

Acknowledgments and Notes of Thanks

We acknowledge and thank the late W. Edwards Deming for his philosophy and guidance in our personal studies of quality improvement and statistics. We thank Edward Popovich (Renaissance Consulting), who helped by reviewing this third edition. Additionally, we thank the individuals who reviewed the second edition: Bruce Christensen (Weber State University, Ogden, Utah), Mark Hanna (Miami University, Oxford, Ohio), Carol Karnes (Clemson University, Clemson, South Carolina), J. Keith Ord (Pennsylvania State University, University Park), and Herbert F. Spirer (University of Connecticut, Stamford). Again, we thank those who helped by reviewing the first edition: Robert F. Hart (University of Wisconsin, Oshkosh), Chandra Das (University of Northern Iowa, Cedar Falls), Donald Holmes (Stochos Incorporated), Peter John (University of Texas, Austin), Sudhakar Deshmukh (Kellogg Graduate School, Northwestern University, Evanston, Illinois), Edwin Saniga (University of Delaware, Newark), Theresa Sandifer (Kimberly-Clark Corporation), and Jeffrey Galbraith (Greenfield Community College, Greenfield, Massachusetts). Finally, we thank Richard Hercher Jr., Executive Editor at McGraw-Hill, Inc., our long-time and patient editor, cheerleader, and friend; Lee Stone, Greta Kleinert, Elizabeth Mavetz, Pat Frederickson, Michael R. McCormick, Artemio Ortiz Jr., Jeremy Cheshareck, Matthew Perry, and Brian Nacik of The McGraw-Hill Companies, Inc., and especially our Project Manager, Deborah J. Pfeiffer, for all their help in producing this book. In the final analysis, of course, we, the authors, accept total responsibility for its content.

Contact Information

hgitlow@miami.edu

oppenheima@mail.montclair.edu

roppenhe@andromeda.rutgers.edu

David_Levine@BARUCH.CUNY.EDU

Howard S. Gitlow

Alan J. Oppenheim

Rosa Oppenheim

David M. Levine

Brief Contents

Contents

Chapter 18
The Fork Model for Quality
Management: Prong 3, or Policy
Management   627

Foundations of Quality Management

Part 1 introduces the fundamental concepts that are necessary to understand and use quality management in an organization. These concepts include a definition of quality and its relationship to costs and productivity, an appreciation of the theory behind quality management, the fundamentals of statistical studies that are used in organizations utilizing quality management principles and practices, and a working knowledge of defining and documenting a process.

Chapter 1 introduces the concept of quality and debunks the notion that high quality means high cost. Rather, it shows that high quality, given a product, service, or process, leads to low cost. Additionally, it presents the relationship between quality and productivity and discusses the benefits of quality management.

Chapter 2 presents the style of management developed by W. Edwards Deming, called the System of Profound Knowledge. It is a practical philosophy of professional management that includes a road map for promoting quality management in an organization, the 14 points for management.

Chapter 3 discusses the basics of statistical studies in order to understand the behavior or products, services, and processes. There are two types of statistical studies, enumerative studies and analytic studies. Enumerative studies are investigations of populations fixed in space and time whose purpose is to estimate the characteristics of the population. Analytic studies are investigations of processes that have a past and present and will have a future, whose purpose is to predict the future output of the process.

Chapter 4 explains how to define and document a process. A process transforms inputs into outputs to accomplish an aim or mission. An analytic study can be performed only on a process that has been defined and documented. The chapter discusses the use of flowcharts and feedback loops for process improvement activities, and how to operationally define each critical step and indicator to increase communication among the stakeholders of the organization.

Chapter 1

Fundamentals of Quality

Sections

Chapter Objectives

- To define a process
- To discuss variation and its causes in processes
- To discuss the difference between common and special causes of variation
- To consider the consequences of treating common causes of variation as special causes of variation (the funnel experiment and the red bead experiment)
- To discuss the quality environment
- To present the goalpost view of quality and the continuous improvement view of quality
- To define and discuss the three types of quality: quality of design or redesign, quality of conformance, and quality of performance
- To discuss the relationship between quality and cost and between quality and productivity
- To present the benefits of improving quality

Introduction

Quality is a term we hear frequently: that is a quality automobile, she is a quality person, this is a quality stock. Most people equate high quality with a big price tag, and low quality with a small price tag. The purpose of this chapter is to debunk this outdated notion of quality and to explain what it really means.

Process Basics

Definition of a Process

A **process** is a collection of interacting components that transform inputs into outputs toward a common aim, called a **mission statement.** It is the job of management to optimize the entire process toward its aim. This may require the suboptimization of selected components of the process; for example, a particular department in an organization may have to give up resources to another department in the short run to maximize profit for the overall organization.

The **transformation,** as shown in Figure 1.1, involves the addition or creation of value in one of three aspects: time, place, or form. An output has "time value" if it is available when needed by a user. For example, you have food when you are hungry, or material inputs are ready on schedule. An output has "place value" if it is available where needed by a user. For example, gas is in your tank (not in an oil field), or wood chips are in a paper mill. An output has "form value" if it is available in the form needed by a user. For example, bread is sliced so it can fit in a toaster, or paper has three holes so it can be placed in a binder.

Processes exist in all facets of organizations, and an understanding of them is crucial. Many people mistakenly think only of production processes. However, administration, sales, service, human resources, training, maintenance, paper flows, interdepartmental communication, and vendor relations are all processes. Importantly, relationships between people are processes. All processes can be studied, documented, defined, improved, and innovated.

An example of a familiar process is the hiring process. Figure 1.2 shows the inputs, process, and outputs of hiring an employee. The inputs (which include the candidate's resume, the information gathered from the interview with the candidate, and other data from references, former employers, and schools attended) are transformed into the output (which is an employee to fill a vacant position). The process involved in this transformation of inputs into outputs includes synthesizing and evaluating the information, making a decision, and hiring the candidate. An important aspect of this process is the **feedback loop** that enables the new employee's supervisor to report back to the

FIGURE 1.1
Basic Process

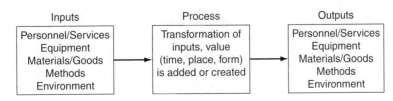

Inputs	Process	Outputs
Personnel/Services Equipment Materials/Goods Methods Environment	Transformation of inputs, value (time, place, form) is added or created	Personnel/Services Equipment Materials/Goods Methods Environment

FIGURE 1.2
Hiring Process

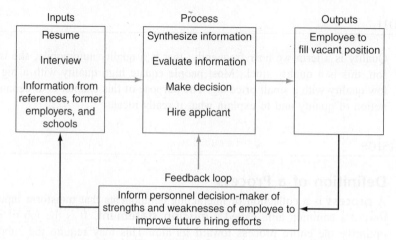

personnel decision-maker on the employee's appropriateness for a given job. The personnel decision-maker (supplier) and supervisor (customer) can use this information to work together to improve the hiring process.

Clerical functions are also processes. Figure 1.3 depicts the process of sending a memo in an organization. The manager inputs the information for the memo and her instructions regarding its distribution. Then the secretary transforms the input, by typing it and distributing it, into the output (communication to the employees). The feedback loop is important because the manager and the employees can work together to improve the communication process.

An example of a generic production process is shown in Figure 1.4. The inputs (component parts, machines, and operators) are transformed in the process of making the final product and shipping it to the customer. The output is the customer receiving the product. Again, the feedback loop (which in this case is the customer's reporting back to the

FIGURE 1.3
**Memo-Sending
Process**

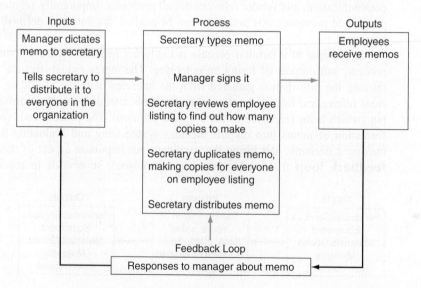

FIGURE 1.4
Production
Process

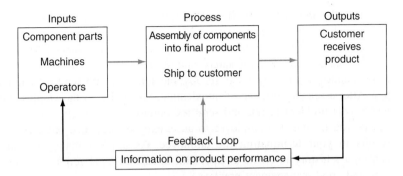

production process manager and/or the supplier on the product's performance) is vital. Communicating this way promotes cooperation on process improvement and innovation.

An organization is a multiplicity of micro subprocesses, all synergistically building to the macro process of that firm. All processes have customers and suppliers; these customers and suppliers can be internal or external to the organization. A customer can be an end user or the next operation downstream. The customer does not even have to be a human; it can be a machine. A vendor can be another firm supplying subassemblies or services, or the prior operation upstream.

Variation in a Process

Common and Special Causes of Variation

The outputs from all processes and their component parts vary over time. Consider a process such as getting ready for work or class in the morning. Some days you are busier than usual, while on other days you have less to do than usual. Your process varies from day to day to some degree. This is **common variation.** However, if a construction project begins on the highway you take to work or school, you might drastically alter your morning routine. This would be **special variation** because it would have been caused by a change external to your "driving to work or school" process. If the traffic patterns had remained as they were, your process would have continued on its former path of common variation.

Common causes of variation are due to the process itself. **Process capability** is determined by inherent common causes of variation, such as poor hiring, training, or supervisory practices; inadequate lighting; stress; management style, policies, and procedures; or design of products or services. Employees cannot control a common cause of variation and should not be held accountable for, or penalized for, its outcomes. Managers must realize that unless a change is made in the process (which only they can make) the process's capability will remain the same. **Special causes of variation** are due to events external to the usual functioning of the system. New raw materials, a broken die, or a new operator can be examples of special causes of variation.

Since unit-to-unit variation decreases the customer's ability to rely on the dependability and uniformity of outputs, managers must understand how to reduce and control variation. Employees should become involved in creating and utilizing statistical methods so that common and special causes of variation can be differentiated, special variation can be resolved, and common variation can be removed by management action, resulting in improvement and innovation of outputs.

The following fictionalized case history demonstrates the need for management to understand the difference between common and special causes of variation in order to take appropriate action. In this case history, an employee comes to work intoxicated. His behavior causes productivity, safety, and morale problems. You, as the supervisor, speak to the employee privately, try to resolve the situation, and send the employee home with pay. After a second instance of intoxication, you speak to the employee privately, try to resolve the problem again, and send the employee home without pay. A third instance causes you to refer the employee to an employee assistance program. A fourth offense results in your terminating the employee. As a good manager, you document the employee's history to create a paper trail in case of legal action. All the above is necessary and good management practice.

It is interesting to note that the **paradigm** behind the above managerial actions is that the employee is the problem. In other words, the employee's behavior is viewed as the special cause of variation from the desired sober state. However, this is true only if there is a statistically significant difference between the employee in question and all other employees. If the employee's behavior is in fact part of a system that allows such behavior to exist, then the problem is not a special cause, but rather a common cause and requires a different solution. In the latter case, the employee must be dealt with as before, but additionally, organizational policies and procedures must be changed to prevent future incidents of intoxication. This new view requires a **paradigm shift.** In the new paradigm, if existing organizational policies and procedures allow employees with drinking problems to be present in the workplace, an intoxicated employee must be dealt with according to the original solution, and policies and procedures must be improved to prevent future incidents of such behavior on the job.

More about the Feedback Loop

An important aspect of any process is a **feedback loop.** A feedback loop relates information about outputs from any stage or stages back to another stage or stages so that an analysis of the process can be made. Figure 1.5 depicts the feedback loop in relation to a basic process. The tools and methods discussed in this book provide vehicles for relating information about outputs to other stage(s) in the process. Decision-making about processes is aided by the transmission of this information. A major purpose of quality management is to provide the information (flowing through a feedback loop) needed to take action with respect to a process.

There are three feedback loop situations: no feedback loop, special-cause-only feedback loop, and special and common cause feedback loop. A process that does not have a feedback loop is probably doomed to deterioration and decay because of the inability of its stakeholders to rejuvenate and improve it on the basis of data from its outputs. An example of a process without a feedback loop is a relationship between two people (manager and subordinate, husband and wife, or buyer and seller) that contains no vehicle (feedback loop) to discuss issues and problems with the intention of establishing a better relationship in the future. A process in which all feedback information is treated as a special cause will exhibit enormous variation in its output. This will be

FIGURE 1.5

Feedback Loop

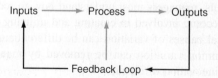

discussed in detail in the next section, which uses a teaching tool called the **funnel experiment.** An example of a process with a special-cause-only feedback loop can again be seen in a relationship between two people, but in this case, the relationship deteriorates through a cycle of successive overreactions to problems that are perceived as special by both members of the relationship. In fact, the problems are probably repetitive in nature, as a result of the structure of the relationship itself and common causes of variation. Finally, a process in which feedback information is separated into common and special causes, special causes are resolved, and common causes are removed will exhibit continuous improvement of its output. For example, relationship problems can be classified as either special or common; statistical methods can be used to resolve special causes and to remove common causes, thereby improving the relationship in the future.

Consider a real-life example. John is 30 years old, healthy, financially stable, intelligent, humorous, good looking, personable, but unhappy because he wants to be married with children. He thinks about his relationships with women with the intention of analyzing the reasons they ended. He determines that over a period of 10 years, the average length of his relationships with women was about six months, so that he had approximately 20 relationships.

John thinks about why each relationship ended. Initially, he thought each ended for its own reason(s) (special cause feedback). He writes down the reason(s) for the breakup for as many of the relationships as he can remember (about 16).

However, after thinking about himself from the perspective of common and special causes, he realizes his relationships with women were not independent events (special causes); rather, they were a repetitive process, and the reasons for the breakups could be classified into common cause categories. He is surprised to see that the 16 reasons collapse down to four basic reasons: jealousy, incompatibility, boredom, and money issues, with one reason, boredom, accounting for 75 percent of all breakups. Armed with this insight, he enters therapy and works on resolving the biggest common cause category for his unsuccessful relationships. He is now happily married with two lovely children.

The Funnel Experiment

W. Edwards Deming has stated, "If anyone adjusts a stable process (one exhibiting only common causes of variation) to try to compensate for a result that is undesirable, or for a result that is extra good, the output that follows will be worse than if he had left the process alone." [See Reference 3, p. 327.] This is called overcontrol of the process, or **tampering.** If management tampers with a process without profound knowledge of how to improve the process through statistical thinking, they will increase the process's variation and reduce their ability to manage that process.

As Deming has pointed out, "A common example is to take action on the basis of a defective item, or a complaint of a customer. The result of his efforts to improve future output (only doing his best) will be to double the variance of the output, or even cause the system to explode. What is required for improvement is a fundamental change in the system, not tampering." [See Reference 3, p. 327.]

Loss to an organization results from overcontrol of its processes, which include safety, training, hiring, supervision, union-management relations, policy formation, production,

FIGURE 1.6
Funnel
Experiment
Equipment

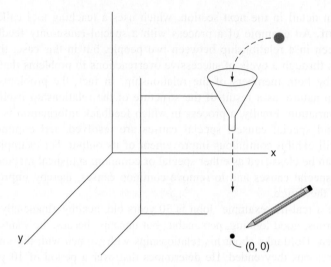

maintenance, shipping, purchasing, administration, and customer relations. This loss can be demonstrated by an experiment utilizing a funnel. [See Reference 4, pp. 194–209.] We will describe the apparatus and procedure for conducting the experiment and then demonstrate its relationship to management's pursuit of continual reduction of variation.

To conduct the experiment, shown in Figure 1.6, we need (1) a funnel, (2) a marble that will fall through the funnel, (3) a flat surface (e.g., a table top), (4) a pencil, and (5) a holder for the funnel.

The experiment involves five steps. (1) Designate a point on the flat surface as a target and consider this target to be the point of origin in a two-dimensional space, where x and y represent the axes of the surface; hence, at the target (x,y) = (0,0). (2) Drop a marble through the funnel. (3) Mark the spot where the marble comes to rest on the surface with a pencil. (4) Drop the marble through the funnel again and mark the spot where the marble comes to rest on the surface. (5) Repeat step 4 through 50 drops.

A rule for adjusting the funnel's position in relation to the target is needed to perform the fourth step. There are four possible rules, and the second rule can be handled in two different ways.

Rule 1

Set the funnel over the target at (0,0) and leave the funnel fixed through all 50 drops. This rule will produce a stable pattern of points on the surface; this pattern will approximate a circle, as shown in Figure 1.7. [See Reference 1, p. 1.] Further, as we will see, the variance of the diameters of all circles produced by repeated experimentation using Rule 1 will be smaller than the variance resulting from any other rule used in the fourth step of the experiment.

Management's use of the first rule demonstrates an understanding of the distinction between special and common variation and between the different types of managerial action required for each type of variation. Rule 1 implies that the process is being managed by people who know how to reduce variation.

FIGURE 1.7
Rule 1

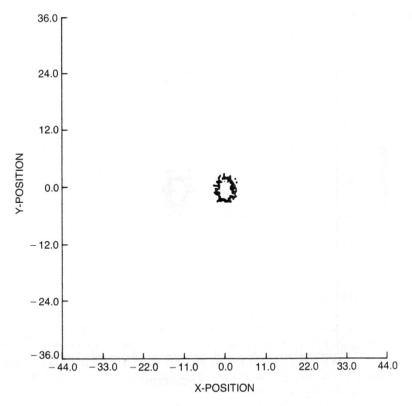

Rule 2

The funnel is set over the target at (0,0) prior to the initial drop. Let (x_k, y_k) represent the point where the kth marble dropped through the funnel comes to rest on the surface. Rule 2 states that the funnel should be moved the distance $(-x_k, -y_k)$ from its last resting point. In essence, this is an adjustment rule with a memory of the last resting point. This rule will produce a stable pattern of resting points on the surface, which will approximate a circle. However, the variance of the diameters of all circles produced by repeated experimentation using Rule 2 will have double the variance of the circular pattern produced using Rule 1, as Figure 1.8 shows. [See Reference 1, p. 1.]

In terms of its application to management actions, Rule 2 implies that the process is being tampered with by people with inadequate knowledge of how to manage the process to reduce its variation. It implies acting on common variation as if it were special variation. Rule 2 is commonly used as a method of "attempting" to make things better in a process. Here are three examples.

• *Automatic process control.* The automatic adjustment of a process to hold output within specified tolerance limits is an example of Rule 2, assuming adjustments to the process are made from the last process measurement. This type of process adjustment procedure is frequently called rule-based process control (RPC). RPC is widely used in industry.

FIGURE 1.8
Rule 2

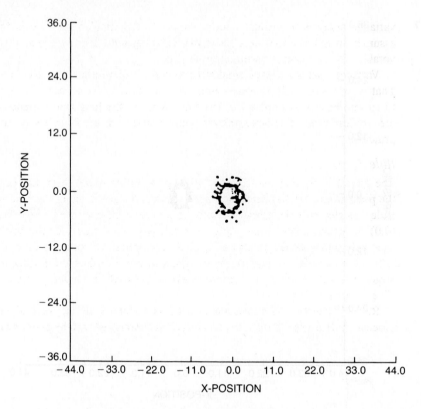

• *Operator adjustment.* Operator adjustment to compensate for a unit of output's not being on target, or nominal, is an example of Rule 2, assuming adjustments to the process are made from the last process measurement. [See Reference 3, pp. 359–360.] This type of overcontrol frequently leads to a sawtooth-type pattern on an $\bar{x}$ chart, as we will see in Chapter 9.

• *Stock market.* The stock market's reaction to good or bad news is often an overreaction to a phenomenon, which follows Rule 2.

Rule 2a

A variant on Rule 2 is often employed in industry. Rule 2a states if (x_k, y_k) is within a circle centered at (0,0) with diameter d_{spec}, do not adjust the funnel. But if (x_k, y_k) is outside the circle centered at (0,0) with diameter d_{spec}, use the adjustment rule specified in Rule 2. Rule 2a creates a "dead band" in which no process adjustment takes place. Research results obtained by Gitlow, Kang, and Kellogg [see Reference 7, pp. 239–310] demonstrate that Rule 2a, with any size dead band, yields the same result of doubling the variation of the process as does Rule 2 when compared with Rule 1.

An example of Rule 2a can be seen in **variance analysis** in cost accounting. One method of monitoring performance in an organization is the use of efficiency and spending variances for the areas of direct labor, direct materials, and overhead. This is called "variance analysis." Traditionally, manufacturers in the United States have relied on variance analysis to evaluate performance. If a particular variance is favorable, it is assumed to indicate that excellent work is being done. If a particular variance is unfavorable, the converse is assumed to be true.

Variance analysis causes employees to react inappropriately to accounting variances. That is, variance analysis forces employees to react to variances as if they are due only to special causes as opposed to system causes. In the long run, variance analysis doubles the variation of a stable process being managed in accordance with cost accounting principles.

Rule 3

The funnel is set over the target at (0,0) prior to the initial drop. Let (x_k, y_k) represent the point where the kth marble dropped through the funnel comes to rest on the surface. Rule 3 states that the funnel should be moved a distance $(-x_k, -y_k)$ from the target (0,0). In essence, this is an adjustment rule with no memory of the last resting point. This rule will produce an unstable, explosive pattern of resting points on the surface; as k increases without bound, the pattern will move farther and farther away from the target in some symmetrical pattern, such as the bow-tie-shaped pattern in Figure 1.9. [See Reference 1, p. 1.]

Rule 3, like Rule 2, is commonly used as a method of "attempting" to improve the process. Rule 3 implies that the process is being tampered with by people with inadequate

FIGURE 1.9
Rule 3

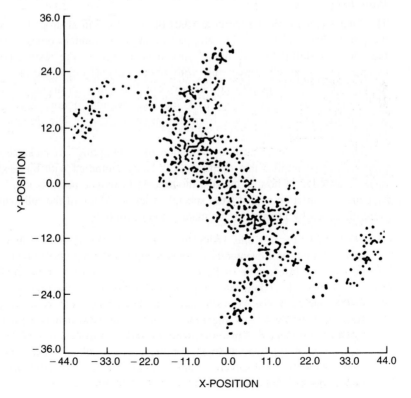

knowledge of how to manage the process to reduce its variation. It implies acting on common variation as if it were special variation. Here are five examples of Rule 3.

• *Automatic process control.* The automatic adjustment of a process to hold output within specified tolerance limits is an example of Rule 3, assuming adjustments to the process are made from the target and not the last process measurement.

• *Operator adjustment.* Operator adjustment to compensate for a unit of output's not being on target, or nominal, is an example of Rule 3, assuming adjustments to the process are made from the target and not the last process measurement.

• *Setting the current period's goal on the basis of last period's overage or underage.* A sales quota policy that states that if you're short of this month's goal by $25,000, you must increase next month's goal by $25,000 is an example of Rule 3.

• *Setting the inspection policy for the kth batch on the basis of the k − 1st batch's record.* An inspection policy that recommends tightened or loosened inspection for a batch of material based on the history of the prior batch is an example of Rule 3. A better policy would be to use the kp rule, as discussed in Chapter 13, in conjunction with a control chart to estimate process capability.

• *Making up the previous period's shortage during the current period.* A production policy that requires production personnel to make up any shortages from last month's production run in this month's production run is an example of Rule 3.

Rule 4

The funnel is set over the target at $(0,0)$ prior to the initial drop. Let (x_k, y_k) represent the point where the kth marble dropped through the funnel comes to rest on the surface. Rule 4 states that the funnel should be moved to the resting point, (x_k, y_k). In essence, this is an adjustment rule with no memory of either the last resting point or the position of the target at $(0,0)$. This rule will produce an unstable, explosive pattern of resting points on the surface as k increases without bound, and it will eventually move farther and farther away from the target at $(0,0)$ in one direction, as shown in Figure 1.10. [See Reference 1, p. 1.]

Rule 4 is commonly used as a method of "attempting" to make things better in a process. Rule 4 implies that the process is being tampered with by people with inadequate knowledge of how to manage the process to reduce its variation. It implies acting on common variation as if it were special variation. Many of the following 10 examples were discussed by Deming in his management seminars.

1. *Make it like the last one.* Using the last unit of output as the standard for the next unit of output will eventually produce material bearing no resemblance to the original piece—an example of Rule 4. A possible solution to this problem is to use a master piece as a point of comparison. A common complaint is that "we sold the master (model) piece" so a standard is no longer available for comparison purposes. Another example of this phenomenon is "a man who matches color from batch to batch for acceptance of material, without reference to the original swatch." [See Reference 3, p. 329.] Two possible solutions to this problem are to use a standard color chip or to use the original color sample, assuming the color chip or the original color sample doesn't fade over time.

FIGURE 1.10
Rule 4

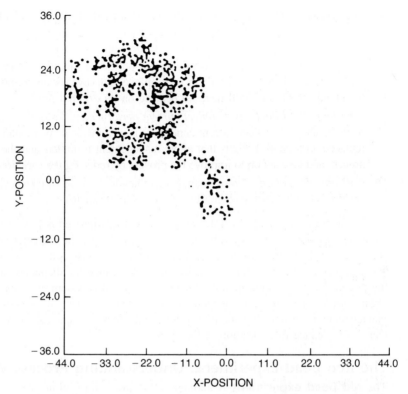

2. *On-the-job training.* Deming cites [see Reference 3, p. 329] "A frightening example of rule 4 . . . where people on a job train a new worker. This worker is then ready in a few days to help to train a new worker. The methods taught deteriorate without limit. Who would know?" Possible solutions to this problem are to formalize training with a video presentation or to utilize a master in the subject matter to do the training, to get a consistent and desired message to the trainees.

3. *Budgeting.* Setting the next period's budget as a percentage of the last period's budget is an example of Rule 4.

4. *Policy setting.* If they lack a mission statement to guide them and a theory of management, then executives meeting to establish policy for an organization will set policies that become increasingly less consistent and more confusing, so that eventually their policies will damage the organization.

5. *The telephone game.* The telephone game small children play, where the first child whispers something to the second, the second whispers the same thing to the third child, and so on, until the last child announces what he has just heard, is an example of Rule 4. The message gets continually more confusing, and after a time the current message bears no resemblance to the original message.

6. *The grapevine.* People who take action in their personal and professional lives based on information from the "grapevine" or "rumor mill" are using Rule 4 as a basis for action. Their next action is a function of only the most recent past action.

7. *Engineering changes.* Engineering changes to a product or process based on the latest version of a design without regard to the original design are made in accordance with Rule 4. Eventually, the current design will bear no resemblance to the original design.

8. *Policy surveys.* An executive who changes policy on the basis of results of the latest employee survey, in a stream of employee surveys, is operating under Rule 4. Eventually the policy will have no bearing on its original intended purpose.

9. *Adjusting work standards to reflect current performance.* An organization that adjusts work standards to reflect current conditions is using Rule 4. Work standards should be replaced with control charts that allow management to understand the capability of a process and take action to improve the process by reducing the variation in the process.

10. *Collective bargaining.* Union-management negotiations in which successive contracts are a reaction to current conditions is an example of Rule 4.

The funnel experiment illustrates how a system is improved not by overcontrol but by reducing variation. In the experiment, this means reducing the diameter of the circle created under Rule 1 either by moving the funnel closer to the surface or by straightening and lengthening the tube portion of the funnel to reduce the dispersion among the resting points. Note that both methods for improvement are system changes. In terms of an organization, the corresponding reduction of variation also involves system changes. As management is responsible for the system, only management can make the necessary changes to reduce this variation in the system.

The Red Bead Experiment: Understanding Process Variability

The **red bead experiment** is another well-known illustration of the negative effects of treating common variation as special variation. It is discussed in this section to further enhance your understanding of common causes and special causes of variation.

The experiment involves using a paddle to select beads from a box that contains 4,000 beads, as shown in Figure 1.11. The box contains 3,200 white beads and 800 red beads. This fact is unknown to the participants in the experiment. One possible variant of the red bead experiment is discussed below.

The Experiment

In the experiment, a foreman in the Quality Bead Company hires, trains, and supervises: (1) four "willing workers" to produce white beads, (2) two inspectors of the willing workers' output, (3) one chief inspector to inspect the findings of the inspectors, and (4) one recorder of the chief inspector's findings. A willing worker's job consists of using a paddle that has five rows of ten bead-size holes to select 50 beads from the box of beads.

Once the employees of the Quality Bead Company have been hired, the foreman trains them in their appropriate job responsibilities and procedures. The job of the workers is to produce white beads, since red beads are unacceptable to customers. Strict procedures are to be followed. Work standards call for the production of 50 beads by each worker (a strict quota system): no more and no less than 50. Management has established a standard that no more than two red beads (4 percent) per worker are permitted on any given day. The paddle is dipped into the box of beads so that when it is removed, each of the 50 holes contains a bead. Once this is done, the paddle is carried to each of the two inspectors, who independently record the count of red beads. The chief inspector

FIGURE 1.11
Bead Box with
Paddle

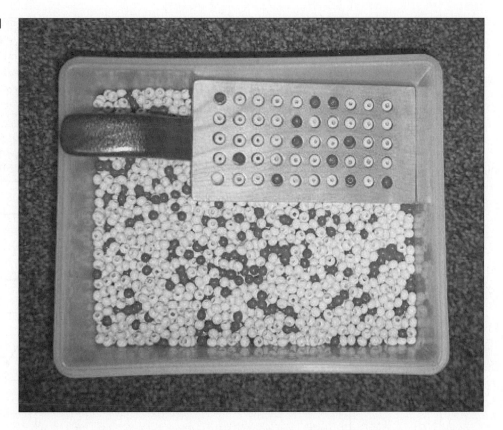

compares their counts and announces the results to the recorder who writes down the number and percentage of red beads next to the name of the worker.

Once all the people know their jobs, "production" can begin. Suppose that on the first "day," the number of red beads "produced" by the four workers (call them Alyson, David, Peter, and Sharyn) was 9, 12, 13, and 7, respectively. How should management react to the day's production when the standard says that no more than two red beads per worker should be produced? Should all the workers be reprimanded, or should only David and Peter be given a stern warning that they will be fired if they don't improve?

Suppose that production continues for an additional 2 days; Table 1.1 summarizes the results for all three days.

From Table 1.1, we can observe several phenomena. On each day, some of the workers were above the average and some below the average. On day 1, Sharyn did best, but on day 2, Peter (who had the worst record on day 1) was best, and on day 3, Alyson was best.

How then can we explain all this variation, especially given all the training provided to employees by the foreman? An answer can be provided by using a tool called a **control chart,** which will be introduced in Chapter 6. A control chart is an effective tool for distinguishing special causes of variation from common cause of variation. Without dwelling on the details of the construction of a control chart, we can nevertheless

TABLE 1.1
Red Bead
Experiment
Results for 4
Workers over
3 Days

Name	Day 1	Day 2	Day 3	All 3 Days
Alyson	9 (18%)	11 (22%)	6 (12%)	26 (17.33%)
David	12 (24%)	12 (24%)	8 (16%)	32 (21.33%)
Peter	13 (26%)	6 (12%)	12 (24%)	31 (20.67%)
Sharyn	7 (14%)	9 (18%)	8 (16%)	24 (16.00%)
All 4 workers	41	38	34	113
Average ($\bar{X}$)	10.25	9.5	8.5	9.42
Proportion	20.5%	19%	17%	18.83%

FIGURE 1.12
Control Chart
Obtained from
Minitab of Red
Beads by
Worker by Day

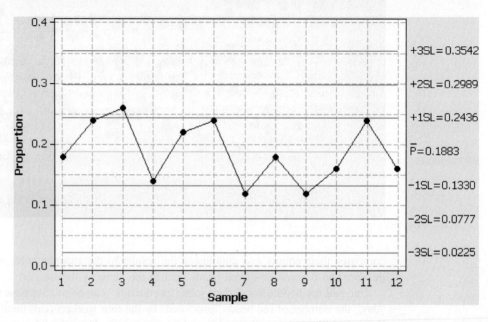

see from Figure 1.12 that the worker-to-worker variation in the proportion of red beads over the 3 days forms a stable and predictable system of variation. In other words, there are no differences between the willing workers over the 3 days other than random noise (common causes of variation) in the system used to produce white beads. All the proportions of red beads randomly bounce around an average proportion of red beads of 0.1883, and lie between the statistical signal limits of 0.3542 and 0.02246. This interesting conclusion will become clearer as you better understand control charts, and hence common and special causes of variation. Granted, the system of production of white beads in the Quality Bead Company is very noisy. If the management is not satisfied with the results, then they must improve the system, not blame the willing workers. One way management could improve the system of production in the Quality Bead Company is to use a different bead supplier, one that delivers beads with a lower proportion of red beads in its shipments.

In conclusion, there are five lessons to be learned from the red bead experiment, as shown in Exhibit 1.1:

EXHIBIT **1.1** *Lessons of the Red Bead Experiment*	1. Common variation is an inherent part of any process.
	2. Managers are responsible for the common variation in a system; they set the policies and procedures.
	3. Workers are not responsible for the problems of the system, that is, common causes of variation. The system primarily determines the performance of workers.
	4. Only management can change the system.
	5. Some workers will always be above the average, and some workers will always be below the average.

Definition of Quality

Goalpost View of Quality

Quality is an emerging concept. In the past, quality meant "conformance to valid customer requirements"—that is, as long as an output fell within acceptable limits, called **specification limits,** around a desired value, called the **nominal value** (denoted by m) or **target value,** it was deemed conforming, good, or acceptable. We refer to this as the goalpost definition of quality. The nominal value and specification limits are based on the perceived needs and wants of customers.

Figure 1.13 shows the goalpost view of losses arising from deviations from the nominal value. That is, losses are zero until the **lower specification limit (LSL)** or

FIGURE 1.13 **Goalpost View of Losses Arising from Deviations from the Nominal Value**

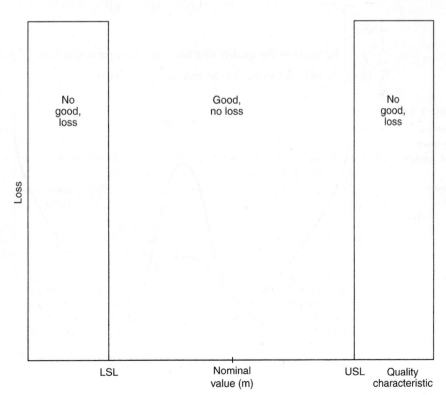

upper specification limit (USL) is reached. Then, suddenly, they become positive and constant, regardless of the magnitude of the deviation from the nominal value.

As an example of the goalpost view, the desired diameter of stainless steel ball bearings is 25 mm (the nominal value). A tolerance of 5 mm above or below 25 mm is acceptable to purchasers. Thus, if a ball bearing diameter measures between 20 mm and 30 mm (inclusive), it is deemed conforming to specifications. If a ball bearing diameter measures less than 20 mm or more than 30 mm, it is deemed not conforming to specifications, and is scrapped at a cost of $1.00 per ball bearing.

Continuous Improvement Definition of Quality

As the definition of quality has emerged, its meaning has shifted. A more current definition of quality states that: "**Quality** is a predictable degree of uniformity and dependability, at low cost and suited to the market." [See Reference 2, p. 229.] Figure 1.14 shows a more realistic loss curve, in which losses begin to accrue as soon as a quality characteristic of a product or service deviates from the nominal value. As with the goalpost view of quality, once the specification limits are reached, the loss suddenly becomes positive and constant, regardless of the deviation from the nominal value beyond the specification limits.

The above view of quality was articulated by Dr. Genichi Taguchi [see Reference 11, pp. 7–11]. The **Taguchi loss function,** called the loss curve in Figure 1.14, expresses the loss of deviating from nominal within specifications: the left-hand vertical axis is "loss" and the horizontal axis is the measure, y, of a quality characteristic. The loss associated with deviating $(y - m)$ units from the nominal value, m, is:

$$L(y) = k(y - m)^2$$

where

    y = the value of the quality characteristic for a particular item of product or service

    m = the nominal value for the quality characteristic

FIGURE 1.14
Continuous Improvement View of Losses from Deviations from the Nominal Value

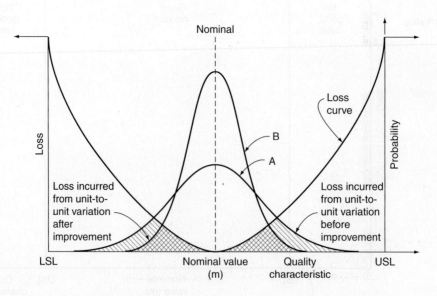

k = a constant, C/d^2

C = the loss (cost) of exceeding specification limits (e.g., the cost to scrap a unit of output)

d = the allowable tolerance from the nominal value that is used to determine specification limits

Under this Taguchi loss function, the continuous reduction of unit-to-unit variation around the nominal value is the most economical course of action. [See Reference 11, pp. 7–9.] In Figure 1.14, the right-hand vertical axis is probability and the horizontal axis is the measure, y, of a quality characteristic. The distribution of output from a process before improvement is shown in curve A, while the distribution of output after improvement is shown in curve B. The loss incurred from unit-to-unit variation before process improvement (the lined area under the loss curve for distribution A) is greater than the loss incurred from unit-to-unit variation after process improvement (the hatched area under the loss curve for distribution B). This definition of quality promotes continual reduction of unit-to-unit variation (uniformity) of output around the nominal value.

Note that this new definition of quality implies that specifications should be surpassed, rather than merely met, because there is a loss associated with products that deviate from the nominal value, even when they conform to specifications.

To illustrate the continuous definition of quality, return to our example of the production of stainless steel ball bearings. Every millimeter higher or lower than 25 mm causes a loss that can be expressed by the following Taguchi loss function:

$$L(y) = k(y - m)^2 = (C/d^2)(y - m)^2$$
$$= (\$1.00/5 \text{ mm}^2)(y - 25 \text{ mm})^2 = (.04)(y - 25 \text{ mm})^2$$

Table 1.2 shows the values of L(y) for values of the quality characteristic (diameter of ball bearings).

TABLE 1.2
Loss Arising from Deviations in Diameters of Ball Bearings

Diameter of Ball Bearing (y)	Value of Taguchi Loss Function L(y)
18	1.00
19	1.00
20	1.00
21	0.64
22	0.36
23	0.16
24	0.04
25	0.00
26	0.04
27	0.16
28	0.36
29	0.64
30	1.00
31	1.00
32	1.00

Under the above loss curve, it is always economical to continually reduce the unit-to-unit variation in the diameter of stainless steel ball bearings.

More Quality Examples

An individual buying a container of milk expects the milk to remain fresh at least until the expiration date stamped on the container, and wants to purchase it at the lowest possible price. If the milk spoils before the expiration date, the customer's expectation will not have been met, and he will perceive the milk's quality as poor. Further, if this happens repeatedly, the customer will lose confidence in the milk provider's ability to supply fresh milk; in other words, the customer will feel he cannot predict with a high degree of belief that the milk will be uniformly and dependably fresh.

If an assembly line worker receives parts that are predictably dependable and uniform from the worker immediately upstream, her needs will be met and she will perceive the quality of those parts as good.

If a hotel guest finds a clean, comfortable room containing all of the amenities promised, he will feel that his expectations were met. But if the room is not made up properly or lacks soap, the guest will perceive that the quality is poor.

The Quality Environment

The pursuit of quality requires that organizations globally optimize their **system of interdependent stakeholders.** This system includes employees, customers, investors, suppliers and subcontractors, regulators, the environment, and the community. The organization, which consists of employees and investors, must work together with suppliers and subcontractors to satisfy the needs of all stakeholders.

At one end of the system of interdependent stakeholders are an organization's external customers (its market segments). Each market segment's needs and wants must be communicated to the organization. This is accomplished through an ongoing process that conveys how an organization's products and services are performing in the marketplace and what improvements and innovations would optimize the system of interdependent stakeholders. The concept of customer also includes regulatory agencies, the community, and investors, and should be applied to all areas and people within the organization; for example, customers are areas and people downstream.

At the other end of the system of interdependent stakeholders are the organization's suppliers and subcontractors. The organization communicates its customers' needs to its suppliers and subcontractors so that they can aid in the pursuit of quality for all stakeholders.

Employees are the most critical stakeholders of an organization. According to quality expert Kaoru Ishikawa: "In management, the first concern of the company is the happiness of people who are connected with it. If the people do not feel happy and cannot be made happy, that company does not deserve to exist. . . . The first order of business is to let the employees have adequate income. Their humanity must be respected, and they must be given an opportunity to enjoy their work and lead a happy life." [See Reference 9, p. 97.]

Types of Quality

Three types of quality are critical to the production of products and services with a predictable degree of uniformity and dependability, at low cost, which are suited to the market. They are (1) quality of design or redesign, (2) quality of conformance, and (3) quality of performance. [See Reference 10, pp. 2–4 to 2–9.] In this text, product will mean either product or service.

Quality of Design

Quality of design focuses on determining the quality characteristics of products that are suited to the needs and wants of a market at a given cost; that is, quality of design develops products from a customer orientation. Quality of design studies begin with consumer research, service call analysis, and sales call analysis and lead to the determination of a product concept that meets the consumer's needs and wants. Next, specifications are prepared for the product concept, as shown in Figure 1.15.

The process of developing a product concept involves establishing and nurturing an effective interface between all areas of an organization, for example, between marketing, service, and design engineering. Design engineering is one of marketing's customers, and vice versa.

Continuous, never-ending improvement and innovation of an organization's product and service concept require that consumer research and sales/service call analysis be an ongoing effort. Consumer research is a collection of procedures whose purpose is to understand the customer's needs and wants, both present and future. Consumer research procedures include both nonscientific and scientific studies. An example is a study of the reasons why purchasers buy or do not buy a particular brand of dog food. The investigation's goal is to determine the customer's needs and wants and redesign the package size, make the package resealable, or alter the composition of the dog food. Consumer research should be ongoing so that the firm will always be in touch with changing customer needs and wants.

FIGURE 1.15
Quality of Design/ Redesign

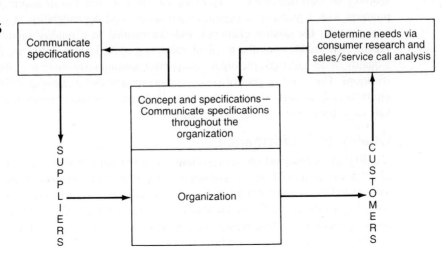

Consumer research can also be performed internally within an organization. For example, employees are the customers of some management policy decisions. Hence, employee surveys are a form of consumer research that could lead to improved management policy.

Sales call analysis involves the systematic collection and evaluation of information concerning present and future customer needs and wants. Information is collected during sales interactions with customers. The analysis helps determine customer needs and wants by examining the questions and concerns people express about products or services at the time of purchase. Sales call analysis is an important window into the customer's needs and wants. An example of sales call analysis is a formal investigation into salesperson-customer interactions at a personal computer distributorship. The investigation's purpose may be to collect information about the questions customers most frequently ask and to use this data to improve the selling protocol.

Service call analysis is the systematic investigation of the problems customers/users have with the product's performance. Service call analysis provides an opportunity to understand which product features must be changed to surpass the customer's present and future needs and wants. An example is Sony Corporation's formal collection of information from field service technicians of customers' problems with Sony KV-32 XBR450 TV sets. The basic source document for the service call analysis data is the service ticket, which indicates the problem and the work done to resolve it. This information is collected and over time may indicate problems that could require changes to work methods and/or materials; for example, redesigning the TV tuner or reducing the time between a customer's request for service and the completed service call.

Service call analysis can also be performed within an organization. For example, an area supervisor may examine the problems the next operation encounters using the parts/service forms that his area delivers to them. The purpose of the analysis could be to learn what the supervisor must do to pursue process improvement and innovation within his own area.

Quality of Conformance

Quality of conformance is the extent to which a firm and its suppliers can produce products with a predictable degree of uniformity and dependability, at a cost that is in keeping with the quality characteristics determined in a quality of design study. As Figure 1.16 shows, once the nominal value and specification limits are determined via a quality of design study, the organization must continuously strive to surpass those specifications. The ultimate goal of process improvement and innovation efforts is to create products and services whose quality is so high that consumers (both external and internal) extol them.

Quality of Performance

Quality of performance studies focus on determining how the quality characteristics identified in quality of design studies, and improved and innovated in quality of conformance studies, are performing in the marketplace, as shown in Figure 1.17. The major tools of quality of performance studies are consumer research and sales/service call analysis, to study after-sales service, maintenance, reliability, and logistical support and to determine why consumers do not purchase the company's products.

FIGURE 1.16
Quality of
Conformance

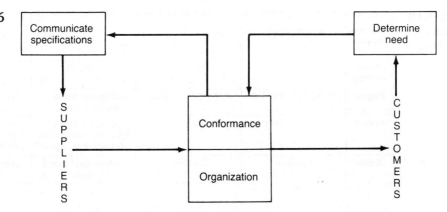

FIGURE 1.17
Quality of
Performance

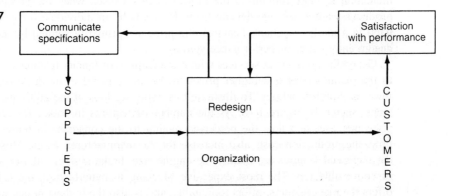

Relationship between Quality and Cost

Consumers can be grouped into market segments once the product characteristics (features) they desire are known and defined. Features and price determine whether a consumer will initially enter a market segment; hence features and price determine market size. After the initial purchase, consumers' decisions to extol a product or purchase it again are based on their experience with the product, that is, the product's dependable and uniform performance. Dependability and uniformity determine a product's success, and therefore its market share, within a market segment. Ultimately features, dependability, uniformity, and price determine market size and market share.

Features

A loss in quality occurs when a process generates products whose features deviate from the needs and wants of the individual (or group of individuals in a market segment), that is, when the products and/or price do not suit the market. This type of loss can be remedied by tailoring the product to the consumer's requirements and/or by modifying the product's price. For example, shirt neck sizes may be marketed in tenths of an inch rather

FIGURE 1.18
2002 Mustang
Feature Price
Options

Mustang Model	 COUPE	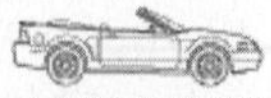 CONVERTIBLE	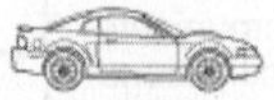 GT	 GT CONVERTIBLE
Price (MSRP)	$18,100	$23,625	$23,845	$28,100
Engine	90-hp, 3.8L OHV V-6	90-hp, 3.8L OHV V-6	260-hp and 302 lb.-ft. of torque, the 4.6L V-8	260-hp and 302 lb.-ft. of torque, the 4.6L V-8
Brakes	Standard brakes	Standard brakes	Anti-Lock Braking System to monitor wheel slippage at any speed	Anti-Lock Braking System to monitor wheel slippage at any speed
Seats	Standard	Standard	Leather sport bucket seats	Leather sport bucket seats

than in half inches, or Velcro may be used in shirt collars instead of buttons. This segmentation strategy minimizes the loss in quality caused when the nominal levels of a product's feature package deviate from the needs of an individual (or group of individuals) in a market segment. Features and price are primarily studied by using quality of design and quality of performance studies.

Generally, products or services with more features or fancier features have higher costs to the manufacturer and higher prices to the consumer than products or services with fewer or simpler features. To illustrate this point, we look at the 2002 line of Ford Mustangs, shown in Figure 1.18. As the number of features increases for each model, the price increases and thus the perceived quality to the consumer increases. At the same time, the production costs also increase for the manufacturer. In the Mustang example, the increased features are mainly the engine size, brake system, interior and a hard top or convertible top. The most expensive Mustang to manufacture, the GT Convertible, offers the most features, offers top quality, and is also the highest priced of all Mustangs currently available.[1]

Dependability and Uniformity

A loss in quality also results when a process generates products whose quality characteristics lack a predictable degree of uniformity and dependability; that is, when there is high unit-to-unit variation, causing customers to lose confidence in that product. For example, if shirt neck sizes are manufactured to be 15 inches and customers notice variation from shirt to shirt, then this shirt-to-shirt variation will cause a loss in quality. The loss in quality can be reduced by understanding and resolving the causes of process variation. Uniformity and dependability are primarily studied by using quality of conformance studies.

Uniformity and dependability create an inverse relationship between quality and cost. When the degree of uniformity and dependability of a product is high, the quality of the product is high, and the overall cost to both the manufacturer and the consumer is less. This relationship is explained by the Taguchi loss function. An example of the relationship between uniformity and dependability, cost and quality can be seen by looking at the ball bearing example discussed earlier in this chapter.

[1] Information for this paragraph was provided by Leah Gregg, Fernando Guerrero, Melissa Hopkins, and Scott Hopkins.

Managers must balance the cost of having many market segments with the benefits of high consumer satisfaction caused by small deviations between an individual consumer's needs and the product characteristic package for that consumer's market segment. Also, managers must continually strive to reduce variation in product characteristics for all market segments.

Relationship between Quality and Productivity

Why should organizations try to improve quality? If a firm wants to increase its profits, why not raise **productivity?** For years, W. Edwards Deming worked to change the thinking in organizations that operate with the philosophy that if productivity increases, profits will increase. The following example illustrates the folly of such thinking.

For the past 10 years the Universal Company has produced an average of 100 widgets per hour, 20 percent of which are defective, yielding 80 good widgets per hour. The board of directors now demands that top management increase productivity by 10 percent. The directive goes out to the employees, who are told that instead of producing 100 widgets per hour, they must produce 110. Responsibility for producing more widgets falls on the employees, creating stress, frustration, and fear. They try to meet the new demands, but must cut corners to do so. Pressure to raise productivity creates a defect rate of 25 percent and only increases production to 104 units, yielding 78 good widgets, two fewer than the original 80, as shown in Table 1.3a.

Stressing productivity often has the opposite effect of what management desires. The following example demonstrates a new way of looking at productivity and quality.

TABLE 1.3
Productivity versus Quality Approach to Improvement

Source: H. Gitlow and S. Gitlow (1987), *The Deming Guide to Quality and Competitive Position* (Prentice Hall, Englewood Cliffs, NJ), pp. 29–31.

	(a) Universal Company Output	
	Before Demand for 10% Productivity Increase (Defect Rate = 20%)	After Demand for 10% Productivity Increase (Defect Rate = 25%)
Widgets produced	100	104*
Widgets defective	20	26
Good widgets	80	78

	(b) Dynamic Factory Output		
	Before Improvement (Defect Rate = 20%)		After Improvement (Defect Rate = 10%)
Widgets produced	100	→	100
Widgets defective	20	Process	10
Good widgets	80	improvement	90
		→	

*Only reached 104, not required 110, but defect rate rose 20 percent to 25 percent. More widgets were produced; but more were defective, yielding less productivity.

The Dynamic Factory produces an average of 100 widgets per hour with 20 percent defectives. Top management is continually trying to improve quality, thereby increasing productivity. Top management realizes that Dynamic is making 20 percent defectives, which translates into 20 percent of the total cost of production being spent to make bad units. If Dynamic's managers can improve the process, they can transfer resources from the production of defectives to the manufacture of additional good products. Management can improve the process by making some changes at no additional cost, so that only 10 percent of the output is defective on average. This results in an increase in productivity, as shown in Table 1.3b. Here management's ability to improve the process results in a decrease in defectives, yielding an increase in good units, quality, and productivity.

Benefits of Improving Quality

Deming's approach to the relationship between quality and productivity stresses improving quality to increase productivity. Promoting quality unleashes the **chain reaction of quality.** Several benefits result from improving a process: rework decreases, productivity rises, quality improves, cost per good unit is decreased, price can be cut, and workers' morale goes up because they are not seen as the problem. This last aspect leads to further benefits: less employee absence, less burnout, more interest in the job, and increased motivation to improve work. This is the chain reaction of quality.

In sum, stressing productivity only may mean sacrificing quality and possibly decreasing output. Employee morale plunges, costs rise, customers are unhappy, and stockholders become concerned. On the other hand, stressing quality can produce all the desired results: less rework, greater productivity, lower unit cost, price flexibility, improved competitive position, increased demand, larger profits, more jobs, and more secure jobs. Customers get high quality at a low price, vendors get predictable long-term sources of business, and investors get profits. Everybody wins!

Summary

This chapter introduced some fundamental notions in the study of quality. A process is the transformation of inputs into outputs. The transformation involves the addition or creation of value in one of three aspects: time, place, or form. Processes exist in all aspects of organizations, and our understanding of them is crucial.

We saw that the outputs from all processes and their component parts vary over time. There are two causes of variation in a process, common causes and special causes. Common causes of variation are due to the process itself. Special causes of variation are external to the process. Managers must realize that unless a change is made in the process (which only they can make) the process's capability will remain the same. This capability is determined by common variation. Employees cannot control a common cause of variation and should not be held accountable for, or penalized for, its outcomes. Understanding and controlling variation leads to improvement and innovation of outputs.

A feedback loop relates information about outputs from any stage or stages back to another stage or stages so that an analysis of the process can be made. There are three feedback loop situations: no feedback loop, special-cause-only feedback loop, and special and common cause feedback loop. A process that does not have a feedback loop is probably doomed to deterioration and decay because of the inability of its stakeholders to rejuvenate and improve it on the basis of data from its outputs. A process in which all feedback information is treated as a special cause will exhibit enormous variation in its output. Finally, a process in which feedback information is separated into common and special causes, where special causes are resolved and common causes are removed, will exhibit continuous improvement of its output.

If management tampers with a process without profound knowledge of how to improve the process through statistical thinking, they will increase the process's variation and reduce their ability to manage that process. This is called overcontrol of the process, or tampering. Loss to an organization results from overcontrol of its processes. This loss can be demonstrated by the funnel experiment and its four rules. Rule 1 demonstrates the effect of recognizing common variation and not confusing it with special variation. Rules 2, 3, and 4 demonstrate the effects of confusing common variation with special variation. The funnel experiment illustrates how a system is improved not by overcontrol but by reducing variation. The modern definition of quality promotes continual reduction of unit-to-unit variation (uniformity) of output around the nominal value.

Pursuit of quality requires that organizations globally optimize their system of interdependent stakeholders. This system includes employees, customers, investors, suppliers and subcontractors, regulators, and the community. The organization, which consists of employees and investors, must work together with suppliers and subcontractors to satisfy the needs of all stakeholders.

The chapter also discussed three types of quality which are critical to the production of products and services with a predictable degree of uniformity and dependability, at low cost, which are suited to the market: (1) quality of design or redesign, (2) quality of conformance, and (3) quality of performance. The role of features and price and the role of uniformity and cost were also discussed; there is a positive relationship between the features/price aspect of quality and cost: the fancier the features, the higher the cost. There is a negative relationship between the uniformity/dependability aspect of quality and cost: the higher the uniformity/dependability, the lower the cost.

We also saw that stressing productivity only may mean sacrificing quality and possibly decreasing output. Employee morale plunges, costs rise, customers are unhappy, and stockholders become concerned. On the other hand, stressing quality can produce all the desired results: less rework, greater productivity, lower unit cost, price flexibility, improved competitive position, increased demand, larger profits, more jobs, and more secure jobs. Customers get high quality at a low price, vendors get predictable long-term sources of business, and investors get profits.

Key Terms

chain reaction of quality, *26*
common cause of variation, *5*
common variation, *5*
control chart, *15*

feedback loop, *3*, *6*
funnel experiment, *7*
lower specification limit (LSL), *17*
mission statement, *3*
nominal value, *17*

paradigm, *6*
paradigm shift, *6*
process, *3*
process capability, *5*
productivity, *25*
quality, *18*

quality of conformance, *22*	special variation, *5*	target value, *17*
quality of design, *21*	specification limits, *17*	transformation, *3*
quality of performance, *22*	system of interdependent	upper specification limit
red bead experiment, *14*	stakeholders, *20*	(USL), *18*
special cause of	Taguchi loss function, *18*	variance analysis, *10*
variation, *5*	tampering, *7*	

Exercises

1.1. Define a process. What is the purpose of a process?

1.2. Explain the different types of feedback loops.

1.3. Explain the two causes of variation in a process and give examples of each.

1.4. Explain the goalpost view of quality and illustrate it.

1.5. Explain the continuous improvement view of quality and illustrate it.

1.6. Define quality of design, quality of conformance, and quality of performance.

1.7. Explain the relationship between the features aspect of quality and cost and the uniformity aspect of quality and cost.

1.8. Describe the relationship between quality and productivity and process improvement.

1.9. What is the chain reaction of quality?

References

1. T. J. Boardman and H. Iyer (1986), *The Funnel Experiment* (Fort Collins, CO: Colorado State University).

2. W. Edwards Deming (1982), *Quality, Productivity, and Competitive Position* (Cambridge, MA: Massachusetts Institute of Technology).

3. W. Edwards Deming (1986), *Out of the Crisis* (Cambridge, MA: Massachusetts Institute of Technology Center for Advanced Engineering Study).

4. W. Edwards Deming (1993), *The New Economics for Industry, Government, Education* (Cambridge, MA: Massachusetts Institute of Technology Center for Advanced Engineering Study).

5. A. Feigenbaum (1951), *Total Quality Control* (New York: McGraw-Hill).

6. H. Gitlow and S. Gitlow (1987), *The Deming Guide to Quality and Competitive Position* (Englewood Cliffs, NJ: Prentice Hall).

7. H. Gitlow, K. Kang, and S. Kellogg, "Process Tampering: An Analysis of On/Off Deadband Process Controlling," *Quality Engineering,* Vol. 5, No. 2, 1992–93, pp. 239–310.

8. H. J. Harrington, "Quality's Footprints in Time," IBM Technical Report, TR02.1064, September 20, 1983.

9. K. Ishikawa and D. Lu (1985), *What Is Total Quality Control? The Japanese Way* (Englewood Cliffs, NJ: Prentice Hall).

10. J. Juran (1979), *Quality Control Handbook,* 3rd ed. (New York: McGraw-Hill).

11. G. Taguchi and Y. Wu (1980), *Introduction to Off-Line Quality Control* (Nagoya, Japan: Central Japan Quality Control Association).

Chapter 2

W. Edwards Deming's Theory of Management

Sections

Chapter Objectives

- To explain W. Edwards Deming's theory of management
- To present and discuss Deming's 14 points for management
- To explain the relationship between Deming's 14 points and variation in a system
- To discuss the paradigm shift in management caused by Deming's theory of management

Introduction

The concept of quality has existed since ancient times. However, it took people like Walter Shewhart and W. Edwards Deming to operationally define quality. Deming took the idea of quality and grew it into a practical philosophy of management, called the System of Profound Knowledge. He also provided a roadmap for pursuing quality in a system, called the 14 points for management. This chapter presents and explains how quality, the

29

System of Profound Knowledge, and the 14 points provide the theory and practice required for professional management.

A Brief History of Quality

Issues of quality have existed since tribal chiefs, kings, and pharaohs ruled. One of the first recorded uses of statistics was by Narmer, King of the North, in ancient Egypt around the year 3200 B.C., the Narmer Palette, as shown in Figure 2.1. The Narmer Palette is a soft greenish piece of slate about 65 centimeters tall with hieroglyphics chiseled on the front and back. On the side of the Narmer Palette, shown on the left side of Figure 2.1, a falcon rests atop six papyrus plants. This symbol is a pictograph of Pharaoh Narmer capturing 6,000 enemies, where each papyrus plant represents 1,000 enemies. On the other side of the Narmer Palette, shown on the right side of Figure 2.1, one of the figures preceding Narmer in the procession is a vizier. A pharaoh's vizier was charged with keeping records of the varying levels of the Nile, controlling the reservoirs and food supplies, and assessing crop production and consumption along with other necessary agricultural statistics. Narmer's vizier is one of the first references to an individual doing statistical work.

Another example of a quality issue in ancient times is found in the Code of Hammurabi dating from as early as 2000 B.C. Item 229 states, "If a builder has built a house for a man, and his work is not strong, and the house falls in and kills the householder, that builder shall be slain." Phoenician inspectors eliminated any repeated violations of quality standards by chopping off the hand of the maker of the defective product. Inspectors accepted or rejected products and enforced government specifications. The emphasis was on equity of trade and complaint handling. In ancient Egypt, approximately 1450 B.C., inspectors checked stone blocks' squareness with a string as the stonecutter watched. This method was also used by the Aztecs in Central America.

FIGURE 2.1
Narmer Palette

Sources: *http://www. ptahhotep.com/articles/ Narmer_palette.html* and *http://asia. geocities.com/atennz/ iunytVizer.htm.*

In thirteenth-century Europe, apprenticeships and guilds developed. Craftsmen were both trainers and inspectors. They knew their trades, their products, and their customers, and they built quality into their goods. They took pride in their work and in training others to do quality work. The government set and provided standards, such as weights and measures, and, in most cases, an individual could inspect all the products and establish a single quality standard. If the world had remained small and localized, this idyllic state of quality could have thrived and endured. However, as the world became more populated, more products were needed.

During the nineteenth century the modern industrial system began to emerge. In the United States, Frederick Taylor pioneered scientific management in the late nineteenth and early twentieth centuries, removing work planning from the purview of workers and foremen and placing it in the hands of industrial engineers. The twentieth century ushered in a technological era that enabled the masses to avail themselves of products previously reserved for only the wealthy. Henry Ford introduced the moving assembly line into Ford Motor Company's manufacturing environment. Assembly line production broke down complex operations that could be performed by unskilled labor. This resulted in the manufacture of highly technical products at low cost. As part of this process, an inspection operation was instituted to separate good and bad products. Quality, at this point, remained under the purview of manufacturing.

It soon became apparent that the production manager's priority was meeting manufacturing deadlines; achieving product quality was not a priority. Managers knew they would lose their jobs if they did not meet production demands, whereas they would only be reprimanded if quality was poor. Upper management eventually realized that quality was suffering as a result of this system, so a separate position of "chief inspector" was created.

Between 1920 and 1940 industrial technology changed rapidly. The Bell System and Western Electric, its manufacturing arm, led the way in quality control by instituting an Inspection Engineering Department to deal with problems created by defects in their products and lack of coordination between their departments. George Edwards and Walter Shewhart, as members of this department, provided leadership in this area. According to George Edwards, "Quality control exists when successive articles of commerce have their characteristics more nearly like its fellows would and more nearly approximating the designer's intent, than would be the case if the application were not made. To me, any procedure, statistical or otherwise, which has the results I have just mentioned, is quality control, and any procedure which does not have these results is not quality control." [See Reference 13, p. 7.]

Edwards coined the term **quality assurance** and advocated quality as part of management's responsibility. He said:

> This approach recognizes that good quality is not accidental and that it does not result
> from mere wishful thinking, that it results rather from the planned and interlocked activi-
> ties of all the organizational parts of the company, that it enters into design, engineering,
> technical and quality planning specification, production layouts, standards, both workman-
> ship and personnel, and even into training and fostering the point of view of administra-
> tive, supervisory, and production personnel. This approach means placing one of the
> officers of the company in charge of the quality control program in a position at the same
> level as the controller or as the other managers in the operation. Its objective would be

elimination of the hunch factors that at present so largely determine the product quality of too many companies. It puts a man at the head of the quality control program in a position to establish and make effective a company-wide policy with respect to quality, to direct the actions to be taken where it is necessary and to place responsibility where it belongs in each instance. [See Reference 13, p. 8.]

In 1924, Walter Shewhart introduced **statistical quality control.** This provided a method for economically controlling quality in mass production environments. In his book of lectures at the graduate school of the U.S. Department of Agriculture, he asked the reader to write several letter A's as carefully as possible. He then suggested that the reader observe them for variations. Clearly, no matter how carefully one formed the letters, variations occurred. This was a simple yet powerful example of variation in a process. Although Shewhart's primary interest was statistical methods, he was very aware of principles of management and behavioral science.

World War II quickened the pace of quality technology development. The need to improve the quality of products being manufactured resulted in increased study of quality control technology and more sharing of information. In 1946 the American Society for Quality Control (ASQC) was formed, and George Edwards was elected its president. He stated at the time:

Quality is going to assume a more and more important place alongside competition in cost and sales price, and the company which fails to work out some arrangement for securing effective quality control is bound, ultimately, to find itself faced with a kind of competition it can no longer meet successfully. [See Reference 13, p. 8.]

In this environment, basic quality concepts expanded rapidly. Many companies implemented vendor certification programs. Quality assurance professionals developed failure analysis techniques to problem-solve, quality engineers became involved in early product design stages, and environmental performance testing of products was initiated. But, as World War II ended, progress in quality control began to wane. Many companies saw it as a wartime effort and felt that it was no longer needed in the booming postwar market.

In 1950, W. Edwards Deming, a statistician who had worked at the Bell System with George Edwards and Walter Shewhart, was invited by the Union of Japanese Scientists and Engineers (JUSE) to speak to Japan's leading industrialists. They were concerned with rebuilding Japan after the war, developing foreign markets, and improving Japan's reputation for producing low-quality goods. Deming convinced them, despite their reservations, that by instituting his methods, Japanese quality could become the best in the world. The industrialists took Deming's teaching to heart. Over the following years, Japanese quality, productivity, and competitive position were improved and strengthened enormously. Deming was awarded the Second Order Medal of the Sacred Treasure by Emperor Hirohito for his contribution to Japan's economy. The coveted Deming Prize is awarded each year in Japan to the company that has achieved the greatest gain in quality and to an individual for developments in statistical theory [see Reference 8, p. 7]. Prize-winning Japanese companies include Nissan, Toyota, Hitachi, and Nippon Steel. In 1989, Florida Power & Light Company became the first non-Japanese company to receive the Deming Prize.

Deming's ideas have spread in the United States and the rest of the world. His clients have included automobile companies, paper companies, railways, telephone companies, consumer researchers, hospitals, law firms, government agencies, and university research organizations. While a professor at the New York University Graduate School of Business Administration and at Columbia University, he wrote extensively on statistics and management.

Armand V. Feigenbaum published *Total Quality Control* in 1951. It advanced the concept of quality control in all areas of business, from design to sales [see Reference 6]. Until then, quality efforts had been primarily directed toward corrective activities, not prevention.

The Korean War sparked increased emphasis on reliability and end-product testing. However, all of the additional testing did not enable firms to meet their quality and reliability objectives, so quality awareness and quality improvement programs began to emerge in manufacturing and engineering areas. Service Industry Quality Assurance (SQA) also began to focus on the use of quality methods in hotels, banks, government, and other service systems. By the end of the 1960s quality programs had spread throughout most of America's major corporations. But American industry was still enjoying the top position in world markets as Europe and Japan continued to rebuild.

Foreign competition began to threaten U.S. companies in the 1970s. The quality of Japanese products such as cars and TVs began to surpass American-made goods. Consumers began to consider the long-term life of a product in purchase decisions. Foreign competition and consumers' increased interest in quality forced American management to become more concerned with quality. The late 1970s through the present have been marked by striving for quality in all aspects of businesses and service organizations including finance, sales, personnel, maintenance, management, manufacturing and service. The focus is on the entire system, not just the manufacturing line. Reduced productivity, high costs, strikes, and high unemployment have caused management to turn to quality improvement as the means to organizational survival.

Motorola introduced **Six Sigma management** in the mid-1980s. This is a style of quality management that endeavors to improve or innovate processes to reduce the number of defects to no more than 3.4 per million to affect the bottom-line results of an organization. In 1987, the **ISO 9000** (International Organization for Standardization) series quality standards were published and they have spread worldwide. These standards promote standardization of activities within an organization. They are standards for governing quality management systems. In 1986, ANSI (American National Standards Institute) and ASQC (American Society for Quality Control) announced the ANSI/ASQC Q90 Series of standards. The ANSI/ASQC standards are the technical equivalents of the ISO 9000 series standards. The Malcolm Baldrige National Quality Award (MBNQA) was established in the United States in 1988 by the Malcolm Baldrige National Quality Improvement Act of 1987. The first winners of the MBNQA award included Motorola, Globe Metallurgical, and the Nuclear Fuel Division of Westinghouse Electric.

The 1990s and the beginning of the twenty-first century have seen an explosion in interest in quality management, especially ISO 9000 and Six Sigma management. Motorola, General Electric, Dupont, Allied Signal, and other well-known organizations have done much to popularize the success of Six Sigma management.

Some of the quality leaders in the United States have been W. Edwards Deming, Joseph Juran, and Armand Feigenbaum [see Reference 13, pp. 29–31]. In this book we focus largely on the ideas of W. Edwards Deming.

W. Edwards Deming's Theory of Management

W. Edwards Deming was born in Sioux City, Iowa, on October 14, 1900, and died in Washington, D.C., on December 20, 1993. He developed a theory of management that will be described in the remainder of this chapter. A photograph of Deming is shown in Figure 2.2.

Deming's System of Profound Knowledge

Deming developed a theory of management that promotes "joy in work" through the acquisition of process knowledge (learning) gained from experience and coordinated by theory. This theory is called the **System of Profound Knowledge** [see References 5,11].

The System of Profound Knowledge is appropriate for leadership in any culture. However, applying this theory in a particular culture requires a focus on issues that are unique to that culture. For example, in the Western world, managers have frequently operated using the following assumptions (often without realizing it):

- Rewards and punishments are the most effective motivators for people.
- Optimization of every area in an organization leads to optimization of the entire organization.
- Results are achieved by setting objectives.
- Quality is inversely related to quantity.
- Rational decisions can be made on the basis of guesswork and opinion.
- Organizations can be improved by fighting fires.
- Competition is a necessary aspect of life.

Leaders who manage in the context of the above assumptions are lost in the twenty-first century. They have no idea of how to manage their organizations because they do not know the assumptions required for success in tomorrow's marketplace. Such leaders need a theory from which they can understand the assumptions of quality management.

FIGURE 2.2
W. Edwards
Deming

Purpose of Deming's Theory of Management

Deming's theory of management promotes **joy in work** for all of the stakeholders of an organization. Deming believed that joy in work will "unleash the power of human resource contained in **intrinsic motivation.** Intrinsic motivation is the motivation an individual experiences from the sheer joy of an endeavor." [See Reference 3.]

Paradigms of Deming's Theory of Management

Deming's theory of management is based on four **paradigms** or belief systems that an individual or group uses to interpret data about conditions and circumstances. You can think of each of Deming's paradigms as a shift in assumptions for the practice of management, designed to create the environment required to promote joy in work, and hence, release the power contained in intrinsic motivation.

Paradigm 1

People are best inspired by a mix of intrinsic and extrinsic motivation, not only extrinsic motivation. Intrinsic motivation comes from the sheer joy of performing an act. It releases human energy that can be focused into improvement and innovation of a system. It is management's responsibility to create an atmosphere that fosters intrinsic motivation. This atmosphere is a basic element of Deming's theory of management. Extrinsic motivation comes from the desire for reward or the fear of punishment. It restricts the release of energy from intrinsic motivation by judging, policing, and destroying the individual. Management based on extrinsic motivation will "squeeze out from an individual, over his lifetime, his innate intrinsic motivation, self-esteem, dignity, and build into him fear, self-defense." [See Reference 5.]

Paradigm 2

Manage using both a process and a results orientation, not only a results orientation. Management's job is to improve and innovate the processes that create results, not just to manage results. This paradigm shift allows management to define the capabilities of processes, and consequently, to predict and plan the future of a system to achieve organizational optimization. This type of optimization requires that managers make decisions based on facts, not on guesswork and opinion. It is critical that top management change the culture of their organization from "management by guts" (called KKD in Japan) to "management by data." It is easy to refute an argument based on guesswork or opinion, but it is difficult to refute an argument based on solid, scientific data. Managers must consider visible figures, as well as unknown and unknowable figures (for example, the cost of an unhappy customer or the benefit of a proud employee).

Paradigm 3

Management's function is to optimize the entire system so that everyone wins, not to maximize only its components of the system. Managers must understand that individuals, organizations, and systems of organizations are interdependent. Optimization of one component may cause suboptimization of another component. Management's job is to optimize the entire system toward its aim. This may require the managers of one or more components of a system to knowingly suboptimize their component(s) of the system in order to optimize the entire system.

Paradigm 4

Cooperation works better than competition. In a cooperative environment, everybody wins. Customers win products and services they can brag about. The firm wins returns for investors and secure jobs for employees. Suppliers win long-term customers for their products. The community wins an excellent corporate citizen.

In a competitive environment, most people lose. The costs resulting from competition are huge. They include the costs of rework, waste, and redundancy, as well as the costs for warranty, retesting, reinspection, customer dissatisfaction, schedule disruptions, and destruction of the individual's joy in work. Individuals and organizations cannot reap the benefits of a win-win point of view when they are forced to compete.

Is competition ever the preferred paradigm? The answer is "yes," if and only if the aim of the system is to win. If the aim of the system is anything other than to win, for example, to improve or have fun, then competition is not the preferred paradigm. Cooperation is the preferred paradigm in all systems with noncompetitive aims.

According to Deming, if leaders practice these four paradigms, they will reap enormous benefits.

Components of Deming's Theory of Management

Deming's theory of management consists of four components: appreciation of a system, theory of variation, theory of knowledge, and psychology. [See Reference 5.] All four components are interdependent. This discussion presents some of the highlights of Deming's theory of management.

Appreciation of a System

A system is a collection of components that interact and have a common purpose or aim. It is the job of top management to optimize the entire system toward its aim. It is the responsibility of the management of the components of the system to promote the aim of the entire system; this may require that they suboptimize some components.

Theory of Variation

Variation is inherent in all processes. As discussed in Chapter 1 in "Variation in a Process," there are two types of variation, special and common. Special causes of variation are external to the system. It is the responsibility of local people and engineers to determine and resolve special causes of variation. Common causes of variation are due to the inherent design and structure of the system; they define the system. It is the responsibility of management to isolate and reduce common causes of variation. A system that does not exhibit special causes of variation is stable; that is, it is a predictable system of variation. Its output is predictable in the near future.

There are two types of mistakes that can be made in the management of a system. (1) Treating a common cause of variation as a special cause of variation; this is by far the more frequent of the two mistakes—it is called **tampering** and will invariably increase the variability of a system. (2) Treating a special cause of variation as a common cause of variation. Shewhart developed the control chart to provide an economic rule for minimizing the loss from both types of mistakes.

Management requires knowledge about the interactions between the components of a system and its environment. Interactions can be positive or negative; they must be managed.

Theory of Knowledge

Information, no matter how speedy or complete, is not knowledge. Knowledge is indicated by the ability to predict future events with a quantifiable risk of being wrong and the ability to explain past events without fail. Knowledge is developed by stating a theory, using the theory to predict a future outcome, comparing the observed outcome with the predicted outcome, and supporting, revising, or even abandoning the theory.

Experience is of no value without the aid of theory. Theory allows people to understand and interpret experience. It allows people to ask questions and to learn.

All plans are based on assumptions. An assumption is the future output of a process. If the process underlying an assumption is not stable with an acceptable degree of predictability, then the assumption required for the plan cannot be relied upon with any degree of comfort. Consequently, the plan must be changed or abandoned, or the process must be improved to enhance the likelihood of the assumption being valid when called for by the plan.

Communication is possible when people share **operational definitions.** Operational definitions are statistical clarifications of the terms people use to communicate with each other. A term is operationally defined if the users of the term agree on a common definition.

Success cannot be copied from system to system. The reason for success in one system may not be present in another system. The theory underlying a success in one system can be used as a basis for learning in another system.

Psychology

Psychology helps us understand people, the interactions between people, and the interactions between people and the system of which they are part. Management must understand the difference between intrinsic motivation and extrinsic motivation. All people require different amounts of intrinsic and extrinsic motivation. It is the job of a manager to learn the proper mix of the two types of motivation for each person.

Overjustification occurs when an extrinsic motivator is used to reward a person who did something for the sheer joy of it. The result of overjustification is to throttle future desire to do an act.

People are different. They learn in different ways and at different speeds. A manager of people must use these differences to optimize the system of interdependent stakeholders of an organization.

Deming's 14 Points for Management

The System of Profound Knowledge generates an interrelated set of **14 points** for leadership in the Western world. [See References 2, 7, and 14.] These 14 Points provide guidelines, or a road map, for the shifts in thinking required for organizational success. They form a highly interactive system of management; no one point can be studied in isolation.

Point 1:

Create constancy of purpose toward improvement of product and service, with the aim to become competitive, stay in business, and provide jobs.

Leaders must state their organization's values and beliefs. They must create statements of vision and mission for their organizations based on these values and beliefs. Values and beliefs are the fundamental operating principles that provide guidelines for organizational behavior and decision-making. A vision statement seeks to communicate the desired future state of the organization to the stakeholders. A mission statement serves to inform stakeholders of the current reason for the existence of the organization. The values and beliefs plus the vision and mission statements provide a frame of reference for focused, consistent behavior and decision-making by all stakeholders of an organization. This framework permits stakeholders to feel more secure because they understand where they fit into the organization.

Point 2:

Adopt the new philosophy. We are in a new economic age. Western management must awaken to the challenge, learn its responsibilities, and take on leadership for change.

Point 2 encompasses the paradigm shifts that leaders must accept as a consequence of Deming's System of Profound Knowledge.

Point 3:

Cease dependence on inspection to achieve quality. Eliminate the need for inspection on a mass basis by building quality into the product in the first place.

There is a hierarchy of views on how to pursue predictable dependability and uniformity at low cost: (1) **defect detection,** (2) **defect prevention,** and (3) **continuous improvement.**

1. *Defect detection* involves dependence upon mass inspection to sort conforming material from defective material. Mass inspection does not make a clean separation of good from bad. It involves checking products with no consideration of how to make them better. Management must eliminate the need for inspection on a mass basis and build quality into the processes that generate goods and services. Mass inspection does nothing to decrease the variability of the quality characteristics of products and services. Dependence on mass inspection to achieve quality forces quality to become a separate subsystem (called *quality assurance*) whose aim is to police defects without the authority to eliminate the defects. As the Quality Assurance department optimizes its efforts, it causes other departments to view quality as someone else's responsibility.

2. *Defect prevention* involves improving processes so that all output is predictably within specification limits; this is often referred to as **zero defects.** Defect prevention leaves employees with the impression that their job (with respect to reducing variation) is accomplished if they achieve zero defects. Unfortunately, zero defects will be eroded by a force similar to the concept of entropy in thermodynamics, or the natural tendency of a system to move toward disorder or chaos. This force makes a stable and capable process eventually stray out of specification limits. Further, when people are rewarded for zero defects, they may attempt to widen specification limits, rather than improve the process's ability to predictably create output within specification limits. Defect prevention is illustrated by the goalpost view of quality, shown in Figure 1.13.

3. *Continuous improvement* is the ongoing reduction of process (unit-to-unit) variation, even within specification limits. Products, services, and processes are improved in a relentless and continuous manner. It is always economical to reduce unit-to-unit variation around the nominal value, even when a process is producing output within specification limits, absent capital investment. Continuous improvement is illustrated in Figure 1.14.

kp Rule Deming advocated a plan that minimizes the total cost of incoming materials and final product. Simply stated, the rule is an "inspect all-or-none" rule. Its logical foundation has statistical evidence of quality as its base. The rule for minimizing the total cost of incoming materials and final product is referred to as the **kp rule,** discussed in Chapter 13. It specifies when mass inspection of all items should be performed and when only routine monitoring of a sample of items should be done. This method facilitates the collection of process or product data such that variation can be continually reduced; this means progressing from defect detection to continuous improvement.

Point 4:

End the practice of awarding business on the basis of price tag. Instead, minimize total cost. Move toward a single supplier for any one item on a long-term relationship of loyalty and trust.

Buyers and vendors form a system. If each individual player in this system attempts to optimize his own position, the system will be suboptimized. Optimization requires that policy makers understand the three scenarios in which purchasing can take place. Deming called these three scenarios World 1, World 2, and World 3.

World 1 is characterized by a purchasing situation in which the customer knows what she wants and can convey this information to a supplier. In this scenario, purchase price is the total cost of buying and using the product (for example, no supplier provides better service than any other supplier); several suppliers can precisely meet the customer's requirements; and the only difference between suppliers is the price. In this world, purchasing on lowest price is the most rational decision.

In World 2 the customer knows what she wants and can convey this information to a supplier. The purchase price is not simply the total cost of buying and using the product (for example, one supplier may provide better service than any other supplier); several suppliers can precisely meet the customer's requirements, and all suppliers quote identical prices. In this world, purchasing based on best service is the most rational decision. World 2 frequently includes the purchasing of commodities.

In World 3 the customer thinks she knows what she wants and can convey this information to a supplier. However, she will listen to advice from the supplier and make changes based on that advice. Purchase price is not the total cost of buying and using the product; for example, there is also a cost to use the purchased goods. Several suppliers tender their proposals (all of which are different in many ways) and all suppliers quote different prices. In this world, selecting a supplier will be difficult.

Some purchasing agents buy as if all purchases were World 1 scenarios; that is, they purchase solely on the basis of price, without adequate measures of quality and service.

In World 3, after careful and extensive research, it makes sense for customers and suppliers to enter into long-term relationships based on trust (that is, relationships without the fear caused by threat of alternative sources of supply) and statistical evidence of quality. Such long-term relationships promote continuous improvement in the predictability of uniformity and reliability of products and services, and, hence, lower costs. The ultimate extension of reducing the supply base is moving to a single supplier and purchasing agent for a given item. [See Reference 14, pp. 131–136.] Single-supplier relationships should include contingencies on the part of the supplier and customer for disasters.

The concept of single supplier extends beyond the purchasing function. For example, employees should focus on improvement of existing information channels, rather than create additional information channels when the main channel does not yield the desired information. [See Reference 14, pp. 131–136.]

Point 5:

Improve constantly and forever the system of production and service to improve quality and productivity, and thus constantly decrease costs.

Improvement of a system requires statistical and behavioral methods. Management should understand the difference between special and common causes of variation and the capability of a system. It must realize that only when a system is stable (that is, when it exhibits only common causes of variation) can management use process knowledge to predict the output of the system in the near future. This allows management to plan the future state of the system. Further, management of a system requires knowledge of the interrelationships between all functions and activities in the system; this includes the interactions between people and the system, as well as between people.

Operational Definitions   Any two people may have different ideas about what constitutes knowledge of an event. This leads to the need for people to agree on the definitions of characteristics that are important about a system. Operational definitions increase communication between people and help to optimize a system; they require statistical and process knowledge. Operational definitions are fully discussed in Chapter 4.

SDSA Cycle   The **standardize-do-study-act (SDSA) cycle** is a technique that helps employees standardize a process. It includes four steps:

1. *Standardize:* Employees study the process and develop **best-practice** methods with key indicators of process performance. The best-practice method is characterized by a flowchart. It is important for all employees doing a job to agree on (operationally define) a best-practice method. If multiple employees perform the same job differently, there will be increased variation in output and problems will result for the customer(s) of those outputs. Consider, for example, the medical records department in a hospital, which receives, processes, and files patients' medical records. The director of such a department decided to standardize the medical records process. First, she trained all of her personnel on how to construct a flowchart. Second, she asked each employee to create a detailed flowchart of the medical records process. Third, she reviewed all of the flowcharts with her entire staff and created a best-practice flowchart. The best-practice flowchart incorporated all of the strengths and eliminated all of the weaknesses of each employee's flowchart. Fourth, she identified the key objectives and indicators for the medical records department. The key objective is: file more than 80 percent of all medical records within 30 days of a patient's checking out of the hospital. This is a state-mandated objective. The key indicator is: percentage of medical records filed within 30 days of a patient checking out of the hospital.

2. *Do:* Employees conduct planned experiments using the best-practice methods on a trial basis. In the case of the medical records department, the director collected baseline data on the key indicator for a period of months.

3. *Study:* Employees collect and analyze data on the key indicators to determine the effectiveness of the best-practice methods. Again, in the case of the medical records department, the director studied the key indicator data and determined that the

percentage of medical records filed within 30 days of a patient leaving the hospital was a predictable process with an average of 35 percent per month that would rarely go above 45 percent per month or below 25 percent per month. She knew that this was woefully inadequate given her state-mandated key objective.

4. *Act:* Managers establish standardized best-practice methods and formalize them through training. In the case of the medical records department, the director formalized the best-practice method by training all employees in the method and putting it in the department's training manual for the training of all future employees. Finally, she prepared to move onto the PDSA cycle to improve the best-practice method.

The Japanese developed a method to promote good housekeeping practices; it is called the **5-S movement** [see Reference 1, pp. 56–59; Reference 13; Reference 14; and Reference 15, p. 233–234]. "In a 5S environment there is a place for everything, and everything in its place. Time spent searching for items is essentially eliminated, and out of place or missing items are immediately obvious in a properly functioning 5S facility." [See Reference 1, p. 56.]

The name 5-S movement is derived from five Japanese words that begin with the letter S. The words are: *seiri* (sort), *seiton* (set in order), *seiso* (shine), *seiketsu* (standardize), and *shitsuke* (sustain). The five words are part of a very basic management system that focuses employees' attention on the following:

Seiri (sort). Simplify a process by omitting unnecessary work-in-progress, unnecessary tools, unused machinery, defective product, and unnecessary documents and papers.

Seiton (set in order). Label things so they are easy to identify; for example, label storage locations with tape on the floor so that one glance identifies missing or improperly stored items. Keep things organized and ready for their next use by putting them in their proper place; for example, put tools and materials in their assigned places.

Seiso (shine). Maintain a clean workplace; promote a proactive system for maintenance.

Seiketsu (standardize). Be a clean and neat person; assist in the development of best-practice methods for your area. The first three S's (seiri, seiton, and seiso) prevent backsliding in seiketsu.

Shitsuke (sustain). Be disciplined and adhere to best-practice methods.

Some employees at Motorola Corporation added a sixth S to the list: *shituke.*

Shituke. Be well mannered.

Deming (PDSA) Cycle   The **Deming cycle** [see Reference 2, pp. 86–89] can aid management in improving and innovating processes; that is, in helping to reduce the difference between customers' needs and process performance. The Deming cycle consists of four stages: **plan-do-study-act (PDSA).** Often, the Deming cycle is referred to as the *PDSA cycle.* Initially, a plan is developed to improve or innovate the standardized best-practice method developed using the SDSA cycle. The revised best-practice method is characterized by a revised flowchart. Hence, a process improvement team *plans* to modify

FIGURE 2.3
Plan Portion of the PDSA Cycle

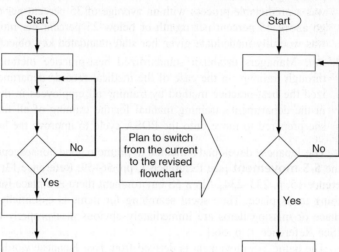

Current best-practice flowchart   Revised best-practice flowchart

Plan to switch from the current to the revised flowchart

a process from operating under the existing best-practice flowchart to operating under a revised and improved best-practice flowchart, as shown in Figure 2.3.

The revised best-practice method is identified using three possible methods:

- Statistically analyzing key indicator data on the components of the process under study to identify an effective change concept.
- Benchmarking the process under study against another organization's process that is considered excellent to identify an effective change concept. The other organization should be one that is known for the quality of the process under study. Benchmarking is accomplished by comparing your flowchart with another organization's flowchart to determine if anything in their flowchart makes sense in your organization. If it does, utilize the new information to improve your flowchart.
- Utilizing a list of tried and proven improvement concepts to identify an effective change concept and determining if any of them make sense within the context of your process. This list of change concepts is discussed in Chapter 10.

In the case of the medical records department, cycle time data were collected for the length of time from when a physician ordered a medical report until the medical records department received (in the inbox) the patient's medical report, from each of 16 departments, such as EEG, EKG, and laboratory. Statistical analysis showed that 15 of the 16 departments' cycle times were stable and predictable processes with cycle times measured in hours. However, the laboratory department had cycle times measured in weeks, with an average of 6 weeks. From this analysis it was obvious that a huge proportion of medical records could not be filed within 30 days if one of the component reports took an average of 6 weeks to get to the medical records department.

The director of the medical records department went to the laboratory department and was greeted by the director with the comment: "We grow cultures and they can't be rushed." The director of the medical records department asked if she could visit the laboratory department anyway. The laboratory director agreed. After poking around the lab, the medical records director noticed that each lab report required three signatures before it could be released. She asked the first signer how often he refused to sign a lab report. He replied, "Never." She asked the second signer how often he refused to sign a lab report. The second signer had seen the director's interaction with the first signer and said: "It happens." She asked, "Does it happen every day?" He said, "No." She asked, "Every week?" He said, "No." She asked, "Every month?" He said, "No." She asked, "Every quarter?" He said, "No." She asked, "Every year?" He said, "No."

The director of medical records asked the director of the laboratory department if he would eliminate the need for the two signatures since they were no screen for quality. The laboratory director agreed, with a modicum of irritation. The average cycle time for the laboratory reports fell from 6 weeks to 3.75 weeks. The percentage of medical records filed on time rose from an average of 35 percent to an average of 60 percent. This was better, but still woefully inadequate for the state-mandated goal of 80 percent per month.

The plan is then tested using an experiment on a small scale or trial basis (*do*), the effects of the plan are studied using measurements from key indicators (*study*), and appropriate corrective actions are taken (*act*). These corrective actions can lead to a new or modified plan, and are formalized through training. The PDSA cycle continues forever in an uphill progression of continuous improvement.

Empowerment   **Empowerment** is a term commonly used by managers in today's organizational environment [see Reference 13]. However, empowerment has not been operationally defined, and its definition varies from application to application. Currently the prevailing definition of empowerment relies loosely on the notion of dropping decision-making down to the lowest appropriate level in an organization. Empowerment's basic premise is that if people are given the authority to make decisions, they will take pride in their work, be willing to take risks, and work harder to make things happen. While this sounds ideal, frequently employees are empowered until they make a mistake, and then the hatchet falls. Most employees know this and treat the popular definition of empowerment without too much respect. Consequently, empowerment in its current form is destructive to quality management.

Empowerment in a quality management sense has a dramatically different aim and definition. The aim of empowerment in quality management is to increase joy in work for all employees. Empowerment can be defined so as to translate the preceding aim into a realistic objective. Empowerment is a process that provides employees with:

1. The opportunity to define and document their key systems.
2. The opportunity to learn about systems through training and development.
3. The opportunity to improve and innovate the best-practice methods that make up systems.
4. The latitude to use their own judgment to make decisions within the context of best-known methods.
5. An environment of trust in which superiors will not react negatively to the latitude taken by people in decision-making within the context of a best-practice method.

Empowerment starts with leadership, but requires the commitment of all employees. Leaders need to provide employees with all five of the preceding conditions. Item 5 requires that the negative results emanating from employees using their judgment within the context of a best-practice method lead to improvement or innovation of best-practice methods, not to judgment and punishment of employees. Employees need to accept responsibility for (1) increasing their training and knowledge of the system; (2) participating in the development, standardization, improvement, and innovation of best-known methods that make up the system; and (3) increasing their latitude in decision-making within the context of best-practice methods.

Individual workers must be educated to understand that increased variability in output will result if each worker follows his own best-practice method. They must be educated about the need to reach consensus on one best-practice method. Management should understand the differences between workers and channel these differences into the development of the best-practice method in a constructive, or team-building, manner.

The best-practice method will consist of generalized procedures and individualized procedures. Generalized procedures are standardized procedures that all workers must follow. The generalized procedures can be improved or innovated through team activities. Individualized procedures are procedures that afford each worker the opportunity to utilize his individual differences. However, the outputs of individualized procedures must be standardized across individuals. The individualized procedures can be improved through individual efforts. In the beginning of a quality improvement effort, management may not have the knowledge to allow for individualized procedures.

Note that latitude to make decisions within the context of a best-practice method refers to the options an employee has in resolving problems within the confines of a best-practice method, not to modification of the best-practice method. Differentiating between the need to change the best-practice methods and latitude within the context of the best-practice methods must take place at the operational level.

Teams must work to improve or innovate best-practice methods. Individuals can also work to improve or innovate best-practice methods; however, the efforts of individuals must be shared with and approved by the team. Empowerment can exist only in an environment of trust that supports planned experimentation concerning ideas to improve and innovate best-practice methods. Ideas for improvement and innovation can come from individuals or from the team, but tests of ideas' worthiness must be conducted through planned experiments under the auspices of the team. Anything else will result in chaos because everybody will "do his own thing."

Empowerment is operationalized at two levels. First, employees are empowered to develop and document best-practice methods using the SDSA cycle. Second, employees are empowered to improve or innovate best-practice methods through application of the PDSA cycle.

Point 6:

Institute training on the job.

Employees are an organization's most important asset. Organizations must make long-term commitments to employees that include their opportunity to take joy in their work. This requires training in job skills.

FIGURE 2.4
Distribution of Job Skills

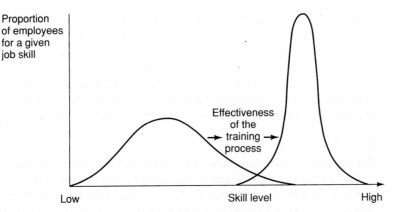

Training in job skills is a system. Effective training changes the skill distribution for a job skill, as shown in Figure 2.4. Management must understand the capability of the training process and the current distribution of job skills to improve the future distribution of job skills. Data, not guesswork or opinion, should be used to guide the training plans for employees.

Training is a part of everyone's job and should include formal class work, experiential work, and instructional materials. Training courseware must take into consideration how the trainee learns and the speed at which she learns. It should utilize statistical methods that indicate when an employee reaches a state of statistical control; that is, only common causes of variation are present in the key indicator(s) used to measure the employee's output. If an employee is not in statistical control with respect to a job characteristic, then more training of the type she is receiving will be beneficial. However if an employee is in a state of statistical control with respect to a job characteristic, then more training of that type will not be beneficial; the employee has learned all that is possible from the training program.

Point 7:

Institute leadership. The aim of supervision should be to help people and machines and gadgets to do a better job. Supervision of management is in need of overhaul, as well as supervision of production workers.

A leader [see Reference 5, pp. 125–128] must see the organization as a system of interrelated components, each with an aim, but all focused collectively to support the aim of the organization. This type of focus may require suboptimization of some system components.

According to Deming, "A leader uses plots of points and statistical calculations, with knowledge of variation, to try to understand both his performance and that of his people." [See Reference 5, p. 127.]

Leaders know when employees are experiencing problems that make their performance fall outside of the system, and leaders treat the problems as special causes of variation. These problems could be common causes to the individual (e.g., long-term alcoholism), but special causes to the system (an alcoholic works differently from his peers).

A leader must understand that experience without theory does not facilitate prediction of future events. For example, a leader cannot predict how a person will perform in a new job based solely on experience in the old job. A leader must have a theory to predict how an individual will perform in a new job.

A leader must be able to predict the future to plan the actions necessary to pursue the organization's aim. Prediction of future events requires that the leader continuously work to create stable processes with low variation to facilitate rational prediction.

Point 8:

Drive out fear so that everyone may work effectively for the company.

There are two kinds of negative reactive behaviors: fear and anxiety. Fear is a reaction to a situation in which the person experiencing the fear can identify its source. Anxiety is a reaction to a situation in which the person experiencing the anxiety cannot identify its source. We can remove the source of fear because it is known, which is not the case with anxiety. Thus, Point 8 focuses on driving out fear.

Fear has a profound impact on those working in an organization, and consequently, on the functioning of the organization. On an individual level, fear can cause physical and physiological disorders such as a rise in blood pressure or an increase in heart rate. Behavioral changes, emotional problems, and physical ailments often result from fear and stress generated in work situations, as do drug and alcohol abuse, absenteeism, and burnout. These maladies impact heavily on any organization. An employee subjected to a climate dominated by fear experiences poor morale, poor productivity, stifling of creativity, reluctance to take risks, poor interpersonal relationships, and reduced motivation to optimize the system of interdependent stakeholders. The economic loss to an organization from fear is immeasurable, but huge.

A statistically based system of management will not work in a fear-filled environment. This is because people in the system will view statistics as a vehicle for policing and judging, rather than a method that provides opportunities for improvement.

Fear emanates from lack of job security, possibility of physical harm, ignorance of company goals, shortcomings in hiring and training, poor supervision, lack of operational definitions, failure to meet quotas, blame for the problems of the system (fear of being below average and being punished), and faulty inspection procedures, to name a few causes. Management is responsible for changing the organization to eliminate the causes of fear.

Point 9:

Break down barriers between departments. People in research, design, sales, and production must work as a team to foresee problems of production and in use that may be encountered with the product or service.

Management's job is to optimize the system of interdependent stakeholders of an organization. This may require suboptimization of some parts of the system. An example of suboptimization of a part, which leads to optimization of the whole, is a supermarket's "loss leader" product (a product carrying an extremely low price). The aim of a loss leader is to entice buyers into a store. Once in the store, buyers purchase other products, thereby creating a greater profit for the store. Profit from the loss leader is suboptimized to optimize store profit. Managers must remove incentives for optimization of areas if they want to optimize the organization. For example, rating departments or divisions with respect to profit alone will usually foster suboptimization of the organization.

Barriers between the areas of an organization thwart communication and cooperation. The greater the interdependence between the components of a system, the greater is the need for communication and cooperation between them.

Point 10:

Eliminate slogans, exhortations, and targets for the workforce that ask for zero defects and new levels of productivity without providing methods.

Slogans, exhortations, and targets do not help to form a plan or method to improve or innovate a process, product, or service. They do not operationally define process variables in need of improvement or innovation. They do not motivate individuals or clarify expectations. Slogans, exhortations, and targets are meaningless without methods to achieve them.

Generally, targets are set arbitrarily by someone for someone else. If a target does not provide a method to achieve it, it is a meaningless plea. Examples of slogans, exhortations, and targets that do not help anyone do a better job are:

Do it right the first time.

Safety is job number 1.

Zero defects.

Just say no.

These kinds of statements do not represent action items for employees; rather, they show management's wishes for a desired result. How, for example, can an employee "do it right the first time" without a method? People's motivation can be destroyed by slogans.

Slogans, exhortations, and targets shift responsibility for improvement and innovation of the system from management to the worker. The worker is powerless to make improvements to the system. This causes resentment, mistrust, and other negative emotions.

Point 11a:

Eliminate work standards (numerical quotas) on the factory floor. Substitute leadership.

Work standards, measured day work, and **piecework** are names given to a practice that can have devastating effects on quality and productivity. A work standard is a specified level of performance determined by someone other than the worker who is actually performing the task.

The effects of work standards are, in general, negative. They do not provide a road map for improvement, and they prohibit good supervision and training. In a system of work standards, workers are blamed for problems beyond their control. In some cases, work standards actually encourage workers to produce defectives to meet a production quota. This robs workers of their pride and denies them the opportunity to produce high-quality goods and thus to contribute to the stability of their employment.

Work standards are negotiated values that have no relationship to the capability of a process. When work standards are set too high or too low, there are additional devastating effects. Setting work standards too high increases pressure on workers and results in the production of more defectives. Worker morale and motivation are diminished because the system encourages the production of defectives. Setting work standards too low also has negative effects. Workers who have met their quota spend the end of the day doing nothing; their morale is also destroyed.

Work standards are frequently used for planning, budgeting, and scheduling, and to provide management with invalid information on which to base decisions. Planning, budgeting, and scheduling would improve greatly if they were based on process capability studies as determined by statistical methods. These will be discussed in Chapter 11.

Point 11b:

Eliminate management by objective. Eliminate management by numbers and numerical goals. Substitute leadership.

The Old Way   Setting arbitrary goals and targets is a dysfunctional form of management. Numerical goals are frequently set without understanding a system's capability. They do not include methods, and hence, do not provide a mechanism for improvement of a process. In a stable system, the proportion of the time an individual is above or below a specified quota/goal is a random lottery. This causes people below the quota to copy the actions of those above the quota even though they are both part of the same common cause system. This increases the variability of the entire system because of inappropriate copying of actions.

Deploying arbitrary goals and targets causes problems in most organizations. Managers use **management by objectives (MBO)** to systematically break down a "plan" into smaller and smaller subsections. Next, managers assign the subsections to individuals or groups who are accountable for achieving results. This is considered fair because subsection goals emerge out of a negotiation between supervisor and supervisee. For example, an employee may negotiate a 3 percent increase in output instead of a 3.5 percent increase as long as the subsection's goals yield the goals of the plan. Note that employees are not being given any new tools, resources, or methods to achieve the 3 percent increase. Consequently, they must abuse the existing system to meet the goal. This type of behavior may allow an employee to meet a goal, but the system will fail somewhere else because of a lack of resources. Arbitrary numerical goals hold people accountable for the problems of the system, and consequently, steal their pride of workmanship.

The New Way   The types of relationships that managers establish between the aim of a system, methods, and goals, or targets, can define a functional style of management. A group of components come together to form a system with an aim. The aim requires that the components organize in such a way that they create subsystems. The subsystems are complex combinations of the components. The subsystems require certain methods to accomplish the aim. Resources are allocated between the methods by setting goals or targets that may be numerical and that optimize the overall system, not the subsystems, with respect to the aim. For example, a group of individuals form a team with an aim. The individuals must combine their efforts to form subsystems. These combinations may require complex interactions between the individuals. The subsystems require methods, and the methods require resources. Resources are allocated between the methods and, ultimately, the subsystems and individuals by setting goals that optimize the team's aim. The aim, methods, and goals are all part of the same system; they cannot be broken into three separate entities. Separation of the aim, methods, and goals destroys them because they are defined by their interactions.

Variation can cause a good method to yield undesirable results. Therefore, one should not overreact (tamper) and change methods by considering negative results in the absence of theory.

Point 12:

Remove barriers that rob the hourly worker of his right to pride of workmanship. The responsibility of supervisors must be changed from stressing sheer numbers to quality. Remove barriers that rob people in management and engineering of their right to pride of workmanship. This means abolishment of the annual merit rating and of management by objective.

People are born with the right to find joy in their work; it provides the impetus to perform better and to improve quality for the worker's self-esteem, for the company, and ultimately for the customer. People enjoy taking joy in their work, but very few are able to do so, because of poor management. Management must remove the barriers that prevent employees from finding joy in their work.

In the current system of management there are many such barriers:

1. Employees not understanding their company's mission and what is expected of them with respect to the mission
2. Employees being forced to act as automatons who are not allowed to think or use their skills
3. Employees being blamed for problems of the system
4. Hastily designed products and inadequately tested prototypes
5. Inadequate supervision and training
6. Faulty equipment, materials, and methods
7. Management systems that focus only on results, such as daily production reports
8. The traditional performance appraisal process, which will be discussed in Chapter 17

Organizations will reap tremendous benefits when management removes barriers to joy in work.

Point 13:

Institute a vigorous program of education and self-improvement.

Education and self-improvement are important vehicles for continuously improving employees, both professionally and personally. Leaders are obligated to educate and improve themselves and their people to optimize the system of interdependent stakeholders. Education for leaders may have to come from outside the system.

Remember, training (Point 6) is to improve job skills, while education (Point 13) is to improve the individual, regardless of his job.

Point 14:

Take action to accomplish the transformation.

The transformation of an organization from its current paradigm of management to the System of Profound Knowledge cannot occur without the expenditure of energy by its stakeholders. Top management will expend this energy in response to a variety of causes—for example, if they are confronted with a crisis or if they have a vision or aim that they want to pursue. Other stakeholders will expend this energy if stimulated by top management. The transformation cannot take place without a critical mass of stakeholders. The critical mass must include some policy makers.

Individuals have different reasons for wanting to, or not wanting to, accomplish the transformation. Individuals will have different interpretations of what is involved in the transformation. To be able to plan, control, and improve the transformation, a leader must know (1) each of his/her people's reasons for wanting (or not wanting) the transformation and (2) how each of those different reasons interact with each other and with the aim of the transformation. A model to promote Point 14 is presented in Chapters 14 through 19.

Deming's 14 Points and the Reduction of Variation

In this section, each of the 14 points is restated with a brief discussion of how it related to the reduction of variation in a process.

Point 1:

Create constancy of purpose toward improvement of product and service with the aim to become competitive, stay in business, and provide jobs. Establishing a mission statement is synonymous with setting a process's nominal or target level. Getting all employees (management, salaried, and hourly), members of the board of directors, and shareholders to behave in accordance to the common interpretation of a mission statement is a problem of reducing variation. [See Reference 18, pp. 133–134.]

Point 2:

Adopt the new philosophy. We can no longer live with commonly accepted levels of delays, mistakes, defective material, and defective workmanship. All people in an organization should embrace the System of Profound Knowledge as the focus of all action. As everyone uniformly embraces the System of Profound Knowledge, variation in how people view the organization—and in how they interpret their job responsibilities—will decrease.

Point 3:

Cease dependence on mass inspection. Require, instead, statistical evidence that quality is built in to eliminate the need for inspection on a mass basis. Dependence on mass inspection does nothing to decrease variation. Moreover, inspection does not create a uniform product within specification limits—rather, product is bunched around specification limits, or, at best, product is distributed within specification limits with large variance and tails truncated at the specification limits.

Point 4:

End the practice of awarding business on the basis of price tag. Instead, depend on meaningful measures of quality, along with price. Move toward a single supplier for any one item on a long-term relationship of loyalty and trust. Multiple-supplier processes, each of which has small variations, combine to create a process with large variation. This means an increase in the variability of inputs to the organization, which is counter to the reduction of variation. Consequently, reducing the supply base from many suppliers to one supplier is a rational action. This idea applies to both external and internal suppliers.

Point 5:

Improve constantly and forever the system of production and service, to improve quality and productivity, and thus constantly decrease costs. The Taguchi loss function explains the need for the continuous reduction of variation in a system, as illustrated in Chapter 1. Management must realize that when a system is stable, or exhibits only common causes of variation, it is able predict the system's future condition. This allows management to plan the future state of the system and use the PDSA cycle to decrease the difference, or variation, between customer needs and process performance. The PDSA cycle is a procedure for improving process by reducing variation.

Point 6:

Institute training on the job. Statistical methods should be used to determine when training is finished. In chaos, more training of the same type is effective. In stability, more training of the same type is not effective; management may have to find the trainee a new job for which he is trainable.

Point 7:

Institute leadership. A leader must understand that variation in a system can come from the individual, the system, or the interaction between the system and the individual. A leader must not rank the people who perform within the limits of a system's capability.

Point 8:

Drive out fear, so that everyone may work effectively for the company. Managers who do not understand variation rank individuals within a system; that is, they hold individuals accountable for system problems. This causes fear, which stifles the desire to change and improve a process. Fear creates variability between an individual's or team's actions and the actions required to surpass customer needs and wants.

Point 9:

Break down barriers between departments. Everyone must work as a team to foresee and solve problems. Barriers between departments result in multiple interpretations of a given message. This increases variability in the actions taken with respect to a given message.

Point 10:

Eliminate slogans, exhortations, and targets for the workforce. Slogans and exhortations try to shift the responsibility for common causes of variation to the worker without providing methods.

Point 11:

Eliminate work standards (numerical quotas). If a work standard is between a system's upper natural limit (UNL) and lower natural limit (LNL), there is a possibility that the standard can be met, but meeting the standard this way is simply a random lottery. If a work standard is above the system's UNL, then there is little chance that the standard will be met unless management changes the system. Rather than focus on the standard as a means to productivity, management should focus on stabilizing and improving the process to increase productivity.

Point 12:

Remove barriers that rob people of their pride of workmanship. Performance appraisal systems can increase variability in employee performance, resulting from actions such as rewarding everyone who is above average and penalizing everyone who is below average. In such a situation, below-average employees try to emulate above-average employees. However, as the employees who are above average and those who are below average are part of the same system (only common variation is present), the below-average ones are adjusting their behavior on the basis of common variation.

Point 13:

Institute a vigorous program of education and self-improvement. The education and training of employees will lower variability in processes, products, and jobs, continuing the never-ending cycle of improvement. [See Reference 18, p. 126.]

Point 14:

Take action to accomplish the transformation. The current paradigm of Western management is shaped by reactive forces. Therefore, it has an explosive and high degree of variation in its application. The transformation must emanate out of a new paradigm shaped by the System of Profound Knowledge, not reactive forces. This new paradigm will have a stable, reducible degree of variation in its application.

Transformation, or Paradigm Shift

Transformation of Management

The issues involved in understanding the transformation of people and organizations from management's prevailing style to the System of Profound Knowledge are presented in Figure 2.5, which displays: (1) the prevailing paradigm of leadership and the business and education systems it creates, (2) the System of Profound Knowledge and the business and education systems it creates, and (3) the 14 points' role in the transformation process from the prevailing style of management to the System of Profound Knowledge.

The Prevailing Paradigm of Leadership

According to Deming, "The prevailing style of management was not born with evil intent. It grew up little by little by reactive behavior, unsuited to any world, and especially unsuited to the new kind of world of dependence and interdependence that we are in now." [See Reference 12, foreword by W. Edwards Deming, p. vii.] The prevailing paradigm of management, shown on the left side of Figure 2.5, is not based on any holistic or comprehensive theory; it is just the cumulative result of assorted theories and experiences.

The New Paradigm of Leadership

The System of Profound Knowledge allows leadership to change and to develop a new basis for understanding the interrelationships between themselves and their environment.

FIGURE 2.5

Issues Involved in Transformation

Source: Darrell Schroeder of Process Management International, Bloomington, IL, 1991.

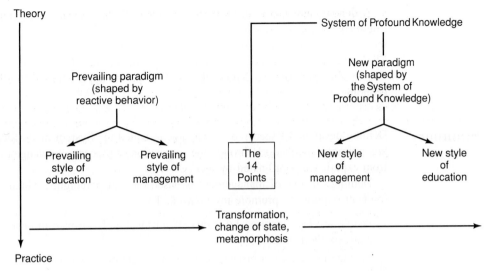

The environment includes people, systems, and organizations. It is based on a holistic and comprehensive theory of management.

Transformation

It is not easy to move from the prevailing style of leadership to the new style of leadership. The 14 points provide a framework that helps explain the relationship between the prevailing style and the System of Profound Knowledge. They provide a window for managers operating under the prevailing techniques to compare and contrast their business practices with business practices in the System of Profound Knowledge. The real work of transformation comes from understanding the System of Profound Knowledge. According to Deming, "Transformation of American style of management is not a job of reconstruction, nor is it revision. It requires a whole new structure, from foundation upward." [See Reference 2, flyleaf cover.]

Managers in one organization should not use the experiences of managers in another organization to focus their transformation efforts. This is because organizations are unique, having their own idiosyncrasies and nuances. Conditions that led to the experiences of managers in one organization may not exist for managers of the other organization. However, this is not to say that managers' experiences in one organization cannot stimulate development of theories for improvement and innovation on the part of another organization's managers.

Quality in Service, Government, and Education

The U.S. Census shows that the overwhelming majority of Americans work in service, government, or educational organizations or perform service functions in manufacturing organizations. Thus, improvement in our standard of living is highly dependent on better quality and productivity in these sectors of the economy. [See Reference 19.]

A denominator common to all organizations is that mistakes and defects are costly. The further a mistake goes without correction, the greater the cost to correct it. A defect that reaches the consumer or recipient may be costliest of all. [See Reference 2, p. 190.] The principles and methods for process improvement are the same in all organizations. The System of Profound Knowledge and 14 points apply equally to all sectors of the economy.

Summary   Deming developed a theory of management, called the System of Profound Knowledge, that promotes joy in work through the acquisition of process knowledge (learning) gained from experience coordinated by theory.

Deming's theory of management is based on four paradigms, which create the environment required to promote joy in work. They are:

1. People are best inspired by a mix of intrinsic and extrinsic motivation, not only by extrinsic motivation.
2. Manage using both a process and results orientation, not only a results orientation.
3. Management's function is to optimize the entire system so that everyone wins, not to optimize only one component of the system.
4. Cooperation works better than competition.

Deming's theory of management comprises four components: appreciation of a system, theory of variation, theory of knowledge, and psychology. All four components are interdependent and will not stand alone. Fortunately, it is not necessary to be expert in any of the components to understand and apply the System of Profound Knowledge.

The System of Profound Knowledge generates an interrelated set of 14 points for leadership in the Western world. These 14 points provide a road map for the shifts in thinking required for organizational success. They form a highly interactive system of management; no one point should be studied in isolation.

The System of Profound Knowledge allows leadership to change and to develop a new basis for understanding the interrelationships between themselves and their environment. The environment includes people, systems, and organizations. It is based on a holistic and comprehensive theory of management.

The U.S. Census shows that the overwhelming majority of Americans are employed in service, government or educational organizations or perform service functions in manufacturing organizations. Hence, improvement in our standard of living is highly dependent on better quality and productivity in these sectors of the economy.

Key Terms

best practice, *40*	empowerment, *43*	joy in work, *34*
continuous improvement, *38*	5-S movement, *41*	kp rule, *39*
defect detection, *38*	14 points, *37*	management by objectives (MBO), *48*
defect prevention, *38*	intrinsic motivation, *34*	operational definition, *37*
Deming cycle, *41*	ISO 9000, *33*	paradigm, *35*

Exercises

2.1. Explain the purpose of Deming's theory of management, called the System of Profound Knowledge.

2.2. List the four assumptions of the System of Profound Knowledge and provide an example for each assumption.

2.3. Briefly discuss the role of systems theory with respect to the System of Profound Knowledge. Be sure to include the following and provide a business or personal example demonstrating your understanding of each topic:

a. Definition of a system.

b. Responsibility for establishing the aim of a system.

c. Significance of optimizing the entire system, not just one component of the system.

2.4. Briefly discuss the role of the theory of variation (statistical theory) with respect to the System of Profound Knowledge. Be sure to include the following and provide a business or personal example demonstrating your understanding of each topic:

a. Define the two types of variation in a system (special variation and common variation). Who is responsible for each type of variation?

b. Define stability in a system.

c. Under what condition is a system predictable into the near future?

2.5. Briefly discuss the role of the theory of knowledge with respect to the System of Profound Knowledge. Be sure to include the following and provide a business or personal example demonstrating your understanding of each topic:

a. Discuss the relationship between theory and learning.

b. Comment on planning, assumptions, and process improvement.

c. Discuss operational definitions.

d. Discuss the dangers of learning from experience.

e. Discuss the dangers of copying other people's or organizations' successful process improvements.

2.6. Briefly discuss the role of psychology with respect to the System of Profound Knowledge. Be sure to include the following and provide a business or personal example demonstrating your understanding of each topic:

a. Discuss extrinsic motivation, intrinsic motivation, and overjustification.

b. Discuss the managerial significance of the idea that people are different from each other. What does this imply about training and education?

2.7. Briefly describe the 14 points for management.

2.8. Describe the PDSA cycle and discuss its role in continuous improvement.

2.9. Define empowerment in the quality management sense.

References

1. K. E. Bullington, "5S for Suppliers," *Quality Progress,* January 2003, pp. 56–59.

2. W. E. Deming (1982), *Quality, Productivity, and Competitive Position* (Cambridge, MA: Massachusetts Institute of Technology).

3. W. E. Deming (1986), *Out of the Crisis* (Cambridge, MA: Massachusetts Institute of Technology Center for Advanced Engineering Studies).

4. W. E. Deming, "Foundation for Management of Quality in the Western World," revised April 1, 1990, delivered at a meeting of The Institute of Management Sciences in Osaka, July 24, 1989.

5. W. E. Deming (1993), *The New Economics for Industry, Government, Education* (Cambridge, MA: Massachusetts Institute of Technology).

6. W. E. Deming (1994), *The New Economics for Industry, Government, Education,* 2nd ed., (Cambridge, MA: Massachusetts Institute of Technology).

7. A. Gabor (1990), *The Man Who Discovered Quality* (New York: Time Books).

8. H. Gitlow and S. Gitlow (1987), *The Deming Guide to Quality and Competitive Position* (Englewood Cliffs, NJ: Prentice Hall).

9. H. Gitlow, "Total Quality Management in the United States and Japan," *APO Productivity Journal,* Asian Productivity Organization, Tokyo, Winter 1993–1994, pp. 3–27.

10. H. Gitlow, "A Comparison of Japanese Total Quality Control and Dr. Deming's Theory of Management," *The American Statistician,* Vol. 48, No. 3, August 1994, pp. 197–203.

11. H. Gitlow, "Understanding Total Quality Creation (TQC): The Japanese School of Thought," *Quality Engineering,* Vol. 7, No. 3, 1995, pp. 523–542.

12. H. Gitlow (2000), *Quality Management Systems* (Boca Raton, FL: St. Lucie Press).

13. H. Hirano (1996), *5S for Operators: 5 Pillars of the Visual Workplace* (Productivity Press).

14. H. Hirano (1990), *5 Pillars of the Visual Workplace* (Productivity Press).

15. M. Imai (1986), *KAIZEN: The Keys to Japan's Competitive Success* (New York: Random House Business Division).

16. H. Neave (1990), *The Deming Dimension* (Knoxville, TN: SPC Press, 1990).

17. D. Pietenpol and H. Gitlow, "Empowerment and the System of Profound Knowledge," *International Journal of Quality Science,* Vol. 1, No. 3, 1996.

18. W. Scherkenbach (1986), *The Deming Route to Quality and Productivity: Road Maps and Roadblocks* (Washington, DC: CeePress).

19. W. A. Shewhart, *Economic Control of Quality of Manufactured Products* (New York: Van Nostrand and Company, 1931; reprinted by the American Society for Quality Control, Milwaukee, 1980).

20. W. A. Shewhart and W. E. Deming, *Statistical Methods from the Viewpoint of Quality Control* (Washington, DC: Graduate School, Department of Agriculture, 1939; Dover Press, 1986).

21. Q. R. Skrebec, "Ancient Process Control and Its Modern Implications," *Quality Progress,* Vol. 25, 1990, pp. 49–52.

22. U.S. Census Bureau, American Fact Finder, "Quick Tables: QT-03. Profiles of Selected Economic Characteristics: 2000, Census 2000 Supplementary Survey Summary Tables," 2000.

23. M. Walton (1986), *The Deming Management Method* (New York: Perigee Books, Putnam Publishing Group).

24. M. Walton (1990), *Deming Management at Work* (New York: Putnam).

Chapter 3

Fundamentals of Statistical Studies

Sections

Chapter Objectives

- To define statistics and the two types of statistical studies
- To discuss the purpose of an enumerative study
- To describe and illustrate how to select a simple random sample for an enumerative study
- To describe and illustrate how to conduct a basic enumerative study
- To discuss the purpose of an analytic study
- To describe and illustrate how to conduct a basic analytic study
- To discuss the distinction between enumerative and analytic studies

Introduction

Statistics is the study of numeric data to improve decision-making. The study of numeric data incorporates operationally defining variables (for example, shape = round, color = red, weight = 5 pounds, satisfaction = very dissatisfied) so that all stakeholders of the definition agree as to its meaning, understanding the sources of variation in process or population variables and understanding interactions between variables (for example, do bake time and oven temperature interact to affect the taste of a cake). There are two types of statistical studies: enumerative studies and analytic studies. Enumerative studies are investigations of populations fixed in space and time, whose purpose is to estimate the characteristics of the population, for example, determining the quality of the coal on a particular barge to establish a worthy price for that barge of coal. Analytic studies are investigations of processes that have a past and present and will have a future, whose purpose is to predict the future output of the process, for example, determining the future quality of barges of coal from a particular coal supplier. In this chapter we discuss appropriate approaches to the two types of statistical studies.

Purpose and Definition of Statistics

The purpose of **statistics,** according to Deming, is to study and understand variation in processes and populations, interactions among the variables in processes and populations, and operational definitions (definitions of process and population variables that promote effective communication between people), and ultimately to take action to reduce variation in a process or population. Hence, statistics can be broadly defined as the study of data to provide a basis for action on a population or process. [See Reference 3, p. 247.]

Types of Statistical Studies

Statistical studies can be either of two types: enumerative or analytic. **Enumerative studies** are statistical investigations that lead to action on a static population (that is, a group of items, people, etc. that exist in a given time period and/or at a given location). An example of an enumerative study is the estimation of the number of residents in Florida left homeless by a hurricane and the number of tents required to temporarily house them. This estimation might be performed to determine how much food must be shipped in to feed the residents. This is an enumerative study because it investigates the number of people in need at a specific point in time. Dynamic questions such as why the people are where they are or why they need the supplies that they need are not considered in an enumerative study. [See Reference 3, pp. 247–8.]

Other examples of enumerative studies are determining market share for "Rice Crispies" in households with a certain demographic profile; calculating statistics on births, deaths, income, education, and occupation, by area; estimating the incidence of AIDS in a given city; and assaying samples from a barge of coal to determine an appropriate price. All of these examples are time-specific and static; there is no reference to the past or the future.

Analytic studies are statistical investigations that lead to action on a dynamic process. They focus on the causes of patterns and variations that take place from year to year, from area to area, from class to class, or from one treatment to another [see Reference 3, p. 249]. An example is determining why grain production in an area is low and how it can be increased in the future. Other examples of analytic studies are testing varieties of wheat to determine the optimal type for a particular area's future production; comparing the output of two machine types over time to determine if one is more productive; comparing ways of advertising a product or service to increase market share; and measuring the effects of an action, such as change in speed, temperature, or ingredients, on an industrial process output. [See Reference 5, p. 26.] All of these examples focus on the future, not on the present. The information gathered is used to make dynamic decisions about a process: What type of wheat should be grown to achieve an optimal yield? Should we replace machine A with machine B to raise production? Is TV advertising more effective than print media for increasing market share? If we change the ingredients in our product, can we improve its quality and lower its cost?

Since this is a text on quality improvement, the primary focus will be on analytic studies.

Enumerative Studies

Basic Concepts

Enumerative studies are statistical investigations that lead to action on static populations. A **population** (or **universe**) is the totality of units, items, or people of interest that exist in a given time period and/or given location. If a population is to be studied, it must be operationally defined by listing all of its units, items, people, and so on. This list is called a **frame.** It is assumed that the population and frame are identical. If they are not, then bias and error will occur in any study results. There are many reasons that a frame may differ from the population it is supposed to define, for example, omissions, errors, or double counting. Regardless of the type of error, the difference between the frame and the population is called the **gap.**

A **sample** is a portion of the frame under investigation, and is selected so that information can be drawn from it about the frame. For example, 100 randomly selected accounts receivable drawn from a list, or frame, of 10,000 accounts receivable constitute a sample. There are two basic types of samples: nonrandom and random.

Nonrandom samples are selected on the basis of convenience (**convenience sample**), the opinion of an expert (**judgment sample**), or a quota to ensure proportional representation of certain classes of items, units, or people in the sample (**quota sample**). All nonrandom samples have the same shortcoming: they are subject to an unknown degree of bias in their results. This bias is caused by the absence of a frame. The sampled items are not selected from an operationally defined population via a frame; hence, classes of items or people in the population may be systematically denied representation in the sample. This may cause bias in the results. Consequently nonrandom samples should be used only when better information is too costly to obtain.

To demonstrate the bias of a nonrandom sample, suppose we wish to estimate the average salary in a manufacturing firm. The list of names is organized by work crews.

Every fifth name is selected as part of the sample. But since the list is organized by work crews, it first lists the foreman and then 4 workers. Thus the sample will contain either all foremen or all workers, depending on the starting point. This creates bias in the results—the average salary will not reflect the true average because of the method of selecting the sample.

Random samples are selected so that every element in the frame has a known probability of selection. Types of random samples include simple, stratified, and cluster. [See References 2, 7, 8, 9.] All random samples allow generalized statements to be made about the frame from the sample. These generalized statements form the basis for action on the population under study.

A random sample is selected by operationally defining a procedure that utilizes random numbers in the selection of the sampled items from the frame to eliminate bias and hold uncertainty within known limits. Seven steps are involved in selecting a simple random sample:

Step 1. Count the number of elements in the frame, N.

Step 2. Number the elements in the frame from 1 through N. If N is 25, then the elements in the frame should be numbered from 01 through 25, as in Table 3.1. All elements must receive an identification number with the same number of digits.

Step 3. Select a page in Table B.2 in Appendix B, a table of random numbers. For example, select page 787.

Step 4. On the selected page of random numbers, randomly select a column of numbers, randomly select a starting point in that column, and use as many digits as there are digits in N (two digits in the case of N = 25). For example, beginning with the first column in Table B.2 on page 787, selecting the seventh row of that column as the starting point, and using the first two digits of each number in that column, the first random number is 19. Table 3.2a shows a list of 39 consecutive random numbers obtained in this way.

Step 5. Determine the necessary sample size. This calculation is discussed in sampling texts and basic statistics texts [see References 2, 7, 8, 9]. Let n be this number. Assume n = 6 in this example.

Step 6. From the chosen column on the selected page, select the first six two-digit numbers between 01 and 25, inclusive. If a number is encountered that is smaller than 01

TABLE 3.1	Item	Identification Number
Identification		
Frame	A	01
	B	02
	C	03
	D	04
	E	05
	F	06
	.	.
	.	.
	.	.
	Y	25

TABLE 3.2
**Random
Sample
Selection**

(a) Random Numbers from Page 787 of Table B.2 in Appendix B		
19	30	40
09	28	78
31	13	98
67	60	69
61	13	39
04	34	62
05	28	56
73	59	90
54	87	09
42	29	34
27	62	12
49	38	69
29	40	93

(b) Random Sample of Size n = 6 from Frame of Size N = 25		
Sample Number	Identification Number	Items
1	19	S
2	09	I
3	04	D
4	05	E
5	13	M
6	12	L

(e.g., 00) or larger than 25 (e.g., 31), ignore the number and continue down the column. If an acceptable number appears more than once, ignore every repetition and continue moving down the column until six unique numbers between 01 and 25 have been selected. If the bottom of the page is reached before six unique random numbers are obtained, go to the top of the page and move down the next two-digit column. Table 3.2b shows the six random numbers selected and the corresponding items comprising the sample.

Step 7.   Finally, analyze the information as a basis for action.

Two important points to remember are: (1) different samples of size six will yield different results, and (2) different methods of measurement will also yield different results. Random samples, however, do not have bias, and the sampling error can be held to known limits by increasing the sample size. These are the advantages of random sampling over nonrandom sampling.

Conducting an Enumerative Study

The following 13 steps present a guide for conducting an enumerative study. The steps are the same whether the study is based on a complete count of the population or a sample. [See Reference 3, pp. 4–9.]

Step 1.   Specify the reason(s) you want to conduct the study (for example, to estimate the average number of sick days per employee in the XYZ Company in 2003). If this average is greater than 8.0 days, then a preventive health care plan will be instituted. If it is less than or equal to 8.0 days, the current plan will be maintained.

Step 2. Specify the population to be studied. In our example, the population would be all full-time employees in the XYZ Company in 2003. An employee is considered full-time in 2003 if he had full-time status designation at any time during the year.

Step 3. Construct the frame (a list of all full-time employees). All who will use the study's results as a basis for action must agree that the frame represents the population upon which they want to take action.

Step 4. Perform secondary research (such as the examination of prepublished data) to determine how much information is already available about the problem under investigation. For example, check the Human Resources Department's records.

Step 5. Determine the type of study to be conducted, such as mail survey, personal interviews, or chemical analysis of units. In this example, we would survey employee absentee cards for 2003.

Step 6. Make it possible for respondents to give clear, understandable information and/or for the researcher to elicit clear, understandable information. For example, the method for analyzing absentee cards should be clear and straightforward. Consider the problem of nonresponse: refusal to answer, no one at home, and missing items to be studied are all possible causes of nonresponse. How significant is the nonresponse? Will it impair the study results? What can be done to reduce it? Establish a procedure for dealing with and reducing nonresponse problems. In this example, be sure no absentee cards are missing, and make sure the data gatherers know how to interpret the absentee cards.

Step 7. Establish the sampling plan to be used, determine the amount of allowable error in the results, and calculate the cost of the sampling plan. At this stage, Steps 1 and 2 may need revisions because of cost considerations. For example, we may decide to draw a simple random sample of employee absentee cards using random numbers, at a cost of $1 per card, assuming an allowable error of one-quarter of a day in the estimate.

Step 8. Establish procedures to deal with nonresponse problems and differences between interviewers, testers, inspectors, and so on. For example, be able to assess differences in collected data due to differences in the data gatherers' abilities.

Step 9. Prepare unambiguous instructions for the data gatherers that cover all phases of data collection. Supervisors may require special additional instructions. Train all data gatherers and supervisors. Use statistical methods to determine when their training is complete, as discussed in Deming's Point 6 in Chapter 2.

Step 10. Establish plans for data handling including format of tables, headings, and number of classes.

Step 11. Pretest the data-gathering instrument and data-gathering instructions. If pretests show a high refusal rate or generate unsatisfactory-quality data, the study may be modified or abandoned. Conduct a dry run with the data gatherers to ensure that they understand and adhere to established procedures. Revise the data-gathering instrument and instructions on the basis of the information collected during the pretest. Finalize all aspects of the study's procedure.

Step 12. Conduct the study and the tabulations. It is critical that the study be carried out according to plans. From the gathered data, calculate the sampling errors of interest. This is important so that the study's users can understand the degree of uncertainty present in the study results. In our example, we would calculate the standard error for the average number of days absent per employee.

Step 13. Interpret and publish the results so that decision makers can take appropriate action. For example, if the average number of days absent per employee is greater than eight, then establish the preventive health care program.

In conducting an enumerative study, note that Step 7 requires random sampling rather than nonrandom sampling, so that the information can serve as a basis for action with a known degree of uncertainty. The result of a nonrandom sample in an enumerative study is worth no more than the reputation of the person who signs the report, because the margin of uncertainty in the estimate reported depends entirely on that person's knowledge and judgment, rather than on objective, quantifiable methods. [See Reference 5, p. 29.]

Analytic Studies

Basic Concepts

Analytic studies are statistical investigations that lead to actions on the cause-and-effect systems of a process (that is, the systems creating the past, present, and future output of a process). [See Reference 8, pp. 54–55.] An analytic study's aim is the prediction of a process's future state so that it can be improved and/or innovated over time.

Recall that in an enumerative study, a population is the total number of units, items, or people of interest that exist in a given time period and/or location. The concept of a population does not exist for an analytic study because future process output, which does not yet exist, cannot be part of the population. A frame cannot exist without a population. Lack of a population and frame makes it impossible to draw a random sample to study the cause-and-effect systems that dictate a process's behavior.

The inability to study a process in an enumerative sense seemingly creates difficulty in understanding its underlying cause-and-effect systems. However, models can be used to study these cause-and-effect systems. These models include simulations of the process, prototypes of a product, flowcharts of a process, operational definitions of process or product quality characteristics, and cause-and-effect diagrams describing the factors and conditions that influence quality characteristics. [See Reference 10, p. 55.] Unfortunately, it is impossible to consider all of the factors that will influence the process's output. Conditions will change. There will always be some uncertainty. In an analytic study (unlike an enumerative study), there is no underlying statistical theory that enables quantification of this uncertainty.

Expert opinion is invaluable in understanding the magnitude of the uncertainty caused by changes to a process (changes from, for example, new equipment, new workers, new tools, new methods, or different operating conditions). Generally, this uncertainty is best explained by an expert who is involved with the process under study: the individuals directly involved with a process know more about it than anyone else.

Conducting an Analytic Study

Improvement or innovation of a process is accomplished using the plan-do-study-act (PDSA) cycle. The **PDSA cycle** is used to narrow the difference between process performance and customer (either internal or external) needs and wants.

In the *plan* stage of the PDSA cycle, the aim is to determine an improvement or innovation to a process that will narrow the difference between process performance and customer needs and wants. In the plan stage, where we study and understand a process, the many tools and methods used include (but are not limited to) flowcharts (discussed in Chapter 4) and cause-and-effect diagrams (discussed under "Diagnostic Tools and Techniques" in Chapter 10).

A plan involves modifying a process from its existing structure or flowchart to a revised structure or revised flowchart. The revised structure or revised flowchart incorporates an improvement or innovation to the process under study. Think of a plan as follows: I plan to change the process under study from operating as shown in the existing flowchart to operating as shown in the revised flowchart.

In analytic studies, **judgment samples** can be drawn from a stable process to study its output. Judgment samples are samples selected on the basis of an expert's opinion. Generally, if a process is stable, any slice of process output (a set of judgment samples) will be very revealing about the process's future behavior. The use of judgment samples to study a process's output will be discussed in detail in Chapters 6 through 9.

The *do* stage of the PDSA cycle requires that experiments be conducted to determine the effectiveness of the plan, or revised flowchart, established in the previous stage. Experiments should be conducted on a small scale, using a laboratory, an office or plant site, or, with consent, even a customer's location. The results of the work in the do stage are examined in the study stage.

The aim of the *study* stage is to determine if the plan has been effective in decreasing the difference between process performance and customer needs and wants. If the plan has not been effective, we return to the plan stage to attempt to devise a new course of action. However, if the plan has been effective, the process owner should move on to the act stage.

In the *act* stage, the plan should be integrated into the process. This may involve anything from minor alterations to the process to a major overhaul of an entire operating procedure. Regardless, the act stage includes training all relevant personnel with respect to the details of the revised process and putting the revised flowchart into relevant training manuals. Keep in mind that actions to improve a process's future functioning are rational only if the process is stable. **Process stability** means that there are no special sources of variation present in the process. Methods for discovering special sources of variation will be discussed in Chapters 6 through 9. Stability allows a process expert to predict the process's future performance with a high degree of belief.

Errors in Analytic Studies

Two types of errors can occur in any study. A **type I error** occurs when action is taken on a process when it should have been left alone. A **type II error** occurs when we fail to take action on a process when action is appropriate. It is impossible to calculate the probability of either type of error in an analytic study because we cannot know how things would have turned out if an alternative action, other than the one chosen, had been selected. Without the benefit of a quantifiable degree of belief of making type I and type II errors, we need a methodology for combining expertise with statistical notions.

Design of Analytic Studies

We can increase our degree of belief in a prediction from an analytic study by considering:

1. Building of knowledge in a sequential fashion
2. Testing over a wide range of conditions
3. Selection of units for the study

Building of Knowledge in a Sequential Fashion

Deming's theory of management requires that an organizational, or team, focus be given to quality improvement efforts. In other words, improvement efforts should be based on an organizational belief that these efforts will decrease the difference between customer needs and process performance. Given the selection of a process for improvement efforts, the process must be described by documenting and defining it, as discussed in Chapter 4. The PDSA cycle can then be used to decrease the difference between customer needs and process performance. Experiments performed in the iterations of the PDSA cycle, in combination with theory about the process from subject matter experts, may increase the degree of belief in predictions about the future behavior of the process under study. This degree of belief is increased as sequential predictions about the process's future behavior come closer to the actual performance of the process.

Note that there can be no significant prediction about the future behavior of a process without knowledge of that process. Further, knowledge of the process is continually improved and increased through successive iterations of the PDSA cycle. It is the predictive ability of knowledge that is the ultimate measure of its value.

Testing over a Wide Range of Conditions

The degree of belief in the predictive value of the knowledge gained from an analytic study is increased if the analytic study yields the same results over a wide range of conditions. Only an expert in the subject matter under study can answer questions such as how wide a range of conditions is adequate to have a degree of belief sufficient to make a prediction, or how close to actual conditions the experimental conditions must be to have a degree of belief high enough to make predictions. These questions cannot be answered solely by statistical theory—but statistical methods can provide guidance for increasing the degree of belief in the knowledge gained from analytic studies.

Selection of the Units for the Study

Since there is no frame in an analytic study, there can be no random sample and quantifiable degree of uncertainty in a prediction about the future. Judgment samples are used to conduct analytic studies. [See Reference 4, pp. 146–152.] The judgment of a subject matter expert determines both the conditions under which a process will be studied and the measurements that will be taken for each set of conditions. Moreover, it is the expert who judges whether the results of an analytic study provide a sufficient degree of belief to take action on a process.

In analytic studies, judgment samples are almost always superior to random samples. For example, consider an analytic study to determine which of two machines is less sensitive to worker-to-worker variation. We need this information to purchase whichever machine yields more uniform output, regardless of operator. Suppose we have funds to include only 10 of 50 operators in the study. In this case, a random sample of the 10 operators would yield a quantifiable degree of uncertainty in the measurement variation, but the conditions under which the operators were studied will never be seen again; in the future, there will be new operators, new materials, and different training. For this study, a judgment sample is more appropriate. For example, a judgment sample might include the five most experienced operators and the five least experienced operators. Suppose both machines perform best when used by an experienced operator and worst when used by an inexperienced operator. The degree of belief that the machine with the lower worker-to-worker variation is the machine to purchase will be greater if the variation is estimated from a judgment sample rather than from a sample of 10 randomly selected workers.

Analysis of Data from Analytic Studies

The purpose of an analytic study is to improve knowledge so that predictions can be made about the future behavior of a process. Yet Deming stated of analytic studies, "Analysis of variance, t-tests, confidence intervals, and other statistical techniques taught in the books, however interesting, are inappropriate because they provide no basis for prediction and because they bury the information contained in the order of production." [See Reference 6.] Thus, most techniques that are useful in enumerative studies are inappropriate for analytic studies. The reader should be aware that this is a minority point of view among statisticians, shared by adherents to Deming's view of statistics.

The **standard deviation** of a stable process (a process exhibiting only common causes of variation) can be used to distinguish past common variation from past special variation. But calculation of the standard deviation based on the assumption of a stable process does not consider the most important source of uncertainty in an analytic study— predicting the process's future behavior.

A Stable Process

When a process is stable, it is easier to determine the effect that changes to the process have on the process's future behavior. Hence, a stable process provides a forum for a subject matter expert to conduct experiments to gain knowledge to predict the future behavior of the process. Unfortunately, stability in the past does not guarantee stability in the future. Past conditions that created the stable process may never be seen again. As a result, responsibility for prediction still rests with the subject matter expert.

Graphical Analysis

Because the distribution of a process that existed in the past cannot be used to predict the distribution of a future process, we need an approach to prediction that does not rely on past distribution statistics.

The general approach for conducting analytic studies relies on graphical techniques, such as control charts, discussed in Chapters 6, 7, and 8, which utilize both statistical knowledge and subject matter knowledge to learn about the process to predict its future behavior. Knowledge of the process gives meaning to control chart patterns and helps distinguish common variation from special variation. For example, knowledge of a process might lead researchers to expect that when eight or more points in a row increase in value, tool wear is the likely special source of variation. This prediction about the process's behavior is generally a combination of subject matter knowledge and statistical knowledge.

Interactions between process variables can dramatically alter process behavior. For example, one machine might be better when used by an experienced operator, while another machine might be better when used by an inexperienced operator. Graphical techniques will allow a process and its interactions to be studied in a dynamic fashion over a wide range of conditions.

Distinction between Enumerative and Analytic Studies

A simple rule exists for deciding whether a study should be enumerative or analytic. If a 100 percent sample of the frame answers the question under investigation, the study is enumerative; if not, the study is analytic. [See Reference 5, p. 26.] A 100 percent sample can be obtained in an enumerative problem because items are drawn from the frame, which is composed of all the elements in the population. A 100 percent sample cannot be obtained in an analytic problem because there is no frame. We are merely studying the output of a dynamic process with an eye to taking action on the process that created the output data.

Statistical studies are critical components of quality improvement efforts. When conducting research for the improvement of quality of design, quality of conformance, and quality of performance, an understanding of the different types of statistical studies allows the information generated by the study to be used rationally as a basis for quality improvement or innovation action.

Summary

In this chapter, we discussed the purpose of statistics: to study and understand variation in processes and populations, interactions among the variables in processes and populations, operational definitions (definitions of process and population variables that promote effective communication between people), and ultimately to take action to reduce variation in a process or population.

There are two types of statistical studies: enumerative and analytic. Enumerative studies are statistical investigations that lead to action on a static population (that is, a group of items, people, etc. that exist in a given time period and/or at a given location). Analytic studies are statistical investigations that lead to action on a dynamic process. They focus on the causes of patterns and variations that take place from year to year, from area to area, from class to class, or from one treatment to another.

Enumerative studies investigate populations. A population (or universe) is the totality of units, items, or people of interest that exist in a given time period and/or given location. If a population is to be studied, it must be operationally defined by listing all of its units, items, people, and so on. This list is called a frame. The difference between the frame and the population is called the gap. A sample is a portion of the frame under investigation, and is selected so that information can be drawn from it about the frame.

Nonrandom samples are selected on the basis of convenience (convenience sample), the opinion of an expert (judgment sample), or a quota to ensure proportional representation of certain classes of items, units, or people in the sample (quota sample). All nonrandom samples have the same shortcoming: they are subject to an unknown degree of bias in their results. This bias is caused by the absence of a frame.

Random samples are selected so that every element in the frame has a known probability of selection. Types of random samples include simple, stratified, and cluster. All random samples allow generalized statements to be made about the frame from the sample. These generalized statements form the basis for action on the population under study. A random sample is selected by operationally defining a procedure that utilizes random numbers in the selection of the sampled items from the frame to eliminate bias and hold uncertainty within known limits.

Analytic studies investigate processes. Improvement or innovation of a process is accomplished using the plan-do-study-act (PDSA) cycle. The PDSA cycle is used to narrow the difference between process performance and customer (either internal or external) needs and wants.

Two types of errors can occur in any study. A type I error occurs when action is taken on a process when it should have been left alone. A type II error occurs when we fail to take action on a process when action is appropriate. It is impossible to calculate the probability of either type of error in an analytic study because we cannot know how things would have turned out if an alternative action, other than the one chosen, had been selected. Without the benefit of a quantifiable degree of belief of making type I and type II errors, we need a methodology for combining expertise with statistical notions.

We can increase our degree of belief in a prediction from an analytic study by considering building of knowledge in a sequential fashion, testing over a wide range of conditions, and selection of units for the study.

It is necessary to distinguish between enumerative and analytic studies, because they require different sampling and computational techniques. A simple rule to distinguish between enumerative and analytic studies is: if a 100 percent sample of the frame answers the question under investigation, the study is enumerative; if not, the study is analytic. We must also understand the different types of statistical studies so that the results can be used for quality improvement and innovation actions.

Key Terms

analytic study, *59*	PDSA cycle, *63*	standard deviation, *66*
convenience sample, *59*	population, *59*	statistics, *58*
enumerative study, *58*	process stability, *64*	statistical studies, *58*
frame, *59*	quota sample, *59*	type I error, *64*
gap, *59*	random sample, *60*	type II error, *64*
judgment sample, *59, 64*	sample, *59*	universe, *59*
nonrandom sample, *59*		

Exercises

3.1. Define both types of statistical studies. List two examples of each type of study in quality improvement efforts.

3.2. Define the following terms: population, frame, gap, random sample, simple random sample.

3.3. Define the following terms: convenience sample, judgment sample, quota sample.

3.4. List the steps required to draw a simple random sample.

3.5. List the steps required to perform an enumerative study.

3.6. Discuss why judgment samples cannot be used as a rational basis for action in enumerative studies.

3.7. Discuss why judgment samples can be used as a rational basis for action in analytic studies.

3.8. Specify a rule to distinguish between enumerative and analytic studies.

References

1. M. Berenson, D. Levine, and T. Krehbiel (2004), *Basic Business Statistics: Concepts and Applications,* 9th ed. (Upper Saddle River, NJ: Prentice Hall).

2. W. Cochran (1963), *Sampling Techniques,* 2nd ed. (New York: John Wiley & Sons).

3. W. Edwards Deming (1950), *Some Theory of Sampling* (New York: John Wiley & Sons).

4. W. Edwards Deming, "On Probability as a Basis for Action," *The American Statistician,* Vol. 29, No. 4, November 1975, pp. 146–152.

5. W. Edwards Deming, "On the Use of Judgment-Samples," *Reports of Statistical Applications,* Vol. 23, March 1976, p. 26.

6. W. Edwards Deming (1986), *Out of the Crisis* (Cambridge, MA: Massachusetts Institute of Technology Center for Advanced Engineering Study).

7. H. Gitlow and R. Oppenheim (1982), *STATCITY: Understanding Statistics Through Realistic Applications* (Homewood, IL: Irwin).

8. M. Hansen, W. Hurwitz, and W. Madow (1953), *Sample Survey Method and Theory: Vol. 1— Methods and Applications* (New York: John Wiley & Sons).

9. W. Mendenhall, R. Scheaffer, and L. Ott (1996), *Elementary Survey Sampling,* 5th ed. (Belmont, CA: Duxbury Press).

10. R. Moen, T. Nolan, and L. Provost (1991), *Improving Quality through Experimentation* (New York: McGraw-Hill).

Chapter 4

Defining and Documenting a Process

Sections

Chapter Objectives

- To define and document a process in an analytic study
- To discuss the concept of feedback in a process
- To discuss the construction and use of a flowchart for communication and process improvement
- To discuss the importance of operational definitions in defining and documenting a process

Introduction

Almost every aspect of life is a process: the aging process, the business life cycle process, and the educational process, among others. A process transforms inputs into outputs to accomplish an aim or mission. For example, a basic business statistics course (process) transforms students (inputs) into professional users of data (outputs) to create knowledgeable business people (mission). We saw in Chapter 3 that an analytic study is a statistical investigation of a process with the purpose of predicting the future nature of its output. However, an analytic study can only be performed on a process that has a known identity; that is, the process must be defined and documented. We will see in this chapter that processes can be documented and defined with flowcharts, or pictorial summaries that clarify the steps and decisions in a process. Data from the process are then generated through feedback loops, enabling further process improvement activities.

Empowerment Revisited

We saw in Chapter 2 that **empowerment** provides an employee with:

1. The opportunity to define and document processes
2. The opportunity to learn about processes through training and development
3. The opportunity to improve and innovate best-practice methods that make up processes
4. The latitude to use her own judgment to make decisions within the context of best-practice methods
5. An environment of trust in which superiors will not react negatively to the latitude taken by people making decisions within the context of best-practice methods.

The operational definition of empowerment has two parts. In the first part, employees are empowered to develop and document best-practice methods using the SDSA cycle. In the second part, employees are empowered to improve or innovate best-practice methods through application of the PDSA cycle.

SDSA Cycle Revisited

Recall from Chapter 1 that the **SDSA cycle** is a tool that helps employees define and document a process; it helps to create an identity for a process. It includes four steps:

Standardize. Employees develop best-practice methods using tools such as flowcharts.

Do. Employees conduct experiments using the proposed best-practice methods.

Study. Employees research the effectiveness of the best-practice methods, as measured through key indicators.

Act. Managers standardize best-practice methods and formalize them through training.

Analytic Studies Revisited

Analytic studies are statistical investigations that lead to action on a dynamic process. Consequently, they are the vehicle for using the SDSA cycle in the context of the first level of empowerment to define and document a process.

Process Basics

A **process** is the transformation of inputs (personnel/services, equipment, materials/goods, methods, and environment) into outputs (personnel/services, equipment, materials/goods,

FIGURE 4.1
Basic Process

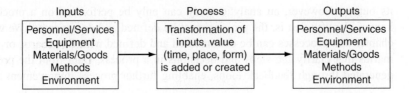

Inputs	Process	Outputs
Personnel/Services Equipment Materials/Goods Methods Environment	Transformation of inputs, value (time, place, form) is added or created	Personnel/Services Equipment Materials/Goods Methods Environment

methods, and environment), as shown in Figure 4.1. The transformation involves the addition or creation of value in one of three aspects: **time, place,** or **form:**

Time value. Something is available when it is needed. For example, you have food when you are hungry, or material inputs are ready on time.

Place value. Something is available where it is needed. For example, gas is in your tank (not in an oil field), or wood chips are in a paper mill.

Form value. Something is available in the way it is needed. For example, bread is sliced so it can fit in a toaster, or paper has three punched holes so it can be placed in a binder.

Processes exist in all aspects of organizations, and our understanding of them is crucial. Many people mistakenly think of only production processes. However, administration, sales, service, human resources, training, maintenance, paper flows, interdepartmental communication, and vendor relations are all processes as well, which can all be studied, documented, defined, improved, and innovated.

An organization is a multiplicity of micro subprocesses, all synergistically building to the macroprocess of that firm. It is important to realize that all processes have customers and suppliers who can be internal or external to the organization. A customer can be an end user or the next operation downstream. The customer does not have to be a human—it can be a machine. Similarly, a vendor can be another firm supplying subassemblies or services, or the prior operation upstream.

The Feedback Loop

An important aspect of a process is a **feedback loop,** which relates information about outputs back to the input stage and/or process stage. This information can be studied to help identify potential improvements and innovations to a process. A major purpose of analytic studies is to provide the information (flowing through feedback loops) needed to take action with respect to a process. Figure 4.2 depicts the feedback loops for a basic process.

Examples of Processes

An example of a process that most people are familiar with is the hiring process, as shown in Figure 4.3. The figure shows the **inputs, process,** and **outputs** of hiring an employee. The inputs (which include the candidate's resume, the information gathered from the interview with the candidate, and other data from references, former employers, and schools attended) are transformed into the output (which is an employee to fill a vacant position).

FIGURE 4.2
Feedback Loop

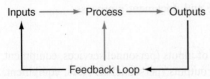

Inputs → Process → Outputs
Feedback Loop

FIGURE 4.3
Hiring Process

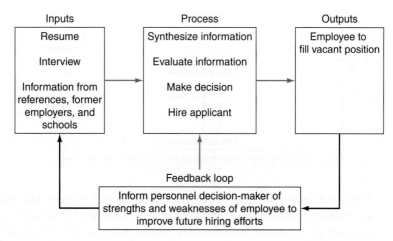

Inputs

| Resume |
| Interview |
| Information from references, former employers, and schools |

Process

| Synthesize information |
| Evaluate information |
| Make decision |
| Hire applicant |

Outputs

| Employee to fill vacant position |

Feedback loop

Inform personnel decision-maker of strengths and weaknesses of employee to improve future hiring efforts

The process involved in this transformation of inputs into output includes synthesizing and evaluating the information, making a decision, and hiring the candidate. An important aspect of this process is the feedback loop that enables the new employee's supervisor to report back to the personnel decision-maker as to the employee's suitability. The personnel decision-maker (supplier) and supervisor (customer) can use this information to work together to improve the hiring process.

Clerical functions are also processes. Figure 4.4 depicts the process of sending a memo in an organization. First, the manager inputs the information for the memo and her instructions regarding its distribution. Then the administrative assistant transforms the input, by typing it and distributing it, into the output (communication to the employees). The feedback loop is important because the manager and the employees can work together to improve the communication process.

FIGURE 4.4
Memo-Sending Process

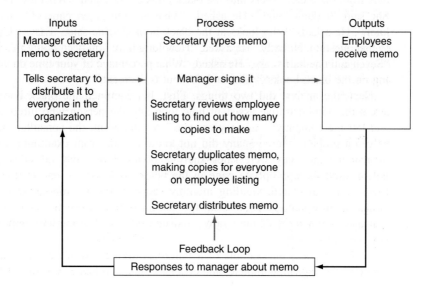

Inputs

| Manager dictates memo to secretary |
| Tells secretary to distribute it to everyone in the organization |

Process

| Secretary types memo |
| Manager signs it |
| Secretary reviews employee listing to find out how many copies to make |
| Secretary duplicates memo, making copies for everyone on employee listing |
| Secretary distributes memo |

Outputs

| Employees receive memo |

Feedback Loop

Responses to manager about memo

FIGURE 4.5
**Production
Process**

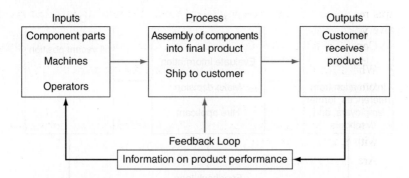

Figure 4.5 shows an example of a generic production process. The inputs (component parts, machines, and operators) are transformed in the process of making the final product and shipping it to the customer. The output is the customer's receipt of the product. Again, the feedback loop (which in this case is the customer's reporting back to the supplier on the product's performance) is vital. Communicating this way promotes cooperation on process improvement and innovation.

Defining and Documenting a Process

Defining and documenting a process is an important step toward improvement and/or innovation of the process. The following example demonstrates this point. In a study of an industrial laundry, an analyst began to diagram the flow of paperwork using a flowchart. While walking the green copy of an invoice through each step of its life cycle, he came upon an administrative assistant feverishly transcribing information from the green invoice copy into large black loose-leaf books. The analyst asked, "What are you doing?" so that he could record it on his flow diagram. She responded, "I'm recording the numbers from the green papers into the black books." He asked, "What are the black books?" She said, "I don't know." He asked, "What are the green papers?" She said, "I don't know." He asked, "Who looks at the black books?" She said, "Easy. I know the answer to that question. Nobody." He asked, "How long have you been doing this job?" She said, "Seven and one-half years." He asked, "What percentage of your time do you spend working on the black books?" She said, "About 60 percent."

Next, the analyst did two things. First, he examined the black books. Second, he asked the administrative assistant how long ago the person who hired and trained her had left the company: "Seven years ago." At this point, the consultant realized he had solved a problem the company did not know it had. From examining the black books he realized that they were sales analysis books. Every day all sales, by item, were entered into the appropriate page in the black book. At the end of each month, page totals were calculated, yielding monthly sales by items. Nobody was looking at the books because nobody knew what the administrative assistant was doing. The current manager assumed the administrative assistant was doing something important. After all, she seemed so busy.

This problem is an example of a failure to define and document a process to make sure that it is logical, complete, and efficient. As an epilogue, the administrative assistant was reassigned to other needed duties because the sales analysis had been computerized five years earlier.

Considering the following questions will help you define and document a process:

- Who owns the process? Who is responsible for the process's improvement?
- What are the boundaries of the process?
- What is the flow of the process?
- What are the process's objectives? What measurements are being taken on the process with respect to its objectives?
- Are process data valid?

Who Owns the Process?

Every process must have an owner (an individual who is responsible for the process). Process owners may have responsibilities extending beyond their departments, called **cross-functional responsibilities;** they must be high enough in the organization to influence the resources necessary to take action on a cross-functional process. In such cases, a process owner is the focal point for the process, but each function of the process is controlled by the line management within that function. The process owner will require representation from each function; these representatives are assigned by the line managers. They provide functional expertise to the process owner and are the promoters of change within their functions. A process owner is the coach and counsel of her process in an organization.

What Are the Boundaries of the Process?

Boundaries must be established for processes. These boundaries make it easier to establish process ownership and highlight the process's key interfaces with other (customer/vendor) processes. **Process interfaces** frequently are the source of process problems, which result from a failure to understand downstream requirements. Process interfaces must be carefully managed to prevent communication problems. Construction of operational definitions for critical process characteristics that are agreed upon by process owners on both sides of a process boundary will go a long way toward eliminating process interface problems. Operational definitions will be discussed in depth later in this chapter.

What Is the Flow of the Process?

A **flowchart** is a pictorial summary of the flows and decisions that comprise a process. It is used for defining and documenting the process. Figure 4.6 shows an example of a

FIGURE 4.6 **Quality of Design Study**

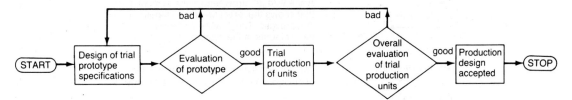

flowchart for one type of quality of design study, a production design study. In the design phase, design engineers determine detailed specifications for the product. Next, they prepare a prototype of the product. Then the prototype is tested and evaluated. It can be judged as good or bad. If it is bad, it returns to the design stage for redesign. If it is good, it moves to the next phase, trial production. After this stage, the product is again evaluated. If it is bad, it returns to the design stage. If it is good, the production design is accepted and full-scale production begins.

A flowchart can help a manager, designer, analyst, or anyone else understand, define, document, study, improve, or innovate a process.

Flowchart Symbols

The American National Standards Institute, Inc. (ANSI) has approved a standard set of flowchart symbols that are used for defining and documenting a process. The shape of the symbol and the information written within the symbol provide information about that particular step or decision in a process. Figure 4.7 shows the basic symbols for flowcharting that standardize the definition and documentation of a process. [See Reference 5, pp. 142–147.]

Types of Flowcharts

This section describes two types of flowcharts. [See Reference 3.]

FIGURE 4.7
Flowchart Symbols

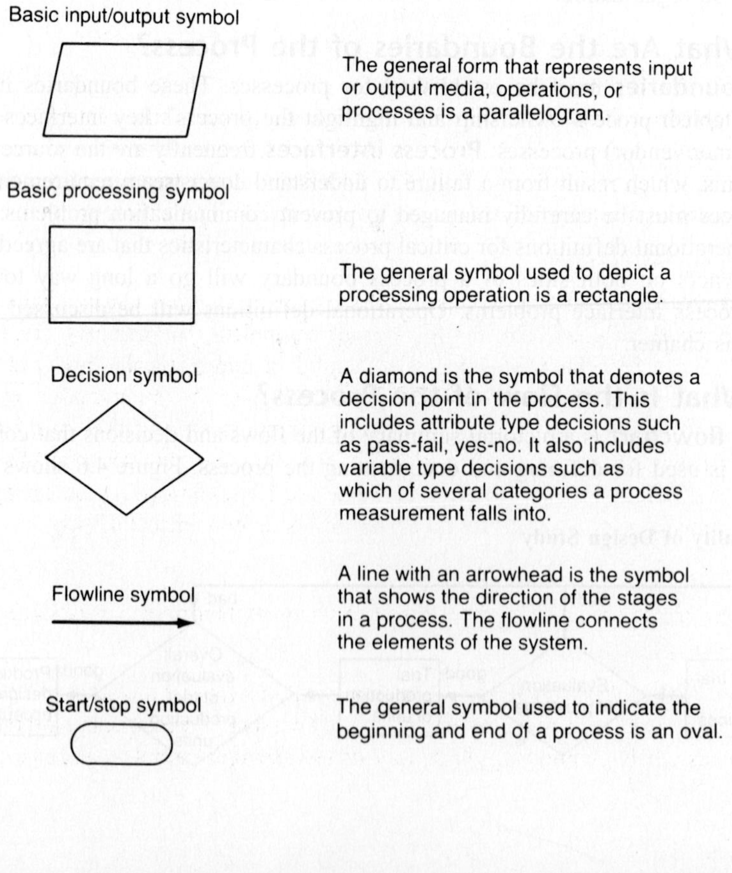

Basic input/output symbol

The general form that represents input or output media, operations, or processes is a parallelogram.

Basic processing symbol

The general symbol used to depict a processing operation is a rectangle.

Decision symbol

A diamond is the symbol that denotes a decision point in the process. This includes attribute type decisions such as pass-fail, yes-no. It also includes variable type decisions such as which of several categories a process measurement falls into.

Flowline symbol

A line with an arrowhead is the symbol that shows the direction of the stages in a process. The flowline connects the elements of the system.

Start/stop symbol

The general symbol used to indicate the beginning and end of a process is an oval.

FIGURE 4.8
Layout
Flowchart

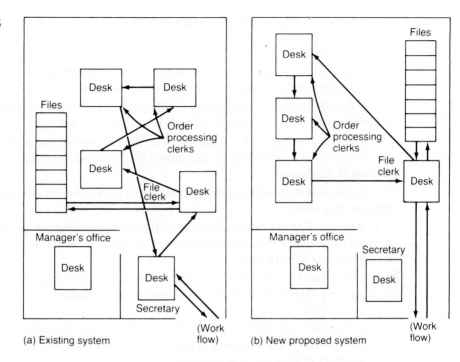

(a) Existing system   (Work flow)   (b) New proposed system   (Work flow)

Systems Flowchart

A **systems flowchart** is a pictorial representation of the sequence of operations and decisions that make up a process. It shows what is being done in a process. See Figure 4.6 again for an example of a systems flowchart. It represents each phase or stage in the process of a quality of design study using standard flowcharting symbols.

Layout Flowchart

A **layout flowchart** depicts the floor plan of an area, usually including the flow of paperwork or goods and the location of equipment, file cabinets, storage areas, and so on. These flowcharts are especially helpful in improving the layout to more efficiently utilize a space. Figure 4.8 shows a layout flowchart before and after flowcharting analysis and flow improvement. The existing system is shown in Figure 4.8a; the new proposed system appears in Figure 4.8b. This flowchart includes the flow of work along with the floor plan and location of desks and files. Comparing the existing and proposed systems is simple when the process's flow is documented this way.

Advantages of a Flowchart

Flowcharting a process, as opposed to using written or verbal descriptions, has several advantages:

• A flowchart functions as a communications tool. It provides an easy way to convey ideas between engineers, managers, hourly personnel, vendors, and others in the extended process. It is a concrete, visual way of representing complex systems.

• A flowchart functions as a planning tool. Designers of processes are greatly aided by flowcharts. They enable a visualization of the elements of new or modified processes and their interactions while still in the planning stages.

• A flowchart provides an overview of the system. The critical elements and steps of the process are easily viewed in the context of a flowchart.

• A flowchart removes unnecessary details and breaks down the system so designers and others get a clear, unencumbered look at what they're creating.

• A flowchart defines roles. It demonstrates the functions of personnel, workstations, and subprocesses in a system. It also shows the personnel, operations, and locations involved in the process.

• A flowchart demonstrates interrelationships. It shows how the elements of a process relate to each other.

• A flowchart promotes logical accuracy. It enables the viewer to spot errors in logic. Planning is facilitated because designers have to clearly break down all of the elements and operations of the process.

• A flowchart facilitates troubleshooting. It is an excellent diagnostic tool. Problems in the process, failures in the system, and barriers to communication can be detected by using a flowchart.

• A flowchart documents a system. This record of a system enables anyone to easily examine and understand the system. Flowcharts facilitate changing a system because the documentation of what exists is available.

Flowcharts can be applied in any type of organization to aid in defining and documenting a process, and ultimately improving and innovating that process. Flowcharts are simple to use, provided that appropriate following guidelines are followed, in keeping with standard practices. [See Reference 3.] These guidelines are shown in Exhibit 4.1.

EXHIBIT 4.1

Guidelines for Systems-Type Flowcharts

1. Flowcharts are drawn from the top of a page to the bottom and from left to right.
2. The activity being flowcharted should be carefully defined, and this definition should be made clear to the reader.
3. Where the activity starts and where it ends should be determined.
4. Each step of the activity should be described using "one-verb" descriptions (e.g., "prepare statement" or "design prototype").
5. Each step of the activity should be kept in its proper sequence.
6. The scope or range of the activity being flowcharted should be carefully observed. Any branches that leave the activity being charted shouldn't be drawn on that flowchart.
7. Use the standard flowcharting symbols.

Constructive Opportunities to Change a Process

When you use a flowchart, changing a process is facilitated by:

1. Finding the sections of the process that are weak (for example, parts of the process that generate a high defect rate).

2. Determining the parts of the process that are within the process owner's control.

3. Isolating the elements in the process that affect customers.

If these three conditions exist simultaneously, an excellent opportunity to constructively modify a process has been found. In general, process improvements have a greater chance of success if they are either nonpolitical or have the appropriate political support, and either do not require capital investment or have the necessary financial resources.

What Are the Process's Objectives?

A key responsibility of a process owner is to clearly state **process objectives** that are consistent with **organizational objectives.** An example of an organizational objective is "Strive to continually provide our customers with higher-quality products/services at an attractive price that will meet their needs." Each process owner can find meaning and a starting point in the adaptation of this organizational objective to his process's objectives. For example, a process owner in the purchasing department could translate the preceding organizational objective into the following subset of objectives:

1. Continuously monitor the purchasing department's customers (e.g., maintenance department, administration department) to determine their needs with respect to:
   a. Number of days from purchase request to item/service delivery
   b. Ease of filling out purchasing forms
   c. Satisfaction with purchased material
2. Continuously train and develop purchasing personnel with respect to job requirements. For example, take measurements on the following as a basis for process improvement:
   a. Number of errors per purchase order
   b. Number of minutes to complete a purchase order

Whatever the objectives of a process are, all involved persons must understand them and devote their efforts toward those objectives. A major benefit of clearly stating the objectives of a process is that everybody works toward the same aim.

Are Process Data Valid?

Management's (process owners') attempts to define and document a process must include precise definitions of process objectives and subobjectives, specifications, products and services, and jobs. [See Reference 1, pp. 323–324.] Such definitions are a prerequisite for understanding between process members. **Operational definitions** used to collect data must have the same meaning to everyone so that the data can be used as a basis for action.

It is useful to illustrate the confusion that can be caused by the absence of operational definitions. The label on a shirt reads "75 percent cotton." What does this mean? Three-quarters cotton, on the average, over this shirt, or three-quarters cotton over a month's production? What is three-quarters cotton? Three-quarters by weight? If so, at what humidity? By what method of chemical analysis? How many analyses? Does 75 percent cotton mean that there must be some cotton in any random cross section the size of a silver dollar? If so, how many cuts should be tested? How do you select them? What criteria must the average satisfy? And how much variation between cuts is permissible? Obviously, the meaning of 75 percent cotton must be stated in operational terms; otherwise confusion results. [See Reference 2, pp. 287–289.]

TABLE 4.1
Identification
of Burrs

Part Number	Inspector				
	A	B	C	D	E
1	0	1	1	1	0
2	0	1	1	0	0
3	1	1	1	1	0
4	1	1	1	0	0
5	0	1	1	1	0
6	0	1	1	0	0
7	1	1	1	1	0
8	1	1	1	0	0
9	0	1	1	1	0
10	0	1	1	0	0

Legend: 0 = No burr on part.
         1 = Burr on part.

As another example, one operation in a production process is a deburring operation. Clearly, it is reasonable to ask for the definition of a burr. The supervisor in charge of the deburring operation was asked for a definition and stated that a burr is a bump or protrusion on a surface. "And," he added, "Deburring's five inspectors all have at least 15 years' experience and certainly know a burr when they see one."

A test was conducted to determine if the definition of a burr was consistent among all five inspectors. Ten parts were drawn from the production line and placed into a tray so that each part could be identified by a number; each of the inspectors was shown the tray and asked to determine which parts had burrs. Table 4.1 shows the results.

Although inspectors B and C always agree, they always disagree with inspector E. Inspector A agrees with inspectors B and C 40 percent of the time, with inspector E 60 percent of the time, and with inspector D 50 percent of the time. Inspector D also agrees with inspectors B, C, and E 50 percent of the time. This information does not paint a pretty picture. Absence of an operational definition of a burr creates mayhem. Deburring's manager (the process owner) and inspectors have no consistent concept of their jobs. This creates fear (Deming's Point 8) and steals their pride of workmanship (Deming's Point 12).

More on Operational Definitions

Major problems can arise when process measurement definitions are inconsistent over time, or when their applications and/or interpretations are different over time. Employees may be confused about what constitutes their jobs. Major problems between customers and suppliers may result from the absence of agreed-upon operational definitions. Endless bickering and ill will are inevitable results.

Operational definitions establish a language for process improvement and innovation. An operational definition puts communicable meaning into a process, product, service, job, or specification. For example, specifications like defective, safe, round, 5 inches long, reliable, hot, cold, and tired have no communicable meaning until they are operationally defined. Everyone concerned must agree on an operational definition before action can be taken on a process. A given operational definition is neither right nor wrong: its significance is that there is agreement between the stakeholders involved with the definition. As conditions change, the operational definition may change to meet new needs.

An operational definition consists of (1) a criterion to be applied to an object or to a group; (2) a test of the object or group; and (3) a decision as to whether the object or group did or did not meet the criterion. [See Reference 2, p. 277.] The three components of an operational definition are best understood through some examples.

A firm produces washers. One of the critical quality characteristics is roundness. The following procedure is one way to arrive at an operational definition of roundness, as long as the buyer and seller agree on it.

Step 1: Criterion for roundness.

Buyer: "Use calipers that are in reasonably good order." (You perceive at once the need to question every word.)

Seller: "What is 'reasonably good order'?" (We settle the question by letting you use your calipers.)

Seller: "But how should I use them?"

Buyer: "We'll be satisfied if you just use them in the usual way."

Seller: "At what temperature?"

Buyer: "The temperature of this room."

Buyer: "Take six measures of the diameter about 30 degrees apart. Record the results."

Seller: "But what is 'about 30 degrees apart'? Don't you mean exactly 30 degrees?"

Buyer: "No, there's no such thing as exactly 30 degrees in the physical world. So try for 30 degrees. We'll be satisfied."

Buyer: "If the range between the six diameters doesn't exceed 0.007 centimeters, we'll declare the washer to be round." (They have determined the criterion for roundness.)

Step 2: Test of roundness.

1. Select a particular washer.

2. Take the six measurements and record the results in centimeters: 3.365, 3.363, 3.368, 3.366, 3.366, and 3.369.

3. The range is 3.369 to 3.363, or a 0.006 difference. They test for conformance by comparing the range of 0.006 with the criterion range of 0.007 (Step 1).

Step 3: Decision on roundness. Because the washer passed the prescribed test for roundness, they declare it to be round.

If a seller has employees who understand what round means and a buyer who agrees, many of the problems the company may have had satisfying the customer will disappear. [See Reference 4, pp. 138–139.]

As another illustration, a salesperson is told that her performance will be judged with respect to the percent change in this year's sales over last year's sales. What does this mean? Average percent change each month? Each week? Each day? For each product? Percent change between December 31, 2001, and December 31, 2002, sales?

How are we measuring sales? Gross, net, gross profit, net profit? Is the percent change in constant or inflated dollars? If it is in constant dollars, is it at last year's prices or this year's prices? Under what economic conditions?

A loose definition of percent change can only lead to confusion, frustration, and ill will between management and the sales force—which is hardly the way to improve productivity. How should management operationally define a percent change in sales?

Step 1: Criterion for percent change in sales. A percent change in sales is the difference between 2002 sales and 2001 sales divided by 2001 sales:

$$\text{Percentage change } (01, 02) = (S_{02} - S_{01})/S_{01} \qquad \textbf{(4.1)}$$

where:

S_{02} = dollar sales volume for the period January 1, 2002, through December 31, 2002

S_{01} = dollar sales volume for the period January 1, 2001, through December 31, 2001

S_{01} is measured in constant dollars, with 2000 as the base year, using June 15, 2000, and June 15, 2001, prices to derive the constant dollar prices, and total unit sales less returns (due to any cause) as of December 31, 2001, for each product.

$$S_{01} = \sum_{i=1}^{m} [(P_{i00}/P_{i01})(TS_{i01} - R_{i01})] \qquad \textbf{(4.2)}$$

where:

m = number of products in the product line

P_{i00} = price of product i as of June 15, 2000

P_{i01} = price of product i as of June 15, 2001

TS_{i01} = total unit sales for product i between January 1, 2001, and December 31, 2001

R_{i01} = total unit returns (for any reason) for product i between January 1, 2001, and December 31, 2001

R_{i01} recognizes that products sold late in 2001 that may be returned will be reflected in R_{i02}, next year's return for product i.

S_{02} is measured in constant dollars, with 2000 as the base year, using June 15, 2000, and June 15, 2002, prices to derive the constant dollar prices, and total unit sales less returns (for any reason) as of December 31, 2002, for each product. (P_{i00} remains the same for all products.)

$$S_{02} = \sum_{i=1}^{m} [(P_{i00}/P_{i02})(TS_{i02} - R_{i02})] \qquad \textbf{(4.3)}$$

where all items are defined as in Equation (4.2) with the appropriate shift in time frame.

This procedure for computing the percentage change in sales between 2001 and 2002 will be in effect regardless of the economic conditions. Further, management may revise the definition after the 2002 sales evaluation, but not before, unless the sales force and management agree.

Step 2: Test on percent change in sales. The sales manager will use all 2001 and 2002 invoices and sales return slips to compute the net number of units sold for each product in 2001 and 2002. The sales manager will record the computations and results.

Step 3: Decision on percent change in sales. The sales manager communicates the percentage change in sales to the salesperson.

The prior definition of sales might not suit another manager and sales force. However, if the sales manager adopts it, and the sales force understands and accepts it, it is an operational definition.

Operational definitions are not trivial; if management does not operationally define terms so that employees and customers agree, serious problems will result. Statistical methods become useless tools in the absence of operational definitions.

Summary

This chapter discussed defining and documenting a process. A process is defined as the transformation of inputs into outputs, and it involves the addition of value in time, place, or form. Processes exist in all aspects of all organizations, including administration, sales, training, vendor relations, and production. Two important characteristics of processes are (1) they all have customers and suppliers and (2) process improvement requires feedback loops, which enable information about outputs to be communicated back to the input stage.

Before a process can be improved or innovated, it must be defined and documented. This is accomplished by answering the questions: Who owns the process? Who is responsible for the process's improvement? What are the boundaries of the process? What is the flow of the process? What are the process's objectives? What measurements are being taken on the process with respect to its objectives? Are process data valid?

Flowcharts provide a structured means to define and document a process. This enables enhanced communication, planning, simplification and clarity of the process elements, identification of roles and interrelationships, logical accuracy, and effective troubleshooting.

Operational definitions bring about increased communication between the stakeholders of a process because they provide precise meanings for specifications, products and services, and jobs; that is, they establish a language for improvement and innovation of a process. Operational definitions consist of a criterion to be applied to an object or to a group, a test of the object or group, and a decision as to whether the object or group did or did not meet the criterion. If operational definitions are not used or are not agreed upon by all concerned, serious problems can occur.

Key Terms

boundaries, *75*
cross-functional responsibilities, *75*
empowerment, *71*
feedback loop, *72*
flowchart, *75*
form value, *72*

input, *72*
layout flowchart, *77*
operational definition, *79*
organizational objectives, *79*
output, *72*
place value, *72*

process, *71, 72*
process interface, *75*
process objectives, *79*
SDSA cycle, *71*
systems flowchart, *77*
time value, *72*

Exercises

4.1. Give an example of a process with no feedback loop.

4.2. Give an example of a process with a "special cause only" feedback loop.

4.3. Give an example of a process with a "special and common cause" feedback loop.

4.4. Set up a flowchart for studying for an examination.

4.5. Set up a flowchart for a person performing her job responsibilities who is concerned about starting time, stopping time, and lunch time.

4.6. Set up a flowchart for selecting a course from your university.

4.7. Set up a flowchart for a preoperative evaluation process.

4.8. Construct an operational definition for a product quality characteristic.

4.9. Construct an operational definition for a service quality characteristic.

References

1. W. Edwards Deming (1982), *Quality, Productivity, and Competitive Position* (Cambridge, MA: Massachusetts Institute of Technology Center for Advanced Engineering Study).

2. W. Edwards Deming (1986), *Out of the Crisis* (Cambridge, MA: Massachusetts Institute of Technology Center for Advanced Engineering Study).

3. J. M. Fitzgerald and A. F. Fitzgerald (1987), *Fundamentals of Systems Analysis,* 3rd ed. (New York: John Wiley and Sons).

4. H. Gitlow and P. Hertz, "Product Defects and Productivity," *Harvard Business Review,* September–October 1983, pp. 138–139.

5. G. A. Silver and J. B. Silver (1976), *Introduction to Systems Analysis* (Englewood Cliffs, NJ: Prentice Hall).

Part 2

Tools and Methods for Analytic Studies

Part 2 presents and discusses the tools and methods needed to conduct analytic studies. These techniques, when used in conjunction with the PDSA cycle, form a powerful arsenal that can be used to pursue continuous, never-ending improvement.

Chapter 5 examines the issues of quantifying probabilities and characteristics of data taken from a population or process. It also introduces the types of data that may be encountered in a statistical study and how they are classified; methods for visually displaying data; and the calculation of numerical measures to describe data.

Chapter 6 provides an overview of procedures for stabilizing and improving a documented and defined process. The chapter includes and illustrates the general theory of statistical control charts for the purpose of distinguishing special and common causes of variation.

Chapter 7 discusses and illustrates attribute control charts, used for defect prevention. For attribute data based on classifying items as conforming or nonconforming, or counting the number of occurrences, such as defects, per item, appropriate charts are presented: p charts (for both constant and variable sample sizes), np charts, c charts, and u charts.

Chapter 8 discusses and illustrates variables control charts, used in the never-ending spiral of process improvement. For variables, or measurement, data, appropriate charts are presented: $\bar{x}$ and R charts, $\bar{x}$ and s charts, and individuals and moving range charts. The logic for the rational subgrouping of control chart data is presented.

Chapter 9 discusses specific control chart patterns that can be used to detect special sources of variation. It also provides statistical rules for detecting special sources of variation.

Chapter 10 presents other tools and methods for determining the causes of special and common sources of variation in order to resolve special causes and reduce common causes of variation. The diagnostic tools and techniques include brainstorming, affinity diagrams, cause-and-effect diagrams, interrelationship diagraphs, check sheets, Pareto diagrams, stratification, systematic diagrams, matrix diagrams, program decision process charts (PDPC analyses), and Gantt charts. The change concepts are 70 proven ideas for improving processes.

Chapter 11 presents process capability and improvement stories. Performance and technical specifications are discussed and illustrated, as is the fallacy of defining quality as conformance to specifications. Process capability studies, to verify process stability, are shown to compare the output of a process (the voice of the process) with the customer's specification limits for the outputs (the voice of the customer). Process improvement studies are presented, in order to decrease the difference between customer needs and process performance.

Chapter 12 presents experimental design, a collection of statistical methods for studying the relationships between independent variables, also called factors, input variables, or process variables, and their interactions on a dependent variable, also called the outcome or response variable. Flawed designs, one-factor designs, factorial designs, and fractional factorial designs are discussed and illustrated.

Chapter 13 discusses policies and procedures for inspection of incoming, intermediate, and final goods and services, and presents the three options for inspection of goods and services: no inspection, 100 percent inspection, and sampling inspection. Three types of acceptance sampling plans are discussed: lot-by-lot plans, continuous plans, and special plans. The chapter also presents a theoretical argument against using acceptance sampling plans, followed by a discussion of the kp rule, an alternative inspection procedure that minimizes the total cost of inspection for incoming, intermediate, and final goods and services.

Chapter **5**

Basic Probability and
Statistics

Sections

Chapter Objectives

- To define probability
- To define and illustrate attribute and variables (measurement) data
- To discuss and illustrate visual (tabular and graphical) displays of data
- To discuss and illustrate numerical methods of describing data
- To interpret the standard deviation as a measure of variation
- To calculate probabilities under the normal distribution

Introduction

Almost everyone makes statements such as "It will probably rain tomorrow" or "Chances are that Bert will outperform Ernie at this new task." These are simple, intuitive statements of likelihood that usually do not require further explanation. However, there are situations for which we may make more precise likelihood statements—for example, "the probability that a coin lands on heads when tossed is ½" or "the probability of this same coin landing on heads twice in a row when tossed is ¼." Understanding some simple probability concepts can help us conceptualize process performance.

In this chapter we look at the issues of quantifying probabilities and characteristics of data taken from a population or process. We discuss the types of data that may be encountered and how they are classified, methods for visually displaying data, and the calculation of numerical measures to describe the data.

Probability Defined

There are two popular definitions of probability: the **classical definition** and the **relative frequency definition**.

The Classical Definition of Probability

We say that two events are **mutually exclusive** if they cannot occur simultaneously; that is, if the occurrence of one event precludes the occurrence of the other. For example, if A is the event that a randomly selected person is two years old and B is the event that the person is President of the United States, events A and B are mutually exclusive.

The classical approach to probability states that if an experiment has N equally likely and mutually exclusive outcomes, and if n of those outcomes correspond to the occurrence of event A, then the probability of event A is:

$$P(A) = \frac{n}{N} \tag{5.1}$$

where:

    n = the number of experimental outcomes that correspond to the occurrence of event A

    N = the total number of experimental outcomes

For example, tossing a fair die results in one of six equally likely and mutually exclusive outcomes: 1, 2, 3, 4, 5, or 6, so N = 6. If our event of interest is tossing an even number (2, 4, or 6), then n = 3 and the probability of tossing an even number on a die is:

$$P(\text{even}) = \frac{3}{6} = 0.5$$

The Relative Frequency Definition of Probability

The relative frequency approach to probability states that if an experiment is conducted a large number of times, then the probability of event A occurring is:

$$P(A) = \frac{k}{M} \tag{5.2}$$

where:

k = the number of times A occurred during these experiments

M = the maximum number of times that event A could have occurred during these experiments

For example, suppose in the die-tossing example that a fair die was tossed 100,000 times and that a 2, 4, or 6 appeared in 50,097 throws. Consequently, the relative frequency probability of tossing an even number on a fair die is:

$$P(even) = \frac{50,097}{100,000} = 0.50097$$

The classical definition of the probability of an even toss and the relative frequency definition of an even toss differ as a result of the methods used in their respective calculations.

Calculating Classical and Relative Frequency Probabilities

As an illustration, a bin contains 4,000 screws; 3,000 are good and 1,000 are defective. We will use this bin of screws to compare the two definitions of the probability of selecting a defective screw.

Calculating the Classical Probability

The classical definition of the probability of drawing a defective screw is, from Equation (5.1),

$$P(defective\ screw) = 1,000/(1,000 + 3,000) = 0.250$$

This is a reasonable conclusion if the screws are selected through a random sampling plan, such as using a table of random numbers. This would involve labeling each screw, clearly an impractical procedure. Since in the real world screws are not selected through a random sampling plan, the classical probability of a defective screw is of little value for process improvement work.

Calculating the Relative Frequency Probability

The relative frequency definition of the probability of drawing a defective screw is very different. Suppose we place the screws in the bin, mix them thoroughly (a mechanical procedure meant to approximate a random procedure), and draw one screw at random. We record the status of the screw (0 if good and 1 if defective) and replace the screw in the bin. We again thoroughly mix the screws, draw another screw, and record the number 0 or 1. Suppose we repeat this process 1,250 times. Further, suppose we put the observations into groups of 50 and record the number of defective screws in each such group, or **subgroup,** as shown in the first four columns of Table 5.1 (see ☛ SCREWS).

If we examine more samples of size 50, we will note that the fluctuations in the cumulative fraction defective diminish because the estimate of the cumulative fraction of defective screws is based on a larger sample. The last three columns of Table 5.1 and the graph in Figure 5.1 illustrate this. From Figure 5.1, we see that after accumulation of 23 subgroups the fraction defective of screws appears to have stabilized around 0.208. This number is the relative frequency estimate of the probability of drawing a defective screw. We use the term *stabilized* to be synonymous with the

TABLE 5.1
Cumulative Samples of 50 Screws

1 Subgroup Number	2 Subgroup Size	3 Number of Defective Screws in Subgroup	4 Fraction of Defective Screws in Subgroup	5 Cumulative Number of Defective Screws	6 Cumulative Number of Screws	7 Cumulative Fraction of Defective Screws
1	50	10	.20	10	50	.200
2	50	9	.18	19	100	.190
3	50	15	.30	34	150	.227
4	50	7	.14	41	200	.205
5	50	9	.18	50	250	.200
6	50	17	.34	67	300	.223
7	50	13	.26	80	350	.229
8	50	8	.16	88	400	.220
9	50	10	.20	98	450	.218
10	50	7	.14	105	500	.210
11	50	7	.14	112	550	.204
12	50	11	.22	123	600	.205
13	50	9	.18	132	650	.203
14	50	9	.18	141	700	.201
15	50	8	.16	149	750	.199
16	50	9	.18	158	800	.198
17	50	12	.24	170	850	.200
18	50	17	.34	187	900	.208
19	50	8	.16	195	950	.205
20	50	7	.14	202	1000	.202
21	50	17	.34	219	1050	.209
22	50	9	.18	228	1100	.207
23	50	11	.22	239	1150	.208
24	50	11	.22	250	1200	.208
25	50	10	.20	260	1250	.208
		Total: 260				

concept of a constant system of variation. In other words, the subgroup fraction defective is within stable and predictable limits. Chapters 6 through 8 discuss the concept of **stability** in detail.

Comparing the Probabilities

Figure 5.2 compares the two definitions of probability. We have seen that the classical probability of selecting a defective screw from the bin is 0.250. The relative frequency probability of selecting a defective screw—or the long-run cumulative fraction defective—is 0.208. In the absence of a complete frame, and hence, in the absence of the classical fraction defective in the bin, the best we can do is to use the most recent cumulative fraction defective.

It is important to consider why the relative frequency approach did not yield a 0.250 probability of selecting a defective screw. The difference between the two probabilities

FIGURE 5.1
Cumulative Fraction of Defective Screws

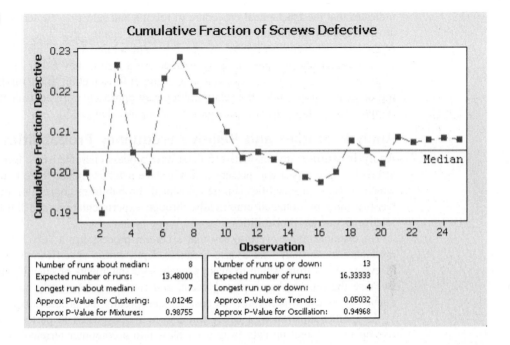

Number of runs about median:	8	Number of runs up or down:	13
Expected number of runs:	13.48000	Expected number of runs:	16.33333
Longest run about median:	7	Longest run up or down:	4
Approx P-Value for Clustering:	0.01245	Approx P-Value for Trends:	0.05032
Approx P-Value for Mixtures:	0.98755	Approx P-Value for Oscillation:	0.94968

FIGURE 5.2
Comparison of the Two Definitions of the Probability of a Defective Screw

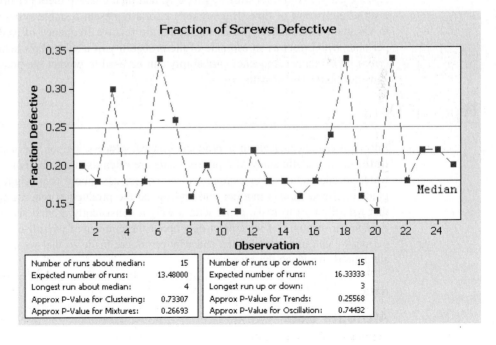

Number of runs about median:	15	Number of runs up or down:	15
Expected number of runs:	13.48000	Expected number of runs:	16.33333
Longest run about median:	4	Longest run up or down:	3
Approx P-Value for Clustering:	0.73307	Approx P-Value for Trends:	0.25568
Approx P-Value for Mixtures:	0.26693	Approx P-Value for Oscillation:	0.74432

indicates that the mechanical procedure of mixing and selecting the screws under the relative frequency definition must have been biased against defective screws; it was not equivalent to random sampling. A possible explanation for this bias is that defective screws are broken and consequently smaller. As a result, they either fall to the bottom of the bin during mixing or present a smaller target for selection. If the mixing and selecting procedure used under the relative frequency approach were equivalent to a random sampling procedure, the two probabilities would be identical.

Analytic Studies and Relative Frequency Probabilities

Analytic studies are conducted to determine process characteristics. But process characteristics have a past and present and will have a future; hence there is no frame from which classical probabilities can be calculated. Probabilities concerning process characteristics must be obtained empirically, through experimentation, and must therefore be relative frequency probabilities.

For example, if we were to say that a certain process has a very high likelihood of producing a camshaft with a case hardness depth within specification limits, no frame of events exists from which to make probabilistic statements or quantify the probability. Because the process has a past, present, and future, we must rely on the relative frequency approach to probability to describe and predict the process's behavior.

As another illustration, a newly hired worker is expected to perform an administrative operation, entering data from sales slips into a computer terminal. Is it possible to predict the percentage of entries per hour that will be in error? Unfortunately not; the best we can do is to train workers properly, and then observe them performing their jobs over a long period of time. If a worker's efforts represent a stable system (more on this in Chapters 6 through 8), we can compute the relative frequency of sales slips entered per hour with errors as an estimate of the probability of a sales slip's being entered with errors. This relative frequency probability can be used to predict the percentage of sales slips per hour entered with errors.

Types of Data

Information collected about a product, service, process, person, or machine is called **data.** In an analytic study of a process, data are often used as a basis for predictions on which to take actions. For example, if we collect data about the weight of a particular grade of paper, we can monitor and understand the production process and take actions that will allow us to make paper with a weight consistently around some desired value. As another example, if we collect data about the number of payroll entry errors by pay period, we can understand when and why errors are made so that we can take appropriate actions to reduce the error rate.

We classify data into two types: **attribute data** and **variables,** or **measurement, data.**

Attribute Data

Attribute data arise from (1) the classification of items, such as products or services, into categories; (2) counts of the number of items in a given category or the proportion in a given category; and (3) counts of the number of occurrences per unit.

TABLE 5.2
Attribute
Data:
Classification
of 2003 Union
Grievances
into Four
Categories

Grievance Number	Grievance Level
1	1
2	1
3	1
4	2
5	4
6	1
7	1
8	1
9	3
10	1
11	1

Classification of Items into Categories

Often data are classified into two categories or grades, representing conformity or non-conformity with some quality characteristic. Whether a purchase order is filled out properly, whether a bearing in a piece of equipment has excessive vibration, whether the seal on a jar of instant coffee is broken, whether a 9-volt battery is operating, and whether a car radio is defective are all examples of attributes.

Items may be similarly classified into three or more categories or grades. Classifying the grade of a stick of butter as grade AA, grade A, or grade B; classifying employees by department; and classifying the type of defect in a roll of paper as dished, crushed core, or wrinkled are all examples of attribute data.

As another illustration, union grievances are classified as first level, second level, third level, or fourth level; a first-level grievance can be resolved by a foreman, whereas a fourth-level grievance must be handled by a special arbitration board. That is, the higher the level of the union grievance, the more serious the grievance. Table 5.2 lists 11 union grievances and their classifications for 2003.

Counts of the Number of Items in a Given Category, or Proportion in a Given Category

The number of items in a given category also represents attribute data. For example, the second column of Table 5.3 shows the number of union grievances in each of the four categories discussed in the preceding example.

The proportion of items in a given category is also an attribute. From the last column of Table 5.3, we see that the proportion of second-level grievances can be calculated as:

$$\text{Proportion of second level union grievances} = \frac{\text{Number of second level union grievances}}{\text{Number of union grievances}}$$

$$= \frac{1}{11} = 0.09$$

Counts of the Number of Occurrences per Unit

An attribute of interest in some quality studies is the number of defects per unit, where a unit can be a single item, a batch of the item under question, or a unit of time or space.

TABLE 5.3
Attribute Data: Number of 2003 Union Grievances per Level

Category	Number of Grievances	Proportion of Grievances
First Level	8	8/11 = .73
Second Level	1	1/11 = .09
Third Level	1	1/11 = .09
Fourth Level	1	1/11 = .09

The number of customer complaints per week, the number of defects per reel of paper, the number of errors per typed page, the number of accidents per month, the number of union grievances per week, and the number of blemishes per square yard of fabric are all examples of count-type attribute data.

As an illustration, in the production of stainless steel washers, the manufacturing process occasionally results in a defective product. Four types of defects are observed: cracks, dents, scratches, and discoloration. An individual washer may have some, all, or none of these defects. Every hour, 10 washers are examined for defects. Table 5.4 shows the number of defects for each washer examined in an eight-hour day.

TABLE 5.4
Attribute Data: Number of Defects per Washer in Eight Hourly Samples of 10 Stainless Steel Washers

Hour #	Item #	Number of Defects	Hour #	Item #	Number of Defects	Hour #	Item #	Number of Defects
1	1	1		8	0		5	1
	2	0		9	3		6	0
	3	0		10	0		7	0
	4	2	4	1	1		8	0
	5	1		2	1		9	3
	6	0		3	0		10	2
	7	0		4	4	7	1	0
	8	0		5	0		2	1
	9	4		6	1		3	0
	10	0		7	0		4	0
2	1	1		8	0		5	1
	2	0		9	3		6	0
	3	0		10	1		7	0
	4	3	5	1	0		8	2
	5	1		2	2		9	0
	6	0		3	0		10	0
	7	2		4	0	8	1	1
	8	0		5	0		2	0
	9	0		6	3		3	0
	10	0		7	0		4	0
3	1	1		8	0		5	1
	2	0		9	1		6	0
	3	0		10	2		7	0
	4	2	6	1	1		8	0
	5	4		2	1		9	2
	6	0		3	0		10	0
	7	1		4	0			

Variables (Measurement) Data

Variables (measurement) data arise (1) from the measurement of a characteristic of a product, service, or process and (2) from the computation of a numerical value from two or more measurements of variables data.

Measurement of a Characteristic

When we make precise measurements of quality characteristics—such as the length of time to resolve a customer complaint (in seconds), the outside diameter of stainless steel washers (in centimeters), the weights of boxes of detergent (in ounces), or the lifetimes of incandescent bulbs (in hours)—we are recording variables, or measurement, data. As an illustration, in a logging operation, trees are cut at age 20 years. Table 5.5 records the length, in centimeters, of each such log as measured in 19 daily samples of five trees each (see ☛ LOGS).

TABLE 5.5
Variables Data: Length of Logs in a Sample of 95 Trees

Day #	Log #	Length (cm)	Day #	Log #	Length (cm)	Day #	Log #	Length (cm)
1	1	783.2		3	1393.9		5	1719.7
	2	1322.8		4	1968.6	14	1	638.8
	3	1012.5		5	1561.2		2	1834.0
	4	1408.6	8	1	1908.7		3	730.0
	5	1589.6		2	1612.2		4	1338.5
2	1	400.2		3	1585.6		5	1621.4
	2	1456.1		4	1510.4	15	1	1192.1
	3	1126.7		5	898.7		2	1542.6
	4	1563.8	9	1	1087.8		3	1886.1
	5	1362.5		2	938.1		4	1688.2
3	1	1537.8		3	1472.3		5	1069.7
	2	505.4		4	1072.0	16	1	1835.3
	3	1686.7		5	489.7		2	1485.2
	4	1508.0	10	1	1208.6		3	1521.4
	5	1235.8		2	1868.5		4	2104.4
4	1	1827.2		3	1321.7		5	1225.2
	2	2148.3		4	2067.7	17	1	929.4
	3	1175.2		5	835.9		2	1732.1
	4	1657.5	11	1	1830.6		3	1340.2
	5	410.3		2	1227.1		4	1445.5
5	1	1577.7		3	1423.3		5	460.7
	2	827.6		4	1022.2	18	1	1021.8
	3	1353.1		5	1690.0		2	1515.2
	4	1410.2	12	1	625.6		3	753.6
	5	1050.2		2	1131.1		4	1117.3
6	1	1468.7		3	1193.9		5	1490.0
	2	1229.2		4	1252.8	19	1	572.5
	3	1346.3		5	1551.8		2	1436.8
	4	1725.6	13	1	1481.4		3	1356.6
	5	693.1		2	1763.6		4	1112.6
7	1	1639.9		3	1392.2		5	1512.7
	2	1786.3		4	1498.9			

TABLE 5.6 Variables Data: Calculation of the Variable Miles per Gallon	Truck	Miles since Refueling	Gallons of Fuel Consumed	Miles per Gallon
	1	308	17.3	17.8
	2	256	15.3	16.7
	3	274	16.5	16.6
	4	310	16.9	18.3
	5	302	17.1	17.7
	6	296	17.3	17.1

*Computation of a Numerical Value from Two or
More Measurements of Variables Data*

Table 5.6 shows the recorded values of two variables for each of six trucks: the number of miles driven since the last refueling, and the number of gallons of fuel consumed since the last refueling.

From these measurements, we may calculate another variable, miles per gallon for each truck, by calculating the ratio of the number of miles driven since the last refueling divided by the number of gallons of fuel consumed since the last refueling. This computed ratio, shown in the last column of Table 5.6, is an illustration of variables data computed from two other measurements of variables data.

As another illustration, the computation of the volume of a rectangular container from the product of the measurements of its length, width, and height results in a new computed variable value.

In any quality study we usually want to rearrange and/or manipulate data to gain some insight into the characteristics of the process under study. The remainder of this chapter discusses ways of interpreting and appropriately describing data, both visually and numerically.

Characterizing Data

Enumerative Studies

A complete census of the frame in an **enumerative study** provides all the information needed to take action on the frame. For example, suppose a lumber supplier must determine how much to charge for a particular large shipment to a lumberyard. The total charge is based on the lengths of the logs in the shipment (the frame). Thus, if we knew the length of each log in the shipment (that is, 100 percent sampling in an enumerative study), we would know exactly how much to charge for the shipment, assuming accuracy in the measurement process.

As discussed in Chapter 3, we often sample rather than perform a complete census; we then use that information to develop visual and/or numerical measures that enable us to take action on the frame. As we are examining only a portion of the frame, the possibility of taking an incorrect action does exist. In our example, suppose the lumber supplier bases the charge on the average of the 95 log lengths shown in Table 5.5. Two types of error are possible in this procedure: (1) the charge is higher by an amount C than what it would be if she had measured every log (often called the **consumer's risk**) or (2) the charge is lower by an amount C′ than what it would be if she had measured every log (the **producer's risk**).

As another illustration, consider the sample of stainless steel washers examined for defects in Table 5.4. If all the washers produced in this eight-hour day make up a single lot to be shipped (the frame), in an enumerative study the manufacturer may wish to determine the number of defects in the entire lot to decide whether or not to ship the lot. In using the sample data as a basis for action, again there are two possible errors: (1) he decides to ship a lot that, in fact, has an unacceptably large number of defects (the consumer's risk) or (2) he decides to reject a lot that, in fact, has an acceptably small number of defects (the producer's risk).

If the information used as the basis for action constitutes a **random sample** from the frame, these errors can be quantified, and valid statistical inferences can be made on the frame in question. Chapter 3 discussed the nature of and procedures for selecting a random sample. This chapter discusses how to describe and characterize such data to ultimately make appropriate inferences.

Analytic Studies

A complete census of the frame is impossible in an analytic study, for a frame consists of all past, present, and future observations, and future observations cannot be measured. As we are dealing with an ongoing process, we wish to characterize the data to take action on that process for the future. For example, in the manufacture of washers, suppose we are not interested, as before, in one particular day's output but instead are interested in the process itself. That is, we wish to determine the necessity for action: whether the process should be left unchanged for the future or modified in some way. A sample selected from the process, such as that in Table 5.4, may lead to two types of errors: (1) decide to retain the process, even though it should be modified or (2) decide to modify the process, although it is actually unnecessary to do so.

Unlike the enumerative study, since the frame is unknown (the future cannot be measured) it is not possible to quantify these errors. Any inferences we make in an analytic study are conditional on the environmental state when the sample was selected; that environmental state will never again exist. Information on such a problem can never be complete. If, however, knowledge of the process and the environment and an analysis of the data indicate that the process is stable and predictable, and will remain so in the near future, the visual and numerical characterizations discussed in this chapter can be used to make inferences and take action in the near future.

Visually Describing Data

Tabular Displays

Frequency Distributions

A **frequency distribution** shows us, in tabular form, the number of times, or the frequency with which, a given value or group of values occurs. For example, when analyzing variables data, we generally group the data into class intervals and count the number of items whose values fall within each interval. Thus, Table 5.7 shows a frequency distribution for the data of Table 5.5, where the class intervals are 400 but less than 700 cm, 700 but less than 1,000 cm, 1,000 but less than 1,300 cm, 1,300 but less than 1,600 cm, 1,600 but less than 1,900 cm, and 1,900 but less than 2,200 cm. The class limits are the endpoints of each interval; in our example, the lower class limits are the

TABLE 5.7

Frequency
Distribution of
Lengths of
Logs in a
Sample of 95
Trees

Length (cm)	Class Midpoint	Absolute Frequency	Relative Frequency (percent)
400 but less than 700	550	9	9.5%
700 but less than 1,000	850	8	8.4
1,000 but less than 1,300	1,150	20	21.1
1,300 but less than 1,600	1,450	35	36.8
1,600 but less than 1,900	1,750	18	18.9
1,900 but less than 2,200	2,050	5	5.3

TABLE 5.8

Frequency
Distribution of
Number of
Defects in a
Sample of 80
Stainless Steel
Washers

Number of Defects	Absolute Frequency	Relative Frequency (percent)
0	46	57.50%
1	18	22.50
2	8	10.00
3	5	6.25
4	3	3.75

lower limits of each interval: 400, 700, 1,000, 1,300, 1,600, and 1,900. The upper class limits are 700, 1,000, 1,300, 1,600, 1,900, and 2,200. The midpoint of each class is the value halfway between the class limits.

Table 5.7 indicates **absolute frequencies** (the actual number of observations in each class) as well as **relative frequencies** (the percentage of the total number of observations in each class). Especially in situations where we want to compare two frequency distributions with unequal total numbers, we often use relative frequencies—or the class frequencies divided by the total number of observations—expressed as a percentage.

For attribute data, we may construct frequency distributions by counting the number of items possessing a particular attribute. Table 5.8 shows a frequency distribution of the number of defects in 80 stainless steel washers shown in Table 5.4.

As a general rule, we select anywhere from 5 to 20 classes when constructing a frequency distribution for variables data; too few or too many classes may fail to reveal patterns of interest. For example, taking the data of Table 5.5 and constructing a frequency distribution consisting of two classes (400 but less than 1,300, with 37 observations, and 1,300 but less than 2,200, with 58 observations) offers little insight in comparison with the distribution of Table 5.7. Where possible, we make the class widths the same for all intervals. This allows us to logically compare frequencies in different classes. For example, if we are measuring the lifetimes of 100 special-purpose incandescent bulbs and count 3 bulbs in a class interval of 1 to 5 hours and 35 bulbs in a class interval of 5.1 to 20 hours, we could not easily determine whether the large difference in frequency results from actual variations in bulb lifetime or simply from the huge difference in class widths. Sometimes, however, we use an open-ended interval to include a small number of highly dispersed values at the top and/or bottom of the distribution. Using the same example, if 1 or 2 of the 100 bulbs burned for 90 hours, while all the rest burned for

50 hours or less, it might make sense to specify the top interval to be "more than 50 hours." The number of classes in a frequency distribution for attribute data is determined by the number of values the attribute can assume; for example, an attribute frequency distribution depicting the gender of employees would have two classes.

Cumulative Frequency Distributions

For many processes, we are interested in the frequency of items with a value less than some numerical measurement. For example, how many of the 100 incandescent bulbs burned for less than 30 hours, how many burned for less than 40 hours, and so on. This information is presented in a **cumulative frequency distribution.** Table 5.9a shows the cumulative frequencies for the data of Table 5.5, calculated by adding the successive frequencies in the distribution of Table 5.7. For example, the number of logs with a length of less than 1,600 cm is the sum of the frequencies for all the class intervals up to and including "1,300 but less than 1,600," or $9 + 8 + 20 + 35 = 72$. Relative cumulative frequency, or the percentage of the items with a value less than the upper limit of each class interval, is calculated as the absolute cumulative frequency divided by the sample size. Thus, for example, 75.8 percent of the logs in the sample have lengths of less than 1,600 cm. Table 5.9b shows the cumulative frequency distribution for the number of defects in the 80 washers.

Limitations of Frequency Displays

It is important to note that the frequency displays we have discussed do not include information on the time-ordering of data. Recall that the diameters of our 80 stainless steel washers were actually measured by examining 10 washers every hour over a period

TABLE 5.9
Cumulative Frequency Distributions

(a) Cumulative Frequency Distribution of Lengths of Logs in a Sample of 95 Trees		
Log Length (cm) Less than or Equal to	Cumulative Frequency	Relative Cumulative Frequency (percent)
700	9	9.5%
1,000	17	17.9
1,300	37	38.9
1,600	72	75.8
1,900	90	94.7
2,200	95	100.0

(b) Cumulative Frequency Distribution of Number of Defects in a Sample of 80 Stainless Steel Washers		
Washers with Number of Defects Less than or Equal to	Cumulative Frequency	Relative Cumulative Frequency (percent)
0	46	57.50%
1	64	80.00
2	72	90.00
3	77	96.25
4	80	100.00

TABLE 5.10
Inside
Diameters of
Brass Nuts

(a) Hourly Observations

Hour #	Inside Diameter (in)	Hour #	Inside Diameter (in)	Hour #	Inside Diameter (in)
1	1.00	8	1.11	15	1.25
2	1.01	9	1.12	16	1.28
3	1.03	10	1.14	17	1.32
4	1.05	11	1.16	18	1.36
5	1.07	12	1.18	19	1.41
6	1.08	13	1.20	20	1.46
7	1.09	14	1.22		

(b) Frequency Distribution

Inside Diameter (in)	Absolute Frequency
1.00 but less than 1.10	7
1.10 but less than 1.20	5
1.20 but less than 1.30	4
1.30 but less than 1.40	2
1.40 but less than 1.50	2

of eight consecutive hours, as shown in Table 5.4. But the frequency distribution in Table 5.8 does not indicate that the observations were made in any particular sequence. In an analytic study, where we examine the sample to take action on the process, a frequency display would fail to show trends that may be occurring over time. This loss of information can be critical.

Consider the production of brass nuts. The process, as a result of equipment wear, is producing nuts with an inside diameter actually increasing over time. Every hour, for 20 consecutive hours, a nut is selected randomly and its inside diameter is recorded. The observations are shown in Table 5.10a. A frequency distribution is shown in Table 5.10b.

If the nuts manufactured during this 20-hour period constitute a population, the frequency distribution indicates all pertinent information about the lot. However, if we are conducting a study of a manufacturing process with the aim of improving its performance in the future, we must detect the trend over time and look for the cause; the frequency distribution in this case gives us an incomplete picture. We will see in the following section that run charts can detect and highlight such trends.

Graphical Displays

Data are often represented in graphical form. Such displays offer a composite picture of the relationships and/or patterns at a glance. Frequency distributions of variables data are commonly presented in **frequency polygons** or **histograms.** Frequency distributions of attribute data are commonly presented in **bar charts.** In all these displays, the class intervals are drawn along the horizontal axis, and the absolute or relative frequencies along the vertical axis.

Frequency Polygon

In a frequency polygon, we plot the midpoint of each class interval on the horizontal axis against the frequency of that class on the vertical axis. We then connect these points with a series of line segments. To complete the polygon, we add two more classes to the distribution—one class preceding the smallest class and one class following the largest class, both with a "0" frequency at their midpoints. In Figure 5.3a the frequency distribution of the data in Table 5.7 is presented as a frequency polygon.

FIGURE 5.3
Graphical
Displays of
Data

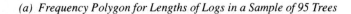

(a) Frequency Polygon for Lengths of Logs in a Sample of 95 Trees

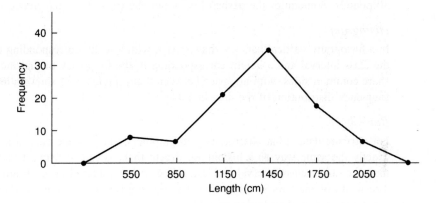

(b) Frequency Polygon for Product Weights of 10 Items

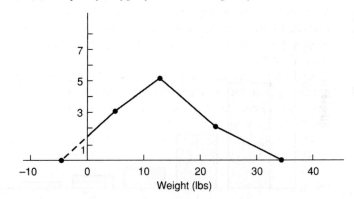

(c) Histogram for Lengths of Logs in a Sample of 95 Trees

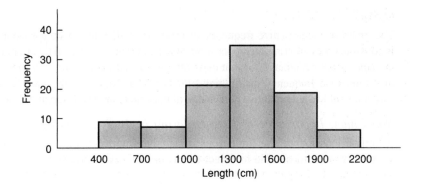

In the particular case where the lower class limit of the smallest class is 0, adding a class preceding the smallest class results in negative values for that class (and its midpoint) on the horizontal axis. To indicate that such values could not really occur, we use a dashed line for the portion of the polygon corresponding to negative observations. Figure 5.3b illustrates this procedure for a frequency distribution of 10 product weights, in which three observations are between 0 and less than 10 pounds, five observations are between 10 and less than 20 pounds, and two observations are between 20 and less than 30 pounds. Sometimes the dashed line is not shown on the final frequency polygon.

Histogram

In a histogram, vertical bars are drawn, each with a width corresponding to the width of the class interval and a height corresponding to the frequency of that interval. The bars share common sides, with no space between them. Figure 5.3c shows a histogram of the frequency distribution of the data in Table 5.7.

Bar Chart

For attribute data, a bar chart is used to graphically display the data. It is constructed in exactly the same way as a histogram, except that instead of using a vertical bar spanning the entire class interval, we use a line or bar centered on each attribute category. The width of the bars in a bar chart has no significance. Figure 5.4 shows a bar chart for the frequency distribution in Table 5.8.

FIGURE 5.4
Bar Chart for Number of Defects in a Sample of 80 Stainless Steel Washers

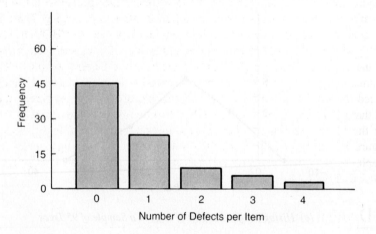

Ogive

The graph of a cumulative frequency distribution, called an **ogive** (pronounced "ohjive"), is constructed by plotting the upper limit of each class interval on the horizontal axis against the cumulative percentage for that class on the vertical axis. Figure 5.5 shows the ogive for the cumulative frequency distribution of Table 5.9a. Note that the lower limit of the first class interval has a cumulative percentage of 0, as there are no observations below that value.

Run Chart: Importance of Time-Ordering in Analytic Studies

As our discussion of the limitations of tabular frequency displays showed, in analytic studies we want to be able to detect trends or other patterns over time to take action on

FIGURE 5.5
Ogive for
Lengths of
Logs in a
Sample of 95
Trees

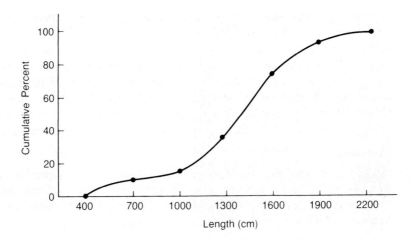

a process in the near future. The graphical displays we have examined do not incorporate the time-ordering of the data; hence they are sometimes of limited value in such studies. In a **run chart** (also called a **tier chart**), this information is preserved by plotting the observed values on the vertical axis and the times they were observed on the horizontal axis. For example, suppose we are studying a process in which chocolate rectangles are cut from larger blocks of chocolate and then packaged as 6-ounce bars. Every 15 minutes, three chocolate bars are weighed, prior to packaging. Table 5.11 shows the weights for each bar examined in a seven-hour day (see ☘ CHOCOLATE).

Figure 5.6a (on page 105) is a histogram of the data, indicating, at a glance, that most of the chocolate bars weigh slightly more than the labeled weight of 6 ounces. In an enumerative study, in which we are interested only in the batch of chocolate bars produced during this seven-hour day, such information may be sufficient for taking action on that batch. But in an analytic study, where we seek to take action on the process itself for the future, we will see that the information gained from Figure 5.6a is incomplete. Figure 5.6b is a run, or tier, chart that shows the observed weights plotted over time. The graph clearly shows an upward drift in the weights of chocolate bars throughout the day and it indicates the need for action on the process.

Numerically Describing Data

Measures of Central Tendency

While tabular and graphical representations give a broad overview, we often need quantitative measures that summarize important characteristics of a population or a process. One such property is **central tendency,** or the behavior of the typical value of a characteristic of the population or process data.

The Mean

In trying to convey the underlying character of variables data by somehow representing the typical value of the data, the most common numerical representation is the arithmetic average or **mean:** the sum of the numerical values of the measurement divided by the

TABLE 5.11
Weights of Chocolate Bars Examined at 15-Minute Intervals

Time	Observation #	Weight (oz)	Time	Observation #	Weight (oz)
9:15	1	6.01	12:45	1	6.03
	2	5.99		2	6.02
	3	6.02		3	6.03
9:30	1	5.98	1:00	1	6.03
	2	5.99		2	6.00
	3	6.01		3	6.01
9:45	1	6.03	1:15	1	6.04
	2	6.02		2	6.02
	3	6.02		3	6.03
10:00	1	6.02	1:30	1	6.05
	2	6.03		2	6.02
	3	6.02		3	6.04
10:15	1	6.00	1:45	1	6.03
	2	5.99		2	6.04
	3	6.01		3	6.01
10:30	1	5.99	2:00	1	6.02
	2	6.00		2	6.02
	3	6.00		3	6.02
10:45	1	6.02	2:15	1	6.04
	2	6.01		2	6.05
	3	6.00		3	6.03
11:00	1	6.01	2:30	1	6.06
	2	6.03		2	6.03
	3	6.01		3	6.04
11:15	1	6.01	2:45	1	6.05
	2	6.02		2	6.04
	3	6.00		3	6.02
11:30	1	6.00	3:00	1	6.05
	2	6.02		2	6.04
	3	6.01		3	6.03
11:45	1	6.04	3:15	1	6.04
	2	6.02		2	6.06
	3	6.03		3	6.05
12:00	1	6.02	3:30	1	6.05
	2	6.01		2	6.03
	3	6.00		3	6.04
12:15	1	6.03	3:45	1	6.03
	2	6.02		2	6.04
	3	6.04		3	6.03
12:30	1	6.02	4:00	1	6.06
	2	6.02		2	6.06
	3	6.03		3	6.05

FIGURE 5.6
**Weights of
Chocolate Bars
Examined at
15-Minute
Intervals:
(a) Histogram
(b) Run Chart**

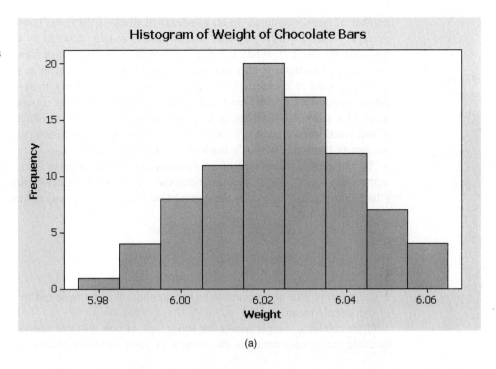

(a)

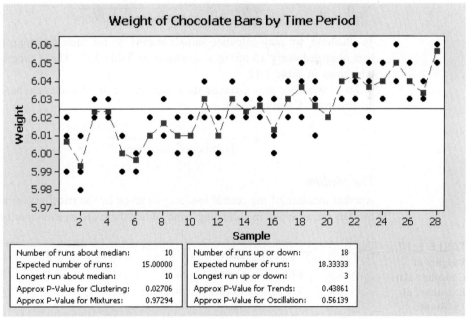

(b)

number of items examined. In an enumerative study, if the items constitute a frame, the average is called the **population mean** and is usually denoted by the Greek letter μ (pronounced "mew"). When the items constitute a sample drawn from a frame, we call the average a **sample mean** and denote it as $\bar{x}$ ("x-bar"). Thus, in an enumerative study, we might make reference to either μ or $\bar{x}$. In an analytic study, there is no frame, since future output does not yet exist, and hence we cannot describe a population mean. The mean of a sampled subgroup, such as four items from a day's production, is denoted as $\bar{x}$, and when we average the $\bar{x}$ values for different subgroups to estimate a process mean, we denote that value as $\bar{\bar{x}}$ ("x bar-bar" or "x double-bar").

To communicate this type of information in compact, precise form, we identify each numerical value as an "x" measurement; the sum of all the measurements is denoted Σx ("the sum of x"), where Σ is the capital Greek letter sigma and represents, mathematically, "summation."

The sample mean, $\bar{x}$, can be calculated as:

$$\bar{x} = \frac{\Sigma x}{n} \qquad (5.3)$$

where n is the size of the sample or the number of items included in the determination of the sample mean.

If we calculate sample means for subgroups of size n in the past and present, we can estimate the process mean as the average of these subgroup means:

$$\bar{\bar{x}} = \frac{\Sigma \bar{x}}{\text{Number of subgroups}} \qquad (5.4)$$

To illustrate, we may calculate sample means, $\bar{x}$, for each subgroup of three chocolate bars observed every 15 minutes, as shown in Table 5.11. These subgroup sample means are shown in Table 5.12.

From these, we may estimate the mean weight of all chocolate bars produced by this process from Equation (5.4):

$$\bar{\bar{x}} = \frac{\Sigma \bar{x}}{\text{Number of subgroups}} = \frac{168.68}{28} = 6.02$$

The Median

Another measure of the central tendency is given by the **median,** or middle value when the data are arranged in ascending order. When there are an even number of observations,

TABLE 5.12
Weights of Chocolate Bars Examined at 15-Minute Intervals: Sample Means of Subgroups of Size 3

Time	$\bar{x}$	Time	$\bar{x}$	Time	$\bar{x}$	Time	$\bar{x}$
9:15	6.01	11:00	6.02	12:45	6.03	2:30	6.04
9:30	5.99	11:15	6.01	1:00	6.01	2:45	6.04
9:45	6.02	11:30	6.01	1:15	6.03	3:00	6.04
10:00	6.02	11:45	6.03	1:30	6.04	3:15	6.05
10:15	6.00	12:00	6.01	1:45	6.03	3:30	6.04
10:30	6.00	12:15	6.03	2:00	6.02	3:45	6.03
10:45	6.01	12:30	6.02	2:15	6.04	4:00	6.06

the median value is the arithmetic average of the middle two values. Symbolically, if n is the number of data points and the data points are arranged in ascending order, the median can be calculated as

$$M_e = [(n + 1)/2]\text{th data point if n is odd or}$$
$$= \text{average of (n/2)th data point and (n/2 + 1)th data point if n is even}$$

(5.5)

Given an ogive, or the graph of the cumulative frequencies for a given set of data points, the median may also be approximated by reading the data value corresponding to a cumulative frequency of 50 percent. That is, since the median is the middle value, 50 percent of the data points must have values less than the median.

The central tendency of some data is not adequately represented by an arithmetic average. Consider the measurement of burning times (in minutes) of small birthday candles from a production lot. Seven candles are randomly selected from the lot. Burning times are found to be 3 minutes, 2 minutes, 4 minutes, 6 minutes, 19 minutes, 5 minutes, and 3 minutes. As these data points are a sample from the population of all such candles in this production lot, and we are only interested in making some inference on the burning characteristics of this lot, this is an enumerative problem. We may calculate the sample mean from Equation (5.3):

$$\bar{x} = \frac{3 + 2 + 4 + 6 + 19 + 5 + 3}{7} = \frac{42}{7} = 6 \text{ minutes}$$

Note, however, that for six of the seven candles in the sample, the burning time was six minutes or less, so that the average value as a measure of central tendency is somewhat misleading. If we look at a frequency polygon for the data points, as shown in Figure 5.7, we see that it is asymmetrical, or **skewed** to the right; only one data point, x = 19, has a high value.

The median burning time is the middle data point in the sequence of burning times written in ascending order (from lowest value to highest value): 2, 3, 3, 4, 5, 6, 19, or a median of 4 minutes. Note that half the data points have a value lower than the median, and half have a value higher than the median. The median is not as influenced by the magnitude of the extreme items as is the mean. That is, if the largest data point had been 500 minutes instead of 19 minutes, the median would still be 4 minutes, although the mean would increase by a great deal. Hence the median is particularly appropriate in an enumerative example such as ours, where a single extreme value appears to be atypical.

FIGURE 5.7
Frequency Polygon for Burning Time of Small Birthday Candles

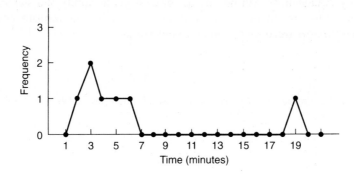

The interpretation of the median in an analytic study, however, can be misleading. Where extreme data points are observed in a sample, we have seen that they do not affect the computation of the median. In an analytic study, where we are concerned with the process itself, the existence of extreme data points is a critical factor in our analysis. That is, extreme data points may indicate process disturbances and instability, and the need for corrective action on the process. A measure like the median, which is insensitive to extreme data points, must be used with caution in an analytic study.

The Mode

The **mode** of a distribution is the value that occurs most frequently, or the value corresponding to the highest point on a frequency polygon or histogram. Like the median, and unlike the mean, it is not affected by extreme data points. A frequency distribution with one such high point is called **unimodal;** distributions with two high points of concentration are called **bimodal.** For the data of Table 5.4, an examination of the frequency distribution in Table 5.8 shows that the mode, or modal number of defects, is 0, for that value has the largest frequency. This is a unimodal distribution.

In the sample of the burning times of seven randomly selected birthday candles discussed earlier, we found that the mean was 6 minutes and the median was 4 minutes. The mode in this example is the most frequently occurring value (3 minutes). As in the case of the median, had the longest observation been 500 minutes instead of 19 minutes, the mode would remain 3 minutes, although the mean would increase.

Like the median, an important characteristic of the mode is that it is not affected by extreme data points. In analytic studies, where extreme data points may reveal a great deal about the process under investigation, the mode must therefore be used with caution.

The Proportion

Often data are classified into two non-numerical conditions, such as broken–not broken, operating–not operating, or defective–conforming. The **proportion** or fraction of the data possessing one of two such conditions is then a meaningful measure of central tendency.

The data of Table 5.13 represent the classification of 38 radios as defective or non-defective in an analytic study of a production process. As in the computation of a sample mean in an analytic study, if the process is not a stable one, the proportion defective computed from this particular sample of 38 radios may be misleading because of process variability. Although we will not discuss process predictability and stability until Chapter 6, under the assumption that the process is stable, the **sample proportion,** or **sample fraction defective,** can be calculated as:

$$p = \frac{x}{n} \qquad\qquad (5.6)$$

where x is the number of defective items and n is the total number of items in the sample. Thus,

$$p = \frac{8}{38} = 0.21$$

TABLE 5.13
Defective Units in a Sample of 38 Radios

Item #	Condition	Item #	Condition
1	Nondefective	20	Defective
2	Defective	21	Nondefective
3	Nondefective	22	Nondefective
4	Nondefective	23	Nondefective
5	Nondefective	24	Nondefective
6	Nondefective	25	Nondefective
7	Nondefective	26	Defective
8	Defective	27	Nondefective
9	Nondefective	28	Nondefective
10	Nondefective	29	Nondefective
11	Nondefective	30	Nondefective
12	Nondefective	31	Nondefective
13	Nondefective	32	Nondefective
14	Defective	33	Defective
15	Nondefective	34	Defective
16	Nondefective	35	Nondefective
17	Nondefective	36	Nondefective
18	Nondefective	37	Defective
19	Nondefective	38	Nondefective

TABLE 5.14
Defective Units in Daily Samples of 38 Radios

Day #	# Radios Inspected	# Defective Units
1	38	8
2	38	6
3	38	0
4	38	2
5	38	5
6	38	8
7	38	3
	Total: 266	32

Often, in analytic studies of processes that operate over long periods of time, data on defectives are taken on a continuing basis to provide information on the necessity for action on the process. Table 5.14 shows such data for the manufacture of radios over a seven-day period, where the data of Table 5.13 were taken on the first day.

If the process is a stable one, the average fraction defective can be obtained by treating the data as a single sample, so that

$$\bar{p} = \frac{\Sigma x}{\Sigma n} \qquad (5.7)$$

$$= \frac{32}{266} = 0.12$$

Measures of Variability

All populations and processes have some degree of variability, given appropriate sensitivity of the measuring instrument; not all items in a population or process are identical. Thus we must be able to quantify not only the central tendency but also the degree of variability in a set of data. To illustrate the need for this additional numerical measure, consider the three sets of data in Table 5.15, which represent the output from three different processes. For each process, the mean weight is 8.0 gram. If we limited ourselves to reporting this measure of central tendency only, we would actually fail to adequately characterize the three sets of measurements. While the three groups have the same mean, they differ with respect to how the data are spread around that mean, which we call the **variability** or **dispersion.** The outputs from processes A and B weigh between 5 and 10.5 grams, while those from process C weigh between 7.6 and 8.4 grams. Further, the weights from processes B and C are clustered around the mean, while those from process A are more widely dispersed away from the mean. The two commonly used quantitative measures of such variability are the **range** and the **standard deviation.**

The Range

The range is the simplest measure of dispersion; for raw data from an enumerative or an analytic study, it is defined as the difference between the largest data point and the smallest data point in a set of data:

$$R = x_{max} - x_{min} \tag{5.8}$$

Thus, for process A the range is $10.5 - 5.0 = 5.5$ grams; for process B the range is $10.5 - 5.0 = 5.5$ grams; and for process C it is $8.4 - 7.6 = 0.8$ grams. The larger the range, the more dispersed the data. In our illustrations, the outputs from processes A and B have more variability than the output from process C.

The Standard Deviation

The standard deviation as a measure of dispersion takes into account each of the data points and their distances from the mean. The more dispersed the data points, the larger the standard deviation will be; the closer the data points to the mean, the smaller the standard deviation will be.

In an enumerative study, the **population standard deviation** is computed as the square root of the average squared deviations from the mean and is denoted by the lowercase Greek letter σ ("sigma").

TABLE 5.15	Weight (g)					
Weights of Ball Bearings from Three Manufacturing Processes	**Item #**	**Process A**	**Item #**	**Process B**	**Item #**	**Process C**
	1	5.0	1	5.0	1	7.6
	2	5.3	2	7.8	2	7.8
	3	8.0	3	7.9	3	8.0
	4	9.2	4	8.0	4	8.1
	5	10.0	5	8.8	5	8.1
	6	10.5	6	10.5	6	8.4

$$\sigma = \sqrt{\frac{\Sigma(x - \mu)^2}{N}} \qquad (5.9)$$

For both enumerative and analytic studies, we calculate the standard deviation of a sample (or subgroup) of n observations, called the **sample standard deviation, s:**

$$s = \sqrt{\frac{\Sigma(x - \bar{x})^2}{n - 1}} \qquad (5.10)$$

The square of the population standard deviation is called the **population variance, σ^2.** The square of the sample standard deviation is the **sample variance, s^2.**

For the data in Table 5.15, we can calculate the sample standard deviation for process A. From Equation (5.10),

x	$(x - \bar{x})$	$(x - \bar{x})^2$
5.0	−3.0	9.00
5.3	−2.7	8.10
8.0	0.0	0.00
9.2	1.2	1.44
10.0	2.0	4.00
10.5	2.5	6.25

$$\Sigma(x - \bar{x}) = 28.79$$

$$s = \sqrt{\frac{28.79}{5}} = 2.37 \text{ grams}$$

Similarly, the sample standard deviation from process B is 1.79 grams, and from process C is 0.28 grams. The standard deviation, then, clearly shows not only that the output from process C is less variable than that from the other two processes but that the overall variability for process B is smaller than that for process A, a distinction that the range did not exhibit, because it considered only the maximum and minimum values of the data.

Measures of Shape

In addition to the measures of central tendency and variability that we have discussed, a population or the output of a process can also be characterized by its shape.

Skewness

We have already mentioned one property of shape in our discussion of the median, the **skewness,** or lack of symmetry, of a set of data. Many variables are naturally skewed, such as surface areas, volumes, warpage, and incomes. The frequency distributions in Figure 5.8 illustrate different degrees of skewness.

A numerical measure of skewness, **Pearson's coefficient of skewness,** is defined as

$$\text{Skewness}_P = \frac{3(\bar{x} - M_e)}{s} \qquad (5.11)$$

Note that for a symmetric distribution, as in Figure 5.8a, where the mean, the median, and the mode are the same, Pearson's coefficient of skewness will be 0; for a **positively**

FIGURE 5.8
Skewness of
Frequency
Distributions

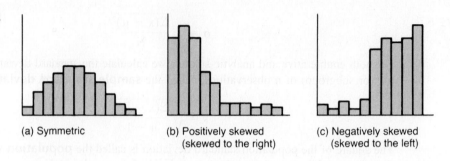

(a) Symmetric   (b) Positively skewed   (c) Negatively skewed
                          (skewed to the right)   (skewed to the left)

skewed distribution, as in Figure 5.8b, where the mean is larger than the median, which is larger than the mode, Pearson's coefficient of skewness will be positive; and for a **negatively skewed** distribution, as in Figure 5.8c, where the mode is larger than the median, which is larger than the mean, Pearson's coefficient of skewness will be negative.

For our 95 log lengths, examination of the frequency displays in Figure 5.3a and c (on page 101) indicates approximate symmetry. The mean length, from Equation (5.3), is $\bar{x} = 1336.2$ cm. The median, from Equation (5.5), is 1408.6 cm, and the standard deviation, from Equation (5.10), is 402.8 cm. Using these statistics, we can calculate Pearson's coefficient of skewness to be

$$\text{Skewness}_P = \frac{3(1336.2 - 1408.6)}{402.8} = -0.539$$

Another way to view skewness is as a measure of the relative sizes of the tails of the distribution. In symmetric distributions (where the two tails are the same), the coefficient of skewness will be zero. In skewed distributions (where the difference between the frequencies in the two tails is large), the magnitude of the coefficient of skewness will be large.

Kurtosis

Another characteristic of the shape of a frequency distribution is its peakedness, or **kurtosis.** A distribution with a relatively high concentration of data in the middle and at the tails, but low concentration in the shoulders, has a large kurtosis; one that is relatively flat in the middle, with fat shoulders and thin tails, has little kurtosis. Figure 5.9 illustrates three curves with the same mean and standard deviation, 0 skewness, and different degrees of kurtosis.

A numerical measure of kurtosis is given by:

$$\text{Kurtosis} = \frac{\Sigma(x - \bar{x})^4}{ns^4} - 3 \qquad \textbf{(5.12)}$$

The bell-shaped frequency distribution (called a **normal curve**) is labeled curve a in Figure 5.9; it has a kurtosis of 0 and is called **mesokurtic.** A more peaked curve, curve b in Figure 5.9, is called **leptokurtic** and has a positive numerical kurtosis; the flatter curve c is called **platykurtic** and has a negative kurtosis.

Necessary Sample Sizes for Estimating Measures of Shape

The measures of shape we have discussed depend largely upon the tails of the distribution. As the central portion of most distributions usually contains a sizable fraction

FIGURE 5.9
Kurtosis

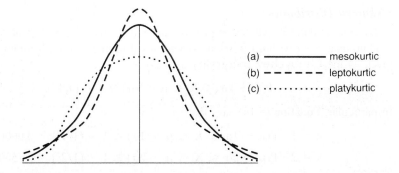

(a) ——————— mesokurtic
(b) – – – – – – leptokurtic
(c) ·············· platykurtic

of the observed data points, measures of skewness and kurtosis are often based on the relatively small fraction of the data in the tails. Hence, some statisticians suggest large sample sizes for estimating skewness and kurtosis for populations or stable processes.

Interpretation of the Standard Deviation

The standard deviation is interpreted by determining the proportion of data that lies within k standard deviations of the mean for a distribution. This proportion is a function of the shape of the distribution. In an analytic study, the distribution must be stable to interpret the standard deviation. There are four classic scenarios for distributions of data: a normal (bell-shaped) distribution, shown in Figure 5.8a; a skewed-to-the-right distribution, shown in Figure 5.8b; a skewed-to-the-left distribution, shown in Figure 5.8c; and an unknown distribution.

Normal Distribution

In the case of data that are normally distributed, the probability of obtaining a random data point within k standard deviations of the mean is:

$$k = 1 \quad P(\mu - 1\sigma < X < \mu + 1\sigma) = 0.6826$$
$$k = 2 \quad P(\mu - 2\sigma < X < \mu + 2\sigma) = 0.9544$$
$$k = 3 \quad P(\mu - 3\sigma < X < \mu + 3\sigma) = 0.9973$$

Skewed Distribution (Right or Left)

In the case of data that are unimodal and skewed to the right or the left, the probability of obtaining a random data point within k standard deviations from the mean is given by the **Camp-Meidel inequality** as follows:

$$P(\mu - k\sigma < X < \mu + k\sigma) \geq 1 - (1/[2.25]k^2) \qquad \textbf{(5.13)}$$

In particular, Equation (5.13) says that:

$$k = 1 \quad P(\mu - 1\sigma < X < \mu + 1\sigma) \geq 1 - [1/(2.25)1^2] = 0.5556$$
$$k = 2 \quad P(\mu - 2\sigma < X < \mu + 2\sigma) \geq 1 - [1/(2.25)2^2] = 0.8889$$
$$k = 3 \quad P(\mu - 3\sigma < X < \mu + 3\sigma) \geq 1 - [1/(2.25)3^2] = 0.9506$$

Unknown Distribution

In the case of data for which the distribution is unknown, the probability of obtaining a random data point within k standard deviations from the mean, assuming that $k \geq 1$, is given by the **Chebychev inequality** as follows:

$$P(\mu - k\sigma < X < \mu + k\sigma) \geq 1 - (1/k^2) \qquad \textbf{(5.14)}$$

In particular, Equation (5.14) says that:

$$k = 1 \quad P(\mu - 1\sigma < X < \mu + 1\sigma) \geq 1 - (1/1^2) = 0.0000$$
$$k = 2 \quad P(\mu - 2\sigma < X < \mu + 2\sigma) \geq 1 - (1/2^2) = 0.7500$$
$$k = 3 \quad P(\mu - 3\sigma < X < \mu + 3\sigma) \geq 1 - (1/3^2) = 0.8889$$

For the data in Table 5.15, the average, μ, for process A is 8.00 grams and the standard deviation, σ, is 2.37 grams. Choosing a value for k of 2, our interval will extend $2(2.37) = 4.74$ on either side of the mean. The interval thus extends from $8 - 4.74$ to $8 + 4.74$, or from 3.26 to 12.74. According to Chebychev's inequality, at least $1 - 1/2^2 = 3/4$ of the data points will fall in this interval. The Chebychev inequality provides us with a lower bound on the fraction of the data falling within k standard deviations of the mean. In this example, all six of the data points actually fall within the boundaries. Often, data are more closely concentrated near the mean than this rule suggests.

Thus, if the standard deviation of a distribution is small, we do not have to go very far on either side of the mean to include a large portion of the data in the distribution, even if we do not know anything about the shape of the distribution.

More Details on the Normal Distribution

We often wish to calculate the probabilities under the normal distribution between two values of the random variable X, or the probabilities under the normal distribution above and/or below one value of the random variable X. For example, Figure 5.10a shows the probability of selecting a value of X between x_1 and x_2, given a stable normal distribution with a mean of μ and a standard deviation of σ.

Suppose we consider normally distributed fuse lifetimes with a mean $\mu = 10,000$ hours and a standard deviation $\sigma = 170$ hours. If we wish to calculate the probability that a particular electric fuse lasts between 10,100 hours and 10,200 hours, we would need to calculate the probability under a normal curve with mean 10,000 and standard

FIGURE 5.10
Probabilities under the Normal Distribution

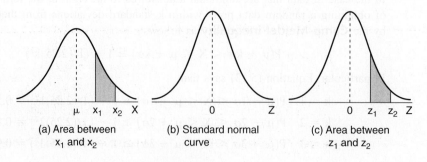

(a) Area between x_1 and x_2

(b) Standard normal curve

(c) Area between z_1 and z_2

deviation 170 between $x_1 = 10,100$ and $x_2 = 10,200$. This probability is the shaded region in Figure 5.10a.

We can calculate such probabilities by standardizing our random variable X and using a table of areas under a standard normal curve or by using Minitab, as discussed in Appendix A5.3. To use the table of areas under a standard normal curve, we define a new random variable Z as the number of standard deviations between the value of the random variable X and the mean of the distribution μ:

$$Z = (X - \mu)/\sigma \qquad (5.15)$$

The random variable Z has a normal distribution with a mean of 0 and a standard deviation of 1, as shown in Figure 5.10b.

Any value on the x-axis will correspond with exactly one z-value. Thus, using Equation (5.15), $x_1 = 10,100$ hours corresponds to a z-value of:

$$z_1 = (10,100 - 10,000)/170 = 0.59$$

That is, $x_1 = 10,100$ is 0.59 standard deviation from the mean of 10,000 hours, while $x_2 = 10,200$ hours corresponds to a z-value of:

$$z_2 = (10,200 - 10,000)/170 = 1.18$$

That is, $x_2 = 10,200$ is 1.18 standard deviations from the mean of 10,000 hours.

The probability under the standard normal distribution between $z_1 = 0.59$ and $z_2 = 1.18$, shown in Figure 5.10c, is identical to the desired area in Figure 5.10a.

Thus, given a single table that allows us to find the probability between different values of Z under the standard normal curve, we could find the probability between any two values of any normally distributed X by first standardizing to z-values.

Table B.3 in Appendix B provides the areas between 0 and positive values of Z. To use the table, values of Z should always be read to two digits after the decimal point. The units and tenths portion are found in the column on the extreme left side of the table. For $z_1 = 0.59$ this is the 0.5 row of the table. The hundredths digit, or second digit after the decimal point, is found in the top row, or the column headed 0.09 in our example. The value in the body of the table corresponding to z = 0.59 is found at the intersection of the 0.5 row and the 0.09 column, or 0.2224. This means that the probability of randomly selecting a value between z = 0 and z = 0.59 under the standard normal distribution is 0.2224, as shown in Figure 5.11a. For $z_2 = 1.18$, the value in the table at the intersection of the 1.1 row and the 0.08 column is 0.3810. Thus, the probability of

FIGURE 5.11
Calculating Probabilities under the Normal Distribution

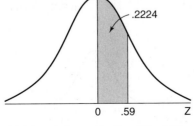
(a) Area between Z = 0 and Z = 0.59

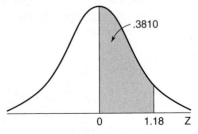
(b) Area between Z = 0 and Z = 1.18

randomly selecting a value between z = 0 and z = 1.18 under the standard normal distribution is 0.3810, as shown in Figure 5.11b.

In our example, we see from Figure 5.10c that the desired probability is the difference between the probabilities in Figures 5.11b and 5.11a; or, the probability that Z is between 0.59 and 1.18 is 0.3810 − 0.2224 = 0.1586. Symbolically, we can write:

$$P(10{,}100 < X < 10{,}200) = P(0.59 < Z < 1.18)$$
$$= P(0 < Z < 1.18) - P(0 < Z < 0.59)$$
$$= 0.3810 - 0.2224$$
$$= 0.1586$$

Thus, 15.86 percent of all electric fuses from this process will have lifetimes between 10,100 and 10,200 hours.

To further illustrate how Table B.3 can be used to find any area under a normal distribution, consider the probabilities in Figure 5.12 for our normal distribution with a mean of 10,000 hours and a standard deviation of 170 hours.

1. To calculate the probability that a fuse lasts between 9,850 and 10,050 hours, or the probability that X is between 9,850 and 10,050, we standardize the two x-values using Equation (5.15):

$$z_1 = (x_1 - \mu)/\sigma = (9{,}850 - 10{,}000)/170 = -0.88$$
$$z_2 = (x_2 - \mu)/\sigma = (10{,}050 - 10{,}000)/170 = 0.29$$

FIGURE 5.12
Probabilities under the Normal Distribution with μ = 10,000 and σ = 170

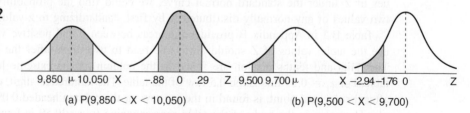

(a) P(9,850 < X < 10,050) (b) P(9,500 < X < 9,700)

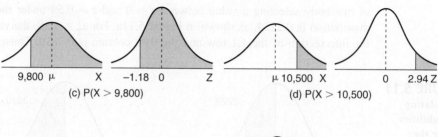

(c) P(X > 9,800) (d) P(X > 10,500)

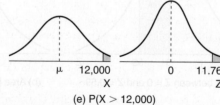

(e) P(X > 12,000)

Thus, we need to find the probability under the standard normal distribution between $z_1 = -0.88$ and $z_2 = 0.29$, since $P(9,850 < X < 10,050) = P(-0.88 < Z < 0.29)$. This probability can be written as $P(-0.88 < Z < 0) + P(0 < Z < 0.29)$.

But as the standard normal distribution is symmetric about its mean of 0, the area under the curve between any negative value of Z and 0 is identical to the value in Table B.3 corresponding to the absolute (or positive) value of Z. Thus, $P(-0.88 < Z < 0.29) = 0.3106 + 0.1141 = 0.4247$.

2. The probability that a fuse lasts between 9,500 and 9,700 hours, or $P(9,500 < X < 9,700) = P(-2.94 < Z < -1.76)$. Again, because of symmetry, this can be written as $P(0 < Z < 2.94) - P(0 < Z < 1.76) = 0.4984 - 0.4608 = 0.0376$.

3. The probability that a fuse lasts longer than 9,800 hours, or $P(X > 9,800) = P(Z > -1.18)$. Recall that the probability to the right of the mean in any normal distribution is 0.5000. Thus, $P(Z > -1.18) = (-1.18 < Z < 0) + 0.5000$, or, because of symmetry, $P(0 < Z < 1.18) + 0.5000 = 0.3810 + 0.5000 = 0.8810$.

4. The probability that a fuse lasts longer than 10,500 hours, or $P(X > 10,500) = P(Z > 2.94)$. Again, because the probability to the right of the mean is 0.5000, $P(Z > 2.94) = 0.5000 - P(0 < Z < 2.94) = 0.5000 - 0.4984 = 0.0016$.

5. The probability that a fuse lasts longer than 12,000 hours, or $P(X > 12,000) = P(Z > 11.76) = 0.5000 - P(0 < Z < 11.76)$. However, Table B.3 only shows values of Z up to 3.09. This is because, as we have indicated, almost all of the probability under the normal distribution is within three standard deviations of the mean; or, in terms of the standard normal distribution, $P(-3.00 < Z < 3.00)$ is 0.9973. From Table B.3, we see that $P(0 < Z < 3.09) = 0.4990$. Thus, $P(Z > 3.09) = 0.5000 - 0.4990 = 0.0010$; the probability that Z is larger than 11.76 is even smaller. Thus, $P(Z > 11.76)$ is approximately 0.0000.

Normal Probability Plot

A **normal probability plot** is a graphical tool that can be used to determine if a distribution of data approximates a normal distribution. A normal probability plot uses special graph paper called normal probability paper, which has the numerical value of x on the horizontal axis (x-axis), and the cumulative distribution for that value of x, $P(X < x)$, on the vertical, or y-axis. If the plotted data fall on a straight line, then the distribution is normally distributed. If the plotted data do not fall on a straight line, the distribution is not normally distributed. For example, returning to the chocolate bar example in Table 5.11, we can construct the normal probability plot in Figure 5.13.

Figure 5.13 shows that the distribution of chocolate bar weights is approximately normally distributed because the plotted points lie on a straight line.

Table 5.16 shows data concerning the "days from order to delivery" for a particular item (see ❀ DELIVERY). We wish to know whether the data are normally distributed.

Figure 5.14 shows a dotplot of the supplier delivery data.

Figure 5.15 shows the normal probability plot for the supplier delivery data. Clearly, the plotted data do not lie on the straight line. This indicates that the distribution of supplier delivery data is not normally distributed.

In fact, Figure 5.14 shows that the supplier delivery data are not normally distributed; rather, it follows a bimodal distribution, as discussed above under "Measures of Central Tendency." One possible cause for this distribution is that there are two suppliers, one

FIGURE 5.13
Normal
Probability
Plot of
Chocolate Bar
Data

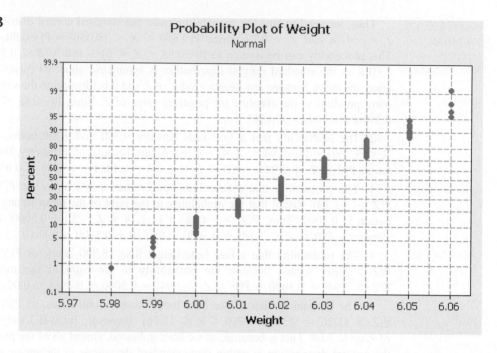

TABLE 5.16
Supplier
Delivery Data:
(Data Are
Listed across
the Rows)

3	4	4	8	3	2	4	5	6	7	3	2	6	11	2
3	6	4	5	3	5	4	3	6	4	4	8	6	3	6
4	4	4	7	5	3	1	7	10	3	8	3	6	1	0
2	4	6	10	6	23	21	26	26	25	24	28	24	26	22
30	26	19	22	24	31	19	22	24	32	21	30	29	25	20
23	27	18	30	28	27	18	14	31	19	30	27	31	26	23
25	22	20	22	27	20	26	28	23	15					

with a mean delivery time around 5 days and the other with a mean delivery time around 25 days. Note that once we observe this, we can improve the supplier delivery process by buying only from the supplier with the shorter delivery time distribution.

An Empirical Rule for Analytic Studies

In enumerative studies we often have the opportunity to know something about the shape of our data. The data points may tend to follow one of a great variety of distributional forms. Unfortunately, in analytic studies, we usually do not have the luxury of such information for future output. Even if we do know the distributional form of historical data, there is no guarantee that the form will remain operational in the future. Nevertheless, it is not necessary to make assumptions about the distribution of future output. W. A. Shewhart demonstrated that the means and standard deviations computed from

FIGURE 5.14
Dotplot of Supplier Delivery Data

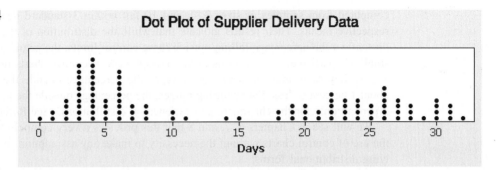

FIGURE 5.15
Normal Probability Plot of Supplier Delivery Data

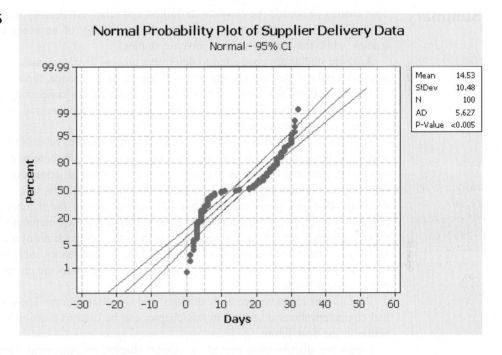

25 samples of four observations each drawn from normal, uniform, and triangular distributions all were within 3 standard deviations of their respective means. In Shewhart's words, "In each case all of the points are within the limits as we should expect them to be under the controlled conditions supposed to exist in drawing these samples." [See Reference 1, p. 318.] Wheeler and Chambers expand on this point, arguing "Control charts work well even if the data are not normally distributed . . . [when data from a process are stable] no matter how the data 'behave,' virtually all of the data will fall within three sigma units of the average." [See Reference 2, p. 65.] Their **Empirical Rule** states that for a stable process: "Approximately 99% to 100% of the data will be located within a distance of three sigma units on either side of the average." [See Reference 2, p. 61.] They show that for six widely differing distributions, virtually all of the means and ranges

computed from samples of sizes 2, 4, and 10 fall within 3 standard deviations of their respective means. Their results indicate that while the distribution of the measurements does affect the percentage falling outside these control limits, the actual effects are quite small. Of particular interest to us in the development of control charts in Chapters 6, 7, and 8, they show that for subgroup averages the percentage outside the limits remains about 1 percent or less. For subgroup ranges, the percentage outside the limits goes above 2 percent only for the chi-square and exponential distributions. [See Reference 2, p. 76.]

We will see in Chapters 6, 7, and 8 that this provides a very compelling argument for the use of control charts without the necessity to make any assumptions regarding underlying distributional forms.

Summary

This chapter presented the classical definition and relative frequency definition of probability. The former allows us to calculate the probability of an event for enumerative studies, while the latter is used in analytic studies.

Analytic studies are conducted to determine process characteristics. But process characteristics have a past and present and will have a future; hence, there is no frame from which classical probabilities can be calculated. Probabilities concerning process characteristics must be obtained empirically, through experimentation, and must therefore be relative frequency probabilities.

We have also looked at how to describe the characteristics of data taken from a population or process. We may classify data into two types: attribute and variables (measurement). Attribute data arise (1) from the classification of items, such as products or services, into categories, (2) from counts of the number of items in a given category or the proportion in a given category, and (3) from counts of the number of occurrences per unit. Variables (measurement) data arise (1) from the measurement of a characteristic of a product, service, or process and (2) from the computation of a numerical value from two or more measurements of variables data. In any quality study we usually want to rearrange and/or manipulate data to gain some insight into the characteristics of the process under study.

Data may be characterized by both visual and numerical means. The visual and numerical characterizations discussed in this chapter can be used to make inferences and take action in the near future.

Frequency distributions provide a tabular display of numerical data grouped into nonoverlapping intervals. Graphical displays offer a composite picture of the relationships and/or patterns in the data at a glance. A frequency distribution shows us, in tabular form, the number of times, or the frequency with which, a given value or group of values occurs. Frequency distributions of variables data are commonly represented graphically in frequency polygons or histograms. Frequency distributions of attribute data are commonly represented in bar charts. In analytic studies we want to be able to detect trends or other patterns over time to take action on a process in the near future. A run chart (also called a tier chart) preserves information concerning the time-ordering of data by plotting the data on the vertical axis and time on the horizontal axis.

Numerical measures summarize important characteristics of a population or process in a more quantitative way. Data can vary with respect to central tendency, variability, and shape.

The mean, median, and mode are used to describe the central tendency of variables data; the median and mode are not affected by extreme values in a data set; the mean is affected by extreme values in a data set. The proportion is a useful measure for attribute data.

All populations and processes have some degree of variability, given appropriate sensitivity of the measuring instrument; not all items in a population or process are identical. Thus we must be able to quantify not only the central tendency but also the degree of variability in a set of data. The range and standard deviation provide useful characterizations of the variability.

The skewness and kurtosis of a frequency distribution are numerical measures of the shape. Skewness is a measure of the lack of symmetry of a set of data. Kurtosis is a measure of the peakedness of a frequency distribution.

A distribution of data is characterized by its center (mean, median, mode, or proportion), variation (range or standard deviation), shape (histogram or bar chart, skewness, kurtosis), and, in an analytic study, whether it comes from a stable process.

Interpretation of the standard deviation was discussed for three cases: normally distributed data, skewed data, and data with an unknown distribution. Rules were given for each case that permit the estimation of the proportion of data in a population or a stable process that lies within k standard deviations from the mean.

We often wish to calculate the probabilities under the normal distribution between two values of the random variable X, or the probabilities under the normal distribution above and/or below one value of the random variable X. We can calculate such probabilities by standardizing our random variable X and using a table of areas under a standard normal curve or by using Minitab.

An Empirical Rule was presented that states that virtually all output for a stable process will be contained within a three-sigma interval around the mean, providing us with a basis for constructing control charts in Chapters 6, 7, and 8.

Key Terms

absolute frequency, *98*
analytic study, *92*
attribute data, *92*
bar chart, *100*
bimodal, *108*
Camp-Meidel inequality, *113*
central tendency, *103*
Chebychev inequality, *114*
classical definition of probability, *88*
consumer's risk, *96*
cumulative frequency distribution, *99*
data, *92*

dispersion, *110*
Empirical Rule, *119*
enumerative study, *96*
frequency distribution, *97*
frequency polygon, *100*
histogram, *100*
kurtosis, *112*
leptokurtic, *112*
mean, *103*
measurement data, *92*
median, *106*
mesokurtic, *112*
mode, *108*
mutually exclusive, *88*
negatively skewed, *112*

normal curve, *112*
normal probability plot, *117*
ogive, *102*
Pearson's coefficient of skewness, *111*
platykurtic, *112*
population mean, *106*
population standard deviation, *110*
population variance, *111*
positively skewed, *111*
producer's risk, *96*
proportion, *108*
random sample, *97*

Exercises

5.1. You have just been appointed plant manager in a sock factory. On your first day you are presented with the following production history.

Grade	Number of Socks Produced January 2001–December 2003	
Firsts (good)	73,197	(72.21%)
Seconds (sell at lower price)	17,877	(17.64%)
Scrap (junk)	10,286	(10.15%)
Total	101,360	

a. What does the table tell you about the factory's capability to produce good socks (firsts) in the future?

b. Would more information about the table's figures improve its usefulness? What information?

5.2. The accompanying table provides seven years of departmental accident data for an industrial laundry. The data have been analyzed chronologically, by day, and found to exhibit stable patterns of variation with respect to accidents per day.

Department	Number of Accidents					
	Mon.	Tues.	Wed.	Thurs.	Fri.	Total
Receiving/Shipping	12	8	9	8	13	50
Washroom	30	19	21	27	33	130
Drying	10	10	11	9	9	49
Ironing/Folding	22	20	21	19	20	102
Total	74	57	62	63	75	331

a. What is the probability that an accident will occur in the Washroom on Monday?

b. What is the probability that an accident will occur in Ironing/Folding on Thursday?

c. What is the probability that an accident will occur on Friday?

d. What is the probability that an accident will occur in Receiving/Shipping?

5.3. An accounting clerk is responsible for computing the effective number of hours worked daily [regular time + (1.5 × overtime)] for each of 500 production workers and for recording the number of days absent each week on the time sheet for each worker. These two functions (computing effective daily hours per worker and recording number of days absent each week per worker) are the job characteristics upon which she is judged. The accounting supervisor draws weekly random samples of 50 time sheets to monitor and help improve the clerk's performance. The following chart reflects 30 weeks of analysis.

Recorded Number of Days Absent per Week	Computation of Effective Hours per Week		Total
	Correct (no mistakes)	**Incorrect** (one or more mistakes)	
Correct (recorded properly)	1,235	190	1,425
Incorrect (recorded improperly)	65	10	75
Total	1,300	200	1,500

a. Can the accounting supervisor use this information to help the clerk improve her performance? Why?

b. What assumptions are required for the supervisor to be able to use those figures in supervisory efforts?

Assuming that the accounting clerk's work is in statistical control in relation to both quality characteristics:

c. What is the probability that the effective hours will be computed correctly?

d. What is the probability that the number of days absent will be recorded correctly?

e. What is the probability that a time sheet will be completed correctly? Incorrectly?

5.4. A consumer protection testing agency wants to study the life expectancy of a particular job lot of a new radial tire (see 🎯 TIRES). Ten tires were randomly selected from the job lot. Achieved mileages before the minimum tread depth was reached (and the tires were declared worn out) were: 32,800, 41,700, 35,200, 39,000, 36,200, 35,600, 35,700, 45,200, 42,800, and 35,700.

a. Construct a frequency distribution and cumulative frequency distribution for these data.

b. Using the frequency distribution in part a, draw a histogram of the recorded mileages for the 10 new radial tires.

c. Is a run chart an appropriate display for these data? Explain why or why not, and if so, construct a run chart.

d. Calculate the mean life expectancy for this sample of 10 tires.

e. Calculate the median life expectancy for this sample of 10 tires.

f. Calculate the modal life expectancy for this sample of 10 tires.

g. Calculate the standard deviation of the life expectancy of the sample of 10 tires.

h. Calculate the range for these data.

5.5. A machine shop manager wishes to study the time it takes an assembler to complete a given small subassembly (see ASSEMBLY). Measurements, in minutes, are made at 15 consecutive half-hour intervals. The times to complete the task are 12, 10, 18, 16, 4, 16, 11, 15, 15, 13, 19, 10, 15, 17, and 11.

   a. Construct a frequency distribution and cumulative frequency distribution for these data.

   b. Using the preceding frequency distribution, draw a frequency polygon for the times to complete the task. Comment on the skewness of the data.

   c. Is a run chart an appropriate display for these data? Explain why or why not, and if so, construct a run chart.

   d. Calculate the mean time to complete the task on the basis of this sample of 15 observations.

   e. Calculate the median time to complete the task on the basis of this sample of 15 observations.

   f. Calculate the modal time to complete the task on the basis of this sample of 15 observations.

   g. Calculate the standard deviation of the time to complete the task for the sample.

   h. Calculate the range for these data.

   i. Calculate Pearson's coefficient of skewness for these data.

5.6. A buyer for a large chain of restaurants is about to purchase a large number of chicken breasts (see CHICKEN). According to the supplier, the breasts weigh an average of 1 pound each. The buyer selects a random sample of 10 breasts and weighs them, finding the following weights, in pounds: 1.04, 1.00, 0.94, 1.10, 1.02, 0.90, 0.97, 1.03, 1.05, and 0.95.

   a. Calculate the mean weight for this sample of 10 chicken breasts.

   b. Calculate the median weight for this sample of 10 chicken breasts.

   c. Calculate the standard deviation of the weight of chicken breasts in this sample.

   d. Calculate the range of weights of chicken breasts, based upon the sample of 10 chicken breasts.

   e. Calculate the kurtosis for these data.

5.7. The ABC Company is planning to analyze the average weekly wage distribution of its 58 employees during fiscal year 2003 (see WAGES). The 58 weekly wages are available as raw data corresponding to the alphabetic order of the employees' names:

241	253	312	258	264	265
316	242	257	251	282	305
298	276	284	304	285	307
263	301	262	272	271	265
249	229	253	285	267	250
288	248	276	280	252	258
262	314	241	257	250	275
275	301	283	249	288	275
281	276	289	228	275	
170	289	262	282	260	

a. Calculate the mean, median, and mode of the data.

b. Calculate the range of the data.

c. Calculate the standard deviation of the data.

d. Calculate the skewness of the data.

e. Calculate the kurtosis of the data.

f. Construct a frequency distribution for the data.

g. Draw a histogram for the frequency distribution in part f.

5.8. The following frequency distribution shows the distance covered (in miles) by a sample of 80 trucks belonging to a long-distance moving company during one year.

Distance Covered (in miles)	Number of Trucks
30,000 but less than 40,000	2
40,000 but less than 50,000	3
50,000 but less than 60,000	7
60,000 but less than 70,000	12
70,000 but less than 80,000	18
80,000 but less than 90,000	24
90,000 but less than 100,000	14

a. Plot a histogram for this frequency distribution.

b. Plot a frequency polygon for this frequency distribution.

5.9. The following frequency distribution shows the number of minutes spent on an elementary task in a customer service center performed by 35 employees over a one-month period:

Number of Minutes	Number of Employees
2 but less than 4	3
4 but less than 6	8
6 but less than 8	20
8 but less than 10	4

a. Plot a frequency polygon for this frequency distribution.

b. Plot a histogram for this frequency distribution.

5.10. Given the ordered arrays in the accompanying table dealing with the lengths of life (in hours) of a sample of forty 100-watt light bulbs produced by manufacturer A and a sample of forty 100-watt light bulbs produced by manufacturer B (see BULBS):

Manufacturer A					Manufacturer B				
684	697	720	773	821	819	836	888	897	903
831	835	848	852	852	907	912	918	942	943
859	860	868	870	876	952	959	962	986	992
893	899	905	909	911	994	1,004	1,005	1,007	1,015
922	924	926	926	938	1,016	1,018	1,020	1,022	1,034
939	943	946	954	971	1,038	1,072	1,077	1,077	1,082
972	977	984	1,005	1,014	1,096	1,100	1,113	1,113	1,116
1,016	1,041	1,052	1,080	1,093	1,153	1,154	1,174	1,188	1,230

a. Form the frequency distribution for each brand according to the following schema: manufacturer A: 650 but less than 750, 750 but less than 850, and so on; manufacturer B: 750 but less than 850, 850 but less than 950, and so on.

b. Plot the histograms for each manufacturer on separate graphs.

c. Plot the percentage polygons for the two manufacturers on one graph.

d. Compute the mean and median for each manufacturer.

e. Compute the range and standard deviation for each manufacturer.

f. Are the data skewed? If so, how?

g. Which manufacturer has bulbs with a longer life? Explain.

h. Can you predict which manufacturer will have a longer life bulb on average in the near future from the above data? If no, why not? If yes, why?

5.11. The following data represent the amount of soft drink filled in a sample of 50 consecutive 2-liter bottles (see DRINK). The results, listed horizontally in the order of being filled, are:

2.109	2.086	2.066	2.075	2.065	2.057	2.052	2.044	2.036	2.038
2.031	2.029	2.025	2.029	2.023	2.020	2.015	2.014	2.013	2.014
2.012	2.012	2.012	2.010	2.005	2.003	1.999	1.996	1.997	1.992
1.994	1.986	1.984	1.981	1.973	1.975	1.971	1.969	1.966	1.967
1.963	1.957	1.951	1.951	1.947	1.941	1.941	1.938	1.908	1.894

a. Construct the frequency distribution and the percentage distribution.

b. Plot a histogram.

c. Plot a frequency polygon.

d. On the basis of the results of parts a to c, does there appear to be any concentration of the amount of soft drink filled in the bottles around specific values?

e. Plot a run chart. What conclusions about the filling process can you make from the run chart?

f. If you had to make a prediction of the amount of soft drink filled in the next bottle, what value would you predict? Why?

5.12. The viscosity (resistance to flow) of a chemical product produced in batches over time was examined to determine if each batch conforms to specifications. The data for 120 batches are in the data file CHEMICAL. Assume that the viscosity of the chemical needs to be between 13 and 18 to meet company specifications.

[**Source:** Holmes and Mergen, "Parabolic Control Limits for the Exponentially Weighted Moving Average Control Charts," *Quality Engineering* 4, No. 4, 1992, pp. 487–495.]

    a. Construct a frequency distribution.

    b. Plot the histogram.

    c. Compute the mean and median for the data.

    d. Compute the range, variance, and standard deviation.

    e. Are the data skewed? If so, how?

    f. Is a run chart appropriate for this data set? If yes, construct the run chart. If no, why not?

    g. What conclusions can you draw from examining the run chart? Are they different from your examination of the histogram?

5.13. The operations manager of a plant that manufactures tires wishes to compare the actual inner diameter of two grades of tires, each of which has a nominal value of 575 millimeters. A sample of five tires of each grade is selected, and the results representing the inner diameters of the tires, ordered from smallest to largest, are as follows:

Grade X	Grade Y
568, 570, 575, 578, 584	573, 574, 575, 577, 578

    a. Compute the mean, median, and standard deviation for each grade of tire.

    b. What would be the effect on your answers in parts a and b if the last value for grade Y was 588 instead of 578? Explain.

    c. Which grade of tire is providing better quality? Explain. (*Hint:* Is the process stable?)

5.14. A manufacturer of flashlight batteries took a sample of 13 batteries from a day's production and used them continuously until they were drained (see BATTERIES). The numbers of hours they were used until failure were:

    342, 426, 317, 545, 264, 451, 1049, 631, 512, 266, 492, 562, 298

    a. Compute the mean, median, mode, range and standard deviation for the time to failure.

    b. Are the above statistics useful to the production manager? If yes, why? If no, why not?

    c. Using the information above, what would you advise if the manufacturer wanted to be able to say in advertisements that these batteries "should last 400 hours"?

5.15. A bank branch of the Bank of New Jersey, located in a commercial district of a city, has developed an improved process for serving customers during the

12:00 P.M. to 1 P.M. peak lunch period (see 🖭 BANK1). The waiting time in minutes (operationally defined as the time the customer enters the line until she is served) of all customers during this hour is recorded over a period of 1 week. A random sample of 15 customers is selected and the results are as follows:

4.21, 5.55, 3.02, 5.13, 4.77, 2.34, 3.54, 3.20, 4.50, 6.10, 0.38, 5.12, 6.46, 6.19, 3.79

a. Compute the mean, median, range and standard deviation for these data.

b. As a customer walks into the branch office during the lunch hour, she asks the branch manager how long she can expect to wait. The branch manager replies, "Almost certainly not longer than five minutes." On the basis of the results of part a, evaluate this statement. Can the manager make this claim on the basis of the statistics in part a? If no, why not? If yes, why?

 5.16. Suppose that another branch of the Bank of New Jersey located in a residential area is most concerned with the Friday evening hours from 5 P.M. to 7 P.M (see 🖭 BANK2). The waiting time in minutes (operationally defined as the time the customer enters the line until she is served) of all customers during these hours is recorded over a period of 1 week. A random sample of 15 customers is selected and the results are as follows:

9.66, 5.90, 8.02, 5.79, 8.73, 3.82, 8.01, 8.35, 10.49,
6.68, 5.64, 4.08, 6.17, 9.91, 5.47

a. Compute the mean, median, range, and standard deviation for this data.

b. As a customer walks into the branch office during the lunch hour, he asks the branch manager how long he can expect to wait. The branch manager replies, "Almost certainly not longer than five minutes." On the basis of the results of part a, evaluate this statement. Can the manager make this claim based on the statistics in part a? If no, why not? If yes, why?

c. What arguments can be raised that would make it inappropriate to compare the waiting times in Exercise 5.15 with those in this exercise?

5.17. In New York State, savings banks are permitted to sell a form of life insurance called Savings Bank Life Insurance (SBLI) (see 🖭 INSURANCE). The approval process consists of underwriting, which includes a review of the application, a medical information bureau check, possible requests for additional medical information and medical exams, and a policy compilation stage where the policy pages are generated and sent to the bank for delivery. The ability to deliver approved policies to customers in a timely manner is critical to the profitability of this service to the bank. During a one-month period, a random sample of 27 approved policies was selected and the total processing time in days was recorded with the following results:

73, 19, 16, 64, 28, 28, 31, 90, 60, 56, 31, 56, 22, 18, 45, 48,
17, 17, 17, 91, 92, 63, 50, 51, 69, 16, 17

a. Compute the mean and median for these data.

b. Compute the range and standard deviation for these data.

c. What would you tell a customer who enters the bank to purchase this type of insurance policy and asks how long the approval process takes?

5.18. One of the major measures of the quality of service provided by any organization is the speed with which it performs its services (see ☛ FURNITURE). A large family-held department store selling furniture and flooring, including carpeting, had undergone a major expansion in the past several years. In particular, the flooring department had expanded from two installation crews to an installation supervisor, a measurer, and 15 installation crews. The following data represent the number of days between the receipt of an order and the installation of the order for the first 50 customers under the new departmental structure.

54	5	35	137	31	27	152	2	123	81	74	27
11	19	126	110	110	29	61	35	94	31	26	5
12	4	165	32	29	28	29	26	25	1	14	13
13	10	5	27	4	52	30	22	36	26	20	23
33	68										

a. Compute the mean and median for these data.

b. Compute the range and standard deviation for these data.

c. Are the data skewed? If so, how?

d. Construct a run chart for these data.

e. On the basis of the results of parts a to d, if you had to tell the president of the company how long a customer should expect to wait to have an order installed, what would you say? Explain.

 5.19. A telephone line on which a customer is unable to receive or make calls is disconcerting to both the customer and the telephone company (see ☛ PHONE). This can be caused by either problems inside a central office or problems on lines between the central office and the customer's equipment. The following data represent the first 20 problems reported to two different offices of a telephone company (Central Office I and Central Office II) on January 21, 2003, and the time to clear these problems (in minutes) from the customers' lines:

Central Office I Time to Clear Problems (minutes)									
1.48	1.75	0.78	2.85	0.52	1.60	4.15	3.97	1.48	3.10
1.02	0.53	0.93	1.60	0.80	1.05	6.32	3.93	5.45	0.97

Central Office II Time to Clear Problems (minutes)									
7.55	3.75	0.10	1.10	0.60	0.52	3.30	2.10	0.58	4.02
3.75	0.65	1.92	0.60	1.53	4.23	0.08	1.48	1.65	0.72

For each of the two central office locations,

a. Compute the mean and median for these data.

b. Compute the range and standard deviation for these data.

c. Are the data skewed? If so, how?

d. Construct run charts for each office using the same y-axis scale.

  e. On the basis of the results of parts a to d, are there any differences between the two central offices? Explain.

  f. What would be the effect on your results and your conclusions if the first value for Central Office II was incorrectly recorded as 27.55 instead of 7.55?

5.20. In many manufacturing processes there is a term called "work-in-process" (see WIP). In a book manufacturing plant this represents the time it takes for sheets from a press to be folded, gathered, sewn, tipped on end-sheets, and bound. The following data represent the time in minutes that it takes to make the first 20 books at each of two production plants.

Plant A									
5.62	5.29	16.25	10.92	11.46	21.62	8.45	8.58	5.41	11.42
11.62	7.29	7.50	7.96	4.42	10.50	7.58	9.29	7.54	8.92

Plant B									
9.54	11.46	16.62	12.62	25.75	15.41	14.29	13.13	13.71	10.04
5.75	12.46	9.17	13.21	6.00	2.33	14.25	5.37	6.25	9.71

For each of the two plants,

  a. Compute the mean and median for these data.

  b. Compute the range, variance, and standard deviation for these data.

  c. Are the data skewed? If so, how?

  d. Construct run charts for each plant using the same y-axis scale.

  e. On the basis of the results of parts a to d, are there any differences between the two plants? Explain.

5.21. Given a standardized normal distribution (with a mean of 0 and a standard deviation of 1, as in Table B.3) what is the probability that

  a. Z is less than 1.43?

  b. Z exceeds 1.64?

  c. Z is between 1.43 and 1.64?

  d. Z is less than 1.43 or greater than 1.64?

  e. Z is between -1.43 and 1.64?

  f. Z is less than -1.43 or greater than 1.64?

  g. What is the value of Z if 50.0 percent of all possible Z values are larger?

  h. What is the value of Z if only 2.5 percent of all possible Z values are larger?

  i. Between what two values of Z (symmetrically distributed around the mean) will 68.26 percent of all possible Z-values be contained?

5.22. Given a normal distribution with $\mu = 20$ and $\sigma = 4$, what is the probability that

  a. $X > 13$?

  b. $X < 12$?

  c. $12 < X < 18$?

  d. $X > 27.5$?

e. X < 10 or X > 25?

f. 5 percent of the values are less than what X value?

g. 70 percent of the values are between what two X values (symmetrically distributed around the mean)?

h. 75 percent of the values will be above what X value?

5.23. An industrial sewing machine uses ball bearings that are targeted to have a diameter of 0.75 inch. The specification limits under which the ball bearings can operate are 0.74 inch (lower) and 0.76 inch (upper). Past experience has indicated that the actual diameter of the ball bearings is approximately normally distributed with a mean of 0.753 inch and a standard deviation of 0.004 inch. What is the probability that a ball bearing diameter will be

a. Between the target and the actual mean?

b. Between the lower specification limit and the target?

c. Above the upper specification limit?

d. Below the lower specification limit?

e. Above which value in diameter will 93 percent of the ball bearings be?

f. What assumption is critical to using the probabilities in parts a to e?

5.24. Suppose that the fill amount of bottles of soft drink has been found to be normally distributed with a mean of 2.0 liters and a standard deviation of 0.05 liter. Bottles that contain less than 95 percent of the listed net content (1.90 liters in this case) can result in the manufacturer being subject to a penalty by the state Office of Consumer Affairs, whereas bottles that have a net content above 2.10 liters may cause excess spillage upon opening. What proportion of the bottles will contain

a. Between 1.90 and 2.0 liters?

b. Between 1.90 and 2.10 liters?

c. Below 1.90 liters?

d. Below 1.90 liters or above 2.10 liters?

e. Above 2.10 liters?

f. Between 2.05 and 2.10 liters?

g. 99 percent of the bottles would be expected to contain at least how much soft drink?

h. 99 percent of the bottles would be expected to contain an amount that is between which two values (symmetrically distributed)?

i. Explain the difference in the results in parts g and h.

j. Suppose that in an effort to reduce the number of bottles that contain less than 1.90 liters, the bottler sets the filling machine so that the mean is 2.02 liters. Under these circumstances, what would be your answers in parts a to i?

k. What assumption is critical to your answers in parts a to j?

References

1. W. A. Shewhart (1931), *Economic Control of Quality of Manufactured Product* (New York: Van Nostrand).

2. Donald J. Wheeler and David S. Chambers (1992), *Understanding Statistical Process Control*, 2nd ed. (Knoxville, TN: SPC Press).

Appendix **A5.1**

Using Windows

The step-by-step instructions for using Minitab require that you are familiar with basic Windows procedures and objects. You can use this section to learn or review these concepts.

You point and select objects on screen by using a **mouse** or other pointing device in Microsoft Windows. The graphical user interface of Windows expects pointing devices to contain two buttons, one designated as the **primary button,** the other as the **secondary button.** Moving the pointing device and pressing and releasing these buttons in different ways determines which one of the standard mouse operations is executed, as shown in Exhibit A5.1.

EXHIBIT A5.1 *Standard Mouse Operations*	**Click:** Move the mouse pointer over an object and press the primary button. For some objects, the verb **select** is used to describe this action, as in the phrase "select the entry for the program." **Drag:** Move the mouse pointer over an object. Then while pressing and holding down the primary button, move the mouse pointer somewhere else on the screen and release the primary button. Dragging either moves objects to another screen location or allows you to select multiple items. **Double-click:** Move the mouse pointer over an object and click the primary button twice in rapid succession. **Right-click:** Move the mouse pointer over an object and click the secondary button.

By default, Microsoft Windows defines the left mouse button as the primary button and the right button as the secondary button (this gives rise to the phrase "right-click"), but the definitions can be reversed by changing the appropriate Windows user settings.

Opening Programs

Microsoft Windows includes three methods of using a mouse to open a program, as shown in Exhibit A5.2. Which way you choose is partly personal preference and partly determined by how the program has been set up.

When you open a program, Microsoft Windows opens an **application window.** The application window of Minitab contains a title bar, resize and close application window buttons, a menu bar containing a list of pull-down menus, a toolbar that contains icons representing menu shortcuts, and a worksheet area of rows and columns for making entries, as shown in Figure A5.1.

You operate the program directly in the application window by making entries and selecting choices from the pull-down menus. Data entries are made directly into worksheet cells to which you navigate by either using the mouse or the cursor keys. Some menu selections directly perform a function or task, but many more lead to **dialog boxes** in which you enter information and settings for a procedure. The Open Worksheet and

EXHIBIT A5.2	**Program icon click:** Double-click the Windows desktop icon representing the program (in some Windows versions this requires only a single click).
Methods of Opening Programs in Microsoft Windows	**Start menu entry selection:** Press the Windows key (or click the on-screen Start button) and select the "Programs" or "All Programs" choice. From the menu list that appears, select the entry for the program. Sometimes, you will find the program entry on a submenu, so several selections may be required.
	File icon click: Double-click the Windows desktop icon representing a file of a type that Windows associates with a specific program. For example, if you click an icon for an .mtw workbook file, both Minitab and the Minitab worksheet open.

Throughout this text, the procedures for using the statistical programs are written presuming that you will be using either the first or second method because these two methods *always* allow you to verify program settings before you use your data. Should you choose to use the third method, you will still be able to use those procedures.

FIGURE A5.1 **Application Window for Minitab**

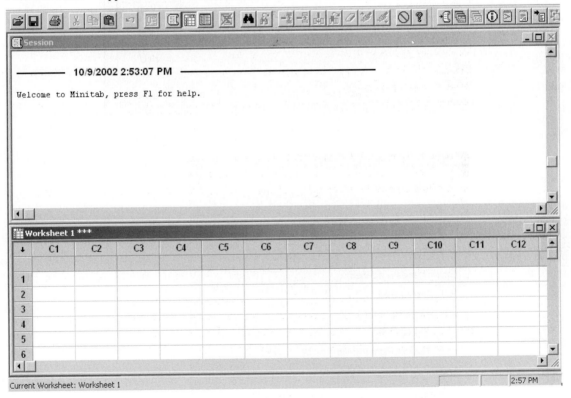

Print Worksheet dialog boxes from Minitab are shown in Figure A5.2. Exhibit A5.3 further explains the dialog boxes.

Note that in the Open Worksheet dialog box, the Files of type: drop-down list box by default lists Minitab (*.mtw). To change the selection to another type of file, click the down arrow and select the desired file type [such as Excel (*.xls)].

FIGURE A5.2
(a) Minitab Open Worksheet Dialog Box;
(b) Minitab Print Options Dialog Box

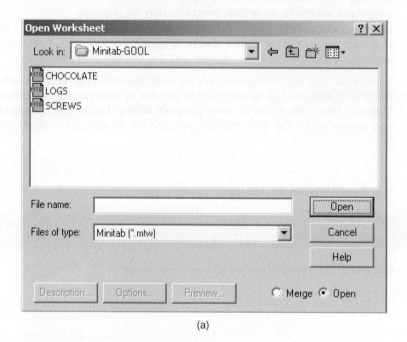

(a)

(b)

EXHIBIT A5.3

Common Dialog Box Objects

Drop-down list box: Displays a list of choices when the drop-down button, located on the right edge of the box, is clicked.

List box: Displays a list of choices for selection. Should the list exceed the dimensions of the list box, the list box will include **scroll buttons** and a **slider** that you can click to display the other choices of the list.

Edit box: Provides an area into which a value can be edited or typed. Edit boxes are often combined with either a drop-down list or **spinner buttons** to provide alternatives to the direct typing of a value.

Option buttons: Represent a set of mutually exclusive choices. Selecting an option button always deselects, or clears, the other option buttons in the set, thereby allowing only one choice to be made for that set.

Check box: Allows the selection of optional actions. Unlike option buttons, more than one check box can be selected at a time.

OK command button: Causes the program to execute some action using the current values and settings of the dialog box. As in the File Open dialog box shown in Figure A5.2a, this button sometimes contains a different label such as Open, Save, or Finish.

Cancel command button: Closes a dialog box and cancels the operation represented by the dialog box. In most contexts, clicking the Cancel button is equivalent to clicking the **Close button** on the title bar.

Help command button: Displays a help message or help window for the dialog box. Many dialog boxes also include the **Question mark button** on the title bar that performs a similar function.

Making Mistakes and Correcting Entries

If you make an error while entering data, you can usually do one of the following three things to correct the error.

- Press the Escape key to cancel the current entry.
- Press the Backspace key to erase typed characters to the left of the cursor one character at a time.
- Press the Delete key to erase characters to the right of the cursor one character at a time.

For errors in the middle of an entry, you can also drag the mouse over the in-error text and then type the replacement text. Selecting Delete from the Edit menu will undo any typing as well.

How This Text Represents Multiple Menu Selections

From this point forward, when this text describes a procedure that involves two or more consecutive menu selections, the selections appear in boldfaced type and chained together with the vertical slash character |. For example, the phrase "selecting the Open Worksheet choice from the File pull-down menu" would, in subsequent pages, be written as "select **File | Open Worksheet.**"

Appendix A5.2 presents the basic operating procedures for the Minitab statistical program that is featured in this text.

Appendix A5.2

Introduction to Minitab

Minitab is a set of computer programs designed to perform statistical analyses. It is used in many large corporations.

In Minitab, you create and open **Projects** to store all of your data and results. A **session** (or log of activities) is managed using a **Project Manager.** A project manager summarizes the project contents, and any worksheets or graphs used are the components that form a project. Project components are displayed in separate windows *inside* the Minitab application window. By default, you will see only the session and one worksheet window when you begin a new project in Minitab. (You can bring any window to the front by selecting the window in the Minitab Windows menu.) You can open and save an entire project or, as is done in this text, open and save worksheets.

Using Minitab Worksheets

You use a Minitab worksheet to enter data for statistical analysis. Minitab worksheets are organized as numbered rows and columns, as shown in Figure A5.3. The columns are labeled C1, C2, C3, etc. Data for a quality characteristic of interest are entered into a column. You enter the "name" for a quality characteristic in a special unnumbered row that precedes row 1. For example, if the "cycle time to process a customer account" is the quality characteristic of interest and 2 customer accounts are selected a day for 5 days,

FIGURE A5.3 **Minitab Worksheet**

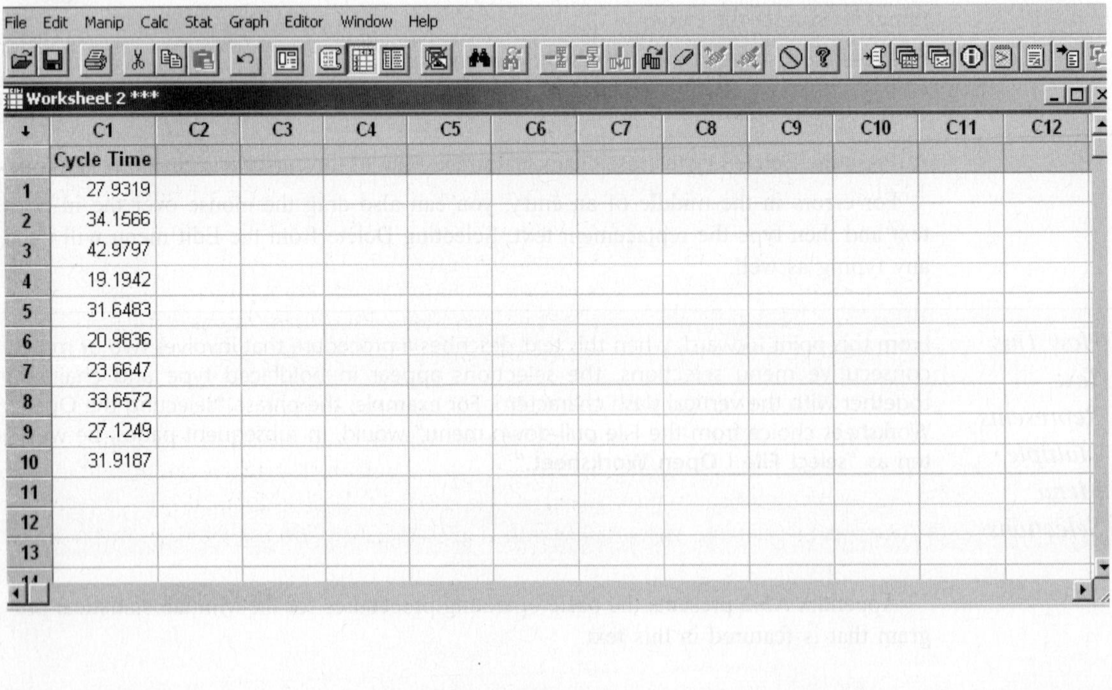
File Edit Manip Calc Stat Graph Editor Window Help
Worksheet 2 ***
C1 C2 C3 C4 C5 C6 C7 C8 C9 C10 C11 C12
Cycle Time
1 27.9319
2 34.1566
3 42.9797
4 19.1942
5 31.6483
6 20.9836
7 23.6647
8 33.6572
9 27.1249
10 31.9187
11
12
13

then the cell directly under C1 would be labeled "Cycle Time" and 10 data points (2 points per day $\times$ 5 days) would be entered into the C1 column.

Unlike worksheets in programs such as Microsoft Excel, Minitab worksheets do not accept formulas and do not automatically recalculate themselves when you change the values of the supporting data.

By default, Minitab names opened worksheets serially in the form of Worksheet1, Worksheet2, and so on. Better names are ones that reflect the content of the worksheets, such as CHOCOLATE for a worksheet that contains data for the weights of chocolate bars. To give a sheet a descriptive name, open the Project Manager window, right-click the icon for the worksheet and select **Rename** from the shortcut menu and type in the new name.

Opening and Saving Worksheets and Other Components

You open worksheets to use data that have been created by you or others at an earlier time. To open a Minitab worksheet, first select **File | Open Worksheet.** As shown in Figure A5.2, in the Open Worksheet dialog box that appears:

1. Select the appropriate folder (also known as a **directory**) from the Look in drop-down list box.
2. Check, and select, if necessary, the proper Files of type value from the drop-down list at the bottom of the dialog box. Typically, you will not need to make this selection as the default choice Minitab will list all Minitab worksheets. However, to list all project files, select Minitab Project; to list all Microsoft Excel files, select Excel (*.xls); to list every file in the folder, select All.
3. If necessary, change the display of files in the central files list box by clicking the rightmost (View Menu) button on the top row of buttons and selecting the appropriate view from the drop-down list.
4. Select the file to be opened from the files list box. If the file does not appear, verify that steps 1, 2, and 3 were done correctly.
5. Click the OK button.

To open a Minitab Project that can include the session, worksheets, and graphs, select Minitab Project in step 2 above or select the similar **File | Open Project.** Individual graphs can be opened as well by selecting **File | Open Graph.**

You can save a worksheet individually to assure its future availability, to protect yourself against a system failure, or to later import it into another project. To save a worksheet, select the worksheet's window and then select **File | Save Worksheet As.** As shown in Figure A5.4, in the Save Worksheet As dialog box that appears:

1. Select the appropriate folder from the Save in drop-down list box.
2. Check, and select, if necessary, the proper Save as type value from the drop-down list at the bottom of the dialog box. Typically, you will want to accept the default choice, Minitab, but select "Minitab Portable" to use the data on a different type of computer system or select an earlier version such as "Minitab 13" to use the data in that earlier version.
3. Enter (or edit) the name of the file in the File name: edit box.

**FIGURE
A5.4
Minitab Save
Current
Worksheet As
Dialog Box**

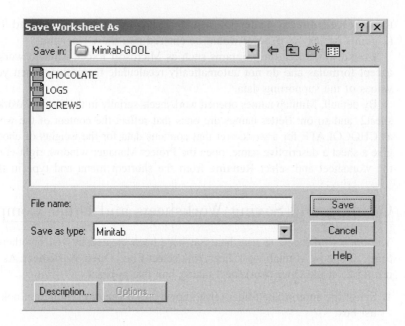

4. Optionally, click the Description button and in the Worksheet Description dialog box (not shown), enter documentary information and click the OK button.
5. Click the OK button (in the Save Worksheet As dialog box).

To save a Minitab Project, select the similar **File | Save Project As.** The Save Project As dialog box (not shown) contains an Options button that displays the Save Project— Options dialog box in which you can specify which project components other than worksheets (session, dialog settings, graphs, and Project Manager content) will be saved.

Individual graphs and the session can also be saved separately by first selecting their windows and then selecting the similar **File | Save Graph As** or **File | Save Session As,** as appropriate. Minitab graphs can be saved in either a Minitab graph format or any one of several common graphics formats, and Session files can be saved as simple or formatted text files.

You can repeat a save procedure and save a worksheet, project, or other component using a second name as an easy way to create a backup copy that can be used should some problem make your original file unusable.

Printing Worksheets, Graphs, and Sessions

Printing components gives you the means to study and review data and results away from the computer screen. To print a specific worksheet, graph, or session:

1. Select the window of the worksheet, graph, or session to be printed.
2. Select **File | Print** *object,* where *object* is either Worksheet, Graph, or Session Window, depending on the component window you selected.

**FIGURE
A5.5**
**Minitab Data
Window Print
Options Dialog
Box**

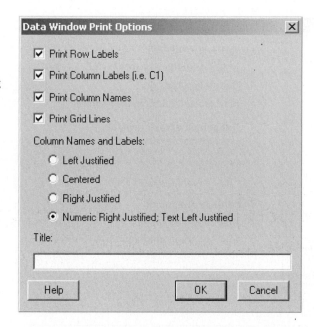

3. If you are printing a worksheet, select formatting options and add a title in the Data Window Print Options dialog box that appears and then click the OK button in that dialog box, as shown in Figure A5.5.

4. In the Print dialog box that appears select the printer to be used, set the Number of copies to the proper value, and click the OK button.

After printing, you should verify the contents of your printout. Most printing problems or failures will trigger the display of an informational dialog box. Click the OK button of any such dialog box and correct the problem noted before attempting a second print operation.

Appendix **A5.3**

Using Minitab for Charts, Descriptive Statistics, and Normal Probabilities

Minitab is used in this appendix to create some commonly used charts and to calculate some basic statistics and probabilities. If you have not already read Appendix A5.2, Introduction to Minitab, you should do so now.

Obtaining a Run Chart

To obtain the run chart in Figure 5.6b on page 105, open the ☘ **CHOCOLATE** file. Select **Stat | Quality Tools | Run Chart.** Then,

FIGURE A5.6
Run Chart Dialog Box

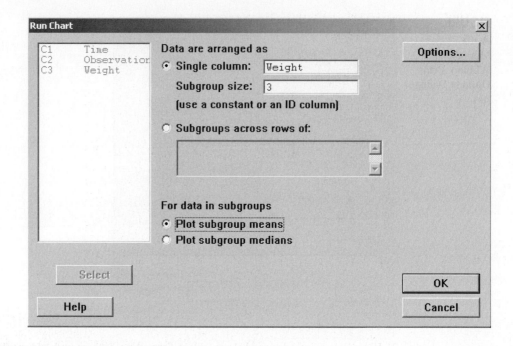

1. In the Run Chart dialog box, shown in Figure A5.6, select the Single column: option button. Enter **C3** or **Weight** in the edit box.
2. In the Subgroup size edit box enter **3.** Click the **OK** button.

Obtaining a Histogram

To obtain the histogram in Figure 5.6a on page 105, open the 🍫 **CHOCOLATE** file. Select **Graph | Histogram.**

1. In the Histogram dialog box shown in Figure A5.7, select Simple. Click the **OK** button.
2. In the Histogram—Data Source dialog box, shown in Figure A5.8, enter **C3** or **Weight** in the Graph variables: edit box. Click the **OK** button.

To select colors for the bars and borders in the histogram,

1. Right-click on any of the bars of the histogram.
2. Select Edit Bars.
3. In the Attributes tab of the Edit bars dialog box enter selections for Fill pattern and Border and Fill Lines. Figure A5.9 illustrates one possible set of selections.

Obtaining Descriptive Statistics

To obtain the descriptive statistics for the weights of chocolate bars, open the 🍫 **CHOCOLATE** file. Select **Stat | Basic Statistics | Display Descriptive Statistics.** In the Display Descriptive Statistics dialog box, as shown in Figure A5.10, enter **C3** or

**FIGURE
A5.7**
**Histogram
Dialog Box**

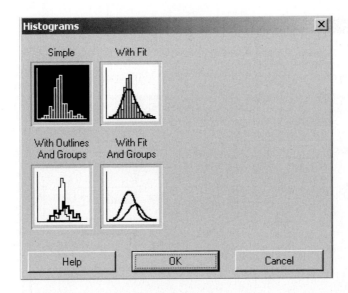

**FIGURE
A5.8**
**Histogram—
Data Source
Dialog Box**

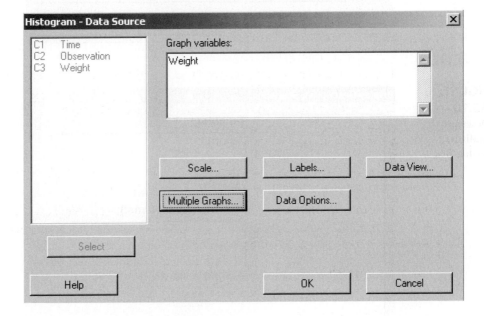

Weight in the Variables: edit box. (If you want to obtain descriptive statistics for each time period, select the **By variable:** check box, and enter **C1** or **Time** in the By variable: edit box.) Click the **OK** button. The session window should now contain the descriptive summary measures, as illustrated in Figure A5.11. Minitab has provided the sample size (labeled as N), the mean, median, standard deviation (labeled as StDev), the standard error of the mean (labeled as SE Mean), the minimum and maximum values, and the first quartile and third quartiles.

**FIGURE
A5.9**
**Attributes Tab
of the Edit
Bars Dialog
Box**

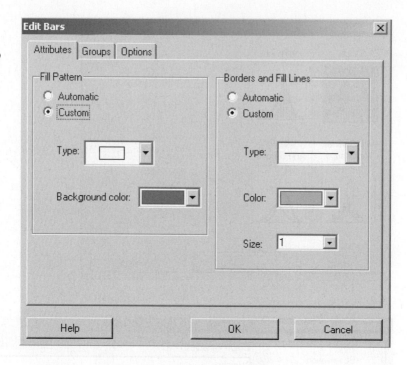

**FIGURE
A5.10**
**Descriptive
Statistics
Dialog Box**

FIGURE A5.11

Descriptive Statistics for the Weights of Chocolate Bars

Variable	N	N*	Mean	SE Mean	StDev	Minimum	Q1	Median	Q3
Weight	84	0	6.0242	0.0020	0.0181	5.9800	6.0100	6.0200	6.0400

Variable	Maximum
Weight	6.0600

To obtain a histogram of the weights of the chocolate bars with a superimposed normal curve, before clicking the OK button, click the **Graphs** button. In the Display Descriptive Statistics—Graphs dialog box, as shown in Figure A5.12, select the **Histogram of data, with normal curve** check box. The histogram appears in Figure A5.13. Click the **OK** button to return to the Display Descriptive Statistics dialog box.

FIGURE A5.12

Display Descriptive Statistics— Graphs Dialog Box

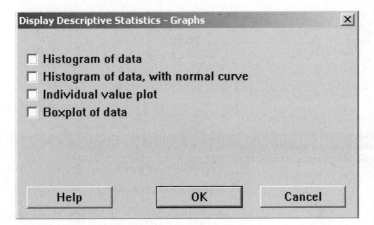

Using Minitab to Obtain Normal Probabilities

Minitab can be used in place of Equation (5.15) and Table B.3 to compute normal probabilities. Referring to the example in "More Details on the Normal Distribution," on page 114, in which $\mu = 10,000$ and $\sigma = 170$, to find the probability that a fuse will last less than 10,100 hours:

1. Enter **10,100** in the first row of column C1.
2. Select **Calc | Probability Distributions | Normal.**
3. In the Normal Distribution dialog box shown in Figure A5.14, select **Cumulative probability.** Enter **10000** in the Mean edit box and **170** in the Standard Deviation edit box. Enter **C1** in the Input column edit box. Click the **OK** button.

The output is displayed in Figure A5.15.

**FIGURE
A5.13**
**Histogram
with Normal
Curve
Superimposed
for the Weights
of Chocolate
Bars**

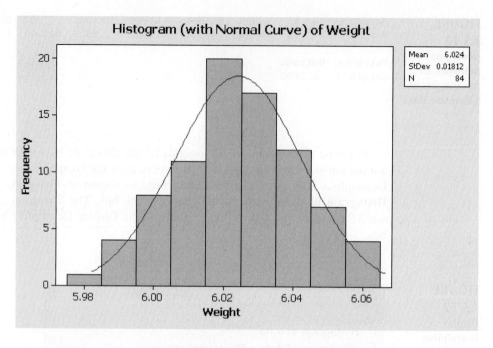

**FIGURE
A5.14**
**Normal
Distribution
Dialog Box**

**FIGURE
A5.15
Obtaining a
Normal
Probability
Using Minitab**

```
Normal with mean = 10000 and standard deviation = 170

    x  P( X <= x )
10100     0.721813
```

Using Minitab to Obtain a Normal Probability Plot

To obtain a normal probability plot using Minitab, open the 🍫 **CHOCOLATE** worksheet. Select **Graph | Probability Plot,** and then do the following:

1. In the Probability Plots dialog box, shown in Figure A5.16, select the **Single** choice.
2. In the Probability Plot—Data Source dialog box, shown in Figure A5.17, in the Graph variables: edit box enter **C3** or **Weight.**

**FIGURE
A5.16
Probability
Plots Dialog
Box**

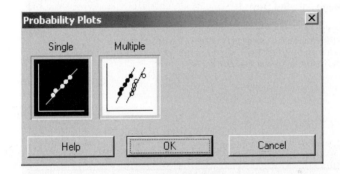

**FIGURE
A5.17
Probability
Plot—Data
Source Dialog
Box**

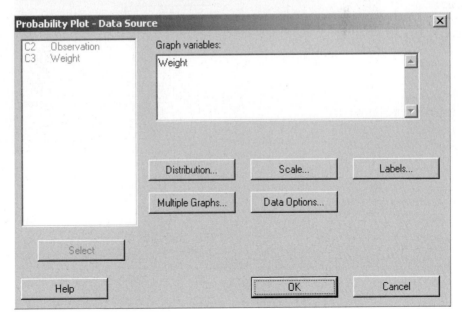

3. Select the Distribution option button. In the Probability Plot—Distribution dialog box, shown in Figure A5.18, in the Distribution: drop-down list box, select **Normal.** Click the **OK** button to return to the Probability Plot—Data Source dialog box.

4. Click the **OK** button.

5. To remove the plotted lines from the normal probability plot, move the cursor to one of the lines and right-click. Select Delete from the Menu.

FIGURE A5.18
Probability Plot— Distribution Dialog Box

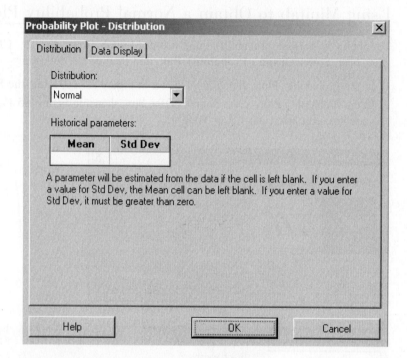

Chapter 6

Stabilizing and Improving a Process with Control Charts

Sections

Chapter Objectives

- To discuss the need for continual reduction of variation, even when the quality characteristic is within specifications
- To discuss and illustrate the use of control charts to stabilize and improve a process
- To discuss the consequences of over- and under-adjustment of a process
- To illustrate the detection of out-of-control behavior
- To describe how attribute control charts can be used for defect prevention
- To describe how variables control charts can be used for never-ending improvement
- To discuss the purposes of studying control charts

147

Introduction

A process that has been defined and documented can be stabilized and then improved. In great measure this can be accomplished through the use of statistical control charts, discussed in this chapter and in Chapters 7 through 9, as well as other techniques that will be introduced in Chapter 10. Without valid measurements, process improvements are difficult if not impossible, and perhaps the best means of measuring process performance is a statistical control chart.

Control charts and the other tools and methods we describe must be used in an environment that provides a positive atmosphere for process improvement; top management must sincerely desire real process improvement. W. E. Deming points out that "any attempt to use statistical techniques under conditions that rob the hourly worker of his pride in workmanship will lead to disaster." [See Reference 3, p. 116.] With this caveat, we may begin to consider the issues of stabilizing and improving a documented and defined process.

Process Variation

Recall from Chapter 1 that we can classify process variation as the result of either **common causes** or **special causes.** Common variation is inherent in every process. It is composed of myriad small sources that are always present in a process and affect all elements of the process. Management should not hold workers responsible for such system problems; the system is management's responsibility. If management is unhappy with the amount of common variation in the system, it must act to reduce or eliminate it. Special variation is created by causes that lie outside the system. Frequently their detection, possible avoidance, and rectification are the responsibility of the people directly involved with the process. But sometimes management must try to find these special causes. When found, policy must be set so that if these special causes are undesirable, they will not recur. If, on the other hand, these special causes are desirable, policy must be set so that they do recur.

Control Charts and Variation

In this chapter we will see that control charts are used to identify and differentiate between common and special causes of variation. When a process no longer exhibits special variation, but only common variation, it is said to be **stable.**

When only common causes of variation are present in a process, management must take action to reduce the difference between customer needs and process performance by endeavoring to move the centerline of the process closer to a desired level **(nominal)** and/or by reducing the magnitude of common variation. These types of changes will aid in the quest for never-ending improvement.

The Need for the Continual Reduction of Variation

During the past two centuries, most mass production concerned itself with meeting engineering specifications most of the time; variation was not the central focus. As long as an item or a part served its intended purpose, it was classified as "good" and passed on to its next operation or final use. When excessive variation caused an item to be nonconforming, it was classified as "bad" and downgraded, reworked, discarded, or somehow removed from the mainstream of output. Little if any effort was made to investigate the causes of such variation; it was accepted as a way of life. High output was maintained by overproducing and then sorting the output into items that met specifications and items that did not. It is still common to find firms increasing output by relaxing engineering specifications to include marginally defective items with good ones. [See Reference 11, pp. 1–7.] Many have come to accept this sort of process output as a fact of life and continue on in this practice until a superior supplier demonstrates the folly of their ways.

Deming has written, "It is good management to reduce the variation in any quality characteristic, whether this characteristic be in a state of control or not, and even when few or no defectives are being produced." [See Reference 2, pp. 1–15.] When variation is reduced, parts will be more nearly alike, and services rendered will be more predictable. Finished products and services will work better and be more reliable. Customer satisfaction will increase because customers will know what to expect. Process output and capability will be known with greater certainty, and the results of any changes to the process will be more predictable.

Therefore, management must constantly attempt to reduce process variation around desired characteristic specification levels (or nominal levels) to achieve the degree of uniformity required for products and services to function during their life cycle as promised to the customer.

Donald J. Wheeler and David S. Chambers clarify the rationale for the continual reduction of process variation. [See Reference 11, pp. 1–7.] A process can be described as existing in one of four states: chaos, the brink of chaos, the threshold state, and the ideal state.

When a process is in a state of **chaos,** it is producing some nonconforming product and it is not in a state of statistical control; that is, special causes of variation are present. There is no way to know or predict the percentage of nonconforming product that the process will generate.

A process on the **brink of chaos** produces 100 percent conforming product; however, the process is not stable: there is variation resulting from special causes. Hence, there is no guarantee that the process will continue to produce 100 percent conforming product indefinitely. Since it is unstable, the process may wander and the product's characteristics may change at any time, entering a state of chaos.

The **threshold state** describes a stable process that produces some nonconforming product; process variation results from common causes that are an inherent part of the system. The only way to reduce this variation is to improve the process itself.

The **ideal state** describes a stable process producing 100 percent conforming product. It is not a natural state; forces will always exist to push the process away from the ideal state. Wheeler and Chambers liken this phenomenon to entropy, in that there is similarly a trend toward disorder in the universe. It may help to visualize a process in the ideal state as a perfectly swept lawn. There will always be winds to mar its perfect appearance by depositing leaves, twigs, or other debris. Keeping the lawn perfectly swept is a never-ending challenge. In the same way, striving toward an ideal state for a process requires constant attention on management's part.

Control charts are statistical tools that make possible the distinction between common and special causes of variation. Consequently, control charts permit management to relentlessly pursue the continuous reduction of process variation and strive toward the ideal state for a process.

The Structure of Control Charts

Control charts are statistical tools used to analyze and understand process variables, to determine a process's **capability** to perform with respect to those variables, and to monitor the effect of those variables on the difference between customer (internal and/or external) needs and process performance. Control charts accomplish this by allowing a manager to identify and understand the sources of variation in a process and hence to manipulate and control those sources to decrease the difference between customer needs and process performance. This decrease can be managed only if the process under study is stable and capable of improvement.

All control charts have a common structure. As Figure 6.1 shows, they have a **centerline,** representing the process average, and upper and lower **control limits** that provide information on the process variation.

Control charts are constructed by drawing samples and taking measurements of a process characteristic. Each set of measurements is called a **subgroup.** Control limits are based on the variation that occurs within the sampled subgroups. In this way, variation between the subgroups is intentionally excluded from the computation of the control limits; the common process variation becomes the variation on which we calculate the control limits. The control limit computations assume that there are no special causes of variation affecting the process. If a special cause of variation is present, the control chart, based solely on common variation, will highlight when and where the special cause occurred. Consequently, the control chart makes possible the distinction between common and special variation and provides management and workers with a basis on which to take corrective action on a process.

Control limits are often called **three-sigma limits.** Recall that the lowercase Greek letter σ ("sigma") is used in enumerative studies to denote the population standard deviation, as described in Chapter 5. In analytic studies, this notation is used to denote a process standard deviation.

When Walter Shewhart described creating a range for allowable variation (common variation), he proposed using as an acceptable economic value the mean of the process characteristic of interest, plus and minus three times its standard deviation (called the **standard error**). [See Reference 9, pp. 276–277.] In practice, as pointed out in Chapter 5, virtually all of the process output will be located within a three-sigma interval of the process mean, provided that the process is stable. Further, virtually all of the sample means for a given subgroup size will be located within a three-standard-error interval

FIGURE 6.1
Structure of a
Control Chart

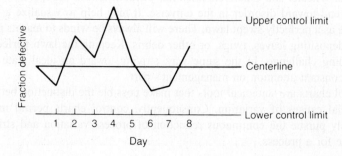

around the process mean, provided that the process is stable. This provides us with a basis for distinguishing between common and special variation for the process characteristics to be discussed here and in Chapters 7 and 8.

In general, the centerline of a control chart is taken to be the estimated mean of the process; the upper control limit is the mean plus three times the estimated standard error; and the lower control limit is the mean minus three times the estimated standard error. These are computed from the process output, assuming that no special sources of variation are present. Subgroup means that behave nonrandomly with respect to these control limits will be said to be indications of the presence of special causes of variation.

Stabilizing a Process with Control Charts

As an example of the use of control charts to detect special variation, consider a data entry operation that makes numerous entries daily. [See Reference 6, pp. 131–141.] On each of 24 consecutive days, subgroups of 200 entries are inspected. Table 6.1 shows the resulting raw data (see 💿 DATAENTRY); Figure 6.2 is a plot of the fraction of defective

TABLE 6.1
Data Entry Operation

	Raw Data for Construction of Control Chart		
Day	Number of Entries Inspected	Number of Defective Entries	Fraction of Defective Entries
1	200	6	.030
2	200	6	.030
3	200	6	.030
4	200	5	.025
5	200	0	.000
6	200	0	.000
7	200	6	.030
8	200	14	.070
9	200	4	.020
10	200	0	.000
11	200	1	.005
12	200	8	.040
13	200	2	.010
14	200	4	.020
15	200	7	.035
16	200	1	.005
17	200	3	.015
18	200	1	.005
19	200	4	.020
20	200	0	.000
21	200	4	.020
22	200	15	.075
23	200	4	.020
24	200	1	.005
Total	4,800	102	

FIGURE 6.2

Plot of Fraction of Defective Entries over Time

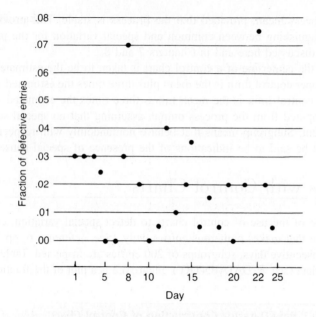

entries as a function of time. Table 6.1 seems to indicate that on days 5, 6, 10, and 20 something unusually good happened (0 percent defectives), and on days 8 and 22 something unusually bad happened. A simple control chart will help to determine whether these points were caused by common or special variation.

When the data consist of a series of fractions that are defective or possess some other characteristic of interest, the appropriate control chart is a **p chart.** This is a depiction of the process output in terms of an attribute of interest—in our example, the fraction defective.

The centerline for a p chart is the mean of the fraction defective, $\bar{p}$, which we calculate as

$$\bar{p} = \left[\frac{\text{Total number of defectives in all subgroups under investigation}}{\text{Total number of units examined in all subgroups under investigation}}\right] \quad \textbf{(6.1)}$$

Control limits are calculated as $\bar{p}$ plus and minus three times the standard error. The standard error for the average proportion, $\sigma_{\bar{p}}$, is given by the expression

$$\sigma_{\bar{p}} = \sqrt{\frac{\bar{p}(1 - \bar{p})}{n}} \quad \textbf{(6.2)}$$

where n is the subgroup size.

Using this value, the upper and lower control limits for a p chart are given by:

$$\text{UCL(p)} = \bar{p} + 3\sqrt{\frac{\bar{p}(1 - \bar{p})}{n}} \quad \textbf{(6.3)}$$

$$\text{LCL(p)} = \bar{p} - 3\sqrt{\frac{\bar{p}(1 - \bar{p})}{n}} \quad \textbf{(6.4)}$$

We can now use Equations (6.1) to (6.4) to find the numerical values for constructing our p chart:

$$\bar{p} = \frac{102}{4{,}800} = 0.021$$

Centerline (p) = 0.021

$$UCL(p) = 0.021 + 3\sqrt{\frac{(0.021)(1 - 0.021)}{200}}$$

$$= 0.02125 + 3(0.0101)$$

$$= 0.052$$

Upper control limit = 0.052

$$LCL(p) = 0.021 - 3\sqrt{\frac{(0.021)(1 - 0.021)}{200}}$$

$$= -0.009$$

Lower control limit = 0.00

Notice that since a negative fraction defective is not possible, the lower control limit is set at 0.00.

Figure 6.3 shows the completed p chart. Clearly on days 8 and 22 there is some special variation. Note, however, that the fractions defective on days 5, 6, 10, and 20 are not beyond the control limits. Days with no defectives are not out of control; we have

FIGURE 6.3
Minitab
p Chart for
Defectives

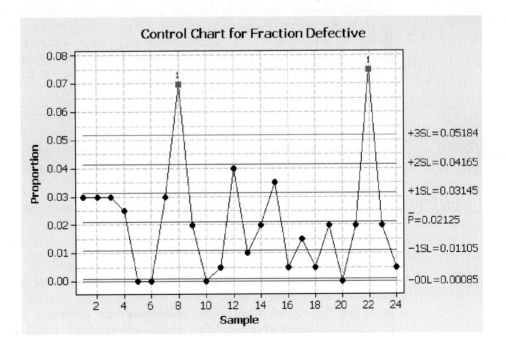

merely observed that the process is capable of producing zero defectives some of the time. The observations on days 8 and 22 indicate that the process exhibits a lack of statistical control.

When a manager or worker determines that the cause of variation is special, he should search for and resolve the causes that may be attributable to such factors as a specific machine, worker, or group of workers, or a new batch of raw materials. After the causes of special variation have been identified and rectified, a stable process that is in statistical control will result.

In our example, to bring the process under control, management investigates the observations that are out of control (days 8 and 22) in an effort to discover and remove the special causes of variation in the process. In this case, management finds that on day 8 a new operator was added to the workforce without any training. The logical conclusion is that the new environment probably caused the unusually high number of errors. To ensure that this special cause does not recur, the company adds a one-day training program in which data entry operators are acclimated to the work environment.

A team of managers and workers conduct an investigation of the circumstances occurring on day 22. Their work reveals that on the previous night one of the data entry terminals malfunctioned and was replaced with a standby unit. The standby unit is older and slightly different from the ones currently used in the department. Repairs on the regular terminal were not expected to be completed until the morning of day 23. To correct this special source of variation, the team recommends developing a proactive program of preventive maintenance on the terminals to decrease the likelihood of future breakdowns. Employees then implement the solution with the policy commitment of management.

Detrimental special causes of variation can be eliminated from a process, or beneficial special causes of variation can be incorporated into a process, by setting and enforcing policy changes. Once this is done, the process has, in essence, been changed.

The action taken on the process stemming from investigations of days 8 and 22 should change the process so that the special causes of variation will be eliminated. Consequently, the data from days 8 and 22 may now be deleted. After eliminating the data for the days in which the special causes of variation are found (see ✿ DATAENTRY2), the control chart statistics are recomputed:

$$\bar{p} = \frac{73}{4,400} = 0.017$$

$$UCL(p) = 0.017 + 3\sqrt{\frac{(0.017)(1 - 0.017)}{200}} = 0.045$$

$$LCL(p) = 0.017 - 3\sqrt{\frac{(0.017)(1 - 0.017)}{200}} = -0.010$$

$$= -0.010$$

and, hence, the lower control limit = 0.00.

Figure 6.4 shows the revised control chart. The process appears to be stable and in statistical control. Notice that the revised control chart has somewhat narrower control limits than the original. When special causes have been eliminated, the narrower limits that occur may reveal other points that are now out of control. It will then be necessary

FIGURE 6.4
Minitab
Revised
Control Chart
for Fraction
Defective

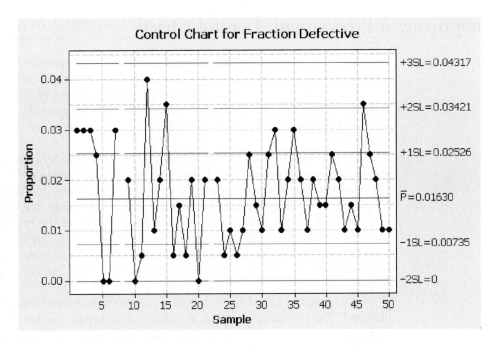

to again search for special causes. Several such iterations may be required until the process is stable and in statistical control. At least 20 subgroups should remain to determine that the process is indeed stable. If the elimination of subgroups has left fewer than 20 subgroups remaining, additional data should be collected to ensure that the process is in a state of statistical control.

In this example, the control limits are extended into the future, as shown on the right half of Figure 6.4, and more data are collected and compared to the revised control limits. The process is found to be stable and consequently capable of being improved.

Advantages of a Stable Process

A stable process is a process that exhibits only common variation, or variation resulting from inherent system limitations. The advantages of achieving a stable process are:

• Management knows the process capability and can predict performance, costs, and quality levels.

• Productivity will be at a maximum, and costs will be minimized.

• Management will be able to measure the effects of changes in the system with greater speed and reliability.

• If management wants to alter specification limits, it will have the data to back up its decision.

A stable process is a basic requirement for process improvement efforts.

Improving a Process with Control Charts

Once a process is stable, it has a known capability. A stable process may, nevertheless, produce an unacceptable number of defects (threshold state) and continue to do so as long as the system, as currently defined, remains the same. Management owns the system and must assume the ultimate responsibility for changing the system to reduce common variation and to reduce the difference between customer needs and process performance.

There are two areas for action to reduce the difference between customer needs and process performance. First, action may be taken to change the process average. This might include action to reduce the level of defects or process changes to increase production or service. Second, management can act to reduce the level of common variation with an eye toward never-ending improvement of the process. Procedures and inputs (such as composition of the workforce, training, supervision, materials, tools and machinery, and operational definitions) are the responsibility of management. The workers can only suggest changes; they can not effect changes to the system.

In our example of the data entry firm, an employee-suggested training program was instituted. The program was aimed at reducing the average fraction of errors and the common variation, which would result in narrower control limits. Figure 6.5 shows the data entry control chart after management instituted the new training program (see ❧ DATAENTRY3). The average proportion of entries with errors decreased from 0.017 to 0.008, and the process variation decreased as well.

FIGURE 6.5
Minitab Control Chart for Fraction Defective after Institution of a New Training Program

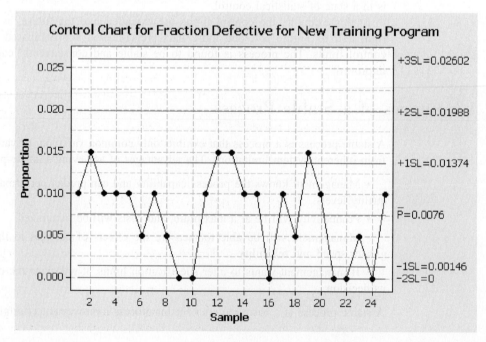

Causes of Variation Out of the Control of the Process Owner

Sometimes the people working in a process detect a cause of variation that is out of the control of the process owner. If this happens, and it surely will happen sooner or later, the people working within the process should look for similar processes, either internal or external to their organization, that have successfully dealt with the special cause of variation. If they find such a process, they can study its flowchart as a starting point for modifying their process: perhaps the similar process will yield a solution to the special cause of variation that makes sense within the context of the process under study.

As an example, Miami, Florida, has the second highest incidence of lightning in the world. Tampa, Florida, has the highest. In the late 1980s, Florida Power and Light Company wanted to improve, or decrease, the minutes of interrupted service per month. A control chart revealed a stable process with an unacceptably high average and standard deviation. Pareto analysis, to be discussed in Chapter 10, revealed that the biggest cause, by far, of interrupted services was electrical poles knocked out of service by lightning strikes. The next biggest cause of interrupted service created only a small fraction of the problems caused by lightning strikes. Dr. Noriaki Kano, a professor at the Science University of Tokyo, suggested that FPL be broken up into small geographic regions to determine if any region had an effective process for dealing with lightning strikes.

The employees studying the problem discovered that Southeastern Dade County had a significantly higher average lightning strike outage rate than any other area, while Western Broward County had a significantly lower average than any other area. Employees wondered what would cause such a disparity in the averages. Pareto analysis revealed that the age distribution of line maintainers (the people who repair electric lines) in Southeastern Dade, with a mean in the mid-50s, was much older than the age distribution is Western Broward County, where the mean was in the mid-20s. A brainstorming session (discussed in detail in Chapter 10) revealed that the line maintainers in Southeastern Dade County had been trained in the standards for grounding electrical poles established in the 1950s, while the line maintainers in Western Broward County had been trained in the standards for grounding electrical poles established in the early 1980s. Employees discovered that the standards for grounding electrical poles had been dramatically improved between the 1950s and 1980s. Consequently, the line maintainers in Southeastern Dade County (as well as all other line maintainers) were trained in the grounding standards established in the 1980s. As a result of this training, the time in minutes of interrupted service was dramatically decreased throughout the Florida Power and Light system. The important point is that a special cause of variation may seem to be out of the control of a process owner, but may be successfully resolved using knowledge from another system.

Two Possible Mistakes in Using Control Charts

There are two types of mistakes that the user of a control chart may make: **over-adjustment** and **under-adjustment**. Proper use of control charts will minimize the total economic consequences of making either of these types of errors.

Over-Adjustment

An over-adjustment error occurs when the user reacts to swings in the process data that are merely the result of common variation, such as adjusting a process downward if its past output is above average or adjusting a process upward if its past output is below average. When a process is over-adjusted, it resembles a car being over-steered, veering back and forth across the highway. In general, processes should be adjusted not on the basis of time-to-time observations, but on the basis of information provided by a statistical control chart.

Examining a frequently used demonstration device known as a **Quincunx board,** as shown in Figure 6.6, one can see the effects of over-adjustment. The Quincunx board is

FIGURE 6.6
A Quincunx Board

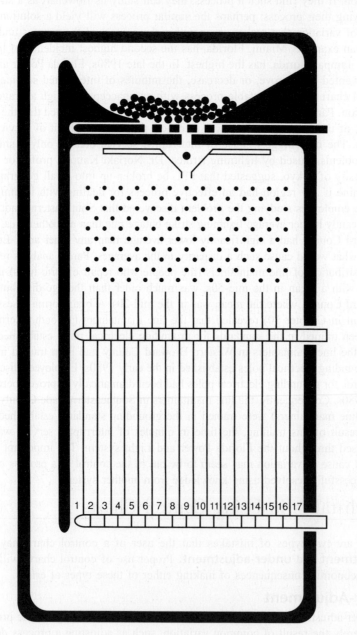

a rectangular box with an upper chamber containing a large number of beads. A horizontal sliding bar feeds one or more beads at a time into a triangular hopper which then allows the beads to fall at a specified lateral point directly above 10 rows of pegs. Each time a bead hits a peg, it will bounce right or left so that its position after falling through the 10 rows of pegs is a result of 10 random events. It does not seem unreasonable to expect that many beads would tend to fall almost directly beneath the point at which they were released. But some beads may tend to wander a bit and end up to the right or left of their release point.

Note that in Figure 6.6 the beads will fall into a series of slots after passing through the rows of pegs. The slots have been numbered from 1 to 17 for purposes of illustration. Note also that the opening of the triangular hopper is set to release the beads directly above the number 9 slot. Provided that the hopper is not moved, the process output (i.e., the slot position of the beads) will be stable.

The slots themselves are divided into two portions: a short upper and a longer lower one. The short portion is used to observe subgroups, while the longer portion is used for the accumulation of subgroups. Figures 6.6 through 6.9 viewed as a sequence show how the Quincunx board is used.

The collection of data may be simulated by allowing small groups of beads to pass through the triangular hopper and fall into the upper portion of the slots. Each small group of beads represents a subgroup of data points. In Figure 6.7 we can see the result of allowing a subgroup of five beads to pass through the hopper. The bottom of the hopper is centered directly above slot number 9, and beads have fallen into slots 7 through 12.

When the data have been examined and recorded, the five beads are allowed to fall into the lower chamber, where all beads will be accumulated. Figure 6.8 shows not only this group but the results of several subgroups accumulated in the bottom chamber. If the position of the hopper is not changed, the accumulated beads in the lower chamber will usually follow an approximately normal curve. In Figure 6.8 we can see that the process average seems to be about 8.5, and the range of the process is 8.

Now suppose that instead of having the good sense to leave the hopper alone, we were to adjust it after each bead dropped. This is adjusting for common variation, or overadjusting.

After each bead passes through the pegs, we count the number of slots above or below the target of 9, and adjust the hopper that many slots in the opposite direction in an attempt to compensate. This will result in a dramatic increase in the process variation indicated by a greatly increased range. Figure 6.9 (on page 162) shows the results for the collection of several subgroups with the hopper being moved in this manner. While the process average still appears to be approximately the same, the range is now 16. This is the penalty for adjusting on the basis of common variation. This dangerous situation is illustrated by Rule 2 of the funnel experiment discussed in Chapter 1.

Under-Adjustment

Under-adjustment, or lack of attention, results when a process is out of control and no effort is made to provide the necessary regulation. The process swings up and down in response to one or more special causes of variation, which may have compounding effects.

FIGURE 6.7
Quincunx
Bead Falling
Beads being
released from
the hopper of a
Quincunx
board. Notice
that most beads
end up below
the release
point.

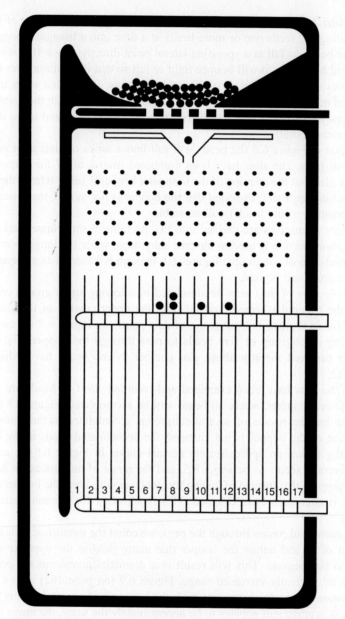

Avoiding both of these mistakes all of the time is an impossible task. That is, never adjusting the process—so that we never make the mistake of over-adjusting—could result in severe under-adjustment. On the other hand, if we made very frequent adjustments to avoid the problem of under-adjustment, we would probably be over-adjusting. Control charts provide an economical means to minimize the total loss that results from these two errors. Consequently, control charts provide management with guidance on when to take action on a process and when to leave it alone.

FIGURE 6.8
Quincunx
Subgroups

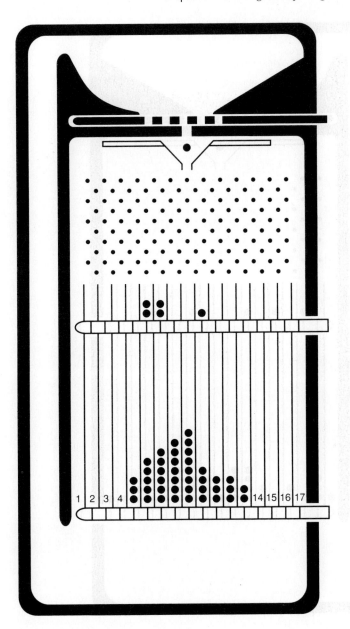

Some Out-of-Control Evidence

We know that a process exhibits a lack of statistical control if a subgroup statistic falls beyond either of the control limits. But it is possible for all subgroup statistics to be within the control limits while there are other factors that indicate a lack of control in the process. Stable processes always exhibit random patterns of variation. Accordingly, most data points will tend to cluster about the mean value, or centerline, with an approximately equal

FIGURE 6.9
Results of Compensating for Bead Motion from Trial to Trial

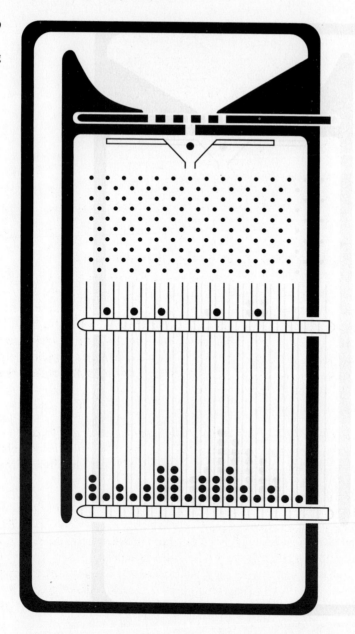

number of points falling above and below the mean. A few of the values will lie close to the control limits. Points will rarely fall beyond a control limit. Also there will seldom be prolonged runs upward or downward for a number of subgroups. If one or more of these conditions is violated in a control chart, the chart does not exhibit statistical control. Hence, for a process that is out of control, there will be an absence of points near the centerline, an absence of points near the control limits, one or more points located beyond the control limits, or runs or nonrandom patterns among the points.

FIGURE 6.10
A, B, and C
Zones for a
Control Chart

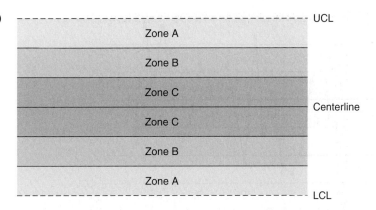

Rules for Identifying Out-of-Control Points

So that we can examine patterns indicating a lack of control, the area between the control limits is divided into six bands, each band one standard error wide. As Figure 6.10 shows, bands within one standard error of the centerline are called the C zones; bands between one and two standard errors from the centerline are called B zones; and the outermost bands, which lie between two and three standard errors from the mean, are A zones.

Seven simple rules based on these bands are commonly applied to determine if a process is exhibiting a lack of statistical control. Any out-of-control points found are marked directly on the control chart.

Rule 1

A process exhibits a lack of control if any subgroup statistic falls outside of the control limits. As we have already seen, this is the first criterion—and the most obvious one. Figure 6.3 on page 153 exhibits points that are out of control by virtue of this rule.

Rule 2

A process exhibits a lack of control if any two out of three consecutive subgroup statistics fall in one of the A zones or beyond on the same side of the centerline. This means that if any two of three consecutive subgroup statistics are in the A zone or beyond, the process exhibits a lack of control when the second A zone point occurs. The two points must be in zone A or beyond on the same side of the centerline; the third point can be anywhere. Figure 6.11 illustrates a process exhibiting a lack of control by virtue of Rule 2 at two points in time: at observations 6 (relating to observations 5 and 6) and 21 (relating to observations 19 and 21).

In applying Rule 2 or any other indicator of a lack of control, it is always best to look for patterns demonstrating evidence of a lack of control by looking backward along the control chart. This makes any patterns or trends more obvious and makes it easier to find the beginning of a pattern or trend.

Consider subgroup statistics 21, 20, and 19. Point 21 is in the upper zone A, point 20 in zone C, and point 19 in the upper zone A again. Point 21 is thus the second of two out of three consecutive points in zone A, so it is marked as demonstrating a lack of control. Next, notice that observation number 6 is in zone A, preceded by observation number 5 (also in zone A) and then observation number 4 (in zone B). This makes

FIGURE 6.11
Lack of
Control by
Virtue of
Rule 2

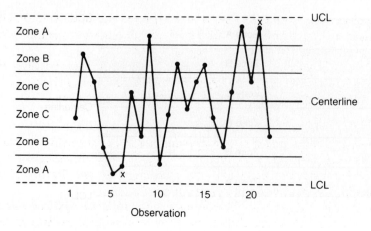

FIGURE 6.12
Lack of
Control by
Virtue of
Rule 3

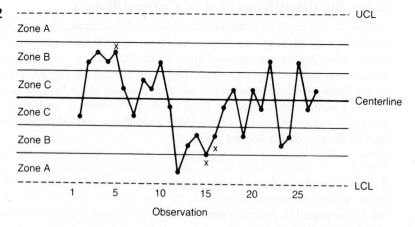

observation number 6 the second of two out of three consecutive points in the A zone. Therefore observation number 6 is marked with an X as evidence of a lack of control. The analysis began by looking from right to left on the control chart, so more recent indications of a lack of control are the first to be found.

Rule 3

A process exhibits a lack of control if four out of five consecutive subgroup statistics fall in one of the B zones or beyond on the same side of the centerline. This means that if any four out of five consecutive subgroup statistics are in either one of the B zones or beyond on the same side of the centerline while the fifth is not, the fourth point in the B zone or beyond is deemed to be providing evidence of a lack of control. It should be marked with an X.

Figure 6.12 illustrates several possible patterns by which a process may be out of control via Rule 3. Observation number 15 is in zone B; number 14 is in zone B; number 13 is also in zone B; number 12 is in zone A (beyond zone B), while number 11 is in zone C. This means that observation number 15 is an indication of a lack of control. Notice that observation 16 lies in zone B also, so it too should be considered out of control because it is the fourth of a different set of five consecutive points (points 12, 13, 14, 15, and 16) that lie in zone B or beyond.

Subgroup statistics 5, 4, 3, and 2 all lie in zone B. They constitute four points in a row in this zone (point 1 can be considered the fifth point because it is in zone C); so the fourth point in zone B, point number 5, is marked with an X.

Rule 4

A process exhibits a lack of control if eight or more consecutive subgroup statistics lie on the same side of the centerline. The eighth and subsequent subgroup statistics are said to provide evidence of a lack of control by virtue of this rule. Figure 6.13 shows a process exhibiting a lack of control by virtue of this rule.

Note that in Figure 6.13, observation number 10 is the eighth of a string of points on one side of the centerline and can therefore be considered evidence of lack of control.

Rules 1 through 4 assume that the distribution of the control chart statistic is continuous, stable, and normally distributed. However, we really do not require the assumption of normality to apply Rules 1 through 4, because of the Empirical Rule discussed earlier in Chapter 5. For example, if the control chart statistic is continuous, stable, and non-symmetrically distributed, as is frequently the case with the range chart, the Empirical Rule still justifies the use of Rules 1 through 4 to detect out-of-control points.

Rule 5

A process exhibits a lack of control if eight or more consecutive subgroup statistics move upward in value or if eight or more consecutive subgroup statistics move downward in value. The eighth and subsequent subgroup statistics that continue moving up (or down) are said to provide evidence of a lack of control. Figure 6.14 shows a process exhibiting a lack of control by virtue of this rule.

Rule 6

A process exhibits a lack of control if an unusually small number of runs above and below the centerline are present (a sawtooth pattern). Figure 6.15 shows a process exhibiting a lack of control by virtue of this rule.

FIGURE 6.13
Lack of Control by Virtue of Rule 4

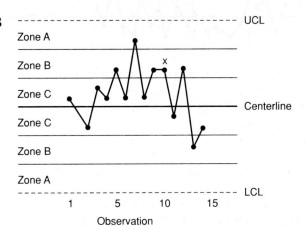

FIGURE 6.14
Lack of
Control by
Virtue of
Rule 5

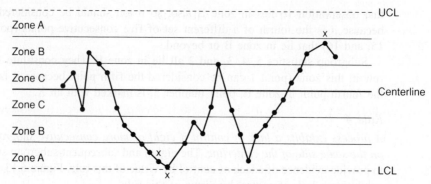

FIGURE 6.15
Lack of
Control by
Virtue of
Rule 6

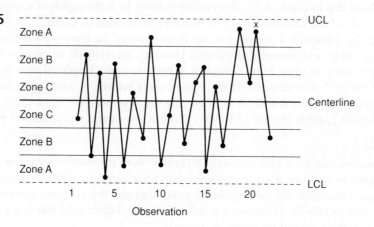

FIGURE 6.16
Lack of
Control by
Virtue of
Rule 7

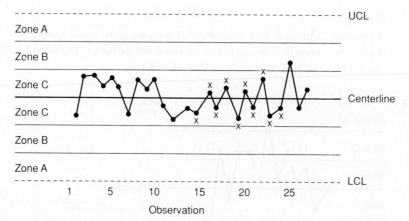

Rule 7

A process exhibits a lack of control if 13 consecutive points fall within zone C on either side of the centerline. The thirteenth and subsequent subgroup statistics are said to provide evidence of a lack of control by virtue of this rule. Figure 6.16 shows such a process.

It should be pointed out that Rules 6 and 7 are used to determine whether a process is unusually noisy (high variability) or unusually quiet (low variability).

False Out-of-Control Signals

Occasionally, a control chart presents out-of-control signals, one or more of which are "false" signals. Table 6.2 presents data from a service center indicating the number of improperly handled calls from a daily sample of 100 calls to the center (see SERVICE). The data are arranged horizontally in five rows. The data point for the first day was 8 defective calls and the data point for the fiftieth day was 4 defective calls.

Figure 6.17 shows a p chart for the data in Table 6.2. There is one data point above the upper control limit (violation of Rule 1, signified by a 1) and many data points that are 8 or more points in a row above or below average (violation of Rule 4, signified by a 2).

TABLE 6.2
Number of Defective Calls to a Service Center

8	9	10	7	6	10	9	10	10	10
7	8	9	6	6	9	10	5	8	5
6	5	12	7	5	1	4	4	2	4
2	0	1	4	0	0	3	0	2	0
3	4	1	1	2	0	2	0	2	4

FIGURE 6.17
Minitab p Chart for Defective Calls to the Service Center

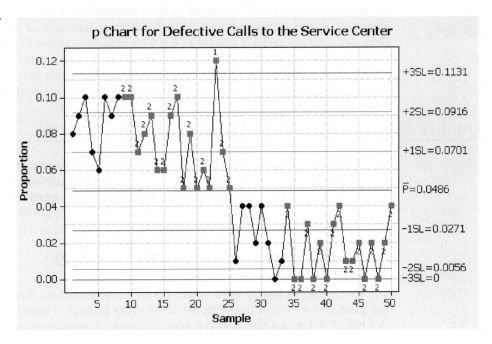

FIGURE 6.18
Minitab
Revised
p Chart for
Defective Calls
to the Service
Center

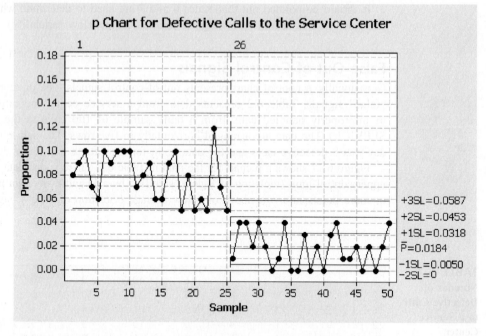

Many analysts might begin to search for both types of special causes (indicated by 1 and 2) shown in Figure 6.17. However, this would be a mistake. In this case, the out-of-control point above the upper control limits is a false signal caused by the shift down in the process average at point 26 caused by the introduction of a training program for staff answering phones. A revised control chart that takes into account the change in the processes from one without training to one with training is shown in Figure 6.18.

We can now see that the out-of-control point above the upper control limit disappears when only the before-training process is considered. The lesson here is that a process expert may have to be consulted when searching for special causes of variation.

Quality Consciousness and Types of Control Charts

Quality consciousness should typically follow a logical pattern. It generally begins with a lack of quality consciousness, moves on to **defect detection,** moves from there to **defect prevention,** then through the **never-ending improvement** of current products and services, and ultimately leads to the realization that the only path to continued prosperity must include **innovations** in future products and services.

No Quality Consciousness: Accept Everything without Question

The lowest level of quality consciousness is to accept everything from a vendor, without question. For example, most people do not count to check if there are 144 toothpicks in a box or if there are 500 sheets of paper in a ream as stated on the package. This type of quality consciousness is borne out of a lack of awareness of quality, or past satisfaction and a consequent lack of concern about poor quality.

Defect Detection: Mass Inspection to Sort Conforming and Nonconforming Output

The purpose of defect detection is to sort conforming and nonconforming products or services through mass inspection (Deming's Point 3, discussed in Chapter 2). Defect detection assumes that defects will be produced; they are expected and anticipated. In this stage of quality consciousness, no feedback loops or tools are available for correcting the factors that created the defectives in the first place. Once a defect is produced, it is too late to do anything but remove it from the process output. The costs associated with its production, its distribution, and, perhaps most important of all, worker morale and good will are usually unrecoverable. Worse yet, if the product or service has found its way to an internal or external customer, the good reputation of the supplier has been tarnished.

Defect Prevention: Attribute Control Charts

The purpose of defect prevention is to achieve **zero defects.** This stage of quality consciousness assumes that if all products and services are within specification limits, then all output will meet customers' needs and wants. This is the goalpost view of quality, discussed in Chapter 1. The initial entry into defect prevention generally involves the use of control charts based on attribute data, such as conforming versus nonconforming with respect to some specification limit.

The most common types of **attribute control charts** are:

• **p chart:** Used to examine the fraction of units with some characteristic (such as the fraction defective).

• **np chart:** Used to study the number of units with some characteristic (such as the number of defectives per batch).

• **c chart:** Used to consider the number of events (such as defects) in some fixed area of opportunity (such as a single unit).

• **u chart:** Used to examine the number of events (such as defects) in a changeable area of opportunity (such as square yards of paper drawn from an operational paper machine).

Attribute control charts, which will be discussed in detail in Chapter 7, can help move processes toward a zero percent defective rate. However, they do not provide specific information on the cause of the defectives. Furthermore, as the percent defective approaches zero, larger and larger sample sizes will be needed to detect defective process output. For example, if a process is generating an average of one defective in every million units produced, then the average sample size needed to find one defective is 1 million units. Hence attribute control charts become ineffective as the proportion of defective output approaches zero. Control charting must continue, but in the face of the limitations of attribute control charts, a better means of process improvement and evaluation is required. This should lead management to the next level of quality consciousness—never-ending improvement.

Never-Ending Improvement: Variables Control Charts

The purpose of never-ending improvement is to modify current processes used for products and services to continuously reduce the difference between customer needs and process performance. This is the Taguchi loss function view of quality, discussed in Chapter 1. Never-ending improvement necessitates using control charts based on variables data. These types of control charts allow for the never-ending reduction of unit-to-unit variation, even though all output is well within specification limits. For example, in the manufacture of steel push rods, all may come from a stable process and all may conform to specifications; an attribute control chart would show zero percent defective in almost every sample. However, by taking actual measurements on rod lengths (variables data), management is able to collect information that will enable them to consistently strive for the reduction of unit-to-unit variation.

The most common types of **variables control charts** are:

- **x̄ chart:** Used to control the process average for subgroups of two or more data points.
- **I (individuals) chart:** Used to control the process average for subgroups of one data point per subgroup.
- **R chart:** Used to control the process range when between 2 and 10 data points exist per subgroup.
- **MR (moving range) chart:** Used to control the process range when only one data point exists per subgroup.
- **s chart:** Used to control the process standard deviation when more than 10 data points exist per subgroup.

Using variables control charts, management may continuously seek to reduce variation, center a process on nominal, and decrease the difference between customer needs and process performance. Chapter 8 discusses in detail the uses and applications of these variables control charts.

Innovation (Quality Creation)

Innovation can be thought of as having two primary purposes: to create a dramatic breakthrough in decreasing the difference between customer needs and process performance, and to discover customers' future needs. Ideas for innovation with respect to customers' future needs generally cannot come from direct queries to customers; rather, they must come from the producer. In this regard, consumer research is backward-looking; that is, asking customers what they want can only help producers improve existing products or services—it cannot help producers anticipate the customer's future needs. As a rule, consumers do not know what innovations they will want in the future. For example, consumers did not know that they wanted a fax machine or an automatic-loading camera before such products existed. The producer studying the problems customers have when using products and services must discover these types of breakthroughs.

In 1974, the camera market was saturated with cameras that satisfied customers' current needs; cameras were reliable, were relatively inexpensive to use, and produced good pictures. This created a nightmare for the camera industry. Consequently Konica decided to ask consumers what more they would like in a camera. Consumers replied that they were satisfied with their cameras; asking consumers what more they would like in a camera did not yield the information Konica needed to create a breakthrough. In response to this situation, Konica studied negatives at film processing laboratories and discovered that often the first few pictures on rolls of film were overexposed, indicating that users had difficulty in loading cameras. This presented an opportunity to innovate camera technology. In response to this analysis, Konica developed the automatic-loading camera. This is an excellent example of innovation of a product or service. The customer could not have been expected to think of this innovation. Digital cameras are now rapidly replacing cameras that use conventional film, presenting another set of challenges for this industry—yet consumers have never asked for these products.

Three Uses of Control Charts

As we have seen, control charts fall into two broad categories: attribute and variables. In both cases, a particular quality characteristic is measured and then examined. That examination can be used (1) to evaluate the history of the process, (2) to evaluate the present state of the process, or (3) to predict the near future state of a process in conjunction with the opinion of a process expert.

Evaluating the Past

The retrospective examination of the process's completed output using a control chart answers the question of whether the process has been in statistical control. A lack of control, or the presence of special causes of variation, is indicated when one or more of the control chart points is beyond the control limits or is otherwise in violation of one of the several rules introduced in this chapter. Chapter 9 more fully discusses patterns indicating a lack of control. When no special causes of variation are present, the characteristic measured is said to be in statistical control or stable.

Evaluating the Present

Control charts have two main functions when evaluating the present condition of a process. The first function is to maintain a state of statistical control during a process's operation. Control charts can be used to generate "special cause" signals during normal operation. The signal might, for example, call attention to tool wear or changes in humidity that might require intervention in the process. In this sense, control charts are useful in maintaining an existing state of process stability. The second function is to stop management from overreacting to common causes of variation and treating them as special causes of variation for aggregated data. If a control chart is computed from aggregated data (data from multiple sources such as multiple production lines), then it is not an effective tool to detect special causes of variation. Rather, a control chart for aggregate data serves the purpose of stopping management of the process being control-charted from tampering with the process.

Predicting the Near Future

Finally, control charts can be used to predict the near future condition of a process, based on statistical evidence of a process's stability and process knowledge concerning future conditions that could affect the process. For example, if a process is stable and a process expert foresees no future sources of special variation, then the expert can predict that the process will remain stable in the near future.

Tips on Using Control Charts

There are two means commonly employed by consultants to determine if control charts are being used on the shop floor or the service center area of an organization. The first is to determine if any dust appears on a control chart: the presence of dust usually indicates that the control charts are not being used by employees. The second is to identify the last plotted point on a control chart: if the last plotted point is not the most recently completed time period, then the control chart is probably not being used by employees.

Summary

In this chapter, we have focused on the importance of stabilizing and improving a process, and presented an overview of the techniques for accomplishing this.

All processes exhibit variation. We can distinguish between common causes of variation, affecting all elements of a process, and special variation, created by causes outside the system. In general, only management can reduce common variation, while workers and others more directly involved with the process are best suited to identifying sources of special variation.

Control charts enable us to identify and differentiate between these two sources of variation. As a result, we are able to eliminate special variation, stabilizing the process, and then focus on reducing common variation and hence improving the process. The continual reduction of variation, even within specifications, is critical to increasing quality, predictability, and customer satisfaction.

A process can be described as existing in one of four states: chaos, the brink of chaos, the threshold state, and the ideal state. When a process is in a state of chaos, it is producing some nonconforming product and it is not in a state of statistical control. A process on the brink of chaos produces 100 percent conforming product; however, the process is not stable. The threshold state describes a stable process that produces some nonconforming product; process variation results from common causes that are an inherent part of the system. The ideal state describes a stable process producing 100 percent conforming product.

All control charts have a centerline, representing the process average, and upper and lower control limits that provide information on the process variation. Control charts are constructed by drawing samples and taking measurements of a process characteristic. Each set of measurements is called a subgroup. Control limits, often called three-sigma limits, are based on the variation that occurs within the sampled subgroups. In this way, variation between the subgroups is intentionally excluded from the computation of the control limits; the common process variation becomes the variation on which we calculate the control limits.

When the observations are plotted on the control chart, points exhibiting nonrandom behavior, such as falling outside the control limits, are indications of special causes of variation. Once these causes are identified and eliminated from the system, the corresponding data points can be deleted and the control limits recalculated. This iterative procedure is continued until there are no indications of special variation, so that we now have a stable process.

The advantages of achieving a stable process are: management knows the process capability and can predict performance, costs, and quality levels; productivity will be at a maximum, and costs will be minimized; management will be able to measure the effects of changes in the system with greater speed and reliability; and if management wants to alter specification limits, it will have the data to back up its decision. A stable process is a basic requirement for process improvement efforts.

Once we have a stable process, there are two areas for action to reduce the difference between customer needs and process performance. First, action may be taken to change the process average. This might include action to reduce the level of defects or process changes to increase production or service. Second, management can act to reduce the level of common variation with an eye toward never-ending improvement of the process.

There are two types of mistakes that the user of a control chart may make: over-adjustment and under-adjustment. Proper use of control charts will minimize the total economic consequences of making either of these types of errors.

Stable processes always exhibit random patterns of variation. Accordingly, most data points will tend to cluster about the mean value, or centerline, with an approximately equal number of points falling above and below the mean. A few of the values will lie close to the control limits. Points will rarely fall beyond a control limit. Also there will seldom be prolonged runs upward or downward for a number of subgroups. If one or more of these conditions is violated in a control chart, the chart does not exhibit statistical control. By dividing the control chart into one-sigma-width bands, called the A, B, and C zones, seven rules can be articulated that enable us to identify points that are out of control. Any out-of-control points found are marked directly on the control chart.

In moving from no quality consciousness to never-ending improvement and innovation, we pass through several stages. Defect detection uses mass inspection to sort good units from bad units. Defect prevention uses attribute control charts to promote the goal-post view of quality. Never-ending improvement uses variables control charts to promote the Taguchi loss function view of quality. The only path to continued prosperity must include innovations in future products and services. Innovation can be thought of as having two primary purposes: to create a dramatic breakthrough in decreasing the difference between customers' needs and process performance, and to discover customers' future needs.

The retrospective examination of the process's completed output using a control chart answers the question of whether the process has been in statistical control. In evaluation of the present condition of a process, control charts have two main functions: to maintain a state of statistical control during a process's operation, and to stop management from over-reacting to common causes of variation and treating them as special causes of variation for aggregated data. For the near future, control charts can be used to predict the condition of a process, based on statistical evidence of a process's stability and process knowledge concerning future conditions that could affect the process.

Key Terms

attribute control charts, *169*	common causes of variation, *148*	ideal state, *149*
brink of chaos, *149*		innovation, *168*
capability, *150*	control limits, *150*	MR chart, *170*
c chart, *169*	defect detection, *168*	never-ending improvement, *168*
centerline, *150*	defect prevention, *168*	
chaos, *149*	I chart, *170*	nominal, *148*

Exercises   The control charts in Exercises 6.1 through 6.6 have been divided into zones. In each exercise, identify any points that indicate a lack of control, and explain why.

6.1.

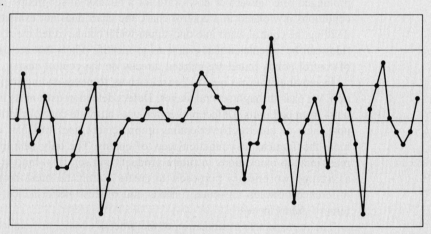

6.2.

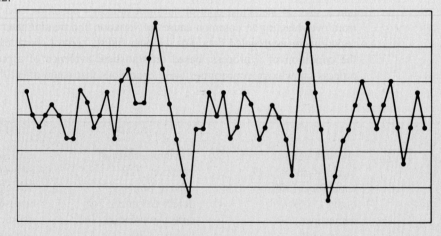

6.3.

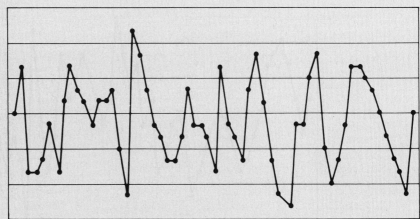

6.4.

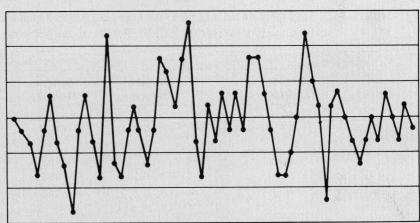

6.5.

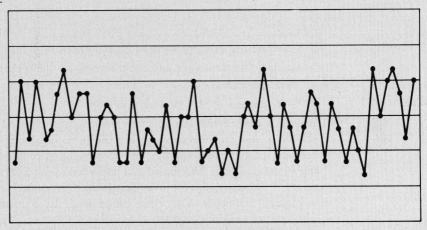

6.6.

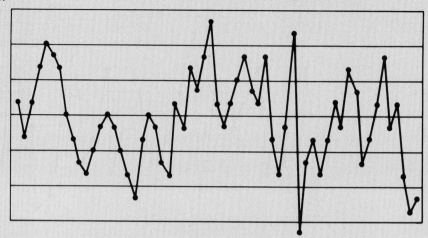

6.7. Steel pails are manufactured at a high rate. Periodic samples of 50 pails are selected from the process (see PAILS). Results of that sampling are:

Sample Number	n	Number Defective	Sample Number	n	Number Defective
1	50	5	11	50	4
2	50	6	12	50	4
3	50	3	13	50	3
4	50	6	14	50	5
5	50	8	15	50	4
6	50	5	16	50	2
7	50	4	17	50	4
8	50	5	18	50	5
9	50	6	19	50	1
10	50	7	20	50	6

a. Calculate the string of successive proportions of defective pails.

b. Calculate the centerline and control limits for the p chart.

c. Draw the p chart.

d. Is the process stable? How do you know?

 6.8. A medical transcription service enters medical data on patient files for hospitals. The service is studying ways to improve the turnaround time (defined as the time between receiving data and time the client receives completed files). Upon studying the process, it is determined that turnaround time is increased by transmission errors. A transmission error is defined as data transmitted that does not go through as planned, and needs to be retransmitted. Each day a sample of 125 record transmissions are randomly selected and evaluated for errors. The table below presents the number and proportion of transmissions with errors in samples of 125 records transmitted (see ☛ TRANSMIT).

Date	Number of Errors	Proportion of Errors
August		
1	6	0.048
2	3	0.024
5	4	0.032
6	4	0.032
7	9	0.072
8	0	0.000
9	0	0.000
12	8	0.064
13	4	0.032
14	3	0.024
15	4	0.032
16	1	0.008
19	10	0.080
20	9	0.072
21	3	0.024
22	1	0.008
23	4	0.032
26	6	0.048
27	3	0.024
28	5	0.040
29	1	0.008
30	3	0.024
September		
3	14	0.112
4	6	0.048
5	7	0.056
6	3	0.024
9	10	0.080
10	7	0.056
11	5	0.040
12	0	0.000
13	3	0.024

a. Construct a p chart.

b. Is the process in a state of statistical control? Why?

6.9. The following 32 days of data represent the findings from a study conducted at a factory that manufactures film canisters (see ☛ CANISTER). Each day 500 film canisters were sampled and inspected. The number of defective film canisters (nonconforming items) was recorded each day as follows:

Day	Number Nonconforming
1	26
2	25
3	23
4	24
5	26
6	20
7	21
8	27
9	23
10	25
11	22
12	26
13	25
14	29
15	20
16	19
17	23
18	19
19	18
20	27
21	28
22	24
23	26
24	23
25	27
26	28
27	24
28	22
29	20
30	25
31	27
32	19

a. Construct a p chart using the first 25 data points to calculate trial limits.

b. Is the process in a state of statistical control? Why?

c. If the process is in control, extend the limits and record the data for days 26 through 32.

6.10. A jewelry manufacturing company has a data processing department with 115 terminals in various locations in its building. A technician is responsible for investigating and correcting problems with the terminals. She is concerned with the rate at which terminals develop problems; she collects the following data to see if the system is in a state of statistical control (see ☞ JEWELRY).

Day	Number with Problems	Proportion with Problems
1	2	0.0174
2	5	0.0435
3	3	0.0261
4	13	0.1130
5	8	0.0696
6	6	0.0522
7	12	0.1043
8	1	0.0087
9	1	0.0087
10	5	0.0435
11	7	0.0609
12	10	0.0870
13	5	0.0435
14	6	0.0522
15	9	0.0783
16	3	0.0261
17	4	0.0348
18	8	0.0696
19	4	0.0348
20	2	0.0174
21	2	0.0174
22	4	0.0348
23	7	0.0609
24	10	0.0870
25	6	0.0522
26	5	0.0435
27	5	0.0435
28	9	0.0783
29	1	0.0087
30	4	0.0348

a. Construct a control chart for these data.

b. Is the process in a state of statistical control? Why?

c. If the process is not in a state of control, eliminate out-of-control points and recalculate the control limits.

6.11. A commuter railroad in a large northeastern city runs 122 trains from suburban areas into the city each weekday. A survey of rider satisfaction indicates that commuters are very concerned with trains arriving on time. Before making changes to the system to increase the proportion of on-time arrivals, the railroad wants to know whether the proportion of on-time arrivals is in a state of statistical control. The number of late trains for 30 weekdays is as follows (see ☞ RRLATE):

Day	Number Late	Day	Number Late
1	3	16	7
2	1	17	3
3	1	18	4
4	4	19	7
5	5	20	5
6	4	21	2
7	6	22	6
8	3	23	2
9	4	24	4
10	5	25	4
11	6	26	5
12	1	27	4
13	7	28	6
14	4	29	1
15	4	30	2

a. Construct a p chart for these data.

b. Is the process in a state of statistical control? Why?

c. If the process is not in a state of control, eliminate out-of-control points and recalculate the trial control limits.

References

1. Mark Berenson, David Levine, and T. Krehbiel (2004), *Basic Business Statistics: Concepts and Applications,* 9th ed. (Upper Saddle River, NJ: Prentice Hall).

2. W. Edwards Deming, "On Some Statistical Aids toward Economic Production," *Interfaces,* 5, August 1975, pp. 1–15.

3. W. Edwards Deming (1982), *Quality, Productivity and Competitive Position* (Cambridge, MA: Massachusetts Institute of Technology Center for Advanced Engineering Study).

4. W. Edwards Deming (1986), *Out of the Crisis* (Cambridge, MA: Massachusetts Institute of Technology Center for Advanced Engineering Study).

5. Howard S. Gitlow, "Definition of Quality," *Proceedings—Case Study Seminar—Dr. Deming's Management Methods: How They Are Being Implemented in the U.S. and Abroad* (Andover, MA: G.O.A.L.), November 6, 1984, pp. 4–18.

6. Howard S. Gitlow and Paul Hertz, "Product Defects and Productivity," *Harvard Business Review,* September/October 1983, pp. 131–41.

7. Kaoru Ishikawa (1985), *What Is Total Quality Control? The Japanese Way* (Englewood Cliffs, NJ: Prentice Hall).

8. W. Scherkenbach (1986), *The Deming Route to Quality and Productivity: Road Maps and Roadblocks* (Washington, DC: Ceepress Books).

9. Walter A. Shewhart (1980), *Economic Control of Quality of Manufactured Product* (Milwaukee, WI: American Society for Quality Control).

10. Genichi Taguchi and Yu-In Wu (1980), *Off-Line Quality Control* (Nagoya, Japan: Central Japan Quality Control Association).

11. Donald J. Wheeler and David S. Chambers (1992), *Understanding Statistical Process Control,* 2nd ed. (Knoxville, TN: SPC Press).

Appendix **A6.1**

Using Minitab for Control Charts: An Overview[1]

In this chapter the concept of a control chart has been introduced and various rules for detecting evidence of out-of-control patterns have been listed. In the control charts that will be developed in subsequent chapters of this text, the Minitab statistical software package will be used to perform the computations.

To use Minitab to obtain a control chart, select **Stat | Control Charts.** The list of different types of control charts available is displayed in Figure A6.1.

FIGURE A6.1
List of Control Charts Available in Minitab

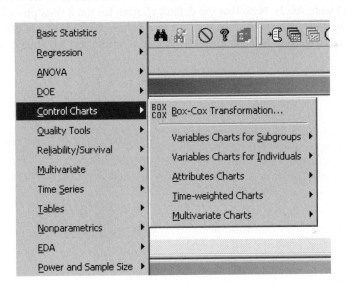

---

[1] The instructions and dialog boxes are based on the beta version of Minitab 14. Subsequent versions of Minitab may differ slightly from what is presented in this appendix.

FIGURE A6.2

Tests Tab of the x̄ and R Chart— Options Dialog Box

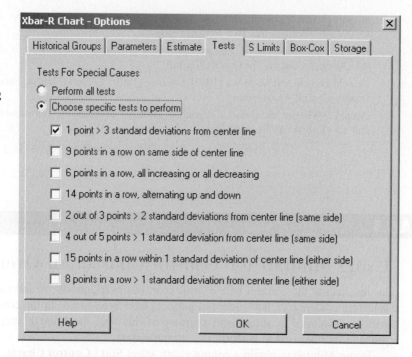

Each control chart provides tests for special causes, usually in the Options box for the test (see Figure A6.2). Note that the default choices for the 8 tests provided are not identical to the rules given in this chapter. The new values provided stay in effect until Minitab is restarted. Note that Minitab currently does not have a test for Rule 6 on page 165.

Chapter 7

Attribute Control Charts

Chapter Objectives

- To discuss when to use the different types of attribute control charts
- To construct the different types of attribute control charts: p chart, np chart, c chart, and u chart
- To analyze and interpret attribute control charts
- To discuss the limitations of attribute control charts

Introduction

Attribute data are data based on counts, or the number of times we observe a particular event. The events may be the number of nonconforming items, the fraction of nonconforming items, the number of defects, or any other distinct occurrence that is operationally defined. Attribute data may include such classifications as defective or conforming, go or no-go, acceptable or not acceptable, or number of defects per unit.

In Chapter 6 we saw that the first step on the ladder of quality consciousness consists of sorting conforming from nonconforming product: shipping conforming items and discarding, reworking, or downgrading nonconforming ones. In the first step, efforts focus on defect detection and on trying to inspect quality in by removing defective items. This stage is characterized by dependence on mass inspection to achieve quality rather than statistical process control. Even today, many firms consider this quality control.

Attribute control charts represent the second step on the ladder of quality consciousness, when organizations move toward defect prevention in a drive toward zero percent defective. At the second step, statistical process control is initiated using attribute control charts. However, information that output failed to meet a given specification does not answer the question of why the specification was not met. Total (100 percent) conformance to specifications does not provide a mechanism for never-ending process improvement. As we will see in Chapter 8, the third step on the ladder leads to continuous, never-ending improvement through the use of variables control charts.

Types of Attribute Control Charts

There are two basic types of attribute control charts: **classification charts** and **count charts.**

Classification Charts

Classification charts deal with either the fraction of items or the number of items in a series of subgroups that have a particular characteristic.

p Chart

The **p chart** is used to control the fraction of items with the characteristic. Subgroup sizes in a p chart may remain constant or may vary. A p chart might be used to control defective versus conforming, go versus no-go, or acceptable versus not acceptable.

np Chart

The **np chart** serves the same function as the p chart except that it is used to control the number rather than the fraction of items with the characteristic and is used only with constant subgroup sizes.

Count Charts

Count charts deal with the number of times a particular characteristic appears in some given **area of opportunity.** An area of opportunity can be a radio, a crate of radios, a hospital room, an airline reservation, a roll of paper, a section of a roll of paper, a time period, a geographical region, a stretch of highway, or any delineated observable region in which one or more events may be observed.

c Chart

A **c chart** is used to control the number of times a particular characteristic appears in a constant area of opportunity. A constant area of opportunity is one in which each subgroup used in constructing the control chart provides the same area or number of places in which the characteristic of interest may occur. For example, defects per air conditioner, accidents per work week in a factory, and deaths per week in a city all provide an approximately constant area of opportunity for the characteristic of interest to occur. The area of opportunity is the subgroup, whether it be the air conditioner, the factory work week, or the week in the city.

u Chart

A **u chart** serves the same basic function as a c chart, but it is used when the area of opportunity changes from subgroup to subgroup. For example, we may examine varying square footage of paper selected from rolls for blemishes, or carloads of lumber for damage when the contents of the rail cars varies.

Manual Construction of Attribute Control Charts

Standard forms exist for the construction of attribute control charts. Although there may be some slight individualizing from firm to firm, certain standard areas are almost always provided on the forms. Figure 7.1 shows an example of an attribute control chart form.

In the upper left corner the plant/factory/office location is entered; then just to the right the type of control chart is noted. The next box requires information on the part name and number. Other identifying entries include the department and the operation number and name. The next two boxes provide space to enter the process average, UCL, and LCL plus the date on which they were calculated.

At the bottom of the page are spaces for entering the total number of discrepancies (or defects), the percentage (or fraction) of discrepancies, and the sample (subgroup) size, n. Also included is a process log to help identify possible sources of variation. There are 10 cells directly above these for listing the type of discrepancy, usually by code number because of space constraints on the form.

The large open area on the left is for calibration and identification of the control chart's scale. The scale should be created to accommodate all observed and anticipated data entries. The control limits should fall well within the created scale so that there's room left for any points beyond the control limits to be entered on the graph.

Notice that the larger, upper portion of the cells (the ones on which the control chart will actually be drawn) is offset by exactly one-half cell width from those below. This is to avoid any confusion as to which vertical bar corresponds to which data entry.

Just above this larger area is a single row of boxes for noting the date, time, or other identifying information for each observation.

Computerized Construction of Attribute Control Charts Using Minitab

Attribute control charts can be created using Minitab. Appendix A7.1 provides detailed instructions on how to use Minitab to create attribute control charts.

FIGURE 7.1   A Typical Attribute Control Chart Form

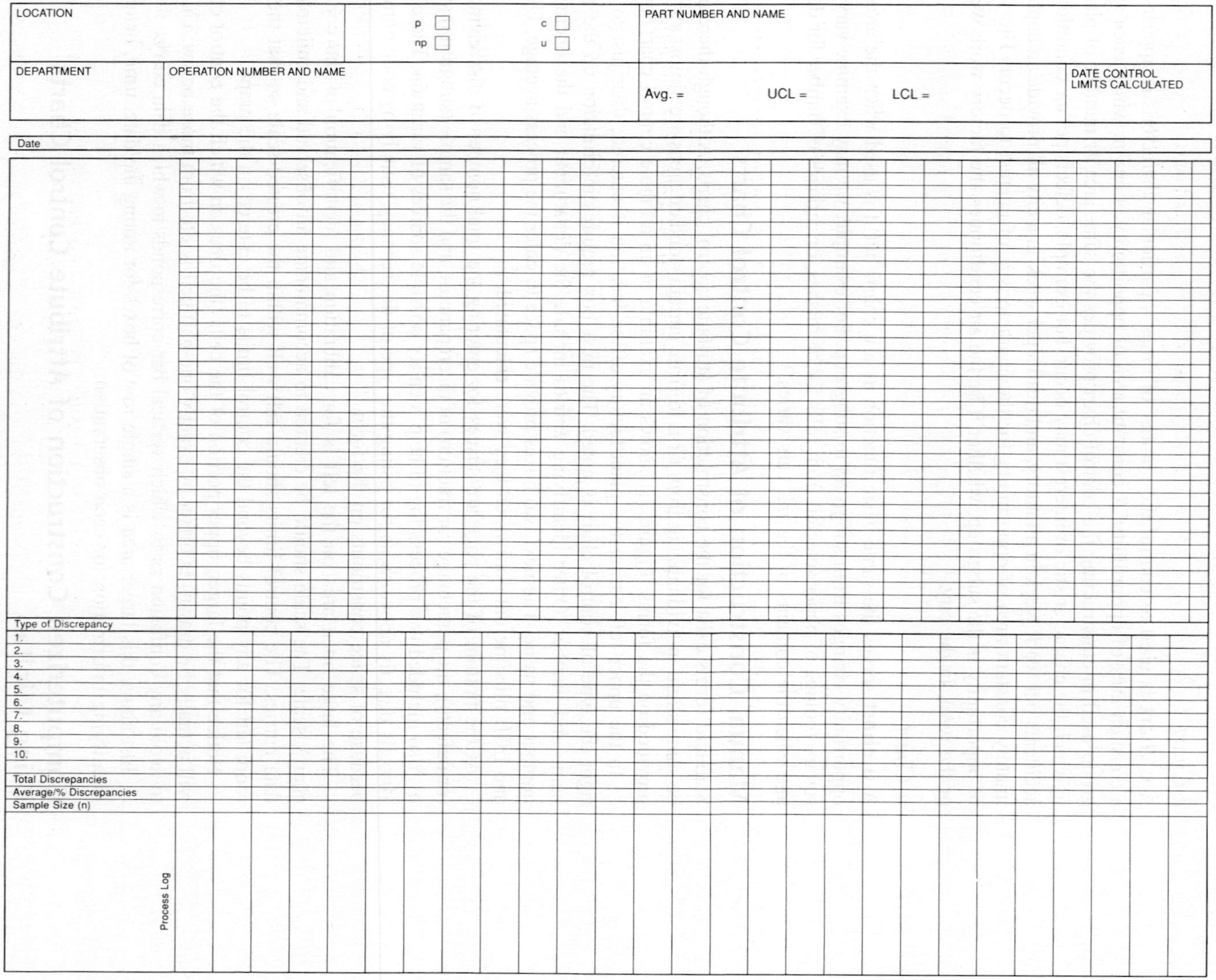

LOCATION		PART NUMBER AND NAME
DEPARTMENT	OPERATION NUMBER AND NAME	DATE CONTROL LIMITS CALCULATED

p   c
np   u

Avg. =　　UCL =　　LCL =

Date

Type of Discrepancy
1.
2.
3.
4.
5.
6.
7.
8.
9.
10.
Total Discrepancies
Average/% Discrepancies
Sample Size (n)

Process Log

Classification Charts

Defect prevention, the second step in the journey toward quality consciousness, relies on the use of attribute control charts to help to begin to reduce the difference between customer specifications and process performance. When the data are in the form of classifications, either a p chart or an np chart is used.

Conditions for Use

When each unit can be classified as either conforming or nonconforming (or having some characteristic of interest or not), a classification chart is appropriate. Samples of n items are periodically selected from process output. For these n distinct units comprising a subgroup:

1. Each unit must be classifiable as either possessing or not possessing the characteristic of interest. For example, each unit in a subgroup might be classified as either defective or nondefective, or conforming or nonconforming. The number of units possessing the characteristic of interest is called the **count,** X.

2. The probability that a unit possesses the characteristic of interest is assumed to be stable from unit to unit.

3. Within a given area of opportunity, the probability that a given unit possesses the characteristic of interest is assumed to be independent of whether any other unit possesses the characteristic.

For data satisfying these conditions, we may use a p chart or np chart. But we must exercise caution to avoid using either of these control charts inappropriately.

When Not to Use p Charts or np Charts

Occasionally data based on measurements (variables data) are downgraded into data in terms of conformance or nonconformance (attribute data). This is not a good practice because the data based on measurements can provide more information than the data based on conformance or nonconformance.

It is also important that the denominator in the fraction being charted is the proper area of opportunity. If it is not, then the data are not truly a proportion but a ratio. For example, the fraction of defectives found on the second shift will be a useful proportion only if it is computed by dividing the number of defectives found on the second shift by the proper area of opportunity, the number of units produced on the second shift. If a ratio is created using the number of defectives found on the second shift divided by the number of items shipped by the second shift, there is no way of knowing that the items shipped during the second shift were all produced on the second shift. Some items shipped on the second shift may have been produced during the first shift and therefore this may be an inappropriate area of opportunity.

Last, we must exercise caution to ensure that the control chart is being created for a single process. Control charting output from combined different processes will result in irrational subgroups or subgroups that will not enable us to identify process problems. Little if anything can be learned from such charts, and the net effect may be a masking of special causes of variation.

Constructing Classification Charts

An adaptation of the **Deming Cycle,** discussed in Chapter 2, may be used to construct and interpret a p chart or np chart.

1. Plan
   a. The process to be studied using the control chart must be named and flowcharted.
   b. The purpose of the chart must be determined.
   c. The characteristic to be charted must be selected and operationally defined.
   d. The manner, size, and frequency of subgroup selection must be established.
   e. The type of chart (i.e., p chart or np chart) must be established.
   f. Forms for recording and constructing the control chart must be established.
2. Do
   a. Data must be recorded either manually onto control chart paper or electronically onto a Minitab worksheet; see Appendix A7.1 for instructions on using Minitab to create attribute control charts.
   b. The fraction of items with the characteristic of interest must be calculated for each of the subgroups, either manually or electronically by Minitab.
   c. The average value must be calculated, either manually or electronically by Minitab.
   d. The control limits and zone boundaries must be calculated and plotted onto the control chart, either manually or electronically by Minitab.
   e. The data points must be entered on the control chart, either manually or electronically by Minitab.
3. Study
   a. The control chart must be examined for indications of a lack of control, either manually or electronically using the **Test** option in Minitab.
   b. All aspects of the control chart must be reviewed periodically and appropriate changes made when required.
4. Act
   a. Actions must be undertaken to bring the process under control by eliminating any special causes of variation.
   b. Actions must be undertaken to reduce the causes of common variation for the purpose of never-ending improvement of the process.
   c. Specifications must be reviewed in relation to the capability of the process.
   d. The purpose of the control chart must be reconsidered by returning to the Plan stage.

The Plan Stage

The first step in the plan stage is to name and flowchart the process to be studied using the control chart.

The second step in the plan stage is to determine the purpose of the chart.

1. For data at the process level, a p chart or np chart may be created to search for special causes of variation in a chaotic system.
2. For data that have been aggregated over two or more processes, a p chart or np chart may be used to stop management from over-reacting to common causes of variation.

The third step in the plan stage is to select and operationally define the characteristic for control charting. Very often a single item possesses several characteristics, any of which may cause the item to be considered defective or nonconforming. Generally, a single chart will be kept for the entire item, but frequently separate charts will be kept for individual characteristics. It is usually efficient to concentrate initial efforts on control charts for the characteristics that cause problems for the customer and are within control of the process owner studying the problem. Some of the techniques to be discussed in Chapter 10, such as brainstorming, may be useful in selecting the characteristics to be charted.

The fourth step in the plan stage is to determine the manner, size, and frequency for the selection of subgroups. The **subgroup size** is the number of items to be observed at each sampling to determine the fraction conforming or nonconforming. As we will see in Chapter 8, **rational subgroups** should be selected to minimize within-subgroup variation. Frequently subgroups are selected in the order of production. The decisions concerning the method of selection and the factors to be isolated will require careful planning by those individuals with knowledge of, and experience with, the process. Early efforts may need revision as a result of unexpected factors that may be revealed while developing the control chart. This may lead to the creation of several charts where only one was initially contemplated, but this may be of use in resolving special causes of variation and reducing common variation in the areas charted.

The necessary subgroup size will be discussed later in this chapter, under "Subgroup Size" on page 197.

The frequency with which the subgroups are selected is generally specific to each situation and depends upon factors such as the rate of production, elapsed time, and shift duration. The frequency should be logical in terms of shifts, time periods, or any other rational grouping. The shorter the intervals between subgroups, the more quickly information may be fed back for possible action. Cost will naturally be a factor, but after process stability has been established, frequency of subgroup selection can often be decreased and efforts focused elsewhere.

The fifth step in the plan stage is to decide whether to use a p chart or np chart. There is no substantive difference between these two charts. The information portrayed is essentially the same; only the form is different. The p chart displays the *fraction* with the characteristic of interest, while the np chart displays the *number* of items with that characteristic of interest. From a technical standpoint, they may be used interchangeably. Nevertheless, as the np chart permits the data to be entered as whole numbers (rather than as the ratio of the number of nonconforming items to the subgroup size), the np chart may be preferable. However, as we will discuss later in this chapter, if subgroup size varies from subgroup to subgroup, a p chart is typically used.

The final step in the plan stage is to select the control chart form. Standard forms are available from the American Society for Quality for attribute control charts. [See Reference 1.] Many firms have developed their own forms, such as the one in Figure 7.1. Alternatively, Minitab may be used to construct the control chart form, as described in Appendix A7.1.

Occasionally, supplemental forms **(check sheets)** are used to collect the initial data, as shown in Figure 7.2. The data are then transferred to a control chart. This technique may be especially convenient if the control chart is to be drawn at another time or with the aid of a computer or if the work environment is not suitable for drawing the chart.

FIGURE 7.2 **Sample Data Collection Form for p Charts and np Charts**

DATA SHEET FOR p CHART OR np CHART

Department: _____

Part Name: _____ Part Number: _____

Date	Time	Inspected by	Number Inspected	No. of Defectives	Fraction Defective	Comments

The Do Stage

The do stage begins with the recording of the required data for each subgroup either on the data collection sheet, directly on the control chart paper, or onto a Minitab worksheet. Any abnormalities or unusual occurrences should be recorded in the space provided for comments on the control chart form, or on a special **log sheet.** Log sheets are diaries that record historical data by subgroup and are used to provide clues to special causes of variation, should a lack of control be found. Hence, they are critical to the proper use of a control chart that is constructed for data at the process level. Recall that this type of control chart is created to search for special causes of variation in a chaotic system.

If the chart is a p chart, the fraction of items with the characteristic of interest must be calculated for each subgroup, either manually or by Minitab. After the data for each subgroup have been collected (using at least 20 subgroups), the average value for p is calculated using Equation (6.1), either manually or using Minitab. This value provides a **centerline** for the control chart and is the basis for the calculation of the standard error used to determine the control limits and zone boundaries.

Next, the **control limits** and **zone boundaries** are computed—using the equations introduced in Chapter 6 and discussed later in this chapter—and are then drawn onto the control chart, either manually or using Minitab.

Last in the do stage, the p values (or np values for the np chart) are plotted onto the control chart, either manually or using Minitab.

It is usually desirable to complete the control chart promptly and display it for those individuals working with the process. It is not unusual for such a display to have immediate beneficial results, especially if those involved have been educated about the purpose and meaning of control charts.

The Study Stage

Using the rules introduced in Chapter 6 and detailed in Chapter 9, we either manually examine the control chart from right to left (looking backward in time) for indications of a lack of control, or use Minitab to examine the data for a lack of control. Any special causes are appropriately noted on the control chart.

Periodically the centerline, control limits, and zone boundaries should be reviewed. Timing of the review, of course, depends on the process and its history. Typically p charts and np charts are kept for long periods of time. Any change in the process is cause to consider a review of chart parameters.

The Act Stage

Indications of special sources of variation may be revealed during the study stage. If any special sources of variation are found, steps must be initiated to remove the sources if they are bad, or incorporate them into the process if they are good. This is accomplished by creating a revised flowchart of the process that utilizes the modifications required to resolve any special causes of variation. It is not uncommon for supervisors or group leaders to already be aware of problem areas; the control chart helps to discover the cause and reinforce arguments for improvement. Furthermore, control charts help focus attention on areas needing immediate help.

If it appears there is a lack of control on the desirable side of the chart, it is a good practice to examine the inspection procedures; faulty inspection procedures may be to blame. On the other hand, perhaps a special cause is responsible for points on the desirable side of the chart that should be formally incorporated into the process—that is, improvements may have spontaneously occurred in the process that, once discovered, should be incorporated.

Although a control chart may reveal no indications of special causes of variation, the overall level of the fraction or number of items with the characteristic of interest may not be at a satisfactory level **(threshold state).** Other tools and techniques, such as cause-and-effect diagrams and Pareto analysis, to be discussed in Chapter 10, may be used in an attempt to reduce the high fraction of nonconforming items as the Deming cycle rolls as a wheel up the hill of never-ending process improvement.

In the drive toward never-ending improvement, no level of defectives is low enough; nevertheless, as the proportion of defectives shrinks as a result of efforts at process improvement, subgroups will often contain no defectives at all. This will make the use of p charts or np charts difficult if not impossible because of the large subgroup sizes needed to detect even a single defective item. This leads to the use of variables control charts, which we discuss in Chapter 8.

Last in the act stage is the reconsideration of the purpose of the control chart. We return to the beginning of the plan stage, where the cycle begins again.

The p Chart for Constant Subgroup Sizes

In Chapter 6 we saw an example of a p chart with a **constant subgroup size.** Constant subgroup size implies that the same number of items is sampled and then classified for each subgroup on the chart. We use a discrete, countable characteristic of output to construct a p chart; for example, the fraction of customers who pay their bills in fewer than 30 days, the fraction of correspondence sent electronically, or the fraction of an airline's flights that arrive within 15 minutes of their scheduled arrival time.

The Centerline and Control Limits

For a stable process, categorization of data into two classes suggests that every item has approximately the same probability of being in one of the two categories. We say approximately because even stable processes exhibit variation.

The centerline for the p chart is established at $\bar{p}$, the overall fraction of output that is nonconforming, as given by Equation (6.1). The upper control limit and the lower control limit are found by adding and subtracting three times the standard error [given by Equation (6.2)] from the centerline value using Equations (6.3) and (6.4).

To reiterate,

$$\text{Centerline(p)} = \bar{p} = \left[\frac{\text{Total number of defectives in all subgroups under investigation}}{\text{Total number of units examined in all subgroups under investigation}} \right] \quad \textbf{(7.1)}$$

$$\text{UCL(p)} = p = \bar{p} + 3\sqrt{\frac{\bar{p}(1 - \bar{p})}{n}} \quad \textbf{(7.2)}$$

$$\text{LCL(p)} = p = \bar{p} - 3\sqrt{\frac{\bar{p}(1 - \bar{p})}{n}} \quad \textbf{(7.3)}$$

Construction of a p Chart: An Example

As an illustration, consider the case of an importer of decorative ceramic tiles. Some tiles are cracked or broken before or during transit, rendering them useless scrap. The fraction of cracked or broken tiles is naturally of concern to the firm. Each day a sample of 100 tiles is drawn from the total of all tiles received from each tile vendor. Table 7.1 presents the sample results for 30 days of incoming shipments for a particular vendor (see ❀ TILES).

The average fraction of cracked or broken tiles can be calculated from these data using Equation (7.1). This is the centerline for the control chart.

$$\text{Centerline(p)} = \bar{p} = 183/3000 = 0.061$$

The upper and lower control limits can then be computed using Equations (7.2) and (7.3).

$$\text{UCL(p)} = 0.061 + 3\sqrt{\frac{0.061(1 - 0.061)}{100}} = 0.133$$

$$\text{LCL(p)} = 0.061 - 3\sqrt{\frac{0.061(1 - 0.061)}{100}} = -0.011$$

Recall from our discussion in Chapter 6 that a negative lower control limit in a p chart is meaningless; instead we use a value of 0 for the lower control limit.

For a stable process, the probability that any subgroup fraction will be outside the three-sigma limits is small. Also, if the process is stable, the probability is small that the data will demonstrate any other indications of the presence of special causes of variation

TABLE 7.1
Daily Cracked
Tiles

Day	Sample Size	Number Cracked or Broken	Fraction
1	100	14	0.14
2	100	2	0.02
3	100	11	0.11
4	100	4	0.04
5	100	9	0.09
6	100	7	0.07
7	100	4	0.04
8	100	6	0.06
9	100	3	0.03
10	100	2	0.02
11	100	3	0.03
12	100	8	0.08
13	100	4	0.04
14	100	15	0.15
15	100	5	0.05
16	100	3	0.03
17	100	8	0.08
18	100	4	0.04
19	100	2	0.02
20	100	5	0.05
21	100	5	0.05
22	100	7	0.07
23	100	9	0.09
24	100	1	0.01
25	100	3	0.03
26	100	12	0.12
27	100	9	0.09
28	100	3	0.03
29	100	6	0.06
30	100	9	0.09
Totals	3,000	183	

by virtue of the other rules discussed in Chapters 6 and 9. But if the process is not in a state of statistical control, the control chart provides an economical basis upon which to search for and identify indications of this lack of control.

For this p chart—or, in fact, for any of the attribute control charts—the exact probabilities that a stable process will generate points indicating a lack of control are impossible to calculate because even a stable process exhibits variation in its mean, dispersion, and shape. Nevertheless, the exact value of these probabilities is not too important for ordinary applications; what is important is the fact that they are small. Therefore, if a point does lie beyond the upper or lower control limits, we will infer that it indicates a lack of control. Additionally, for p charts, the six other rules for out-of-control points described in Chapter 6 can all be applied. In order to do so, we need to compute the boundaries for the A, B, and C zones.

Recall from Chapter 6 that the width of each zone is one standard error, or one-third of the distance between the upper control limit and the centerline. Thus the boundaries between zones B and C are one standard error on either side of the centerline. Here they are found by adding and subtracting the quantity $\sqrt{\bar{p}(1-\bar{p})/n}$ from the centerline, $\bar{p}$.

$$\sqrt{\frac{p(1-p)}{n}} = \sqrt{\frac{0.061(1-0.061)}{n}} = 0.024$$

So that

$$\text{Boundary between upper zones B and C} = \bar{p} + \sqrt{\frac{\bar{p}(1-\bar{p})}{n}} \tag{7.4}$$

In our example this value is $0.061 + 0.024 = 0.085$ and

$$\text{Boundary between lower zones B and C} = \bar{p} - \sqrt{\frac{\bar{p}(1-\bar{p})}{n}} \tag{7.5}$$

In our example this value is $0.061 - 0.024 = 0.037$.

We find the upper and lower boundaries between zones A and B by adding and subtracting, respectively, two standard errors from the centerline, $\bar{p}$.

$$\text{Boundary between upper zones A and B} = \bar{p} + 2\sqrt{\frac{\bar{p}(1-\bar{p})}{n}} \tag{7.6}$$

and

$$\text{Boundary between lower zones A and B} = \bar{p} - 2\sqrt{\frac{\bar{p}(1-\bar{p})}{n}} \tag{7.7}$$

Using these in our example gives

$$0.061 + 2(0.024) = 0.109$$

and

$$0.061 - 2(0.024) = 0.013$$

Figure 7.3 shows the completed control chart.

Examining it, we find a process that is out of control. On day 1, the mean fraction value is above the upper control limit. The sample mean for day 14 is also above the upper control limit, another indication of lack of control. None of the other rules presented in Chapter 6 appears to be violated. That is, there are no instances when two out of three consecutive points lie in zone A on one side of the centerline; there are no instances when four out of five consecutive points lie in zone B or beyond on one side of the centerline; there are no instances when eight consecutive points move upward or downward; nor are there eight consecutive points on one side of the centerline. There does not appear to be a lack of runs; there are no instances of 13 consecutive points in zone C.

Nevertheless, the incoming flow of ceramic tiles needs further examination. The special causes of these two erratic shifts in the fraction of cracked or broken tiles should be eliminated so that expectations for usable portions can be stabilized. Only after this is done can improvements be made in the process.

FIGURE 7.3

Minitab
p Chart for
Fraction of
Cracked Tiles

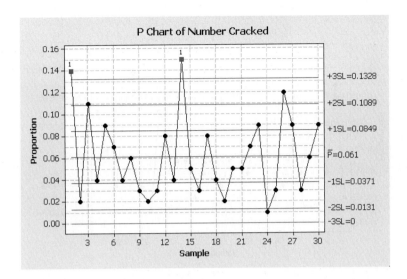

Further study reveals that on both day 1 and day 14 the regular delivery truck operator was absent because of illness. Another employee loaded and drove the delivery truck on those days. That individual had never been instructed in the proper care of the product, which requires special handling and treatment. To solve this problem and eliminate this special cause of variation, management created and implemented a training program using the regular driver's experience for three other employees. Any one of these three employees can now properly fill in and perform satisfactorily. Thus the system has been changed to eliminate this special cause of variation.

After the process has been changed so that special causes of variation have been removed, the out-of-control points are removed from the data. The points are removed from the control chart, and the graph merely skips over them.

Removing these points also changes the process average and standard error. Therefore the centerline, control limits, and zone boundaries must be recalculated.

The new centerline and control limits are:

$$\bar{p} = 154/2800 = 0.055$$

$$\text{UCL(p)} = 0.055 + 3\sqrt{\frac{(0.055)(0.945)}{100}} = 0.123$$

$$\text{LCL(p)} = 0.055 - 3\sqrt{\frac{(0.055)(0.945)}{100}} = -0.013 \text{ (use 0.000)}$$

The new upper and lower boundaries between zones B and C are calculated using Equations (7.4) and (7.5):

$$\text{Boundary between upper zones B and C} = 0.055 + \sqrt{\frac{(0.055)(0.945)}{100}} = 0.078$$

$$\text{Boundary between lower zones B and C} = 0.055 - \sqrt{\frac{(0.055)(0.945)}{100}} = 0.032$$

FIGURE 7.4
Minitab
Revised
p Chart for
Fraction of
Cracked Tiles

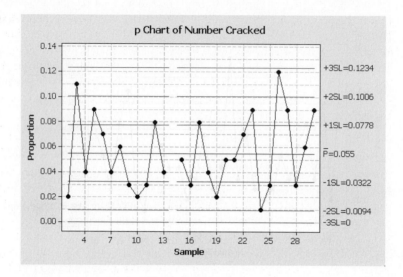

The new upper and lower boundaries between zones A and B are calculated using Equations (7.6) and (7.7):

$$\begin{array}{c} \text{Boundary between} \\ \text{upper zones A and B} \end{array} = 0.055 + 2\sqrt{\frac{(0.055)(0.945)}{100}} = 0.101$$

$$\begin{array}{c} \text{Boundary between} \\ \text{lower zones A and B} \end{array} = 0.055 - 2\sqrt{\frac{(0.055)(0.945)}{100}} = 0.009$$

The entire control chart is redrawn, as shown in Figure 7.4. None of the seven rules discussed in Chapter 6 is violated, so there does not appear to be a lack of control. The process now appears to be stable and in a state of statistical control. Management may now look for ways to reduce the overall process average of the number of cracked or broken tiles to raise the usable number of tiles per shipment and effectively increase the process output.

Iterative Reevaluations

It is possible—and not at all uncommon—that by changing the process, removing points that were out of control, and recomputing the control limits and zone boundaries, points that initially exhibited only common variation will now indicate a lack of control. If and when this happens, the system must again be reevaluated to eliminate the newly revealed special causes of variation.

This may once again uncover even more indications of a lack of control, which also must be removed from the system. Analysis of the process will continue to iterate in this manner until there no longer appears to be a lack of control. Keep in mind that in the course of these iterations, some of the data will be discarded. Hence the database will shrink, and the control chart will be based on fewer and fewer subgroups. Furthermore, as changes are made, the process may no longer resemble the original process.

We must also keep in mind that if control limits are recalculated too frequently (as might be the temptation with automatic data processing available with many computer control routines), it becomes possible to mistake common variation for special variation. This effect parallels the over-steering many new drivers experience when first learning to drive a car. Knowledge and experience with the process are the best guides here.

At some point a decision must be made to stop analyzing the original data and collect new data. There is no explicit rule for the point at which this should be done; only knowledge and experience with the process can dictate when to stop analyzing previous data and begin collecting and analyzing new data.

Subgroup Size

When constructing a p chart, the subgroup size is much larger than that required for variables control charts. This is because the sample size must be large enough that some nonconforming items are likely to be included in the subgroup. If, for example, a process produces 1.0 percent defectives, sample subgroups of size 10 will only occasionally contain a nonconforming item. As a general rule of thumb, control charts based on classification count data should have sample sizes large enough so that the average count per subgroup is at least 2.00. This allows the A, B, and C zones to be wide enough to provide a reasonable working region into which data points may fall for analysis. This is true for both the p chart and the np chart, which we discuss later in this chapter.

Consider, for example, a process producing 5 percent of its output with a particular characteristic of interest (i.e., $\bar{p} = 0.05$). Subgroups of size 20 yield an average count of only $20(0.05) = 1.0$. Further, each subgroup would have an integer number of counts, yielding fractions in increments of 5 percent. The centerline would be at 0.050, the lower control limit would be at 0.000, and the upper control limit would be at

$$0.05 + 3\sqrt{\frac{(0.05)(1 - 0.05)}{20}} = 0.196$$

Only fractions of 0.00, 0.05, 0.10, and 0.15 would fall within the control limits. Examining patterns such as runs up or down would not be practical; finding eight points moving upward or downward would almost always be redundant because the beginning or end of the run would be beyond the upper control limit and would indicate a lack of control for that reason. Clearly we would not be able to learn too much from a p chart based on a subgroup size of 20 items with its centerline at 0.05. Similarly, samples taken from a process producing nonconforming items at a rate of only 1 percent would require samples of 200 to have an average count of 2.00. Even with samples of size 200, samples would provide counts of 0, 1, 2, and so on for subgroup fractions in increments of 0.005. With a centerline at 0.01, the p chart would not be very detailed and might not provide satisfactory indications of a lack of control.

Average subgroup counts of less than 2.00 present problems that can become extreme, especially if the average count per subgroup falls below 1.00. Hence, subgroups must be made large enough so that the average count is at least 2.00.

Ideally, subgroup sizes should remain the same for all subgroups, but occasionally circumstances require variations in subgroup size. Whether the subgroup size for a p chart varies or remains constant, the larger the subgroup size, the narrower the control limits will be. This is because the subgroup size, n, appears in the denominator of the expression for the standard error; the larger the value for n, the narrower the width of the control limits and zones A, B, and C around the process average will be.

Subgroup Frequency

Every process goes through physical cycles, such as shifts and ordering sequences. p chart and np chart calculations must be based on a sufficient number of subgroups to encompass all of the cycles of a process in order to include all possible sources of variation. Subgroup data should be collected at a frequency greater than the frequency at which the process can change. This frequency is determined by a process expert.

Number of Subgroups

As a rule of thumb, the number of subgroups should be at least 25 for p charts and np charts.

Subgroups Not Based on Time

It is possible to construct control charts for rational subgroups that do not represent chronological events. For example, a p chart for the fraction defective produced by a battery of 100 machines performing the same task (such as spot welding) might be kept on a single control chart. In these situations the number of subgroups must encompass all machines to encompass all possible sources of variation. Additionally, the rules concerning indications of a lack of control by virtue of trends over time in the data—such as two out of three consecutive points in zone A or four out of five consecutive points in zone B or beyond—should be ignored.

Construction of a p Chart: Another Example

An injection molding process provides a bracket to be used on aircraft passenger seats. Daily samples of 500 brackets are selected from the production output and examined carefully for cracks, splits, or other imperfections that will render them defective. Table 7.2 lists the results (see ❀ MOLDING).

The centerline, control limits, and zone boundaries are calculated from Equations (7.1) through (7.7):

$$\text{Centerline(p)} = \bar{p} = 504/12500 = 0.040$$

$$\text{UCL(p)} = 0.040 + 3\sqrt{\frac{(0.040)(0.960)}{500}} = 0.066$$

$$\text{LCL(p)} = 0.040 - 3\sqrt{\frac{(0.040)(0.960)}{500}} = 0.014$$

$$\text{Boundary between lower zones A and B} = 0.040 - 2\sqrt{\frac{(0.040)(0.960)}{500}} = 0.022$$

$$\text{Boundary between lower zones B and C} = 0.040 - \sqrt{\frac{(0.040)(0.960)}{500}} = 0.031$$

TABLE 7.2
Defective
Aircraft Seat
Brackets

Date	Sample Size	No. of Defectives	Fraction Defective
July 5	500	12	0.024
6	500	9	0.018
7	500	8	0.016
8	500	10	0.020
9	500	17	0.034
12	500	33	0.066
13	500	15	0.030
14	500	46	0.092
15	500	22	0.044
16	500	13	0.026
19	500	9	0.018
20	500	15	0.030
21	500	4	0.008
22	500	37	0.074
23	500	20	0.040
26	500	15	0.030
27	500	14	0.028
28	500	18	0.036
29	500	45	0.090
30	500	25	0.050
Aug 2	500	27	0.054
3	500	33	0.066
4	500	17	0.034
5	500	28	0.056
6	500	12	0.024
Totals	12,500	504	

$$\text{Boundary between upper zones B and C} = 0.040 + \sqrt{\frac{(0.040)(0.960)}{500}} = 0.049$$

$$\text{Boundary between upper zones A and B} = 0.040 + 2\sqrt{\frac{(0.040)(0.960)}{500}} = 0.058$$

Figure 7.5 illustrates the p chart for these data. Many points indicate that this process is not in a state of statistical control. The operator running the molding process initiates a study that reveals that the mold is poorly designed, so consistent parts cannot be fabricated. The operator suggests a redesign of the mold that may eliminate most of the special causes of variation and reduce the average fraction defective. The out-of-control points would then be eliminated and the control limits and zone boundaries recalculated. For any new out-of-control points, sources of special variation would have to be identified and removed; the process continues until no further evidence of special variation can be found.

FIGURE 7.5
Minitab
p Chart for
Fraction of
Defective
Aircraft Seat
Brackets

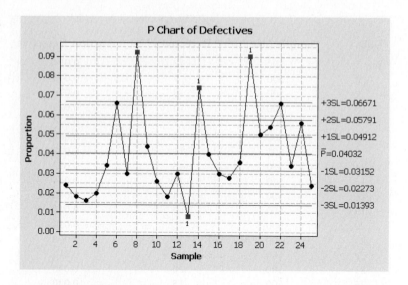

The p Chart for Variable Subgroup Sizes

Sometimes subgroups vary in size. This makes the construction of a p chart somewhat more tedious, although circumstances may make this situation unavoidable. Common among these is when data initially collected for some purpose other than the creation of a control chart are later used to construct a control chart.

The standard error, $\sqrt{\bar{p}(1 - \bar{p})/n}$, varies inversely with the sample size. That is, as the sample size increases, the standard error decreases, and vice versa. Control limits and zone boundaries are calculated on the basis of the standard error. Consequently, as the sample size changes so will the control limits and the zone boundaries.

Using Varying Control Limits: An Example

When sample sizes vary from subgroup to subgroup, we calculate new zone boundaries and control limits for each subgroup.

Consider, for example, the case of a highway toll barrier with two types of toll collection: by automatic machine and by human operator. The automatic lanes require exact change or a transponder while the human operator lanes do not. The fraction of vehicles arriving with exact change or a transponder is examined using a control chart for a series of rush hour intervals on consecutive weekdays. As the number of vehicles passing through the toll barrier varies from day to day, the control limits change day to day. One-hour periods (7:30 to 8:30 A.M.) for 20 consecutive weekdays yield the data in Table 7.3 (see ☛ TOLL).

From these data, $\bar{p}$, the centerline, can be calculated from Equation (7.1) as

$$\text{Centerline(p)} = \bar{p} = 2569/6421 = 0.400$$

We can also calculate each UCL, LCL, and zone boundary using Equations (7.2) through (7.7).

TABLE 7.3
Number of Vehicles Using Exact Change

Day	n	Number with Exact Change	Day	n	Number with Exact Change
1	465	180	11	406	186
2	123	38	12	415	149
3	309	142	13	379	90
4	83	20	14	341	148
5	116	35	15	258	107
6	306	108	16	270	84
7	333	190	17	480	185
8	265	106	18	350	184
9	354	94	19	433	210
10	256	116	20	479	197
			Totals	6,421	2,569

For example, for the first data point,

$$\text{UCL(p)} = 0.40 + 3\sqrt{\frac{(0.40)(1 - 0.40)}{465}} = 0.468$$

$$\text{LCL(p)} = 0.40 - 3\sqrt{\frac{(0.40)(1 - 0.40)}{465}} = 0.332$$

$$\text{Boundary between lower zones A and B} = 0.40 - 2\sqrt{\frac{(0.40)(1 - 0.40)}{465}} = 0.355$$

$$\text{Boundary between lower zones B and C} = 0.40 - \sqrt{\frac{(0.40)(1 - 0.40)}{465}} = 0.377$$

$$\text{Boundary between upper zones A and B} = 0.40 + 2\sqrt{\frac{(0.40)(1 - 0.40)}{465}} = 0.445$$

$$\text{Boundary between upper zones B and C} = 0.40 + \sqrt{\frac{(0.40)(1 - 0.40)}{465}} = 0.423$$

Since subgroup sizes vary, these control limits and zone boundaries are only valid for the first observation, where n = 465. Each subgroup will have its own control limits and zone boundaries. Table 7.4 shows the results of calculating these in the same manner as for the first point.

We use these values to draw the control limits and zone boundaries in Figure 7.6. The process indicates many instances of a lack of control. Fully 25 percent of the subgroup proportions are out of control, and the data seem to be behaving in an extremely erratic pattern. Days 19, 18, 13, 9, and 7 are all beyond the control limits. Day 5 also indicates a lack of control because it is the second of three consecutive points falling in zone C or beyond on the same side of the centerline.

Careful study is warranted to determine the cause or causes of this special variation. Removing the special causes of variation may require some fundamental changes in the way this system operates. Nevertheless, we must eliminate all of the special sources of variation before attempting to reduce the common causes of variation in the process.

TABLE 7.4   Control Limits and Zone Boundaries for Vehicles with Exact Change

Subgroup Number	n	Fraction Defective	UCL	LCL	Upper Zone C	Lower Zone C	Upper Zone B	Lower Zone B
1	465	0.387	0.468	0.332	0.423	0.377	0.446	0.354
2	123	0.309	0.533	0.267	0.444	0.356	0.488	0.312
3	309	0.460	0.484	0.316	0.428	0.372	0.456	0.344
4	83	0.241	0.561	0.239	0.454	0.346	0.508	0.292
5	116	0.302	0.536	0.264	0.445	0.355	0.491	0.309
6	306	0.353	0.484	0.316	0.428	0.372	0.456	0.344
7	333	0.571	0.481	0.319	0.427	0.373	0.454	0.346
8	265	0.400	0.490	0.310	0.430	0.370	0.460	0.340
9	354	0.266	0.478	0.322	0.426	0.374	0.452	0.348
10	256	0.453	0.492	0.308	0.431	0.369	0.461	0.339
11	406	0.458	0.473	0.327	0.424	0.376	0.449	0.351
12	415	0.359	0.472	0.328	0.424	0.376	0.448	0.352
13	379	0.237	0.475	0.325	0.425	0.375	0.450	0.350
14	341	0.434	0.480	0.320	0.427	0.373	0.453	0.347
15	258	0.415	0.491	0.309	0.430	0.370	0.461	0.339
16	270	0.311	0.489	0.311	0.430	0.370	0.460	0.340
17	480	0.385	0.467	0.333	0.422	0.378	0.445	0.355
18	350	0.526	0.479	0.321	0.426	0.374	0.452	0.348
19	433	0.485	0.471	0.329	0.424	0.376	0.447	0.353
20	479	0.411	0.467	0.333	0.422	0.378	0.445	0.355

FIGURE 7.6
Minitab
p Chart for
Vehicles with
Exact Change

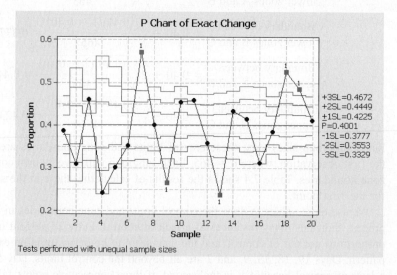

Changing the Process

Management decides it would be advantageous to remove the erratic patterns in the preceding process. They could better serve the public by having adequate toll lanes of either the automatic or human operator type available during rush hours. As a result of brainstorming, management institutes the sale of tokens that can be used in the exact change lanes. These are sold at a discount (to encourage their purchase) to motorists in the human operator lanes. Because the process has now been changed, a new set of observations is made. After a period of two months, to allow for transient effects to die down, the same sample selection method is again employed. Results for those subgroups appear in Table 7.5 (see TOLL2). Their corresponding control limits and zone boundaries are shown in Table 7.6.

TABLE 7.5
Number of
Vehicles Using
Exact Change,
Transponders,
or Tokens

Day	n	Number with Exact Change	Day	n	Number with Exact Change
1	421	171	11	401	199
2	466	197	12	384	165
3	389	192	13	428	213
4	254	107	14	352	149
5	186	89	15	444	193
6	456	189	16	357	158
7	411	211	17	283	147
8	322	139	18	424	207
9	287	136	19	337	143
10	262	131	20	326	157
			Totals	7,190	3,293

TABLE 7.6   Control Limits and Zone Boundaries for Vehicles with Exact Change

Subgroup Number	n	Fraction Defective	UCL	LCL	Upper Zone C	Lower Zone C	Upper Zone B	Lower Zone B
1	421	0.406	0.531	0.385	0.482	0.434	0.507	0.409
2	466	0.423	0.527	0.389	0.481	0.435	0.504	0.412
3	389	0.494	0.534	0.382	0.483	0.433	0.509	0.407
4	254	0.421	0.552	0.364	0.489	0.427	0.521	0.395
5	186	0.479	0.568	0.348	0.495	0.421	0.531	0.385
6	456	0.415	0.528	0.388	0.481	0.435	0.505	0.411
7	411	0.513	0.532	0.384	0.483	0.433	0.507	0.409
8	322	0.432	0.541	0.375	0.486	0.430	0.514	0.402
9	287	0.474	0.546	0.370	0.487	0.429	0.517	0.399
10	262	0.500	0.550	0.366	0.489	0.427	0.520	0.396
11	401	0.496	0.533	0.383	0.483	0.433	0.508	0.408
12	384	0.430	0.534	0.382	0.483	0.433	0.509	0.407
13	428	0.498	0.530	0.386	0.482	0.434	0.506	0.410
14	352	0.423	0.538	0.378	0.485	0.431	0.511	0.405
15	444	0.435	0.529	0.387	0.482	0.434	0.505	0.411
16	357	0.443	0.537	0.379	0.484	0.432	0.511	0.405
17	283	0.519	0.547	0.369	0.488	0.428	0.517	0.399
18	424	0.488	0.531	0.385	0.482	0.434	0.506	0.410
19	337	0.424	0.539	0.377	0.485	0.431	0.512	0.404
20	326	0.482	0.541	0.375	0.486	0.430	0.513	0.403

FIGURE 7.7

Minitab Revised Control Chart for Vehicles with Exact Change

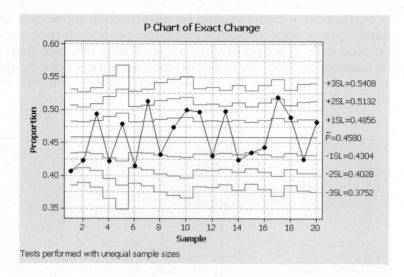

Figure 7.7 illustrates the control chart for the revised process. The process now appears stable, with no indications of a lack of control. Furthermore, the process is now improved: not only is the proportion of motorists using the exact change lanes stable and predictable, but the proportion of those motorists has risen from 0.400 to 0.458, which results in a smoother flow of traffic at the toll barrier.

The np Chart

Classification data can sometimes be more easily understood if the data appear as counts rather than fractions. This is especially true when attribute control charts are used to introduce control charting and some members of the affected community are reluctant to deal with fractions rather than whole numbers, such as the number of defects.

The quantity np is the number of units in the subgroup with some particular characteristic, such as the number of nonconforming units. Traditionally, np charts are used only when subgroup sizes are constant. As the information used is the same as for p charts with constant subgroup sizes, these two charts are interchangeable.

Just as for the p chart, the categorization of data into two classes suggests, for a stable process, that every item must have approximately the same probability of being in one of the two categories. In a series of subgroups of constant size n, the mean or expected number of nonconforming items is approximated by np, and the associated standard error is given by $\sqrt{n\bar{p}(1 - \bar{p})}$. This enables us to construct the np chart.

Constructing the np Chart

Data collected for an np chart will be a series of integers, each representing the number of nonconforming (or conforming) items in its subgroup. Computations for the centerline, the control limits, and the zone boundaries are similar to those of the p chart with constant sample sizes.

The centerline is the overall average number of nonconforming (or conforming) items found in each subgroup of the data. For the ceramic tile importer discussed earlier in this chapter (the data appear in Table 7.1), there are a total of 183 cracked or broken tiles in the 30 subgroups examined; this represents an average count of $183/30 = 6.1$ tiles per day; equivalently,

$$\text{Centerline (np)} = n\bar{p} = (100)\left[\frac{183}{3000}\right] = 6.100 \qquad \textbf{(7.8)}$$

The standard error is

$$\sqrt{n\bar{p}(1-\bar{p})} = \sqrt{(100)(0.061)(1-0.061)} = 2.393$$

Adding or subtracting three times the standard error from the centerline, respectively, yields the upper and lower control limits:

$$\text{UCL(np)} = n\bar{p} + 3\sqrt{n\bar{p}(1-\bar{p})} \qquad \textbf{(7.9)}$$

$$\text{LCL(np)} = n\bar{p} - 3\sqrt{n\bar{p}(1-\bar{p})} \qquad \textbf{(7.10)}$$

For the tile importer this yields values of

$$\text{UCL(np)} = (100)(0.061) + 3\sqrt{(100)(0.061)(1-0.061)} = 13.280$$

$$\text{LCL(np)} = (100)(0.061) - 3\sqrt{(100)(0.061)(1-0.061)} = -1.080$$

As the LCL value is negative (-1.080), and a negative value is meaningless, a value of 0 is used instead.

As for the p chart, the upper and lower boundaries between zones B and C are found by adding and subtracting one standard error from the centerline, $n\bar{p}$:

$$\begin{array}{l} \text{Boundary between} \\ \text{upper zones B and C} \end{array} = n\bar{p} + \sqrt{n\bar{p}(1-\bar{p})} \qquad \textbf{(7.11)}$$

$$\begin{array}{l} \text{Boundary between} \\ \text{lower zones B and C} \end{array} = n\bar{p} - \sqrt{n\bar{p}(1-\bar{p})} \qquad \textbf{(7.12)}$$

The upper boundary between zones B and C for this example is given by

$$6.1 + \sqrt{(100)(0.061)(1-0.061)} = 8.493$$

and the lower boundary between zones B and C is given by

$$6.1 - \sqrt{(100)(0.061)(1-0.061)} = 3.707$$

Upper and lower boundaries between zones B and A are found by adding and subtracting two standard errors from the centerline, $n\bar{p}$:

$$\begin{array}{l} \text{Boundary between} \\ \text{upper zones A and B} \end{array} = n\bar{p} + 2\sqrt{n\bar{p}(1-\bar{p})} \qquad \textbf{(7.13)}$$

$$\begin{array}{l} \text{Boundary between} \\ \text{lower zones A and B} \end{array} = n\bar{p} - 2\sqrt{n\bar{p}(1-\bar{p})} \qquad \textbf{(7.14)}$$

The results for this example are

$$6.1 + 2\sqrt{(100)(0.061)(1-0.061)} = 10.887$$

$$6.1 - 2\sqrt{(100)(0.061)(1-0.061)} = 1.313$$

FIGURE 7.8
Minitab
np Chart for
Cracked Tiles

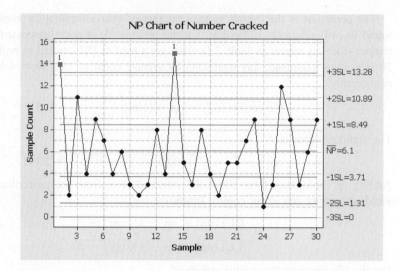

Figure 7.8 illustrates the np chart for this process. A comparison of Figures 7.3 and 7.8 reveals that these two control charts are mathematically equivalent and present the same information. The only reason that one is preferred to the other is the form in which the data are presented, or the way in which the user prefers to visualize the control chart. Subsequent actions to stabilize the process are identical to those for the p chart.

Count Charts

A **defective** item is a nonconforming unit. It must be discarded, reworked, returned, sold, scrapped, or downgraded. It is unusable for its intended purpose in its present form. A **defect,** on the other hand, is an imperfection of some type that is undesirable, although it does not necessarily render the entire good or service unusable. One or more defects may not make an entire good or service defective. For example, we would not scrap or discard a computer, a washing machine, or an air conditioner because of a small scratch in the paint.

An assembled piece of machinery such as a car, dishwasher, or air conditioner may have one or more defects that may not render the entire unit defective but may cause it to be downgraded, or may necessitate its being reworked. Additionally, any product produced in sheets or rolls, such as paper, fabric, or plastic, may have several defects in a sheet or roll and still need not be scrapped as totally defective. A hotel room or airline reservation may have one or more defects, but may serve most of the intended purposes. In fact, there are many instances where more than one defect is the norm rather than the exception; this has created situations where products or services may not even be downgraded as a result of having several flaws. Naturally, in the quest for improvement, our goal is no defects in our output. Control charting is one of the tools to help achieve this end.

When there are multiple opportunities for defects or imperfections in a given unit (such as a large sheet of fabric), we call each such unit an area of opportunity; each area of opportunity is a subgroup. When areas of opportunity are discrete units and a single defect will make the entire unit defective, a p chart or np chart is appropriate. But when areas of opportunity are continuous or very nearly so, and more than one defect may occur in a given area of opportunity, a c chart or u chart should be used. The c chart is used when the areas of opportunity are of constant size, while the u chart is used when the areas of opportunity are not of constant size.

Conditions for Use

Area of opportunity charts have wide applicability. If we are counting defects, the enamel on an appliance represents a continuous area of opportunity; a roll of cloth or plastic film is a continuous area of opportunity. If we are measuring the number of accidents recorded per month, a month represents a continuous area of opportunity. Measurements of the number of errors per hour in data entry or the number of typographical errors made per page have areas of opportunity (an hour or a page) that present enough opportunities for multiple defects to be considered nearly continuous. Imperfections in a complex piece of machinery, such as a computer, have areas of opportunity that are not strictly continuous; but the large number of individual pieces involved makes the areas of opportunity very nearly so, and they are often taken to be continuous.

Both the c chart and u chart are concerned with counts of the number of occurrences of an event over a continuous (or virtually continuous) area of opportunity. Those counts will be whole numbers such as 0, 1, 2, 3, ... The principle behind both types of charts is the same; the primary difference between the two charts is whether the size of the areas of opportunity remains constant from subgroup to subgroup.

If we are to use the c charts or u charts, the events we are studying must be describable as discrete events; these events must occur randomly within some well-defined area of opportunity; they should be relatively rare; and they should be independent of each other. Exact conformance to these conditions is not always easy to verify. Usually, it is not too difficult to tell whether the events are discrete and whether there is some well-defined area of opportunity. But whether the events are relatively rare is somewhat subjective and requires process knowledge and experience. The issue of independence is generally revealed by the control chart. That is, if the events are not random and independent, they will tend to form the identifiable patterns that we introduced in Chapter 6 and will discuss further in Chapter 9, revealing indications of a lack of control on the control chart.

c Charts

Areas of opportunity that are constant in size are easier to manage than those that vary, in much the same way as constant subgroup sizes in a p chart are easier to manage than those that vary. Constant areas of opportunity might be such things as one unit of a particular model of a TV set, a particular type of hospital room, one printed circuit board, one purchase order, one aircraft canopy, five square feet of paper board, or five linear feet of wire. When all conditions for an area of opportunity chart are met, and when the subgroup sizes remain constant, a c chart is used.

The number of events in an area of opportunity is denoted by c, the count for each area of opportunity. The sequence of successive c values, taken over time, is used to construct the control chart.

The centerline for the chart is the average number of events observed. It is calculated as

$$\text{Centerline(c)} = \bar{c} = \frac{\text{Total number of events observed}}{\text{Number of areas of opportunity}} \qquad (7.15)$$

The standard error is the square root of the mean, $\sqrt{\bar{c}}$. Adding and subtracting three times the standard error from the centerline, $\bar{c}$, yields the upper and lower control limits. Thus

$$UCL(c) = \bar{c} + 3\sqrt{\bar{c}} \qquad (7.16)$$

$$LCL(c) = \bar{c} - 3\sqrt{\bar{c}} \qquad (7.17)$$

Counts, Control Limits, and Zones

As we have already seen with p charts and np charts, when a process is in a state of control, only very rarely will points fall beyond the control limits. Therefore, when a point does fall outside the control limits, we will consider it an indication of a lack of control and take appropriate action. When the lower control limit is calculated to be negative, we will use 0 as the lower control limit because, just as with p charts and np charts, negative numbers of events (such as -3 defects on a radio) are meaningless.

Consider a firm that has decided to use a c chart to help keep track of the number of telephone requests received daily for information on a given product. Each day represents an area of opportunity. Over a 30-day period, 1,206 requests are received, or an average of 40.2 per day. This value is $\bar{c}$, the centerline. The upper and lower control limits can be found using Equations (7.16) and (7.17):

$$UCL(c) = 40.2 + 3\sqrt{40.2} = 59.2$$

$$LCL(c) = 40.2 - 3\sqrt{40.2} = 21.2$$

Actual counts occurring in an area of opportunity will always be whole numbers. Thus a count of 59 is within the control limits, while a count of 60 is beyond the UCL. The A, B, and C zone boundaries are constructed at one and two standard errors from the centerline, respectively. The zone boundaries are:

$$\begin{array}{l} \text{Boundary between} \\ \text{lower zones B and C} \end{array} = 40.2 - \sqrt{40.2} = 33.9$$

$$\begin{array}{l} \text{Boundary between} \\ \text{lower zones A and B} \end{array} = 40.2 - 2\sqrt{40.2} = 27.5$$

$$\begin{array}{l} \text{Boundary between} \\ \text{upper zones A and B} \end{array} = 40.2 + 2\sqrt{40.2} = 52.9$$

$$\begin{array}{l} \text{Boundary between} \\ \text{upper zones B and C} \end{array} = 40.2 + \sqrt{40.2} = 46.5$$

Because the actual counts are whole numbers, the observations would fall into zones as follows:

Zone	Counts
Upper A	53, 54, 55, 56, 57, 58, 59
Upper B	47, 48, 49, 50, 51, 52
Upper C	41, 42, 43, 44, 45, 46
Lower C	34, 35, 36, 37, 38, 39, 40
Lower B	28, 29, 30, 31, 32, 33
Lower A	22, 23, 24, 25, 26, 27

The zones each contain a reasonable number of whole numbers and are close enough in size to be workable. But consider the problem that would have been encountered if the process average had been $\bar{c} = 2.4$. Here we would get

$$UCL(c) = 2.4 + 3\sqrt{2.4} = 7.0$$

$$LCL(c) = 2.4 - 3\sqrt{2.4} = -2.2 \quad \text{(use 0.0)}$$

$$\text{Boundary between lower zones B and C} = 2.4 - \sqrt{2.4} = 0.9$$

$$\text{Boundary between lower zones A and B} = 2.4 - 2\sqrt{2.4} = -0.7 \quad \text{(use 0.0)}$$

$$\text{Boundary between upper zones A and B} = 2.4 + 2\sqrt{2.4} = 5.5$$

$$\text{Boundary between upper zones B and C} = 2.4 + \sqrt{2.4} = 3.9$$

As before, because the counts are whole numbers, the observations will fall into zones as follows:

Zone	Counts
Upper A	6, 7
Upper B	4, 5
Upper C	3
Lower C	1, 2
Lower B	0
Lower A	0

These zones are so small that they are practically meaningless. The upper zone C, for example, only has one possible count, 3. When the average count is small, we generally do not make use of the zones in seeking indications of a lack of control. Rather, we focus on points beyond the control limits, runs of points above or below the centerline, and runs upward or downward in the data as indicators of a lack of stability. The exact value of the centerline, below which the use of A, B, and C zones becomes impractical, requires knowledge of, and experience with, the particular process involved. As a rule of thumb, the zone boundaries should not be used for c charts with average counts of less than 20.0. Once again, there is no substitute for process knowledge and experience; however, as the observable count shrinks, the use of variables control charts must be instituted for continued process improvement.

Furthermore, keep in mind that when the average count is small, larger and larger areas of opportunity will be needed to detect imperfections. This will occur as a natural consequence of improved quality through the use of control charts. When the areas of opportunity needed to find imperfections grow unacceptably large, attribute control charts must be abandoned in favor of variables control charts. This usually solves the problem of small values for c and is another step on the ladder of quality consciousness.

Construction of a c Chart: An Example

Consider the output of a paper mill: the product appears at the end of a web and is rolled onto a spool called a reel. Every reel is examined for blemishes, which are imperfections. Each reel is an area of opportunity. Results of these inspections produce the data in Table 7.7 (see ❀ REEL).

The assumptions necessary for using the c chart are well met here, as the reels are large enough to be considered continuous areas of opportunity; imperfections are discrete events and seem to be independent of one another, and they are relatively rare. Even if these conditions are not precisely met, the c chart is fairly robust, or insensitive to small departures from the assumptions, so we may safely use it.

In this example the average number of imperfections per reel is

$$\text{Centerline(c)} = \bar{c} = \frac{150}{25} = 6.00$$

and the standard error is $\sqrt{6.00} = 2.45$.

Equations (7.16) and (7.17) yield upper and lower control limits:

$$\text{UCL(c)} = 6.00 + 3(2.45) = 13.35$$
$$\text{LCL(c)} = 6.00 - 3(2.45) = -1.35 \qquad \text{(use 0.00)}$$

The control chart is shown in Figure 7.9.

Small Average Counts

Even though the control chart in Figure 7.9 is useful, frequently, when average counts are small, data appearing as counts will tend to be asymmetric. This may lead to **over-adjustment (false alarms)** or **under-adjustment** (too little sensitivity).

False alarms are indications that the process is exhibiting special variation when no special variation can be found. Most often, these indications will be points on the control

TABLE 7.7
Number of Blemishes Found in 25 Reels of Paper

Reel	Number of Blemishes	Reel	Number of Blemishes
1	4	14	9
2	5	15	1
3	5	16	1
4	10	17	6
5	6	18	10
6	4	19	3
7	5	20	7
8	6	21	4
9	3	22	8
10	6	23	7
11	6	24	9
12	7	25	7
13	11	Total	150

FIGURE 7.9
Minitab
c Chart for
Blemishes

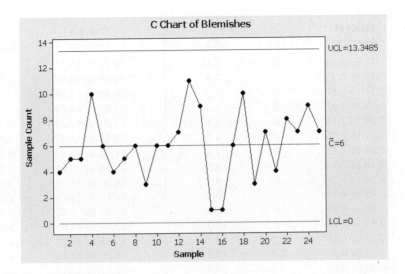

chart that are just beyond the upper control limit. False alarms, in and of themselves, can destabilize a stable process. Employees searching for special sources of variation will generally fix something that does not need fixing. That is, they will adjust the process to compensate for nonexistent special sources of variation. This may send the system into a complete state of chaos. Also, false alarms may demoralize employees who may begin to feel that many of their efforts do not result in process improvements.

In some cases, control limits calculated using Equations (7.16) and (7.17) may not provide sufficient sensitivity to an indication of a special source of variation. This can result in a loss of opportunity for process improvement.

To avoid both of these problems, we may use a set of **fixed control limits** for the c chart. These fixed control limits are sometimes called **probability control limits** and provide an excellent and economical rule for separating special and common variation when average counts are less than 20. Table 7.8 gives values for upper and lower control limits that can be used when average counts are less than 20.

In the example of the reels of paper, the centerline is 6.00. Therefore, for this application of the c chart the control limits should properly have come from Table 7.8. As 6.00 is in the 5.59 to 6.23 range, the values for the lower and upper control limits respectively are 0.5 and 13.5. These values have been used to draw the c chart in Figure 7.10. Note that this control chart has been drawn by hand because Minitab does not incorporate fixed probability limits.

Notice that these control limits are almost the same as those created using Equations (7.16) and (7.17): 13.35 and 0.00. In general, because the number of events is a whole number, both control charts may show the same indications of a lack of control. In this particular case, the resulting control charts are similar, but a count of 0 will indicate a lack of control using the fixed limits, and will not indicate a lack of control using the three-sigma limits.

It is not too unusual to find that the control limits resulting from computations using Equations (7.16) and (7.17) and those resulting from Table 7.8 are similar, and some

TABLE 7.8
c Chart Using
Fixed Control
Limits

Process Average	LCL	UCL	Process Average	LCL	UCL
0 to 0.10	0	1.5	9.65 to 10.35	2.5	19.5
0.11 to 0.33	0	2.5	10.36 to 10.97	2.5	20.5
0.34 to 0.67	0	3.5	10.98 to 11.06	3.5	20.5
0.68 to 1.07	0	4.5	11.07 to 11.79	3.5	21.5
1.08 to 1.53	0	5.5	11.80 to 12.52	3.5	22.5
1.54 to 2.03	0	6.5	12.53 to 12.59	3.5	23.5
2.04 to 2.57	0	7.5	12.60 to 13.25	4.5	23.5
2.58 to 3.13	0	8.5	13.26 to 13.99	4.5	24.5
3.14 to 3.71	0	9.5	14.00 to 14.14	4.5	25.5
3.72 to 4.32	0	10.5	14.15 to 14.74	5.5	25.5
4.33 to 4.94	0	11.5	14.75 to 15.49	5.5	26.5
4.95 to 5.29	0	12.5	15.50 to 15.65	5.5	27.5
5.30 to 5.58	0.5	12.5	15.66 to 16.24	6.5	27.5
5.59 to 6.23	0.5	13.5	16.25 to 17.00	6.5	28.5
6.24 to 6.89	0.5	14.5	17.01 to 17.13	6.5	29.5
6.90 to 7.43	0.5	15.5	17.14 to 17.76	7.5	29.5
7.44 to 7.56	1.5	15.5	17.77 to 18.53	7.5	30.5
7.57 to 8.25	1.5	16.5	18.54 to 18.57	7.5	31.5
8.26 to 8.94	1.5	17.5	18.58 to 19.36	8.5	31.5
8.95 to 9.27	1.5	18.5	19.37 to 20.00	8.5	32.5
9.28 to 9.64	2.5	18.5			

users merely ignore these table values. The danger in doing so, however, is that when average counts are small, the three-sigma limits may generate false indications of a lack of control or fail to signal a lack of control. This can lead to over-adjustment or under-adjustment of a process, which in and of itself may cause the process to become out of control or may lead to frustration on the part of those employees trying to search for special causes of variation where none exist.

A note of caution when dealing with c charts: those charged with determining the number of imperfections must be clear and consistent in the definition of an imperfection. Operational definitions, as discussed in Chapter 4, are extremely important, and the individuals identifying imperfections must be properly trained so that they understand the nature of the process; if they are not, some identified imperfections may not actually be imperfections, while some actual imperfections may go undetected—hence the independence of observations of the occurrence of imperfections may suffer. This, in turn, may result in violations of the underlying assumptions used for the c chart, resulting in either the generation of many false alarms, or in undetected out-of-control behavior.

Stabilizing a Process: An Example

An industrial washing machine manufacturer inspects completed units for defects. Table 7.9 lists counts of defects found on 24 machines (see 🐁 WASHING).

FIGURE 7.10   c Chart Using Fixed Probability Limits for Number of Blemishes

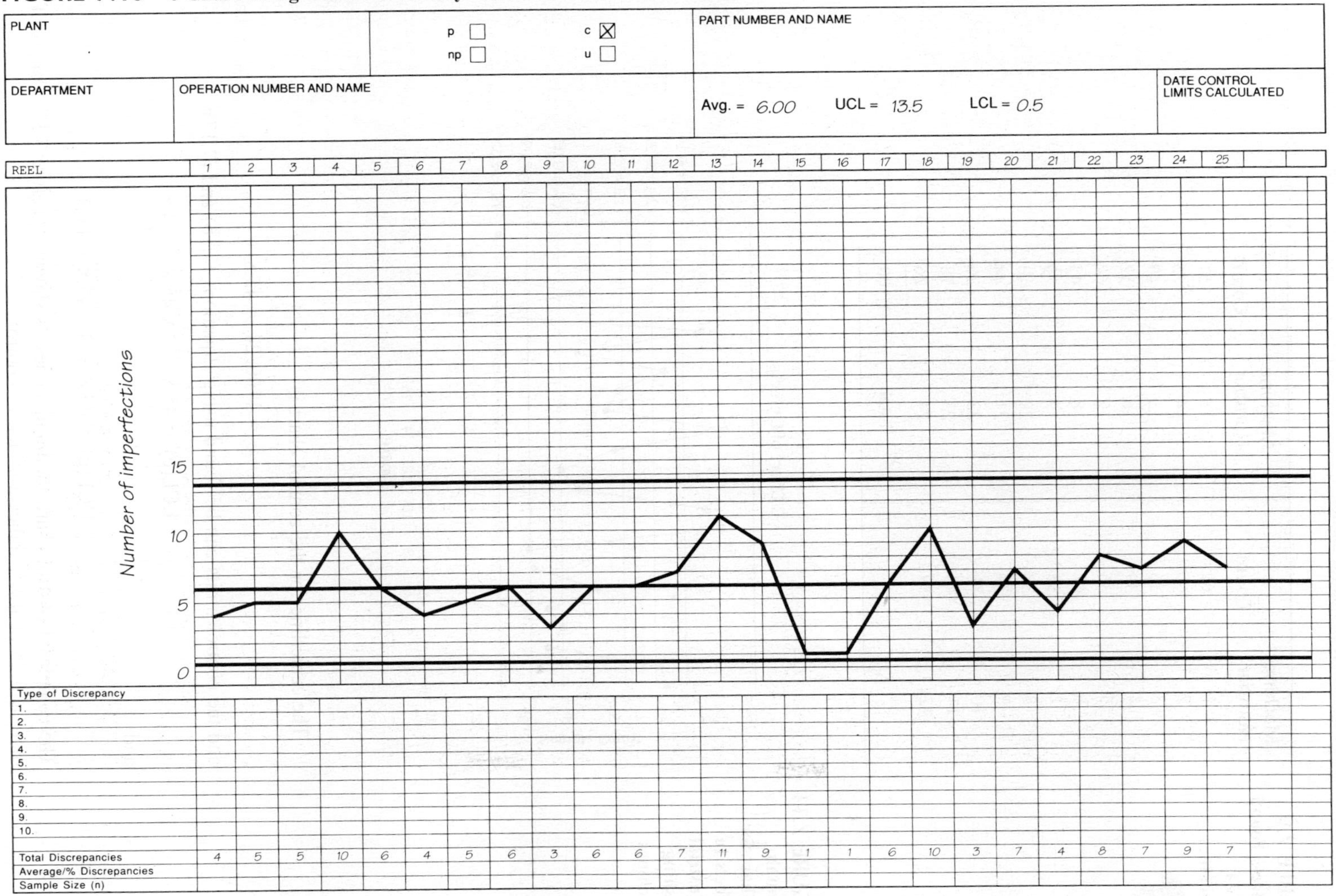

PLANT

PART NUMBER AND NAME

DEPARTMENT

OPERATION NUMBER AND NAME

p ☐   c ☒
np ☐   u ☐

Avg. = 6.00   UCL = 13.5   LCL = 0.5

DATE CONTROL
LIMITS CALCULATED

REEL | 1 | 2 | 3 | 4 | 5 | 6 | 7 | 8 | 9 | 10 | 11 | 12 | 13 | 14 | 15 | 16 | 17 | 18 | 19 | 20 | 21 | 22 | 23 | 24 | 25

Number of imperfections

15
10
5
0

Type of Discrepancy
1.
2.
3.
4.
5.
6.
7.
8.
9.
10.

Total Discrepancies	4	5	5	10	6	4	5	6	3	6	6	7	11	9	1	6	10	3	7	8	4	7	9	7
Average/% Discrepancies																								
Sample Size (n)																								

TABLE 7.9
Defects Found on 24 Machines

Machine Number	Count	Machine Number	Count
1	62	13	51
2	60	14	75
3	36	15	49
4	39	16	52
5	36	17	62
6	47	18	43
7	33	19	70
8	32	20	18
9	74	21	44
10	71	22	20
11	43	23	18
12	39	24	26
		Total	1,100

FIGURE 7.11
Minitab c Chart for Defects in Industrial Washing Machines

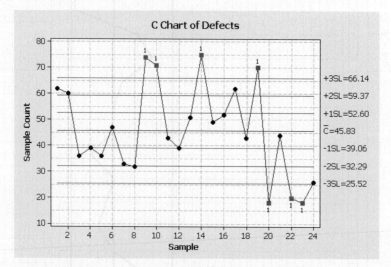

The centerline for the control chart is

$$\bar{c} = 1100/24 = 45.8$$

and the control limits can be found using Equations (7.16) and (7.17):

$$LCL(c) = 45.8 - 3\sqrt{45.8} = 25.5$$

and

$$UCL(c) = 45.8 + 3\sqrt{45.8} = 66.1$$

The completed control chart, including zones, is shown in Figure 7.11. Counts of 67 or more and 25 or fewer indicate a lack of control.

The process is not in control. Special causes of variation are present. Let us assume that the local operators responsible for the final inspection act so that the special causes of variation for points 9, 10, 14, 19, 20, 22, and 23 are identified and the appropriate corrections are made. The data for points affected by known special causes that have been eliminated are deleted from the data set, and the centerline and control limits are recomputed:

$$\bar{c} = \frac{754}{17} = 44.4$$

$$\text{LCL}(c) = 44.4 - 3\sqrt{44.4} = 24.4$$

$$\text{UCL}(c) = 44.4 + 3\sqrt{44.4} = 64.4$$

The new limits are so close to the old limits that the old limits are used for the next 24 machines produced; Table 7.10 presents the data.

The first five data points for these next 24 machines are well below the lower control limit. Investigation by the local operators reveals that a substitute for the regular inspector counted the defects on those five machines. The substitute was not properly trained and did not identify all the defects correctly. The operators informed management, and management made appropriate changes in policy so that this situation would not recur. These points can now be eliminated from the data. Beginning with machine number 30, all counts are below the process average. Local operators decided that the process has been changed, so a revised control chart is constructed beginning with point number 30, as shown in the data file ✿ WASHING2.

$$\bar{c} = \frac{674}{19} = 35.5$$

$$\text{LCL}(c) = 35.5 - 3\sqrt{35.5} = 17.6$$

$$\text{UCL}(c) = 35.5 + 3\sqrt{35.5} = 53.4$$

TABLE 7.10
Defects Found on Next 24 Industrial Washing Machines

Machine Number	Number of Defects	Machine Number	Number of Defects
25	21	37	46
26	18	38	31
27	7	39	42
28	12	40	44
29	18	41	26
30	32	42	37
31	32	43	26
32	37	44	29
33	39	45	31
34	39	46	34
35	34	47	36
36	39	48	40

FIGURE 7.12
Minitab
Revised
c Chart for
Defects in
Industrial
Washing
Machines

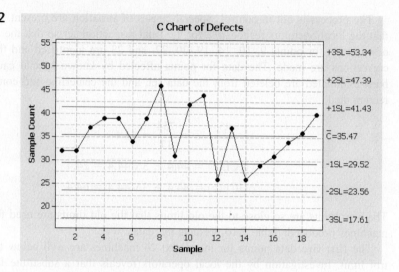

Figure 7.12 illustrates the revised control chart. The process, as it stands, now appears to be in a state of control.

Construction of a c Chart: Another Example

Consider the case of a mill with a constant work force of 450 employees that has a sign posted at the employee entrance reading "SAFETY IS BETTER THAN COMPENSATION." Informal conversations with employees reveal they consider the sign a reminder to be careful. But management has not simultaneously made the work environment safer. There are still cluttered aisles, and spills and leaks of liquids on the floor are not attended to rapidly. The workers know this but have long ago stopped their fruitless efforts at getting management to allocate the resources necessary to create a safer workplace.

To examine the problem, a control chart of the number of accidents per month is constructed. Table 7.11 shows the data for the past 26 months (see 🐾 ACCIDENTMILL).

Note that as the number of labor hours per month remains constant, the area of opportunity is considered constant month to month. The centerline for the c chart is:

$$\bar{c} = \frac{26}{26} = 1.00$$

From Table 7.8, the fixed control limits are:

$$LCL(c) = 0 \text{ and } UCL(c) = 4.5$$

Figure 7.13 displays the control chart for the past 26 months. Note that this control chart has been drawn by hand because Minitab does not incorporate fixed probability limits. As there are no indications of any special variation, we can conclude that the process is stable and in a state of statistical control. The company may not realize it, but it is in the business of producing accidents at the stable rate of one per month. It will continue to do so until some effort is made to change the underlying process. If no change in the process is made, accidents will continue to be produced at this rate. Consequently,

TABLE 7.11
Accidents per
Month

Month	Number of Accidents	Month	Number of Accidents
Jan.	3	Feb.	2
Feb.	2	Mar.	0
Mar.	0	Apr.	0
Apr.	2	May	3
May	1	June	2
June	1	July	0
July	1	Aug.	1
Aug.	0	Sept.	0
Sept.	0	Oct.	1
Oct.	1	Nov.	0
Nov.	1	Dec.	0
Dec.	3	Jan.	1
Jan.	0	Feb.	1
		Total	26

the "SAFETY IS BETTER THAN COMPENSATION" sign is unfair: employees are not empowered to make system changes that would lower the average number of accidents per month; the sign subtly and unjustly shifts the burden of responsibility for safety from management to the employees.

Construction of a c Chart: Another Example

A national company opens a sales office with six sales people in Cleveland, Ohio. [See Reference 2, pp. 124–125.] The office has been open for just over six months. All sales people have the same responsibilities and opportunities. The number of new accounts generated by each sales person in the first six months of operation is recorded in Table 7.12.

The company's policy calls for a semiannual review of performance to determine who should be rewarded or punished. According to traditional thinking, it appears that the company should reward Fred and punish David.

Examining the above data from the perspective of the System of Profound Knowledge and statistical thinking results in the following c chart statistics:

$$\bar{c} = 174/6 = 29$$
$$\text{UCL} = 29 + 3[\sqrt{29}] = 45.2 \rightarrow 45$$
$$\text{LCL} = 29 - 3[\sqrt{29}] = 12.8 \rightarrow 13$$

According to the above calculations, the number of new accounts generated by a sales person in a six-month period can be predicted to be between 13 and 45 new accounts. This large amount of variation is attributable to the sales system. All sales people are in the same sales system, and they all deserve the percentage pay raise. No one should be rewarded, and no one should be punished. Sales management should focus their attention on improvement of the sales system, not on rewarding and punishing salesmen.

FIGURE 7.13 Control Chart for Accidents per Month

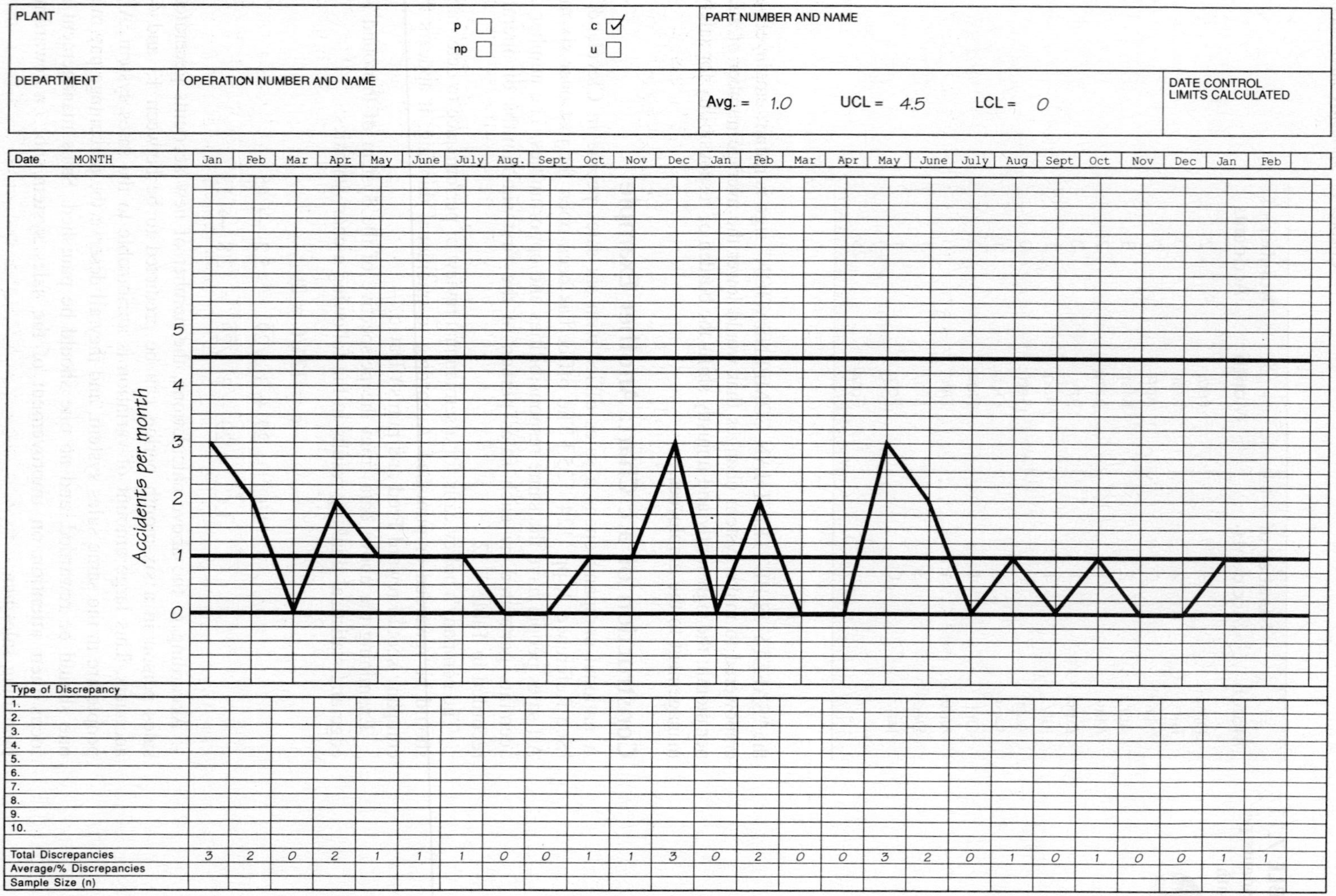

PLANT		PART NUMBER AND NAME	
	p ☐ np ☐ c ☑ u ☐		DATE CONTROL LIMITS CALCULATED

DEPARTMENT	OPERATION NUMBER AND NAME		
	Avg. = 1.0	UCL = 4.5	LCL = 0

Accidents per month (vertical axis: 0, 1, 2, 3, 4, 5)

Date	MONTH	Jan	Feb	Mar	Apr	May	June	July	Aug.	Sept.	Oct.	Nov	Dec	Jan	Feb	Mar	Apr	May	June	July	Aug	Sept	Oct	Nov	Dec	Jan	Feb

Type of Discrepancy
1.
2.
3.
4.
5.
6.
7.
8.
9.
10.

| Total Discrepancies | 3 | 2 | 0 | 2 | 1 | 1 | 0 | 0 | 1 | 0 | 3 | 0 | 2 | 0 | 0 | 3 | 2 | 0 | 1 | 0 | 0 | 1 | 1 |
| Average/% Discrepancies |
| Sample Size (n) |

TABLE 7.12
Number of
New Accounts

Name of Sales Person	Number of New Accounts
Allan	27
Fred	36
Mark	28
David	24
John	29
Phil	30
Total	174

If Fred had generated 66 new accounts (instead of 36) the sales system's statistics would be:

$$\bar{c} = 204/6 = 34$$

$$UCL = 34 + 3[\sqrt{34}] = 51.5 \rightarrow 51$$

$$LCL = 34 - 3[\sqrt{34}] = 16.5 \rightarrow 17$$

In this scenario, Fred is outside the sales system on the high side (he is above 51). Investigation by Fred's manager leads to the realization that Fred has developed a better telephone procedure for screening potential customers. Fred should receive special recognition because he is outside the sales system on the high side and because his efforts provide guidance for improvement for all sales people in the sales system.

u Charts

In some applications the areas of opportunity vary in size. Generally, the construction and interpretation of control charts are easier when the area of opportunity remains constant, but from time to time variation may be unavoidable. For example, samples taken from a roll of paper may need to be manually torn from rolls, so that the areas sampled—the areas of opportunity—will vary; continuous welds in heat exchangers will have varying areas of opportunity depending on the total number and lengths of the welds present in different units; and the number of word processing errors in a document will have areas of opportunity that will vary with the length of the document. When the areas vary, the appropriate control chart to be used is a u chart.

The u chart is similar to the c chart in that it is a control chart for the count of the number of events, such as the number of nonconformities over a given area of opportunity. The fundamental difference lies in the fact that during construction of a c chart, the area of opportunity remains constant from observation to observation, while this is not a requirement for the u chart. Instead, the u chart considers the number of events (such as blemishes or other defects) as a fraction of the total size of the area of opportunity in which these events were possible, thus circumventing the problem of having different areas of opportunity for different observations.

The characteristic used for the control chart, u, is the ratio of the number of events to the area of opportunity in which the events may occur. For observation i, we call the number of events (such as imperfections) the observed c_i, and the area of opportunity a_i. Thus, u_i is the ratio

$$u_i = \frac{c_i}{a_i} \tag{7.18}$$

for each point.

The average of all the u_i values, $\bar{u}$, provides a centerline for the control chart:

$$\text{Centerline (u)} = \bar{u} = \frac{\Sigma c_i}{\Sigma a_i} \tag{7.19}$$

Control limits are usually placed at three standard errors on either side of the centerline for each individual subgroup. The standard error is given by the square root of the average u value divided by the subgroup's area of opportunity, $\sqrt{\bar{u}/a_i}$. Since the area of opportunity varies from subgroup to subgroup, so does the standard error. This results in control limits that vary from subgroup to subgroup:

$$\text{LCL(u)} = \bar{u} - 3\sqrt{\frac{\bar{u}}{a_i}} \tag{7.20}$$

$$\text{UCL(u)} = \bar{u} + 3\sqrt{\frac{\bar{u}}{a_i}} \tag{7.21}$$

When the lower control limit is negative, a value of 0.0 is used instead.

Construction of a u Chart: An Example

Consider the case of the manufacture of a certain grade of plastic. The plastic is produced in rolls, with samples taken five times daily. Because of the nature of the process, the square footage of each sample varies from inspection lot to inspection lot. Hence the u chart should be used here. Table 7.13 shows the data on the number of defects, c_i, for the past 30 inspection lots (see ❦ PLASTIC). The number of defects per 100 square feet is calculated from Equation (7.18).

Using Equation (7.19) we find the centerline to be:

$$\text{Centerline(u)} = \text{Average number of defects/100 sq.ft.} = \bar{u} = \frac{120}{47.90} = 2.51$$

The control limits are different for each of the subgroups and must be computed individually for each subgroup using Equations (7.20) and (7.21). Table 7.14 shows the resulting values.

For u charts, the manual calculation of zone boundaries is computationally cumbersome; however, Minitab easily incorporates these zones. Figure 7.14 shows the Minitab control chart, with zones, for this process. No points indicate a lack of control, so there is no reason to believe that any special variation is present. If sources of special variation were detected, we would proceed as we did with the c chart—that is, we would identify the source or sources of the special variation, eliminate them from the system if detrimental, or incorporate them into the system if beneficial; drop the data points from the data set; and reconstruct and reanalyze the control chart.

TABLE 7.13
Defects in
Rolls of Plastic

Inspection Lot (i)	Square Feet of Plastic	Area of Opportunity (in 100 square feet) a_i	Number of Defects in Lot c_i	Defects per 100 Square Feet u_i
1	200	2.00	5	2.50
2	250	2.50	7	2.80
3	100	1.00	3	3.00
4	90	0.90	2	2.22
5	120	1.20	4	3.33
6	80	0.80	1	1.25
7	200	2.00	10	5.00
8	220	2.20	5	2.27
9	140	1.40	4	2.86
10	80	0.80	2	2.50
11	170	1.70	1	0.59
12	90	0.90	2	2.22
13	200	2.00	5	2.50
14	250	2.50	12	4.80
15	230	2.30	4	1.74
16	180	1.80	4	2.22
17	80	0.80	1	1.25
18	100	1.00	2	2.00
19	140	1.40	3	2.14
20	120	1.20	4	3.33
21	250	2.50	2	0.80
22	130	1.30	3	2.31
23	220	2.20	1	0.45
24	200	2.00	5	2.50
25	100	1.00	2	2.00
26	160	1.60	4	2.50
27	250	2.50	12	4.80
28	80	0.80	1	1.25
29	150	1.50	5	3.33
30	210	2.10	4	1.90
Totals	4,790	$\Sigma a_i = 47.90$	$\Sigma c_i = 120$	

Limitations of Attribute Control Charts

As processes improve and defects or defectives become rarer, the number of units that must be examined to find one or more of these events increases. If we consider a p chart where the average fraction of nonconforming items is 0.005, then on average we would need to examine 200 units to have an average count of just 1.00. In the extreme, to maintain a reasonable average count as the area of opportunity grows, 100 percent inspection becomes the rule. This implies inspecting all of the items and sorting those that conform to some specification from those that do not. Not only is this inspection costly, but it is

TABLE 7.14 **Control Limits for Defects in Rolls of Plastic**

Inspection Lot i	Number of Inspection Units a_i	LCL	UCL	Inspection Lot i	Number of Inspection Units a_i	LCL	UCL
1	2.0	0	5.9	16	1.8	0	6.1
2	2.5	0	5.5	17	0.8	0	7.8
3	1.0	0	7.3	18	1.0	0	7.3
4	0.9	0	7.5	19	1.4	0	6.5
5	1.2	0	6.8	20	1.2	0	6.8
6	0.8	0	7.8	21	2.5	0	5.5
7	2.0	0	5.9	22	1.3	0	6.7
8	2.2	0	5.7	23	2.2	0	5.7
9	1.4	0	6.5	24	2.0	0	5.9
10	0.8	0	7.8	25	1.0	0	7.3
11	1.7	0	6.2	26	1.6	0	6.3
12	0.9	0	7.5	27	2.5	0	5.5
13	2.0	0	5.9	28	0.8	0	7.8
14	2.5	0	5.5	29	1.5	0	6.4
15	2.3	0	5.6	30	2.1	0	5.8

FIGURE 7.14
Minitab
u Chart for
Number of
Defectives in
Rolls of Plastic

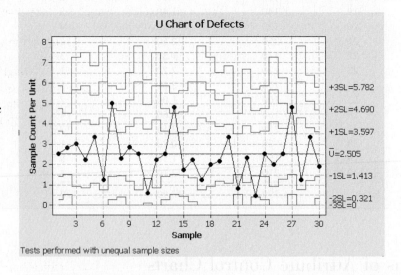

Tests performed with unequal sample sizes

equivalent to accepting the fact that the process is producing a constant fraction of its output as defective and will continue to do so. Hence, attribute control charts are limited in terms of the level of process improvement they enable. Additional process improvement, however, is possible with variables control charts, to be discussed in Chapter 8.

Another disadvantage of using attribute control charts is that if special variation from several different sources is present, it is difficult to identify and isolate the special sources individually. One or more of these special sources may mask another, resulting in a process that appears to be stable but is really operating under the influence of several special sources of variation. As the number of special sources of variation increases, their tendency to mask one another can grow, resulting in further difficulties in the future. On the other hand, variables control charts use numerical measurements, which make them more revealing and powerful than attribute control charts. Attribute data indicate only whether a given unit conforms; they fail to reveal by how much a unit is beyond an upper or lower specification limit. Therefore, attribute data will not provide as clear a direction for process improvement as will variables data.

Summary

Attribute control charts can be broadly categorized into two groups: (1) p charts and np charts based on classification and (2) u charts and c charts based on counts over areas of opportunity.

The p chart can help stabilize a process by indicating a lack of statistical control in some characteristic of interest measured as a proportion of output, such as fraction defective. Subgroup sizes may be constant or may vary from subgroup to subgroup.

The np chart is mathematically equivalent to a p chart; however, the number, rather than the proportion of items, with the characteristic of interest is charted. Subgroup sizes are always held constant for each subgroup for the np chart.

A c chart is used when a single unit of output may have multiple events, such as the number of defects in an appliance or in a roll of paper. The c chart helps stabilize the number of events when the area of opportunity in which the events may occur remains the same for each unit of output from the system.

The u chart is used when the area of opportunity varies from unit to unit, and counts of the number of events are to be control charted.

While attribute control charts help identify special process variation, as the process improves and the number of defectives or defects becomes smaller, the subgroup size necessary to detect these events becomes prohibitively large. Hence, the use of attribute charts is only a milestone on the road to never-ending improvement. To continue on the journey, variables control charts must be instituted and used.

Key Terms

area of opportunity, *184*
c chart, *185*
centerline, *190*
check sheets, *189*
classification charts, *184*
control limits, *190*
constant subgroup size, *191*
count, *187*
count charts, *184*

defect, *206*
defective, *206*
Deming cycle, *188*
false alarms, *210*
fixed control limits, *211*
log sheet, *190*
np chart, *184*
over-adjustment, *210*
p chart, *184*

probability control
limits, *211*
rational subgroups, *189*
subgroup size, *189*
threshold state, *191*
u chart, *185*
under-adjustment, *210*
zone boundaries, *190*

Exercises

7.1. A manufacturer of wood screws periodically examines screw heads for the presence or absence of burrs. Subgroups of 300 screws are selected and examined using a carefully designed procedure. The data appear below (see 🖝 BURR):

Observation	Number of Screws with Burrs	Observation	Number of Screws with Burrs
1	19	11	7
2	16	12	13
3	11	13	17
4	6	14	29
5	22	15	1
6	2	16	2
7	4	17	19
8	7	18	28
9	5	19	24
10	27	20	23

a. Find the centerline and standard error.

b. Find the control limits and zone boundaries.

c. Are there any special causes of variation? Which observations?

7.2. A large metropolitan hospital processes many samples of blood daily. Some occasionally get mislabeled or lost, so new samples are required (rework). Subgroups of 50 samples are tracked each day for a 30-day period (see 🖝 BLOOD). Construct a control chart to search for special sources of variation.

Sample Number	n	Missing or Lost	Sample Number	n	Missing or Lost
1	50	4	16	50	3
2	50	4	17	50	5
3	50	6	18	50	1
4	50	5	19	50	6
5	50	2	20	50	5
6	50	0	21	50	3
7	50	6	22	50	1
8	50	1	23	50	0
9	50	2	24	50	4
10	50	0	25	50	3
11	50	4	26	50	5
12	50	2	27	50	6
13	50	3	28	50	2
14	50	0	29	50	3
15	50	2	30	50	1

7.3. A firm with 248 vehicles at one location keeps track of the number out of service each day (see ☞ VEHICLE). Out of service is defined as unavailable for normal use for four or more hours.

Day	Number Out of Service	Proportion	n
1	7	0.028	248
2	3	0.012	248
3	6	0.024	248
4	2	0.008	248
5	1	0.004	248
6	0	0.000	248
7	12	0.048	248
8	3	0.012	248
9	6	0.024	248
10	4	0.016	248
11	3	0.012	248
12	2	0.008	248
13	7	0.028	248
14	6	0.024	248
15	2	0.008	248
16	5	0.020	248
17	8	0.032	248
18	9	0.036	248
19	3	0.012	248
20	1	0.004	248
21	0	0.000	248
22	2	0.008	248
23	4	0.016	248
24	6	0.024	248
25	4	0.016	248

a. Determine the centerline and control limits for the appropriate control chart.

b. Are there any indications of a lack of control? What are the indications, and why do they indicate a lack of control?

7.4. A bank is studying the proportion of transactions made using an automated teller machine (ATM). The following represents a series of days and the number of transactions using the ATM (see 🖸 ATM):

Day	Total Number of Transactions	Number of ATM Transactions
1	320	87
2	356	92
3	280	75
4	325	109
5	344	69
6	410	99
7	385	120
8	324	86
9	367	111
10	312	90
11	276	86
12	342	106
13	387	65
14	312	91
15	390	131
16	354	78
17	322	89
18	353	98
19	317	81
20	374	58
21	409	104
22	366	81
23	298	87
24	311	72
25	339	84

a. Determine the centerline and control limits for the appropriate control chart.

b. Are there any indications of a lack of control? What are the indications, and why do they indicate a lack of control?

7.5. A company manufactures 2,000 lawn mowers per day. Every day 40 lawn mowers are randomly selected from the production line. If a mower fails to start on the first pull, it's labeled "nonconforming." Results for 22 days are shown below (see ☛ MOWER):

Day	n	Number Nonconforming
1	40	2
2	40	3
3	40	1
4	40	4
5	40	3
6	40	2
7	40	1
8	40	1
9	40	0
10	40	3
11	40	2
12	40	4
13	40	7
14	40	2
15	40	3
16	40	3
17	40	2
18	40	8
19	40	0
20	40	1
21	40	3
22	40	2

a. Find the centerline for the appropriate control chart.
b. Determine the control limits and zone boundaries.
c. Find any indications of a lack of control.

7.6. A given model of a large radar dish represents an area of opportunity in which nonconformities may occur. Results for 25 such assemblies are (see ☞ RADAR):

Assembly Number	Number of Nonconformities	Assembly Number	Number of Nonconformities
1	25	14	75
2	60	15	24
3	28	16	50
4	65	17	70
5	91	18	56
6	56	19	21
7	40	20	88
8	54	21	34
9	90	22	82
10	44	23	53
11	62	24	102
12	81	25	64
13	70		

a. Determine the centerline and control limits for the appropriate control chart.

b. Are there any indications of a lack of control? What are the indications, and why do they indicate a lack of control?

7.7. Samples of 90 retainer rings are examined for the number nonconforming. The results for 30 consecutive days are (see ☞ COPPER):

Day	Number Nonconforming	Day	Number Nonconforming	Day	Number Nonconforming
1	11	11	14	21	11
2	8	12	13	22	11
3	3	13	12	23	8
4	7	14	1	24	7
5	13	15	8	25	1
6	5	16	14	26	4
7	15	17	16	27	14
8	13	18	6	28	11
9	14	19	2	29	15
10	15	20	10	30	12

a. Determine the centerline and control limits.

b. Are there any indications of a lack of control? On which days?

7.8. A large publisher counts the number of keyboard errors that make their way into finished books. The number of errors and the number of pages in the past 26 publications are (see ☛ BOOK):

Book Number	Number of Errors	Number of Pages	Book Number	Number of Errors	Number of Pages
1	49	202	14	48	612
2	63	232	15	50	432
3	57	332	16	41	538
4	33	429	17	45	383
5	54	512	18	51	302
6	37	347	19	49	285
7	38	401	20	38	591
8	45	412	21	70	310
9	65	481	22	55	547
10	62	770	23	63	469
11	40	577	24	33	652
12	21	734	25	14	343
13	35	455	26	44	401

a. Determine the centerline and control limits for the appropriate control chart.

b. Are there any indications of a lack of control? For which books?

7.9. Lots of cloth produced by a manufacturer are inspected for defects. Because of the nature of the inspection process, the size of the inspection sample varies from lot to lot (see ☛ CLOTH).

Lot Number	100's of Square Yards	Number of Defects
1	2.0	5
2	2.5	7
3	1.0	3
4	0.9	2
5	1.2	4
6	0.8	1
7	1.4	0
8	1.6	2
9	1.9	3
10	1.5	0
11	1.7	2
12	1.7	3
13	2.0	1
14	1.6	2
15	1.9	4

a. Calculate the centerline and upper and lower control limits for the appropriate control chart.

b. Are any special causes of variation present in the data? For which lots?

7.10. A firm manufactures high-voltage capacitor film for the electronics industry. They are concerned with the yield on a slitter process that produces reels of film. Reels that are nonconforming must be scrapped. Reels were sampled and inspected each week for 38 weeks (see REELS). The number of reels of film in each sample, number of scrap reels, and proportion of scrap reels are as follows:

Week	Number of Total Reels	Number of Scrap Reels	Proportion of Scrap Reels
1	1,145	142	0.1240
2	1,013	55	0.0543
3	1,275	125	0.0980
4	686	57	0.0831
5	984	58	0.0589
6	717	37	0.0516
7	1,408	57	0.0405
8	1,254	38	0.0303
9	890	60	0.0674
10	1,155	99	0.0857
11	969	121	0.1249
12	858	69	0.0804
13	832	100	0.1202
14	839	101	0.1204
15	1,230	123	0.1000
16	843	49	0.0581
17	1,102	99	0.0898
18	1,039	111	0.1068
19	1,385	125	0.0903
20	1,352	142	0.1050
21	903	43	0.0476
22	976	64	0.0656
23	695	81	0.1165
24	1,123	82	0.0730
25	1,252	102	0.0815
26	857	113	0.1319
27	1,277	74	0.0579
28	1,182	97	0.0821
29	440	41	0.0932
30	916	123	0.1343

a. Construct an appropriate control chart for these data.

b. Is the process in a state of statistical control? Why?

7.11. A computer system team is concerned about a data management system. Each day decisions need to be made that relate to the way in which records and data files are to be maintained. Some information is required to be maintained for one day, some for seven days, some for thirty days, some for a year, and some for perpetual storage. Data that are to be maintained for more than seven days must be stored remotely on disk cartridges off the production site. The data cartridges used for the remote off-site storage involve both an acquisition expense and the cost of maintaining and managing the remote storage system. In an effort to study the stability of the process, weekly reports for the past six months are obtained. The number of data cartridges sent for remote storage each week during this period are presented in the table below (see ☞ CARTS):

Week	Data Cartridges Sent
1	123
2	116
3	115
4	116
5	115
6	120
7	140
8	137
9	141
10	142
11	164
12	148
13	160
14	134
15	162
16	174
17	174
18	176
19	193
20	173
21	147
22	159
23	147
24	147

a. Construct an appropriate control chart for these data.

b. Is the process in a state of statistical control? Why?

c. If the process is not in a state of control, eliminate out-of-control points and recalculate the trial control limits.

7.12. A medical transcription service enters medical data on patient files for hospitals. The service studied ways to improve the turnaround time (defined as the time between receiving the data and the time the client receives the completed files). After studying the process, it is determined that turnaround time is increased by transmission errors. A transmission error is defined as data transmitted that does not go through as planned, and needs to be retransmitted. Each day a sample of 125 record transmissions is randomly selected and evaluated for errors. The table below presents the number and proportion of transmissions with errors in samples of 125 records transmitted (see ☞ TRANSMIT):

Date	Number of Errors	Proportion of Errors
August		
1	6	0.048
2	3	0.024
5	4	0.032
6	4	0.032
7	9	0.072
8	0	0.000
9	0	0.000
12	8	0.064
13	4	0.032
14	3	0.024
15	4	0.032
16	1	0.008
19	10	0.080
20	9	0.072
21	3	0.024
22	1	0.008
23	4	0.032
26	6	0.048
27	3	0.024
28	5	0.040
29	1	0.008
30	3	0.024
September		
3	14	0.112
4	6	0.048
5	7	0.056
6	3	0.024
9	10	0.080
10	7	0.056
11	5	0.040
12	0	0.000
13	3	0.024

a. Construct a p chart if you did not already do so for Exercise 6.8.

b. Is the process in a state of statistical control? If not, when is it out of control?

c. Construct an np chart.

d. Compare the results of the np chart with the results obtained with the p chart and explain any similarities or differences.

7.13. The following 32 days of data represent the findings from a study conducted at a factory that manufactures film canisters. Each day 500 film canisters were sampled and inspected. The number of defective film canisters (nonconforming items) were recorded each day as follows (see CANISTER):

Day	Number Nonconforming
1	26
2	25
3	23
4	24
5	26
6	20
7	21
8	27
9	23
10	25
11	22
12	26
13	25
14	29
15	20
16	19
17	23
18	19
19	18
20	27
21	28
22	24
23	26
24	23
25	27
26	28
27	24
28	22
29	20
30	25
31	27
32	19

a. Construct an np control chart using the first 25 data points to calculate trial limits.

b. Is the process in a state of statistical control? If not, when is it out of control?

c. If the process is in control, extend the limits and record data for days 26 through 32.

d. Is the process in control for days 26 through 32? If not, when is it out of control?

e. Construct a p chart using the first 25 data points if you did not already do so in Exercise 6.9.

f. Compare the results of the np chart with the results obtained with the p chart and explain any similarities or differences for the first 25 days.

7.14. The information systems department of a hospital is concerned with the time it takes for patients' medical records to be processed after discharge. They determine that all records should be processed within five days; any record not processed within five days of discharge is considered nonconforming. The number of patients discharged and the number and proportion of records not processed within the five-day standard are recorded (see ☞ MEDREC):

Day	Number of Discharges	Number of Medical Records Not Processed within 5 Days	Proportion of Nonconforming Items
1	54	13	0.241
2	63	23	0.365
3	110	38	0.345
4	105	35	0.333
5	131	40	0.305
6	137	44	0.321
7	80	16	0.200
8	63	21	0.333
9	75	18	0.240
10	92	24	0.261
11	105	27	0.257
12	112	43	0.384
13	120	25	0.208
14	95	21	0.221
15	72	11	0.153
16	128	24	0.188
17	126	33	0.262
18	106	38	0.358
19	129	39	0.302
20	136	74	0.544
21	94	31	0.330
22	74	15	0.203
23	107	45	0.421
24	135	53	0.393
25	124	57	0.460
26	113	28	0.248
27	140	38	0.271
28	83	21	0.253
29	62	10	0.161
30	106	45	0.425

a. Construct an appropriate control chart for these data.

b. Is the process in a state of statistical control? Why?

c. If the process is not in a state of statistical control, eliminate out-of-control points and recalculate the trial control limits.

 7.15. A company fills bulk orders of electronic telephones and is concerned about the number of units that were returned. As part of their investigation of the problem they sample orders and record order size and the number of telephones returned (see ✿ PHONES).

Order	Order Size	Number Returned	Fraction Returned
1	350	12	0.034
2	420	29	0.069
3	384	23	0.060
4	840	33	0.039
5	405	20	0.049
6	752	40	0.053
7	409	13	0.032
8	385	28	0.073
9	780	24	0.031
10	820	46	0.056
11	392	25	0.064
12	818	24	0.029
13	399	23	0.058
14	355	21	0.059
15	414	22	0.053
16	754	44	0.058
17	366	24	0.066
18	839	34	0.041
19	411	28	0.068
20	387	26	0.067
21	353	18	0.051
22	415	28	0.068
23	390	17	0.044
24	358	28	0.078
25	411	22	0.053

a. Construct an appropriate control chart for these data.

b. Is the process in a state of statistical control? If not, which orders are out of control?

7.16. A large metropolitan hospital provides laboratory services to physicians in the community. A physician who submits a specimen for analysis must fill out a form indicating the services requested, the types of analyses requested, and billing information. These lab slips also contain demographic information on the patient. Incomplete slips must be returned and resubmitted. This process is costly and may increase the time required to complete analyses. In an effort to establish whether the process is in a state of statistical control, data are collected for a 30-day period. The number of lab slips, the number of slips missing demographic information, and the fraction of incomplete slips are as follows (see 💿 LABSLIP):

Date	Number of Lab Slips Received	Number of Lab Slips Missing Demographics	Fraction Incomplete Lab Slips
September			
16	187	11	0.0588
17	216	15	0.0694
18	144	9	0.0625
19	166	7	0.0422
20	192	16	0.0833
23	158	10	0.0633
24	146	9	0.0616
25	199	7	0.0352
26	221	10	0.0452
27	159	4	0.0252
30	222	6	0.0270
October			
1	230	16	0.0696
2	214	15	0.0701
3	198	8	0.0404
4	147	8	0.0544
7	159	7	0.0440
8	145	4	0.0276
9	202	8	0.0396
10	217	11	0.0507
11	204	16	0.0784
14	229	13	0.0568
15	219	8	0.0365
16	211	5	0.0237
17	154	9	0.0584
18	188	13	0.0691
21	146	7	0.0479
22	172	12	0.0698
23	158	7	0.0443
24	148	6	0.0405
25	190	8	0.0421

a. Construct an appropriate control chart for these data.

b. Is the process in a state of statistical control? If not, on which dates is it out of control?

7.17. A commuter railroad in a large northeastern city runs 122 trains from suburban areas into the city each weekday. A survey of rider satisfaction indicates that commuters are very concerned with trains arriving on time. Before making changes to the system to increase the proportion of on-time arrivals, the railroad wants to know whether the proportion of on-time arrivals is in a state of statistical control. The number of late trains for 30 weekdays is as follows (see ☞ RRLATE):

Day	Number Late	Day	Number Late
1	3	16	7
2	1	17	3
3	1	18	4
4	4	19	7
5	5	20	5
6	4	21	2
7	6	22	6
8	3	23	2
9	4	24	4
10	5	25	4
11	6	26	5
12	1	27	4
13	7	28	6
14	4	29	1
15	4	30	2

a. Construct an appropriate control chart for these data if you have not already done so in Exercise 6.11.

b. Is the process in a state of statistical control? If not, on which days is it out of control?

c. Construct an alternative control chart for these data.

d. Is the process in a state of statistical control? If not, on which days is it out of control?

7.18. The management of a city rapid transit system is concerned about the number of accidents reported and would like to know if the number of accidents is in a state of statistical control before instituting changes in procedure. The number of accidents reported each week for a 52-week period is as follows (see 🢝 ACCIDENTS):

Month	Week	Number of Accidents	Month	Week	Number of Accidents
January	1	175	August	31	101
	2	111		32	67
	3	77		33	98
	4	106		34	96
February	5	116	September	35	94
	6	57		36	82
	7	119		37	135
	8	109		38	95
March	9	106	October	39	86
	10	128		40	73
	11	104		41	101
	12	107		42	113
April	13	113		43	124
	14	99	November	44	110
	15	119		45	124
	16	99		46	108
May	17	112		47	81
	18	99	December	48	93
	19	76		49	111
	20	88		50	123
	21	76		51	103
June	22	98		52	169
	23	109			
	24	100			
	25	85			
July	26	134			
	27	141			
	28	98			
	29	55			
	30	85			

a. Construct a control chart for these data.

b. Is the process in a state of statistical control? If not, when is the process out of control?

7.19. The manager of a regional office of a telephone company has the responsibility of processing requests for additions, changes, or deletions of telephone service. A service improvement team studies such orders in terms of central office equipment and facilities required to process orders. They find that errors requiring correction should be reduced. Before suggesting changes in the process, they monitor the number of errors to determine whether or not the system is stable. Their data collected over a 30-day period are as follows (see ☞ CORRECT):

Day	Number of Orders	Number Corrections	Day	Number of Orders	Number Corrections
1	600	80	16	831	91
2	676	88	17	816	80
3	896	74	18	701	96
4	707	94	19	761	78
5	694	70	20	851	85
6	765	95	21	678	65
7	788	73	22	915	74
8	794	103	23	698	68
9	694	100	24	821	72
10	784	103	25	750	101
11	812	70	26	600	91
12	759	83	27	744	64
13	781	64	28	698	67
14	682	64	29	820	105
15	802	72	30	732	112

a. Construct a control chart for these data.

b. Is the process in a state of statistical control? If not, on which days is it out of control?

7.20. A private mail delivery service has a policy of guaranteeing delivery by 10:30 A.M. of the morning after a package is picked up. Suppose that management wishes to study delivery performance in a particular geographic area over a four-week time period based on a five-day work week. The total number of packages delivered daily and the number of packages that were not delivered by 10:30 A.M. are recorded. The results are as follows (see ☞ MAILSPC):

Day	Packages Delivered	Packages Not Arriving Before 10:30 A.M.	Day	Packages Delivered	Packages Not Arriving Before 10:30 A.M.
1	136	4	11	157	6
2	153	6	12	150	9
3	127	2	13	142	8
4	157	7	14	137	10
5	144	5	15	147	8
6	122	5	16	132	7
7	154	6	17	136	6
8	132	3	18	137	7
9	160	8	19	153	11
10	142	7	20	141	7

a. Set up an appropriate control chart for the proportion of packages that are not delivered before 10:30 A.M.

b. Does the process give an out-of-control signal?

 7.21. The owner of a dry-cleaning business, in an effort to measure the quality of the services provided, would like to study the number of dry-cleaned items that are returned for rework per day. Records are kept for a four-week period (the store is open Monday–Saturday) with the following results (see ☞ DRYCLEAN):

Day	Items Returned for Rework	Day	Items Returned for Rework
1	4	13	5
2	6	14	8
3	3	15	3
4	7	16	4
5	6	17	10
6	8	18	9
7	6	19	6
8	4	20	5
9	8	21	8
10	6	22	6
11	5	23	7
12	12	24	9

a. Construct an appropriate control chart for the number of items per day that are returned for rework.

b. Is the process in a state of statistical control?

c. Should the owner of the dry-cleaning store take action to investigate why 12 items were returned for rework on day 12? Explain. Would your answer be the same if 20 items were returned for rework on day 12?

 7.22. The branch manager of a savings bank has recorded the number of errors of a particular type that each of 12 tellers has made during the past year. The results are as follows (see ☞ TELLER):

Teller	Number of Errors
Anita	4
Carla	7
George	12
Jed	6
Linda	2
Matthew	5
Mitchell	6
Ned	3
Ron	5
Susan	4
Tamara	7
Victor	5

a. Do you think the bank manager will single out George for any disciplinary action regarding his performance in the last year? Why?

b. Construct an appropriate control chart for the number of errors committed by the 12 tellers. Is the number of errors in a state of statistical control?

c. On the basis of the control chart developed in part b, do you now think that George should be singled out for special attention regarding his performance? Does your conclusion agree with what you expected the manager to do in part a?

 7.23. Falls are one source of preventable hospital injury. Although most patients who fall are not hurt, a risk of serious injury is involved. The following data represent the number of patient falls per month over a 28-month period in a 19-bed AIDS unit at a major metropolitan hospital (see ✈ PTFALLS):

Month	Number of Patient Falls	Month	Number of Patient Falls
1	2	15	6
2	4	16	5
3	2	17	3
4	4	18	8
5	3	19	6
6	3	20	3
7	1	21	9
8	4	22	4
9	5	23	5
10	11	24	0
11	8	25	2
12	7	26	6
13	9	27	5
14	10	28	7

a. Construct an appropriate control chart for the number of patient falls per month.

b. Is the process of patient falls per month in a state of statistical control?

c. If not, during which months is it out of control?

7.24. The funds transfer research department of a bank is concerned with turnaround time for investigations of funds-transfer payments. A payment may involve the bank as a remitter of funds, a beneficiary of funds, or an intermediary in the payment. An investigation is initiated by a payment inquiry or query by a party involved in the payment or any department affected by the flow of funds. Once a query is received, an investigator reconstructs the transaction trail of the payment and verifies that the information is correct and the proper payment is transmitted. The investigator then reports the results of the investigation and the transaction is considered closed. It is important that investigations are closed rapidly, preferably within the same day. The number of new investigations and the number and proportion closed on the same day that the inquiry was made are as follows (see ❧ FUNDTRAN):

Day	New Investigations	Number Closed
1	240	96
2	296	88
3	309	113
4	293	138
5	253	119
6	254	94
7	245	75
8	331	125
9	303	134
10	278	83
11	256	90
12	273	102
13	276	115
14	291	98
15	204	83
16	263	79
17	311	116
18	248	104
19	287	110
20	238	107
21	280	131
22	271	139
23	237	121
24	258	94
25	289	128
26	226	90
27	287	106
28	263	81
29	282	107
30	194	75

a. Construct an appropriate control chart for these data.

b. Is the process in statistical control? If not, on which days is it out of control?

7.25. The manager of a retail sales branch of a brokerage office is concerned with the number of undesirable trades made by the sales staff. A trade is considered undesirable if there is an error on the trade ticket. Trades that are in error must to be cancelled and resubmitted. The cost of correcting errors is billed to the brokerage. In studying the problem, the manager wants to know whether the proportion of undesirable trades is in a state of statistical control so he can plan the next step in a quality improvement process. Data are collected for a 30-day period with the following results (see ☞ TRADE):

Day	Undesirable Trades	Total Trades
1	2	74
2	12	85
3	13	114
4	33	136
5	5	97
6	20	115
7	17	108
8	10	76
9	8	69
10	18	98
11	3	104
12	12	98
13	15	105
14	6	98
15	21	204
16	3	54
17	12	74
18	11	103
19	11	100
20	14	88
21	4	58
22	10	69
23	19	135
24	1	67
25	11	77
26	12	88
27	4	66
28	11	72
29	13	118
30	15	138

a. Construct an appropriate control chart for these data.

b. Is the process in a state of statistical control? If not, on which days is it out of control?

7.26. Rochester-Electro-Medical Inc. is a manufacturing company based in Tampa, Florida, that produces medical products. Recently, management felt the need to improve the safety of the workplace and began a safety sampling study. The data that follow represent the number of unsafe acts observed by the company safety director over an initial time period in which the study was carried out (see SAFETY):

Tour	Number of Unsafe Acts
1	10
2	6
3	6
4	10
5	8
6	12
7	2
8	1
9	23
10	3
11	2
12	8
13	7
14	6
15	6
16	11
17	13
18	9
19	6
20	9

Source: H. Gitlow, A. R. Berkins, and M. He, "Safety Sampling: A Case Study," *Quality Engineering,* 14, 2002, pp. 405–419.

a. Construct an appropriate control chart for the number of unsafe acts.

b. According to the results of part a, is the process in a state of statistical control?

c. If not, when is the process out of control?

References

1. American Society for Quality, 310 West Wisconsin Ave., Milwaukee, WI 53203.

2. H. Gitlow and S. Gitlow (1987), *The Deming Guide to Quality, Productivity and Competitive Position* (Englewood Cliffs, NJ: Prentice Hall).

Appendix **A7.1**

Using Minitab for Attribute Charts[1]

Using Minitab for the p Chart

To illustrate how to obtain a p chart, refer to the data of Table 7.1 on page 193 concerning the number of broken tiles. Open the ❀ **TILES.MTW** worksheet.

1. Select **Stat | Control Charts | Attribute Charts | P.** In the P Chart dialog box, shown in Figure A7.1, enter **C3** or **'Number Cracked'** in the Variable(s): edit box. Since the subgroup sizes are equal, select **Size** in the **Subgroup** drop-down list box and enter **100** in the edit box. Select the **P Chart Options** button.

2. In the P Chart-Options dialog box, click on the Tests tab, shown in Figure A7.2. Select the **perform all tests** option button. Click the **OK** button to return to the P Chart dialog box. These values will stay intact until Minitab is restarted.

3. If there are points that should be omitted when estimating the centerline and control limits, click the **Estimate** tab in the P Chart-Options dialog box, as shown in Figure A7.3. Enter the points to be omitted in the edit box shown. Click the **OK** button to return to the P Chart dialog box. In the P Chart dialog box, click the **OK** button to obtain the p chart.

To illustrate an example in which the subgroups sizes differ, open the ❀ **INSULATOR. MTW** file. Select **Stat | Control Charts | Attribute Charts | P.**

1. In the P Chart dialog box, shown in Figure A7.4 on page 247, enter **C3** or **Nonconforming** in the Variable(s): edit box.

FIGURE A7.1
Minitab p Chart Dialog Box

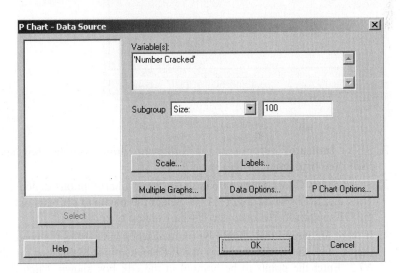

[1] The instructions and dialog boxes are based on the beta version of Minitab 14. Subsequent versions of Minitab may differ slightly from what is presented in this appendix.

FIGURE A7.2
Minitab p Chart-Options Dialog Box, Tests Tab

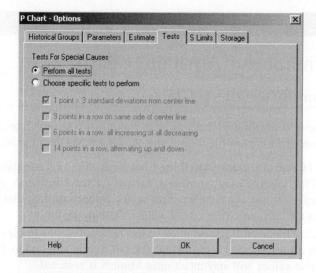

FIGURE A7.3
Minitab p Chart-Options Dialog Box, Estimate Tab

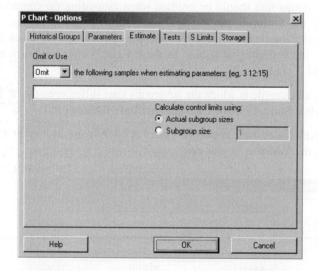

2. Select **Indicator column** in the **Subgroup** drop-down list box and enter **C2** or **'Number Inspected'** in the edit box.

3. Select the **P Chart Options** button. In the P Chart-Options dialog box, click on the Tests tab, as shown in Figure A7.2. Select the **perform all tests** option button. Click the **OK** button to return to the P Chart dialog box.

4. If there are points that should be omitted when estimating the centerline and control limits, click the **Estimate** tab in the P Chart-Options dialog box, as shown in Figure A7.3. Enter the points to be omitted in the edit box shown. Click the **OK** button to return to the P Chart dialog box. In the P Chart dialog box, click the **OK** button to obtain the p chart.

**FIGURE
A7.4
Minitab p
Chart Dialog
Box for
Unequal
Sample Sizes**

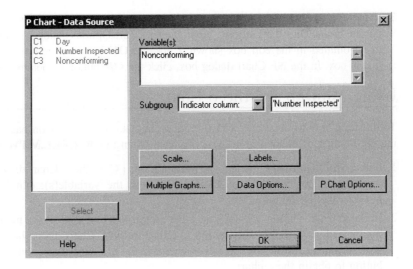

Using Minitab for the np Chart

To illustrate how to obtain an np chart, refer to the data of Table 7.1 on page 193 concerning the number of cracked tiles. Open the ☻ **TILES.MTW** worksheet.

1. Select **Stat | Control Charts | Attribute Charts | NP.** In the NP Chart dialog box, shown in Figure A7.5, enter **C3** or **'Number Cracked'** in the Variable(s): edit box. Select **Size** in the **Subgroup** drop-down list box and enter **100** in the edit box. Select the **NP Chart Options** button.

2. In the NP Chart-Options dialog box, click on the Tests tab. Select the **perform all tests** option button. Click the **OK** button to return to the NP Chart dialog box. These values will stay intact until Minitab is restarted.

**FIGURE
A7.5
Minitab np
Chart Dialog
Box**

3. If there are points that should be omitted when you are estimating the centerline and control limits, click the **Estimate** tab in the NP Chart-Options dialog box. Enter the points to be omitted in the edit box shown. Click the **OK** button to return to the NP Chart dialog box. In the NP Chart dialog box, click the **OK** button to obtain the np chart.

Using Minitab for the c Chart

To illustrate how to obtain a c chart, refer to the data of Table 7.7 on page 210 concerning the number of blemishes in reels of paper. Open the ☀ **REEL.MTW** worksheet.

1. Select **Stat | Control Charts | Attribute Charts | C.** In the C Chart dialog box, shown in Figure A7.6, enter **C2** or **BLEMISHES** in the Variable(s): edit box. Click the C Chart Option button.

2. In the C Chart-Options dialog box, click on the Tests tab. Select the **perform all tests** option button. Click the **OK** button to return to the C Chart dialog box. These values will stay intact until Minitab is restarted. In the C Chart dialog box, click the **OK** button to obtain the c chart.

3. If there are points that should be omitted when estimating the centerline and control limits, click the **Estimate** tab in the C Chart Options dialog box. Enter the points to be omitted in the edit box shown. Click the **OK** button to return to the C Chart dialog box.

FIGURE A7.6
Minitab c Chart Dialog Box

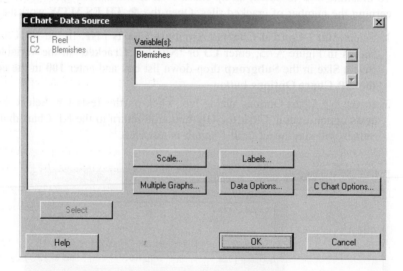

Using Minitab for the u Chart

To illustrate how to obtain a u chart, refer to the data of Table 7.13 on page 221 concerning the number of defects in a lot of plastic. Open the ☀ **PLASTIC.MTW** worksheet.

1. Select **Stat | Control Charts | Attribute Charts | U.** In the U Chart dialog box, shown in Figure A7.7, enter **C3** or **DEFECTS** in the Variable(s): edit box. In the Subgroups: drop-down list box, select Indicator column: and enter **C2** or **'Square Feet (00)'** in the edit box. Click the U Chart Options button.

**FIGURE
A7.7**
**Minitab u
Chart Dialog
Box**

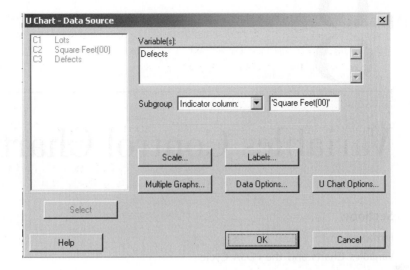

2. In the U Chart-Options dialog box, click on the Tests tab. Select the **perform all tests** option button. Click the **OK** button to return to the U Chart dialog box. These values will stay intact until Minitab is restarted. In the U Chart dialog box, click the **OK** button to obtain the u chart.

3. If there are points that should be omitted when estimating the centerline and control limits, click the **Estimate** tab in the U Chart Options dialog box. Enter the points to be omitted in the edit box shown. Click the **OK** button to return to the U Chart dialog box.

Using Minitab to Obtain Zone Limits

To plot zone limits on any of the control charts discussed in this appendix, open to the initial dialog box for the control chart being developed and do the following:

1. Click the **Scale** button. Click the **Gridlines** tab. Select the **Y major ticks, Y minor ticks,** and **X major ticks** check boxes. Click the **OK** button to return to the previous dialog box.

2. Select the **Options** button. Select the **S limits** tab. In the Display control limits at these multiples of the standard deviation: edit box, enter **1 2 3.** Click the **OK** button to return to the previous dialog box.

Chapter 8

Variables Control Charts

Sections

Chapter Objectives

- To distinguish between attribute data and variables data
- To discuss variables charts and the PDSA cycle
- To discuss the determination of subgroup size and the frequency of subgroup selection
- To discuss and illustrate the construction and interpretation of x̄ and R charts
- To discuss and illustrate the construction and interpretation of x̄ and s charts
- To discuss and illustrate the construction and interpretation of individuals and moving range charts
- To discuss the conditions for revision of control limits for variables charts
- To discuss rational subgrouping of data

Introduction

Variables (measurement) data consist of numerical measurements such as weight, length, width, height, time, temperature, and electrical resistance. Variables data contain more information than attribute data, which either classify a process's output as conforming or nonconforming, or count the number of imperfections. Furthermore, because variables control charts deal with measurements themselves, they do not mask valuable information and therefore are more powerful than attribute charts. They use all the information contained in the data; this alone makes variables charts preferable when a choice is possible.

There are three principal types of variables control charts: the $\bar{x}$ and R chart, the $\bar{x}$ and s chart, and the individuals and moving range chart. All are used in the never-ending spiral of process improvement.

Quality consciousness must increase in order for a firm to continue to reduce the difference between customer needs and process performance. Early efforts to control the quality of output will often find firms segregating nonconforming product from conforming product. Nonconforming product is then reworked, discarded, downgraded, or otherwise removed from the mainstream of the process output. Each item so removed incurs a greater overall cost to the firm than the production of a conforming item. This is because special attention is required that is, more often than not, labor-intensive and costly. Furthermore, the firm cannot measure the harm done to its reputation and self-esteem by even occasionally shipping a defective item.

As a greater awareness of the need to improve quality grows, organizations will use attribute control charts to control and stabilize factors such as the proportion of defectives or the number of defects. However, as that proportion becomes smaller as a result of these efforts, as discussed in Chapter 7, a controlled process producing a very low fraction of defective units will require very large subgroups to detect those defectives. The only way to overcome the need for larger and larger subgroups is to continue upward on the spiral of quality consciousness through the use of variables measurements and variables control charts.

Variables Charts and the PDSA Cycle

As with attribute control charts, the **PDSA cycle** provides both an important guideline for proceeding with variables control charts on **variables (measurement) data** and the mechanism for improved quality through continued process improvement.

Plan

The purpose of the control chart must be carefully delineated to effectively use it as a vehicle to reduce the difference between customer needs and process performance. A plan must be established that clearly shows what will be control charted, why it will be control charted, where it will be control charted, when it will be control charted, who will do the control charting, and how it will be control charted. Consequently, the personnel in an organization must decide which variables to measure. These decisions require the cooperation and input of all those directly or indirectly involved with the process, including operators, group leaders, supervisors, and engineers. Some of the techniques discussed in Chapter 10, such as brainstorming, cause-and-effect diagrams, check sheets, or Pareto diagrams, may be useful in determining the process variables that will decrease the difference between customer needs and process performance. Often some feature of the process that has been a source of trouble (resulting in extra cost in scrap or rework) and has failed to yield to corrective efforts is a good place to start. Starting far upstream, or near the beginning of a process, will often produce the most dramatic results and may offer the greatest opportunity to alter the factors at the root of downstream special causes of variation.

Subgroup selection is crucial to the proper use of the control chart. Subgroups should be chosen rationally, as discussed later in this chapter. The choice should minimize the variation within the subgroups. This will allow isolation of special variation between the subgroups while capturing the inherent process variation within the subgroups. The frequency with which subgroups are selected will help minimize the amount of variation between the subgroups by isolating batches, shifts, production runs, machines, or people. This enables the special variation to be captured, isolated, observed, and analyzed. Decisions concerning **rational subgroups** often require the combined knowledge of those directly involved with the process and an experienced statistician. Rational subgroup selection may require a trial-and-error solution, may produce several false starts, and may very well require a great deal of patience.

The method by which the measurements are to be made must be studied carefully. **Operational definitions,** as discussed in Chapter 4, must be constructed and communicated to people involved with the data collection. At this point any forms to be used for data collection should be selected or designed and the responsibility for construction of the charts assigned.

Do

Data collection and the calculation of control chart statistics constitute the do stage for constructing variables control charts. It is usually best to collect at least 20 subgroups before beginning to construct a control chart. On rare occasions fewer than 20 subgroups may be used, but a control chart should almost never be attempted with fewer than 10 subgroups.

Variables charts consist of two parts: one charts the **process variability,** and one charts the **process location.** For instance, in the $\bar{x}$ and R chart, the R values, or subgroup ranges, are used to track variability. The $\bar{x}$ values, or subgroup averages, are used for the process location. As the control limits of the portion of the control chart measuring location are based on the average variability (R in the $\bar{x}$ and R chart), the variability-measuring portion of the control chart must be constructed and evaluated first. Only if there is stability in the variability portion can the location portion of the control chart be constructed. For each of the variables control charts, the estimate of the process standard deviation is based on the average value of the measure of variability used for the subgroups. If the process is not stable, its variability will not be predictable, leading to unreliable estimates of the process standard deviation. If these estimates are used to construct control limits, those limits will also be unreliable and may not reveal special sources of variation when they exist.

After the initial data set has been collected, the centerline, control limits, and zone boundaries (if applicable) should be computed for both portions of the control chart. These should be entered onto the control charts along with the collected set of data points. First, the variability portion of the control chart should be examined for indications of special variation. Any special causes of variation must be studied and the process must be stabilized before the location portion of the control chart is analyzed. This means skipping ahead to the study stage of the PDSA cycle before completing the do stage. If there are no indications of a lack of control in the control chart's variability portion, the location portion of the chart can be analyzed in the study stage of the PDSA cycle. This completes the do stage.

Study

Indications of a lack of control, such as patterns of the type introduced in Chapter 6, are identified in the study stage of the PDSA cycle. These indications of special sources of variation may be found in the chart dealing with variability, in the chart dealing with location, or in both. Whether the variation is common process variation or special process variation, once we have found and identified the sources, we proceed to the act stage to set policy to formalize process improvements resulting from analysis of the control chart.

We must periodically review all aspects of the control chart and make changes where appropriate. If the process itself has been changed in some way, the control limits should certainly be recomputed and the analysis of the process begun anew.

Act

If the variation found in the study stage results only from common causes, then efforts to reduce that variation must focus on changes in the process itself. When indications of special causes of variation are present, the cause or causes of that special variation should be removed if the variation is detrimental or incorporated into the process if the variation is beneficial.

The focus of the act stage is on formalizing policy that results directly from the prior study of the causes of process variation. This will lead to a reduction in the difference between customer needs and process performance.

Last, the purpose of the control chart must be reconsidered by returning to the plan stage. This will help to maintain a focus on improvement and on those areas that can be most beneficial in reducing the difference between customer needs and process performance.

Subgroup Size and Frequency

The selection of an appropriate control chart depends, in part, on the **subgroup size.** In turn, many factors affect the decision of ideal subgroup size. Large subgroups are, of course, more expensive than small ones; nevertheless, large subgroups lead to tighter control limits so long as the subgroups are selected rationally to minimize the within-group variation.

Subgroups should be large enough to detect points or patterns indicating a lack of control when a lack of control exists. Both statistical expertise and process expertise are required to determine the proper subgroup size for a control chart. **Individuals and moving range charts** are used when only one variables measurement is available or appropriate as a subgroup, for example, monthly labor expense or hours per week devoted to repair calls. $\bar{x}$ and range charts (**$\bar{x}$ and R charts**) are used with a subgroup size of two or three when the cost of sampling is relatively high; they are also typically used with subgroup sizes of four through nine. $\bar{x}$ and standard deviation charts (**$\bar{x}$ and s charts**) are generally used with subgroup sizes of 10 or more. In general, subgroup sizes of 6 to 14 are frequently used when a control chart is designed to be sensitive to changes in the process average.

Subgroup frequency, or how often subgroups are selected, depends on the particular application. If quick action is required, the frequency should be greater. A stable process merely being monitored will require less frequent subgroup selection than one being studied or being brought into a state of statistical control for the first time. There are no hard and fast rules for determining the frequency of subgroup selection, and decisions are generally made on the basis of knowledge about the process under study and knowledge of statistics.

$\bar{x}$ and R Charts

As the name implies, the $\bar{x}$ and R chart uses the subgroup range, R, to chart the process variability, and the subgroup average, $\bar{x}$, to chart the process location. Stable processes yield subgroups that will behave predictably, enabling us to construct an $\bar{x}$ and R chart. The two characteristics, $\bar{x}$ and R, can be estimated by relatively simple procedures. Estimates of the standard errors of both R and $\bar{x}$ are based on the average subgroup range, $\bar{R}$. This not only simplifies the estimation procedure but directly impacts how the control charts must be constructed and analyzed.

An Example

A large pharmaceutical firm provides vials filled to a nominal value (specification) of 52.0 grams. The firm's management has embarked on a program of statistical process control and has decided to use variables control charts for this filling process to detect special causes of variation. Samples of six vials are selected every five minutes during a 105-minute period (see ✿ VIALS). Each set of six measurements makes up a subgroup.

The appropriate control chart in this instance is an $\bar{x}$ and R chart, since there are six variables measurements per subgroup. The purpose of this chart is to see whether the process output is stable with regard to its variability and its average value. The output of each subgroup is summarized by its sample average and range. $\bar{x}$ is the average for each of the subgroups, as given by Equation (5.3), while R is the range, as calculated using Equation (5.8).

The Range Portion

For our example, the subgroup ranges are shown in Table 8.1. They begin with a range at 9:30 of

$$R = 53.10 - 52.22 = 0.88$$

and continue for all 22 subgroups to the last range at 11:15 of

$$R = 52.16 - 51.67 = 0.49$$

TABLE 8.1
Vial Weights

| Obs. # | Time | Measurement (grams) | | | | | | Nominal Fill: 52.00 grams | |
		1	2	3	4	5	6	R	x̄
1	9:30	52.22	52.85	52.41	52.55	53.10	52.47	0.88	52.60
2	9:35	52.25	52.14	51.79	52.18	52.26	51.94	0.47	52.09
3	9:40	52.37	52.69	52.26	52.53	52.34	52.81	0.55	52.50
4	9:45	52.46	52.32	52.34	52.08	52.07	52.07	0.39	52.22
5	9:50	52.06	52.35	51.85	52.02	52.30	52.20	0.50	52.13
6	9:55	52.59	51.79	52.20	51.90	51.88	52.83	1.04	52.20
7	10:00	51.82	52.12	52.47	51.82	52.49	52.60	0.78	52.22
8	10:05	52.51	52.80	52.00	52.47	51.91	51.74	1.06	52.24
9	10:10	52.13	52.26	52.00	51.89	52.11	52.27	0.38	52.11
10	10:15	51.18	52.31	51.24	51.59	51.46	51.47	1.13	51.54
11	10:20	51.74	52.23	52.23	51.70	52.12	52.12	0.53	52.02
12	10:25	52.38	52.20	52.06	52.08	52.10	52.01	0.37	52.14
13	10:30	51.68	52.06	51.90	51.78	51.85	51.40	0.66	51.78
14	10:35	51.84	52.15	52.18	52.07	52.22	51.78	0.44	52.04
15	10:40	51.98	52.31	51.71	51.97	52.11	52.10	0.60	52.03
16	10:45	52.32	52.43	53.00	52.26	52.15	52.36	0.85	52.42
17	10:50	51.92	52.67	52.80	52.89	52.56	52.23	0.97	52.51
18	10:55	51.94	51.96	52.73	52.72	51.94	52.99	1.05	52.38
19	11:00	51.39	51.59	52.44	51.94	51.39	51.67	1.05	51.74
20	11:05	51.55	51.77	52.41	52.32	51.22	52.04	1.19	51.89
21	11:10	51.97	51.52	51.48	52.35	51.45	52.19	0.90	51.83
22	11:15	52.15	51.67	51.67	52.16	52.07	51.81	0.49	51.92

The average of the R values is called $\overline{R}$, and it is computed by taking the simple arithmetic average of the R values:

$$\overline{R} = \frac{\Sigma R}{k} \qquad (8.1)$$

where k is the number of subgroups.

Thus, the centerline can be computed as

$$\overline{R} = \frac{16.28}{22} = 0.74$$

Using a multiple of three standard errors to construct the upper control limit and the lower control limit, we have

$$UCL(R) = \overline{R} + 3\sigma_R$$
$$LCL(R) = \overline{R} - 3\sigma_R \qquad (8.2)$$

Assuming that the distribution of process output was, and will be, stable and approximately normally distributed, we can derive control limits. (Note that because of the

Empirical Rule discussed in Chapter 5, the assumption of normality is not necessary to interpret the control limits.)

When the characteristic of interest is stable and approximately normally distributed, and the subgroup size is small ($2 \leq n \leq 9$), then the relationship between the range and the process standard deviation is:

$$\overline{R} = d_2\sigma \tag{8.3}$$

and

$$\sigma_R = d_3\sigma = d_3[\overline{R}/d_2] \tag{8.4}$$

where σ is the process standard deviation and the values of d_2 and d_3 are tabulated as a function of subgroup size in Table B.1 in Appendix B.

We can thus replace $\overline{R}$ and σ_R with these functions of the process standard deviation, σ:

$$UCL(R) = d_2\sigma + 3d_3\sigma = d_2\sigma\left(1 + \frac{3d_3}{d_2}\right)$$

$$= \overline{R}\left(1 + \frac{3d_3}{d_2}\right) \tag{8.5}$$

Similarly,

$$LCL(R) = d_2\sigma - 3d_3\sigma = d_2\sigma\left(1 - \frac{3d_3}{d_2}\right)$$

$$= \overline{R}\left(1 - \frac{3d_3}{d_2}\right) \tag{8.6}$$

A more convenient way to represent these control limits is by defining two new constants, D_3 and D_4:

$$D_3 = 1 - \frac{3d_3}{d_2} \tag{8.7}$$

$$D_4 = 1 + \frac{3d_3}{d_2} \tag{8.8}$$

So that

$$UCL(R) = D_4\overline{R} \tag{8.9}$$

and

$$LCL(R) = D_3\overline{R} \tag{8.10}$$

where D_3 and D_4 are tabulated as a function of subgroup size in Table B.1 in Appendix B. For our example,

$$UCL(R) = 2.004(0.740) = 1.48$$

and

$$LCL(R) = 0(0.740) = 0$$

FIGURE 8.1
Minitab $\bar{x}$ and
R Charts for
Filling
Operations

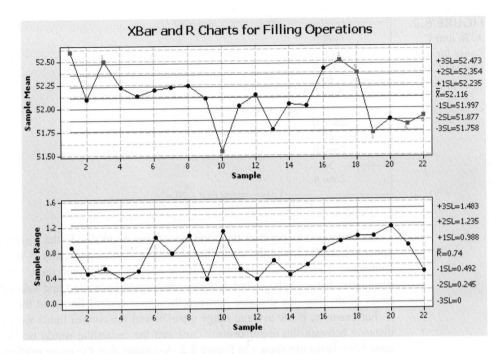

The bottom portion of Figure 8.1 illustrates the resulting average range and upper and lower control limits for the subgroup ranges. The R chart is then examined for signs of special variation. None of the points on the R chart is outside of the control limits, and there are no other signals indicating a lack of control. Thus there are no indications of special sources of variation on the R chart. More will be said later in this chapter and in Chapter 9 about indications of special causes of variation.

In the determination of the upper and lower control limits, three times the estimated standard error of the subgroup ranges, σ_R, was added to and subtracted from the average range value, $\bar{R}$, yielding the factors D_4 and D_3. Recall from Chapter 6 that the **zone boundaries** for zones A, B, and C are positioned at one and two standard errors on either side of the control chart centerline. Using the estimated standard error of $\bar{R}$ from Equation (8.4), the zone boundaries are given by

$$\begin{array}{l}\text{Boundary between}\\ \text{lower zones A and B}\end{array} = \bar{R} - 2d_3(\bar{R}/d_2) = \bar{R}(1 - 2d_3/d_2) \quad \textbf{(8.11)}$$

$$\begin{array}{l}\text{Boundary between}\\ \text{lower zones B and C}\end{array} = \bar{R} - 1d_3(\bar{R}/d_2) = \bar{R}(1 - d_3/d_2) \quad \textbf{(8.12)}$$

When the result of Equation (8.11) or (8.12) is a negative number, 0.00 is used instead, as negative ranges are meaningless. Also,

$$\begin{array}{l}\text{Boundary between}\\ \text{upper zones B and C}\end{array} = \bar{R} + d_3(\bar{R}/d_2) = \bar{R}(1 + d_3/d_2) \quad \textbf{(8.13)}$$

$$\begin{array}{l}\text{Boundary between}\\ \text{upper zones A and B}\end{array} = \bar{R} + 2d_3(\bar{R}/d_2) = \bar{R}(1 + 2d_3/d_2) \quad \textbf{(8.14)}$$

FIGURE 8.2
A, B, and C
Zones for a
Control Chart

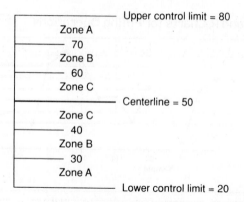

An easy way to position the zone boundaries is to divide the distance between the upper control limit and the centerline by 3. The resulting quantity is then added to and subtracted from the centerline to form the boundaries between the C and B zones. The boundaries between the B and A zones are formed by adding and subtracting twice the result of dividing the distance between the upper control limit and the centerline by 3.

For example, if the average range were 50 and the control limits were 20 and 80, the distance between the upper control limit and the centerline would be 30. The resulting zone boundaries are shown in Figure 8.2. Assuming that the range portion of the control chart is stable, the $\bar{x}$ portion may now be developed.

The $\bar{x}$ Portion

After analyzing the R chart, we may construct the $\bar{x}$ chart. This control chart depicts variations in the averages of the subgroups. To find the average for each subgroup, we add the data points for each subgroup and divide by the number of entries in the subgroup, as given by Equation (5.3). For the pharmaceutical company, the average of the 9:30 subgroup is

$$\frac{52.22 + 52.85 + 52.41 + 52.55 + 53.10 + 52.47}{6} = 52.60$$

This calculation is repeated for each of the subgroups. The $\bar{x}$ results for this example can be found in the last column of Table 8.1.

The centerline of an $\bar{x}$ control chart is found by taking the average of the subgroup averages, $\bar{\bar{x}}$, calculated from Equation (5.4). In our example, the average of the 22 subgroup averages is

$$\bar{\bar{x}} = \frac{1146.55}{22} = 52.12$$

Using a multiple of three standard errors to construct the control limits, we have

$$\text{UCL}(\bar{x}) = \bar{\bar{x}} + 3\sigma_{\bar{x}}$$
$$\text{LCL}(\bar{x}) = \bar{\bar{x}} - 3\sigma_{\bar{x}}$$

(8.15)

Assuming that the distribution of process output was, and will be, stable and approximately normally distributed, we can derive control limits. (Note that because of the

Empirical Rule discussed in Chapter 5, the assumption of normality is not necessary to interpret the control limits.)

Consequently, when the characteristic of interest is stable and approximately normally distributed,

$$\bar{\bar{x}} = \frac{\Sigma\bar{x}}{k} \tag{8.16}$$

where k is the number of subgroups.

$$\sigma_{\bar{x}} = \frac{\sigma}{\sqrt{n}} = \frac{\overline{R}/d_2}{\sqrt{n}} \tag{8.17}$$

that is, since $\overline{R} = d_2\sigma$, $\sigma = \overline{R}/d_2$ and the values of d_2 are tabulated as a function of subgroup size in Table B.1 in Appendix B.

We can thus rewrite the control limits as

$$UCL(\bar{x}) = \bar{\bar{x}} + 3\left[\frac{\overline{R}/d_2}{\sqrt{n}}\right] \tag{8.18}$$

or

$$UCL(\bar{x}) = \bar{\bar{x}} + A_2\overline{R} \tag{8.19}$$

and

$$LCL(\bar{x}) = \bar{\bar{x}} - 3\sigma_{\bar{x}}$$

$$= \bar{\bar{x}} - 3\frac{\sigma}{\sqrt{n}}$$

$$= x - 3\left[\frac{\overline{R}/d_2}{\sqrt{n}}\right] \tag{8.20}$$

or

$$LCL(\bar{x}) = \bar{\bar{x}} - A_2\overline{R} \tag{8.21}$$

where $A_2 = 3/(d_2\sqrt{n})$ and is tabulated as a function of subgroup size in Table B.1 in Appendix B.

For the pharmaceutical company, the upper and lower control limits can now be computed as:

$$UCL(\bar{x}) = 52.12 + (0.483)(0.740) = 52.47$$

and

$$LCL(\bar{x}) = 52.12 - (0.483)(0.740) = 51.76$$

The upper portion of Figure 8.1 on page 257 illustrates the $\bar{x}$ chart. Notice that a total of five points on the $\bar{x}$ chart are outside of the control limits and therefore indicate a lack of control. Further investigation is warranted to determine the source(s) of this special variation.

It is important to recognize that an $\bar{x}$ chart cannot be meaningfully analyzed if its corresponding R chart is not in statistical control. This is because $\bar{x}$ chart control limits are calculated from $\bar{R}$ (i.e., $\bar{\bar{x}} \pm A_2\bar{R}$), and if the range is not stable, no calculations based on it will be accurate.

The product, $A_2\bar{R}$, represents three times the standard error of the subgroup means. This is useful in forming the A, B, and C zones used in this chart as well as in helping to detect patterns indicating a lack of statistical control. Zone boundaries are placed on both sides of the centerline at a distance of one and two times the standard error, respectively. Equivalently, a simple way to position the zone boundaries is to divide the distance between the upper control limit and the centerline by 3. Just as with the range portion, the resulting quantity is then added to and subtracted from the centerline to form the boundaries between the C and B zones. As before, the boundaries between the B and A zones are formed by adding (or subtracting) twice the result of dividing the distance between the upper control limit and the centerline by 3.

$$\text{Boundary between lower zones A and B} = \bar{\bar{x}} - (2/3)A_2\bar{R} \tag{8.22}$$

$$\text{Boundary between lower zones B and C} = \bar{\bar{x}} - (1/3)A_2\bar{R} \tag{8.23}$$

$$\text{Boundary between upper zones B and C} = \bar{\bar{x}} + (1/3)A_2\bar{R} \tag{8.24}$$

$$\text{Boundary between upper zones A and B} = \bar{\bar{x}} + (2/3)A_2\bar{R} \tag{8.25}$$

Another Example

Consider the case of a manufacturer of circuit boards for personal computers. Various components are to be mounted on each board and the boards eventually slipped into slots in a chassis. The boards' overall length is crucial to assure a proper fit, and this dimension has been targeted as an important item to be stabilized. (Note: The width, thickness, hardness, or any other characteristic may also be targeted either simultaneously or at another point in time.) Boards are cut from large sheets of material by a single rotary cutter continuously fed from a hopper. At a customer's request, it is decided to create a control chart for the length of circuit boards produced by the process.

After input from many individuals involved with the process, it is decided to select the first five units every hour from the production output. Each group of five items represents a subgroup. This manner of subgroup selection is most likely to isolate the variation over time between the subgroups and, therefore, capture only common process variation within the subgroups.

Boards are measured using an operationally defined method (see ☞ BOARD); Table 8.2 lists the resulting lengths. The average and the range for each subgroup of five elements in Table 8.2 have been computed and are shown in the last two columns on the right. This arrangement of the data will be used to determine whether special sources of variation between subgroups are evident in measurement-to-measurement changes over time.

TABLE 8.2
Cut Circuit Board Lengths

Time	Sample Number	1	2	3	4	5	Average $\bar{x}$	Range R
9 A.M.	1	5.030	5.002	5.019	4.992	5.008	5.010	0.038
10	2	4.995	4.992	5.001	5.011	5.004	5.001	0.019
11	3	4.988	5.024	5.021	5.005	5.002	5.008	0.036
12	4	5.002	4.996	4.993	5.015	5.009	5.003	0.022
1 P.M.	5	4.992	5.007	5.015	4.989	5.014	5.003	0.026
2	6	5.009	4.994	4.997	4.985	4.993	4.996	0.024
3	7	4.995	5.006	4.994	5.000	5.005	5.000	0.012
4	8	4.985	5.003	4.993	5.015	4.988	4.997	0.030
5	9	5.008	4.995	5.009	5.009	5.005	5.005	0.014
6	10	4.998	5.000	4.990	5.007	4.995	4.998	0.017
7	11	4.994	4.998	4.994	4.995	4.990	4.994	0.008
8	12	5.004	5.000	5.007	5.000	4.996	5.001	0.011
9	13	4.983	5.002	4.998	4.997	5.012	4.998	0.029
10	14	5.006	4.967	4.994	5.000	4.984	4.990	0.039
11	15	5.012	5.014	4.998	4.999	5.007	5.006	0.016
12	16	5.000	4.984	5.005	4.998	4.996	4.997	0.021
1 A.M.	17	4.994	5.012	4.986	5.005	5.007	5.001	0.026
2	18	5.006	5.010	5.018	5.003	5.000	5.007	0.018
3	19	4.984	5.002	5.003	5.005	4.997	4.998	0.021
4	20	5.000	5.010	5.013	5.020	5.003	5.009	0.020
5	21	4.988	5.001	5.009	5.005	4.996	5.000	0.021
6	22	5.004	4.999	4.990	5.006	5.009	5.002	0.019
7	23	5.010	4.989	4.990	5.009	5.014	5.002	0.025
8	24	5.015	5.008	4.993	5.000	5.010	5.005	0.022
9	25	4.982	4.984	4.995	5.017	5.013	4.998	0.035
						Totals	125.029	0.569

Construction of the control chart begins with the range portion. The centerline is found by taking the average of the subgroup ranges using Equation (8.1):

$$\bar{R} = 0.569/25 = 0.023$$

Not only does this value form the centerline for the range portion of the control chart, it also forms the basis for estimating the standard error and hence the control limits and zone boundaries as well. Values for D_3 and D_4, from Table B.1 in Appendix B, are 0.00 and 2.114, respectively. Equations (8.9) and (8.10) yield the control limits:

$$UCL(R) = (2.114)(0.023) = 0.049$$

and

$$LCL(R) = (0)(0.023) = 0.000$$

Equations (8.11), (8.12), (8.13), and (8.14) yield values for the zone boundaries:

Boundary between lower zones A and B = $0.023[1 - 2(0.864)/2.326] = 0.006$

Boundary between lower zones B and C = $0.023[1 - 1(0.864)/2.326] = 0.014$

FIGURE 8.3
Minitab $\bar{x}$ and
R Chart for
Circuit Board
Length

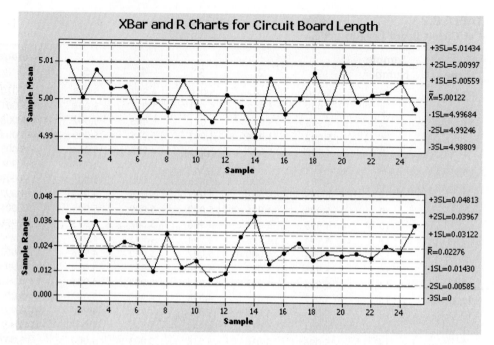

Boundary between upper zones B and C = 0.023[1 + 1(0.864)/2.326] = 0.032

Boundary between upper zones A and B = 0.023[1 + 2(0.864)/2.326] = 0.040

The lower portion of Figure 8.3 displays the control chart. There are no indications of any special sources of variation, and the process appears stable with regard to its range.

Once the stability of the range has been established, the $\bar{x}$ portion of the control chart may be constructed. $\bar{R}$ can be used as a basis for the estimate of the standard error for the $\bar{x}$ portion of the chart if the range is stable. Equation (8.16) yields a centerline of

$$\bar{\bar{x}} = 125.029/25 = 5.001$$

The upper and lower control limits can be found using Equations (8.19) and (8.21). The value for A_2 comes from Table B.1 in Appendix B for a subgroup of size 5.

$$\text{UCL}(\bar{x}) = 5.001 + (0.577)(0.023) = 5.014$$
$$\text{LCL}(\bar{x}) = 5.001 - (0.577)(0.023) = 4.988$$

Zone boundaries are found using Equations (8.22) through (8.25):

Boundary between lower zones A and B = 5.001 − (2/3)(0.577)(0.023) = 4.992

Boundary between lower zones B and C = 5.001 − (1/3)(0.577)(0.023) = 4.997

Boundary between upper zones B and C = 5.001 + (1/3)(0.577)(0.023) = 5.005

Boundary between upper zones A and B = 5.001 + (2/3)(0.577)(0.023) = 5.010

These values are shown in the upper portion of Figure 8.3. There are no indications of any special sources of variation present between the subgroups with respect to time in the $\bar{x}$ portion, so we can conclude that this process is stable and its output is predictable in the near future, assuming continued stability.

Another Example

A manufacturer of high-end audio components buys metal tuning knobs to use in assembling its products. Knobs are produced automatically by a subcontractor using a single machine that is designed to produce them with a constant diameter. Because of persistent final assembly problems with the knobs, management has decided to examine this process output by requesting that the subcontractor construct an $\bar{x}$ and R chart for knob diameter. Beginning at 8:30 A.M. on a Tuesday, the first four knobs are selected every half hour. The diameter of each is carefully measured using an operationally defined technique. The average and range for each subgroup are computed; the data, along with these statistics, are shown in Table 8.3 (see ☉ KNOB).

The data are arranged this way to help us determine whether the differences in the subgroups result from special causes over time. The measurement-to-measurement

TABLE 8.3
Tuning Knob Diameters

Time	Sample Number	1	2	3	4	Average $\bar{x}$	Range R
8:30 A.M.	1	836	846	840	839	840.25	10
9:00	2	842	836	839	837	838.50	6
9:30	3	839	841	839	844	840.75	5
10:00	4	840	836	837	839	838.00	4
10:30	5	838	844	838	842	840.50	6
11:00	6	838	842	837	843	840.00	6
11:30	7	842	839	840	842	840.75	3
12:00	8	840	842	844	836	840.50	8
12:30 P.M.	9	842	841	837	837	839.25	5
1:00	10	846	846	846	845	845.75	1
1:30	11	849	846	848	844	846.75	5
2:00	12	845	844	848	846	845.75	4
2:30	13	847	845	846	846	846.00	2
3:00	14	839	840	841	838	839.50	3
3:30	15	840	839	839	840	839.50	1
4:00	16	842	839	841	837	839.75	5
4:30	17	841	845	839	839	841.00	6
5:00	18	841	841	836	843	840.25	7
5:30	19	845	842	837	840	841.00	8
6:00	20	839	841	842	840	840.50	3
6:30	21	840	840	842	836	839.50	6
7:00	22	844	845	841	843	843.25	4
7:30	23	848	843	844	836	842.75	12
8:00	24	840	844	841	845	842.50	5
8:30	25	843	845	846	842	844.00	4
					Totals	21,036.25	129

differences here are arranged to trap special variation over time between the subgroups and to confine the common process variation within the subgroups.

Using the subgroup range values and Equation (8.1) gives

$$\overline{R} = 129/25 = 5.16$$

From this, the control limits can be calculated using Equations (8.9) and (8.10). Using a subgroup size of 4, Table B.1 in Appendix B gives us values for $D_3 = 0.00$ and $D_4 = 2.282$. Hence,

$$UCL(R) = (2.282)(5.16) = 11.78$$

$$LCL(R) = 0(5.16) = 0.00$$

Zone boundaries are computed using Equations (8.11) through (8.14):

Boundary between lower zones A and B = $5.16[1 - 2(0.880)/2.059] = 0.75$

Boundary between lower zones B and C = $5.16[1 - 1(0.880)/2.059] = 2.95$

Boundary between upper zones B and C = $5.16[1 + 1(0.880)/2.059] = 7.36$

Boundary between upper zones A and B = $5.16[1 + 2(0.880)/2.059] = 9.57$

Figure 8.4 illustrates the control chart for the range. Recall from Chapter 6 that a search for indications of a lack of control should always be made from right to left on the control chart; that is, the search should be made by looking backward in time from the present. Reading from right to left, the range at subgroup number 23 is beyond the upper control limit. Furthermore, subgroup number 16 is the eighth consecutive point below the centerline and therefore indicates a lack of control by virtue of the fourth rule presented in Chapter 6. Hence, there are two indications of a lack of control.

An investigation reveals that at 7:25 P.M. a water pipe burst in the lunchroom. The episode was not serious, but caused water to leak from the lunchroom onto the floor beneath the machinery involved in the process. This disruption seems to have caused the lack of control

FIGURE 8.4
Minitab Initial Range Chart for Tuning Knob Diameters

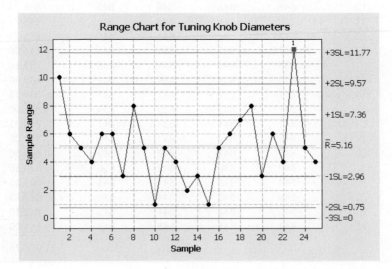

observed at subgroup 23. The operators believe this to be a special cause of variation that should not recur once the plumbing has been repaired. The initial study does not reveal any special source of variation for the indication of a lack of control at subgroup 16.

The data for subgroup 23 are then removed from the data set. The repair of the plumbing has permanently removed the conditions leading to this observation. The data for subgroup 16 are left in place, as no special cause of variation can be isolated and removed that would explain its presence. $\overline{R}$ is recomputed using Equation (8.1) to reflect the deletion of subgroup 23:

$$\overline{R} = 117/24 = 4.88$$

The revised control limits and zone boundaries are computed using Equations (8.9) and (8.10), and Equations (8.11) through (8.14):

$$UCL(R) = (2.282)(4.88) = 11.14$$

$$LCL(R) = (0)(4.88) = 0.00$$

Boundary between lower zones A and B $= 4.88[1 - 2(0.880)/2.059] = 0.71$

Boundary between lower zones B and C $= 4.88[1 - 1(0.880)/2.059] = 2.79$

Boundary between upper zones B and C $= 4.88[1 + 1(0.880)/2.059] = 6.96$

Boundary between upper zones A and B $= 4.88[1 + 2(0.880)/2.059] = 9.05$

The revised R chart appears in the lower portion of Figure 8.5; because the centerline has been shifted, subgroup number 16 is no longer the eighth consecutive point below the centerline. There are no other indications of a lack of control in the data. Changing

FIGURE 8.5
Minitab $\overline{x}$ and
R Chart for
Tuning Knob
Diameters

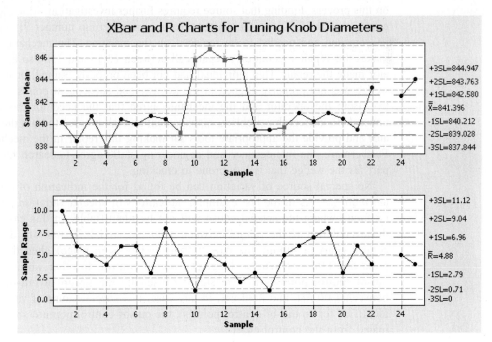

the centerline, control limits, and zone boundaries may uncover other indications of a lack of control, but this is not the case here. Hence, the $\bar{x}$ portion of the chart may be constructed using the average range from the now-stable R portion of the chart.

The centerline of the $\bar{x}$ chart is the average of the subgroup averages, where $\bar{x}$ for subgroup 23 has been subtracted from the total in Table 8.2. Equation (8.16) yields

$$\bar{\bar{x}} = 20,193.50/24 = 841.40$$

The control limits and the zone boundaries can now be computed using Equations (8.19) and (8.21), and Equations (8.22) through (8.25):

$$\text{UCL}(\bar{x}) = 841.40 + (0.729)(4.88) = 844.96$$
$$\text{LCL}(\bar{x}) = 841.40 - (0.729)(4.88) = 837.84$$

Boundary between lower zones A and B $= 841.40 - (2/3)(0.729)(4.88) = 839.03$

Boundary between lower zones B and C $= 841.40 - (1/3)(0.729)(4.88) = 840.21$

Boundary between upper zones B and C $= 841.40 + (1/3)(0.729)(4.88) = 842.59$

Boundary between upper zones A and B $= 841.40 + (2/3)(0.729)(4.88) = 843.77$

The $\bar{x}$ portion of the control chart has been completed using these values and appears in the upper portion of Figure 8.5. Reading from right to left, there are several indications of a lack of control. Four points are beyond the upper control limit. These occurred sequentially from 1:00 P.M. to 2:30 P.M. Also, at 10:00 A.M. (fourth subgroup), the average is 838.00, the second of three consecutive points in the lower zone A. This indicates a lack of control by virtue of Rule 2 of Chapter 6.

There is very little doubt that there is at least one source of special variation acting on this process. Finding that source requires further investigation, which leads to the discovery that at 12:50 P.M. (just after selection of subgroup number 9), a keyway wedge had cracked and needed to be replaced on the machine. The mechanic who normally makes this repair was out on a repair call between 12:45 and 2:45, so the machine operator made the repair. This individual had not been properly trained for the repair, so the wedge was not properly aligned in the keyway and subsequent points were out of control. Both the operator and the mechanic agree that the need for this repair was not unusual. To correct this problem, management and labor agree to train the machine operator and provide the appropriate tools for making this repair in the mechanic's absence. Furthermore, the maintenance and engineering staffs agree to search for a replacement part for the wedge that is less prone to cracking.

No special source of variation can be found for the indication of a lack of control at 10:00 A.M. As in the last example, indications of special variation will occasionally be found where the special cause will not be identifiable. In this case, the operators discovered that if the points between 1:00 P.M. and 2:30 P.M. are deleted from the control chart (assuming the new training policy is in place), then the out-of-control point at 10:00 A.M. will no longer be out of control. In other words, the 10:00 A.M. out-of-control point is a false signal caused by the group of out-of-control points between 1:00 P.M. and 2:30 P.M. In any case, if a special cause of variation cannot be identified for an out-of-control point(s), the out-of-control point(s) should not be eliminated from the control chart.

After the sources of special variation are found and the underlying causes are resolved, the subgroups generated as a result of those sources are dropped from the data. This changes all of the calculated values for centerlines, control limits, and zone boundaries of the control chart. Accordingly, for the control knobs, we delete subgroups 10, 11, 12, and 13. We must recompute the values for the relevant statistics:

$$\bar{\bar{x}} = 16{,}809.25/20 = 840.46$$

$$\bar{R} = 105/20 = 5.25$$

Using these, the control limits and zone boundaries for the revised R chart become

$$UCL(R) = (2.282)(5.25) = 11.98$$

$$LCL(R) = 0(5.25) = 0.00$$

Boundary between lower zones A and B $= 5.25[1 - 2(0.880)/2.059] = 0.76$

Boundary between lower zones B and C $= 5.25[1 - 1(0.880)/2.059] = 3.01$

Boundary between upper zones B and C $= 5.25[1 + 1(0.880)/2.059] = 7.49$

Boundary between upper zones A and B $= 5.25[1 + 2(0.880)/2.059] = 9.74$

The control chart for the range portion is shown in the lower portion of Figure 8.6. Recall that although the previously out-of-control value for point 23 is still on the Minitab control chart, it is no longer in the data set. There are no indications of a lack of control, so the $\bar{x}$ chart may be constructed. The control limits and zone boundaries are:

$$UCL(\bar{x}) = 840.46 + (0.729)(5.25) = 844.29$$

$$LCL(\bar{x}) = 840.46 - (0.729)(5.25) = 836.63$$

FIGURE 8.6
Minitab
Revised $\bar{x}$ and
R Chart for
Tuning Knob
Diameters

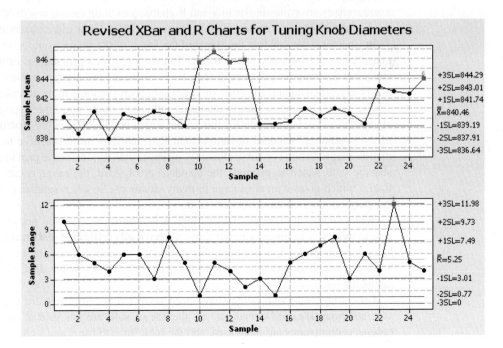

Boundary between lower zones A and B = $840.46 - (2/3)(0.729)(5.25) = 837.91$

Boundary between lower zones B and C = $840.46 - (1/3)(0.729)(5.25) = 839.18$

Boundary between upper zones B and C = $840.46 + (1/3)(0.729)(5.25) = 841.74$

Boundary between upper zones A and B = $840.46 + (2/3)(0.729)(5.25) = 843.01$

The $\bar{x}$ portion of the control chart is shown in the upper portion of Figure 8.6. The last data point, number 25, now indicates a lack of control. That is, if we ignore the now-eliminated entry at data point number 23, data point number 25 is the second of three consecutive points in zone A or beyond, indicating a lack of control by virtue of the second rule of Chapter 6.

At times a conservative approach is warranted—that is, detection of patterns indicating a lack of control will usually be followed by a somewhat costly search for the special cause(s) of variation. A process that has just been altered to eliminate one or more special sources of variation may be allowed to run for a while longer to determine whether additional special sources of variation are really present or whether the indication of a lack of control is only a temporary effect that can be attributed to the removal of some of the data. If special sources of variation are present, the data taken from the process output will soon demonstrate evidence of that variation.

This process can be permitted to run as if it were statistically controlled. However, it must be watched closely to ensure that the special sources of variation have been removed and are no longer affecting the process.

$\bar{x}$ and s Charts

$\bar{x}$ and s charts are quite similar to $\bar{x}$ and R charts, providing the same sort of information—but $\bar{x}$ and s charts are used when subgroups consist of 10 or more observations.

In Chapter 5 we saw that the standard deviation of the process output, σ, could be estimated using s, which is computed from Equation (5.10). s provides an estimate that generally has a smaller standard error than R. The benefits of having a smaller standard error must be weighed against the costs of larger subgroup sizes and more complex calculations.

The $\bar{x}$ and s chart is used with larger subgroup sizes, and larger subgroups are not always desirable. One reason for this is that s may be viewed as a less **robust estimator** of the population standard deviation than R, since R is more sensitive to shifts in population shape than s. For subgroup sizes of fewer than 10, the range provides a reasonable statistic with which to estimate the standard error. Also, the range is easier to calculate than s, which gives it an advantage in many situations. So when subgroup sizes are small, the range is used as an estimator for σ.

When subgroup sizes are 10 or more, s is almost always used because as subgroup size increases, s becomes a much more **statistically efficient estimator** for σ. When the subgroup size is increased, the likelihood of encountering an extreme value increases, so that s, which is less affected than R by extreme values in the data, becomes a better estimator for σ.

Historically, subgroup ranges have been preferred because they are easier to compute than subgroup standard deviations. As the use of software has grown, the need to avoid tedious computations has decreased, and the reluctance to use $\bar{x}$ and s charts has decreased.

The s Portion

The construction of the $\bar{x}$ and s chart parallels that of the $\bar{x}$ and R chart. Both charts begin with an examination of the portion of the chart concerned with the variability of the process. The standard deviation, s, must be calculated for each subgroup. The value for s is the basis for an estimate of the process standard deviation, from which a set of factors for the control limits is developed.

Equation (5.10) is used to compute s for each subgroup:

$$s = \sqrt{\frac{\Sigma(x - \bar{x})^2}{n - 1}}$$

where n is the number of observations in each subgroup (subgroup size). The sequence of s values is then averaged, yielding $\bar{s}$, the centerline for the s chart:

$$\text{Centerline}(s) = \bar{s} = \Sigma s/k \qquad (8.26)$$

where k is the number of subgroups.

$\bar{s}$ is used to form an estimate of the process standard deviation, σ:

$$\sigma = \bar{s}/c_4 \qquad (8.27)$$

where c_4 is a factor that depends on the subgroup size, assumes that the process characteristic is stable and normally distributed, and is given in Table B.1 in Appendix B.

Control limits for the s chart are constructed by adding and subtracting three times the standard error of s from the centerline of the control chart:

$$\text{UCL}(s) = \bar{s} + 3\sigma_\sigma \qquad (8.28)$$

$$\text{LCL}(s) = \bar{s} - 3\sigma_\sigma \qquad (8.29)$$

Assuming that the distribution of the process output was and will be stable, we can derive control limits. (As indicated in Chapter 6, the assumption of normality is not necessary to interpret the control limits; we can use the Empirical Rule instead.)

The sampling distribution of the standard deviation of a stable process has a standard error given by

$$\sigma_\sigma = \sigma\sqrt{1 - c_4^2} \qquad (8.30)$$

Hence, the upper control limit for the s chart is

$$\text{UCL}(s) = \bar{s} + 3\sigma\sqrt{1 - c_4^2} \qquad (8.31)$$

Using $\bar{s}/c_4$ to estimate σ yields

$$\text{UCL}(s) = \bar{s} + \frac{3\bar{s}\sqrt{1 - c_4^2}}{c_4} = \bar{s}\left[1 + \frac{3\sqrt{1 - c_4^2}}{c_4}\right] \qquad (8.32)$$

Similarly,

$$\text{LCL}(s) = \bar{s} - \frac{3\bar{s}\sqrt{1 - c_4^2}}{c_4} = \bar{s}\left[1 - \frac{3\sqrt{1 - c_4^2}}{c_4}\right] \qquad (8.33)$$

A more convenient way to represent these control limits is by defining two new constants, B_3 and B_4:

$$B_3 = 1 - \frac{3\sqrt{1 - c_4^2}}{c_4} \tag{8.34}$$

$$B_4 = 1 + \frac{3\sqrt{1 - c_4^2}}{c_4} \tag{8.35}$$

so that

$$UCL(s) = B_4\bar{s} \tag{8.36}$$

$$LCL(s) = B_3\bar{s} \tag{8.37}$$

Values for B_3 and B_4 depend on subgroup size and can be found in Table B.1 in Appendix B.

Boundaries for zones A, B, and C for the s chart are placed at the usual multiples of one and two times the standard error on either side of the centerline. As negative values are meaningless, the zone boundaries cease to exist below the 0.00 line on the control chart. To find the zone boundaries, we divide the difference between the upper control limit and the centerline by 3. This value provides an estimate for the standard error of $\bar{s}$. Adding and subtracting this value from the centerline yields the upper and lower boundaries between zones B and C, respectively, while adding and subtracting two times this value yields the upper and lower boundaries between zones A and B, respectively. These boundaries can be expressed as

$$\text{Boundary between lower zones A and B} = \bar{s} - (2/3)\bar{s}(B_4 - 1) \tag{8.38}$$

$$\text{Boundary between lower zones B and C} = \bar{s} - (1/3)\bar{s}(B_4 - 1) \tag{8.39}$$

$$\text{Boundary between upper zones B and C} = \bar{s} + (1/3)\bar{s}(B_4 - 1) \tag{8.40}$$

$$\text{Boundary between upper zones A and B} = \bar{s} + (2/3)\bar{s}(B_4 - 1) \tag{8.41}$$

If the s portion of the control chart is found to be stable, the $\bar{x}$ portion may be constructed. However, if the s portion indicates of a lack of statistical control, then the $\bar{x}$ portion cannot be safely evaluated until any special sources of variation have been removed and the process stabilized. As we will see, this is because the estimate of the standard error of the $\bar{x}$ portion is based on the average value of s. Just as with the $\bar{x}$ and R chart, if the variability is not in control, then estimates of the standard error are unreliable, leading to unreliable control limits for $\bar{x}$.

The $\bar{x}$ Portion

The centerline for the $\bar{x}$ chart is the average of the subgroup averages, $\bar{\bar{x}}$, and can be found using Equation (8.16). The control limits are found by adding and subtracting three times the standard error of $\bar{x}$ from the centerline:

$$\bar{\bar{x}} \pm 3\sigma/\sqrt{n} \tag{8.42}$$

Our estimate of the process standard deviation is, from Equation (8.27):

$$\sigma = \bar{s}/c_4$$

so that the control limits become

$$\bar{\bar{x}} \pm 3(\bar{s}/c_4)/\sqrt{n} = \bar{\bar{x}} \pm 3\bar{s}/(c_4\sqrt{n}) \qquad \textbf{(8.43)}$$

Letting the constant $A_3 = 3/(c_4\sqrt{n})$, the control limits for the $\bar{x}$ portion can be expressed as:

$$UCL(\bar{x}) = \bar{\bar{x}} + A_3\bar{s} \qquad \textbf{(8.44)}$$

and

$$LCL(\bar{x}) = \bar{\bar{x}} - A_3\bar{s} \qquad \textbf{(8.45)}$$

where the value for A_3 depends on subgroup size and can be found in Table B.1 in Appendix B.

The zone boundaries are placed at one and two times the standard error on either side of the centerline. The standard error is $\bar{s}/(c_4\sqrt{n})$, so that the zone boundaries are:

$$\text{Boundary between lower zones A and B} = \bar{\bar{x}} - 2\bar{s}/(c_4\sqrt{n}) \qquad \textbf{(8.46)}$$

$$\text{Boundary between lower zones B and C} = \bar{\bar{x}} - \bar{s}/(c_4\sqrt{n}) \qquad \textbf{(8.47)}$$

$$\text{Boundary between upper zones B and C} = \bar{\bar{x}} + \bar{s}/(c_4\sqrt{n}) \qquad \textbf{(8.48)}$$

$$\text{Boundary between upper zones A and B} = \bar{\bar{x}} + 2\bar{s}/(c_4\sqrt{n}) \qquad \textbf{(8.49)}$$

$\bar{x}$ and s Charts: An Example

In a converting operation, a plastic film is combined with paper coming off a spooled reel. As the two come together, they form a moving sheet that passes as a web over a series of rollers. The operation runs in a continuous feed, and the thickness of the plastic coating is an important product characteristic. Coating thickness is monitored by a highly automated piece of equipment that uses 10 heads to take 10 measurements across the web at half-hour intervals. Table 8.4 shows a sequence of measurements taken over 20 time periods (see ✿ COATING).

Arranging the data in this way helps us determine whether there are any special causes of variation from subgroup to subgroup over time. Values for $\bar{x}$ and s, the subgroup means and standard deviations, have been computed for each subgroup. The values for the averages of these subgroup means and standard deviations are computed using Equations (8.16) and (8.26):

$$\bar{\bar{x}} = 42.43/20 = 2.12$$

and

$$\bar{s} = 2.19/20 = 0.11$$

The s chart must be constructed first, and Equations (8.36) and (8.37) provide the upper and lower control limits:

$$UCL(s) = (1.716)(0.11) = 0.189$$
$$LCL(s) = (0.284)(0.11) = 0.031$$

TABLE 8.4
Plastic Coating
Thickness

Head #	8:30	9:00	9:30	10:00	10:30	11:00	11:30
1	2.08	2.14	2.30	2.01	2.06	2.14	2.07
2	2.26	2.02	2.10	2.10	2.12	2.22	2.05
3	2.13	2.14	2.20	2.15	1.98	2.18	1.97
4	1.94	1.94	2.25	1.97	2.12	2.27	2.05
5	2.30	2.30	2.05	2.25	2.20	2.17	2.16
6	2.15	2.08	1.95	2.12	2.02	2.26	2.02
7	2.07	1.94	2.10	2.10	2.19	2.15	2.02
8	2.02	2.12	2.16	1.90	2.03	2.07	2.14
9	2.22	2.15	2.37	2.04	2.02	2.02	2.07
10	2.18	2.36	1.98	2.08	2.09	2.36	2.00
$\bar{x}$	2.14	2.12	2.15	2.07	2.08	2.18	2.06
s	.111	.137	.136	.098	.074	.099	.059

Head #	12:00	12:30	13:00	13:30	14:00	14:30	15:00
1	2.08	2.13	2.13	2.24	2.25	2.03	2.08
2	2.31	1.90	2.16	2.34	1.91	2.10	1.92
3	2.12	2.12	2.12	2.40	1.96	2.24	2.14
4	2.18	2.04	2.22	2.26	2.04	2.20	2.20
5	2.15	2.40	2.12	2.13	1.93	2.25	2.02
6	2.17	2.12	2.07	2.15	2.08	2.03	2.04
7	1.98	2.15	2.04	2.08	2.29	2.06	1.94
8	2.05	2.01	2.28	2.02	2.42	2.19	2.05
9	2.00	2.30	2.12	2.05	2.10	2.13	2.12
10	2.26	2.14	2.10	2.18	2.00	2.20	2.06
$\bar{x}$	2.13	2.13	2.14	2.19	2.10	2.14	2.06
s	.107	.141	.070	.125	.170	.084	.086

Head #	15:30	16:00	16:30	17:00	17:30	18:00
1	2.04	1.92	2.12	1.98	2.08	2.22
2	2.14	2.10	2.30	2.30	2.12	2.05
3	2.18	2.13	2.01	2.31	2.11	1.93
4	2.12	2.02	2.20	2.12	2.22	2.08
5	2.00	1.93	2.11	2.08	2.00	2.15
6	2.02	2.17	1.93	2.10	1.95	2.27
7	2.05	2.24	2.02	2.15	2.15	1.95
8	2.34	1.98	2.25	2.35	2.14	2.11
9	2.12	2.34	2.05	2.12	2.28	2.12
10	2.05	2.12	2.10	2.26	2.31	2.10
$\bar{x}$	2.11	2.10	2.11	2.18	2.14	2.10
s	.101	.136	.115	.121	.113	.106

The zone boundaries are computed using Equations (8.38) through (8.41):

Boundary between lower zones A and B = $0.11 - (2/3)(0.11)(1.716 - 1) = 0.057$

Boundary between lower zones B and C = $0.11 - (1/3)(0.11)(1.716 - 1) = 0.084$

Boundary between upper zones B and C = $0.11 + (1/3)(0.11)(1.716 - 1) = 0.136$

Boundary between upper zones A and B = $0.11 + (2/3)(0.11)(1.716 - 1) = 0.163$

The control chart for the standard deviation is shown in the lower portion of Figure 8.7. As the control chart does not indicate a lack of control, the process variability appears stable. The $\bar{x}$ portion of the chart may now be constructed.

It would not have been correct to analyze the $\bar{x}$ portion before establishing the stability of the process standard deviation. If the standard deviation were not stable, the mean value of the subgroup standard deviations would be unreliable; the control limits on the $\bar{x}$ chart would also be unreliable, as the control limits are based on the value for s. The control chart might then fail to reveal patterns indicating a lack of control when they existed. This is why the estimate of the process standard deviation is not based on the standard deviation taken across all observations.

The average value for x, $\bar{x}$, is 2.12. Equations (8.44) and (8.45) are used to form the upper and lower control limits for the $\bar{x}$ chart:

$$UCL(\bar{x}) = 2.12 + (0.975)(0.11) = 2.227$$
$$LCL(\bar{x}) = 2.12 - (0.975)(0.11) = 2.013$$

FIGURE 8.7
Minitab $\bar{x}$ and s Chart for Plastic Coating Thickness

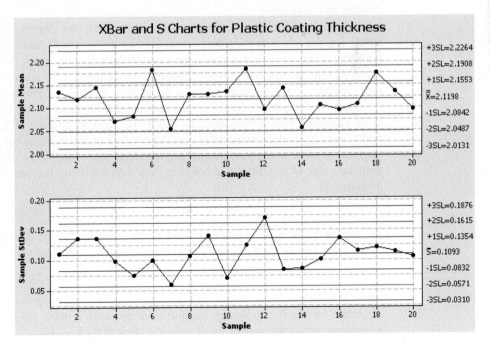

We then use Equations (8.46) through (8.49) to calculate the zone boundaries:

Boundary between lower zones A and B = $2.12 - 2\{0.11/[(0.9727)(3.16)]\} = 2.048$

Boundary between lower zones B and C = $2.12 - 1\{0.11/[(0.9727)(3.16)]\} = 2.084$

Boundary between upper zones B and C = $2.12 + 1\{0.11/[(0.9727)(3.16)]\} = 2.156$

Boundary between upper zones A and B = $2.12 + 2\{0.11/[(0.9727)(3.16)]\} = 2.192$

The $\bar{x}$ chart appears in the upper portion of Figure 8.7 and completes the control chart. There are no indications of a lack of control, so the process can be considered to be stable and the output predictable with respect to time, as long as conditions remain the same.

It is now appropriate to use some of the methods that will be described in Chapter 10 (such as check sheets, Pareto analysis, and brainstorming) to attempt to reduce the common causes of variation in the never-ending quest to decrease the difference between process performance and customer needs.

Individuals and Moving Range Charts

It is not uncommon to encounter a situation where only a single variable value can be periodically observed for control charting. Perhaps measurements must be taken at relatively long intervals, or the measurements are destructive and/or expensive, or perhaps they represent a single batch where only one measurement is appropriate, such as the total yield of a homogeneous chemical batch process. Whatever the case, there are circumstances when data must be taken as individual units that cannot conveniently be divided into subgroups.

Individuals and moving range charts have two parts: one charting the process variability and the other charting the process average for the single measurements. The two parts are used in tandem much as in the $\bar{x}$ and R chart. Stability must first be established in the portion charting the variability, because the estimate of the process variability provides the basis for the control limits of the portion charting the process average.

Single measurements of variables are considered a subgroup of size one. Hence, there is no variability within the subgroups themselves, and an estimate of the process variability must be made in some other way. An estimate of variability is based on the point-to-point variation in the sequence of single values, measured by the moving range (the absolute value of the difference between each data point and the one that immediately preceded it):

$$R = |x_i - x_{i-1}| \qquad \textbf{(8.50)}$$

An average of the moving ranges is used as the centerline for the moving range portion of the chart and as the basis of an estimate of the overall process variation:

$$\text{Centerline(moving range)} = \bar{R} = \Sigma R/(k - 1) \qquad \textbf{(8.51)}$$

where k is the number of single measurements. As it is impossible to calculate the moving range for the first subgroup because none precedes it, there are only $k - 1$ range measurements; so the sum of the R values is divided by $k - 1$.

From Equations (8.3) and (8.4), subgroup ranges have an average given by $\overline{R} = d_2\sigma$, and a standard error of $\sigma_R = d_3\sigma$, where σ is the process standard deviation. The estimate of the process variation is subsequently used to create the 3-sigma control limits for both the moving range portion and the individuals portion of the control chart. As we saw earlier in this chapter, the control limits for a range are given by:

$$\text{UCL(moving range)} = D_4\overline{R} \qquad (8.52)$$

$$\text{LCL(moving range)} = D_3\overline{R} \qquad (8.53)$$

where D_3 and D_4 depend on subgroup size and are given in Table B.1 in Appendix B. In this case D_3 is 0.000 and D_4 is 3.267 because the subgroup size for the moving range portion is 2.

For the individuals portion of the control chart, the centerline is the average of the single measurements. We find the control limits by adding and subtracting three times the standard deviation of the single measurements, estimated by $\overline{R}/d_2$:

$$\text{Centerline}(x) = \overline{x} = \Sigma x/k \qquad (8.54)$$

$$\text{UCL}(x) = \overline{x} + 3(\overline{R}/d_2) \qquad (8.55)$$

Using the factor E_2 to represent $3/d_2$, the expression for the upper control limit becomes

$$\text{UCL}(x) = \overline{x} + E_2\overline{R} \qquad (8.56)$$

where E_2 depends on subgroup size and can be found in Table B.1 in Appendix B. In this case the subgroup size is 2, as we use two observations to calculate each moving range value. Hence, $E_2 = 2.66$, and

$$\text{UCL}(x) = \overline{x} + 2.66\overline{R} \qquad (8.57)$$

Similarly, the lower control limit is found using:

$$\text{LCL}(x) = \overline{x} - 2.66\overline{R} \qquad (8.58)$$

An Example

A chemical company produces 2,000-gallon batches of a liquid chemical product, A-744, once every two days. The product is a combination of six raw materials, of which three are liquids and three are powdered solids. Production takes place in a single tank, agitated as the ingredients are added, and for several hours thereafter. Shipments of A-744 to the customer are made in bins as single lots when the batches are finished. The chemical company is concerned with the density of the finished product, which it measures in grams per cubic centimeter. As batches are constantly stirred during production, the density is assumed to be relatively uniform throughout each batch. Therefore, management decides that density will be measured by only one reading per batch. During a 60-day period, 30 batches of A-744 are produced. Table 8.5 shows the density readings for these batches (see ☞ DENSITY).

Using Equation (8.50), we calculate the moving range by subtracting the previous observation from the next observation and then taking the absolute value. For example, the first moving range is obtained by subtracting the first observation $X_1 = 1.242$ from the second observation $X_2 = 1.289$. Thus, the first moving range is $1.289 - 1.242 = 0.047$.

TABLE 8.5
A-744 Batch
Density

Date	Density	Moving Range		Date	Density	Moving Range
5/6	1.242	—		6/10	1.253	0.018
5/8	1.289	0.047		6/12	1.257	0.004
5/10	1.186	0.103		6/14	1.275	0.018
5/13	1.197	0.011		6/17	1.232	0.043
5/15	1.252	0.055		6/19	1.201	0.031
5/17	1.221	0.031		6/21	1.281	0.080
5/20	1.299	0.078		6/24	1.274	0.007
5/22	1.323	0.024		6/26	1.234	0.040
5/24	1.323	0.000		6/28	1.187	0.047
5/27	1.314	0.009		7/1	1.196	0.009
5/29	1.299	0.015		7/3	1.282	0.086
5/31	1.225	0.074		7/5	1.322	0.040
6/3	1.185	0.040		7/8	1.258	0.064
6/5	1.194	0.009		7/9	1.261	0.003
6/7	1.235	0.041		7/11	1.201	0.060
				Totals	37.498	1.087

This process continues until the next to last observation $X_{29} = 1.261$ is subtracted from the last observation $X_{30} = 1.201$, or a moving range of 0.60. Since there is no moving range for the first observation, there is one fewer moving range than there are observations. The moving ranges are also shown in Table 8.5.

Using Equation (8.51), the average of the 29 moving range values is

$$\text{Centerline(moving range)} = \overline{R} = 1.087/29 = 0.037$$

The control limits for the moving range portion of the control chart can be found using Equations (8.52) and (8.53):

$$\text{UCL(moving range)} = D_4\overline{R} = (3.267)(0.037) = 0.121$$
$$\text{LCL(moving range)} = D_3\overline{R} = (0.000)(0.037) = 0.000$$

The control chart for the moving ranges is shown in the lower portion of Figure 8.8. The moving range appears to be in a state of statistical control, so it is safe to use the average moving range value to construct the single measurements portion of the chart.

Using Equation (8.54), the centerline for the individuals control chart is:

$$\text{Centerline}(x) = \overline{x} = 37.498/30 = 1.250$$

The control limits for the individuals portion are found using Equations (8.57) and (8.58):

$$\text{UCL}(x) = \overline{x} + 2.66\overline{R} = 1.250 + 2.66(0.037) = 1.348$$
$$\text{LCL}(x) = \overline{x} - 2.66\overline{R} = 1.250 - 2.66(0.037) = 1.152$$

The upper portion of Figure 8.8 illustrates the control chart for the individuals portion. The process appears to be in a state of statistical control, since there are no points beyond the control limits and no other signs of any trends or patterns in the data.

FIGURE 8.8
Minitab
Individuals
and Moving
Range Chart
for A-744
Density

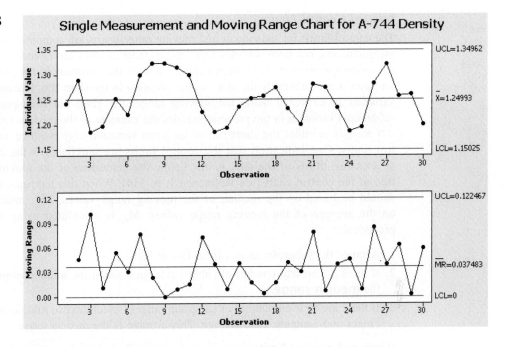

Special Characteristics of Individuals and Moving Range Charts

Because each subgroup consists of only one value, and process variation is estimated on the basis of observation-to-observation changes, individuals and moving range charts have certain unique characteristics that distinguish them from other control charts. For example, for an individuals and moving range chart to be reliable, it is best to have at least 100 subgroups, whereas 25 will suffice for most other control chart forms.

Correlation in the Moving Range

The moving ranges tend to be correlated. For example, a data point near the centerline followed by one in the upper zone A, followed by one in the lower zone C, will result in two large successive moving range points. As a consequence, large moving range values tend to be followed by other large moving range values, and small moving range values tend to be followed by other small moving range values. Because of this, users must be cautious in applying rules for a lack of control dealing with patterns in the data. For example, a false alarm may be created by using the rule designating the second of two out of three consecutive points in zone A or beyond as indicating a lack of control. For this reason, it is usually best to be conservative when applying the rules concerning patterns in the data other than points beyond the control limits that indicate a lack of control in moving range charts. For example, instead of 8 consecutive values above or below the centerline indicating a lack of control, we might require 10 or 12. Knowledge and experience are the best guides in establishing policy in this case.

Inflated Control Limits

The control limits for individuals and moving range charts are computed from individual measurements, not from statistics (e.g., mean, range or standard deviation). The individual measurements will fall within control limits if the variation in the process over the long run is approximately the same as the variation in the short run. Because the process variation is estimated using the moving range, the short-run (between-consecutive-subgroups) variation in the process provides the estimate of the process variation.

Changes in either the short-run or long-run variation may produce unreliable control limits. One indication that the control limits are unreliable is the occurrence of at least two-thirds of the data points below the centerline of the moving range portion of the control chart [see Reference 1, p. 314]. When this happens, control limits should be based on the median of the moving range values, M_{e_R}, rather than based on the average of the moving range values. M_{e_R} is calculated using the following procedure:

1. Arrange the subgroup ranges from low to high.
2. If there are an odd number of subgroup ranges, select the middle subgroup range as the **median range.**
3. If there are an even number of subgroup ranges, select the two middle-most subgroup ranges and compute their average. This average is the median range.

If **inflated control limits** are suspected, control limits based on the median of the moving ranges should be calculated and compared to those based on the average moving range; the narrower of the two sets should be used. Control limits for the moving range portion, based on the median, can be computed using

$$\text{Centerline(median moving range)} = M_{e_R} \qquad \textbf{(8.59)}$$

$$\text{UCL(median moving range)} = D_6 M_{e_R} \qquad \textbf{(8.60)}$$

$$\text{LCL(median moving range)} = D_5 M_{e_R} \qquad \textbf{(8.61)}$$

where values for D_5 and D_6 depend on subgroup size, assume stability and a normal distribution of the process characteristic, and can be found in Table B.1 in Appendix B. For the individuals chart the subgroup size is two, so the values used are $D_6 = 3.865$ and $D_5 = 0.000$. Hence,

$$\text{UCL(median moving range)} = 3.865 M_{e_R} \qquad \textbf{(8.62)}$$

$$\text{LCL(median moving range)} = 0.000 \qquad \textbf{(8.63)}$$

(Again, recall that the assumption of normality is not required to interpret the control limits; the Empirical Rule may be used instead.)

The standard error of the single measurements is estimated using M_{e_R}/d_4, where values for d_4 depend on subgroup size and assume stability of the process characteristic. They can be found in Table B.1 in Appendix B. For subgroup size two, $d_4 = 0.954$. Hence, control limits for the single measurements portion are created by adding and subtracting three times $M_{e_R}/0.954$ from the centerline:

$$\text{UCL}(x) = \bar{x} + 3 M_{e_R}/0.954 = \bar{x} + 3.145 M_{e_R} \qquad \textbf{(8.64)}$$

TABLE 8.6
A-744 Batch Yields

Date	Yield	Moving Range	Date	Yield	Moving Range
5/6	1989.0	—	6/10	2002.3	4.9
5/8	1998.9	9.9	6/12	1999.5	2.8
5/10	2027.4	28.5	6/14	2000.8	1.3
5/13	2001.5	25.9	6/17	2022.4	21.6
5/15	1991.3	10.2	6/19	1998.3	24.1
5/17	2001.3	10.0	6/21	1999.8	1.5
5/20	1997.4	3.9	6/24	2000.9	1.1
5/22	1989.3	8.1	6/26	1994.3	6.6
5/24	1995.5	6.2	6/28	1998.7	4.4
5/27	2014.4	18.9	7/1	2013.5	14.8
5/29	1990.2	24.2	7/3	1998.1	15.4
5/31	1999.6	9.4	7/5	2002.5	4.4
6/3	2008.1	8.5	7/8	2000.2	2.3
6/5	1999.4	8.7	7/9	1996.1	4.1
6/7	1997.4	2.0	7/11	2020.9	24.8
			Totals	60049.0	308.5

Similarly,

$$\text{LCL}(x) = \bar{x} - 3.145 M_{e_R} \qquad \textbf{(8.65)}$$

Consider the example of the manufacturer of chemicals discussed earlier. The chemical, A-744, is used by the manufacturer's customer as an ingredient in another process sensitive to the quantity of A-744. The manufacturer's customer is seeking to reduce costs by using the A-744 in whole bin lots. As the yield of the batches of A-744 can be expected to vary from its 2,000-gallon target, that yield is a likely candidate for the use of an individuals control chart. The yields of the 30 batches of A-744 are each carefully measured, yielding a sequence of 30 single values. The data and the computed moving ranges are shown in Table 8.6 (see ☺ YIELD).

The centerline and control limits for the moving range portion of the control chart are found using Equations (8.51) through (8.53):

$$\bar{R} = 308.5/29 = 10.64$$

$$\text{UCL(moving range)} = D_4\bar{R} = (3.267)(10.64) = 34.76$$

$$\text{LCL(moving range)} = 0.00$$

The control chart for the moving range is shown in the lower portion of Figure 8.9. The moving range appears stable, so the average moving range value can be used to construct the individuals portion of the chart.

Using Equation (8.54), the average of the 30 yields is:

$$\bar{x} = 60,049.0/30 = 2001.63$$

The control limits for the individuals portion are found using Equations (8.57) and (8.58):

$$\text{UCL}(x) = \bar{x} + 2.66\bar{R} = 2001.63 + (2.66)(10.64) = 2029.93$$

$$\text{LCL}(x) = \bar{x} - 2.66\bar{R} = 2001.63 - (2.66)(10.64) = 1973.33$$

FIGURE 8.9
Minitab
Individuals
and Moving
Range Chart
for A-744
Batch Yields

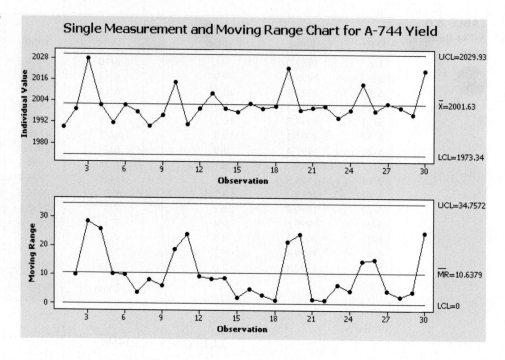

The control chart is shown in the upper portion of Figure 8.9. This portion also appears to be in a state of statistical control. However, an experienced eye detects that more than two-thirds of the data points (20 of the 29 moving ranges) are below the centerline, indicating that the control limits may be artificially inflated and therefore may be hiding indications of special sources of variation.

The median of the 29 moving range values is 8.5. This value can be used to calculate an alternate centerline and set of control limits using Equations (8.59) through (8.61) for the moving range portion of the control chart:

$$\text{Centerline (median moving range)} = 8.5$$

$$\text{UCL (median moving range)} = (3.865)(8.5) = 32.85$$

$$\text{LCL (median moving range)} = 0.00$$

Figure 8.10 represents the control chart using the median moving range. The lower portion shows the new control chart for the moving ranges. The process still appears in a state of statistical control, so the median of the moving ranges may be used to construct a new individuals portion of the chart.

Note that it is essential to establish stability in the moving range portion of the control chart before constructing the individuals portion of the control chart. This is because the control limits for the individuals portion are based on the estimate of the process variability, generated by the moving range portion. A lack of stability in the moving range portion will produce unreliable estimates of the process variation, resulting in the control chart's failure to properly separate special and common variation.

FIGURE 8.10 Individuals and Moving Range Chart (Based on Median Moving Range Value) for A-744 Batch Yields

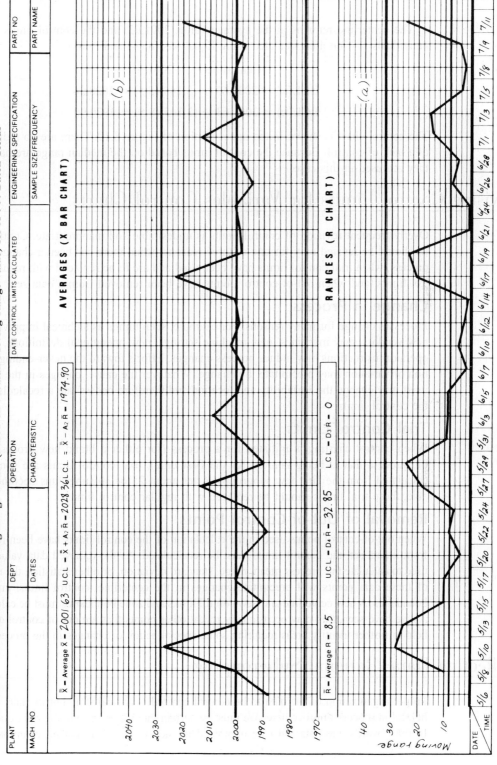

The centerline remains at the average value, 2001.63, and the control limits for the individuals portion are calculated using Equations (8.64) and (8.65):

$$\text{Centerline}(x) = 2001.63$$

$$\text{UCL}(x) = 2001.63 + (3.145)(8.5) = 2028.36$$

$$\text{LCL}(x) = 2001.63 - (3.145)(8.5) = 1974.90$$

The control chart is shown in the upper portion of Figure 8.10. There are no indications of a lack of control. Because the control limits based on the median range are narrower, they are used in this case.

Revising Control Limits for Variables Control Charts

Overly frequent revision of control limits is undesirable and inappropriate. Control limits should be revised only for one of three reasons: when there has been a change in the process, when trial control limits have been used and are to be replaced with regular control limits, and when out-of-control points have been removed from a data set.

Change in Process

Processes change for many reasons. For example, such things as technical improvements, new vendors, new machines, new machine settings, new operational definitions, or new operator instructions may induce process changes. Efforts toward the never-ending reduction of variation may precipitate the change. Whatever the cause, changes in the process itself may change the variability and location and therefore necessitate a recalculation of the control limits.

Trial Control Limits

When control charting is initiated for a process (for either a brand new process or an old process that is being charted for the first time), trial control limits are sometimes calculated from the first few subgroups. After about 25 or 30 subgroups become available, these trial limits should be replaced with regular control limits.

Removal of Out-of-Control Points

When out-of-control points used in the calculation of the control limits have been removed from a data set, the control limits must be recalculated. As the removed data values were used to calculate the process mean, range, standard deviation, or other statistics, the removal of these data points will precipitate changes in the centerline, control limits, and zone boundaries. A new centerline and new control limits and zone boundaries must be calculated. As we have seen, this may occasionally reveal other points that are out of control and will help to further identify areas requiring some special action or changes in the process.

Collecting Data: Rational Subgrouping

Proper organization of the data to be control charted is critical if a control chart is to be helpful in process improvement. We must be certain that we are asking the right questions. In other words, the data must be organized in such a way as to permit examination of variation productively and in a manner that will reveal special sources of variation. The organization of the data defines the question the control chart is addressing to achieve process improvement. Each subgroup should be selected from a small area so that relatively homogeneous conditions exist within each subgroup; this is called rational subgrouping. Wheeler and Chambers [see Reference 2, pp. 111–120] provide an excellent example of rational subgrouping.

Let us consider the case of a manufacturer of industrial paints. One-gallon cans are filled four at a time, each one by a separate filling head. The department manager is interested in learning if the weight of the product is stable and within specification and has decided to use statistical process control as an aid.

The supervisor is asked to take five successive cans from each of the four filling heads every hour. The gross weight (in kilograms) of each can is recorded for 20 measurements each hour. The supervisor continues observations for 8 consecutive hours, yielding 160 individual observations, as shown in Table 8.7 (see ☻ PAINT).

How these observations are arranged may reveal variation from one of three sources: variations over time, variations between measurements, or variations between filling heads. Variation over time (hour-to-hour in this case) is represented by the differences in the groups of 20 cans; variation between measurements is represented by the differences between the five cans selected at each hour regardless of filling head; and variation between filling heads is represented by the differences between the results of the filling heads for each of the five cans selected per head, per hour.

The manager must decide on the proper arrangement of these data; their arrangement will dictate the variation that might be revealed. We will consider an arrangement of the data for each possible source of variation.

Arrangement 1

If the basic subgroup consists of the four head readings for a given measurement and hour, as shown in Table 8.8 (see ☻ PAINT), then the variation within the subgroups will be the variation from head to head. That is, our estimate of the process standard error will be based on the measurements taken across all four filling heads. The control chart will be set up to detect variation between the subgroups due to measurement-to-measurement and hour-to-hour special causes of variation. This means that the process variation is allocated as follows:

Source of Variation	Allocation
Hour-to-hour	Between subgroups
Measurement-to-measurement	Between subgroups
Head-to-head	Within subgroups

For the eight hours, there will be a total of 40 subgroups. The average and range for each subgroup have been computed and appear in Table 8.9 (see ☻ ARR1). The average of the averages, $\bar{\bar{x}}$, has been calculated to be 6.13. The average of the range values, $\bar{R}$, is 0.08. When the data are analyzed via this arrangement, there is some evidence of

TABLE 8.7
Fill Data for 160 Paint Cans

Time: 8 A.M. Measurement

		1	2	3	4	5
H	1	6.09	6.10	6.09	6.09	6.09
E	2	6.09	6.09	6.10	6.09	6.09
A	3	6.10	6.11	6.12	6.11	6.11
D	4	6.16	6.16	6.17	6.17	6.17

Time: 9 A.M. Measurement

		1	2	3	4	5
H	1	6.13	6.13	6.14	6.13	6.11
E	2	6.12	6.12	6.11	6.13	6.10
A	3	6.11	6.13	6.13	6.14	6.14
D	4	6.20	6.20	6.20	6.17	6.17

Time: 10 A.M. Measurement

		1	2	3	4	5
H	1	6.14	6.13	6.12	6.13	6.13
E	2	6.11	6.10	6.11	6.10	6.14
A	3	6.13	6.13	6.11	6.13	6.14
D	4	6.16	6.16	6.19	6.19	6.21

Time: 11 A.M. Measurement

		1	2	3	4	5
H	1	6.10	6.10	6.08	6.15	6.11
E	2	6.08	6.12	6.10	6.11	6.10
A	3	6.13	6.13	6.15	6.15	6.09
D	4	6.20	6.18	6.21	6.21	6.20

Time: 12 Noon Measurement

		1	2	3	4	5
H	1	6.14	6.15	6.14	6.13	6.16
E	2	6.10	6.12	6.15	6.13	6.13
A	3	6.13	6.13	6.14	6.14	6.13
D	4	6.17	6.18	6.18	6.18	6.17

Time: 1 P.M. Measurement

		1	2	3	4	5
H	1	6.12	6.09	6.11	6.10	6.10
E	2	6.16	6.13	6.13	6.09	6.10
A	3	6.16	6.11	6.11	6.13	6.10
D	4	6.19	6.21	6.21	6.19	6.16

Time: 2 P.M. Measurement

		1	2	3	4	5
H	1	6.07	6.07	6.08	6.07	6.08
E	2	6.07	6.08	6.07	6.07	6.09
A	3	6.09	6.09	6.09	6.09	6.10
D	4	6.15	6.15	6.16	6.16	6.14

Time: 3 P.M. Measurement

		1	2	3	4	5
H	1	6.11	6.12	6.13	6.13	6.13
E	2	6.10	6.11	6.13	6.10	6.13
A	3	6.13	6.16	6.14	6.13	6.13
D	4	6.18	6.19	6.20	6.19	6.21

TABLE 8.8
Arrangement 1

Time: 8:00 A.M. Measurement

		1	2	3	4	5
H	1	6.09	6.10	6.09	6.09	6.09
E	2	6.09	6.09	6.10	6.09	6.09
A	3	6.10	6.11	6.12	6.11	6.11
D	4	6.16	6.16	6.17	6.17	6.17

TABLE 8.9
Arrangement 1: 40 Subgroups

		Time: 8 A.M. Measurement							Time: 9 A.M. Measurement			
		1	**2**	**3**	**4**	**5**			**1**	**2**	**3**	**4**	**5**
H	1	6.09	6.10	6.09	6.09	6.09	H	1	6.13	6.13	6.14	6.13	6.11
E	2	6.09	6.09	6.10	6.09	6.09	E	2	6.12	6.12	6.11	6.13	6.10
A	3	6.10	6.11	6.12	6.11	6.11	A	3	6.11	6.13	6.13	6.14	6.14
D	4	6.16	6.16	6.17	6.17	6.17	D	4	6.20	6.20	6.20	6.17	6.17
$\bar{x}$		6.11	6.12	6.12	6.12	6.12	$\bar{x}$		6.14	6.15	6.15	6.14	6.13
R		0.07	0.07	0.08	0.08	0.08	R		0.09	0.08	0.09	0.04	0.07

		Time: 10 A.M. Measurement							Time: 11 A.M. Measurement			
		1	**2**	**3**	**4**	**5**			**1**	**2**	**3**	**4**	**5**
H	1	6.14	6.13	6.12	6.13	6.13	H	1	6.10	6.10	6.08	6.15	6.11
E	2	6.11	6.10	6.11	6.10	6.14	E	2	6.08	6.12	6.10	6.11	6.10
A	3	6.13	6.13	6.11	6.13	6.14	A	3	6.13	6.13	6.15	6.15	6.09
D	4	6.16	6.16	6.19	6.19	6.21	D	4	6.20	6.18	6.21	6.21	6.20
$\bar{x}$		6.14	6.13	6.13	6.14	6.16	$\bar{x}$		6.13	6.13	6.14	6.16	6.13
R		0.05	0.06	0.08	0.09	0.08	R		0.12	0.08	0.13	0.10	0.11

		Time: 12 Noon Measurement							Time: 1 P.M. Measurement			
		1	**2**	**3**	**4**	**5**			**1**	**2**	**3**	**4**	**5**
H	1	6.14	6.15	6.14	6.13	6.16	H	1	6.12	6.09	6.11	6.10	6.10
E	2	6.10	6.12	6.15	6.13	6.13	E	2	6.16	6.13	6.13	6.09	6.10
A	3	6.13	6.13	6.14	6.14	6.13	A	3	6.16	6.11	6.11	6.13	6.10
D	4	6.17	6.18	6.18	6.18	6.17	D	4	6.19	6.21	6.21	6.19	6.16
$\bar{x}$		6.14	6.15	6.15	6.15	6.15	$\bar{x}$		6.16	6.14	6.14	6.13	6.12
R		0.07	0.06	0.04	0.05	0.04	R		0.07	0.12	0.10	0.10	0.06

		Time: 2 P.M. Measurement							Time: 3 P.M. Measurement			
		1	**2**	**3**	**4**	**5**			**1**	**2**	**3**	**4**	**5**
H	1	6.07	6.07	6.08	6.07	6.08	H	1	6.11	6.12	6.13	6.13	6.13
E	2	6.07	6.08	6.07	6.07	6.09	E	2	6.10	6.11	6.13	6.10	6.13
A	3	6.09	6.09	6.09	6.09	6.10	A	3	6.13	6.16	6.14	6.13	6.13
D	4	6.15	6.15	6.16	6.16	6.14	D	4	6.18	6.19	6.20	6.19	6.21
$\bar{x}$		6.10	6.10	6.10	6.10	6.10	$\bar{x}$		6.13	6.15	6.15	6.14	6.15
R		0.08	0.08	0.09	0.09	0.06	R		0.08	0.08	0.07	0.09	0.08

FIGURE 8.11
Minitab
Control
Chart for
Arrangement 1

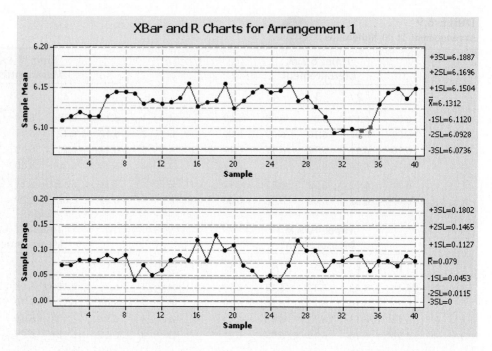

a lack of control, as shown in Figure 8.11. The evidence is the long string of points above the centerline on the $\bar{x}$ portion of the control chart (Rule 4). This, in all likelihood, results from some special source of variation that must be investigated.

Arrangement 2

If the basic subgroup consists of five measurements for a given head and hour, as shown in Table 8.10 (see ☁ ARR2), then the variation from measurement to measurement is the basis for our estimate of the standard error. Our estimate of the process standard error is based on the observations taken across all five measurements for each one of the heads for each hour. The control chart will be set up to detect variation between subgroups due to filling-head-to-filling-head and hour-to-hour special causes of variation. This means that the process variation is allocated as follows:

Source of variation	Allocation
Hour-to-hour	Between subgroups
Measurement-to-measurement	Within subgroups
Head-to-head	Between subgroups

The second arrangement has 32 subgroups each with five measurements. (Note we still have the same 160 measurements.) These five are the measurements taken each hour on each of the four filling heads. The centerline, $\bar{\bar{x}}$, remains 6.13, while the

TABLE 8.10
Arrangement 2

		Time: 8 A.M. Measurement						
		1	**2**	**3**	**4**	**5**	**x̄**	**R**
H	1	6.09	6.10	6.09	6.09	6.09	6.09	0.01
E	2	6.09	6.09	6.10	6.09	6.09	6.09	0.01
A	3	6.10	6.11	6.12	6.11	6.11	6.11	0.02
D	4	6.16	6.16	6.17	6.17	6.17	6.17	0.01

		Time: 9 A.M. Measurement						
		1	**2**	**3**	**4**	**5**	**x̄**	**R**
H	1	6.13	6.13	6.14	6.13	6.11	6.13	0.03
E	2	6.12	6.12	6.11	6.13	6.10	6.12	0.03
A	3	6.11	6.13	6.13	6.14	6.14	6.13	0.03
D	4	6.20	6.20	6.20	6.17	6.17	6.19	0.03

		Time: 10 A.M. Measurement						
		1	**2**	**3**	**4**	**5**	**x̄**	**R**
H	1	6.14	6.13	6.12	6.13	6.13	6.13	0.02
E	2	6.11	6.10	6.11	6.10	6.14	6.11	0.04
A	3	6.13	6.13	6.11	6.13	6.14	6.13	0.03
D	4	6.16	6.16	6.19	6.19	6.21	6.18	0.05

		Time: 11 A.M. Measurement						
		1	**2**	**3**	**4**	**5**	**x̄**	**R**
H	1	6.10	6.10	6.08	6.15	6.11	6.11	0.07
E	2	6.08	6.12	6.10	6.11	6.10	6.10	0.04
A	3	6.13	6.13	6.15	6.15	6.09	6.13	0.06
D	4	6.20	6.18	6.21	6.21	6.20	6.20	0.03

		Time: 12 Noon Measurement						
		1	**2**	**3**	**4**	**5**	**x̄**	**R**
H	1	6.14	6.15	6.14	6.13	6.16	6.14	0.03
E	2	6.10	6.12	6.15	6.13	6.13	6.13	0.05
A	3	6.13	6.13	6.14	6.14	6.13	6.13	0.01
D	4	6.17	6.18	6.18	6.18	6.17	6.18	0.01

(continued)

TABLE 8.10 (concluded)

		Time: 1 P.M. **Measurement**						
		1	**2**	**3**	**4**	**5**	**x̄**	**R**
H	1	6.12	6.09	6.11	6.10	6.10	6.10	0.03
E	2	6.16	6.13	6.13	6.09	6.10	6.12	0.07
A	3	6.16	6.11	6.11	6.13	6.10	6.12	0.06
D	4	6.19	6.21	6.21	6.19	6.16	6.19	0.05

		Time: 2 P.M. **Measurement**						
		1	**2**	**3**	**4**	**5**	**x̄**	**R**
H	1	6.07	6.07	6.08	6.07	6.08	6.07	0.01
E	2	6.07	6.08	6.07	6.07	6.09	6.08	0.02
A	3	6.09	6.09	6.09	6.09	6.10	6.09	0.01
D	4	6.15	6.15	6.16	6.16	6.14	6.15	0.02

		Time: 3 P.M. **Measurement**						
		1	**2**	**3**	**4**	**5**	**x̄**	**R**
H	1	6.11	6.12	6.13	6.13	6.13	6.12	0.02
E	2	6.10	6.11	6.13	6.10	6.13	6.11	0.03
A	3	6.13	6.16	6.14	6.13	6.13	6.14	0.03
D	4	6.18	6.19	6.20	6.19	6.21	6.19	0.03

average range, $\overline{R}$, is now computed as 0.03. Figure 8.12 shows a control chart illustrating this.

Notice that the process can now be seen as being wildly out of control, with many points beyond the control limits. Grouping the measurements by fill head reduced the within-group variation so that the average range was lowered. This subsequently tightened the control limits and revealed the out-of-control points. Undoubtedly, special sources of variation are present, and the control chart indicates where we should begin our investigation; that is, careful examination reveals that many of the out-of-control points on the $\overline{x}$ portion correspond to the number 4 fill head. Its fill values are consistently above the upper control limit. Obviously fill head number 4 is putting more product on average into the containers than the other three fill heads.

The reason the overfilling of head 4 was not revealed by the first arrangement of the data and the first control chart is that the first chart was not constructed to identify differences between the fill heads; it was aimed at examining measurement-to-measurement differences and hour-to-hour differences. The second arrangement was grouped to reveal differences between the fill heads and differences from hour to hour.

FIGURE 8.12
Minitab
Control
Chart for
Arrangement 2

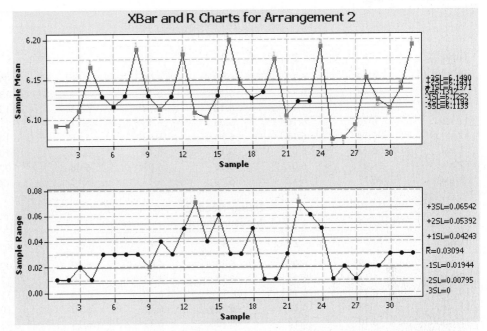

Arrangement 3

Most revealing at this point would be a third arrangement of the data that keeps separate control charts for each fill head. As each filling head has been separated with its own control chart, there is no longer any variation between the filling heads on our control chart. There are, in fact, now four distinct control charts, none of which can detect filling-head-to-filling-head variation. Computationally this third arrangement of the data is shown in Table 8.11 (see ☞ ARR3). Using this arrangement, the process variation is allocated as follows:

Source of Variation for a Head	Allocation
Hour-to-hour	Between subgroups
Measurement-to-measurement	Within subgroups

Note that head-to-head variation is no longer within the control chart and is visible only by comparing the different control charts.

Arranging the data in this way permits the construction of individual sets of $\bar{x}$ and R charts for each filling head. When the four head control charts are drawn on the same scale, as in Figure 8.13a through d, the charts reveal things that may have been obscured earlier: head 4 is significantly different from heads 1, 2, and 3. This information allows management to take appropriate action on the process (that is, fix head 4).

TABLE 8.11
Arrangement 3

Filling Head 1
Measurement

Time	1	2	3	4	5	$\bar{x}$	R
8 A.M.	6.09	6.10	6.09	6.09	6.09	6.09	0.01
9 A.M.	6.13	6.13	6.14	6.13	6.11	6.13	0.03
10 A.M.	6.14	6.13	6.12	6.13	6.13	6.13	0.02
11 A.M.	6.10	6.10	6.08	6.15	6.11	6.11	0.07
12 NOON	6.14	6.15	6.14	6.13	6.16	6.14	0.03
1 P.M.	6.12	6.09	6.11	6.10	6.10	6.10	0.03
2 P.M.	6.07	6.07	6.08	6.07	6.08	6.07	0.01
3 P.M.	6.11	6.12	6.13	6.13	6.13	6.12	0.02

Filling Head 2
Measurement

Time	1	2	3	4	5	$\bar{x}$	R
8 A.M.	6.09	6.09	6.10	6.09	6.09	6.09	0.01
9 A.M.	6.12	6.12	6.11	6.13	6.10	6.12	0.03
10 A.M.	6.11	6.10	6.11	6.10	6.14	6.11	0.04
11 A.M.	6.08	6.12	6.10	6.11	6.10	6.10	0.04
12 NOON	6.10	6.12	6.15	6.13	6.13	6.13	0.05
1 P.M.	6.16	6.13	6.13	6.09	6.10	6.12	0.07
2 P.M.	6.07	6.08	6.07	6.07	6.09	6.08	0.02
3 P.M.	6.10	6.11	6.13	6.10	6.13	6.11	0.03

Filling Head 3
Measurement

Time	1	2	3	4	5	$\bar{x}$	R
8 A.M.	6.10	6.11	6.12	6.11	6.11	6.11	0.02
9 A.M.	6.11	6.13	6.13	6.14	6.14	6.13	0.03
10 A.M.	6.13	6.13	6.11	6.13	6.14	6.13	0.03
11 A.M.	6.13	6.13	6.15	6.15	6.09	6.13	0.06
12 NOON	6.13	6.13	6.14	6.14	6.13	6.13	0.01
1 P.M.	6.16	6.11	6.11	6.13	6.10	6.12	0.06
2 P.M.	6.09	6.09	6.09	6.09	6.10	6.09	0.01
3 P.M.	6.13	6.16	6.14	6.13	6.13	6.14	0.03

Filling Head 4
Measurement

Time	1	2	3	4	5	$\bar{x}$	R
8 A.M.	6.16	6.16	6.17	6.17	6.17	6.17	0.01
9 A.M.	6.20	6.20	6.20	6.17	6.17	6.19	0.03
10 A.M.	6.16	6.16	6.19	6.19	6.21	6.18	0.05
11 A.M.	6.20	6.18	6.21	6.21	6.20	6.20	0.03
12 NOON	6.17	6.18	6.18	6.18	6.17	6.18	0.01
1 P.M.	6.19	6.21	6.21	6.19	6.16	6.19	0.05
2 P.M.	6.15	6.15	6.16	6.16	6.14	6.15	0.02
3 P.M.	6.18	6.19	6.20	6.19	6.21	6.19	0.03

FIGURE 8.13
Minitab
Control
Chart for
Arrangement 3

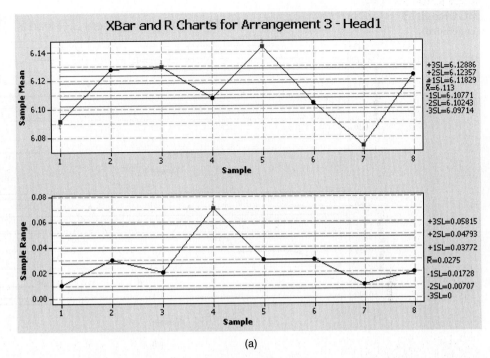

(a)

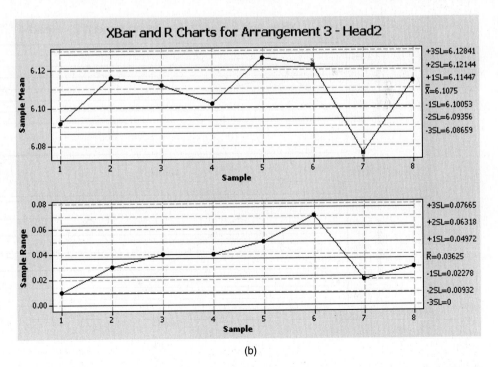

(b)

(continued)

FIGURE 8.13
(concluded)

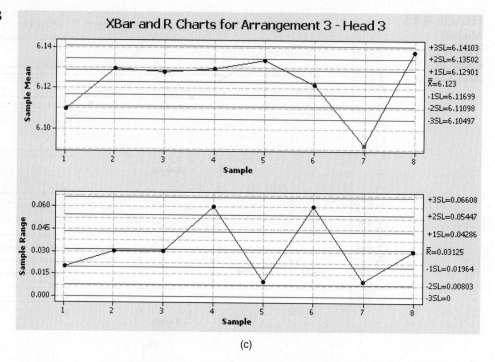

(c)

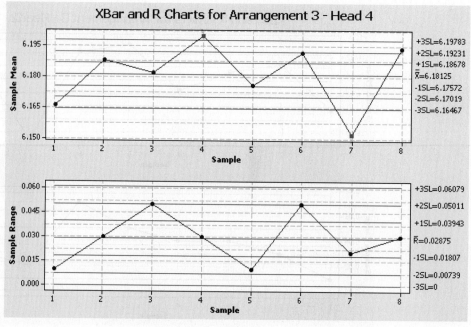

(d)

Thus, proper subgrouping of the data to be control charted is critical to process improvement efforts. Knowledge of the process under study is often the best guide to rational subgrouping of data.

Summary

Variables data consist of numerical measurements such as weight, length, width, height, time, temperature, and electrical resistance. Variables data contain more information than attribute data, which either classify a process's output as conforming or nonconforming, or count the number of imperfections. Furthermore, because variables control charts deal with measurements themselves, they do not mask valuable information and therefore are more powerful than attribute charts. They use all the information contained in the data; this alone makes variables charts preferable when a choice is possible.

There are three principal types of variables control charts: the $\bar{x}$ and R chart, the $\bar{x}$ and s chart, and the individuals and moving range chart. All are used in the never-ending spiral of process improvement.

The following flowchart presents a pictorial view of the different types of variables control charts in relation to subgroup size.

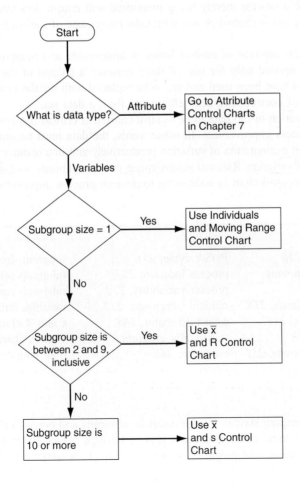

The $\bar{x}$ and R chart uses the subgroup range, R, to chart the process variability, and the subgroup average, $\bar{x}$, to chart the process location when subgroups consist of between two and nine measurements. Stable processes yield subgroups that will behave predictably, enabling us to construct an $\bar{x}$ and R chart.

$\bar{x}$ and s charts use the standard deviation to chart the process variability, and the subgroup average, $\bar{x}$, to chart the process location when subgroups consist of 10 or more observations.

Individuals and moving range charts are used when only a single variable value is measured per subgroup. Single measurements of variables are considered a subgroup of size one.

In general, subgroups should be large enough to detect points or patterns indicating a lack of control when a lack of control exists. Subgroups of two or three are used when the cost of sampling is relatively high. Subgroups of 6 to 14 are used when we want a control chart to be very sensitive to changes in the process average.

For an individuals chart to be reliable, it is best to have at least 100 subgroups, whereas 25 will suffice for most other control charts.

The frequency with which subgroups are selected depends upon the particular application. If quick action is required, the subgroups should be selected more often. On the other hand, a stable process merely being monitored will require less frequent subgroup selection than one being studied or being brought into a state of statistical control for the first time.

Frequent regular revision of control limits is undesirable and inappropriate. Control limits should be revised only for one of three reasons: a change in the process; when trial control limits have been used and are to be replaced with regular control limits; and when points out of control have been eliminated from a data set.

Proper organization of the data to be control charted is critical if a control chart is to be helpful in process improvement. In other words, the data must be organized in such a way as to permit examination of variation productively and in a manner that will reveal special sources of variation. Rational subgrouping, or the organization of the data, defines the question the control chart is addressing to achieve process improvement.

Key Terms

Empirical Rule, *256*	PDSA cycle, *251*	subgroup frequency, *254*
individuals and moving range chart, *253*	process location, *252*	subgroup selection, *252*
	process variability, *252*	subgroup size, *253*
inflated control limits, *278*	rational subgroups, *252*	variables data, *251*
measurement data, *251*	robust estimator, *268*	$\bar{x}$ and R chart, *254*
median range, *278*	statistically efficient estimator, *268*	$\bar{x}$ and s chart, *254*
operational definitions, *252*		zone boundaries, *257*

Exercises

8.1. The housekeeping staff in a large resort hotel cleans and prepares all of the guest-rooms daily. In an effort to improve service through reducing variation in the time required to clean and prepare a room, a series of measurements is taken of the times to service rooms in one section of the hotel. The cleaning times for five rooms for 25 consecutive days are shown below, in minutes (see 🐾 HOTEL):

Cleaning and Preparation Time

Room	Day 1	Day 2	Day 3	Day 4	Day 5	Day 6	Day 7	Day 8	Day 9	Day 10
1	15.6	15.0	16.4	14.2	16.4	14.9	17.9	14.0	17.6	14.6
2	14.3	14.8	15.1	14.8	16.3	17.2	17.9	17.7	16.5	14.0
3	17.7	16.8	15.7	17.3	17.6	17.2	14.7	16.9	15.3	14.7
4	14.3	16.9	17.3	15.0	17.9	15.3	17.0	14.0	14.5	16.9
5	15.0	17.4	16.6	16.4	14.9	14.1	14.5	14.9	15.1	14.2

Room	Day 11	Day 12	Day 13	Day 14	Day 15	Day 16	Day 17	Day 18	Day 19	Day 20
1	14.6	15.3	17.4	15.3	14.8	16.1	14.2	14.6	15.9	16.2
2	15.5	15.3	14.9	16.9	15.1	14.6	14.7	17.2	16.5	14.8
3	15.9	15.9	17.7	17.9	16.6	17.5	15.3	16.0	16.1	14.8
4	14.8	15.0	16.6	17.2	16.3	16.9	15.7	16.7	15.0	15.0
5	14.2	17.8	14.7	17.5	14.5	17.7	14.3	16.3	17.8	15.3

Room	Day 21	Day 22	Day 23	Day 24	Day 25
1	16.3	15.0	16.4	16.6	17.0
2	15.3	17.6	15.9	15.1	17.5
3	14.0	14.5	16.7	14.1	17.4
4	17.4	17.5	15.7	17.4	16.2
5	14.5	17.8	16.9	17.8	17.9

a. Construct a control chart for the data above. Use zone boundaries.

b. Is the process in control? If not, when does the out-of-control behavior occur?

c. Drop the out-of-control points (assuming you have discovered any and changed the process to resolve the special causes) and recompute the control chart. Is the process now in control? If not, when does the out-of-control behavior occur?

8.2. A parcel-sorting facility's management wants to know how much time is needed to sort units in what is termed the primary sort. The variable to be measured is the number of units sorted in a one-minute interval by a given team. Each hour, the first five one-minute intervals are selected (see ☞ SORTED). The results are shown below:

Number of Units Sorted

Subgroup Number	Observation				
	1	2	3	4	5
1	474	386	528	333	465
2	688	367	691	602	569
3	427	500	279	479	721
4	846	506	420	509	409
5	384	365	884	521	562
6	774	889	326	581	270
7	728	902	809	468	318
8	682	614	315	688	594
9	401	418	429	722	781
10	613	394	421	684	675
11	874	546	804	709	469
12	409	591	665	685	540
13	748	818	694	481	290
14	790	796	705	503	710
15	227	409	621	495	891
16	588	789	344	785	724
17	725	802	336	645	782
18	671	691	735	351	853
19	778	795	462	301	549
20	366	691	644	547	705

a. Construct a control chart for the data above. Use zone boundaries.

b. Is the process in control? If not, when does the out-of-control behavior occur?

c. Drop the out-of-control points (assuming you have discovered any and changed the process to resolve the special causes) and recompute the control chart. Is the process now in control? If not, when does the out-of-control behavior occur?

8.3. The drive-up window at a local bank is searching for ways to improve service. One teller keeps a control chart for the service time in minutes for the first four customers driving up to her window each hour for a three-day period (see TELLERTIME). The results of her data collection are shown below:

Drive-Up Teller Service Times

Cust.	9 A.M.	10 A.M.	11 A.M.	12	1 P.M.	2 P.M.	3 P.M.	4 P.M.
				Time				
1	1.4	3.8	3.6	4.3	4.0	1.3	0.9	4.7
2	2.3	5.2	2.5	1.2	5.2	1.1	4.4	5.1
3	1.9	1.9	0.8	3.0	2.7	4.9	5.1	0.9
4	5.1	4.8	2.9	1.5	0.3	2.3	4.6	4.7

Cust.	9 A.M.	10 A.M.	11 A.M.	12	1 P.M.	2 P.M.	3 P.M.	4 P.M.
				Time				
1	2.8	0.5	4.5	0.6	4.8	2.7	4.2	0.9
2	3.0	2.7	1.9	1.2	2.8	2.0	1.1	4.4
3	4.1	4.7	4.2	2.7	1.1	2.6	4.4	0.6
4	4.8	3.6	0.4	2.5	0.4	2.6	3.1	0.4

Cust.	9 A.M.	10 A.M.	11 A.M.	12	1 P.M.	2 P.M.	3 P.M.	4 P.M.
				Time				
1	0.3	3.5	5.2	2.9	3.3	4.0	2.8	0.6
2	2.4	3.4	0.3	1.9	3.7	3.3	0.7	2.1
3	5.0	4.6	2.4	0.8	3.8	5.0	1.6	3.3
4	0.9	3.3	3.9	0.3	2.1	2.8	4.6	2.7

a. Construct a control chart for the data above. Use zone boundaries.

b. Is the process in control? If not, when does the out-of-control behavior occur?

c. Drop the out-of-control points (assuming you have discovered any and changed the process to resolve the special causes) and recompute the control chart. Is the process now in control? If not, when does the out-of-control behavior occur?

8.4. A paper products manufacturer coats one particular paper product with wax. In an effort to control and stabilize the coating process, the employee running the coating machine takes six measurements of coating thickness every 15 minutes during a one-day study period. The results of the data collection are shown below:

Coating Thickness

					Time				
	8 A.M.	8:15	8:30	8:45	9 A.M.	9:15	9:30	9:45	10 A.M.
x̄	2.90	3.30	2.87	0.93	1.43	1.93	2.90	3.03	3.70
R	0.35	0.50	0.32	0.44	0.91	0.42	0.29	0.78	1.01

					Time				
	10:15	10:30	10:45	11 A.M.	11:15	11:30	11:45	12 NOON	12:15
x̄	3.70	3.00	3.20	2.80	2.90	3.53	3.90	3.73	3.23
R	1.09	0.95	0.56	0.42	0.55	0.16	1.04	0.90	0.86

					Time				
	12:30	12:45	1 P.M.	1:15	1:30	1:45	2 P.M.	2:15	2:30
x̄	2.73	3.00	3.33	2.50	2.13	1.97	2.70	3.10	2.63
R	0.19	0.84	0.20	0.71	0.90	0.92	1.00	0.56	0.88

				Time		
	2:45	3 P.M.	3:15	3:30	3:45	4 P.M.
x̄	2.63	3.40	3.20	2.20	2.03	3.23
R	0.89	1.06	0.66	0.93	0.59	0.91

a. Construct a control chart for the data above. Use zone boundaries.

b. Is the process in control? If not, when does the out-of-control behavior occur?

8.5. Groups of customers arriving at a restaurant must wait to be seated by a hostess. Waiting time is short if a table is available, but long if the restaurant is crowded. The hostess records waiting times for the first eight people arriving from 7:00 P.M. each Friday, Saturday, and Sunday evening for a series of 10 consecutive weeks. She then computes the average and range for each subgroup. The results of the data collection and calculations are shown below:

Waiting Times (minutes)

	Date									
	9/2	9/3	9/4	9/9	9/10	9/11	9/16	9/17	9/18	9/23
$\bar{x}$	15.5	23.0	18.0	11.5	12.0	12.3	15.5	13.5	21.5	12.2
R	5.1	6.2	2.6	2.4	4.8	2.6	2.8	4.0	4.8	1.8

	Date									
	9/24	9/25	9/30	10/1	10/2	10/7	10/8	10/9	10/14	10/15
$\bar{x}$	21.5	28.0	16.0	17.0	31.0	21.1	15.0	17.5	17.5	18.0
R	4.0	3.6	3.0	4.4	7.2	2.1	3.6	1.8	1.8	3.6

	Date									
	10/16	10/21	10/22	10/23	10/28	10/29	10/30	11/4	11/5	11/6
$\bar{x}$	17.5	20.2	26.0	17.0	19.0	20.0	16.0	18.0	18.5	19.5
R	3.6	4.8	5.6	3.4	3.4	3.6	3.2	3.8	3.4	3.6

a. Construct a control chart for the data above. Use zone boundaries.

b. Is the process in control? If not, when does the out-of-control behavior occur?

8.6. The production department of a newspaper has embarked upon a quality improvement effort. After several brainstorming sessions, the team has chosen as its first project an issue that relates to the blackness of the print of the newspaper: each day a determination needs to be made concerning how "black" the newspaper print is. This is measured on a densitometer that records the results on a standard scale. Each day, five spots on the first newspaper printed are chosen and the blackness of each spot is measured. The results for 20 consecutive weekdays are presented in the table below (see ☛ BLACK):

Day	_____ Spot _____				
	1	2	3	4	5
1	0.96	1.01	1.12	1.07	0.97
2	1.06	1.00	1.02	1.16	0.96
3	1.00	0.90	0.98	1.18	0.96
4	0.92	0.89	1.01	1.16	0.90
5	1.02	1.16	1.03	0.89	1.00
6	0.88	0.92	1.03	1.16	0.91
7	1.05	1.13	1.01	0.93	1.03
8	0.95	0.86	1.14	0.90	0.95
9	0.99	0.89	1.00	1.15	0.92
10	0.89	1.18	1.03	0.96	1.04
11	0.97	1.13	0.95	0.86	1.06
12	1.00	0.87	1.02	0.98	1.13
13	0.96	0.79	1.17	0.97	0.95
14	1.03	0.89	1.03	1.12	1.03
15	0.96	1.12	0.95	0.88	0.99
16	1.01	0.87	0.99	1.04	1.16
17	0.98	0.85	0.99	1.04	1.16
18	1.03	0.82	1.21	0.98	1.08
19	1.02	0.84	1.15	0.94	1.08
20	0.90	1.02	1.10	1.04	1.08

a. Construct a control chart for the data above. Use zone boundaries.

b. Is the process in control? If not, when does the out-of-control behavior occur?

c. Drop the out-of-control points (assuming you have discovered any and changed the process to resolve the special causes) and recompute the control chart. Is the process now in control? If not, when does the out-of-control behavior occur?

8.7. The manager of a branch of a local bank wants to study waiting times of customers for teller service during the peak 12 noon to 1 P.M. lunch hour. A subgroup of four customers is selected (one at each 15-minute interval during the hour), and the time in minutes is measured from the point each customer enters the line to when his or her service begins. The results over a 4-week period are as follows (see ☚ BANKTIME):

Day	Time in Minutes			
1	7.2	8.4	7.9	4.9
2	5.6	8.7	3.3	4.2
3	5.5	7.3	3.2	6.0
4	4.4	8.0	5.4	7.4
5	9.7	4.6	4.8	5.8
6	8.3	8.9	9.1	6.2
7	4.7	6.6	5.3	5.8
8	8.8	5.5	8.4	6.9
9	5.7	4.7	4.1	4.6
10	1.7	4.0	3.0	5.2
11	2.6	3.9	5.2	4.8
12	4.6	2.7	6.3	3.4
13	4.9	6.2	7.8	8.7
14	7.1	6.3	8.2	5.5
15	7.1	5.8	6.9	7.0
16	6.7	6.9	7.0	9.4
17	5.5	6.3	3.2	4.9
18	4.9	5.1	3.2	7.6
19	7.2	8.0	4.1	5.9
20	6.1	3.4	7.2	5.9

a. Construct a control chart for the data above. Use zone boundaries.

b. Is the process in control? If not, when does the out-of-control behavior occur?

c. Drop the out-of-control points (assuming you have discovered any and changed the process to resolve the special causes) and recompute the control chart. Is the process now in control? If not, when does the out-of-control behavior occur?

8.8. The Director of Radiology at a large metropolitan hospital is concerned about the scheduling of the radiology facilities. 250 patients per day, on average, are transported from wards to the Radiology department for treatment or diagnostic procedures. If patients do not reach their radiology unit at their scheduled time, backups will occur and other patients will experience delays. The time it takes to transport patients from wards to the radiology unit was operationally defined as the time between when the transporter was assigned to the patient and the time the patient arrived at the radiology unit. A sample of $n = 4$ patients was selected each day for 20 days and the time to transport each patient (in minutes) was measured, with the following results (see ☀ TRANSPORT):

		Patient		
Day	1	2	3	4
1	16.3	17.4	18.7	16.9
2	29.4	17.3	22.7	10.9
3	12.2	12.7	14.1	10.3
4	22.4	19.7	24.9	23.4
5	13.5	11.6	14.8	13.5
6	15.2	23.6	19.4	20.0
7	23.1	13.6	21.1	13.7
8	15.7	10.9	16.4	21.8
9	10.2	14.9	12.6	11.9
10	14.7	18.7	22.0	19.1
11	15.6	19.1	22.9	19.4
12	19.8	12.2	26.7	19.0
13	24.3	18.7	30.3	22.9
14	16.5	14.3	19.5	15.5
15	23.4	27.6	30.7	24.0
16	9.7	14.6	10.4	10.8
17	27.8	18.4	23.7	22.8
18	17.4	25.8	18.4	9.0
19	20.5	17.8	23.2	18.0
20	14.2	14.6	11.1	17.7

a. Construct a control chart for the data above. Use zone boundaries.

b. Is the process in control? If not, when does the out-of-control behavior occur?

c. Drop the out-of-control points (assuming you have discovered any and changed the process to resolve the special causes) and recompute the control chart. Is the process now in control? If not, when does the out-of-control behavior occur?

8.9. The Telecommunications department for a county General Services Agency is responsible for the repair of equipment used in radio communications by police, fire, and emergency medical services in the county. The timely repair of the radios is critically important for the efficient operation of these public service units. The following table shows the repair times in minutes for a daily sample of five radios taken over a 30-day period (see ☛ RADIO):

	Radio				
Day	1	2	3	4	5
1	114	499	106	342	55
2	219	319	162	44	87
3	64	302	38	83	93
4	258	110	98	78	154
5	127	140	298	518	275
6	151	176	188	268	77
7	24	183	202	81	104
8	41	249	342	338	69
9	93	189	209	444	151
10	111	207	143	318	129
11	205	281	250	468	79
12	121	261	183	606	287
13	225	83	198	223	180
14	235	439	102	330	190
15	91	32	190	70	150
16	181	191	182	444	124
17	52	190	310	245	156
18	90	538	277	308	171
19	78	587	147	172	299
20	45	265	126	137	151
21	410	227	179	298	342
22	68	375	195	67	72
23	140	266	157	92	140
24	145	170	231	60	191
25	129	74	148	119	139
26	143	384	263	147	131
27	86	229	474	181	40
28	164	313	295	297	280
29	257	310	217	152	351
30	106	134	175	153	69

a. Construct a control chart for the data above. Use zone boundaries.

b. Is the process in control? If not, when does the out-of-control behavior occur?

c. Drop the out-of-control points (assuming you have discovered any and changed the process to resolve the special causes) and recompute the control chart. Is the process now in control? If not, when does the out-of-control behavior occur?

8.10. The workers in a packaging operation shovel 30 kilograms of a granular product from a large pile into sacks that are then sealed and placed on pallets for shipping. The scale used by the workers is accurate, and an effort has been made to educate the workers about the need to measure each weight carefully. A sequence of 25 subgroups, each consisting of the weights of five sacks, has been recorded (see ☛ PACKAGING).

Weight (kilograms)

Subgroup Number	Observation				
	1	2	3	4	5
1	35.4	35.6	34.8	34.7	34.8
2	36.0	35.6	34.9	34.8	35.9
3	35.2	35.0	35.0	35.4	35.1
4	34.8	35.8	35.2	35.0	34.9
5	34.2	35.0	36.1	34.9	35.1
6	36.0	35.0	35.2	34.8	34.9
7	36.1	34.9	34.5	35.0	35.1
8	35.1	35.0	35.6	34.9	36.2
9	35.0	35.6	36.1	34.8	35.6
10	35.4	35.8	36.0	34.2	36.0
11	35.2	35.3	35.2	35.9	34.8
12	35.9	36.0	35.1	35.1	35.6
13	35.2	35.6	35.0	34.9	35.0
14	35.2	35.6	35.8	35.0	35.1
15	34.9	34.8	35.0	35.2	34.9
16	35.2	35.3	35.2	35.6	35.1
17	35.6	35.8	35.2	35.4	34.9
18	35.2	35.6	35.4	35.6	35.2
19	34.7	34.9	35.6	35.2	35.0
20	35.0	35.1	35.6	35.0	35.1
21	35.6	35.0	35.8	35.2	34.6
22	34.9	35.1	35.6	35.0	35.2
23	35.9	36.0	35.2	36.0	35.2
24	35.2	35.1	35.4	34.9	35.1
25	35.2	35.2	35.1	35.6	34.9

a. Construct a control chart for the data above. Use zone boundaries.

b. Is the process in control? If not, when does the out-of-control behavior occur?

c. Drop the out-of-control points (assuming you have discovered any and changed the process to resolve the special causes) and recompute the control chart. Is the process now in control? If not, when does the out-of-control behavior occur?

8.11. A hospital administrator is studying how long an emergency room patient waits to see a physician during the midnight to 8:00 A.M. shift. The study is limited to those patients who actually do see a physician, and the length of waiting time has been carefully operationally defined. Each day, the first 15 records are studied, with the results shown below (see ✿ ERWAIT):

Waiting Time (minutes)

Day 1	Day 2	Day 3	Day 4	Day 5	Day 6	Day 7	Day 8
2	26	19	24	40	31	39	16
32	2	18	33	22	13	41	24
8	40	15	46	23	15	8	27
30	17	18	20	40	4	37	17
38	12	18	32	34	35	17	13
24	14	18	5	7	40	48	30
31	9	44	48	23	41	36	44
46	45	3	20	37	39	32	23
49	13	28	39	31	31	40	50
32	43	47	2	48	17	30	41
32	42	44	16	23	18	38	18
10	33	3	12	45	32	22	14
43	7	13	36	15	8	1	30
27	4	37	47	43	30	33	9
41	34	5	40	5	28	13	44

a. Construct a control chart for the data above. Use zone boundaries.

b. Is the process in control? If not, when does the out-of-control behavior occur?

c. Drop the out-of-control points (assuming you have discovered any and changed the process to resolve the special causes) and recompute the control chart. Is the process now in control? If not, when does the out-of-control behavior occur?

8.12. The food services director of an airline wants to measure the weight of food left over on passenger food trays to measure the difference between product performance and customer expectations. Each day, 12 of the trays returned in the main cabin on a particular flight are set aside, placed into a special container, and sent to a lab for weighing. The average and standard deviation of each of these subgroups over a period of 25 days is as follows:

Weight of Leftovers (grams)

					Day					
	1	2	3	4	5	6	7	8	9	10
$\bar{x}$	44.5	61.5	66.6	64.9	22.9	12.7	44.2	10.4	82.6	55.2
s	23.5	11.2	28.6	31.9	13.3	12.5	32.8	35.1	39.1	10.9

					Day					
	11	12	13	14	15	16	17	18	19	20
$\bar{x}$	92.9	25.5	92.9	27.5	84.8	82.2	24.7	25.8	79.7	19.5
s	35.5	38.3	27.5	21.3	22.5	35.2	20.7	19.4	14.7	23.5

			Day		
	21	22	23	24	25
$\bar{x}$	10.9	47.5	72.2	28.6	90.0
s	36.7	28.6	25.9	22.7	23.4

a. Construct a control chart for the data above. Use zone boundaries.

b. Is the process in control? If not, when does the out-of-control behavior occur?

8.13. A hospital is studying the length of time patients spend in their routine admitting procedure. Samples of 12 are selected each day for a 20-day period. Admitting time (which has been carefully operationally defined) is measured in seconds, with the following subgroup results (see ☛ ADMITTING):

Admitting Time (seconds)

Day 1	Day 2	Day 3	Day 4	Day 5	Day 6	Day 7	Day 8	Day 9	Day 10
362	611	320	621	680	759	372	370	530	494
468	873	944	927	794	665	835	294	881	914
553	768	593	948	650	730	884	480	943	870
390	807	857	817	780	930	930	558	383	272
460	476	710	641	442	369	667	502	316	662
910	816	724	764	372	635	747	595	611	348
707	567	545	986	627	313	390	847	778	447
829	833	526	430	882	843	644	544	531	306
955	521	348	743	756	264	339	853	896	751
705	959	456	451	548	663	664	876	772	415
884	315	576	645	767	991	245	744	719	717
904	414	855	996	745	431	893	816	670	387

Day 11	Day 12	Day 13	Day 14	Day 15	Day 16	Day 17	Day 18	Day 19	Day 20
659	274	797	678	997	242	594	368	806	497
919	754	253	679	205	474	817	850	575	785
603	428	829	351	893	966	381	510	348	806
897	811	857	663	734	823	462	688	298	263
319	916	898	638	474	515	429	201	487	435
499	332	387	928	631	617	786	795	697	337
799	765	918	258	746	894	901	977	249	659
482	961	900	338	642	519	278	715	668	537
615	437	691	446	484	636	472	253	533	786
497	692	600	936	525	547	885	310	985	607
430	380	450	584	685	993	991	412	284	466
765	566	775	535	358	858	557	813	707	564

a. Construct a control chart for the data above. Use zone boundaries.

b. Is the process in control? If not, when does the out-of-control behavior occur?

c. Drop the out-of-control points (assuming you have discovered any and changed the process to resolve the special causes) and recompute the control chart. Is the process now in control? If not, when does the out-of-control behavior occur?

8.14. Specifications for toothpaste call for the amount of active ingredient in each sample to be 7.20 ± 0.08 milligrams. Ten samples are drawn each day and the amount of active ingredient in each sample is determined. The table below shows the mean amount and the standard deviation for 30 samples:

Day	Mean	Standard Deviation
1	7.14	0.163
2	7.14	0.117
3	7.21	0.057
4	7.18	0.162
5	7.14	0.117
6	7.22	0.092
7	7.13	0.074
8	7.20	0.067
9	7.26	0.052
10	7.20	0.082
11	7.25	0.053
12	7.17	0.134
13	7.25	0.071
14	7.24	0.084
15	7.19	0.099
16	7.16	0.126
17	7.21	0.089
18	7.24	0.097
19	7.17	0.142
20	7.16	0.143
21	7.25	0.071
22	7.15	0.127
23	7.19	0.159
24	7.13	0.082
25	7.25	0.097
26	7.18	0.103
27	7.24	0.084
28	7.19	0.088
29	7.24	0.097
30	7.26	0.107

a. Construct a control chart for the data above. Use zone boundaries.

b. Is the process in control? If not, when does the out-of-control behavior occur?

c. Drop the out-of-control points (assuming you have discovered any and changed the process to resolve the special causes) and recompute the control chart. Is the process now in control? If not, when does the out-of-control behavior occur?

8.15. A manufacturer of a special chemical fertilizer is concerned with the pH of finished batches of product. A series of careful measurements reveals (see ➤ PH):

Batch	pH	Batch	pH	Batch	pH	Batch	pH
1	6.5	26	6.1	51	6.6	76	6.4
2	6.2	27	6.8	52	6.1	77	6.7
3	6.7	28	6.6	53	6.3	78	6.4
4	6.7	29	6.4	54	6.8	79	6.2
5	6.2	30	6.0	55	6.3	80	6.1
6	6.1	31	6.5	56	6.7	81	6.4
7	6.8	32	6.0	57	6.1	82	6.2
8	6.4	33	6.5	58	6.6	83	6.7
9	6.0	34	6.8	59	6.6	84	6.5
10	6.6	35	6.2	60	6.6	85	6.8
11	6.7	36	6.0	61	6.7	86	6.2
12	6.9	37	6.6	62	6.2	87	6.7
13	6.2	38	6.3	63	6.5	88	6.5
14	6.9	39	6.2	64	6.0	89	6.1
15	6.1	40	6.7	65	6.8	90	6.5
16	6.5	41	6.2	66	6.2	91	6.7
17	6.3	42	6.4	67	6.0	92	6.0
18	6.2	43	6.3	68	6.1	93	6.0
19	6.9	44	6.7	69	6.8	94	6.6
20	6.6	45	6.1	70	6.7	95	6.2
21	6.7	46	6.3	71	6.8	96	6.4
22	6.6	47	6.0	72	6.3	97	6.1
23	6.3	48	6.6	73	6.6	98	6.5
24	6.6	49	6.8	74	6.3	99	6.1
25	6.2	50	6.5	75	6.6	100	6.9

a. Construct a control chart for the data above. Use zone boundaries.

b. Is the process in control? If not, when does the out-of-control behavior occur?

c. Do the control limits appear inflated? Explain.

d. Drop the out-of-control points (assuming you have discovered any and changed the process to resolve the special causes) and recompute the control chart. Is the process now in control? If not, when does the out-of-control behavior occur?

8.16. A small independent public water utility in the San Francisco area monitored daily usage of water (1 unit = 748,000 gallons) for a period of 10 weeks (Monday to Friday only) during September, October, and November in a recent year. The following table shows the daily water usage for 50 weekdays (see ☛ WATER). Records show that on day 5 a water main broke and a major leak occurred. No other anomalies were recorded.

Day	Water Usage	Day	Water Usage
1	2.50	26	2.39
2	2.67	27	3.51
3	2.73	28	2.23
4	2.64	29	2.55
5	4.45	30	2.64
6	2.74	31	2.58
7	3.31	32	2.98
8	2.49	33	2.43
9	2.76	34	2.39
10	2.63	35	3.22
11	2.47	36	2.33
12	2.59	37	2.27
13	3.20	38	2.30
14	3.02	39	2.29
15	2.31	40	2.20
16	2.30	41	3.31
17	2.50	42	3.45
18	3.31	43	3.23
19	2.48	44	2.29
20	2.22	45	2.33
21	2.61	46	2.34
22	2.64	47	3.31
23	2.92	48	2.31
24	2.10	49	2.64
25	3.18	50	2.24

a. Construct a control chart for the data above. Use zone boundaries.

b. Is the process in control? If not, when does the out-of-control behavior occur?

c. Drop the out-of-control points (assuming you have discovered any and changed the process to resolve the special causes) and recompute the control chart. Is the process now in control? If not, when does the out-of-control behavior occur?

8.17. One of the important quality characteristics of paste ink used in lithographic print-ing presses is viscosity. For ink to flow properly through the press and be applied to the paper, it must be within a limited range of viscosity. If the viscosity is too high, the ink will not flow through the press fast enough, while too low a viscos-ity value will result in too much ink flowing through the press. Either of these conditions will adversely affect the quality of the printed material. A viscosity measure is taken at the end of production of each batch of ink. Viscosity measures for 50 consecutive batches are shown below (see 🖭 PASTEINK):

Sample	Viscosity	Sample	Viscosity
1	305	26	291
2	274	27	301
3	290	28	290
4	314	29	290
5	291	30	308
6	315	31	306
7	301	32	292
8	298	33	279
9	306	34	276
10	305	35	285
11	270	36	296
12	296	37	275
13	307	38	299
14	284	39	301
15	280	40	294
16	264	41	312
17	299	42	289
18	270	43	278
19	275	44	288
20	276	45	299
21	294	46	270
22	313	47	308
23	304	48	298
24	310	49	294
25	271	50	306

a. Construct a control chart for the data above. Use zone boundaries.

b. Is the process in control? If not, when does the out-of-control behavior occur?

c. Drop the out-of-control points (assuming you have discovered any and changed the process to resolve the special causes) and recompute the control chart. Is the process now in control? If not, when does the out-of-control behavior occur?

8.18. The following data represent the amount of soft drink filled in a subgroup of 50 consecutive two-liter bottles. The nominal fill amount is 2.0 liters ± 0.11 liters. The results, listed horizontally in the order of being filled, were (see ✱ DRINK):

2.109	2.086	2.066	2.075	2.065
2.057	2.052	2.044	2.036	2.038
2.031	2.029	2.025	2.029	2.023
2.020	2.015	2.014	2.013	2.014
2.012	2.012	2.012	2.010	2.005
2.003	1.999	1.996	1.997	1.992
1.994	1.986	1.984	1.981	1.973
1.975	1.971	1.969	1.966	1.967
1.963	1.957	1.951	1.951	1.947
1.941	1.941	1.938	1.908	1.894

a. Construct a control chart for the data above. Use zone boundaries.

b. Is the process in control? If not, when does the out-of-control behavior occur?

c. Drop the out-of-control points (assuming you have discovered any and changed the process to resolve the special causes) and recompute the control chart. Is the process now in control? If not, when does the out-of-control behavior occur?

References

1. W. A. Shewhart (1931), *Economic Control of Quality of Manufactured Product* (New York: D. Van Nostrand).
2. Donald J. Wheeler and David S. Chambers (1986), *Understanding Statistical Process Control* (Knoxville, TN: Statistical Process Controls).

Appendix **A8.1**

Using Minitab for Variables Charts[1]

Using Minitab for the $\bar{x}$ and R Charts

$\bar{x}$ and R charts can be obtained from Minitab by selecting **Stat | Control Charts | Variable Charts for Subgroups | $\bar{x}$-R** from the menu bar. The format for entering the variable name depends on whether the data are stacked down a single column or unstacked across a set of columns with the data for each time period in a single row. If the data for the variable of interest are stacked down a single column, choose Single Column in the Data are arranged as drop-down list box and enter the variable name in the edit box below. If the subgroups are unstacked with each row representing the data for a single

[1] The instructions and dialog boxes are based on the beta version of Minitab 14. Subsequent versions of Minitab may differ slightly from what is presented in this appendix.

time period, choose Subgroups as rows in the Data are arranged as drop-down list box and enter the variable names for the data in the edit box below.

To illustrate how to obtain $\bar{x}$ and R charts, refer to the data of Table 8.1 on page 255 concerning the weight of vials. Open the 🐾 **VIALS.MTW** worksheet.

1. Select **Stat | Control Charts | Variable Charts for Subgroups | $\bar{x}$-R.** In the Xbar-R Chart-Data Source Chart dialog box, as shown in Figure A8.1, enter **C3** or **1, C4** or **2, C5** or **3, C6** or **4, C7** or **5,** and **C8** or **6** in the edit box. Click the Xbar-R Options button.
2. In the Xbar-R Chart Options dialog box, click on the Tests tab, as shown in Figure A8.2. Select the **Perform all tests** option button. Click the **OK** button to return to the Xbar-R Data Source Chart dialog box. These values will stay intact until Minitab is restarted.

**FIGURE
A8.1**
Minitab
$\bar{x}$-R Data
Source Chart
Dialog Box

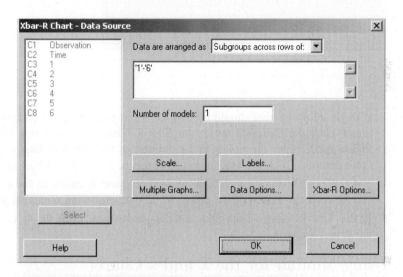

**FIGURE
A8.2**
Minitab
$\bar{x}$-R Chart
Options Dialog
Box, Tests Tab

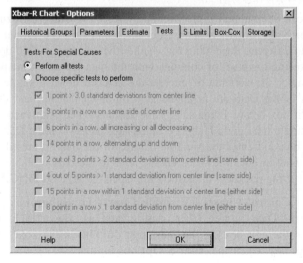

FIGURE A8.3

Minitab $\bar{x}$-R Chart Options Dialog Box, Estimate Tab

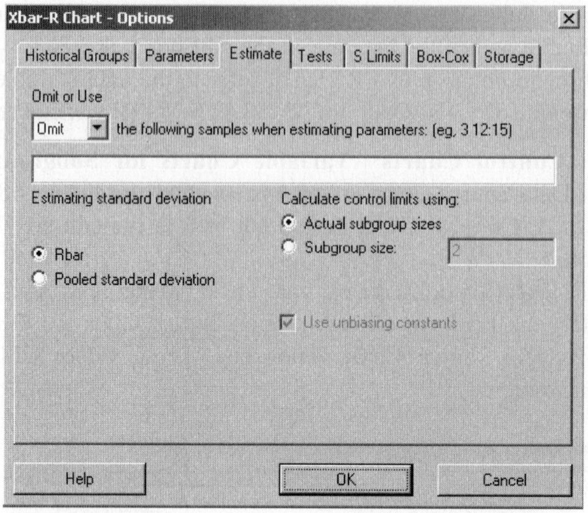

3. If there are points that should be omitted when estimating the centerline and control limits, click the **Estimate** tab in the Xbar-R Chart Options dialog box, as shown in Figure A8.3. Enter the points to be omitted in the edit box shown. Click the Rbar option button. Click the **OK** button to return to the Xbar-R Chart dialog box.

4. Note: When obtaining more than one set of $\bar{x}$ and R charts in the same session, be sure to reset the values of the points to be omitted before obtaining new charts.

5. In the Xbar-R Chart—Data Source Chart dialog box, click the **OK** button to obtain the R and $\bar{x}$ charts.

Using Minitab for the $\bar{x}$ and s Charts

$\bar{x}$ and s charts can be obtained from Minitab by selecting **Stat | Control Charts | Variable Charts for Subgroups | Xbar-S** from the menu bar. The format for entering the variable name is different, depending on whether the data are stacked down a single column or unstacked across a set of columns with the data for each time period in a single row. If the data for the variable of interest are stacked down a single column, choose Single Column in the Data are arranged as drop-down list box and enter the variable name in the edit box below. If the subgroups are unstacked with each row representing the data for a single time period, choose Subgroups as rows in the Data are arranged as drop-down list box and enter the variable names for the data in the edit box below.

To illustrate how to obtain $\bar{x}$ and s charts, refer to the data of Table 8.4 on page 272 concerning the coating thickness of plastic film. Open the ✿ **COATING.MTW** worksheet.

1. Select **Stat | Control Charts | Variable Charts for Subgroups | Xbar-S.** In the Xbar-S Chart—Data Source Chart dialog box, as shown in Figure A8.4, enter **Thickness** in the edit box. In the Subgroup drop-down list box, select **Size.** Enter **10** in the edit box. Click the **Xbar-S Options** button.

FIGURE A8.4
Minitab x̄-s Data Source Chart Dialog Box

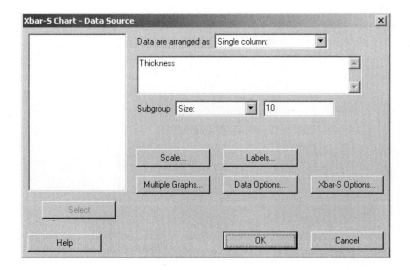

2. In the Xbar-S Chart Options dialog box, click on the Tests tab. Select the **Perform all tests** option button. Click the **OK** button to return to the Xbar-S Data Source Chart dialog box. These values will stay intact until Minitab is restarted.

3. If there are points that should be omitted when estimating the centerline and control limits, click the **Estimate** tab in the Xbar-S Chart Options dialog box. Enter the points to be omitted in the edit box shown. Click the Sbar option button. Click the **OK** button to return to the Xbar-S Chart dialog box.

4. Note: When obtaining more than one set of s and x̄ charts in the same session, be sure to reset the values of the points to be omitted before obtaining new charts.

5. In the Xbar-S Chart—Data Source Chart dialog box, click the **OK** button to obtain the s and x̄ charts.

Using Minitab for the Individuals and Moving Range Charts

Individuals and moving range charts can be obtained from Minitab by selecting **Stat | Control Charts | Variable Charts for Individuals | I-MR** from the menu bar. To illustrate how to obtain Individuals and Moving Range charts, refer to the data of Table 8.5 on page 276 concerning the density of a liquid. Open the ✿ **DENSITY.MTW** worksheet.

1. Select **Stat | Control Charts | Variable Charts for Individuals | I-MR.** In the Individuals-Moving Range Chart—Data Source Chart dialog box (see Figure A8.5) enter **Density** in the variables edit box. Click the **I-MR Options** button.

2. In the I-MR Chart Options dialog box, click on the Tests tab. Select the **Choose specific tests to perform** option button. Select the **1 point > 3 standard deviations from center line** check box. Click the **OK** button to return to the Xbar-S Data Source Chart dialog box. These values will stay intact until Minitab is restarted.

FIGURE A8.5
Minitab I-MR Data Source Chart Dialog Box

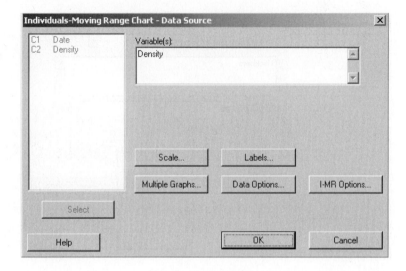

3. If there are points that should be omitted when estimating the centerline and control limits, click the **Estimate** tab in the I-MR Chart Options dialog box. Enter the points to be omitted in the edit box shown. Click the Average moving range option button. (If you prefer to use the Median moving range, click that option button.) Click the **OK** button to return to the I-MR Chart dialog box.

4. Note: When obtaining more than one set of Individuals and Moving Range charts in the same session, be sure to reset the values of the points to be omitted before obtaining new charts.

5. In the I-MR Chart—Data Source Chart dialog box, click the **OK** button to obtain the individuals and moving range charts.

Using Minitab to Obtain Zone Limits

To plot zone limits on any of the control charts discussed in this appendix, open to the initial dialog box for the control chart being developed and do the following:

1. Click the **Scale** button. Click the **Gridlines** tab. Select the **Y major ticks, Y minor ticks,** and **X major ticks** check boxes. Click the **OK** button to return to the previous dialog box.

2. Select the **Options** button. Select the **S limits** tab. In the Display control limits at these multiples of the standard deviation: edit box, enter **1 2 3**. Click the **OK** button to return to the Data Source dialog box.

Chapter 9

Out-of-Control Patterns

Sections

Chapter Objectives

- To define and illustrate two types of special variation: periodic (between-group) variation and persistent (within-group) variation
- To distinguish between within-group variation and common variation
- To discuss and illustrate characteristic control chart patterns, enabling the identification of special variation

Introduction

We have seen that a control chart highlights special (or assignable or exogenous) causes of variation, or special disturbances. Once detected, special causes can be resolved, leaving a stable process with only common (or endogenous) causes of variation. In this chapter, we present different control chart patterns that indicate the presence of these special causes.

Between- and Within-Group Variation

Special (or **assignable** or **exogenous**) **causes of variation** can be classified into two types: **periodic disturbances** and **persistent disturbances**.

Periodic Disturbances

Periodic disturbances create special causes of variation that intermittently affect a process. The intermittent nature of these causes tends to affect sampled observations separated in time and, hence, in different subgroups. This is called **between-group variation.** The effect of between-group variation is to create control chart patterns in which subgroup statistics are beyond the control limits; in other words, its effect is control limits too narrow for the subgroup statistics.

Examples of causes of variation that could generate between-group variation include:

- Chaotic (unstable) functioning of automatic control devices.
- Operator carelessness in setting up machine runs.
- Loose and wobbly braces for holding material in place.
- Over-adjustment of a machine.
- Changes in personnel (such as changes in shift).

As an example of between-group variation, one component part of a certain machine tool is an eccentric cam in which a slot 1/2 inch deep is milled. The milling machine operator places five cams in the jig, tightens them in with an adjusting screw, and cuts five slots simultaneously. During a study of this milling operation, it becomes apparent that the slots are not being held within tolerances. Both the group leader and the operator complain that the milling cutter has to be changed too often and that the slot goes out of tolerance before the cutter needs resharpening. A control chart analysis is made in an attempt to reduce the downtime required for changing cutters and to increase the operation's productivity.

As five slots are cut at one time, it seems logical to use groups of five simultaneous slots as the subgroup for the control chart. Measurements of slot depth therefore are made on each of five simultaneous slots. About 30 minutes elapse between inspections.

Figure 9.1 shows the $\bar{x}$ chart for 18 samples of 5 slots each. The range portion of the chart (not shown) exhibited no indications of a lack of control. Either the process is very erratic or the subgrouping is incorrect. A classification of the possible sources of special variation in the operation reveals:

- Raw materials: variability in hardness of steel.
- Dimensions of cam: variability from preceding operations.
- Positioning of the milling jig: variability resulting from operator skill.
- Wear in the cutting tool: variability caused by slot's growing shallower as cutter dulls.

FIGURE 9.1
$\bar{x}$ **Chart for Milling Slots in Cams**

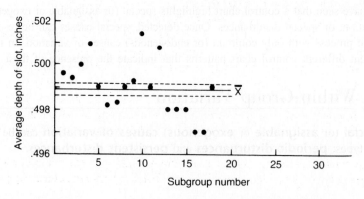

As far as the chosen method of subgrouping is concerned, the cams are thoroughly scrambled, or randomized, before coming to the mills. The first and second sources are therefore included in the subgroups because a cam of any specified hardness or size would be as likely to appear in one subgroup as another. But the third and fourth causes are not included in the subgroups; their effect is *between* the subgroups. Positioning of the jig affects all five cams in the jig in the same way, but the next group of five might be positioned differently. Tool wear, a long-term directional effect, should appear as a trend between successive subgroups and would not affect the range within subgroups. Regarding the third cause, positioning of the jig, some variation between successive jig settings is unavoidable, since jig setting depends on the operator's manual skill. Certainly excessive variations from this cause are undesirable. [See Reference 4, pp. 102–104.]

Persistent Disturbances

Persistent disturbances create special causes of variation that continually affect the process. The constant nature of these causes tends to affect all sampled observations and, hence, sampled items both within and between subgroups. Called **within-group variation,** this is the most difficult type of variation to identify and interpret. Within-group variation creates control chart patterns in which subgroup statistics hug the centerline—in other words, it creates control limits too wide for the subgroup statistics.

Examples of causes of variation that could generate within-group variation include:

- Subcomponents in final assemblies that come from two or more sources.
- Persistent differences in operators, where their work is mixed further down the line.
- Variation in gauges, where measured items are mixed and used in later operations.

As an extreme example of within-group variation, shafts are cut to length by two machines: A and B. Each machine cuts 50 percent of all shafts, and each machine accomplishes its task in approximately the same amount of time. Machine A's shafts are all good, but machine B's shafts are all defective. Figure 9.2 presents a schematic of machines A and B.

As shafts are finished, they are placed on the conveyor belt and fall into a bin, which can hold 100 shafts. Once a bin is filled, a new one is placed at the end of the conveyor to take its place. Consequently, approximately 50 percent of the shafts in any bin are from machine A; the other 50 percent are from machine B.

The bins are then taken to the next operation. Employees at this next operation have started to complain about defective shafts. An inspection station is set up, as shown in Figure 9.3, and control chart limits are calculated from 100 percent inspection of every 20th bin, as shown in Table 9.1, from the data in 🐟 LENGTH.

An examination of the control chart in Figure 9.4 shows that the fraction defective hugs the centerline. Recall that one would expect approximately two-thirds of all subgroup fractions to fall within one standard error of the mean; in this case, 100 percent fall in this region. Stated another way, it is extremely unlikely that a run of 13 or more points (in this case, 15) in a row would all fall within a one-sigma band on either side of the mean. The process is unusually "quiet."

A novice to control chart interpretation might say that this process exhibits a large degree of stability and predictability, although at a very high defect rate; this is erroneous.

FIGURE 9.2
Work Flow of Cut-to-Length Operation

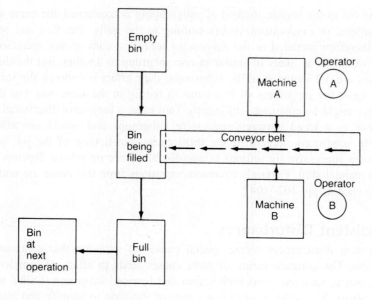

FIGURE 9.3
Work Flow of Cut-to-Length Operation with an Inspection Station

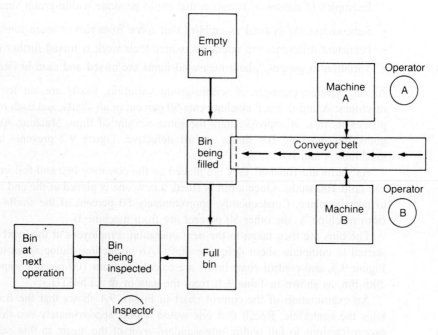

TABLE 9.1
Calculation of Control Limits for Cut-to-Length Data

Bin	Number of Items in Bin	Defective Items in Bin
1	100	48
2	100	53
3	100	46
4	100	47
5	100	50
6	100	53
7	100	48
8	100	53
9	100	47
10	100	49
11	100	53
12	100	47
13	100	51
14	100	49
15	100	48
Totals	1,500	742

$$\bar{p} = .4947$$

$$UCL = .4947 + 3\sqrt{\frac{.4947(.5053)}{100}} = .6447$$

$$LCL = .4947 - 3\sqrt{\frac{.4947(.5053)}{100}} = .3447$$

FIGURE 9.4
Minitab Control Chart for Cut-to-Length Data

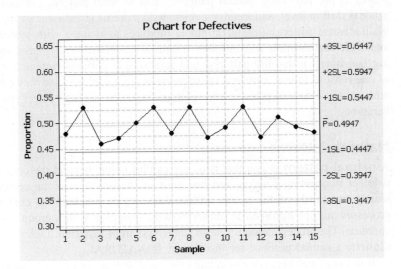

The shaft-cutting process is plagued by within-group variation. Each bin is made up of approximately 50 percent defective and 50 percent good shafts, resulting in large within-group variation and small between-group variation. As Figure 9.4 shows, this generates control limits too wide for the subgroup statistics.

Three issues must be addressed in this shaft problem. First, the subgrouping should be made on a rational basis; that is, samples should be taken separately from machines A and B. Second, the causes of machine B's defective output must be corrected. Last, both machines should be continually improved using statistical methods.

Distinguishing Within-Group Variation from Common Variation

Both within-group special causes of variation and **common** (or **endogenous**) **causes of variation** are persistent. However, the critical distinction is that within-group special sources of variation are external, or exogenous disturbances to the process, while common sources of variation are internal, or endogenous to the process.

We need to realize that both between- and within-group special sources of variation must be resolved before the process can be considered stable. As we have discussed, stability is essential to process improvement.

Types of Control Chart Patterns

Identifiable control chart patterns can occur as a consequence of the presence of between- and/or within-group causes of special variation in a process. Fifteen characteristic patterns have been identified by Western Electric Company engineers [see Reference 1, pp. 161–180]: natural patterns; shift in level patterns (sudden shift in level, gradual shift in level, and trends); cycles; wild patterns (freaks and grouping/bunching); multiuniverse patterns (mixtures: stable mixtures associated with systematic variables and with stratification and unstable mixtures associated with freaks and with grouping/bunching); instability patterns; and relationship patterns (interaction and tendency of one chart to follow another). These patterns are useful because they can be compared with control charts in practice and used as diagnostic tools to detect special sources of variation.

Natural Patterns

A **natural pattern** is one that does not exhibit points beyond the control limits, runs, or other nonrandom patterns and has most of the points near the centerline (approximately two-thirds of the points within a one-sigma band of the centerline). Natural processes are not disturbed by either between-group or within-group special causes of variation. The process demonstrates a stable system of variation. Table 9.2 and Figure 9.5 illustrate a natural process, for the data in ☞ NATURAL.

It is sometimes necessary to create external disturbances (special sources of variation) to a natural process to create improvements—for example, to move a process's average toward nominal or to reduce the number of defects per unit. The purpose of these external disturbances is to alter the process's basic structure.

TABLE 9.2
Data from a
Process
Exhibiting
a Natural
Pattern

Day	Date	Subgroup Numbers				
		1	2	3	4	5
1	8/30	4.9	5.5	5.3	5.6	5.1
2	31	5.8	5.5	5.6	6.3	5.7
3	9/1	5.9	6.2	5.9	5.8	5.4
4	2	5.9	5.9	6.4	5.3	5.2
5	3	6.2	5.9	5.7	4.9	5.9
6	6	6.0	5.7	5.7	6.3	6.0
7	7	5.2	4.6	5.4	6.1	5.2
8	8	5.1	5.8	6.2	5.9	5.6
9	9	5.8	6.1	5.7	6.5	5.2
10	10	5.2	5.4	5.2	5.8	4.6
11	13	5.2	4.6	5.4	6.1	5.2
12	14	6.2	5.8	5.1	5.2	5.4
13	15	4.9	4.9	4.9	4.9	4.8
14	16	6.1	6.2	5.9	4.5	5.6
15	17	5.3	5.4	5.4	5.4	5.2
16	20	6.3	5.6	5.9	4.7	6.2
17	21	5.4	5.3	5.4	5.2	5.2
18	22	5.6	5.0	5.2	4.9	4.7
19	23	4.7	4.7	5.6	5.0	5.2
20	24	6.0	5.3	5.6	5.0	5.2
21	27	5.1	6.2	5.0	5.2	5.7
22	28	5.6	6.1	5.8	5.9	5.8
23	29	5.5	6.0	5.7	5.0	4.9
24	30	4.9	4.8	6.1	5.3	5.2
25	10/1	4.7	4.9	5.2	6.0	5.7
26	4	6.0	5.1	5.3	4.9	6.1
27	5	5.5	5.0	6.0	5.7	5.0
28	6	5.2	4.9	5.2	5.0	5.3
29	7	5.0	5.2	6.0	4.9	6.1
30	8	5.5	5.1	5.3	4.1	5.0

Shift in Level Patterns

There are three types of **shift in level patterns: sudden shift in level, gradual shift in level,** and **trends.**

Sudden Shift in Level Patterns

A sudden shift in level pattern involves a sudden rise or fall in the level of data on a control chart. This is one of the most easily detectable control chart patterns.

Sudden shifts on $\bar{x}$ charts or on charts for individuals frequently result from a special source of variation which first shifts the process's average to a new level, but then has no further effect on the process. Sudden shifts on R charts can indicate the presence of some related variable affecting the process variability. For example, the addition of a new untrained worker to a trained and stable workforce could increase the variability of output.

FIGURE 9.5
Minitab
Natural Pattern
Control Chart

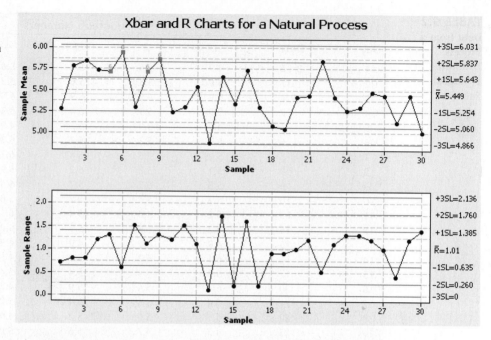

Xbar and R Charts for a Natural Process

Sudden shifts on p charts can indicate such factors as a dramatic change in materials, methods, personnel, or operational definitions. If p is the proportion defective, then sudden shifts up indicate process degeneration, while sudden shifts down indicate process improvement. To illustrate a sudden shift in level on a p chart, daily samples of the first 1,000 medium-sized ratchets produced are taken from a production process and tested for tight levers. The data appear in Table 9.3 and in ● LEVER. Figure 9.6 shows the

TABLE 9.3
Ratchet Tight
Lever Data

Date	Sample Size	Number Defectives	Fraction Defective
Oct. 3	1,000	25	.025
4	1,000	18	.018
5	1,000	16	.016
6	1,000	20	.020
7	1,000	33	.033
10	1,000	65	.065
11	1,000	30	.030
12	1,000	92	.092
13	1,000	45	.045
14	1,000	26	.026
17	1,000	17	.017
18	1,000	30	.030
19	1,000	8	.008
20	1,000	74	.074
21	1,000	41	.041
24	1,000	29	.029
25	1,000	28	.028
26	1,000	35	.035

TABLE 9.3
(concluded)

27	1,000	90	.090
28	1,000	51	.051
Nov. 2	1,000	53	.053
3	1,000	67	.067
4	1,000	34	.034
5	1,000	55	.055
6	1,000	24	.024
9	1,000	60	.060
10	1,000	81	.081
11	1,000	44	.044
12	1,000	50	.050
13	1,000	46	.046
16	1,000	12	.012
17	1,000	28	.028
18	1,000	40	.040
19	1,000	23	.023
20	1,000	29	.029
23	1,000	27	.027
24	1,000	65	.065
25	1,000	55	.055
26	1,000	69	.069
27	1,000	18	.018
30	1,000	51	.051
Dec. 1	1,000	47	.047
2	1,000	40	.040
3	1,000	52	.052
Totals	44,000	1,843	

$$\text{Average fraction defective} = \bar{p} = \frac{1,843}{44,000} = 0.0419$$

$$\bar{p} \pm 3\sqrt{\frac{\bar{p}(1-\bar{p})}{n}} = .0419 \pm 3\sqrt{\frac{.0419(1-.0419)}{1000}}$$

$$= .061 \text{ and } .023$$

FIGURE 9.6
Minitab
p Chart for
Ratchet Tight
Lever Data

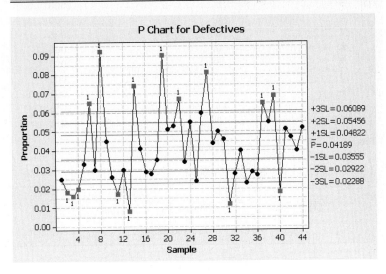

p chart. Variations are much larger than they should be, indicated by many out-of-control points. Some exogenous factor is apparently preventing consistent quality of work. A study of the assembly process soon reveals that the fixture used in welding the lever is designed so poorly that consistent welds cannot be obtained. The fixture is redesigned and more data are collected, as shown in Table 9.4 and 💿 LEVER2. The redesigned fixture has eliminated most of the trouble and reduced the average percentage of tight levers from 4.2 to 0.6 percent. The old and new p charts in Figure 9.7 demonstrate a sudden shift in level.

TABLE 9.4
Redesigned
Ratchet Tight
Lever Data

Date	Number Defectives	Fraction Defective
Dec. 4	8	.008
5	10	.010
7	2	.002
8	5	.005
9	10	.010
10	6	.006
11	7	.007
14	6	.006
15	3	.003
16	1	.001
17	2	.002
18	3	.003
21	0	.000
22	4	.004
23	7	.007
24	12	.012
28	9	.009
29	17	.017
30	15	.015
31	10	.010
Jan. 3	8	.008
4	0	.000
7	6	.006
8	0	.000
9	3	.003
10	0	.000
11	1	.001
14	13	.013
15	12	.012
Total	180	

$$\bar{p} = \frac{180}{29,000} = 0.0062$$

$$\bar{p} \pm 3\sqrt{\frac{\bar{p}(1-\bar{p})}{n}} = .0062 \pm 3\sqrt{\frac{.0062(1-.0062)}{1000}}$$

$$= .0136 \text{ and } .0000$$

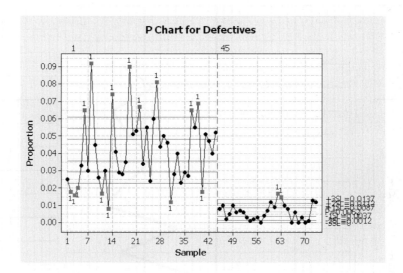

FIGURE 9.7
Minitab
Sudden Shift
in Level:
p Chart for
Old and New
Ratchet Tight
Lever Data

Note in Figure 9.7 that the two points in the latter part of December are out of control as a result of a batch of faulty levers. Nevertheless, the 1.7 percent and 1.5 percent defective pieces found on these two days are fewer than were found most of the time on the old fixture. [See Reference 4, pp. 70–74.]

Gradual Shift in Level Patterns

Gradual shifts in level generally indicate that some portion of the process has been changed and that the effect of this change is a gradual shift in the average level of output from the process. For example, if new employees are put onto the work floor or new machines or maintenance procedures are implemented, as they become integrated into the existing process they will continually and increasingly affect the average level and variation of output. This type of pattern (in the constructive direction) is common in the early stages of quality improvement efforts. Figure 9.8 depicts a gradual shift in level on a p chart.

Trends

Trends are steady changes, increasing or decreasing, in control chart level; they are gradual shifts in level that do not settle down. Trends can result from special sources of variation that gradually affect the process.

Trends on $\bar{x}$ charts or individuals charts result from disturbances that shift the process level up (or down) over time, such as tool wear, loosening of guide rails or holding devices, or operator fatigue. Figure 9.9 shows trend on an $\bar{x}$ chart for slot depth caused by tool wear in a cutting jig. Trends are relatively easy to detect, although people who are inexperienced in control chart diagnosis often see trends when they do not exist. Thus caution is advised.

Cycles

Cycles are repeating waves of periodic low and high points on a control chart caused by special disturbances that appear and disappear with some degree of regularity, such as morning start-ups and periodic shifting of operators on $\bar{x}$ charts; fluctuations in

FIGURE 9.8 Gradual Shift in Level Control Chart

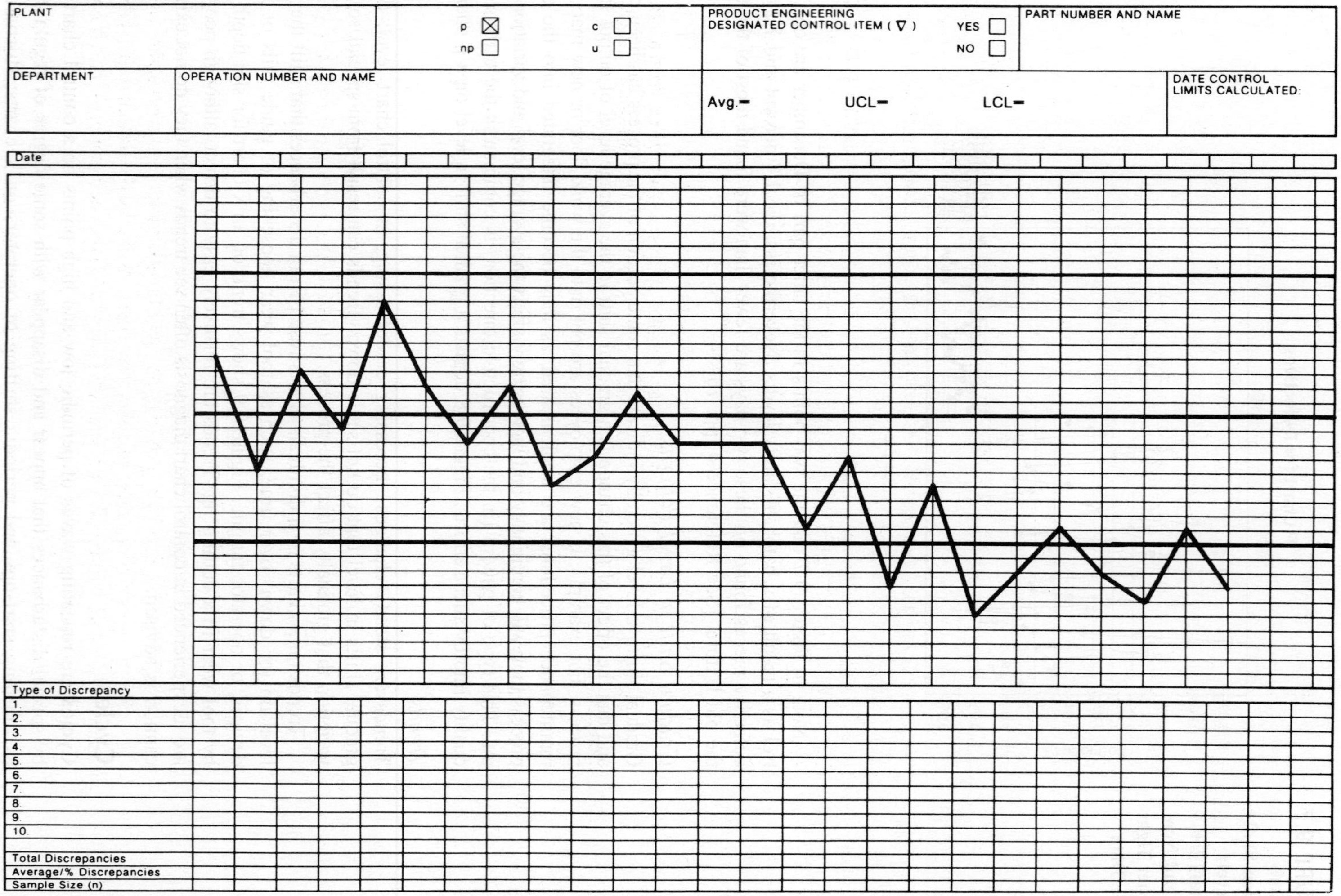

PLANT		PRODUCT ENGINEERING DESIGNATED CONTROL ITEM (▽)	PART NUMBER AND NAME
	p ☒ c ☐	YES ☐	
	np ☐ u ☐	NO ☐	
DEPARTMENT	OPERATION NUMBER AND NAME		DATE CONTROL LIMITS CALCULATED:

Avg.— UCL— LCL—

Date

Type of Discrepancy
1
2
3
4
5
6
7
8
9
10
Total Discrepancies
Average/% Discrepancies
Sample Size (n)

FIGURE 9.9
Trend Pattern
Control Chart
for Slot Depth
Resulting from
Tool Wear in
Cutting Jig

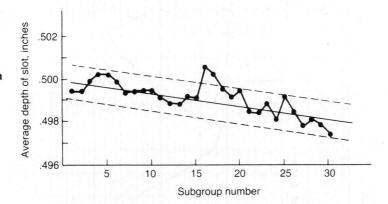

operator fatigue caused by coffee breaks and differences between shifts on R charts; and regular changes in inspectors on a p chart.

If a sampling frequency coincides with the cycle's pattern, sampling may reveal only high or low points; in this case, cycles will not show up on a control chart. The remedy is to sample more frequently to detect the cyclical pattern. Process knowledge is essential to detecting cycles. Figure 9.10 shows a control chart exhibiting cyclical special sources of variation.

Wild Patterns

There are two types of **wild patterns: freaks** and **grouping/bunching.** Both patterns are characterized by one or more subgroups that are very different from the main body of subgroups.

Freaks

Freaks can be caused by calculation errors or by external disturbances that can dramatically affect one subgroup. They appear on a control chart as points significantly beyond the control limits. Freaks are one of the easiest patterns to recognize. Figure 9.11 shows an example of a freak.

Grouping/Bunching

Grouping/bunching is caused by the introduction into a process of a new system of disturbances that affect a "group" or "bunch" of points that are close together. Figure 9.12 illustrates grouping/bunching on an R chart. In this case the grouping/bunching is a good special cause of variation and should be built into the process.

Multiuniverse Patterns

There are three **multiuniverse patterns** and two groups of associated patterns. The three multiuniverse patterns are **mixtures, stable mixtures,** and **unstable mixtures.** The first group of associated patterns are **systematic variables** and **stratification** related to stable mixtures. The second group of associated patterns are **freaks** and **grouping/bunching** related to unstable mixtures.

All multiuniverse patterns are characterized by an absence of points near the centerline (large fluctuations) or by too many points near the centerline (small fluctuations).

FIGURE 9.10　Cycle Pattern Control Chart

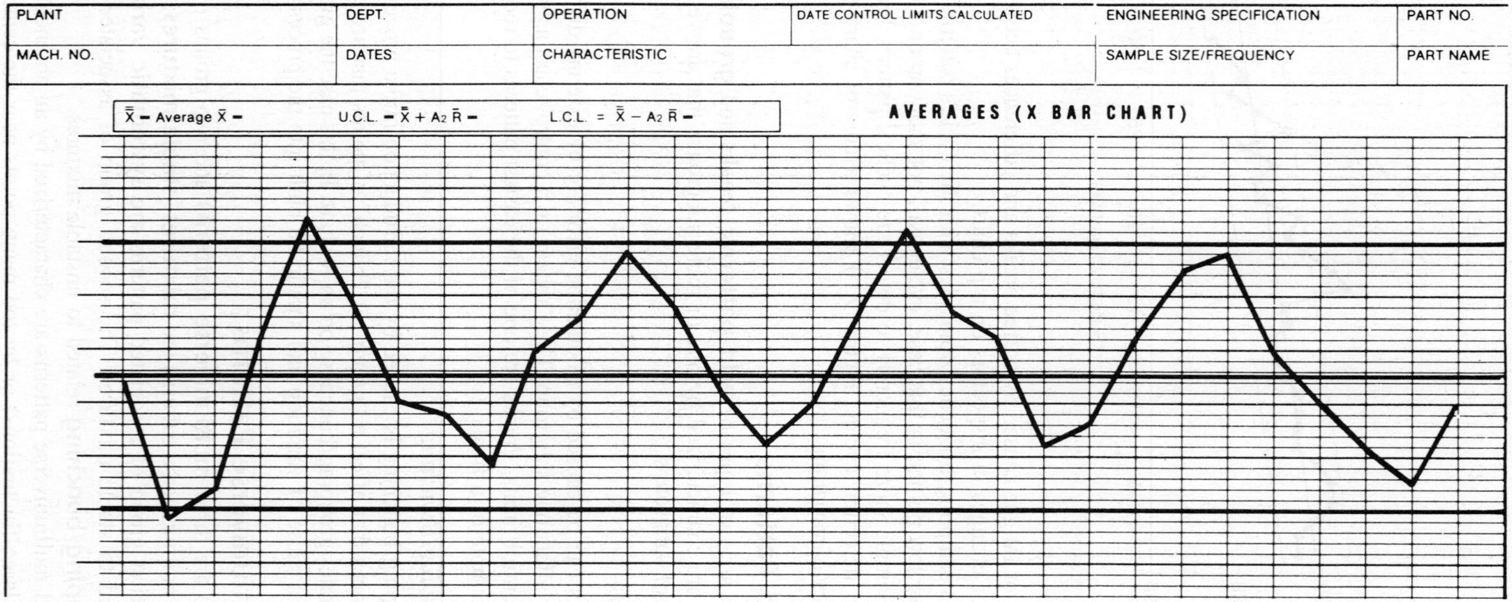

PLANT	DEPT.	OPERATION	DATE CONTROL LIMITS CALCULATED	ENGINEERING SPECIFICATION	PART NO.
MACH. NO.	DATES	CHARACTERISTIC		SAMPLE SIZE/FREQUENCY	PART NAME

$\overline{X}$ – Average $\overline{\overline{X}}$ –

U.C.L. – $\overline{\overline{X}} + A_2 \overline{R}$ –

L.C.L. = $\overline{\overline{X}} - A_2 \overline{R}$ –

AVERAGES (X BAR CHART)

FIGURE 9.11 Freak Pattern Control Chart

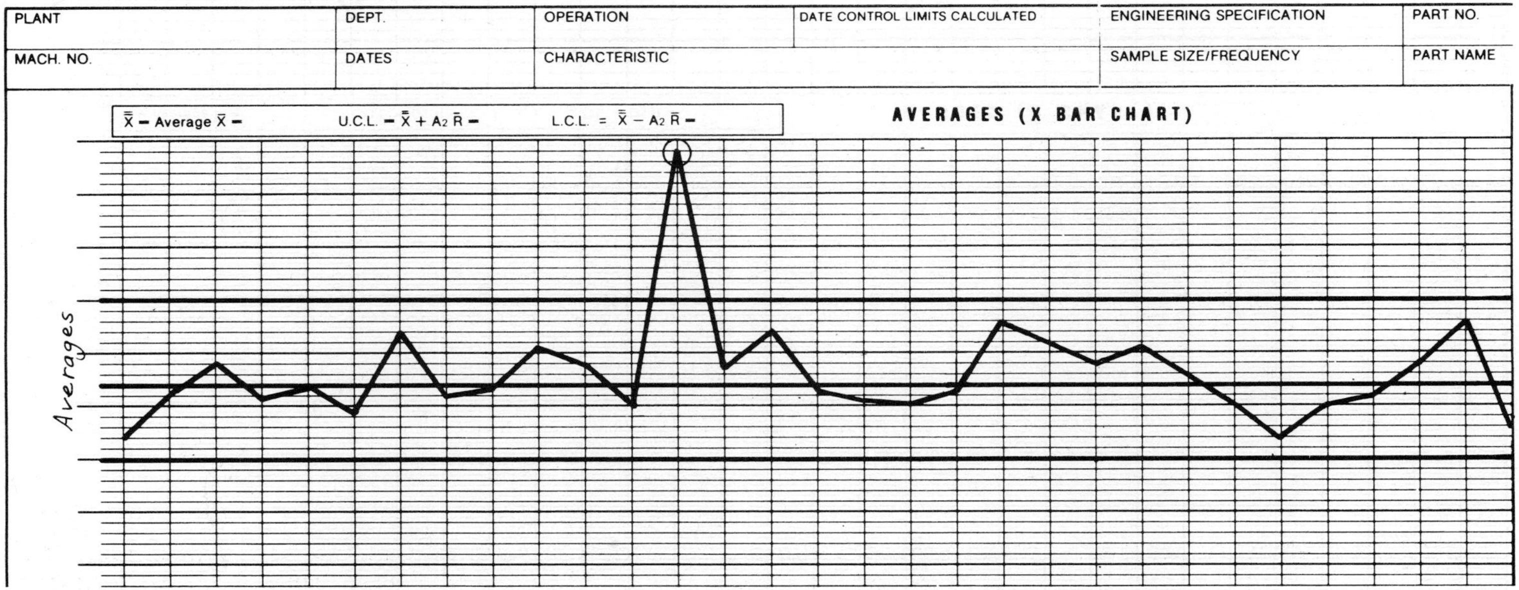

PLANT	DEPT.	OPERATION	DATE CONTROL LIMITS CALCULATED	ENGINEERING SPECIFICATION	PART NO.
MACH. NO.	DATES	CHARACTERISTIC		SAMPLE SIZE/FREQUENCY	PART NAME

$\overline{\overline{X}}$ – Average $\overline{\overline{X}}$ –   U.C.L. = $\overline{\overline{X}}$ + A$_2$ $\overline{R}$ –   L.C.L. = $\overline{\overline{X}}$ – A$_2$ $\overline{R}$ –

AVERAGES (X BAR CHART)

Averages

FIGURE 9.12 Grouping/Bunching Pattern Control Chart

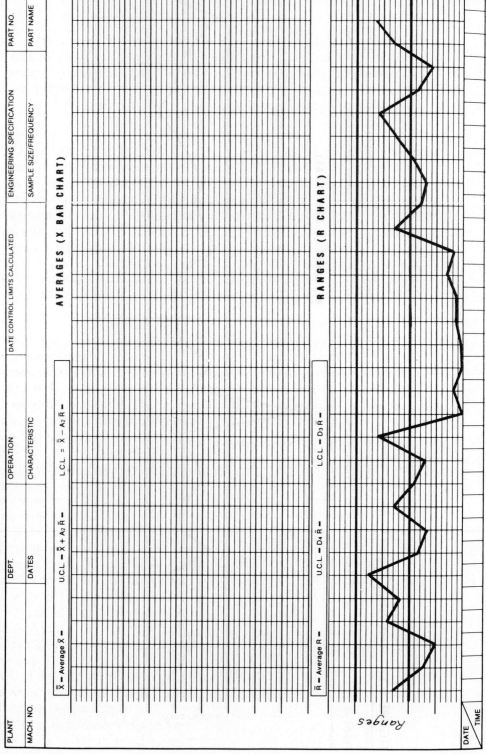

Mixtures

Mixture patterns indicate the presence of two or more distributions for a quality characteristic—for example, two distributions of cycle times to process a bank loan caused by numerous transactions coming from two different loan officers. Mixtures become more apparent the greater the difference between the component distributions. There are two basic forms of mixtures: stable mixtures and unstable mixtures.

Stable Mixtures

Stable mixtures indicate the presence of two or more distributions for a quality characteristic that does not change over time with respect to the proportion of items coming from each distribution and/or the average for each distribution. For example, two vendors supply units to a buyer. Seventy percent of the incoming units are purchased from vendor A and weigh 10 pounds on average; the remaining 30 percent of incoming units are purchased from vendor B and weigh 12 pounds on average. As another example, samples are drawn consistently from two shifts or machines. These are stable mixture problems because the proportion of items coming from each distribution is stable over time.

Stable mixture patterns are characterized by an unusually high presence of control chart points near (or beyond) the upper and lower control limits or near the centerline.

Systematic Variables

If samples are drawn separately from the component distributions, then the stable mixture pattern will appear on the control chart. This is a case of systematic variables. For example, if samples are alternately drawn from the output of two shifts where the outputs are widely different (two distributions), the points on a control chart will sawtooth up and down—shift A high, shift B low, shift A high, shift B low, and so on. This is a systematic variable pattern. An example of the systematic variable form of a stable mixture is differences between tools or differences between shifts, where the data are systematically plotted to bring out these differences. For example, suppose a box plant produces corrugated boxes. These boxes have many quality characteristics. In this example we will focus on "glued tab width." The glue tab is what forms the manufacturer's joint of a corrugated box, as shown in Figure 9.13. The glued tab width is important to ensure proper strength of the final box.

Ten subgroups of the glued tab widths of four corrugated boxes were drawn from the outputs of shift A and shift B. Figure 9.14 presents the data and $\bar{x}$ and R charts. The $\bar{x}$ chart shows a classic sawtooth pattern leading to the unusually high presence of control chart points beyond the control limits. The problem is the presence of a variable that

FIGURE 9.13
Glued Tab Width

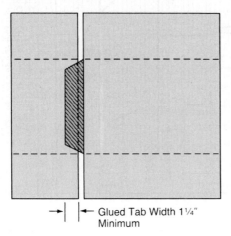

The glue tab is what forms the manufacturer's joint of the box.
The carrier regulations specify that the overlapped width of the joint must be a minimum of 1¼". The glue tab is made 1⅜" wide so as to meet the minimum 1¼" when the box blank is folded and glued.

Glued Tab Width 1¼" Minimum

FIGURE 9.14 Systematic Variable–Stable Mixture Pattern Control Chart

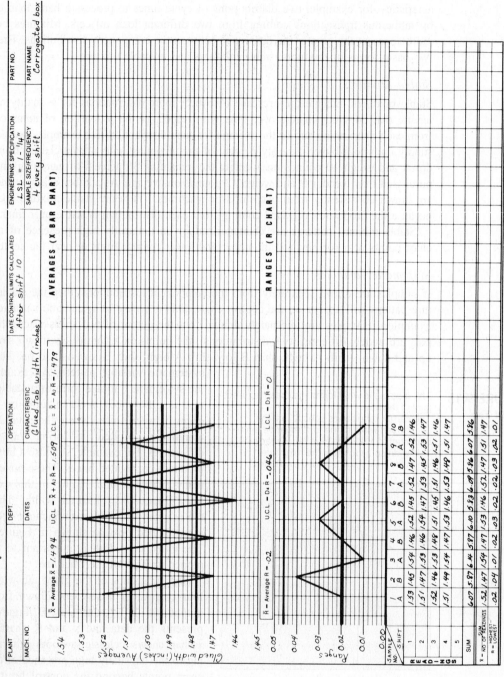

systematically affects the process—in this case, shifts. The control charts in this example should be separated into $\bar{x}$ and R charts for shift A and shift B.

Stratification

If samples are drawn from two or more distributions that have been combined, then the stable mixture pattern can create extremely small differences among statistics on $\bar{x}$, R, individuals, or p charts, resulting in an unusually high presence of control chart points near the centerline. The small differences on $\bar{x}$, R, individuals, or p charts are frequently interpreted by the novice control chart user as representing unusually good control; nothing could be further from the truth.

An excellent example of stratification was shown in Figure 9.4. Note the presence of an unusually high number of control chart points near the average proportion defective. This overly quiescent pattern means that the control chart is not valid for this process. In the presence of stratification, the control chart user must first correct errors in the methods of sampling so that items from component distributions do not get mixed in each sample.

Another illustration of the stratification–stable mixture pattern can be shown via the box plant example discussed in Figures 9.13 and 9.14. Suppose the data on the glued tab width had been collected and recorded by a concerned employee who wanted to make sure he obtained a "representative" sample of output and consequently took two boxes from each shift's output and grouped them together to form one day's sample. The data and $\bar{x}$ and R chart in Figure 9.15 show unnaturally quiet patterns. The control chart in this example is invalid because the concerned operator sampled simultaneously from both shifts. Sampling from both shifts is especially problematic if both shifts are stable with very different means and small standard deviations. This situation causes a stable R chart with a high $\bar{R}$ caused by the differences in the means for the two shifts. Since the control limits for the $\bar{x}$ chart uses $\bar{R}$ ($\bar{\bar{x}} \pm A_2\bar{R}$), the control limits will be very wide, making the subgroup means look very quiet with respect to the control limits. The proper procedure would have been to sample separately from each shift to create a more rational subgrouping.

Unstable Mixtures

Unstable mixtures indicate the presence of two or more distributions for a quality characteristic that changes over time with respect to the proportion of items coming from each distribution and/or the average for each distribution—for example, a buyer has two vendors for an item, and the proportion coming from each vendor and/or the quality characteristic averages for each vendor change over time. Figure 9.16 depicts an unstable mixture pattern.

Freaks and Grouping/Bunching

The nature of an unstable mixture pattern implies that the multiple component distributions that make up the distribution of a quality characteristic are sporadically affected by special disturbances. This will cause a systematic variable effect, but one that will occur unevenly, generating an unusually large number of control chart points near or beyond the control limits. However, those points will be in groups or bunches, depending on the juxtaposition of the various component quality characteristic distributions. This pattern could also result in freaks.

FIGURE 9.15   Stratification—Stable Mixture Pattern Control Chart

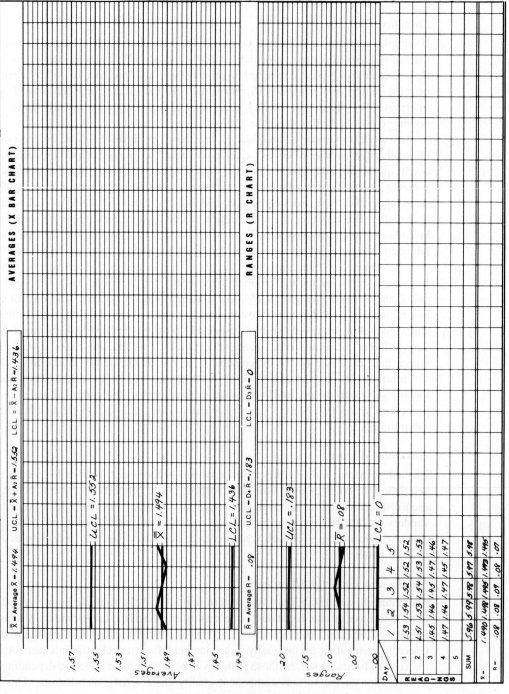

FIGURE 9.16 Unstable Mixture Pattern Control Chart

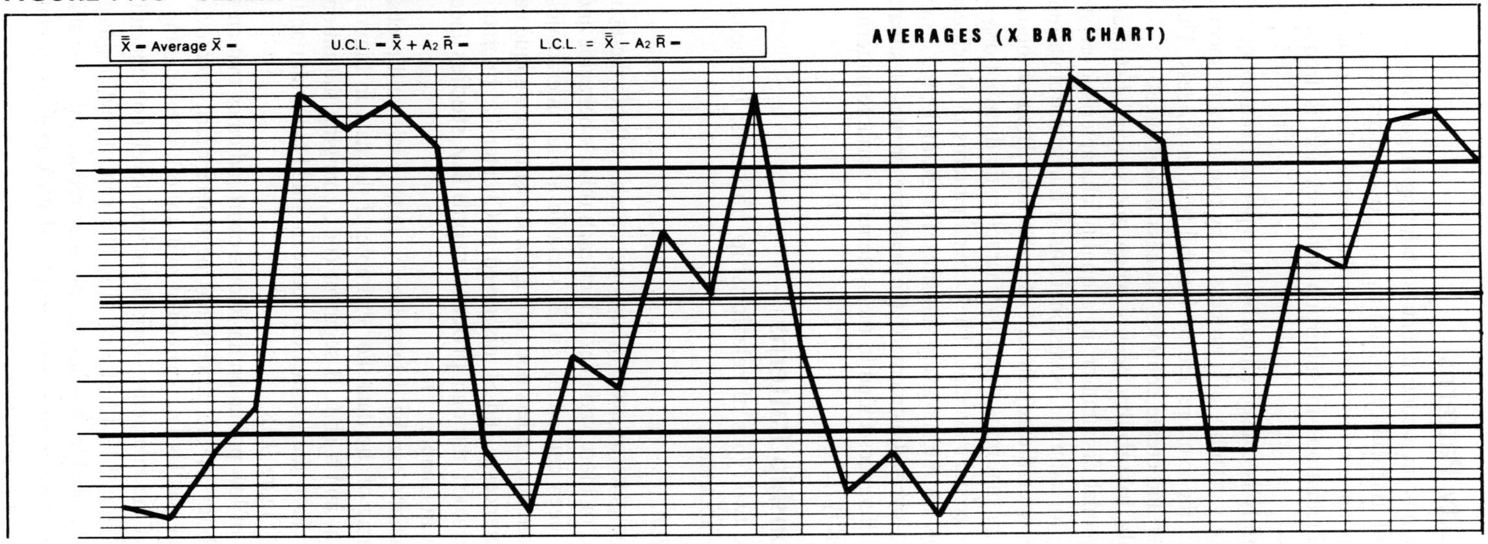

AVERAGES (X BAR CHART)

$\overline{\overline{X}}$ – Average $\overline{\overline{X}}$ –   UCL = $\overline{\overline{X}}$ + A₂ $\overline{R}$ –   LCL = $\overline{\overline{X}}$ – A₂ $\overline{R}$ –

Instability Patterns

Erratic points on a control chart exhibiting large swings up and down characterize a pattern called **instability.** Instability is a possible result of special variation so that the control limits appear too narrow for the control chart. Instability is characterized by large, erratic fluctuations in subgroup statistics and is frequently associated with unstable mixtures.

Instability is caused either by one special disturbance that can sporadically affect the average or variability of a process or by two or more special disturbances, each of which can affect the average and/or variability of a process. These disturbances interact with each other and create complex process disturbances.

Simple instability occurs when one special disturbance creates a wide, bimodal, or multimodal distribution in a quality characteristic or sporadically shifts the process average—for example, occasional lots of material from a supplier that are extremely good or bad, or sporadic adjustment of a machine. Both of these situations create either wide, bimodal, or multimodal quality characteristic distributions or sporadically shift the quality characteristic's average. They create patterns in which control chart limits will appear too narrow for the subgroup statistics. For example, the erratic effect of the bad (or good) lot or the over-adjustment of the machine creates a situation comparable to the shift-to-shift differences found in the systematic variable pattern. Figure 9.17 depicts a pattern of instability.

Relationship Patterns

There are two types of **relationship patterns:** interaction and tendency of one chart to follow another.

Interaction

Interaction patterns occur when one variable affects the behavior of another variable, or when two or more variables affect each other's behavior and create an effect that would not have been caused by either variable alone. Interactions between variables are best investigated and understood through a statistical technique called **experimental design** [see References 2 and 3], discussed in Chapter 12. Interactions can also be investigated and understood through **process capability studies** [see Reference 1, pp. 75–117], discussed in Chapter 11.

Interactions can be detected on $\bar{x}$, individuals, and p charts by changing the rational subgrouping of the data. For example, if the data in Figure 9.14 are broken into a shift A segment and a shift B segment (i.e., changing the rational subgrouping of the data) on the $\bar{x}$ chart, the interaction between glued tab width and shifts becomes apparent, as shown in Figure 9.18.

A run of low points on an R or s chart indicates that an interacting variable affecting the variability of the process has been temporarily removed or held at one level. This realization may lead to permanent removal of the interacting variable or continuous maintenance of the interacting variable at one level, consequently reducing the process variability. Figure 9.19 illustrates this. The run of low points indicates the presence of an interacting variable that has temporarily reduced the variability. It is a matter of experience in the process being studied to identify and manipulate the interacting variable to aid process improvement.

FIGURE 9.17 Simple Instability Pattern Control Chart

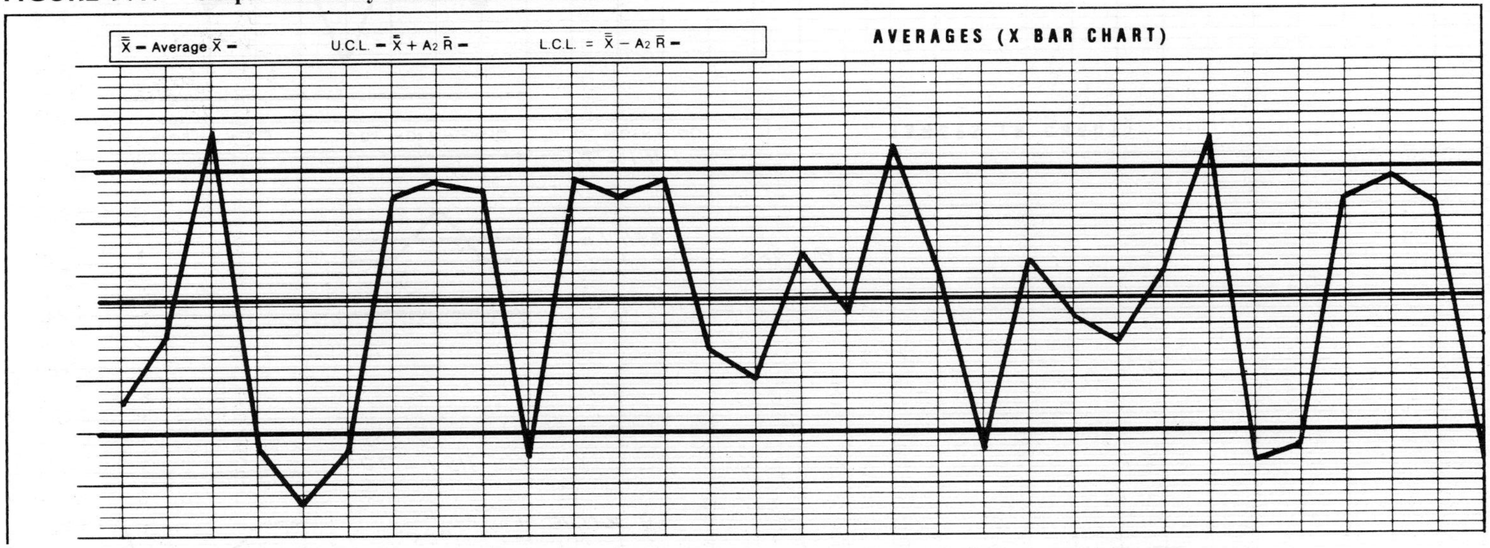

| $\bar{\bar{X}}$ – Average $\bar{X}$ – | UCL – $\bar{\bar{X}}$ + A₂R̄ – | LCL = $\bar{\bar{X}}$ – A₂R̄ – |

AVERAGES (X BAR CHART)

FIGURE 9.18 Interaction Pattern Control Chart

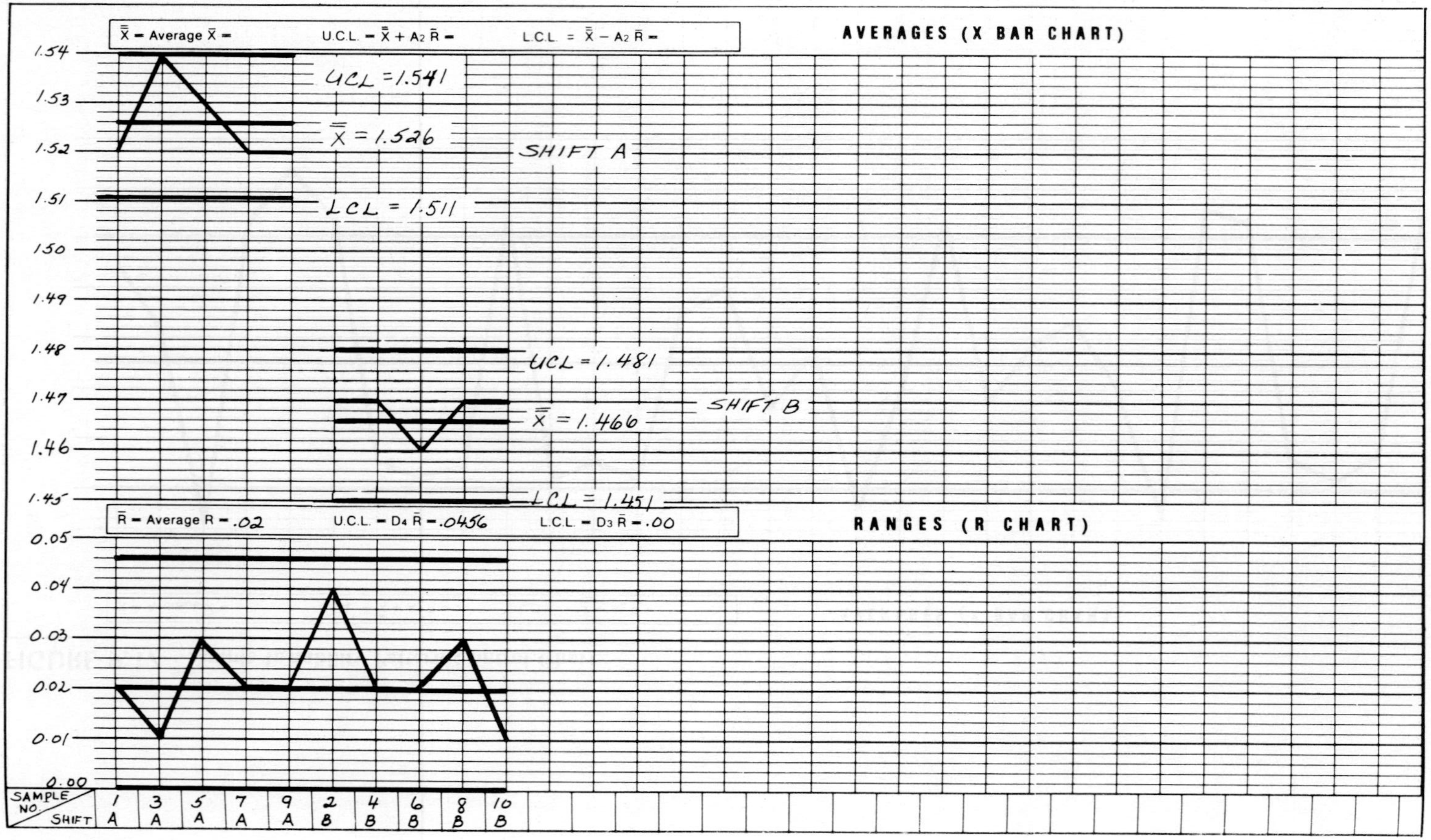

FIGURE 9.19   Run of Low Variation: Interacting Variable Control Chart

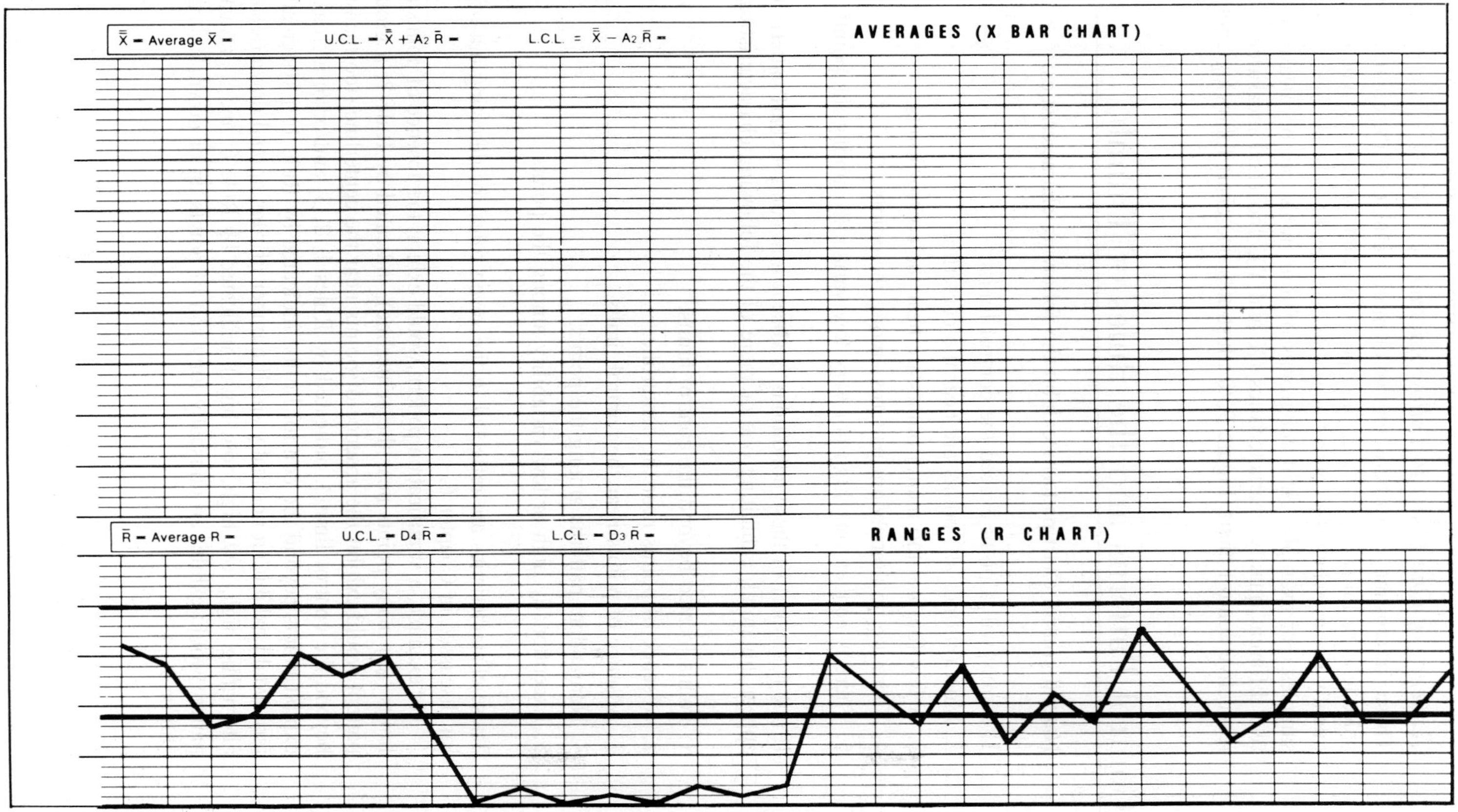

$\bar{X}$ — Average $\bar{X}$ —   UCL — $\bar{\bar{X}}$ + A₂ $\bar{R}$ —   LCL = $\bar{\bar{X}}$ – A₂ $\bar{R}$ —

AVERAGES (X BAR CHART)

$\bar{R}$ — Average R —   UCL — D₄ $\bar{R}$ —   LCL — D₃ $\bar{R}$ —

RANGES (R CHART)

Tendency of One Chart to Follow Another

These patterns may exist between two or more variables if the control charts for the variables tend to follow each other on a point-to-point basis. This type of pattern most frequently occurs when the control charts in question have been constructed from the same samples. For example, eight subgroups of four items can be measured with respect to two different quality characteristics (X and Y), and each measurement plotted on its respective control chart. Figure 9.20 illustrates one chart following another.

Out-of-Control Patterns and the Rules of Thumb

Natural control chart patterns exhibit the following characteristics:

1. Rarely will a point exceed the control limits.
2. Most (but not all) points are near the centerline.
3. A few (but not too many) points are near the control limits.
4. There are no nonrandom patterns among the points.
5. There is neither very high nor very low variability among the points.

If one (or more) of these conditions is absent in a control chart pattern, the pattern will appear unnatural, exhibiting one or more of the following characteristics:

1. Points located beyond the control limits.
2. Absence of points near the centerline.
3. Absence of points near the control limits.
4. Nonrandom patterns among the points.
5. Exceptionally high or low variability among the points.

These characteristics are reflected in the seven rules for detecting out-of-control behavior discussed in Chapter 6.

For example, a stratification pattern would exhibit the absence of points near the control limits (too many points near the centerline), indicated by Rule 7; a grouping/bunching pattern would exhibit the absence of points near the centerline (too many points near or beyond the control limits), indicated by Rules 1, 2, 3, and/or 6; a freak pattern would exhibit points beyond the control limits, indicated by Rule 1; a systematic variable pattern would exhibit an unusually small number of runs up and down (a sawtooth pattern, alternating high, low, high, low, high), indicated by Rule 6; and a gradual shift or trend pattern would exhibit an unusually long run of points up or down, indicated by Rules 4 and/or 5.

FIGURE 9.20 One Chart Following Another Pattern Control Chart

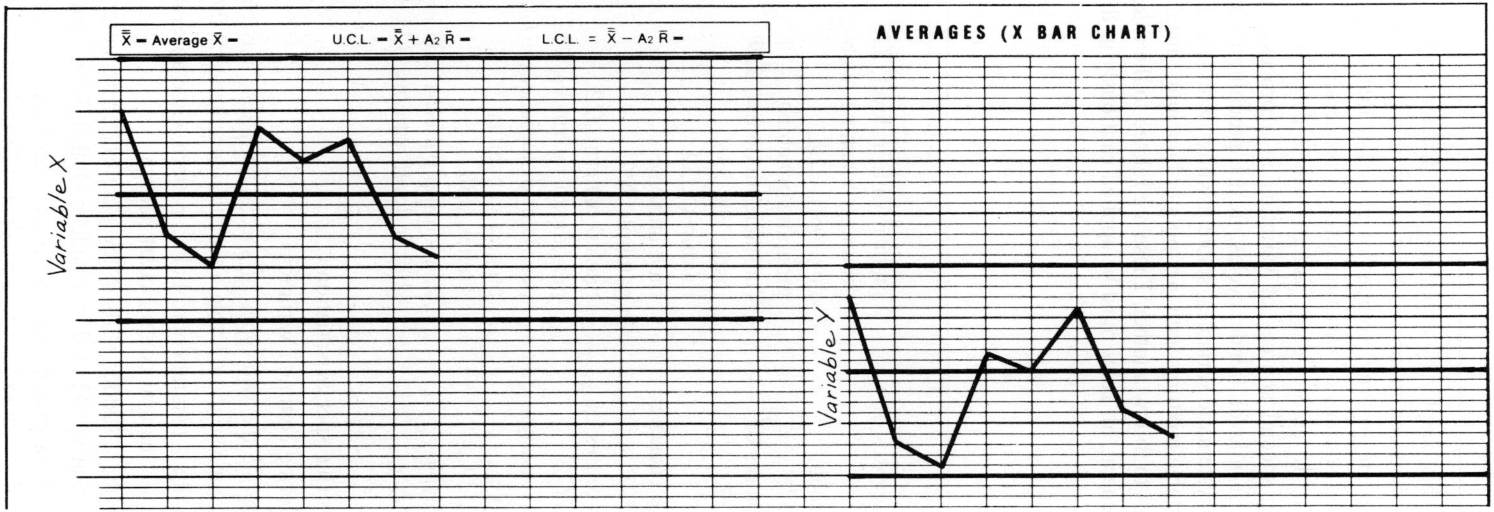

Summary

We began this chapter by explaining the different types of special variation in an analytic study: between-group variation and within-group variation. Between-group sources of variation are external sources of variation that affect a process periodically, while within-group sources of variation affect a process persistently.

There are 15 control chart patterns whose detection is helpful in understanding and eliminating special sources of variation in a process: natural, sudden shift in level, gradual shift in level, trends, cycles, freaks, grouping or bunching, mixtures, stable mixtures with systematic variables, stable mixtures with stratification, unstable mixtures with freaks, unstable mixtures with grouping or bunching, instability, interaction, and tendency of one chart to follow another. These are related to the rules of thumb presented in Chapter 6. In general, all rules must be applied cautiously in the context of the process being analyzed.

Key Terms

assignable causes of variation, *317*
between-group variation, *318*
common causes of variation, *322*
cycles, *327*
endogenous causes of variation, *322*
exogenous causes of variation, *317*
experimental design, *338*
freaks (stable mixtures), *329*
freaks (unstable mixtures), *329*

gradual shift in level, *323*
grouping/bunching (stable mixtures), *329*
grouping/bunching (unstable mixtures), *329*
instability, *338*
mixtures, *329*
multiuniverse patterns, *329*
natural pattern, *322*
periodic disturbances, *317*
persistent disturbances, *317*
process capability studies, *338*
relationship patterns, *338*
shift in level patterns, *323*

simple instability, *338*
special causes of variation, *317*
stable mixtures, *329*
stratification, *329*
sudden shift in level, *323*
systematic variables, *329*
trends, *323*
unstable mixtures, *329*
wild patterns, *329*
within-group variation, *319*

Exercises

9.1. a. Define special variation.

b. Define common variation.

c. Define the two types of special variation: between-group variation and within-group variation. Explain the difference between them and give examples of each.

9.2. Describe a natural control chart pattern. Give an example of a situation that would lead to a natural control chart pattern.

9.3. Describe a sudden shift in level control chart pattern. Give an example of a situation that would lead to a sudden shift in level control chart pattern.

9.4. Describe a gradual shift in level control chart pattern. Give an example of a situation that would lead to a gradual shift in level control chart pattern.

9.5. Describe a trend control chart pattern. Give an example of a situation that would lead to a trend control chart pattern.

9.6. Describe a cycles control chart pattern. Give an example of a situation that would lead to a cycles control chart pattern.

9.7. Describe a freak control chart pattern. Give an example of a situation that would lead to a freak control chart pattern.

9.8. Describe a grouping or bunching control chart pattern. Give an example of a situation that would lead to a grouping or bunching control chart pattern.

9.9. Describe a mixture control chart pattern. Give an example of a situation that would lead to a mixture control chart pattern.

9.10. Describe a stable mixture control chart pattern. Give an example of a situation that would lead to a stable mixture control chart pattern.

9.11. Describe a systematic variables control chart pattern. Give an example of a situation that would lead to a systematic variables control chart pattern.

9.12. Describe a stratification control chart pattern. Give an example of a situation that would lead to a stratification control chart pattern.

9.13. Describe an unstable mixture control chart pattern. Give an example of a situation that would lead to an unstable mixture control chart pattern.

9.14. Describe an instability control chart pattern. Give an example of a situation that would lead to an instability control chart pattern.

9.15. Describe an interaction control chart pattern. Give an example of a situation that would lead to an interaction control chart pattern.

9.16. Describe a tendency of one chart to follow another control chart pattern. Give an example of a situation that would lead to a tendency of one chart to follow another control chart pattern.

References

1. AT&T (1956), *Statistical Quality Control Handbook,* 10th printing, May 1984 (Indianapolis: AT&T).

2. M. Berenson, D. Levine, and T. Krehbiel (2004), *Basic Business Statistics: Concepts and Applications,* 9th ed. (Upper Saddle River, NJ: Prentice Hall).

3. D. M. Montgomery (2001), *Design and Analysis of Experiments,* 5th ed. (New York: John Wiley & Sons).

4. William B. Rice (1947), *Control Charts in Factory Management* (New York: John Wiley & Sons).

Chapter 10

Diagnosing a Process

Sections

Introduction

Diagnostic Tools and Techniques

Change Concepts

Summary

Key Terms

Exercises

References

Appendix A10.1: Using Minitab to Obtain a Pareto Diagram

Chapter Objectives

- To present and discuss diagnostic tools and change concepts to identify and eliminate special causes of variation and stabilize a process
- To present and discuss diagnostic tools and change concepts to reduce common causes of variation and improve a process
- To demonstrate the use of brainstorming as a diagnostic tool to elicit a large number of ideas in a short period of time to resolve special variation and reduce common variation
- To demonstrate the use of affinity diagrams to organize non-numeric data for a problem
- To demonstrate the use of cause-and-effect diagrams to organize the possible causes of a problem and to identify the most probable cause
- To demonstrate the use of interrelationship diagraphs to identify the root effects and root causes of a problem
- To demonstrate the use of check sheets to collect data
- To demonstrate the use of Pareto analysis to identify and prioritize problems
- To demonstrate the use of stratification in understanding a process's structure, identifying root causes, and establishing necessary process improvements

- To demonstrate the use of systematic diagrams to break a problem down into its component parts to determine process improvement actions
- To demonstrate the use of matrix diagrams to express the interrelationships between two or more variables (key indicators)
- To demonstrate the use of a program decision process chart (PDPC) to develop contingency plans
- To demonstrate the use of Gantt charts to schedule the tasks in a project
- To discuss a list of 70 change concepts to improve a process

Introduction

In addition to the quantitative tools discussed earlier in this book in Chapters 6 through 8, a number of techniques can be used in conjunction with control charts to help resolve special causes of variation and to reduce common causes of variation in a process, that is, to improve a process. The techniques and tools discussed in this chapter fall into two categories: diagnostic tools and techniques, and change concepts. [See Reference 4, pp. 293–359.] The diagnostic techniques and tools include brainstorming, affinity diagrams, cause-and-effect diagrams, interrelationship diagraphs, check sheets, Pareto diagrams, stratification, systematic diagrams, matrix diagrams, program decision process charts (PDPC analyses), and Gantt charts. The change concepts consist of 70 proven ideas for improving processes. Both quantitative and qualitative tools are essential to improving a process.

Diagnostic Tools and Techniques

Brainstorming

Brainstorming is a way to elicit a large number of ideas from a group of people in a short period of time. Members of the group use their collective thinking power to generate unrestrained ideas and thoughts. Brainstorming is used for several purposes: to determine relevant problems to address, to find possible causes of a particular problem, to find solutions to a particular problem, and to find ways to implement solutions. For our purposes, brainstorming is used to help resolve special causes of variation and to help reduce common causes of variation.

Brainstorming was fully developed and utilized by the ancient Greeks. Alex Osborn revived brainstorming in the 1940s in his work in advertising; subsequently the technique became popular in industrial applications.

Effective brainstorming normally takes place in a structured session. The group should be small in number, between 3 and 12 participants as a general rule; having too large a group deters participation. The composition of the group depends on the issue being examined. The group should include a variety of people, not all of whom should be technical experts in the particular area under study. The group leader should be experienced in brainstorming techniques. The leader's task is to keep the group focused, prevent distractions, keep ideas flowing, and record the outputs (or ensure that team members record their own outputs). The brainstorming session should be a closed-door meeting with no interruptions that might interfere with the group's creative process or cause distractions. Participants in the brainstorming session should turn off their cell phones and beepers. Seating should promote the free flow of ideas. A U-shape or circle arrangement is recommended. The leader should record the ideas so everyone can see them, preferably on a flip chart, blackboard, or illuminated transparency. Or each participant can write her own ideas on 3 × 5 cards, recording one idea per 3 × 5 card.

Procedure

The following steps are recommended prior to a brainstorming session:

1. Select the topic or problem. Clearly define the topic or problem to avoid confusion and focus the discussion. It is far easier to brainstorm about a well-defined problem than to try to do so for a vaguely defined problem. After the topic or problem has been clearly defined, write it on a flip chart.

2. Conduct research on the topic in a library or on the Internet to identify what is known about the topic. You do not want the participants in the brainstorming session to reinvent the wheel, or, more likely, reinvent part of the wheel.

3. Prepare a list of the ideas identified in the research from step 2 above and provide a copy to each of the participants before the session begins.

4. Establish a time and place for the brainstorming session. Identify between 3 and 12 team members, including a variety of people, not all of whom are technical experts on the product or process problem. For example, a team meeting to study problems encountered in purchasing component parts could consist of a purchasing agent, an engineer, a maintenance person, the operator who uses the component part, and his supervisor. Invite all attendees to the session, and remind all attendees to study the list of ideas provided to them on the topic.

The following steps are recommended at a brainstorming session.

1. Post the topic or problem to be discussed on a flip chart or similar device.

2. Each group member makes a list of ideas about the problem on a piece of paper. This should take no longer than 10 minutes. Remind the group members to add to the list of ideas provided to them prior to the brainstorming session.

3. Each person reads one idea at a time from her list of ideas, sequentially, starting at the top of the list. As ideas are read, they should be recorded and displayed by the group leader, or alternatively, written on a 3 × 5 card by the author of the idea. Group members continue in this circular reading fashion until all the ideas on everyone's list are read.

4. If a member's next idea is a duplication of a previously stated idea, then that member goes on to the subsequent idea on his list.

5. After each idea is read by a group member, the leader requests all other group members to think of new ideas. Hearing others' ideas may result in new ideas. This is called **piggybacking.** The leader continues asking each group member, in turn, for new ideas, until no one can think of any more.

6. Members are free to pass on each go-round but should be encouraged to add something.

7. If the group reaches an impasse, the leader can ask for everyone's "wildest idea." A wild idea can stimulate a valid one from someone else. Alternatively, the group leader can use the **random word technique** [see Reference 2] to stimulate a new flow of ideas. This is a simple technique used to move a thinker from one thinking location to another thinking location, by relying on the brain's ability to connect two entirely unrelated ideas. For example, if a group wanted to generate ideas to improve customer service in the bank, they would say: "Improve customer service in the bank *po* egg." The random word is "egg" and "po" signifies a provocative operation. In other words, team members are being provoked to think about the word "egg" and "improving service in a bank" at the same time. The human brain will eventually connect the two ideas and move team members to a new line of ideas on how to improve service in a bank. For example, eggs come in cartons to protect them, so maybe groups of customers in a bank should be serviced by one teller who protects them from bad service.

Rules

Certain rules should be observed by the participants to ensure that participation is not inhibited.

1. Do not criticize, by word or gesture, any member's ideas.
2. Do not discuss any ideas during the session, except for clarification.
3. Do not hesitate to suggest an idea because it sounds "silly." Many times a silly idea can lead to the problem solution.
4. Do not allow any group member to present more than one idea at a time.
5. Do not allow the group to be dominated by one or two people.
6. Do not let brainstorming become a gripe session.

Aids to Better Brainstorming

A relaxed atmosphere in which people feel free to suggest any kind of idea enhances the brainstorming session. Five techniques may be used to improve brainstorming by encouraging people to come up with new ideas.

1. **Modification** is changing some aspect of an existing product or service. An example is lower-priced movie tickets for senior citizens.
2. **Magnification** is enlarging a product or service, such as giant economy-size packages.
3. **Minification** is altering a product or service so it becomes smaller or less complex. Examples are electronic notebooks, laptop computers, and no-frills airline travel.
4. **Substitution** is using a certain material or service in place of what has traditionally been employed. Examples are using polyester instead of cotton, plastic in place of metal, and nurse-midwives instead of physicians.
5. **Rearrangement** is altering the configuration of basic elements in a product or service—for example, some housing developments use several floor plans but all homes have the same basic features.

An Example

Consider a group of six people, one from each department of an organization, who brainstorm about the problem of excessive employee absenteeism. They have already decided on the topic to be discussed, so they can proceed to making their lists of causes. After completing their lists, they read their ideas, sequentially, one at a time. The designated leader records the ideas on a flip chart. The first person's list of possible causes of excessive employee absenteeism is:

1. Low morale
2. No penalties for absence
3. Boredom with job
4. Personal problems

The second person's list is:

1. Dislike of supervisor
2. Drug problems
3. Performance anxiety
4. Anger over pay
5. Work-related accidents

Other members have similar lists. After all participants have read their lists according to the previously stated rules, and the causes have been recorded, the leader requests any new ideas that have emerged. Piggybacking on one of the first person's causes—"personal problems"—might elicit another cause, "family problems." Asking for wild ideas might generate a response such as "addiction to video games" or "rundown bathroom facilities."

After all of the ideas have emerged, each group member gets a copy of the list to study. The group meets again and evaluates the ideas. They rank them in order of importance and decide that low morale, drug problems, and boredom with job are the three most critical causes of absenteeism. They are then in the position to develop an action plan to deal with these causes.

Another Example

A brainstorming session was conducted at a private university during 2003 to identify crises. Internet and library searches were performed prior to the brainstorming session. The purpose of the searches was to identify crises at other universities. The results of these searches were input into the brainstorming session.

The members of the brainstorming session were top-level administrators from selected divisions within the university. All members were viewed by senior management as being capable of identifying current crises and potential threats to the university.

A list of 74 potential crises was the outcome of that brainstorming session. A subset of the crises on that list is shown in Exhibit 10.1. Team members had to organize and consolidate the 74 outputs from the brainstorming session. An affinity diagram, a technique for accomplishing this task, is discussed in the next section.

**EXHIBIT
10.1**

*Brainstormed
List of
Crises
Facing a
Private
University*

1. Local funding drying up
2. Federal funding drying up
3. State funding drying up
4. Grant dollars as a percentage of applications declining
5. Competition for research awards increasing
6. No mandatory retirement age
7. Some faculty unable to get grants
8. Insufficient teaching load to cover all courses offered
9. Focus on teaching, as opposed to learning
10. Business universities adding competition
11. Students focusing on "getting a job," not education for self-improvement
12. K-12 not doing its job
13. U.S. population is becoming more diversified
14. Drop in number of high school graduates
15. Majority of high school students less able to afford university education
16. Low faculty productivity
17. Some universities have lowered entrance qualifications
18. We are not focusing on the nontraditional students
19. Our schedule is set for the convenience of faculty and traditional students
20. Faculty are not student-focused
21. We need to focus on K-80 education
22. We must use our resources more effectively
23. Security costs are much higher
24. Security is vital to our image
25. The Internet communicates image issues fast and worldwide
26. More money earmarked for federal regulations
27. Insurance rates have increased substantially
28. Need to beef up the use of technology
29. Need to use more interactive instruction
30. Need to educate staff and faculty that "education is a business"
31. Use carrots to drive change—not sticks
32. Need to solicit ideas for change from the staff
33. We need to change our culture here
34. We do not work well together
35. We do not communicate among ourselves
36. We do not have the freedom to change gradually
37. We need to create or plan a crisis to get people moving
38. We can no longer afford to be all things to all people
39. We are good at finding crises, but not good at solving them
40. Academia has difficulty defining its stakeholders
41. It is easier to do something and then apologize than to ask permission

42. University is a culture of asking permission
43. Some colleges within the university have "passé" curriculum
44. Change is talked about, not financially supported
45. We allocate resources in ways that do not reward innovation
46. Funding is not based on strategic planning
47. Getting information technology is a crisis
48. Getting information technology used is a crisis
49. Difficult to change the culture and attitudes of people so they will use technology
50. We need better classrooms for our students
51. We need better dorm rooms for our students
52. Our dorm rooms need to be built with the future in mind
53. Professors view themselves as independent contractors, not as employees
54. Need to build trust with faculty
55. Security for access to scholarly communications is an issue
56. The Internet is changing the definition of publishing
57. Issues of "ownership" of information and charging for access need to be addressed
58. How scholars communicate is changing
59. Technology is changing the need for libraries in current format
60. We have a crisis in our social contract with society
61. People do not trust institutions any more
62. Concerns about research ethics
63. People are bitter about their "contract" with the university
64. Some organizations and people are more "loyal" than others
65. We do not communicate the "depth" we have
66. We do not share or use the capability of one part of the university with other parts of the university
67. We need more entrepreneurial managers
68. Need to shift from "industrial age" to "information age" model
69. People need different skills at different times—JIT (just in time) training
70. Old attitude: "If we sit here—people will come to us"
71. We need larger endowment
72. We need more dollars to use to change things
73. University needs to be more aggressive and open to dollar-generating innovations
74. Poor relationship between our image and what we offer

Limitations of Brainstorming

Sometimes ideas that are generated in a brainstorming session are inappropriate, or not polite, or "politically incorrect." Consequently, people may not verbalize them for fear of criticism or fear of offending someone. This is a weakness of brainstorming. Nevertheless, a very offensive idea could possibly stimulate someone to think of a new and creative idea.

Affinity Diagram

A team can use an **affinity diagram** to organize and consolidate an extensive and disorganized amount of verbal, pictorial, and/or audio data concerning a problem. For our purposes, an affinity diagram is used to help resolve special causes of variation and to help reduce common causes of variation. The data usually consist of facts, opinions, intuition, and experience. Frequently, the input into an affinity diagram is the output of a brainstorming session. The affinity diagram helps organize the data into natural **clusters** that bring out the **latent structure** of the problem under study. The affinity diagram is also called the **KJ method,** named after its founder, Kawakita Jiro.

Current problems may not respond to established thinking patterns. An affinity diagram can help a group break free from such patterns and promote creative, rather than logical, solutions. It is particularly useful if the problem under study has not responded to traditional, or well-established, solutions or requires the involvement of group members to be solved.

Construction

Constructing an affinity diagram begins with identifying a problem. Team composition usually consists of the same people who participated in the brainstorming session about the problem under study.

A team should take the following steps to construct an affinity diagram:

1. Select a team member to serve as the group's facilitator.
2. The facilitator transfers all the ideas generated from a brainstorming session to 3 × 5 cards, recording one idea per 3 × 5 card.
3. The facilitator spreads all the 3 × 5 cards on a table in no particular order, but all cards face the same direction.
4. *In silence,* all group members simultaneously move the 3 × 5 cards into clusters so the 3 × 5 cards in a cluster seem to be related; that is, they have an *unspoken* underlying theme. One team member may move a card to one cluster, and another team member may move the card back to its former cluster; this may go on for a time, but the card will eventually find a home cluster. Group members continue to move the cards until meaningful clusters form. Clustering is finished once group members stop moving cards. If clustering continues for too long, too few piles may remain, thereby hiding the latent structure of the problem. Cards that do not fit into any cluster should be placed in a miscellaneous cluster. Again, it is critical that team members *do not speak* during this step.
5. After the group agrees that the clusters are complete (usually 3 to 15 clusters emerge), the group discusses all the cards in each cluster and prepares a header card that sums up the information for each cluster. The header card should contain a short sentence summing up the theme represented by the cards in the cluster. For example, the header card should not contain a phrase such as "infrastructure." Rather, it should contain a sentence like "Improve the buildings and grounds of the company." The group facilitator prepares the header cards.
6. The facilitator transfers the information from the cards onto a flip chart, or rolled paper 36 inches in width, and draws a circle around each cluster. The transfer of

information involves either rewriting the header cards and ideas from the clusters onto the flip chart or taping the header cards and ideas from the clusters onto the flip chart. Related clusters are joined by using connecting lines. The group then discusses the clusters' relationships to the problem and makes any changes to the affinity diagram.

7. The underlying structure of the problem, usually typified by the names of the header cards, is used to understand the product or process problem.

An Example

A subset of the affinity diagram developed from the brainstormed crises facing a private university in Exhibit 10.1 is shown in Exhibit 10.2.

EXHIBIT 10.2 *Affinity Diagram of Crises Facing a Private University*	**Inadequate Educational System** Poor productivity Insufficient teaching load to cover all courses offered Low faculty productivity Our schedule is set for the convenience of faculty and traditional students No mandatory retirement age Some faculty unable to get grants Ineffective educational philosophy Focus on teaching, as opposed to learning Faculty are not student-focused Need to educate staff and faculty that "education is a business" Use carrots to drive change—not sticks Need to solicit ideas for change from the staff Some colleges within the University have "passé" curriculum **Dysfunctional Culture** We need to change our culture here We do not work well together We do not communicate among ourselves We do not have the freedom to change gradually We are good at finding crises, but not good at solving them It is easier to do something and then apologize than to ask permission University is a culture of asking permission Change is talked about, not financially supported We allocate resources in ways that do not reward innovation Funding is not based on strategic planning Difficult to change the culture and attitudes of people so they will use technology Professors view themselves as independent contractors, not as employees Need to build trust with faculty We have a crisis in our social contract with society We do not communicate the "depth" we have

We do not share the capability between parts of the university
We need more entrepreneurial managers
People need different skills at different times

Ineffective Internal Systems to Support the Future

The Internet communicates image issues fast and worldwide
Need to beef up the use of technology
Security for access to scholarly communications is an issue
The Internet is changing the definition of publishing
Issues of "ownership" of information and charging for access need to be addressed
How scholars communicate is changing
Technology is changing the need for libraries in current format
Need to shift from "industrial age" to "information age" model
We must use our resources more effectively
We need better classrooms for our students
We need better dorm rooms for our students
Our dorm rooms need to be built with the future in mind
Getting information technology is a crisis
Getting information technology used is a crisis

Unclear Understanding of Identity

We need to focus on K-80 education
We are not focusing on the nontraditional students
Need to use more interactive instruction
We need to get people moving
We can no longer afford to be all things to all people
Academia has difficulty defining its stakeholders
Poor relationship between our image and what we offer

Increasingly Hostile External Environment

Safety on campus
Security is an increasing problem
Security costs are much higher
Security is vital to our image
Competitive environment
Business universities adding competition
Some universities have lowered entrance qualifications
Old attitude: "If we sit here—people will come to us"
K-12 not doing its job
Changing stakeholders
Students focusing on "getting a job," not education for self-improvement
U.S. population is becoming more diversified
Drop in number of high school graduates

Majority of high school students less able to afford university education

People do not trust institutions any more

People are bitter about their "contract" with the university

Some organizations and people are more "loyal" than others

Concerns about research ethics

Decreasing Resource Base

Need dollars to change things

Need to be more aggressive and open to dollar-generating innovations

Local funding drying up

Federal funding drying up

State funding drying up

Grant dollars as a percentage of applications declining

Competition for research awards increasing

More money earmarked for federal regulations

Insurance rates have increased substantially

We need larger endowment

The six major themes (crises) in the diagram, and their subthemes (crises), have been organized and reworded to enhance clarity and communicability to stakeholders of the university.

Another Example

A team of employees in a company addressed the question: "What are the problems in achieving a total quality transformation?" The team recorded its ideas on cards. When they placed the cards on a table, all team members took several turns moving the cards. When everyone agreed on the clusters, they found that seven clusters had emerged; one cluster had a single card. Figure 10.1 shows the resulting affinity diagram.

In Figure 10.1 the team's view of the problems in achieving a total quality transformation are given by the header cards:

1. Barriers exist among departments.
2. Management creates a fear-filled environment.
3. Organizational practices hinder the functioning of the organization.
4. Improve policies for working with suppliers.
5. Improve training programs to be more responsive to employees' needs.
6. Empower all employees in the quality management sense.
7. Help employees buy into the quality management transformation.

A detailed study of the seven categories will help the group understand the problems in achieving a total quality transformation.

Cause-and-Effect Diagram

A **cause-and-effect (C&E) diagram** is a tool used to organize the possible causes of a problem, select the most probable cause, and verify the cause-and-effect relationship

FIGURE 10.1 What Are the Problems in Achieving a Total Quality Transformation?

Source: H. Gitlow and Process Management International (1990), *Planning for Quality, Productivity and Competitive Position* (Homewood, IL: Irwin), Fig. 3.4, p. 88.

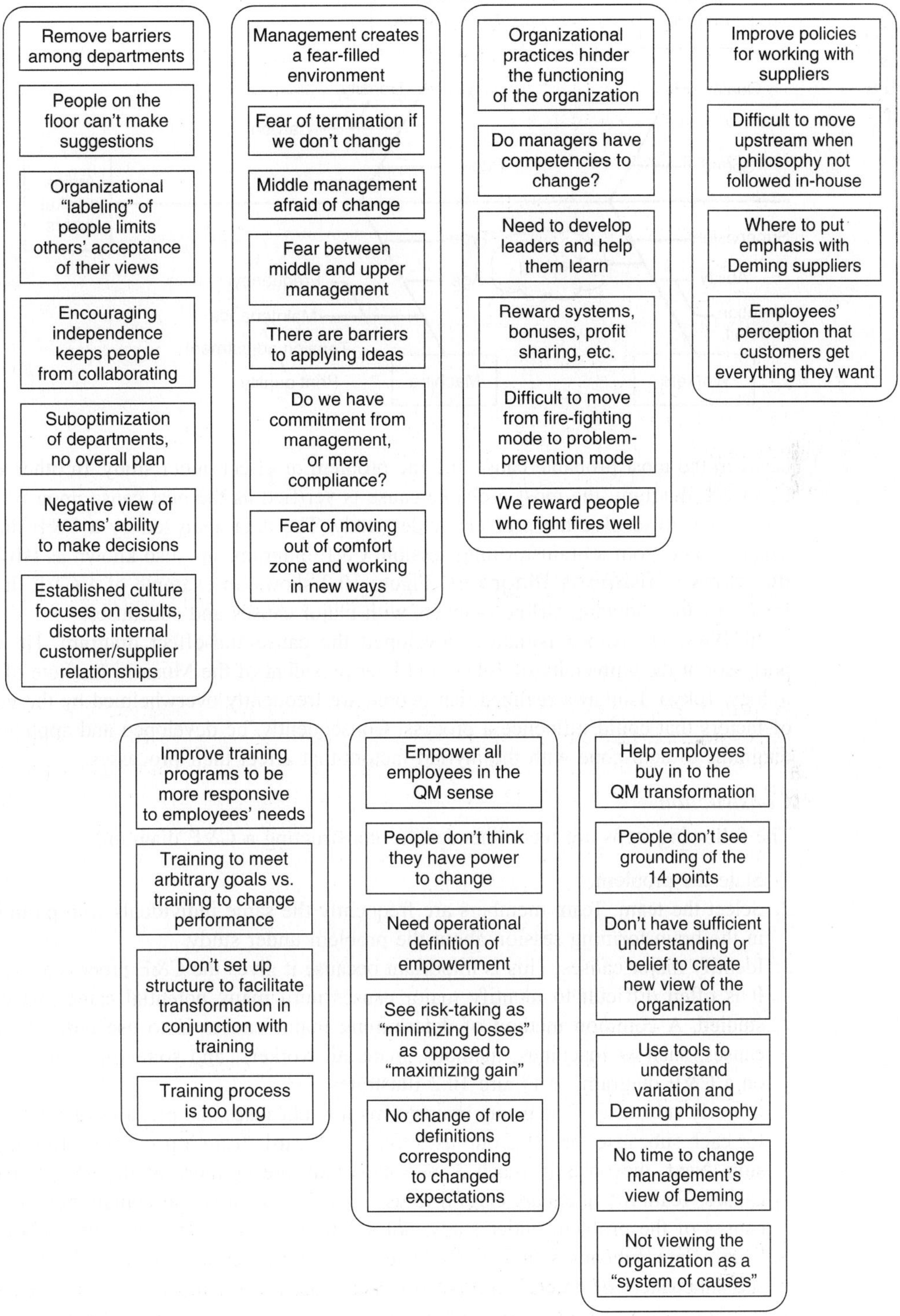

Remove barriers among departments
- People on the floor can't make suggestions
- Organizational "labeling" of people limits others' acceptance of their views
- Encouraging independence keeps people from collaborating
- Suboptimization of departments, no overall plan
- Negative view of teams' ability to make decisions
- Established culture focuses on results, distorts internal customer/supplier relationships

Management creates a fear-filled environment
- Fear of termination if we don't change
- Middle management afraid of change
- Fear between middle and upper management
- There are barriers to applying ideas
- Do we have commitment from management, or mere compliance?
- Fear of moving out of comfort zone and working in new ways

Organizational practices hinder the functioning of the organization
- Do managers have competencies to change?
- Need to develop leaders and help them learn
- Reward systems, bonuses, profit sharing, etc.
- Difficult to move from fire-fighting mode to problem-prevention mode
- We reward people who fight fires well

Improve policies for working with suppliers
- Difficult to move upstream when philosophy not followed in-house
- Where to put emphasis with Deming suppliers
- Employees' perception that customers get everything they want

Improve training programs to be more responsive to employees' needs
- Training to meet arbitrary goals vs. training to change performance
- Don't set up structure to facilitate transformation in conjunction with training
- Training process is too long

Empower all employees in the QM sense
- People don't think they have power to change
- Need operational definition of empowerment
- See risk-taking as "minimizing losses" as opposed to "maximizing gain"
- No change of role definitions corresponding to changed expectations

Help employees buy in to the QM transformation
- People don't see grounding of the 14 points
- Don't have sufficient understanding or belief to create new view of the organization
- Use tools to understand variation and Deming philosophy
- No time to change management's view of Deming
- Not viewing the organization as a "system of causes"

FIGURE 10.2
Cause-and-Effect Diagram for Airline e-Ticket Errors

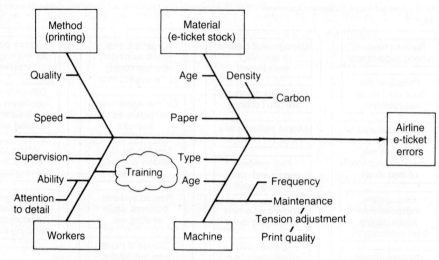

between the most probable cause and the problem or effect under study. In other words, in a C&E diagram, the most probable cause is verified as the best cause upon which to take action to resolve the problem under study. The data analyzed by a C&E diagram usually come from a brainstorming session. C&E diagrams are also known as **Ishikawa diagrams** or **fishbone diagrams.** Figure 10.2 shows an example of a C&E diagram for errors in producing airline e-tickets with major causes and subcauses.

In 1943, Dr. Kaoru Ishikawa developed the cause-and-effect diagram. He was a professor at the University of Tokyo and later president of the Musashi Institute of Technology, Tokyo. Ishikawa realized that people are frequently overwhelmed by the number of factors that could influence a process. Consequently, he developed and applied C&E diagrams to help cope with the myriad factors that affect their processes.

Construction

The following steps are recommended for constructing a C&E diagram.

1. State the problem.
2. Select the team. Team members are frequently the same individuals who participated in the brainstorming session about the problem under study.
3. Identify major causes. This is important because it gives the C&E process a structure. It is often difficult to identify major causes until many potential causes have been studied. A common method of determining major causes is to use universal major causes, such as machines, methods, material, workers, and sometimes environment, on a C&E diagram, as Figure 10.2 illustrates.
4. Classify subcauses. The group brainstorms for subcauses and prepares one 3 × 5 card for each subcause, or the group uses the 3 × 5 cards from a prior brainstorming session. Next, they classify each 3 × 5 card into one or more of the universal major causes. Team members are careful to use only 3 × 5 cards that contain potential subcauses of the problem under study, not solutions. Group members keep subdividing causes into subcauses and sub-subcauses. This procedure creates subclusters and sub-subclusters of potential causes for each major universal cause.

5. Allow time to ponder the subcauses before evaluating them. Questions to consider about each subcause are:

   a. Has the cause been operationally defined?

   b. Are there any data relating the cause to the problem under study?

   c. Does this cause interact with other causes? Should this cause be grouped with any other cause(s) into a subcause cluster?

   This information is valuable because it can aid in better understanding a cause's impact on the problem under study.

6. Circle likely causes. Causes of the problem should be evaluated. The most likely cause or causes should be circled on the C&E diagram. For example, training is circled in a cloud in Figure 10.2.

7. Verify the cause. Analyze the problem's most likely cause by gathering data to see if it has a significant impact on the problem. If the most likely cause does not significantly impact the problem, the group should verify the next most likely choice to determine if it has a significant impact, and so on.

Root Cause Analysis

In some instances, the use of a C&E diagram does not result in finding the problem's actual underlying causes. The group may become aware of this when discussing the cause or when implementing a solution. At either point, the group can examine a cause in more depth; that is, the group can perform cause-and-effect analysis when cause classification does not reach the root of the problem. Each cause originally identified can potentially be examined in a much more detailed manner by asking who, what, where, when, why, and how about each cause. In essence, each cause now becomes an effect or problem in a C&E diagram.

Returning to the example of the C&E diagram for airline e-ticket errors, we can illustrate the use of **root cause analysis.** Some causes identified were quality of printing, training of personnel, age of the e-ticket stock, and type of machine. Training of personnel is selected for further analysis. Figure 10.3 illustrates this concept. This procedure could be used to peel back the layers of a problem—to get to the heart of a problem.

FIGURE 10.3
Root Cause-and-Effect Diagram

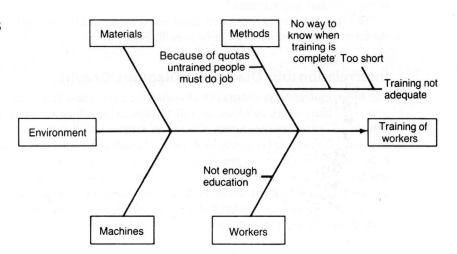

FIGURE 10.4
**Process Cause-
and-Effect
Diagram of
How to
Prepare a
Mousse**

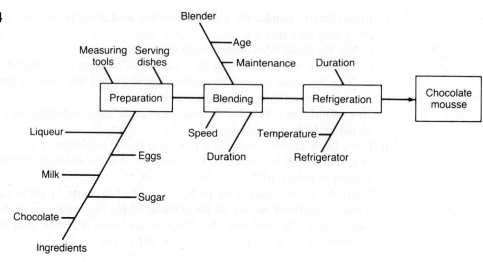

Process Analysis

Another form of a C&E diagram is for **process analysis.** It is used when a series of events or steps in a process create a problem and it is not clear which event or step is the major cause of the problem. Figure 10.4 illustrates a process analysis for making a chocolate mousse. Note that each category or subprocess is examined for possible causes. After discovering causes from each step in the process, we select and verify significant causes of the problem.

Combining a C&E Diagram and an Affinity Diagram

An effective technique for constructing a C&E diagram that is tailor-made for a problem is to combine an affinity diagram and a C&E diagram. This simply involves using the header cards from an affinity diagram as the major causes on a C&E diagram instead of the universal major causes.

An example of a C&E diagram constructed using an affinity diagram to understand the crises facing a university can be seen in Figure 10.5.

Interrelationship Diagraph (Diagram/Graph)

The **interrelationship diagraph** identifies the cause-and-effect relationships between a set of related issues or ideas, as well as identifying which issues or ideas are **root effects** and **root causes.** A root effect is an issue or idea that is affected by many other issues or ideas, and consequently, is not a good candidate for the issue or idea that should be considered as critical to resolving the problem under study. It is interesting to note that root effects are commonly the issues or ideas people think are the best candidates for resolving the problem under study. A root cause issue or idea affects many other issues or ideas, and consequently, is a good candidate for the issue or idea to use to resolve the problem under study.

FIGURE 10.5   Cause-and-Effect Diagram of Crises Facing a Private University

The university is encountering an increasingly hostile external environment

The university needs to improve the functionality of its culture

The university does not have an acceptable set of key indicators

From business universities in medical services market
Increasing competition
Technology is creating a new world
Need to broaden student base
Changing social contract with stakeholders
Increasing chaos in medical services market
Increasing demand to be accountable to stakeholders
Effectively use our capabilities with potential stakeholders
Faculty resists change
Ineffective resources/reward allocation system creates a negative environment does not deal with technology
Need to improve stakeholders' satisfaction
Need to improve productivity
Must have better results

Cause-and-effect diagram of crises facing a private university

The university has an unclear understanding of its identity

The university has a decreasing resource base

The university has ineffective internal systems to keep up with tomorrow's demands

Touchy-feely versus virtual university
Educators versus trainers
Government funding is in short supply
Difficulty cutting costs
Money is getting scarce
Need more and faster innovation
Need to improve infrastructure

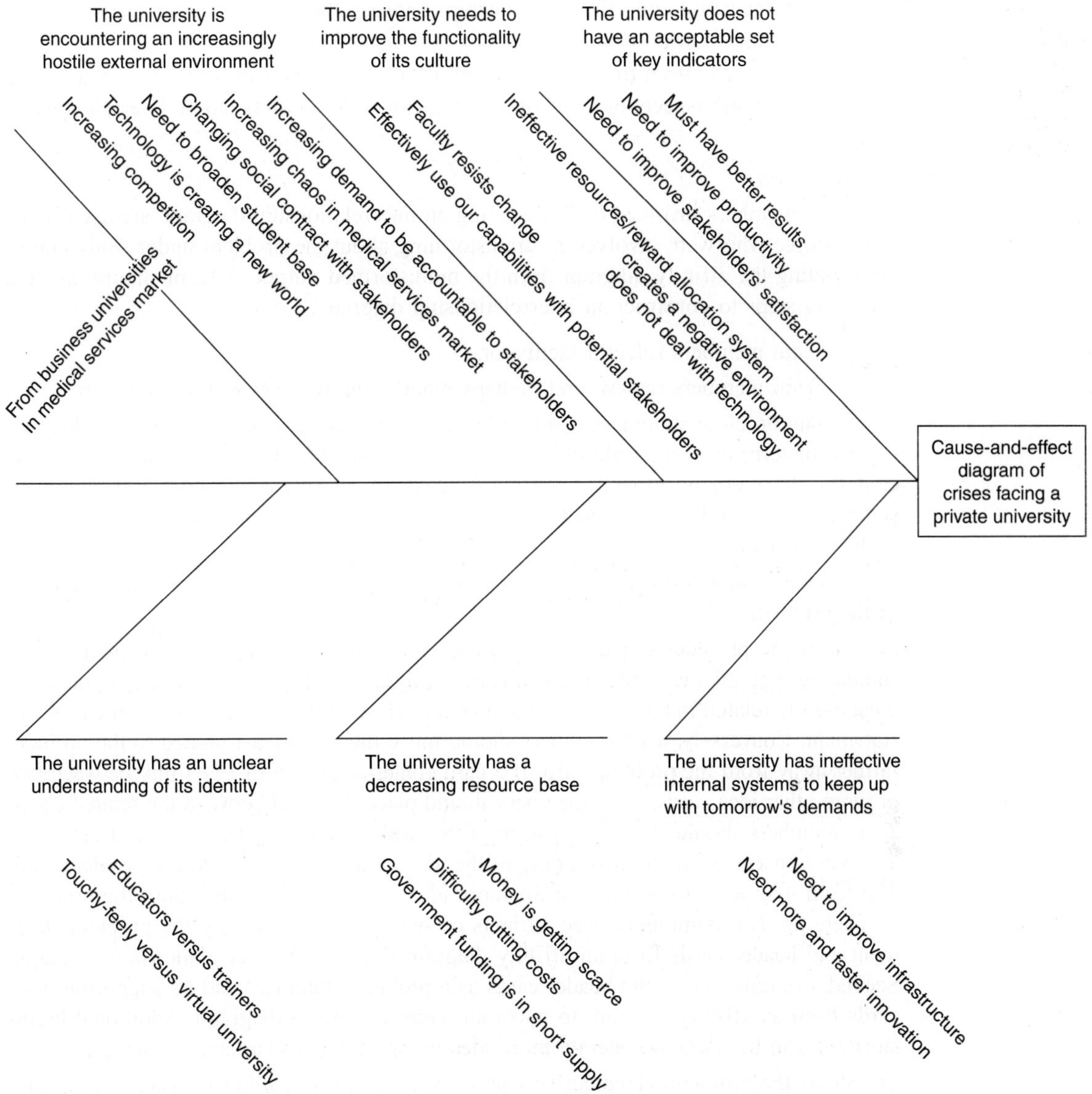

It is common practice to use an affinity diagram as the starting point for constructing an interrelationship diagraph. Three methods for using affinity diagram cards as input into an interrelationship diagraph are:

1. Use only the header cards from the affinity diagram. This method focuses the interrelationship diagraph on the cause-and-effect relationships between the ideas that form the latent structure of the problem.

2. Use the cards under one header card. This method focuses the interrelationship diagraph on the cause-and-effect relationships between the ideas that compose one of the basic building blocks or latent structure of the problem.

3. Use all the cards from the affinity diagram. This method focuses the interrelationship diagraph on all aspects of the problem, but can yield a cumbersome interrelationship diagraph.

Construction

The team members involved in constructing an interrelationship diagraph are usually the same people who were involved in brainstorming about the problem under study and in constructing the affinity diagram from the brainstormed output. A team should take the following steps to construct an interrelationship diagraph:

1. Team members select a facilitator.

2. Team members review, and perhaps modify, the relevant affinity diagram.

3. The problem statement can be placed in the middle of the work space (the centralized pattern) or at the right or left of the work space (the unidirectional pattern). The centralized pattern is utilized when many ideas are closely connected to the problem statement. The unidirectional pattern is used when fewer ideas are closely related to the problem statement.

4. Draw a double-lined circle (also known as double hatching) around the statement of the problem.

5a. If the problem statement was drawn from an affinity diagram, team members should arrange all the cards in the affinity diagram so the cards containing the ideas most closely related to the problem statement are close to the card containing the problem statement. Conversely, team members should move the cards least related to the problem farther away from the problem card. If a card contains an idea that is a link between two or more other idea cards, team members should place this card between the related cards. Team members should shift the position of the cards containing the ideas until the group achieves consensus on the positioning of the idea cards with respect to the problem card. The team may want to brainstorm for more ideas to fill in any gaps about the problem.

There are two commonly used variants of step 5a. First, use only the problem statement and header cards from an affinity diagram to make an interrelationship diagraph. Second, use only *one* of the header cards as a problem statement and its supporting idea cards from an affinity diagram to make an interrelationship diagraph. Additional brainstorming can be done to generate more idea cards with both variants of step 5a.

5b. If the problem statement was derived from a source other than an affinity diagram, the team will need to brainstorm for ideas related to the statement. The facilitator should write the ideas on individual 3×5 cards. Team members need to shift ideas around until they reach consensus, so putting the ideas directly on the flip chart is not recommended. Again, team members should arrange all the cards so those containing the ideas most closely related to the problem statement are close to the card containing the problem statement and those least related to the problem are farther away. If a card contains an idea that is a link between two or more other idea cards, team members should place this card between the related idea cards. Team members should shift the positions of the cards until the group achieves consensus on the positioning of the idea cards. The team may want to brainstorm more to fill in any gaps about ideas relating to the problem.

6. Draw a causal arrow connecting pairs of related idea cards, for all combinations of cards. For example, if 5 header cards (labeled A, B, C, D, and E) are being used in constructing an interrelationship diagram, team members would do the following pairwise comparisons: A-B, A-C, A-D, A-E, B-C, B-D, B-E, C-D, C-E, and D-E.

If two cards are not related, do not draw an arrow between them. An arrowhead (known as a causal arrow) at the end of a line will indicate the direction of the cause-and-effect relationship characterized by the line. The idea card with the arrowhead pointing to it is the effect, while the idea card with the arrow pointing away from it is the cause. Use only one-way arrows. The team must decide which direction is the stronger cause-and-effect direction. Consider the problem statement as just another header or idea card for this part of the analysis.

7. For each card, count the number of arrows moving away from and moving into the card. Place both counts on the top of the card as follows: (number away, number into).

8. Identify the key cause card(s) by determining which card(s) has the most arrows moving away from it. Enclose the key cause card(s) in a double-hatched box.

9. Identify the key effect card(s) by determining which card(s) has the most arrows moving into it.

10. Identify the sequence of intermediate cause card(s) between the key cause card(s), the key effect card(s), and the problem statement.

11. Create a legible copy of the interrelationship diagraph and circulate copies of it to the team members. Incorporate team members' modifications onto the diagraph. Repeat this step several times to achieve consensus on the diagraph.

12. Use the diagraph as an aid in understanding the cause-and-effect relations needed to resolve the problem under study. It is important to begin solving a problem by attacking a root cause, not a root effect.

An Example

The team investigating "What are the problems in achieving a total quality transformation?" wanted a better understanding of the interrelationships underlying the latent structure determined in the affinity diagram in Figure 10.1. To this end, an interrelationship diagraph was constructed using the header cards from the affinity diagram, as shown in Figure 10.6. Figure 10.6 indicates that "training" and "organizational practices" are two root causes that must be addressed in achieving a total quality transformation.

Check Sheets

Check sheets are used for collecting or gathering data in a logical format, called rational subgrouping, as discussed in Chapter 8. The data collected can be used to construct a control chart, a Pareto diagram (to be discussed in the next section), or a histogram. Check sheets have several purposes, the most important being to enable the user(s) to gather and organize data in a format that permits efficient, easy analysis. The check sheet's design should facilitate data gathering.

Process improvement is aided by determining what data or information is needed to reduce the difference between customer needs and process performance. There are

FIGURE 10.6
Interrelation-ship Diagraph:
What Are the Problems in Achieving a Total Quality Transformation?

Source: H. Gitlow and Process Management International (1990), *Planning for Quality, Productivity and Competitive Position* (Homewood, IL: Irwin), Fig. 3.6, p. 95.

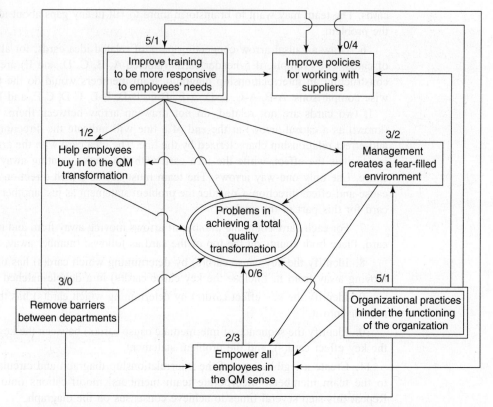

unlimited types of data that can be gathered in any organization, including information on the process, products, costs, vendors, inspection, customers, employees, administrative tasks, paperwork, sales, and personnel. Virtually any aspect of an organization can yield facts or data amenable to improving the interdependent system of stakeholders.

Data can be visible or invisible. **Visible data** are quantifications of product or process characteristics, as either attribute or variables. Visible data are collected with check sheets. **Invisible data** are unknown and/or unknowable; that is, they cannot be quantified. Invisible data include the cost of an unhappy customer or the benefit of a proud employee. They include the most important business data, yet they cannot be studied using check sheets or related tools.

Types of Check Sheets

In designing a check sheet, it is necessary to determine what the user(s) are attempting to learn by collecting the data, and what action the user(s) will take, given the results. This information will facilitate proper design of the check sheet to optimize benefit from the data. We will discuss three types of check sheets: attribute check sheets, variables check sheets, and defect location check sheets.

Attribute Check Sheet

Gathering data about defects in a process is necessary for stabilization, improvement, and innovation of the process. As there are many possible causes for any given defect,

TABLE 10.1   **Attribute Check Sheet of Defects in Corrugated Board Boxes**

Type of Defect	Monday				Tuesday				Total
	8–10 A.M.	10–12 A.M.	12–2 P.M.	2–4 P.M.	8–10 A.M.	10–12 A.M.	12–2 P.M.	2–4 P.M.	
Smeared print	II		III	I	III		I		10
Box not glued properly	I		II	III	II	III	I	III	15
Wrong symbol/ letter	I	IIII	II	HH	II		II		16
Symbol/letter in wrong location	III		HH	II	II	III	HH	II	22
Total	7	4	12	11	9	6	9	5	63

the logical way to collect data is to determine the number or percentage of defects generated by each cause. Depending on the information collected, appropriate action can be taken to improve the process. Table 10.1 shows an **attribute check sheet** for the causes of defects on corrugated board boxes.

This check sheet was created by tallying each type of defect during four two-hour time periods each day; it shows the types of defects and how many of each type occurred during each time period. Keeping track of these data for several days provides management with information on which to base improvements to the process.

Variables Check Sheet

Gathering data about a process also involves collecting information about variables, such as size, length, weight, and diameter. These data are best represented by organizing the measurements into a frequency distribution on a **variables check sheet.**

Table 10.2 is a variables check sheet showing the frequency distribution of the length of logs in a sample of 95 trees discussed in Chapter 5. Recall that the raw data in Table 5.5 could be displayed as a frequency distribution in Figure 5.3. These absolute frequencies appear in Table 10.2. This type of check sheet is a simple way to examine the distribution of a process characteristic and its relationship to the specification limits; for example, the boundaries of what is considered acceptable log lengths, as shown in Table 10.2. The number and percentage of items outside the specification limit is then easy to identify so that appropriate action can be taken to reduce the number of defectives.

TABLE 10.2
Variables Check Sheet for Length of Logs in a Sample of 95 Trees

400 but under 700	HH IIII	9
		Specification = 700
700 but under 1,000	HH III	8
1,000 but under 1,300	HH HH HH HH	20
1,300 but under 1,600	HH HH HH HH HH HH HH	35
1,600 but under 1,900	HH HH HH III	18
		Specification = 1,900
1,900 but under 2,200	HH	5

FIGURE 10.7
Defect Location
Check Sheet

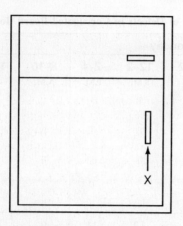

Examiner: *John May*	Date: *8/18/03*	Serial No. **HO 13988**
Remarks: *Bolt holding button of handle is missing. Handle loose.*		

Defect Location Check Sheet

Another way to gather information about defects in a product is to use a **defect location check sheet.** This is a picture of a product or a portion of it on which an inspector indicates the location and nature of the defect. Figure 10.7 shows a defect location check sheet for collecting data regarding defects on the front of a model of refrigerator door. It shows the location of a defect where the handle is attached to the refrigerator door. If this check sheet were used, and we determined that most defects on the refrigerator doors occurred in the same location, we could perform further analysis. After investigation, we could find the cause and implement a plan to eliminate the problem.

Pareto Analysis

Pareto analysis is a tool used to identify and prioritize problems for solution. It is based on the work of Italian economist Vilfredo Pareto (1848–1923). Pareto focused attention on the concept of *"the vital few* versus the *trivial many."* The vital few are the few causes that account for the largest percentage of the problems in a process. The trivial many are the myriad causes that account for a small percentage of the problems in a process. Focusing on the significant few is the important management principle of prioritization, eliminating micromanagement and focusing attention on the important causes of problems in a process.

Several other researchers have popularized this approach to prioritizing problem solving, most notably Joseph Juran and Alan Lakelin [see Reference 1, p. 88]. Lakelin formulated the **80-20 rule** based on an application of the Pareto principle. This rule says that approximately 80 percent of the value or costs come from 20 percent of the elements. For example, 80 percent of sales originate from 20 percent of customers, or 80 percent of phone calls are made by 20 percent of customers, or 80 percent of dollar inventory is accounted for by 20 percent of the items.

The **Pareto diagram** is a simple bar chart of the type discussed in Chapter 5, with the bars representing the frequency of each problem, arranged in descending order. That is, the tallest bars are on the left side of the chart descending to the right side. While Pareto analysis is commonly thought of as a problem-solving tool, it is really a problem-identification tool. The process of arranging the data, classifying it, and tabulating it helps determine the most important problem(s) to be worked on. [See Reference 3, p. 43.]

Constructing a Pareto Diagram

The following steps are recommended for constructing a Pareto diagram. We illustrate with an example concerning sources of defective cards for a particular data entry operator.

1. Establish categories for the data being analyzed. Data should be classified according to defects, products, work groups, size, and other appropriate categories; a check sheet listing these categories should be developed. In the example that follows, data on the type of defects for a data entry operator will be organized and tabulated.

2. Specify the time period during which data will be collected. Three factors important in setting a time period to study are: (1) selection of a convenient time period, such as one week, one month, one quarter, one day, or four hours, (2) selection of a time period that is constant for all related diagrams for purposes of comparison, and (3) selection of a time period that is relevant to the analysis, such as a specific season for a certain seasonal product. In the data entry example, the time period is four months—January through April 2003. In the example, the types of defects are recorded as they occur during the time period and are totaled, as shown in Table 10.3.

3. Construct a frequency table arranging the categories from the one with the largest number of observations to the one with the smallest number of observations. The frequency table should contain a category column; a frequency column indicating the number of observations per category with a total at the bottom of the column; a cumulative frequency column indicating the number of observations in a particular category plus all frequencies in categories above it; a relative frequency column indicating the percentage of observations within each category with a total at the bottom of the column; and a relative cumulative frequency column indicating the cumulative percentage of observations

TABLE 10.3
Record of
Defects for
Data Entry
Operator:
Check Sheet to
Determine the
Sources of
Defects

Major Causes of Defective Entries	Month				Total
	1/03	2/03	3/03	4/03	
Transposed numbers	7	10	6	5	28
Out of field	1		2		3
Wrong character	6	8	5	9	28
Data printed too lightly		1	1		2
Torn document	1	1		2	4
Creased document			1	1	2
Illegible source document			1		1
Total	15	20	16	17	68

TABLE 10.4
Frequency
Table of
Defects for
Data Entry
Operator:
Pareto Analysis
to Determine
Major Sources
of Defects

Major Cause of Defective Entries	Frequency	Relative %	Cumulative Frequency	Cumulative %
Transposed numbers	28	41.2	28	41.2
Wrong character	28	41.2	56	82.4
Torn document	4	5.9	60	88.3
Out of field	3	4.4	63	92.7
Data printed too lightly	2	2.9	65	95.6
Creased document	2	2.9	67	98.5
Illegible source document	1	1.5	68	100.0
Total	68	100.0		

in a particular category plus all categories above it in the frequency table. An "other" category, if there is one, should be placed at the extreme right of the chart. If the "other" category accounts for as much as 50 percent of the total, the breakdown of categories must be reformulated. A rule of thumb is that the "other" bar should be smaller than the category with the largest number of observations.

The frequency table for the data entry example, in Table 10.4, shows that two types of defects (transposed numbers and wrong characters) are causing 82.4 percent of the total number of defective entries.

4. Draw a Pareto diagram:

• Draw horizontal and vertical axes on graph paper and mark the vertical axis with the appropriate units, from zero up to the total number of observations in the frequency table.

• Under the horizontal axis, write the most frequently occurring category on the far left, then the next most frequent to the right, continuing in decreasing order to the right. In the data entry example, "transposed numbers" and "wrong character" are the most frequently occurring defects and are positioned to the far left; "illegible source document" accounts for the fewest defective cards and appears at the far right of the chart.

• Draw in the bars for each category. For some applications, this may provide enough information on which to base a decision, but often the percentage of change between the columns must be determined. Figure 10.8 displays the bars for the data entry example.

• Plot a cumulative percentage line on the Pareto diagram. Indicate an approximate cumulative percentage scale on the right side of the chart and plot a cumulative percentage line on the Pareto diagram. To plot the cumulative percentage line, or **cum line,** start at the lower left (zero) corner and move diagonally to the top right corner of the first column. In our example, the top of the line is now at the 28 level, as in Figure 10.9a. Repeat the process, adding the number of observations in the second column. In our example, the line rests on the 56 level, as in Figure 10.9b. The process is repeated for each column, until the line reaches the total number of observations level that includes 100 percent of the observations, as in Figure 10.9c.

• Title the chart and briefly describe its data sources. Without information on when and under what conditions the data were gathered, the Pareto diagram will not be useful.

FIGURE 10.8
Pareto
Diagram of
Defective Data
Entries for an
Operator

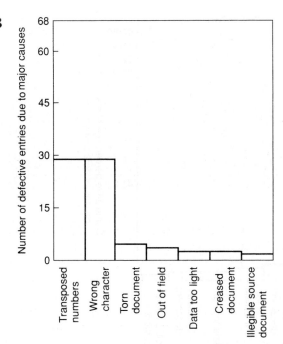

FIGURE 10.9
Pareto
Diagram:
Cumulative
Percentage
Line Plotting

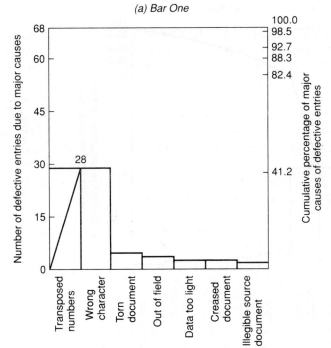

(a) Bar One

(continued)

FIGURE 10.9
(concluded)

(b) Bar Two

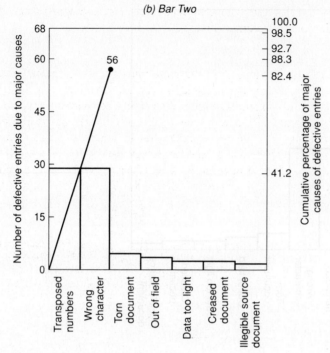

(c) All Bars

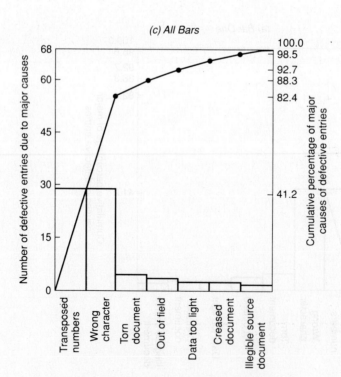

Appendix A10.1 explains how to construct a Pareto diagram using Minitab; Figure 10.9c is redrawn by Minitab in Figure A10.1 in that appendix.

Cost Pareto Diagrams

Sometimes Pareto diagrams can have more impact when problems or defects are represented in terms of their dollar costs. We can calculate the dollar cost for a particular type of defect by evaluating the unit cost each time the particular type of defect occurs, and then multiplying that figure by the number of times the defect occurs. We then construct a Pareto diagram using the dollar cost of a defect, rather than the number of defective units, as the vertical axis. A frequency table with costs per defect and a **cost Pareto diagram** for the data entry example appear in Table 10.5 and Figure 10.10, respectively. When the dollar cost of each defect is considered, a reordering of defect categories occurs.

TABLE 10.5
Frequency
Table of
Causes of
Defective Data
Entries with
Costs

Defect	Number of Defective Entries	Cost per Defective Entry ($)	Dollar Cost for Type of Defect ($)
Transposed numbers	28	$0.05	$1.40
Wrong character	28	$0.05	$1.40
Torn document	4	$1.00	$4.00
Out of field	3	$0.05	$0.15
Data too light	2	$0.05	$0.10
Creased document	2	$1.00	$2.00
Illegible source document	1	$0.05	$0.05
Total	68		

FIGURE 10.10
Cost Pareto
Diagram of
Defective Data
Entries

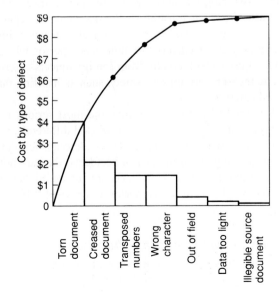

This reordering occurs because of the high cost of some types of defects. For example, although there were only four "torn documents," the cost to the company for each torn document is $1 because of machine jams and downtime. Therefore, the dollar cost is $4, making it the most expensive problem. The 28 cards containing "transposed numbers," although high in number, drop down to a lower bar position in terms of dollar cost ($1.40), because the unit cost to correct an entry containing transposed numbers is only $0.05 per entry; only a replacement entry is required to resolve the "transposed numbers" problem. Note that cost Pareto diagrams consider only visible and known costs; they do not consider invisible and unknown costs such as the cost of an unhappy customer receiving a job containing transposed numbers. This is an important limitation on the effective use of cost Pareto diagrams.

Use of Pareto Diagrams

Pursuing never-ending improvement depends on cooperation between everyone concerned. The Pareto diagram is a tool for prioritizing problems, allocating resources, and stopping micromanagement of the trivial many problems.

As resources, personnel, and time are limited—and the need to improve is critical—it is crucial to concentrate on the most important problems, those represented by the tallest bars on the Pareto diagram. It is often wiser to reduce a tall bar by half than to reduce a short bar to zero. Reducing the tallest bar is a considerable accomplishment, whereas reducing short bars leads to less overall improvement. [See Reference 1, pp. 45–46.]

Use of Pareto Diagrams for Root Cause Analysis

Pareto diagrams can be used to determine the root, or underlying, causes of problems. For example, root cause analysis can be used to improve safety in a mill. First, we construct a Pareto diagram to find out in which department the major injuries occur, as shown in Figure 10.11a, assuming all departments are approximately the same size in terms of personnel. Clearly, from our illustration, the maintenance department accounts for the largest number of accidents. Another Pareto diagram, shown in Figure 10.11b, is constructed to determine how the accidents to maintenance personnel occur. From this chart, we determine that injuries result chiefly from foreign objects entering the eye. We can now take appropriate measures to improve safety, such as insisting that maintenance personnel wear approved safety goggles.

If the safety effort's focus had been to determine the most serious injuries, perhaps those that disable employees, the chart would be constructed differently, as shown in Figure 10.12. This is akin to a cost Pareto diagram. Here, although foreign objects in the eye may have accounted for the greatest number of accidents, they are not the most serious in terms of causing disability—back strains account for the highest number of disabling injuries. The nature of the analysis we perform can yield different priorities for improvement.

Use of Pareto Diagrams to Improve Chaotic Processes

Pareto diagrams can focus attention on the major problem on which a team concentrates its efforts. This is effective when the ordering of problems remains stable over

**FIGURE
10.11
Accident
Pareto
Diagram**

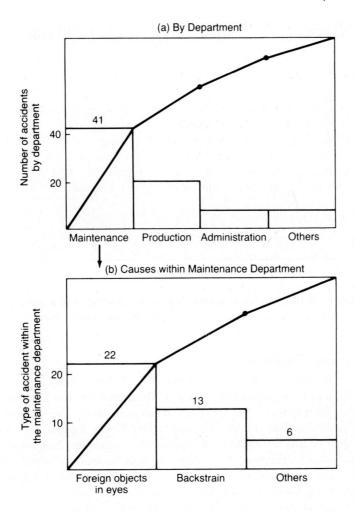

(a) By Department

(b) Causes within Maintenance Department

**FIGURE
10.12
Pareto
Diagram of
Disability
Accidents**

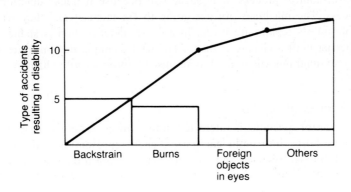

TABLE 10.6
Department Leader's Pareto Diagram

Other Breakdowns	Machine	Spindle Breakdowns
	1	xx
	2	x
x	3	xx
xxxx	4	x
x	5	xxxxxxxx
	6	xxxx
x	7	x
	8	
xx	9	x
	10	xxxxxx
	.	
	.	
	.	
	72	

time—that is, if the process is stable. But if the process is in a state of chaos, Pareto diagrams may not be effective, as the following examples show. [See Reference 5, pp. 316–317.]

A Maintenance Nightmare

The leader of a department, considered one of his factory's worst in terms of downtime, realizes he must try to improve the situation. The department has 72 machines, each with 36 spindles, for a total of 2,592 spindles that can break down. The foreman, trying to deal with a chaotic situation, constructs a rudimentary Pareto diagram, shown in Table 10.6. On this chart he lists the machines by number and creates two categories: spindle breakdowns and other breakdowns. After collecting data, he sees that spindle breakdowns are the major source of problems and he also identifies the machines that are experiencing the spindle breakdowns and therefore need an overhaul. Thus, he can plan for the overhauls in order of priority and work them into his maintenance schedule. After three months, the number of breakdowns is reduced by about 70 percent.

Here the Pareto diagram clarified information that had been muddled in the chaotic day-to-day operations. This is an example of a successful application of a Pareto chart to an out-of-control process. It is successful because it tracks deterioration—a one-way process. The machines are not going to fix themselves—they will continue to deteriorate unless repairs are made. In a sense, deterioration is stable instability; its effects persist until a change is made. The next example demonstrates what happens when Pareto diagrams are applied to an unstable process with changing special causes of variation.

Shifting Causes of Defects

A quality control specialist is interested in the causes of defects in rejected parts. She divides the causes into eight categories, each representing a different reason for rejection. Data are collected and used to create a Pareto diagram for one month. For this month foreign material is found to be the major cause for rejections, followed by damaged edges, others, stress, damaged mounts, bad trim, bubbles, and sinks. According to the Pareto diagram, foreign material and damaged edges account for 45 percent of the defective units, making these problems the logical starting points for process improvement.

Various distractions keep the quality control specialist from beginning work on process improvement after the first month. At the end of the second month she again prepares a Pareto diagram. This time stress and sinks are the two major problems. Yet in the first month, these had been the fourth and eighth largest reasons for rejection. The causes of defects have shifted over time, indicating process instability.

Pareto diagrams will not be effective if used on a chaotic process because the process is not ready for improvement. The process must first be stabilized via control charts, as discussed in Chapters 6 through 9.

Use of Pareto Diagrams to Gauge Improvement

Pareto diagrams can help us determine whether efforts toward process improvement are producing results. If effective actions have been taken, the order of the items on the horizontal axis will change. Figure 10.13 shows Pareto diagrams before and after improvements are implemented on a stable process producing corrugated board boxes. On the basis of the before-improvement chart, the major cause of a defective box is diagnosed as "symbol/letter in wrong location." After improvements are made to the process, "symbol/letter in wrong location" becomes the least frequent source of trouble, demonstrating the improvements' effect through Pareto diagrams. This is a powerful tool when used in this way because it can mobilize support for further process improvement and reinforce continuation of current efforts.

Stratification

Stratification, not to be confused with the stratification control chart pattern discussed in Chapter 9, is a procedure used to describe the systematic subdivision of process data to obtain a detailed understanding of the process's structure. Stratification can be used to break down a problem to discover its root causes and set into motion appropriate process improvement actions, also called **countermeasures.** Stratification is important to the proper functioning of the PDSA cycle. For example, the number of traffic accidents in Japan peaked in 1970. For each accident, the police officer present at the accident scene was required to complete an accident report relating the accident's cause. The most common cause of accidents listed on the report, after analysis, was "careless driving." Unfortunately, this stratification did not yield the root cause of the accidents. Subsequently, a more in-depth stratification of the accident data—particularly the "careless driving" category—yielded specific locations where accidents occurred with high frequency. Determination of these locations gave the police and the Department of Highways information they needed to set appropriate countermeasures to improve road conditions. These actions drastically cut the number of traffic accidents in Japan. Proper stratification showed the root causes of the problem and led the way for establishing proper countermeasures. [See Reference 5.]

FIGURE 10.13

Pareto Diagram Showing Type and Number of Defects in a Corrugated Box Process Before and After Improvement

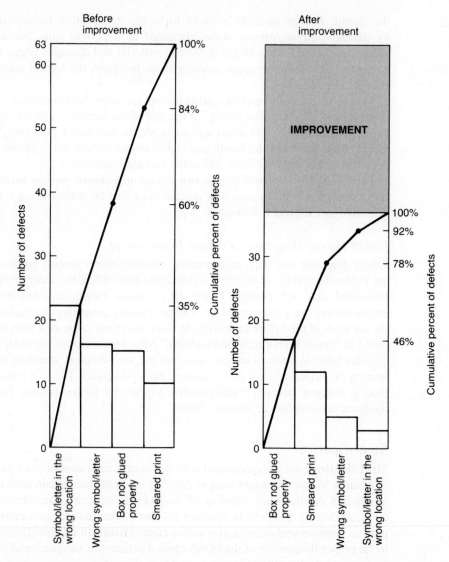

Tools for Stratification

Stratification is illustrated in this section using several of the basic tools described earlier in this chapter.

Stratification and Pareto Diagrams

Figure 10.14 shows how stratification is used when performing root cause analysis with Pareto diagrams. Here 110 observations are made. We see that by breaking down a problem into its subcomponents (stratifying the 110 items into appropriate subcomponents A, B, etc.) and by breaking each subcomponent into its subcomponents (stratifying

**FIGURE
10.14**
**Pareto
Diagrams with
Stratification**

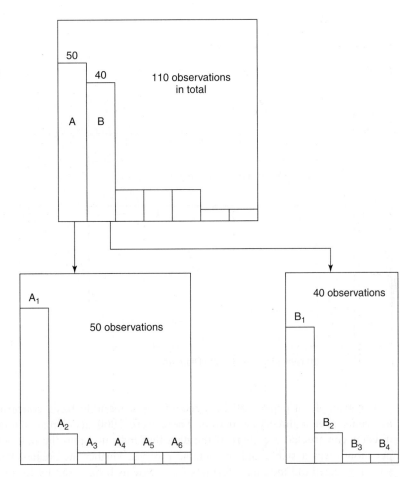

the 50 items in A into A1 through A6 and the 40 items in B into B1 through B4), we can focus on one or more of the root causes of a process or product problem, from which we can establish a countermeasure for resolving the problem.

In general, when all categories in a Pareto diagram are approximately the same size, as in Figure 10.15a, stratifying on another product or process characteristic should be done until a Pareto diagram like the one in Figure 10.15b is found. Figure 10.15a is called an **old mountain stratification** (the mountain is worn flat) because no category or categories emerge as the obvious characteristic(s), the significant few, on which to take process or product improvement action. Figure 10.15b is called a **new mountain stratification** (the mountain is young and has high peaks) because one or two categories emerge as the obvious starting point for process or product improvement action. It is critical that anyone using a Pareto diagram continue to stratify a problem by different characteristics until a new mountain Pareto diagram emerges from the analysis. This may require the development of a hypothesis on which characteristic(s) should be used for stratification in the Pareto diagram. Without a new mountain Pareto diagram there are no significant few categories, and hence, no prioritization.

FIGURE 10.15
Pareto Diagram with Same-Size Categories

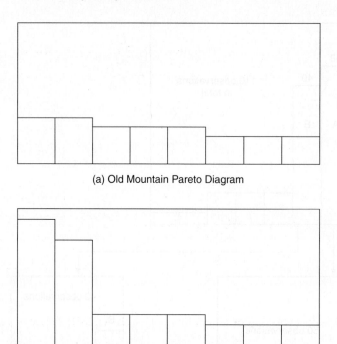

(a) Old Mountain Pareto Diagram

(b) New Mountain Pareto Diagram

For example, a paper mill kept records on a monthly basis concerning industrial accidents over a three-year period. There were 3000 accidents in total. The safety director constructed a c chart of the data that indicated that the number of accidents per month was a stable and predictable process. Further, he created Pareto diagrams which revealed old mountain formats for accidents broken out by location of accident in the mill, age of person injured, and time of day of the accident, as well as several other characteristics. The safety director conducted some research through the trade association for the pulp and paper industry and discovered that body part injured and type of injury are the two most likely characteristics with which to stratify the accident data. Subsequently, he prepared a Pareto diagram that used body part *and* type of injury as the stratifying characteristic. The analysis revealed that 60 percent of all accidents (n = 1800) were due to "strains and sprains to the back." "Strains and sprains to the back" was the significant few category in this example. Further stratification of the 1800 "strains and sprains to the back" accidents by the characteristic "method used to lift during the accident" directed the safety director to his improvement action plan. The action plan was to require a training program on proper lifting techniques, as opposed to giving everyone a back brace, or changing the rules on what can be lifted.

Stratification and Cause-and-Effect (C&E) Diagrams

Figure 10.16 shows how stratification is used in performing root cause analysis with C&E diagrams. We see that second-tier C&E diagrams can be constructed to study in

FIGURE 10.16
Stratification and Cause-and-Effect Diagrams

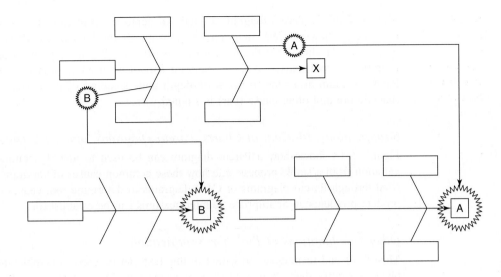

FIGURE 10.17
Stratification with Pareto Diagrams and Cause-and-Effect Diagrams

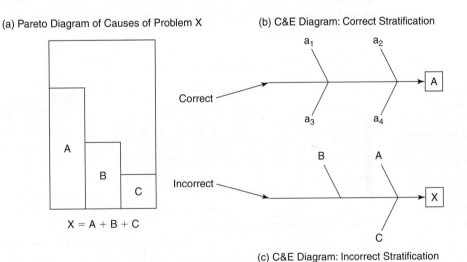

(a) Pareto Diagram of Causes of Problem X

X = A + B + C

(b) C&E Diagram: Correct Stratification

(c) C&E Diagram: Incorrect Stratification

depth any cause shown on a first-tier C&E diagram, and so on. For example, a C&E diagram used to study "Problem X" generated two major possible causes for Problem X: A and B. Consequently, both A and B are studied through their own C&E diagrams. This stratification could go on indefinitely until one or more of the root causes of Problem X are determined and appropriate countermeasures are set that should lead to process or product improvement.

Stratification with Pareto Diagrams and Cause-and-Effect Diagrams
Figure 10.17a shows a Pareto diagram. Figure 10.17b shows a C&E diagram focusing exclusively on one of the bars in the Pareto diagram in Figure 10.17a; this is the correct

way to stratify a Pareto diagram to study in depth the root causes of a problem. Figure 10.17c shows a C&E diagram focusing on all the bars in the Pareto diagram in Figure 10.17a; this is not the correct way to stratify a Pareto diagram to study in depth a problem's root causes. A C&E diagram should be used to stratify one bar from a Pareto diagram at a time to get an in-depth understanding of the corresponding cause (bar) before any other cause (bar) is studied.

Stratification with Control Charts, Pareto Diagrams, and C&E Diagrams

Figure 10.18 shows how a Pareto diagram can be used to identify common causes of variation from a stable process, and how these common causes of variation can be stratified through Pareto diagrams or C&E diagrams to determine root causes of process or product problems so appropriate countermeasures can be established.

Other Combinations of Tools for Stratification

Most tools and techniques presented in this text can be used in combination with each other to stratify data about a process or product problem, enabling us to search for a problem's root cause(s). Once we have determined the root cause(s) of a product or process problem, we can establish appropriate countermeasures leading to process or product improvement(s).

**FIGURE
10.18**
**Stratification
with Control
Charts, Pareto
Diagrams, and
Cause-and-
Effect
Diagrams**

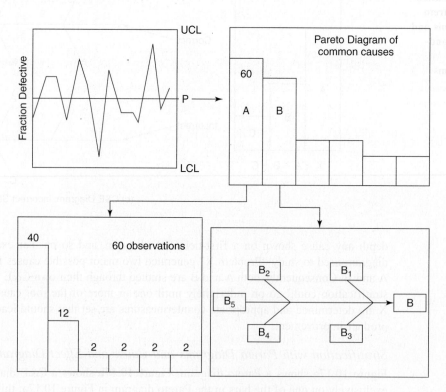

Dangers and Pitfalls of Poor Stratification

Failure to perform meaningful stratification can result in establishing inappropriate countermeasures, which can then result in process or product deterioration. For example, analyzing a random sample of 100 records of repairs performed in a factory by maintenance personnel in which accidents occurred could lead to the isolation of alleged root causes of accidents. Countermeasures designed to prevent future accidents would be established on the basis of these alleged root causes. However, this analysis could lead to the determination of causes that are not unique to repairs resulting in accidents but are typical of both accident and nonaccident repairs. Consequently, the alleged root causes would be ineffective in establishing significant countermeasures to prevent future accidents. Alternatively, if a random sample of 50 records of repairs performed in a factory by maintenance personnel in which accidents occurred were compared with a random sample of 50 records of repairs performed in the same factory (under the same conditions) in which accidents did not occur, this comparison could lead to the isolation of the real root causes of accidents. This alternative procedure would isolate real root causes because stratification focused attention on the differences between accident and nonaccident repairs.

Systematic Diagram

A **systematic diagram** is used to generate the actions needed to solve a problem, as shown in Table 10.7. It is also called a **dendrogram** or **tree diagram.** A systematic diagram

TABLE 10.7
Generic
Systematic
Diagram

Problem	Level A	Level B	Level C
	A	A1	A11
			A12
			A13
		A2	A21
			A22
	B	B1	B11
			B12
		B2	B21
			B22
Problem			B23
	C	C1	C11
			C12
		C2	C2
		C3	C31
			C32
	D	D1	D11
			D12
			D13
			D14
		D2	D2

can help team members ask what events must take place at level B to resolve the problem at level A, and what actions must occur at level C to make level B actions happen, and so on. If the actionable items in the lowest level of detail are accomplished this will lead to the next less specific level of detail, which when accomplished will lead to the next less specific level of detail, and so on. This process is continued until the problem is resolved.

Construction

A systematic diagram is constructed using the following procedure:

1. Management selects a problem and team.
2. The team selects a facilitator to coordinate its activities.
3. If an affinity diagram or interrelationship diagraph have been constructed for the problem, team members use the 3 × 5 cards from them as a starting point for constructing a systematic diagram, but continue to brainstorm for the components and actions needed to resolve the problem.
4. The team evaluates each card (suggested component or action) with one of the following codes:
   a. (0) indicates an actionable component.
   b. (Δ) indicates a component that requires more information to determine if it is actionable.
   c. (X) indicates a nonactionable component. An X should be used only after careful study; do not use an X hastily.
   These code assignments will be helpful for constructing the systematic diagram.
5. The team constructs the systematic diagram by:
   a. Placing the problem card on the left side of a work surface, such as a large conference table.
   b. Locating the cards with ideas most closely related to the problem card by asking questions such as: "_____ must happen to achieve _____" or "_____ causes _____."
   c. Brainstorming for new ideas if no ideas exist that explain a card already on the systematic diagram, having the facilitator write these ideas on cards, and placing them on the systematic diagram where the team agrees.
   d. Placing the cards selected in step b to the right of the problem card in a tree diagram fashion. The idea cards should be assembled so the ideas most related to the problem under study are to the immediate right of the problem card. Careful consideration of the means to an objective or the causes of an effect are the most important part of constructing a systematic diagram.
   e. Repeating the procedure in step d for each of the rightmost idea cards by asking questions such as: "_____ must happen to achieve _____" or "_____ causes _____." Continue this process until all idea cards are placed on the systematic diagram.
6. The team studies the systematic diagram. If there are gaps in the systematic diagram, team members brainstorm to close the gaps. The team continues to brainstorm to close any gaps in the systematic diagram for as long as is necessary to create a complete path between the problem under study and ideas that are specific enough to be action items that will resolve the problem.

An Example

Recall the affinity diagram in Figure 10.1 concerning: "What are the problems in achieving a total quality transformation?" Suppose the team studying this question decides to focus on training. The team identified four main subideas relating to training: (1) structure, (2) instructor, (3) participant, and (4) environment. Figure 10.19 shows the results of the team trying to expand the subissue of environment. The sub-subissues are:

1. Before
2. During
3. After

FIGURE 10.19
Systematic Diagram of How to Achieve Effective Training

Source: H. Gitlow and Process Management International (1990), *Planning for Quality, Productivity and Competitive Position* (Homewood, IL: Irwin), Fig. 3.10, p. 102.

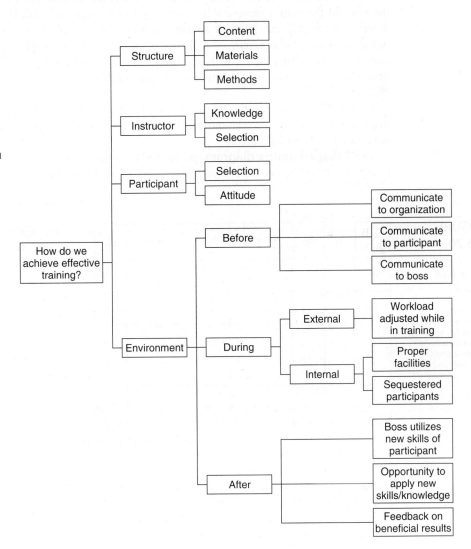

Next, the team expanded "during," which led to "external" and "internal." Finally, the team expanded "external" to "workload adjusted while in training"; this is an actionable item. The level of detail in Figure 10.19 is extended until actionable items are determined, which, if accomplished, will result in a total quality transformation.

Matrix Diagram

The **matrix diagram** is used to arrange large quantities of data relating to two or more aspects of a problem. It helps locate and plug any holes in the information base relating to a problem. There are several types of matrix diagrams. We will discuss only the L and T matrices in this section.

The **L-shaped matrix diagram** explains the interrelationships between two aspects of a problem. The columns of the matrix represent the subcategories of one variable; the rows of the matrix represent the subcategories of a second variable. In the matrix diagram, a variable can indicate almost anything; for example, the actions emanating out of a systematic diagram or a listing of items, such as people, departments, or courses. The resulting matrix cells symbolize possible correlations between the subcategories of the two aspects of the problem. Figure 10.20 shows a generic L-shaped matrix diagram.

Figure 10.21 illustrates the use of part of a systematic diagram in an L-shaped matrix diagram showing the interrelationships between "how to achieve effective training" and organizational areas/individuals.

The **T-shaped matrix diagram** can be used to compare, correlate, or study two aspects of a problem with respect to a third problem. Figure 10.22 on page 386 shows a T-shaped

FIGURE 10.20

Generic L-Shaped Matrix

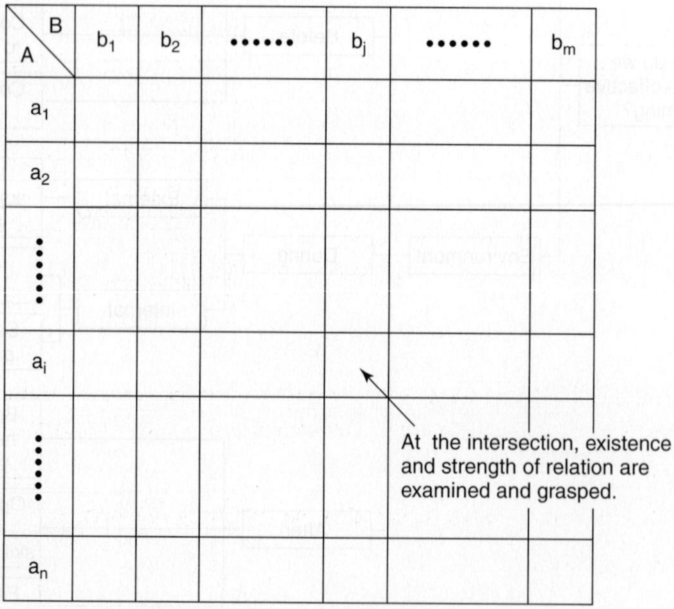

Source: Kaoru Ishikawa, "Reports of Statistical Application Research, Union of Japanese Scientists and Engineers," *Reports of Statistical Application Research, JUSE,* Vol. 33, No. 2, June 1986, p. 14.

At the intersection, existence and strength of relation are examined and grasped.

FIGURE 10.21   L-Shaped Matrix Example: How Do We Achieve Effective Training?

Source: H. Gitlow and Process Management International (1990), *Planning for Quality, Productivity and Competitive Position* (Homewood, IL: Irwin), Fig. 3.13, p. 106.

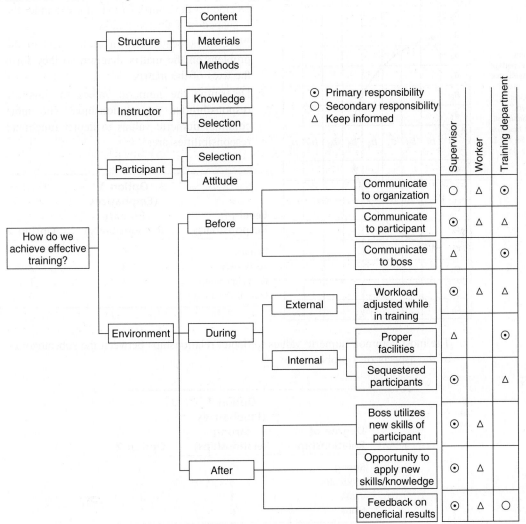

matrix diagram that combines two L-shaped matrix diagrams. A common application of the T-matrix is to pinpoint training requirements, as shown in Figure 10.23 on page 387.

Construction

Matrix diagrams may be constructed in the following manner:

1. Select a problem.
2. Form a team.

FIGURE 10.22

Generic T-Shaped Matrix

Source: Kaoru Ishikawa, "Reports of Statistical Application Research, Union of Japanese Scientists and Engineers," *Reports of Statistical Application Research, JUSE,* Vol. 33, No. 2, June 1986, p. 15.

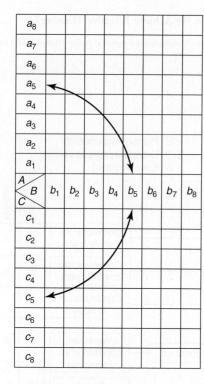

3. Select a facilitator.

4. Identify the aspects of the problem.

5. Decide on the matrix format, for example, the L-shaped or T-shaped matrix.

6. Place the subcategories of each aspect of the problem on the matrix diagram so they form the axes of the matrix.

7. Determine the numeric values to illustrate responsibilities or relationships. The most common numeric values to depict functional responsibilities are:

Level of Responsibility	Option 1 (Emphasizes Primary Responsibility)	Option 2
Primary	9	3
Secondary	3	2
Keep Informed	1	1
Out of the loop	0	0

The most common numeric values to depict relationships between the subcategories of the aspects of a problem are:

Degree of Relationship	Option 1 (Emphasizes Strong Relationships)	Option 2
Strong	9	3
Moderate	3	2
Weak	1	1
None	0	0

8. Enter the appropriate numeric value into each cell of the matrix diagram.

9. Analyze the matrix by: (a) studying and understanding the relationships between the aspects of the problem being studied, or (b) balancing work loads (see example below), or (c) locating and plugging any holes between the aspects of the problem being studied. Use the information gained from the matrix diagram to resolve the problems under study.

An Example

Again, Figure 10.20 shows an L-shaped matrix using the systematic diagram for "How do we achieve effective training?" as the vertical axis and the people needed to resolve

FIGURE 10.23
T-Shaped Matrix Diagram for Training

Source: H. Gitlow and Process Management International (1990), *Planning for Quality, Productivity and Competitive Position* (Homewood, IL: Irwin), Fig. 3.15, p. 108.

TO: Organization	TO: Participant	TO: Boss	Training needs: What needs to be communicated (two-way)	FROM: Training coordinator	FROM: Steering committee	FROM: Boss	FROM: Instructor/S.M.E.
	Δ	Δ	Prerequisites	⊙	Δ		○
Δ	Δ	Δ	Objectives of course	○	Δ		
Δ	Δ	Δ	Objectives of big picture		⊙		
Δ	Δ	Δ	Where this course "fits"		⊙		
Δ	Δ	Δ	Who should attend	○	Δ	⊙	
Δ	Δ	Δ	Benefits		⊙		○
	Δ	Δ	Topics/content	⊙	Δ		○
	Δ	Δ	When	⊙			
	Δ	Δ	Where	⊙			
	Δ	Δ	How long	⊙			
Δ	Δ	Δ	Effect on job		○	⊙	○

⊙ = Responsible
○ = Information source
Δ = Keep informed

the training problem as the horizontal axis. It shows that the supervisor has primary responsibility for "communicate to participant," has secondary responsibility for "communicate to organization," and has to be kept informed about "proper facilities," among other responsibilities relating to achieving effective training. It also shows that the supervisor may not be delegating responsibility to the workers where appropriate. This is called **workload balancing.**

PDPC Analysis

The **Program Decision Process Chart (PDPC)** helps anticipate and develop **contingency plans** to avoid potential problems when executing an action. PDPC is appropriate if the action to be executed requires an unknown amount of time to complete and is set in an unfamiliar environment.

Construction

A PDPC is constructed using the following steps:

1. Select an action in need of a contingency plan.
2. Identify a team.
3. Select a facilitator.

4. Begin with a systematic diagram of the problem.
5. Select one branch from the systematic diagram and brainstorm for the answers to the following two questions with respect to each rightmost action item:
   a. What are the potential problems in accomplishing this action item?
   b. What contingency plans could be developed to avoid the potential problems?

FIGURE 10.24
PDPC Analysis: What Could Happen to Cause an Unsuccessful Training Experience?

Source: H. Gitlow and Process Management International (1990), *Planning for Quality, Productivity and Competitive Position* (Homewood, IL: Irwin), Fig. 3.29. p. 129.

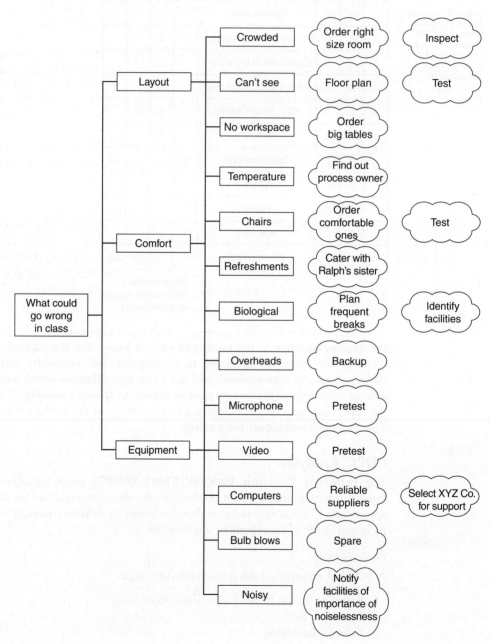

Answering these questions will form the basis of a contingency plan for coping with potential problems. Do not be overwhelmed by the explosion of contingencies that surface.

6. Record the information from the second question on a new branch to the right of the original branch. Enclose these contingencies in "clouds" which are similar to cartoon captions. Draw arrows between the contingencies and the original action items indicating which original action items are affected by a particular contingency plan.

7. Continue steps 5 and 6 on the selected branch of the systematic diagram until brainstorming has been completed.

8. Repeat steps 5 and 6 for each remaining branch on the systematic diagram.

9. Assemble all branches into a final PDPC, review the PDPC, and modify and/or add to the action plan and contingency plans.

10. Analyze the PDPC.

An Example

Figure 10.24 shows a PDPC analysis developed for "What could happen to cause an unsuccessful training experience?" The contingency plan to deal with "Bulb blows" is to have a "spare" bulb on hand.

Gantt Chart

A **Gantt chart** is a simple scheduling tool. It is a bar chart that plots tasks and subtasks against time. Once a list of tasks and subtasks has been created for a project, then responsibilities can be assigned for each. Next, beginning and finishing dates can be scheduled for each task and subtask. Finally, any comments relevant to a task or subtask are indicated on the Gantt chart. A Gantt chart is shown in Figure 10.25.

Construction

Each task or subtask is listed on the vertical axis, as are the person(s) or area(s) responsible for its completion. The horizontal axis is time. It shows the anticipated and actual duration of each task by a bar of the appropriate length. The left end of the bar indicates the beginning time (B) for the task, and the right end indicates the ending time (E) for the task. For example, Figure 10.25 shows that task 3 begins in March and ends in April,

FIGURE 10.25 **Gantt Chart**

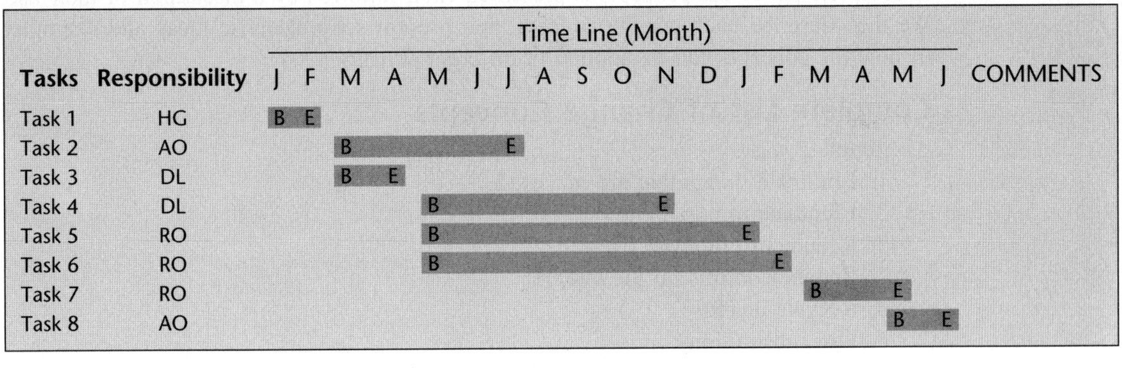

while task 4 begins in May and ends in November. The Gantt chart in Figure 10.25 shows that three tasks begin in May.

Change Concepts

While all changes do not lead to improvement, all improvement requires change. The ability to develop, test, and implement changes is essential for any individual, group, or organization that wants to continuously improve. But what kinds of changes will lead to improvement? Usually, a unique, specific change is required to obtain improvement in a specific set of circumstances. Thus, there are many kinds of changes. But these specific changes are developed from a limited number of change concepts. [See Reference 4, pp. 293–359.]

A concept is a general, abstract notion that is applied through a more specific idea. A **change concept** is a general notion or approach to change that has been found to be useful in developing specific ideas for changes that lead to improvement. Creatively combining these change concepts with knowledge about specific subjects can result in developing changes that lead to improvement. Many change concepts can be used to develop specific changes that do not require trade-offs between costs and quality.

The 70 change concepts listed here are organized into the following nine general groupings:

Grouping	Number of Concepts in Grouping
A. Eliminate waste	11
B. Improve work flow	11
C. Optimize inventory	4
D. Change the work environment	11
E. Enhance the producer/customer relationships	8
F. Manage time	5
G. Manage variation	8
H. Design systems to avoid mistakes	4
I. Focus on the product/service	8

A complete list of the concepts is presented first, followed by a discussion of their use. We then describe each change concept, and present some specific ideas and examples of how the concepts can be applied in different situations.

Complete List of Change Concepts

A. Eliminate waste
1. Eliminate things that are not used
2. Eliminate multiple entry
3. Reduce or eliminate overkill
4. Reduce controls on the system
5. Recycle or reuse
6. Use substitution

7. Reduce classifications
8. Remove intermediaries
9. Match the amount to the need
10. Use sampling
11. Change targets or set points

B. Improve work flow

12. Synchronize
13. Schedule into multiple processes
14. Minimize handoffs
15. Move steps in the process close together
16. Find and remove bottlenecks
17. Use automation
18. Smooth work flow
19. Do tasks in parallel
20. Consider people as in the same system
21. Use multiple processing units
22. Adjust to peak demand

C. Optimize inventory

23. Match inventory to predicted demand
24. Use pull systems
25. Reduce choice of features
26. Reduce multiple brands of same item

D. Change the work environment

27. Give people access to information
28. Use proper measurements
29. Take care of basics
30. Reduce demotivating aspects of the pay system
31. Conduct training
32. Implement cross-training
33. Invest more resources in improvement
34. Focus on core processes and purpose
35. Share risks
36. Emphasize natural and logical consequences
37. Develop alliances/cooperative relationships

E. Enhance the producer/customer relationship

38. Listen to customers
39. Coach customers to use product/service
40. Focus on the outcome to a customer
41. Use a coordinator
42. Reach agreement on expectations
43. Outsource for "free"
44. Optimize level of inspection
45. Work with suppliers

F. Manage time

46. Reduce setup or start-up time
47. Set up timing to use discounts

48. Optimize maintenance
49. Extend specialists' time
50. Reduce wait time

G. Manage variation

51. Standardization (create a formal process)
52. Stop tampering
53. Develop operational definitions
54. Improve predictions
55. Develop contingency plans
56. Sort product into grades
57. Desensitize
58. Exploit variation

H. Design systems to avoid mistakes

59. Use reminders
60. Use differentiation
61. Use constraints
62. Use affordances

I. Focus on the product or service

63. Mass customize
64. Offer the product/service anytime
65. Offer the product/service anyplace
66. Emphasize intangibles
67. Influence or take advantage of fashion trends
68. Reduce the number of components
69. Disguise defects and problems
70. Differentiate product using quality dimensions

How to Use the Change Concepts

The change concepts presented here are not specific enough to be applied directly to making improvements. Rather, the concept must be considered within the context of a particular situation and then turned into an idea. The idea will need to be specific enough to describe how the change can be developed, tested, and implemented in the particular situation. When describing the change concepts, we have tried to be consistent in the degree of specificity or generality of the concepts. Sometimes, a new idea seems at first to be a new change concept, but often, upon further reflection, it is seen to be an application of one of the more general concepts.

The primary purpose of this discussion is to provide help to individuals and teams who are trying to answer the question, What change can we make that will result in improvement? The change concepts can serve to provoke a new idea for an individual or team. This is critical in the Plan stage of the PDSA cycle. A team leader can choose one of the change concepts and then the team can explore some ideas for possible application of this concept to the situation of interest. The list of ideas should be recorded. After the generation of ideas is complete, the ideas can be discussed and critiqued. Any of the ideas that show promise can be further explored by the team to obtain a specific idea for a change.

Some of the change concepts appear to offer conflicting advice for developing changes. For example, concept 25, "reduce choice of features," and concept 63, "mass customize," appear to be aimed in opposite directions. Change concept 4, "reduce controls on the system," and change concept 51, "standardization (create a formal process)," also suggest conflicting directions. The important consideration is the context in which the change concept is being applied.

Eliminate Waste

In a broad sense, any activity or resource in an organization that does not add value to an external customer can be considered waste. This section provides some concepts for eliminating waste.

1. *Eliminate things that are not used.* Constant change in organizations results in less demand for specific resources and activities that were once important to the business. Unnecessary activities and unused resources can be identified through surveys, audits, data collection, and analysis of records. The next step is to take the obvious actions to remove the unused elements from the system.

2. *Eliminate multiple entry.* In some situations, information is recorded in a log or entered into a database more than one time, creating no added value. This practice is also called data redundancy. Changing the process to require only one entry can lead to improvement in productivity and quality by reducing discrepancies.

3. *Reduce or eliminate overkill.* Sometimes, a company's standard or recommended resources are designed to handle special, severe, or critical situations rather than the normal situation. Changing the standard to the appropriate level of resources for the normal situation will reduce waste. Additional resources would be used only when the situation warrants it.

4. *Reduce controls on the system.* Individuals and organizations use various types of controls to make sure a process or system does not stray too far from standards, requirements, or accepted practices. While useful for protection of the organization, these controls can increase costs, reduce productivity, and stifle improvement. Typical forms of controls include a layered management structure, approval signatures, standardized forms, and reports. A regular review of all of the organization's control procedures by everyone working in the system can result in identifying opportunities to reduce controls on the system without putting the organization at risk.

5. *Recycle or reuse.* Once a product is created and used for its intended purpose, it is natural to discard it and the by-products created by its use. However, if other uses can be found for the discarded product or by-products, the cost of producing the product can be spread out over its use and its reuse.

6. *Use substitution.* Waste can often be reduced by replacing some aspect of the product or process with a better alternative. One type of substitution is to include lower-cost components, materials, or methods that do not affect the performance of the process, service, or product (sometimes called **value engineering**). Another type of substitution is to switch to another process with fewer steps or less manual effort.

7. *Reduce classifications.* Classifications are often developed to differentiate elements of a system or to group items with common characteristics, but these classifications can lead to system complexity that increases costs or decreases quality. Classification should be reduced when the complexity caused by the classification is greater than the benefit gained.

8. *Remove intermediaries.* Intermediaries such as distributors, handlers, agents, and carriers may be part of a system. Consider eliminating these activities by linking production directly with the consumer. Some intermediaries add value to a process because of their specialized skills and knowledge. Often, however, eliminating these services can increase productivity without reducing value to the customer.

9. *Match the amount to the need.* Rather than use traditional standard units or sizes, organizations can adjust products and services to match the amount required for a particular situation. This practice reduces waste and carryover inventory. By studying how customers use the product, more convenient package sizes can be developed.

10. *Use sampling.* Reviews, checks, and measurements are made for a variety of reasons. Can these reasons be satisfied without checking or testing everything? Many times, the standard 100 percent inspection and testing results in waste of resources and time. Formal **sampling** procedures are available that can often provide as good or even better information than 100 percent checking. This will be discussed further in Chapter 13.

11. *Change targets or set points.* Sometimes problems go on for years because some piece of equipment is not designed or set up properly. Make sure that process settings are at desirable levels. Investigate places where waste is created, and consider adjustments to targets or set points to reduce the waste.

Improve Work Flow

Products and services are produced by processes. How does work flow in these processes? What is the plan to get work through a process? Are the various steps in the process arranged and prioritized to obtain quality outcomes at low costs? How can the work flow be changed so that the process is less reactive and more planned?

12. *Synchronize.* Production of products and services usually involves multiple stages. These stages operate at different times and at different speeds, resulting in an operation that is not smooth. Much time can be spent waiting for another stage to be reached. By focusing on the flow of the product (or customer) through the process, each of the stages can be synchronized.

13. *Schedule into multiple processes.* A system can be redesigned to include multiple versions of the same process focused on the specific requirements of the situation. Rather than a "one-size-fits-all" large process, multiple versions of the process are available, each tuned to the different types of needs of customers or users. Priorities can be established to allocate and schedule the inputs in order to maximize the performance of the system. The specific processes can then be greatly simplified since they only address a limited range of input requirements.

14. *Minimize handoffs.* Many systems require that elements such as a customer, a form, or a product be transferred to multiple people, offices, or workstations to complete the processing or service. The handoff from one stage to the next can increase time and costs and cause quality problems. The work flow can be rearranged to minimize any handoff in the process. The process can be redesigned so that any worker is involved only once in an iteration of a process.

15. *Move steps in the process close together.* The physical location of people and facilities can affect processing time and cause communication problems. If the physical location of adjacent steps in a process are moved close together, work can be directly

passed from one step to the next. This eliminates the need for communication systems, such as mail, and physical transports, such as vehicles, pipelines, and conveyor belts.

16. *Find and remove bottlenecks.* A **bottleneck** or **constraint** is anything that restricts the throughput of a system. A constraint within an organization would be any resource for which the demand is greater than its available capacity. To increase the throughput of a system, the constraints must be identified, exploited if possible, and removed if necessary. Bottlenecks occur in many parts of daily life; they can usually be identified by looking at where people are waiting or where work is piling up.

17. *Use automation.* The flow of many processes can be improved by the intelligent use of automation. Consider automation to improve the work flow for any process to reduce costs, reduce cycle times, eliminate human slips, reduce repetitive manual tasks, and provide measurement.

18. *Smooth work flow.* Yearly, monthly, weekly, and daily changes in demand often cause work flow to fluctuate widely. Rather than try to staff in order to handle the peak demands, steps can often be taken to better distribute the demand. This distribution results in a smooth work flow rather than in continual peaks and valleys.

19. *Do tasks in parallel.* Many systems are designed so that tasks are done in a series or linear sequence. The second task is not begun until the first task is completed. This is especially true when different groups in the organization are involved in the different steps of a process. Sometimes, improvements in time and costs can be gained from designing the system to do some or all tasks in parallel.

20. *Consider people as in the same system.* People in different systems are usually working toward different purposes, each trying to optimize their own system. Taking actions that help people to think of themselves as part of the same system can give them a common purpose and provide a basis for optimizing the larger system.

21. *Use multiple processing units.* To gain flexibility in controlling the work flow, try to include multiple workstations, machines, processing lines, and fillers in a system. This makes it possible to run smaller lots, serve special customers, minimize the impact of maintenance and downtime, and add flexibility to staffing. With multiple units, the primary product or service can be handled on one line to maximize efficiency and minimize setup time. The less-frequent products and services can be handled by the other units.

22. *Adjust to peak demand.* Sometimes it is not possible to balance the demands made on a system. In these cases, rather than keep a fixed amount of resources (materials, workers, and so on), historical data can be used to predict peak demands. Then methods can be implemented to meet the temporarily increased demand.

Optimize Inventory

Inventory of any type can be a source of waste in organizations. Inventory requires capital investment, storage space, and people to handle and keep track of it. In manufacturing organizations, inventory includes raw material waiting to be processed, in-process inventory, and finished-good inventory. For service organizations, the number of skilled workers available is often the key inventory issue. Extra inventory can result in higher costs with no improvement in performance for an organization. How can the costs associated with the maintenance of inventory be reduced? An understanding of where inventory is stored in a system is the first step in finding opportunities for improvement.

23. *Match inventory to predicted demand.* Excess inventory can result in higher costs with no improvement in performance for an organization. How can the proper amount of inventory to be maintained at any given time be determined? One approach to minimizing the costs associated with inventory is to use historical data to predict the demand. Using these predictions to optimize lead times and order quantities will lead to replenishing inventory in an economical manner. This is often the best approach to optimizing inventory when the process involves lengthy production times.

24. *Use pull systems.* In a "pull system" of production, work at a particular step in the process is done only if the next step in the process is demanding the work. Enough product is ordered or made to replenish what was just used. This is in contrast to most traditional "push systems," in which work is done as long as inputs are available. A pull system is designed to match production quantities with a downstream need. This approach can often result in lower inventories than a schedule-based production system. Pull systems are most beneficial in processes with short cycle times and high yields. Some features of effective pull systems are small lot sizes and container quantities, fast setup times, and minimal rework and scrap.

25. *Reduce choice of features.* Many features are added to products and services to accommodate the desires and wants of different customers and different markets. Each of these features makes sense in the context of a particular customer at a particular time, but taken as a whole, they can have tremendous impact on inventory costs. A review of current demand for each feature and consideration of grouping the features can allow a reduction in inventory without loss of customer satisfaction.

26. *Reduce multiple brands of same items.* If an organization uses more than one brand of any particular item, inventory costs will usually be higher than necessary, since a backup supply of each brand must be kept. Consider ways to reduce the number of brands while still providing the required service.

Change the Work Environment

Changes to the environment in which people work, study, and live can often provide leverage for improvements in performance. As organizations try to improve quality, reduce costs, or increase the value of their products and services, technical changes are developed, tested, and implemented. Many of these technical changes do not lead to improvement because the work environment is not ready to accept or support the changes. Changing the work environment itself can be a high-leverage opportunity for making other changes more effective.

27. *Give people access to information.* Traditionally, organizations have carefully controlled the information available to various groups of employees. Making relevant information available to employees allows them to suggest changes, make good decisions, and take actions that lead to improvements.

28. *Use proper measurements.* Measurement plays an important role in focusing people on particular aspects of a business. Developing appropriate measures, making better use of existing measures, and improving measurement systems can lead to improvement throughout the organization.

29. *Take care of basics.* There are certain fundamentals that must be considered to make any organization successful. Concepts like orderliness, cleanliness, discipline, and

managing costs and prices are examples of such fundamentals. It is sometimes useful to take a fresh look at these basics to see whether the organization is still on track. If there are fundamental problems in the business, changes in other areas may not lead to improvements. Also, when people's basic needs are not being met, meaningful improvements cannot be expected in other areas. The **Five-S movement,** which was the beginning of quality control in Japanese workshops, got its name from the Japanese words for straighten up, put things in order, clean up, personal cleanliness, and discipline.

30. *Reduce demotivating aspects of the pay system.* Pay is rarely a positive motivator in an organization, but it can cause confusion and become a demotivator. Some pay systems can encourage competition rather than cooperation among employees. Another result of some pay systems is the reluctance to take risks or make changes. Review the organization's system for pay to ensure that the current system does not cause unnecessary problems.

31. *Conduct training.* Training is basic to quality performance and the ability to make changes for improvement. Many changes will not be effective if people have not received the basic training required to do a job. Training should include the "why" as well as the "what" and the "how."

32. *Implement cross-training.* Cross-training means training people in an organization to do multiple jobs. Such training allows for flexibility and makes change easier. The investment required for the extra training will pay off in productivity, product quality, and cycle times.

33. *Invest more resources in improvement.* In some organizations, people spend more than a full-time job getting their required tasks completed and fighting the fires created in their work. The only changes made are reactions to problems or changes mandated outside the organization. To break out of this mode, management must learn how to start investing time in developing, testing, and implementing changes that will lead to improvements.

34. *Focus on core processes and purpose.* Core processes are the processes directly related to the purpose of the organization. They can be characterized as those activities that provide value directly to external customers. To reduce costs, consider reducing or eliminating activities that are not part of the core processes.

35. *Share risks.* Every business is faced with taking risks, and reaping their accompanying potential rewards or losses. Many people become more interested in the performance of their organization when they can clearly see how their future is tied to the long-term performance of the organization. Developing systems that allow all employees to share in the risks can lead to an increased interest in performance. Types of plans for sharing risks and gains include profit-sharing, gain-sharing, bonuses, and pay for knowledge.

36. *Emphasize natural and logical consequences.* An alternative approach to traditional reward-and-punishment systems in organizations is to focus on natural and logical consequences. Natural consequences follow from the natural order of the physical world (for example, not eating leads to hunger), while logical consequences follow from the reality of the business or social world (for example, if you are late for a meeting, you will not have a chance to have input on some of the issues discussed). The idea of emphasizing natural and logical consequences is to get all to be responsible for their own behavior rather than to use power, judge others, and force submission. Rather than demand conformance, the use of natural and logical consequences permits choice.

37. *Develop alliances/cooperative relationships.* Cooperative alliances optimize the interactions between the parts of a system and offer a better approach for integration of organizations.

Enhance the Producer/Customer Relationship

To benefit from improvements in quality of products and services, the customer must recognize and appreciate the improvements. Many ideas for improvement can come directly from a supplier or from the producer's customers. Many problems in organizations occur because the producer does not understand the customer's needs, or because customers are not clear about their expectations of suppliers. The interface between the producer/provider and the customer provides opportunities to learn and develop changes that will lead to improvement.

38. *Listen to customers.* It is easy for people to get caught up in the internal functioning of the organization and forget why they are in business: to serve their customers. Time should be invested on a regular basis in processes that "listen" to the customers. Sometimes it is important to figure out how to communicate with customers further down the **supply chain,** or even with the final consumer of the product or service. Talk to customers about their experiences in using the organization's products. Learn about improvement opportunities.

39. *Coach customers to use the product/service.* Customers often encounter quality problems and actually increase their costs because they do not understand all of the intricacies of the product or service. Companies can increase the value of their products and services by developing ways to coach customers on how to use them.

40. *Focus on the outcome to a customer.* Make the outcome (the product or service) generated by your organization the focus of all activities. First, clearly understand the outcomes that customers expect from your organization. Then, to focus improvement efforts on a particular work activity, consider the question, "How does this activity support the outcome to the customer?" Make improvements in such areas as the quality, cost, efficiency, and cycle time of that activity. Organize people, departments, and processes in a way that best serves the customer, paying particular attention to the product/customer interfaces. This change concept can also be described as "begin with the end in mind."

41. *Use a coordinator.* A coordinator's primary job is to manage producer/customer linkages. For example, an expeditor is someone who focuses on ensuring adequate supplies of materials and equipment or who coordinates the flow of materials in an organization. Having someone coordinate the flow of materials, tools, parts, and processed goods for critical processes can help prevent problems and downtime. A coordinator can also be used to work with customers to provide extra services. One example is a case manager, who acts as a buffer between a complex process and the customer.

42. *Reach agreement on expectations.* Many times customer dissatisfaction occurs because the customers feel that they have not received the products or services they were led to expect as a result of advertising, special promotions, and promises by the sales group. Marketing processes should be coordinated with production capabilities. Clear expectations should be established before the product is produced or the service is delivered to the customer.

43. *Outsource for "free."* Sometimes it is possible to get suppliers to perform additional functions for the customer with little or no increase in the price to the customer. A task that is a major inconvenience or cost for the customer can be performed inexpensively and efficiently by the supplier. The supplier might be willing to do this task for "free" in order to secure ongoing business with the customer.

44. *Optimize level of inspection.* What level of inspection is appropriate for a process? All products will eventually undergo some type of inspection, possibly by the user. Options for inspection at any given point in the supply chain are: no inspection, 100 percent inspection, or reduction or increases to the current level of inspection. A study of the level of inspection can potentially lead to changes that increase quality of outcomes to the customers and/or decrease costs. Identifying the appropriate level of inspection for a process is discussed in Chapter 13.

45. *Work with suppliers.* Inputs to a process sometimes control the costs and quality of performance of a process. Working with suppliers to use their technical knowledge can often reduce the cost of using their products or services. Suppliers may even have ideas on how to make changes in a company's process that will surprise its customers.

Manage Time

Cut cycle time as a strategy for improving any organization. An organization can gain a competitive advantage by reducing the time to develop new products, waiting times for services, lead times for orders and deliveries, and cycle times for all functions and processes.

46. *Reduce setup or start-up time.* Setup times can often be cut in half just by getting organized for the setup. Minimizing setup or start-up time allows the organization to maintain lower levels of inventory and get more productivity out of its assets.

47. *Set up timing to use discounts.* The planning and timing of many activities can be coordinated to take advantage of savings and discounts that are available, resulting in a reduction of operating costs. An organization must have a system in place to take advantage of such opportunities. For example, available discounts on invoices offered by suppliers for paying bills within 10 days of the invoice date require a system that can process an invoice and cut a check within the discount period. Opportunities to apply this concept require a flexible process and knowledge of the opportunity to take advantage of the timing.

48. *Optimize maintenance.* Time is lost and quality often deteriorates when production and service equipment break down. A preventive maintenance strategy attempts to keep people and machines in good condition instead of waiting until there is a breakdown. Through proper design and the study of historical data, an efficient maintenance program can be designed to keep equipment in production with a minimum of downtime for maintenance. Learning to observe and listen to equipment before it breaks down is also an important component of any plan to optimize maintenance.

49. *Extend specialists' time.* Organizations employ specialists who have specific skills or knowledge, but not all of their work duties utilize these skills or knowledge. Try to remove assignments and job requirements that do not use the specialists' skills. Find ways to let specialists have a broader impact on the organization, especially when the specialist is a constraint to throughput in the organization.

50. *Reduce wait time.* Reduction in wait time can lead to improvements in many types of services. Ideas for change that can reduce the time that customers have to wait are

especially useful. This refers not only to the time to perform a service for the customer, but the time it takes the customer to use or maintain a product.

Manage Variation

Many quality and cost problems in a process or product are due to variation. Reduction of variation will improve the predictability of outcomes, and may actually exceed customer expectations and help to reduce the frequency of poor results. Many procedures and activities are designed to deal with variation in systems. Consideration of Shewhart's concept of common and special causes opens up opportunities to improve these procedures. By focusing on variation, some ideas for changes can be developed. Three basic approaches can be taken: reduce the variation, compensate for the variation, or exploit the variation.

51. *Standardization (create a formal process).* The use of standards, or **standardization,** has a negative and bureaucratic connotation to many people. However, an appropriate amount of standardization can provide a foundation upon which improvement in quality and costs can be built. Standardization is one of the primary methods for reducing variation in a system. The use of standardization, or creating a more formal process, should be considered for the parts of a system that have big effects on the outcomes, or the leverage points.

52. *Stop tampering.* Tampering is defined as interfering so as to weaken or change for the worse. In many situations, changes are made on the basis of the last result observed or measured. Often these changes actually increase the variation in a process or product, as illustrated by the **funnel experiment,** discussed in Chapter 1. The methods of statistical process control can be used to decide when it is appropriate to make changes based on recent results.

53. *Develop operational definitions.* Reduction of variation can begin with a common understanding of concepts typically used in the transaction of business. The meaning of a concept is ultimately found in how that concept is applied. Simple concepts such as on-time, clean, noisy, and secure need **operational definitions** in order to reduce variation in communications and measurement.

54. *Improve predictions.* Plans, forecasts, and budgets are based on predictions. In many situations, predictions are built from the ground up each time a prediction is required, and historical data are not used. The study of variation from past predictions can lead to alternative ways to improve the predictions.

55. *Develop contingency plans.* Variation in everyday life often creates problems. Reducing the variation may eventually eliminate the problems, but how do people cope in the meantime? One way is to prepare backup plans, or contingencies, to deal with the unexpected problems. When the variation is due to a special cause that can be identified, then contingency plans can be ready when these special causes of variation occur.

56. *Sort product into grades.* Creative ways can be developed to take advantage of naturally occurring variation in products. Ways of sorting the product or service into different grades can be designed to minimize the variation within a grade and maximize the variation between grades. The different grades can then be marketed to different customer needs.

57. *Desensitize.* It is impossible to control some types of variation: between students in a class, among the ways customers try to use a product, in the physical condition of

patients who enter the hospital. How can the impact on the outcome (education, function and health) be minimized when this variation is present? It can be done by desensitizing or causing a nonreaction to some stimulus. This change concept focuses on desensitizing the effect of variation rather than reducing the incidence of variation.

58. *Exploit variation.* It is sometimes not clear how variation can be reduced or eliminated. Instead of just accepting or "dealing with" the variation, ways can be developed to exploit it. This change concept deals with some ways to turn the negative variation into a positive method to differentiate products or services.

Design Systems to Avoid Mistakes

Making mistakes is part of being human; they occur because of the interaction of people with a system. Some systems are more prone to mistakes than others. Mistakes can be reduced by redesigning the system to make their occurrence less likely. This type of system design or redesign is called **mistake proofing** or **error proofing.** Mistake proofing can be achieved by using technology, such as adding equipment to automate repetitive tasks, by using methods to make it more difficult to do something wrong, or by integrating these methods with technology. Methods for mistake proofing are not directed at changing people's behavior, but rather at changing the system to prevent slips. They aim to reduce mistakes from actions that are done almost subconsciously in performing a process or using a product.

59. *Use reminders.* Many mistakes are made as a result of forgetting to do something. Reminders can come in many different forms: a written notice or a phone call, a checklist of things to accomplish, an alarm on a clock, a standard form, or the documented steps to follow for a process.

60. *Use differentiation.* Mistakes can occur when people are dealing with things that look nearly the same. A person may copy a wrong number or grab a wrong part because of similarity or close proximity to other numbers or parts. Mistakes can also occur when actions are similar. A person may end up in the wrong place or use a piece of equipment in the wrong way because the directions or procedures are similar to others they might have used in a different situation. Familiarity that results from experience can sometimes increase the chance of committing mistakes of association. To reduce mistakes, steps should be taken to break patterns. This can be done by, for example, color coding, sizing, using different symbols, or separating similar items.

61. *Use constraints.* A constraint restricts the performance of certain actions. A door that blocks passage into an unsafe area is a constraint. Constraints are an important method for mistake proofing because they can limit the actions that result in mistakes. They do not just make information available in the external world, they also make it available within the product or system itself. To be effective, constraints should be visible and easy to understand. Constraints can be built into a process so that accidental stopping or an unwanted action that will result in a mistake can be prevented. Constraints can also be used to make sure that the steps performed in a process or in using a product are accomplished in the correct sequence.

62. *Use affordances.* An **affordance** provides insight, without the need for explanation, into how something should be used. In contrast to a constraint, which limits the actions possible, an affordance provides visual (or other sensory) prompting for the

actions that should be performed. Once a person sees the fixtures on a door, he or she should be able to determine whether it opens in, opens out, or slides. There should not be a need to refer to labels or to use a trial-and-error approach. If a process or product can be designed to lead the user to perform the correct actions, fewer mistakes will occur.

Focus on the Product or Service

Most of the change concepts in the other categories address the way that a process is performed; however, many of the concepts also apply to improvements to a product or service. This category comprises eight change concepts that are particularly useful for developing changes to a product or service that do not naturally fit into any of the other groupings.

63. *Mass customize.* Most consumers of products and services would agree that quality increases as the product or service is customized to the customer's unique circumstances. Most consumers would also expect to pay more or wait longer for these customized offerings than for a mass-produced version. To **mass customize** means combining the uniqueness of customized products with the efficiency of mass production.

64. *Offer the product or service anytime.* Many products and services are available only at certain times. Such constraints almost always detract from their quality. How can these constraints be removed? In some cases a technology breakthrough, such as the ATM, is needed. In other cases, prediction plays an important role—for example, predicting what type of cars customers will order. However, in many situations the constraint is created because it is more convenient for the provider of the service than for the customer. Offering the product or service anytime is different from just reducing wait time. To achieve this goal often takes a totally new conceptualization of the product or service. For this reason, "anytime" is an important concept for expanding the expectations of customers.

65. *Offer the product or service anyplace.* An important dimension of quality for most products and services is convenience. To make a product or service more convenient, free it from the constraints of space. Make it available anyplace. For products, the constraint of space is often related to the size of the product. Making a product smaller or lighter without adversely affecting any of its other attributes almost always improves the quality of the product. One of the most striking examples is the miniaturization of the computer to the point that it can now be carried in a briefcase and used virtually anywhere.

66. *Emphasize intangibles.* Opportunities for improvement can be found by embellishing a product or service with intangible features. Three ways to accomplish this are by miniaturizing, by providing information (electronically or otherwise), and by developing producer-customer relationships.

67. *Influence or take advantage of fashion trends.* The features and uniformity of a product or service define its quality. Uniformity is often assumed to exist in a product or service, while features can affect customer expectations. Features are frequently subject to fashion trends.

68. *Reduce the number of components.* Reducing handoffs was one of the change concepts for simplifying a process. Similarly, reducing the number of component parts is a way to simplify a product. Components in this context can mean component parts, ingredients, or multiple types of the same component. Reduction in the number of components can be achieved through design of the product so that one component performs

the functions previously performed by more than one; or by standardizing the size, shape, or brand of similar components; or by packaging components into modules.

69. *Disguise defects and problems.* In some instances, especially in the short term, it may be more effective to hide the defect in a product or service than to remove it. However, the longer-term strategy is to remove the defect. Included in this category are actions taken to make the defect more palatable to the customer. This change concept does not include false advertising, in which claims about the product are made that are not true, nor does it include defects that are hidden at the time of sale only to emerge in later use of the product.

70. *Differentiate product using quality dimensions.* Customer satisfaction is improved as the match between process output and customer needs/wants is increased. The degree of matching is determined using customer research. Customer research can provide an understanding of customers' needs and wants.

Case Study of Using a Change Concept to Improve a Process

Undergraduate and graduate students require convenient access to accurate and timely information on their financial accounts with their university. The goals of student account services (SAS) are to first satisfy student account information needs electronically, then by phone, and finally, if necessary, in person. This approach enables a university to improve both customer service quality and employee productivity.

A quality improvement team analyzed the total number of calls and corresponding abandoned calls through the student accounts automated call distributor (ACD). The team studied the list of 70 change concepts and concluded that the thirteenth change concept, "schedule into multiple processes," could be helpful in reducing the percentage of abandoned calls. The team developed this change concept into hiring inexpensive graduate student assistants who could answer basic phone questions and perform triage for complex inquiries. If an inquiry required a higher level of account expertise than that possessed by the graduate assistant, the assistant would forward the call to a full-time student account customer representative. This change took effect during the first week of August. An immediate improvement was realized in the rate of abandoned calls. The abandoned call rate dropped from 44 percent in July 2003 to 10 percent in August 2003. By October 2003, the rate was down to 6 percent, as shown in Figure 10.26.

FIGURE 10.26
Percentage of Abandoned Calls by Month

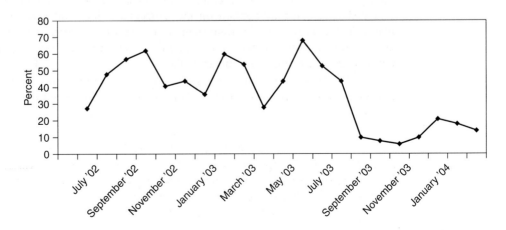

Summary

This chapter presented qualitative techniques that can be used in conjunction with control charts to help resolve special causes of variation and reduce common causes of variation in a process. The techniques discussed in this chapter are brainstorming, affinity diagrams, cause-and-effect diagrams, interrelationship diagraphs, check sheets, Pareto diagrams, stratification, systematic diagrams, matrix diagrams, PDPC analyses, Gantt charts, and change concepts.

Brainstorming is a way to elicit a large number of ideas from a group of people in a short period of time. Brainstorming is used for several purposes: to determine problems to work on; to find possible causes of a problem; to find solutions to a problem; and to find ways to implement solutions. For our purposes, brainstorming is used to help resolve special causes of variation and to help reduce common causes of variation.

An affinity diagram is used to organize and consolidate an extensive and unorganized amount of verbal, pictorial, and/or audio data concerning a problem. Again, for our purposes, an affinity diagram is used to help resolve special causes of variation (usually problems) and to help reduce common causes of variation (problems). The data usually consist of facts, opinions, intuition, and experience. Frequently, the input into an affinity diagram is the output of a brainstorming session. The affinity diagram helps organize and consolidate verbal, pictorial, and/or audio data into natural clusters that bring out the latent structure of the problem under study.

A cause-and-effect (C&E) diagram is a tool used to organize the possible causes of a problem, select the most probable cause, and verify the cause-and-effect relationship between the most probable cause and the problem (effect) under study, in order to direct appropriate action to resolving the problem (effect) under study. The data analyzed by a C&E diagram usually come from a brainstorming session.

An interrelationship diagraph (ID) identifies the cause-and-effect relationships between a set of related issues or ideas, and which issues or ideas are root effects and root causes. A root effect is an issue or idea that is affected by many other issues or ideas, and consequently, is not a good candidate to be considered critical to resolving the problem under study. A root cause affects many other issues or ideas, and consequently, is a good candidate to be considered critical to resolving the problem under study.

Check sheets are used for collecting or gathering data in a logical format. The data collected can be used in constructing a control chart, a Pareto diagram, or a histogram. Pareto diagrams focus attention on the concept of "the vital few versus the trivial many." The vital few are the small number of causes that account for the largest percentage of the problems in a process. The trivial many are the myriad causes that account for only a small percentage of the problems in a process. Focusing on the significant few is the important management principal of prioritization, eliminating micromanagement and focusing everyone's attention on the important causes of problems in a process.

Stratification is a procedure used to describe the systematic subdivision of process data to obtain a detailed understanding of the process's structure. Stratification can be used to break down a problem to discover its root causes and set into motion appropriate corrective actions, called countermeasures.

A systematic diagram is used to generate the actions needed to solve a problem. It can help team members ask what events must take place at level B to resolve the problem at level A, and what actions must occur at level C to make level B actions happen, and so on. This analysis continues until a set of actions is achieved which consists of doable events.

A matrix diagram is used to arrange large quantities of data relating to two or more aspects of a problem. It helps locate and plug any holes in the information base relating to a problem.

The program decision process chart (PDPC) helps anticipate and develop contingency plans to avoid potential problems when executing an action. PDPC analysis is appropriate if the action to be executed requires an unknown amount of time to complete and is set in an unfamiliar environment.

A Gantt chart is a scheduling tool for relatively small projects. It is a bar chart that plots tasks and subtasks against time. Once a list of tasks and subtasks has been created for a project, then responsibilities can be assigned for each task or subtask and beginning and finishing dates can be scheduled for each task and subtask.

Change concepts are general notions or approaches to change that have been found to be useful in developing specific ideas for changes that lead to improvement. Creatively combining these change concepts with knowledge about specific subjects can result in developing changes that lead to improvement. This chapter organized 70 change concepts for ease of reference and use.

Individually, the above tools and techniques are powerful aids for improvement of a process. However, they take on their true strength when they are used as an integrated system of tools and techniques for diagnosing a process.

Key Terms

80-20 rule, *366*
affinity diagram, *353*
affordance, *401*
attribute check sheet, *365*
bottleneck, *395*
brainstorming, *347*
cause-and-effect diagram, *356*
change concept, *390*
check sheet, *363*
cluster, *353*
constraint, *395*
contingency plan, *387*
cost Pareto diagram, *371*
countermeasure, *375*
cum line, *368*
defect location check sheet, *366*
dendrogram, *381*
error proofing, *401*
fishbone diagram, *358*
five-S movement, *397*
funnel experiment, *400*

Gantt chart, *389*
interrelationship diagraph, *360*
invisible data, *364*
Ishikawa diagram, *358*
KJ method, *353*
latent structure, *353*
L-shaped matrix diagram, *384*
magnification, *349*
mass customize, *402*
matrix diagram, *384*
minification, *349*
mistake proofing, *401*
modification, *349*
new mountain stratification, *377*
old mountain stratification, *377*
operational definition, *400*
Pareto analysis, *366*
Pareto diagram, *367*
piggybacking, *348*

process analysis, *360*
Program Decision Process Chart (PDPC analyses), *387*
random word technique, *349*
rearrangement, *349*
root cause, *360*
root cause analysis, *359*
root effect, *360*
sampling, *394*
standardization, *400*
stratification, *375*
substitution, *349*
supply chain, *398*
systematic diagram, *381*
T-shaped matrix diagram, *384*
tree diagram, *381*
value engineering, *393*
variables check sheet, *365*
visible data, *364*
workload balancing, *387*

Exercises

10.1. Conduct a brainstorming session on the "barriers to QM in your organization."

10.2. Construct an affinity diagram from the brainstorming data in Exercise 10.1.

10.3. Construct a cause-and-effect diagram of "the barriers to QM in your organization" using the universal major causes.

10.4. Construct a cause-and-effect diagram of "the barriers to QM in your organization" using the header cards from the affinity diagram in Exercise 10.2.

10.5. Construct an interrelationship diagraph of "the barriers to QM in your organization" using the header cards from the affinity diagram in Exercise 10.2.

10.6. Construct a systematic diagram for the root cause theme discovered in Exercise 10.2.

10.7. Construct a matrix diagram for the actionable items on the right-most branches of the systematic diagram in Exercise 10.6 and people/departments in your organization.

10.8. Construct a PDPC analysis for the actionable items on the right-most branches of the systematic diagram in Exercise 10.6.

10.9. Construct a Gantt chart for the actionable items on the right-most branches of the systematic diagram in Exercise 10.6.

10.10. Explain the relationship between the "change concepts" and the PDSA cycle.

References

1. J. F. Beardsley & Associates, International (1977), *Quality Circles: Member Manual.*
2. E. De Bono (1993), *Serious Creativity: Using the Power of Lateral Thinking to Create New Ideas* (Des Moines: Advanced Practical Thinking).
3. K. Ishikawa (1983), *Guide to Quality Control,* 11th printing (Tokyo: Asian Productivity Organization).
4. J. Langley, K. Nolan, T. Nolan, C. Norman, and L. Provost (1996), *The Improvement Guide* (San Francisco: Jossey-Bass).
5. D. Wheeler and D. Chambers (1992), *Understanding Statistical Process Control,* 2nd ed. (Knoxville, TN: SPC Press).

Appendix A10.1

Using Minitab to Obtain a Pareto Diagram

To obtain a Pareto diagram such as the one displayed in Figure 10.9c on page 370, open the file ☞ OPERATOR4.MTW.

1. Note that this data set contains the causes in column C1 and the frequency of each cause in column C2.
2. Select Stat | Quality Tools | Pareto Chart.
3. Select the Chart defects table option button.
4. In the Labels in: edit box, enter C1 or Cause.
5. In the Frequencies in: edit box, enter C2 or Frequency.
6. Enter 99.9 in the Combine defects after the first % into one: edit box.
7. Click the OK button.

**FIGURE
A10.1**
**Pareto
Diagram
Drawn by
Minitab**

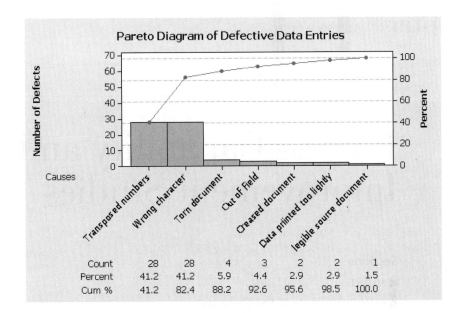

Pareto Diagram of Defective Data Entries

	Transposed numbers	Wrong character	Torn document	Out of field	Creased document	Data printed too lightly	Illegible source document
Count	28	28	4	3	2	2	1
Percent	41.2	41.2	5.9	4.4	2.9	2.9	1.5
Cum %	41.2	82.4	88.2	92.6	95.6	98.5	100.0

If the variable of interest is located in a single column and is in raw form with each row indicating a type of error, the Charts defects data in: option button would be selected and the appropriate column number or variable name would be entered in the Chart defects data in: edit box.

Figure A10.1 shows the Pareto diagram of Figure 10.9c redrawn by Minitab.

Chapter 11

Process Capability and Improvement Studies

Sections

Chapter Objectives

- To discuss the voice of the customer, or customer specification limits for the output of a process
- To define and illustrate performance specifications
- To define and illustrate technical specifications, including individual unit specifications, acceptable quality level (AQL) specifications, and distribution specifications
- To discuss the distinction between performance and technical specifications
- To discuss the fallacy that conformance to technical specifications is sufficient to achieve acceptable quality
- To discuss the voice of the process, or the output of a process
- To discuss the importance and application of process capability studies to compare the voice of the process, or process performance, with the voice of the customer, or customer needs
- To describe and illustrate attribute process capability studies

- To describe and illustrate variables capability studies, and compare natural limits on the output of a stable process with specification limits
- To define and illustrate process capability indices to summarize processes
- To describe and illustrate two types of process improvement studies: attribute improvement studies and variables improvement studies
- To discuss and illustrate the use of quality improvement stories to present process capability and process improvement studies to management

Introduction

Process capability studies determine whether a process is unstable, investigate any sources of instability, determine their causes, and take action to eliminate such sources of instability. After all sources of instability have been eliminated from a process, the natural behavior of the process is called its process capability. Process capability compares the output of a process (called "voice of the process") with the customer's specification limits for the outputs (called "voice of the customer"). A process must have an established process capability before it can be improved. Consequently, a process capability study must be successfully completed before a process improvement study can have any chance for success.

Process improvement studies follow the Deming cycle of Plan, Do, Study, Act. First, managers construct a plan to decrease the difference between customer needs (voice of the customer) and process performance (voice of the process). Recall that a plan is an intention to move from an existing method or flowchart to a revised method or flowchart. Second, they test the plan's validity using a planned experiment (do). Third, they collect data and study the results of the planned experiment to determine if the plan or revised flowchart will decrease the difference between customer needs and process performance (study). Fourth, if the data collected about the plan show that the plan will achieve its objective(s), the revised flowchart is standardized through "best practices" and training (act), and the managers responsible for the plan return to the plan phase of the Deming cycle to find further revisions to the flowchart that will further reduce the difference between customer needs and process performance. If the data collected about the plan show that the plan will not achieve its objective(s), the managers responsible for the plan return to the plan phase of the Deming cycle to find a different revision to the flowchart that will reduce the difference between customer needs and process performance. Hence, the Deming cycle follows a never-ending path of process and quality improvement.

This chapter is divided into four sections: **specifications, process capability studies, process improvement studies,** and **quality improvement stories.** The quality improvement story is an effective format for quality management practitioners to present process capability and process improvement studies to management.

Specifications (Voice of the Customer)

Specifications fall into two broad categories: **performance specifications** and **technical specifications.**

Performance Specifications

Performance specifications address a customer's needs or wants. An example of a performance specification can be seen in restaurants rated by the *Red Michelin Guide*. The customers of these restaurants set their performance specifications as "a perfect dining experience." Perfection is measured in terms of the synergistic experience created by the interaction of food, service, ambience, and price. The *Red Michelin Guide* rates restaurants on a one to three star scale. Only the best restaurants in the world receive Michelin stars. A restaurant receives one Michelin star for consistently serving very good food in a good setting, but it is not considered worthy of a special traveling effort. A restaurant receives two Michelin stars for consistently serving excellent food, including specialties and wines of choice in a great setting. The restaurant is worth a detour from one's existing travel itinerary. A restaurant receives three Michelin stars for serving excellent food and great wine, with impeccable and elegant service and ambience. The restaurant is one of the best restaurants in the world and is worth a special trip. All starred restaurants have a high average level of quality with very little variation around the average. A three star Michelin chef is an artist; it is as if Picasso were painting for your pleasure. Three star Michelin restaurants provide performance specifications. They guarantee satisfaction at the point of delivery. Nothing short of perfection is acceptable.

Technical Specifications

Technical specifications describe the desired values of quality characteristics at delivery. There are three types of technical specifications: **individual unit specifications, acceptable quality level (AQL) specifications,** and **distribution specifications.**

Individual Unit Specifications

Individual unit specifications state a boundary, or boundaries, that apply to individual units of a product or service. An individual unit of product or service is considered to conform to a specification if it is on or inside the boundary or boundaries; this is the **goalpost view of quality.** Individual unit specifications are made up of two parts, which together form a third part. The first part of an individual unit specification is the **nominal value.** This is the desired value for process performance mandated by the customer's needs. Ideally, if all quality characteristics were at nominal, products and services would perform as expected over their life cycle. The second part of an individual unit specification is a **tolerance.** A tolerance is an allowable departure from a nominal value established by design engineers that is deemed nonharmful to the functioning of the product or service over its life cycle. Tolerances are added and/or subtracted from nominal values. The third part of an individual unit specification is a **specification limit,** or the boundaries created by adding and/or subtracting tolerances from a nominal value. It is possible to have either two-sided specification limits:

$$USL = Nominal + Tolerance$$

$$LSL = Nominal - Tolerance$$

where USL is the upper specification limit and LSL is the lower specification limit, or one-sided specification limits (i.e., either USL or LSL only). A nominal value and specification limits form the **voice of the customer.**

An example of an individual unit specification and its three parts can be seen in the specification for the "case hardness depth" of a camshaft. A camshaft is considered to be conforming with respect to case hardness depth if each individual unit is between 7.0 mm $\pm$ 3.5 mm (or 3.5 to 10.5 mm). The nominal value in that specification is 7.0 mm; the two-sided tolerance is 3.5 mm; the lower specification limit is 3.5 mm (7.0 mm $-$ 3.5 mm); and the upper specification limit is 10.5 mm (7.0 mm $+$ 3.5 mm).

From our earlier discussion of the philosophy of continuous reduction of variation, we saw that the goal of modern management should not be 100 percent conformance to specifications **(zero defects)**, but the never-ending reduction of process variation within specification limits so that all products/services are as close to nominal as possible. This is the **Taguchi loss function view of quality.** Specified tolerances become increasingly irrelevant as process variation is reduced so that the process's output is well within specification limits.

Acceptable Quality Level (AQL) Specifications

Acceptable quality level (AQL) specifications state a requirement that must be met by most individual units of product or service, but allow a certain proportion of the units to exceed the requirements. For example, camshafts shall be acceptable if no more than 3 percent of the units exceed the specification limits of 3.5 and 10.5 mm. This type of specification limit is frequently referred to as an acceptable quality level. AQL specifications are much like individual unit specifications, except they have a unique negative feature: they formally support the production of a certain percentage of defective product or service.

Distribution Specifications

Distribution specifications define an acceptable distribution for each product or service quality characteristic. In an analytic study, a distribution is defined in terms of its mean, standard deviation, and shape. However, from the Empirical Rule discussed in Chapter 5, it is not necessary to make any assumptions about the shape of the distribution. That is, virtually all data from a stable process will fall between the mean plus or minus three standard deviations.

As an example of a distribution specification, the case hardness depth of a camshaft shall be stable with an average depth of 7.0 mm and a standard deviation not to exceed 1.167 mm. In other words, individual units shall be distributed around the average with a dispersion not to exceed 3.50 mm on either side of the average, since for a stable process, virtually all of the output will be within three standard deviations on either side of the mean [7.0 mm $\pm$ 3(1.167 mm) = 7.0 mm $\pm$ 3.50 mm = 3.50 to 10.50 mm]. The mean and standard deviation are simply directional goals for management when using distribution specifications. Management must use statistical methods to move the process average toward the nominal value of 7.0 mm and to decrease the process standard deviation as far below 1.167 mm as possible. Distribution requirements are stated in the language of the process and promote the never-ending improvement of a process.

Distinguishing between Performance Specifications and Technical Specifications

Performance specifications are not commonly used in business; instead, technical specifications are used. Unfortunately, this can cause major problems because technical specifications may not produce the performance desired by a customer. As an example, consider a hospital that serves medium (versus rare or well-done) steak to patients who select steak for dinner [see Reference 2]. The performance desired is patient satisfaction within nutritional guidelines. But performance specifications are not used. Instead, a technical specification of 5 ounces of steak is substituted; it is assumed they are equivalent.

A hospital purchasing agent switches from meat vendor A to meat vendor B to secure a lower price, while still meeting the technical specification of 5 ounces. He does not discuss or inform the hospital nutritionist and kitchen staff of the switch in vendors. The hospital nutritionist begins receiving complaints from patients that the steak is tough and well done. She investigates and finds that vendor A's steaks were thick, while vendor B's are thin (but longer and wider). She realizes via statistical monitoring methods that the thinner steaks get hotter more quickly and hence cook faster, given the usual preparation regimen, as shown in Figure 11.1. She concludes, "If I'd known that the steaks had been changed, I could have accommodated the change without creating patient dissatisfaction." The purchasing agent says, "I met the technical specification of 5 ounces." The problem lies in assuming that technical specifications are the same as desired level of performance. This is not necessarily true.

The Fallacy That Conformance to Technical Specifications Defines Quality

Mere conformance to specification limits is insufficient to achieve the quality level required to compete effectively in today's marketplace. Management must constantly try

FIGURE 11.1
Final Cooked Temperature of 5-Ounce Hospital Steaks

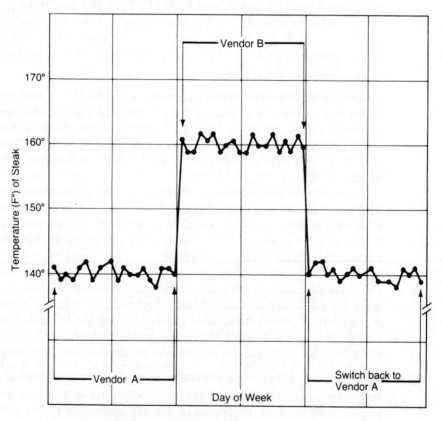

Note: Most patients can detect a 10°F difference in steak temperature. The difference in temperature between vendor A's and vendor B's steak when subjected to the hospital's cooking regimen is approximately 20°F.

to reduce process variation around a nominal value within specification limits (the Taguchi loss function) to achieve the degree of uniformity required to produce products or services that function exactly as promised to the customer over their life cycle.

Created Dimensions

The features of products, services, or processes that are created when the component parts of products or services are assembled are called **created dimensions.** The voice of the customer for created dimensions is discussed in Appendix A11.1 of this chapter.

Process Capability Studies

There are two types of **process capability studies: attribute process capability studies** and **variables process capability studies.**

Attribute Process Capability Studies

Attribute process capability studies determine a process's capability in terms of fraction defective output or counts of defects for a unit of output. The major tools used in attribute process capability studies are attribute control charts, discussed in Chapter 7, and the tools discussed in Chapter 10. The **process capability** for a p chart is $\bar{p}$ (the average fraction defective units generated by the process). The process capability for the np chart is $n\bar{p}$ (the average number of defective units generated by the process for a given subgroup size, n). The process capability for a c chart is $\bar{c}$ (the average number of defects per unit generated by the process for a given area of opportunity). Finally, the process capability for a u chart is $\bar{u}$ (the average number of defects per unit generated by the process where the area of opportunity varies from subgroup to subgroup).

A shortcoming of this type of study is that it begins with a specification, but it is not specific about the reason for failure to meet that specification. The p chart does not indicate if defective units result from the process being off nominal and too close to the specification limit, or because the process has too much unit-to-unit variation, or because the process is not stable with respect to its mean and/or variance. Further, as p charts are relatively insensitive to shifts or trends in the process, problems can go undetected for so long that they cause defectives before they are checked. p charts are frequently based on readily available data.

Variables Process Capability Studies

Variables process capability studies determine a process's ability to meet specifications stated by the customer. The major tools used in variables process capability studies are variables control charts, discussed in Chapter 8, and the tools discussed in Chapter 10. Variables control charts are used to stabilize a process so we can determine meaningful upper and lower natural limits. **Natural limits** are computed for stable processes by adding and subtracting three times the process's standard deviation to the process centerline. In general, for any variables control chart, the upper and lower natural limits are:

$$\text{UNL} = \bar{\bar{x}} + 3\sigma \qquad \textbf{(11.1)}$$

$$\text{LNL} = \bar{\bar{x}} - 3\sigma \qquad \textbf{(11.2)}$$

For $\bar{x}$ and R charts specifically, the upper and lower natural limits are:

$$\text{UNL} = \bar{\bar{x}} + 3(\bar{R}/d_2) \qquad (11.3)$$

$$\text{LNL} = \bar{\bar{x}} - 3(\bar{R}/d_2) \qquad (11.4)$$

where d_2 is a constant factor based on subgroup size that is presented in Table B.1 in Appendix B. $d_2 = (\bar{R}/\sigma)$ for a stable normal distribution.

For $\bar{x}$ and s charts, the upper and lower natural limits are:

$$\text{UNL} = \bar{\bar{x}} + 3(\bar{s}/c_4) \qquad (11.5)$$

$$\text{LNL} = \bar{\bar{x}} - 3(\bar{s}/c_4) \qquad (11.6)$$

where c_4 is a constant factor based on subgroup size that is presented in Table B.1 in Appendix B. $c_4 = (\bar{s}/\sigma)$ for a stable normal distribution.

For individuals charts, the upper and lower natural limits are:

$$\text{UNL} = \bar{x} + 3(\bar{R}/d_2) \qquad (11.7)$$

$$\text{LNL} = \bar{x} - 3(\bar{R}/d_2) \qquad (11.8)$$

where d_2 is a constant factor based on a subgroup size of 2 that is shown in Table B.1 in Appendix B. $d_2 = (\bar{R}/\sigma)$ for a stable normal distribution.

As a rule, natural limits should not be shown on variables control charts because natural limits apply to individual units of output and control limits apply to subgroup statistics. One notable exception to this rule is the individuals control chart for variables. In that case, the subgroups consist of individual units, and natural limits and control limits are the same.

Interpretation of the natural limits requires stability of the process under study and the application of the Empirical Rule discussed in Chapter 5. If the output distribution of a process is stable, then for Equations (11.1) through (11.8) we can say that virtually all process output will be between the natural limits. For example, if samples of four steel ingots are drawn from an ingot-producing process every hour, and the process is stable with a process average subgroup weight of 42.0 pounds ($\bar{\bar{x}} = 42.0$ pounds) and an average range of 0.6856 pounds, we can say the following about the process, using Equations (11.3) and (11.4):

1. The process's upper natural limit is

$$\text{UNL} = \bar{\bar{x}} + 3(\bar{R}/d_2) = 42.0 + 3(0.6856/2.059)$$
$$= 42.0 + 3(0.333) = 42.999 \approx 43.0 \text{ pounds}$$

2. The process's lower natural limit is

$$\text{LNL} = \bar{\bar{x}} - 3(\bar{R}/d_2) = 42.0 - 3(0.6856/2.059)$$
$$= 42.0 - 3(0.333) = 41.001 \approx 41.0 \text{ pounds}$$

3. Virtually all (99.73 percent for a stable normal distribution) of the steel ingots produced will weigh between 41.0 and 43.0 pounds. This is what the steel ingot process is capable of producing; it is the identity of the process.

The disadvantage of variables process capability studies is that they frequently require the collection of special data. The advantages of variables process capability studies are that they provide information such as whether the process is centered on nominal, or exhibiting too much unit-to-unit variation, or unstable with respect to its mean and/or variation. Furthermore, these studies are sensitive to shifts in the process and are helpful in detecting trends or shifts in the process before they cause trouble. Finally, variables process capability studies examine if the specification limits are reasonable.

Data Requirements for Process Capability Studies

Attribute Studies

Attribute process capability studies require a great deal of data. In general, the study should cover at least three distinct time periods, where each time period should contain 20 to 25 samples and each sample should have between 50 and 100 units. This rule of thumb is based on experience as well as statistical theory.

Variables Studies

Variables process capability studies require far less data than attribute studies. However, a separate variables study may be required for each quality characteristic that can cause a unit to be defective. As a rule of thumb, a variables study should cover at least three distinct time periods. The first period should contain about 50 samples of between three and five units each, and the second and third time periods should contain 25 samples of between three and five units each.

Addition of New Data onto a Process Capability Chart

After initial control limits have been calculated, the question arises as to what to do with additional data: should revised control limits be computed, or should the old control limits be extended across the control chart and new points plotted against the old limits? Recall from our discussion in Chapter 8 on revising control limits that if the process is stable and has not changed significantly, new limits should not be calculated because they can stimulate tampering with the process [see Reference 1, pp. 34–37 and 45–73]. In this case, the best procedure is to plot the new data against the old limits and search for a change in the data pattern. If the process has changed significantly, new limits should then be calculated using only the data from the revised process. These new limits allow for analysis of the process's new capability.

Process Capability Studies on Unstable Processes

Process statistics, such as the measures of location, dispersion, and shape discussed in Chapter 5, cannot be estimated from a process capability study performed on an unstable (chaotic) process; nevertheless, useful information is still available. In such cases, the study often reveals information about the sources of special variation that affect the process, and it provides an opportunity to better understand the process. [See Reference 1, pp. 34–37 and 45–73.]

Process Capability Studies on Stable Processes

A process capability study on a stable process sets the stage for the estimation of the process's central tendency, $\bar{\bar{x}}$, and standard deviation, σ. These statistics allow (1) comparisons between the process's performance **(voice of the process)** and specifications **(voice of the customer)**, and (2) the use of centerlines, or process averages, on which to establish budgets and forecasts. [See Reference 4, p. 161.] Note that predicting a stable process's behavior in the near future assumes that the process will remain stable. Unfortunately, it is impossible to know if this will be the case, so caution is advised.

An Example of an Attribute Process Capability Study

The centerline of a stable attribute control chart should be used as an estimate of the overall process capability. But there is one important proviso: an estimate of overall process capability is not specific as to the potential cause or causes of defective output. To identify these, we must separate out all possible sources of defects (such as operators, machines, and vendors) and perform individual process capability studies for each source. In such a case, $\bar{x}$ and R charts are often more cost-effective, in terms of sample size and information, than attribute charts, if they can be used.

To illustrate an attribute capability study, consider the case of a manager of a data entry department who has taken a survey indicating customer dissatisfaction. The manager wants to determine the capability of the data entry operation in her department in terms of the proportion of defective entries produced. [See Reference 5, pp. 131–141.] She decides to take samples of the first 200 lines of code from each day's output, inspect them for defects, and construct an initial p chart. Table 11.1 shows the raw data (see ✷ DATAENTRY), and Figure 11.2 shows the initial process control chart. The latter reveals that on days 8

TABLE 11.1
Attribute
Process
Capability
Study on
Data Entry
Operation

		Raw Data for Construction of Control Chart	
Day	Number of Lines Inspected	Number of Defective Lines	Fraction of Defective Lines
1	200	6	.030
2	200	6	.030
3	200	6	.030
4	200	5	.025
5	200	0	.000
6	200	0	.000
7	200	6	.030
8	200	14	.070
9	200	4	.020
10	200	0	.000
11	200	1	.005
12	200	8	.040
13	200	2	.010
14	200	4	.020
15	200	7	.035
16	200	1	.005
17	200	3	.015
18	200	1	.005
19	200	4	.020
20	200	0	.000
21	200	4	.020
22	200	15	.075
23	200	4	.020
24	200	1	.005
Totals	4,800	102	

FIGURE 11.2
Minitab p
Chart from
Raw Data

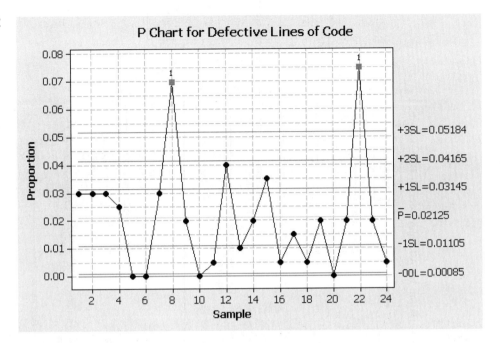

(14 defective lines out of 200 inspected) and 22 (15 defective lines out of 200 inspected) something special happened, not attributable to the system, to cause defective lines to be entered.

The manager calls a meeting of the 10 operators to brainstorm for possible special causes of variation on days 8 and 22. Results of the brainstorming session are put onto the **cause-and-effect diagram** in Figure 11.3. The 10 group members vote that their best guess for the problem on day 8 was a new untrained operator (see cause in Figure 11.3—circled in a cloud) who had been added to the workforce, and that the one day it took the worker to acclimate to the new environment probably caused the unusually high number of errors. To ensure that this special cause will not be repeated, the manager institutes a one-day training program for all new employees. The 10 group members also vote that their best guess for the problem on day 22 was that on the previous evening the department had run out of paper from the regular vendor, did not expect a new shipment until the morning of day 23, and consequently purchased a one-day supply of paper from a new vendor. The operators found this paper was of inferior quality, which caused the large number of defective entries. To correct this special cause of variation, the manager revises the firm's relationship with its regular paper vendor and operationally defines acceptable quality for paper.

After eliminating the days for which special causes of variation are found, the manager recomputes the control chart statistics using Equations (7.1), (7.2), and (7.3):

$$\text{Centerline(p)} = \text{Average fraction of defective lines} = \bar{p}$$

$$\bar{p} = 73/4{,}400 = 0.01659 \cong 0.017$$

$$\text{UCL(p)} = 0.044$$

$$\text{LCL(p)} = 0.000$$

FIGURE 11.3 Cause-and-Effect Diagram to Determine Special Sources of Variation for All Operators on Days 8 and 22

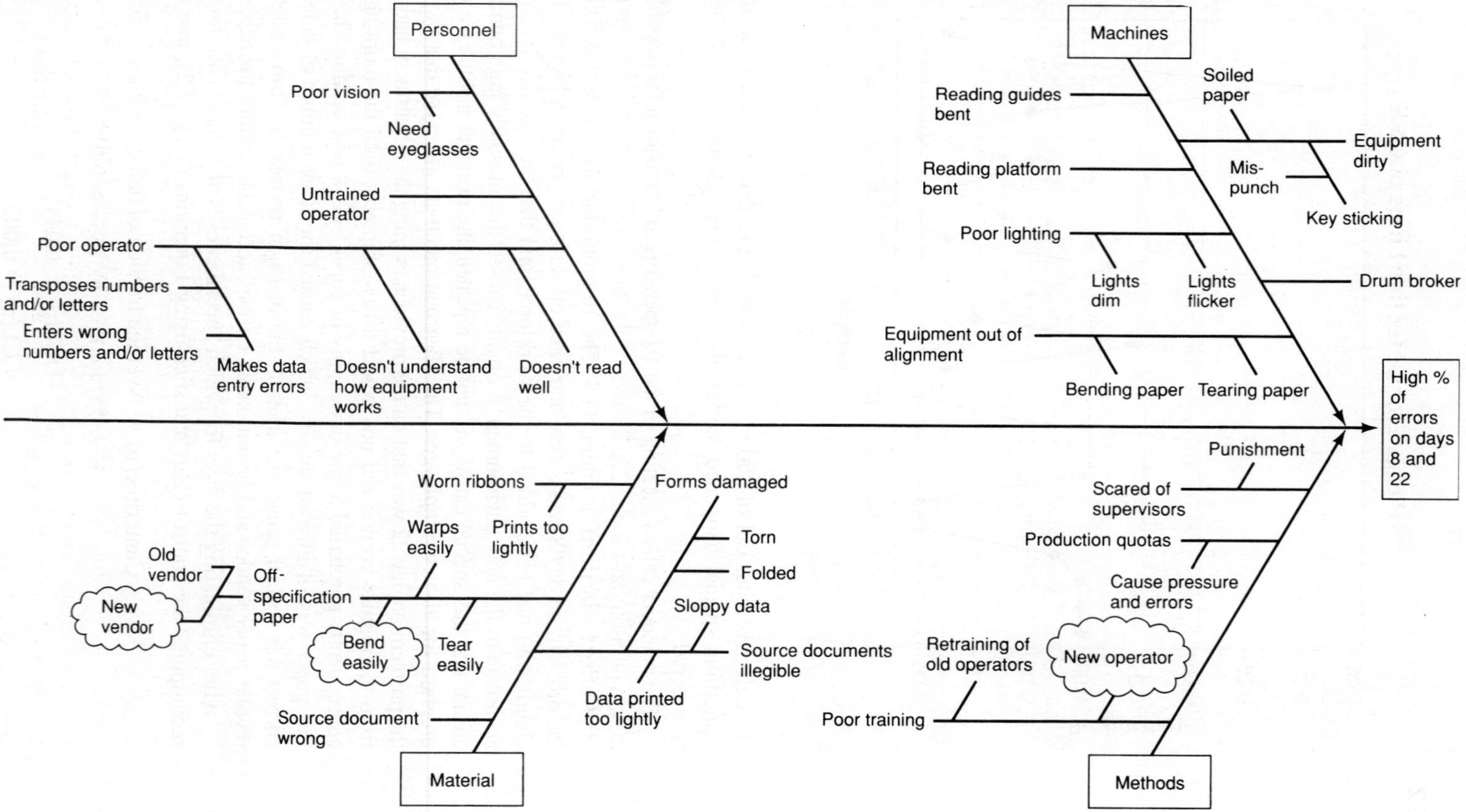

FIGURE 11.4
Minitab
Revised p
Chart
Following
Removal of
Special Causes

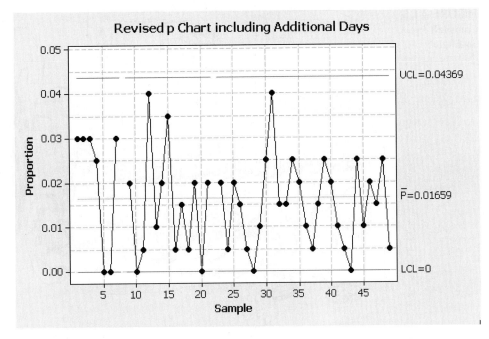

Revised p Chart including Additional Days

Figure 11.4 shows the revised control chart. The process appears stable. The center-line and control limits were extended out into the future for 25 days. Data from daily samples of 200 lines of code were collected for these 25 days and plotted with respect to the forecasted centerline and control limits. The process was found to be stable. The capability of the process is such that it will produce an average of 1.7 percent defective lines per day. Further, the percentage defective will rarely surpass 4.4 percent. Although the process's capability is now known, the manager is not satisfied with its capability and should not stop attempting further improvement. We will see how this is done in this chapter's section on process improvement studies.

An Example of a Variables Process Capability Study

To illustrate a variables process capability study, consider an auto manufacturer that wishes to purchase camshafts from a vendor [see Reference 3, pp. 7.E.9–7.E.18]. The buyer is concerned with the finish grind, diameters, and case hardness as well as other quality characteristics of the camshaft. For illustrative purposes, this discussion will focus only on the case hardness depth of the camshafts. The contract between the auto manu-facturer and camshaft vendor calls for camshafts that have an average case hardness depth of 7.0 mm (nominal) and are distributed around the average with a dispersion not to exceed 3.5 mm either way (tolerance); this is a distribution specification (voice of the customer). Further, the contract requires that the vendor produce a process capability study demonstrating statistical control of the process. Consequently, management's objec-tive is to reduce camshaft-to-camshaft variation for case hardness depth and to move the process's average case hardness depth to the desired nominal of 7.0 mm (voice of the process).

FIGURE 11.5
**Camshaft in
an Engine**

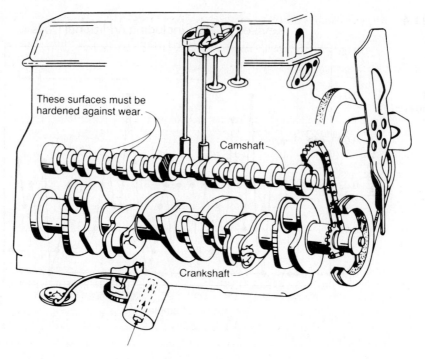

These surfaces must be
hardened against wear.

Camshaft

Crankshaft

A camshaft is a rod with elliptical lobes along its length. As the rod rotates, so do the elliptical lobes, and this ultimately causes intake and exhaust valves to open and close. The intake valves permit a mixture of fuel and air to enter the cylinders, where combustion takes place. The exhaust valves permit the waste gases to exit the cylinders after combustion. The surfaces of the elliptical lobes must be hardened (made brittle) to reduce wear, as in Figure 11.5. This hardening is called case hardening and is accomplished by immersing the camshaft in oil, placing electric bearing coils around the lobes, and passing electric current through the coils. This process heat-treats the lobes and makes them brittle. The depth to which the brittleness extends is called case hardness depth. The case hardness depth must be tightly controlled, since if the case hardness depth is too deep, the lobes will be too brittle and will tend to crack, while if the case hardness depth is too shallow, the lobes will be too soft and will wear quickly.

Pursuant to the terms of the contract calling for a process capability study, a sample of five camshafts is drawn from the vendor's process every day. Each shaft is measured with respect to each of the relevant quality characteristics (see ✿ CAMSHAFT). Figure 11.6 shows the control chart for the initial data collected in the process capability study.

These data reveal that the vendor's process is not in statistical control; this is indicated by points 3, 12, 16, and 30 in the R chart of Figure 11.6. Consequently, corrective action on the process is required by vendor management. An engineer from the vendor's plant forms a brainstorming group comprising workers in the Induction Hardening and Quench department—the department that performs case hardening on the

FIGURE 11.6   **Minitab Control Chart—Process Capability Study of the Camshaft**

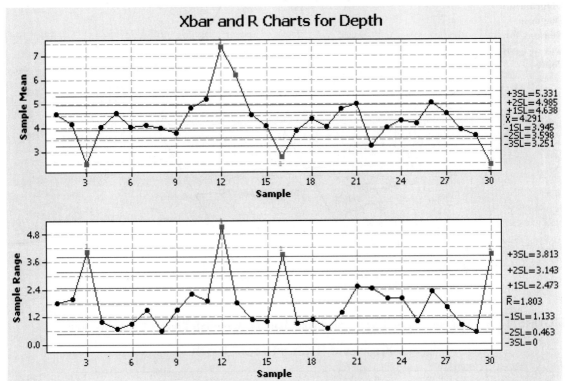

camshafts. The brainstorming group's aim is to determine causes for the out-of-control points in Figure 11.6. The brainstorming session's results appear in the cause-and-effect diagram in Figure 11.7. The group determines that probable causes for out-of-control points were:

1. *Point 3.* Low power in the coil resulted in increased variability and less stable depth in the case hardness, as shown in cloud 1 in Figure 11.7.

2. *Point 12.* A temporary operator was used because the regular operator was sick, as shown in cloud 2 in Figure 11.7.

3. *Point 16.* The case hardness setting on the machine was incorrect, as shown in cloud 3 in Figure 11.7.

4. *Point 30.* Low power in the coil resulted in an out-of-control situation, as shown in cloud 1 in Figure 11.7.

This analysis leads vendor management to take action on the process by repairing the voltage meter on the induction hardening machine (see points 3 and 30) and training all personnel in the proper operation of the machine (see points 12 and 16). After these policies are instituted, the engineer collects 30 additional days of data and draws a new control chart, as shown in Figure 11.8 (see 🐟 CAMSHAFT2).

FIGURE 11.7
Cause-and-Effect Diagram to Diagnose Reasons for Out-of-Control Points

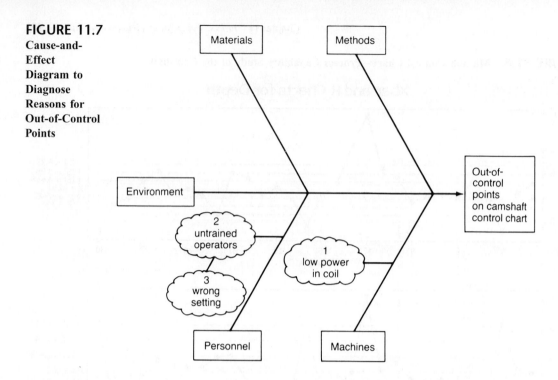

FIGURE 11.8   **Minitab Control Chart—Additional Data for Camshaft Process Capability Study**

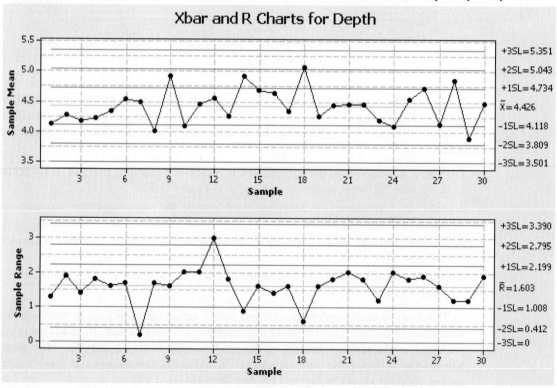

FIGURE 11.9

Fraction of Camshafts Out of Specification

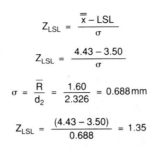

$$Z_{LSL} = \frac{\bar{\bar{x}} - LSL}{\sigma}$$

$$Z_{LSL} = \frac{4.43 - 3.50}{\sigma}$$

$$\sigma = \frac{\bar{R}}{d_2} = \frac{1.60}{2.326} = 0.688 \text{mm}$$

$$Z_{LSL} = \frac{(4.43 - 3.50)}{0.688} = 1.35$$

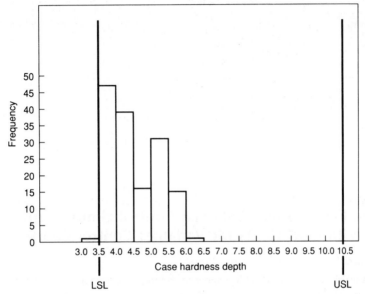

We see that the vendor's process is in statistical control, with values for $\bar{\bar{x}}$ and $\bar{R}$ of 4.43 and 1.6, respectively. Recall from Chapter 8 that $\bar{R} = d_2\sigma$, so we can calculate σ as $\bar{R}/d_2$, where d_2 is found in Table B.1 in Appendix B for a subgroup of size 5. However, from the calculations in Figure 11.9, we see that $Z_{LSL} = 1.35$; that is, the process average is only 1.35 process standard deviations above the lower specification limit. Since Z_{LSL} is less than 3, this indicates that the process may produce some nonconforming product. We determine the proportion of nonconforming product by examining the histogram of actual process output in Figure 11.9. As we see, one camshaft had a case hardness depth less than the lower specification limit. In other words, the process generated 0.67 percent nonconforming camshafts in the study period. It is interesting to note from the histogram that the case hardness depths are not normally distributed—a disproportionate number of values lie near the lower specification limit. Asymmetrical situations like this could imply that there is some form of sorting prior to inspection or possibly that inspectors are accepting unsatisfactory product because they are fearful of failing to meet some production quota.

TABLE 11.2
Relationship between Control Limits and Natural Limits for Variables Location Charts

Chart Type	Control Limits	Natural Limits	Comments
$\bar{x}$ (with R chart)	$\bar{\bar{x}} \pm A_2\bar{R} =$ $\bar{\bar{x}} \pm 3\left(\dfrac{\bar{R}/d_2}{\sqrt{n}}\right)$ $\left(A_2 = \dfrac{3}{d_2\sqrt{n}}\right)$	$\bar{\bar{x}} \pm 3(\bar{R}/d_2)$	If A_2 and/or A_3 are multiplied by the square root of the subgroup size $(\sqrt{n})$, and this new quantity is added or subtracted from $\bar{\bar{x}}$, the new limits are the natural limits.
$\bar{x}$ (with s chart)	$\bar{\bar{x}} \pm A_3\bar{s} =$ $\bar{\bar{x}} \pm 3\left(\dfrac{\bar{s}/c_4}{\sqrt{n}}\right)$ $\left(A_3 = \dfrac{3}{c_4\sqrt{n}}\right)$	$\bar{\bar{x}} \pm 3(\bar{s}/c_4)$	
x (individuals chart with moving range chart)	$\bar{x} \pm E_2\bar{R} =$ $\bar{x} \pm 3(\bar{R}/d_2)$ $(E_2 = 3/d_2)$	$\bar{x} \pm 3(\bar{R}/d_2)$	Control limits and natural limits are equivalent.

The Relationships between Control Limits, Natural Limits, and Specification Limits for Variables Control Charts

Natural Limits and Control Limits

Natural limits are used with respect to individual observations—and consequently on run charts. Control limits are used with respect to subgroup statistics—and consequently on control charts. Table 11.2 shows the relationships between natural limits and control limits. We see that for $\bar{x}$ charts, if A_2 ($\bar{x}$ and R chart) or A_3 ($\bar{x}$ and s chart) is multiplied by the square root of the subgroup size $(\sqrt{n})$, and these new quantities $(A_2\sqrt{n})$ and $(A_3\sqrt{n})$ are added and subtracted from the process average $(\bar{\bar{x}})$, the control limits are transformed into natural limits. In the case of control limits for individuals charts, the control limits and the natural limits are identical because the subgroup size is one.

Natural Limits and Specification Limits

Natural limits (voice of the process) and specification limits (voice of the customer) are comparable quantities for stable processes because they are both measured with respect to the individual units of output generated by the process under study. There are four basic relationships between natural limits and specification limits for normal, stable processes. Each relationship is portrayed using a normal distribution. However, from the Empirical Rule, the assumption of normality is not necessary.

Relationship 1. The process's natural limits are inside the specification limits and the process is centered on nominal. This is illustrated in Figure 11.10a.

Relationship 2. The process's natural limits are inside the specification limits and the process is not centered on nominal. This is illustrated in Figure 11.10b.

FIGURE 11.10
Relationship between Natural Limits and Specification Limits

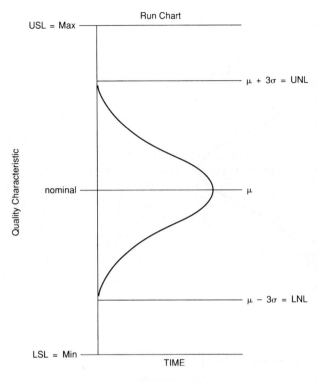

(a) Relationship 1

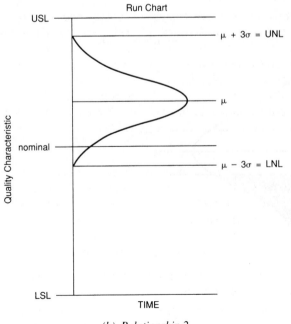

(b) Relationship 2

(continued)

**FIGURE
11.10**
(concluded)

Run Chart

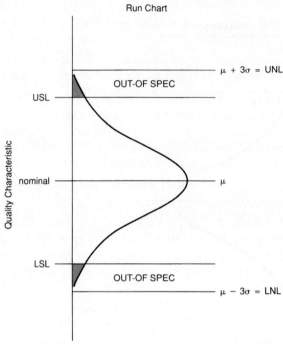

(c) Relationship 3

Run Chart

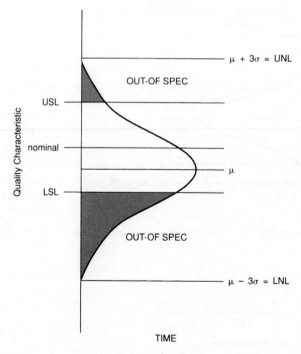

(d) Relationship 4

Relationship 3. The process's natural limits are outside the specification limits and the process is centered on nominal. This is illustrated in Figure 11.10c.

Relationship 4. The process's natural limits are outside the specification limits and the process is not centered on nominal. This is illustrated in Figure 11.10d.

In Chapter 6 we discussed the four states of a process [see Reference 7, pp. 12–21]. Relationships 1 and 2 represent a process in its **ideal state;** given the same variation between relationships 1 and 2, relationship 1 is preferable. Relationships 3 and 4 represent a process in the **threshold state;** given the same variation between relationships 3 and 4, relationship 3 represents the more desirable situation.

Control Limits and Specification Limits

In no case should specification limits be shown on $\bar{x}$ charts. This is because while control limits apply to process statistics ($\bar{x}$), specification limits apply to individual units of process output (or some other quality characteristic). Nevertheless, specification limits are sometimes shown on control charts for individuals because in this special case the control limits are based on subgroups of size one—hence, on individual values.

Process Capability Indices for Variables Data

A common desire of many control chart users is to be able to state a process's ability to meet specifications in one summary statistic [see Reference 6, pp. 41–52]. Such statistics are available and are called process capability indices. We use these indices to summarize internal processes as well as vendor processes.

Assumptions

All the process capability indices we will discuss here require variables data and stability of the process characteristic under study. Additionally, it is common practice to assume that this process characteristic is normally distributed.

Unfortunately, the assumption of normality is not realistic even when dealing with processes that are both stable and capable. This is because capability calculations in this situation are based on the extreme tails of the normal distribution, or the portion of the normal distribution that is beyond the specification limits. Unfortunately, the extreme tails of the normal distribution are mathematical quantities that rarely, if ever, characterize the real world. In the outer 5 percent of each tail, considerable discrepancies will occur between the theoretical fraction nonconforming and the actual fraction nonconforming [see Reference 7, p. 130]. Given this caveat, we may now discuss capability indices.

TABLE 11.3   **Process Capability Indices**

Index	Estimation Equation	Equation No.	Purpose	Assumptions about Process
C_p	$\dfrac{USL - LSL}{UNL - LNL}$	11.9	Summarize process potential to meet acceptable tolerances (USL − LSL).	1. Stable process. 2. Variables data. 3. Centered process. (Process average equals nominal.)
CPU	$\dfrac{USL - \bar{\bar{x}}}{3\sigma}$	11.10	Summarize process potential to meet only a one-sided upper specification limit.	1. Stable process. 2. Variables data.
CPL	$\dfrac{\bar{\bar{x}} - LSL}{3\sigma}$	11.11	Summarize process potential to meet only a one-sided lower specification limit.	(same as CPU)
C_{pk}	$C_p - \dfrac{\lvert m - \bar{\bar{x}}\rvert}{3\sigma}$ where m = Nominal value of the specification	11.12	1. Summarize process potential to meet two-sided specification limits. 2. $\lvert m - \bar{\bar{x}}\rvert/3\sigma$ is a penalty factor for the process's being off nominal. It's stated in terms of the number of natural limit units the process is off nominal.	(same as CPU)

Indices

Four **process capability indices** are commonly used: C_p, CPU, CPL, and C_{pk}. They are summarized in Table 11.3.

C_p The **C_p index** is used to summarize a process's ability (voice of the process) to meet two-sided specification limits (voice of the customer). As we see in Table 11.3, C_p is computed as:

$$C_p = \frac{USL - LSL}{UNL - LNL} = \frac{USL - LSL}{6\sigma} \qquad (11.9)$$

In addition to the general assumptions stated above, the C_p index also assumes that the process average ($\bar{\bar{x}}$) is centered on the nominal value, m.

Recall that a process's capability is defined to be the range in which virtually all of the output will fall; usually, this is described as plus or minus three standard deviations from the process's mean, or within an interval of six standard deviations (6σ); that is, $UNL - LNL = (\bar{\bar{x}} + 3\sigma) - (\bar{\bar{x}} - 3\sigma) = 6\sigma$. Consequently, if a process's USL = UNL = $\bar{\bar{x}} + 3\sigma$ and its LSL = LNL = $\bar{\bar{x}} - 3\sigma$, the process's capability is 1.0:

$$C_p = \frac{USL - LSL}{UNL - LNL} = \frac{USL - LSL}{6\sigma} = \frac{(\bar{\bar{x}} + 3\sigma) - (\bar{\bar{x}} - 3\sigma)}{6\sigma} = \frac{6\sigma}{6\sigma} = 1.0$$

According to the Empirical Rule, a process capability index of 1.0 indicates that a process will generate virtually all of its output within specification limits. According to

**FIGURE
11.11**
**Process
Capability
Indices**

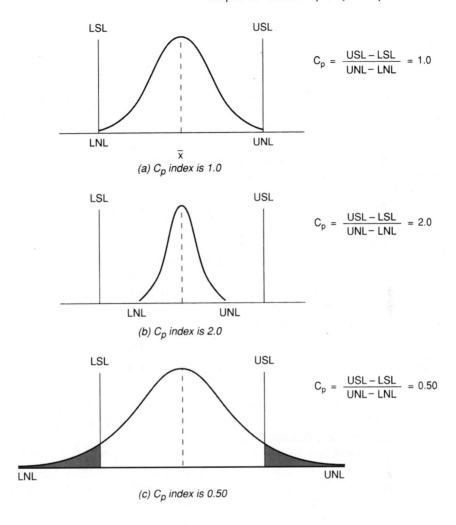

(a) C_p index is 1.0

$$C_p = \frac{USL - LSL}{UNL - LNL} = 1.0$$

(b) C_p index is 2.0

$$C_p = \frac{USL - LSL}{UNL - LNL} = 2.0$$

(c) C_p index is 0.50

$$C_p = \frac{USL - LSL}{UNL - LNL} = 0.50$$

the normal distribution, a process capability index of 1.0 indicates that a process will generate 99.73 percent of its output within specification limits. For centered processes, given the preceding assumptions, Figure 11.11a shows a process with C_p = 1.0, indicating that the UNL = USL, and the LNL = LSL.

Figure 11.11b shows a process with C_p = 2.0, indicating that the UNL is midway between nominal and the USL, and the LNL is midway between the LSL and nominal. To state this another way, the natural limits only take up half the distance between the specification limits. According to the normal distribution, a process capability index of 2.0 indicates that a process will generate 99.9999998 percent of its output within specification limits.

Figure 11.11c shows a process with C_p = 0.5, where the USL is midway between nominal and the UNL, and the LSL is midway between the LNL and nominal. To state this another way, the natural limits are twice as wide as the specification limits. According to the normal distribution, a process capability index of 0.5 indicates that a process will generate 86.64 percent of its output within specification limits.

CPU   The **CPU index** is used to summarize a process's ability to meet a one-sided upper specification limit. In many situations process owners are concerned only that a process not exceed an upper specification limit. For example, for products that can warp in only one direction, there is no LSL for warpage; the lower the warpage the better. However, there is a USL for warpage, the value for warpage that will critically impair the product's ability to meet customer needs. It can also be used in situations where we want to examine one side of a two-sided specification limit.

CPU is computed as:

$$CPU = (USL - \bar{\bar{x}})/(UNL - \bar{\bar{x}}) = \frac{USL - \bar{\bar{x}}}{3\sigma} \qquad (11.10)$$

The CPU index measures how far the process average $(\bar{\bar{x}})$ is from the upper specification limit in terms of one-sided natural tolerance limits $(3\sigma = [UNL - \bar{\bar{x}}] = [\{\bar{\bar{x}} + 3\sigma\} - \bar{\bar{x}}])$. Natural tolerances, when added and subtracted from the process mean $(\bar{\bar{x}})$, yield the range in which a process is capable of operating—the process's capability, $\bar{\bar{x}} \pm 3\sigma = \bar{\bar{x}} \pm$ natural tolerance.

If a process's USL = UNL = $(\bar{\bar{x}} + 3\sigma)$, the CPU is 1.0:

$$CPU = \frac{USL - \bar{\bar{x}}}{3\sigma} = \frac{USL - \bar{\bar{x}}}{UNL - \bar{\bar{x}}} = 1.0$$

From the Empirical Rule, a CPU of 1.0 or more indicates that a process will generate virtually all of its output within the upper specification limit. From the normal distribution, a CPU of 1.0 indicates that a process will generate 99.865 percent of its output within the upper specification limit.

If a process's UNL is greater than the USL, the CPU is less than 1. As UNL − USL increases, the fraction of process output that is out of specification will increase geometrically. Conversely, if a process's UNL is less than the USL, then the CPU is greater than 1. As USL − UNL increases, the fraction of process output that is out of specification will decrease geometrically. To determine the fraction of process output that will be out of specification, we examine the histogram of process output with respect to the upper specification limit, as illustrated earlier.

CPL   The **CPL index** is used to summarize a process's ability to meet a one-sided lower specification limit. The CPL operates just like the CPU. CPL is computed as:

$$CPL = \frac{\bar{\bar{x}} - LSL}{3\sigma} \qquad (11.11)$$

If a process's LNL is greater than the LSL, then CPL is less than 1. As LNL − LSL increases, the fraction of process output that is out of specification will increase geometrically. Conversely, if a process's LNL is less than the LSL, then CPL is greater than 1. As LSL − LNL increases, the fraction of process output that is out of specification will decrease geometrically. To determine the fraction of process output that will be out of specification, we examine the histogram of process output with respect to the lower specification limit.

C_{pk} The **C_{pk} index** is used to summarize a process's ability to meet two-sided specification limits when the process is not centered on nominal. The C_{pk} index uses the C_p index as a starting point for stating a process's capability, but it penalizes C_p if the process is not centered on nominal, m:

$$C_{pk} = C_p - \left\{ \frac{|m - \bar{\bar{x}}|}{3\sigma} \right\} \qquad (11.12)$$

The term in brackets in Equation (11.12) is always positive, and hence lowers the value of C_p, which indicates that the process is less able to produce within specifications. The bracketed term is a measure of how many **natural tolerance units** (3σ) the process mean ($\bar{\bar{x}}$) is from nominal (m). The further off-center the process, the more C_p is penalized by the bracketed factor. Hence, C_{pk} is a two-sided capability index that accounts for process centering.

A firm that exists in a **defect detection** mode will not know the process capability indices for its various processes. On the other hand, a firm operating in a **defect prevention** mode will know the values for its various processes and will be striving for a C_p or C_{pk} approximately equal to or greater than 1.0. Finally, if a firm is pursuing **never-ending improvement,** it will be striving to move C_p and C_{pk} higher and higher. As C_p and C_{pk} become increasingly greater than 1, the specification limits from which they were computed become increasingly irrelevant.

Limitations of Capability Indices

Several potential problems exist when using the C_p and C_{pk} indices. First, if a process is not stable, C_p and C_{pk} are meaningless statistics. Second, not all processes meet the assumption of normality. Hence, the naive user of capability indices may incorrectly assess the actual fraction of process output that will be out of specification. Last, experience shows that naive users of capability indices frequently confuse C_p and C_{pk}; they think they yield the same information about a process. Of course, this can result in a great deal of confusion.

An Example

Each process capability index discussed earlier in this chapter is calculated using the camshaft example in Figures 11.6, 11.8, and 11.9. Figure 11.6 shows the camshaft operation is out of control. After special sources of variation are removed from the process, it becomes stable, as shown in Figure 11.8. From Figure 11.8 we see that the average case hardness depth is 4.43 mm, the average range for case hardness depth is 1.60 mm, the upper specification limit is 10.5 mm, and the lower specification limit is 3.5 mm.

$$\bar{\bar{x}} = 4.43 \text{ mm}$$

$$\bar{R} = 1.60 \text{ mm} \qquad \text{hence } \sigma = \bar{R}/d_2 = 1.60/2.326 = 0.688 \text{ mm}$$

$$USL = 10.5 \text{ mm}$$

$$LSL = 3.5 \text{ mm}$$

Given these figures, the C_p, CPU, CPL, and C_{pk} can be computed and interpreted.

C_p We compute C_p as

$$C_p = \frac{USL - LSL}{6\sigma} = \frac{10.5 - 3.5}{6(0.688)} = 1.70$$

This C_p indicates an extremely capable process that will almost never produce out-of-specification product. However, from Figure 11.8 we see that while virtually all the camshafts have case hardness depths within acceptable tolerances, the C_p index, which assumes the process is centered, has failed to detect that the process, with an average of 4.43, is 2.57 mm off nominal ($|\bar{\bar{x}} - m| = |4.43 - 7.00| = 2.57$ mm).

CPU We compute CPU as:

$$CPU = \frac{USL - \bar{\bar{x}}}{3\sigma} = \frac{10.5 - 4.43}{3(0.688)} = 2.94$$

The CPU accurately indicates that the process is operating well within the USL of 10.5 mm.

CPL We compute CPL as:

$$CPL = \frac{\bar{\bar{x}} - LSL}{3\sigma} = \frac{4.43 - 3.5}{3(0.688)} = 0.45$$

The CPL accurately indicates that the process is not operating within the LSL of 3.5 mm.

C_pk We compute C_{pk} as:

$$C_{pk} = C_{pk} = C_p - \frac{|m - \bar{\bar{x}}|}{3\sigma} = \frac{USL - LSL}{6\sigma} - \frac{|m - \bar{\bar{x}}|}{3\sigma}$$

$$= \frac{10.5 - 3.5}{6(0.688)} - \frac{|7.0 - 4.43|}{3(0.688)} = 1.70 - 1.25 = 0.45$$

This C_{pk} correctly indicates a process that will produce out-of-specification product, because, unlike C_p, it has taken into account that the process is not centered on nominal.

It should be noted that capability indices can sometimes potentially cause more problems than they can provide benefits; consequently, some practitioners recommend that they not be used.

Process Improvement Studies

As with process capability studies, there are two types of process improvement studies: **attribute improvement studies** and **variables improvement studies.** In the pursuit of continuous and never-ending improvement, it is natural that attribute improvement studies lead to variables improvement studies.

Attribute Improvement Studies

Returning to this chapter's data entry example, recall that the percentage of defective entries was stabilized with an average of 1.7 percent defective and would rarely go above 4.4 percent defective. At this point, the manager decides that to improve the process further she must study each operator individually. However, she must determine which operators to work with first. She makes a check sheet to record the number and fraction of defective lines of code by operator for December, as shown in Table 11.4 (see OPERATOR).

Next, she constructs a c chart for the number of defective lines of code per operator for December, shown in Figure 11.12a. From the c chart, she notes that operators 004

TABLE 11.4
Check Sheet of Defective Lines of Code by Operator (12/1–12/31)*

Operator	Frequency	Fraction of Defectives
001	2	.04
002	3	.06
003	1	.02
004	19	.38
005	0	.00
006	2	.04
007	1	.02
008	3	.06
009	17	.34
010	2	.04
Total	50	1.00

*All operators produced approximately the same number of lines of code during the period under study.

FIGURE 11.12
Minitab Control Chart for Number of Defective Lines of Code by Operator

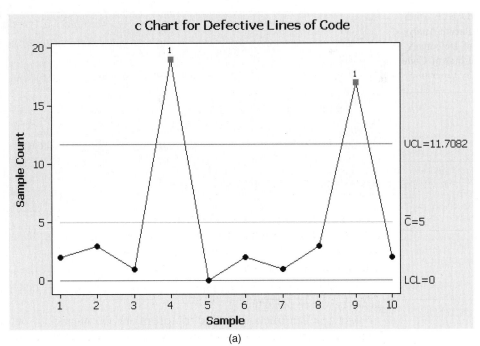

(a)

(continued)

**FIGURE
11.12**
(concluded)

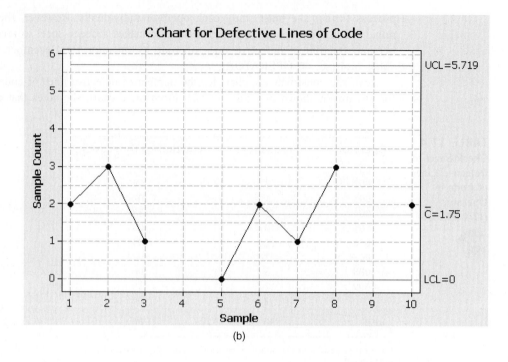

(b)

TABLE 11.5
**Pareto Analysis
of Defective
Lines of Code
by Operator**

Operator	Frequency	Fraction	Cumulative Fraction
004	19	.38	.38
009	17	.34	.72
002	3	.06	.78
008	3	.06	.84
001	2	.04	.88
006	2	.04	.92
010	2	.04	.96
003	1	.02	.98
007	1	.02	1.00
005	0	.00	1.00
Totals	50	1.00	

and 009 are out of control. She revises the c chart to determine if any other operators are out of control after having removed the impact of operators 004 and 009; she finds none, as we see in Figure 11.12b.

Next, she constructs a **Pareto diagram** for the number of defects per operator. Table 11.5 shows the data used, and Figure 11.13 shows the Minitab Pareto diagram

**FIGURE
11.13**
**Minitab Pareto
Diagram of
Defective Lines
of Code**

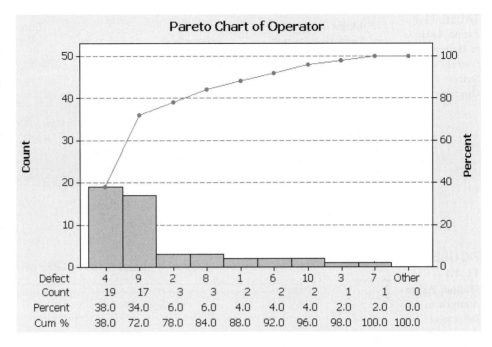

Pareto Chart of Operator

Defect	4	9	2	8	1	6	10	3	7	Other
Count	19	17	3	3	2	2	2	1	1	0
Percent	38.0	34.0	6.0	6.0	4.0	4.0	4.0	2.0	2.0	0.0
Cum %	38.0	72.0	78.0	84.0	88.0	92.0	96.0	98.0	100.0	100.0

TABLE 11.6
**Check Sheet to
Determine
Defects for
Operator 004
(1/1–4/30)**

| Major Causes of | Month | | | | |
Defective Entries	Jan	Feb	Mar	Apr	Totals
Transposed numbers	7	10	6	5	28
Out of field	1		2		3
Wrong character	6	8	5	9	28
Data printed too lightly		1	1		2
Torn document	1	1		2	4
Creased document			1	1	2
Illegible source document			1		1
Totals	15	20	16	17	68

(the construction of a Pareto diagram using Minitab was discussed in Chapter 10, Appendix A10.1). From the Pareto diagram, she determines that 72 percent of all defective lines of code are produced by operators 004 and 009.

The manager decides to perform separate analyses for operators 004 and 009. She begins with operator 004 by setting up a check sheet, as shown in Table 11.6, to determine the sources for operator 004's defects (see ✿ OPERATOR4).

TABLE 11.7
Pareto Analysis to Determine Sources of Defects for Operator 004

Major Causes of Defective Entries	Frequency	Fraction	Cumulative Fraction
Transposed numbers	28	.412	.412
Wrong character	28	.412	.824
Torn document	4	.059	.883
Out of field	3	.044	.927
Data printed too lightly	2	.029	.956
Creased document	2	.029	.985
Illegible source document	1	.015	1.000
Totals	68	100.0	

FIGURE 11.14
Minitab Pareto Analysis to Determine Sources of Defects for Operator 004

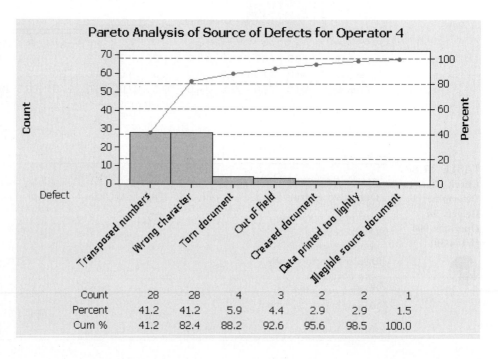

Pareto Analysis of Source of Defects for Operator 4

Count	28	28	4	3	2	2	1
Percent	41.2	41.2	5.9	4.4	2.9	2.9	1.5
Cum %	41.2	82.4	88.2	92.6	95.6	98.5	100.0

The corresponding Pareto diagram, with the data in Table 11.7 and the Minitab diagram in Figure 11.14, shows 82 percent of operator 004's defects resulted from "transposed numbers" and "wrong character."

Subsequently, the manager forms a brainstorming group composed of three select employees to do a cause-and-effect analysis of these two problems, as shown in Figure 11.15. The group members vote to attack both problems simultaneously. The cause-and-effect diagram leads the manager to send operator 004 to have her eyes checked.

FIGURE 11.15
Cause-and-Effect Diagrams for Operator 004

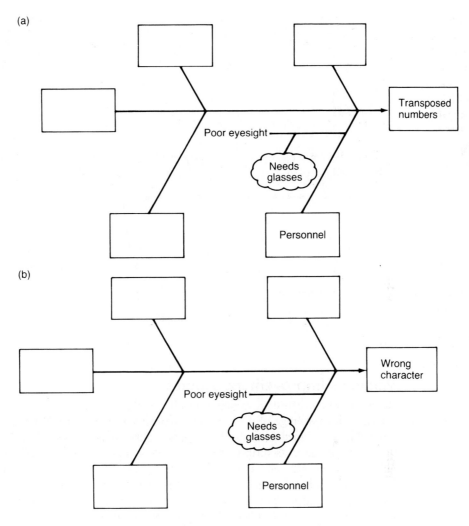

The optometrist finds that operator 004 is legally blind in her right eye. Eyeglasses correct her vision.

Next, the manager collects 25 more daily samples of 200 lines of code and constructs a p chart for the fraction of defectives, as shown in Figure 11.16 (see OPERATOR4ERRORS). From the p chart, the manager finds that operator 004's work is now stable, has an average defective rate of 0.8 percent (8 in 1,000 lines), and rarely goes above 2.6 percent defective. The manager realizes that if she wants to improve operator 004's performance further, she must switch from an attribute process improvement study to a variables process improvement study. Her next step is to plan her future courses of action: (1) study operator 009 and (2) review the entire department.

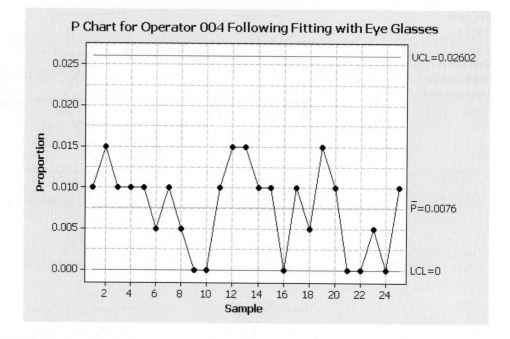

Variables Improvement Studies

Returning to our camshaft example, recall that the camshafts' case hardness depth was stable, with an average of 4.43 mm and standard deviation of 0.688 mm. At this point, the engineer assigned to study the induction quench-and-harden operation decides that to improve the process further, the induction coil must be changed. The old coil is pitted and consequently emits an erratic electrical output, causing increased variability in case hardness depth between camshafts. The induction coil is changed on the evening of August 29, and then 30 more days of data are collected (August 30–October 8) and control charted, as shown in Figure 11.17 (see ● CAMSHAFT3).

The process is in statistical control, with an average case hardness depth of 5.45 mm and a standard deviation of 0.434 mm ($\overline{R}/d_2 = 1.01/2.326 = 0.434$). Note that the process has been shifted toward nominal (7.0 mm) and its unit-to-unit variation has been reduced. Next, the process is studied to determine the number of standard deviations between the specification limits and the process average. This is done by computing Z_{LSL} and Z_{USL}. Remember, if the process average is more than three process standard deviations from both specification limits, then according to the Empirical Rule, virtually all of the process's output will be within the specification limits.

$$Z_{LSL} = \frac{(\overline{\overline{x}} - LSL)}{\sigma} = \frac{(5.45 - 3.50)}{0.434} = 4.49$$

$$Z_{USL} = \frac{(USL - \overline{\overline{x}})}{\sigma} = \frac{(10.5 - 5.45)}{0.434} = 11.6$$

FIGURE 11.17   **Minitab Case Hardness Depth after Coil Change**

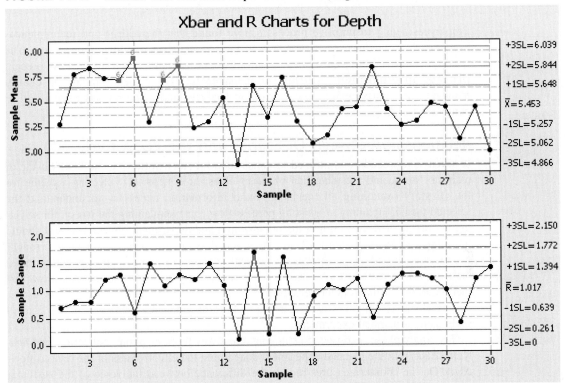

The process is operating well within specification limits. But in the spirit of never-ending improvement (as illustrated by the Taguchi loss function), the engineer assigned to study the induction quench-and-harden operation should continually work to reduce unit-to-unit variation and move the process average toward nominal.

This example highlights the benefits of process improvement. The case hardness process was moved from chaos to the threshold state to the ideal state. The move from the threshold state to the ideal state resulted in:

1. Increased quality.
2. Increased productivity.
3. Lower unit cost. (It costs less to make good items than defective items because good items do not require rework.)
4. Increased price flexibility resulting from lower unit costs.
5. Increased market share resulting from increased quality and price flexibility.
6. Increased profit resulting from lower unit costs and greater market share.
7. More secure jobs for all employees.

Quality Improvement Stories

Employees trying to improve processes have found that their ideas and recommendations are more persuasive when based on facts rather than opinions and guesses. The Quality Improvement (QI) story is an efficient format for employees to present **process improvement studies** to management. QI stories standardize quality management reports, avoid logical errors in analysis, and make reports easy for all to comprehend.

Relationship between QI Stories and the PDSA Cycle

A seven-step procedure is utilized to construct a QI story, following the PDSA cycle of plan, do, study, and act. The Plan phase involves three steps: (1) selecting a theme for the QI story (obtaining all the background information necessary to understand the selected theme, including an existing process flow chart; explaining the reason for selecting the theme; and determining the organization and department objective(s) that should be influenced by the theme); (2) getting a full grasp of the present situation surrounding the theme; and (3) analyzing the present situation to identify appropriate action(s) (called **countermeasures**) to the process—that is, construct a revised process flowchart that incorporates the countermeasures.

The Do phase involves a further step: (4) testing the revised flowchart on a small scale using a planned experiment.

The Study phase involves: (5) studying, creatively thinking about, collecting, and analyzing data from the planned experiment concerning the effectiveness of the revised flowchart. Do the countermeasures reduce the difference between the voice of the customer and the voice of the process? Before and after comparisons of the experimental countermeasures' effects on the targeted department and organization objectives must be presented.

The Act phase requires two final steps: (6) determining if the revised flowchart was effective in pursuing department and organization objectives. If not, we go back to the Plan stage to find other countermeasures that will be effective in pursuing department and organization objectives. If the countermeasures were effective in pursuing department and organization objectives, we either go to the plan stage to seek the optimal settings of the countermeasure(s) or formally establish revised **standard operating procedures** based on the data about the experimental countermeasures and train all relevant personnel in the new best practice method. Further actions must be taken to prevent backsliding for the revised flowchart set into motion. This phase also includes (7) identifying remaining process problems, establishing a plan for further actions, and reflecting on the positive and negative aspects of past countermeasures.

Table 11.8 relates the seven steps of the QI story to the four phases of the PDSA cycle.

Potential Difficulties

Two areas of potential difficulty when applying QI stories are **qualitative** (non-numerical) **themes** and **exogenous problems**. Themes that are difficult to describe with numerical values should be analyzed by focusing on the magnitude of the gap between actual

TABLE 11.8
Relationship between the QI Story and the PDSA Cycle

Steps of the QI Story	Phases of the PDSA Cycle
1. Select a theme for the QI story.	
2. Get a full grasp of the present situation surrounding the theme.	Plan phase
3. Analyze the present situation to identify appropriate countermeasures.	
4. Set the countermeasures into action in a planned experiment.	Do phase
5. Study data concerning the effectiveness of the countermeasures.	Study phase
6. Establish revised standard operating procedures.	Act phase
7. Establish a plan for future actions.	

performance and the desired performance. If a problem's cause (e.g., cold weather or no rain) is beyond the control of anyone in the organization, we do not conclude that it is impossible to take countermeasures to remedy the exogenous problem. Instead, we attempt to determine why there are so many occurrences of the exogenous problem in area A versus area B, given that the areas have equal opportunities for the exogenous problem's occurrence.

Pursuit of Objectives

Unfortunately, QI stories will be initially selected because they are nearly complete resolutions to departmental problems and may not relate to organizational and departmental objectives. However, as employees gain experience with QI stories, they will want to select themes related to organization and department objectives. A **dashboard** is the best vehicle for linking organizational **objectives** and **indicators** to departmental objectives and indicators. Dashboards are used to create a cascading and interlocking system of objectives and indicators, from the organizational level to the departmental level to the area level, that deploys the organization's mission statement throughout the layers of an organization. Ultimately, objectives and their indicators are linked to processes that can be improved to attain the desired levels of the indicator(s) for each objective. Dashboards are discussed in Chapter 18.

Quality Improvement Story Case Study

A QI story drawn from a data processing department demonstrates the role of QI stories in an organization's improvement efforts. Figure 11.18 shows the story in QI story boards 1 through 14.

The QI story goes through two iterations of the PDSA cycle; nevertheless, a never-ending set of PDSA iterations will follow as the data processing department pursues continuous improvement in its daily work. The first iteration of the PDSA cycle focuses on all data entry operators in the data processing department. In this iteration of the PDSA cycle, *Select a Theme* is presented in QI story board 1; this includes showing the background of theme selection and the reason for selecting the theme in relation to the organization's and department's objectives. A *Grasp of the Present Situation* is presented in QI story board 2. An *Analysis of the Present Situation,* in QI story board 3, is performed to determine appropriate countermeasures that pursue the theme and the organization and department objectives. *Set the Countermeasures into Motion* on a trial basis is presented in QI story board 4. The *Effectiveness of the Countermeasures* on the theme and the organization and department objectives is measured as shown in QI story board 5. *Standard Operating Procedure* is a set that formalizes the countermeasures and prevents backsliding in QI story board 6. A *Plan for Future Actions* is presented in QI story board 7. The second iteration of the PDSA cycle focuses attention on an individual data entry operator. In this iteration, *Select a Theme* is accomplished when the data processing manager realizes that future process improvements will require her to identify and train operators whose performance is out of control on the high side, shown in QI story board 8. In this iteration of the PDSA cycle, a *Grasp of the Present Situation* determines that data entry operators 004 and 009 are out of control on the high side and why operator 004 is out of control on the high side; this is presented in QI story board 9. An *Analysis of the Present Situation,* in QI story board 10, determines the countermeasures necessary to improve operator 004's work. The manager *Sets the Countermeasures into Motion,* shown in QI story board 11. The positive *Effectiveness of the Countermeasures* on operator 004 and on the organization and department objectives is confirmed, as shown in QI story board 12. *Standard Operating Procedure* is a set that formalizes the countermeasure to all operators and prevents backsliding, in QI story board 13. Finally, a *Plan for Future Action* is specified in QI story board 14.

FIGURE 11.18   **Quality Improvement Story**
QI STORY BOARD 1

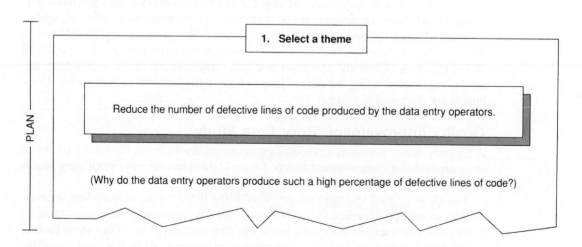

PLAN

1. **Select a theme**

Reduce the number of defective lines of code produced by the data entry operators.

(Why do the data entry operators produce such a high percentage of defective lines of code?)

FIGURE 11.18 (continued)

Background of theme selection (Relationship of the theme to organizational objectives)

ORGANIZATIONAL OBJECTIVES

The organization's mission mandates that every employee must base his/her decisions and actions on the following organizational objectives:

1. Pursuing continuous improvement in customer satisfaction.
2. Respecting and continuously improving all employees.
3. Establishing long-term and trusting relationships with suppliers.
4. Providing stockholders with a reasonable return.
5. Being a good corporate citizen.

DEPARTMENTAL OBJECTIVES

The data processing department's mission mandates that every employee must base his/her decision and actions on the following departmental objectives:

1. Recognizing that customers are both internal and external to the organization and continuously strive to improve data processing services to all customers.
2. Identifying areas in which employees require improvement and establish necessary training programs to bring about the identified improvements.

The data processing department will achieve the first departmental objective by:

1. Entering all data exactly as it appears on the source document.
2. Pursuing continuous reduction in the amount of time it takes to process a data entry job.

The manager of the data processing department realizes that the theme she selected to study is directly affected by the above objectives!

PLAN

FIGURE 11.18   (continued)

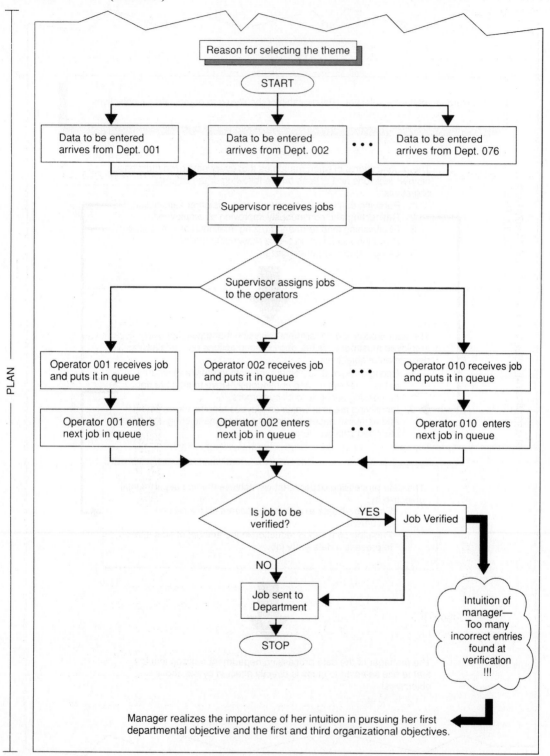

FIGURE 11.18 (continued)
QI STORY BOARD 2

PLAN

2. Grasp of the present situation

Manager's intuition leads her to conduct a survey to determine customer (other departments) satisfaction with her department's performance.

Manager constructs a list of her department's customers.

Administration
Production
Marketing
•
•
•

Manager constructs a questionnaire to determine customer satisfaction.

Department:_____

Supervisor:_____

(1) Do you feel that the error rate that data entry provides your department is:
unsatisfactory [ ]   satisfactory [ ]   excellent [ ]

(2) Approximately what percent of the data entry errors your department receives from our department contain errors attributable to our department? _____ %

FIGURE 11.18 (continued)

PLAN

Questionnaires were sent to all of the departments and all of the departments responded. Analysis of the questionnaires yielded the following results:

Findings:

• Do you feel that the error rate that data
  entry provides your department is:
  unsatisfactory?   (72%)
  satisfactory?   (20%)
  excellent?   (8%)

• Appproximately 2% of the data entry
  errors received by the various departments contain errors attributable to the
  data processing department.

FIGURE 11.18 (continued)

Due to customer dissatisfaction, the manager decided to collect data concerning the daily proportion of defective entry errors.

Day	Number of lines of code inspected	Number of defective lines	Proportion of defective lines
1	200	6	.03
2	200	6	.03
3	200	6	.03
4	200	5	.025
5	200	0	.0
6	200	0	.0
7	200	6	.03
8	200	14	.07
9	200	4	.02
10	200	0	.0
11	200	1	.005
12	200	8	.04
13	200	2	.01
14	200	4	.02
15	200	7	.035
16	200	1	.005
17	200	3	.015
18	200	1	.005
19	200	4	.02
20	200	0	.0
21	200	4	.02
22	200	15	.075
23	200	4	.02
24	200	1	.005
Total	4,800	102	

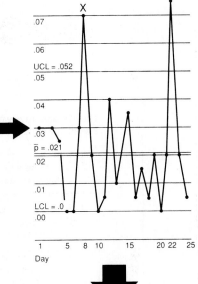

Finding:
The data entry operation is in a state of chaos; it produces an unknown proportion of defectives per day.

PLAN

FIGURE 11.18 (continued)

QI STORY BOARD 3

PLAN

3. Analysis of the present situation

Process must be stabilized. Hence, causes for days 8 and 22 must be found and policy must be set to prevent them from reoccurring.

The manager reviewed her daily comments concerning any unusual events that occurred on days 8 and 22.

Log sheet for data entry operation	
Day	Comment

8	untrained operator used for a rush job

22	ran out of toner from usual vendor
23	
24	

Findings:

• Policy needed for training new operators used for rush jobs.

• Inventory policy need to set safety stock level.

PLAN
ESTABLISHED

FIGURE 11.18 (continued)

QI STORY BOARD 4

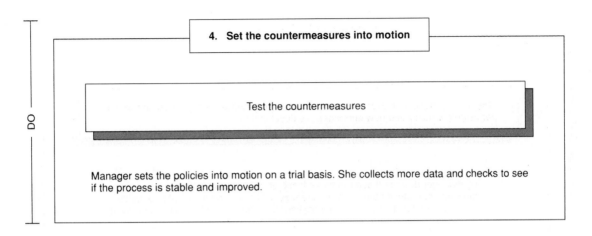

4. Set the countermeasures into motion

DO

Test the countermeasures

Manager sets the policies into motion on a trial basis. She collects more data and checks to see if the process is stable and improved.

QI STORY BOARD 5

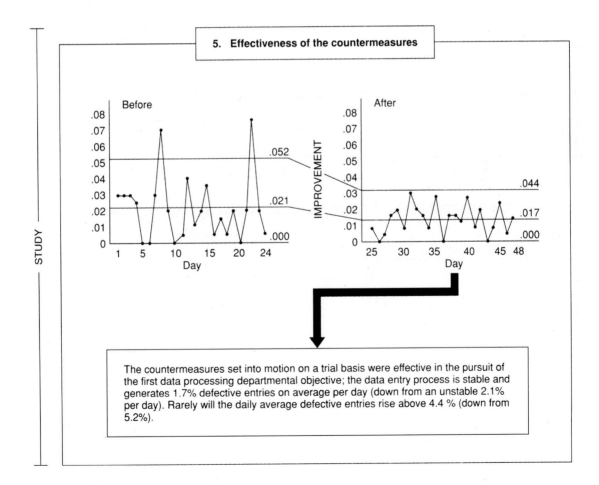

5. Effectiveness of the countermeasures

STUDY

Before

After

IMPROVEMENT

Day

Day

The countermeasures set into motion on a trial basis were effective in the pursuit of the first data processing departmental objective; the data entry process is stable and generates 1.7% defective entries on average per day (down from an unstable 2.1% per day). Rarely will the daily average defective entries rise above 4.4 % (down from 5.2%).

FIGURE 11.18 (continued)
QI STORY BOARD 6

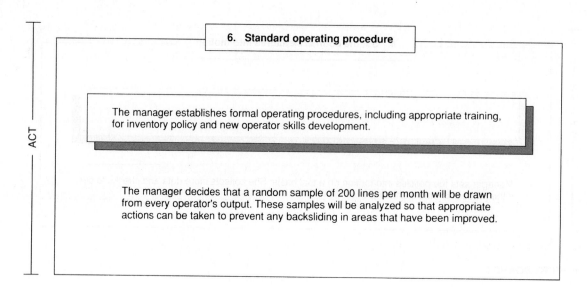

6. Standard operating procedure

The manager establishes formal operating procedures, including appropriate training, for inventory policy and new operator skills development.

The manager decides that a random sample of 200 lines per month will be drawn from every operator's output. These samples will be analyzed so that appropriate actions can be taken to prevent any backsliding in areas that have been improved.

QI STORY BOARD 7

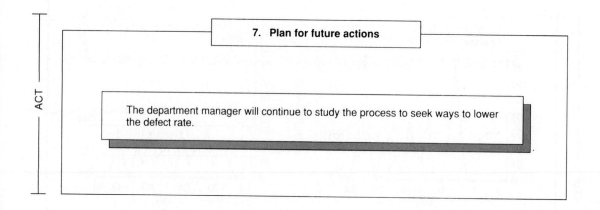

7. Plan for future actions

The department manager will continue to study the process to seek ways to lower the defect rate.

FIGURE 11.18 (continued)

QI STORY BOARD 8

PLAN

1.   Select a theme

Manager realizes that to improve the data entry process she must conduct a separate study for each operator.

QI STORY BOARD 9

PLAN

2.   Grasp of the present situation

Checksheet of defective entries by operator (All operators produced approximately the same number of lines of code during the period under study.) [12/1 - 12/31]

Operator	Tally	Frequency
001	||	2
002	|||	3
003	|	1
004	╫╫ ╫╫ ╫╫ ||||	19
005		0
006	||	2
007	|	1
008	|||	3
009	╫╫ ╫╫ ╫╫ ||	17
010	||	2
TOTAL		50

FIGURE 11.18 (continued)

PLAN

c chart of number of defective lines by operator

Number of defective lines

19
15
10
5
0

X
●

X
●

● ● ● ● ● ● ●

UCL = 11.71

$\bar{c}$ = 5.00

LCL = 0

1 2 3 4 5 6 7 8 9 10

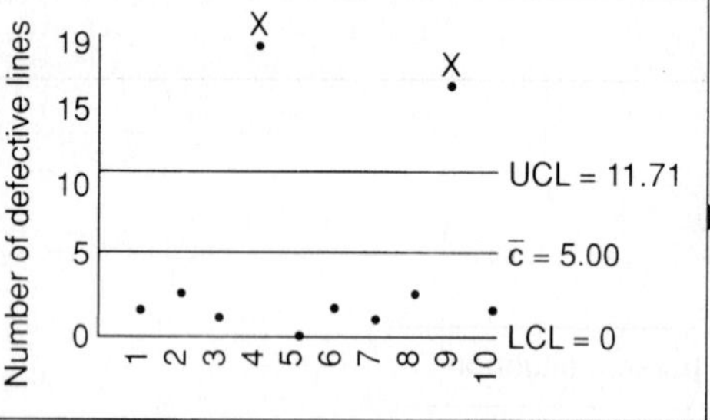

Operators 004 and 009 are out of the lines system.

c chart of number of defective lines by operator (excluding operators 004 and 009)

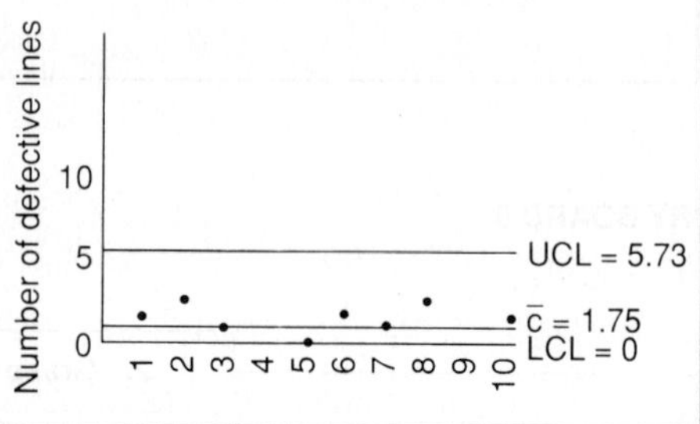

Number of defective lines

10
5
0

● ● ● ● ● ●

UCL = 5.73

$\bar{c}$ = 1.75

LCL = 0

1 2 3 4 5 6 7 8 9 10

Operators are stable without operators 004 and 009.

What percentage of the departmental errors are caused by operators 004 and 009?

Pareto Diagram of defective lines by operator (12/1-31)

Number of defective lines

50
45
40
35
30
25
20
15
10
5
0

100
98
96
92
88
84
78
72

38

Cum. % of defective lines

4 9 2 8 1 6 10 3 7 5

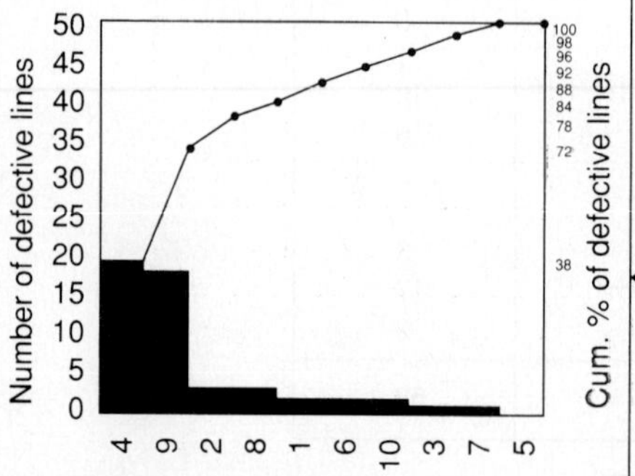

Finding: 72% of all defective lines are produced by operators 004 and 009!!!

Pareto Analysis of defective lines by operator (12/1-31)

Operator	Freq.	%	Cum. %
4	19	38	38
9	17	34	72
2	3	6	78
8	3	6	84
1	2	4	88
6	2	4	92
10	2	4	96
3	1	2	98
7	1	2	100
5	0	0	100
Total	50	100	100

FIGURE 11.18 (continued)

PLAN

Manager decides to study operators 004 and 009; she begins with operator 004.

QI STORY BOARD 10

PLAN

3. **Analysis of the present situation**

Checklist to determine the sources of operator 004's defective lines (Jan-Apr)					
Major causes of defective lines	Month				
	Jan	Feb	Mar	Apr	Total
Transposed numbers	7	10	6	5	28
Out of field	1		2		3
Wrong character	6	8	5	9	28
Data printed too lightly		1	1		2
Torn document	1	1		2	4
Creased document			1	1	2
Illegible source doc.			1		1
TOTAL	15	20	16	17	68

FIGURE 11.18 (continued)

Pareto Analysis to determine major causes of defective lines of code for operator 004 (Jan-Apr)			
Major causes of defective lines	Freq.	%	Cumulative %
Transposed numbers	28	41.2	41.2
Wrong character	28	41.2	82.4
Torn document	4	5.9	88.3
Out of field	3	4.4	92.7
Data printed too lightly	2	2.9	95.6
Creased document	2	2.9	98.5
Illegible source doc.	1	1.5	100.0
TOTAL	68	100.0	

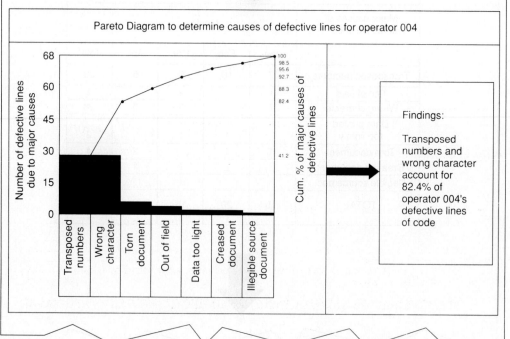

PLAN

FIGURE 11.18 (continued)

PLAN

Manager forms a group for a brainstorming session concerning how to resolve operator 004's problems with transposed numbers and wrong characters.

Brainstorming group votes to work on both problems simultaneously by a unanimous vote of the group.

Materials

Machines

Environment

Poor eyesight

Needs glasses

Methods

Personnel

Transposed numbers and wrong characters

PLAN ESTABLISHED

QI STORY BOARD 11

4. Set the countermeasures in motion

DO

Operator 004 is sent to have her eyes examined by an optometrist. She needs and receives eyeglasses.

FIGURE 11.18 (continued)
QI STORY BOARD 12

STUDY

5. Effectiveness of the countermeasures

Manager collects 25 additional daily samples of 200 lines of code each to determine the effect of operator 004's eyeglasses on her defective rate.

Day	Number Defective	Total Lines of Code	Proportion Defective
1	2	200	0.010
2	3	200	0.015
3	2	200	0.010
.	.	.	.
.	.	.	.
.	.	.	.
25	2	200	0.010
	40	5000	0.008

p charts comparing the proportion of defective lines produced by the "average" operator <u>before</u> improvement efforts with the proportion of defective lines produced by operator 004 <u>after</u> improvement efforts.

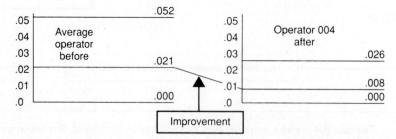

Finding: Operator 004 is stable and producing 8 defective lines per 1,000. Rarely will her defect rate go above 2.6 per 1,000. The countermeasure taken with operator 004 is effective in the pursuit of the first data processing department objective.

FIGURE 11.18 (concluded)
QI STORY BOARD 13

ACT

6. Standard operating procedure

The manager establishes a formal procedure by sending operator 004 for glasses.

The manager formally establishes a policy stating that all operators must have their eyes examined yearly and provide evidence of said examination. If any operator needs glasses, she will receive them. This policy should prevent backsliding in improvement efforts due to poor eyesight.

QI STORY BOARD 14

ACT

7. Plan for future action

		When will future plan be carried out?					Who will carry out plan?
		May	Jun	Jul	Aug	Sep	
Phase 1	Work with operator 009	←→					Manager and 009
Phase 2	Check progress of entire department			←→			Manager plus 001-010
Phase 3	Survey customers to determine satisfaction with data entry department					←→	Manager

Summary   An organization's quality consciousness can be better understood by examining the types of specifications it uses in production and service. If a firm uses individual unit and/or AQL specifications as guidelines to separate good product/service from bad, the firm is operating in a defect detection mode. If a firm uses individual unit specification as guidelines to determine the percentage of its output that is out of specification so that the difference between customer needs and process performance can be decreased, the firm has advanced to a defect prevention mode. Finally, if a firm uses distribution or performance specifications in its never-ending pursuit of total process improvement, it is operating in a never-ending improvement mode. The goals of never-ending improvement are the constant reduction of unit-to-unit variation and the movement of the process average toward nominal. Conformance to technical specifications (zero defects) is not an acceptable form of quality consciousness.

Process capability studies determine if a process is unstable, investigate any sources of instability and determine their causes, and take action to eliminate these sources of instability. After all sources of instability have been eliminated, the natural behavior of the process is called its process capability. We use types of process capability studies: attribute studies and variables studies. For each, we consider data requirements and possible actions that can be taken on the process as a result of the process capability study. For variables process capability studies, we consider the relationship between control limits, natural limits, and specification limits, and process capability indices.

Quality improvement stories provide an efficient format for employees to present process improvement studies to management; they standardize quality management reports, avoid logical errors in analysis, and make reports easy for all to comprehend.

Key Terms

Exercises

11.1. What is the basic function of a performance specification?

11.2. Explain the purpose and describe the construction of the three types of technical specifications: individual unit specifications, acceptable quality level specifications, and distribution specifications.

11.3. (See Created Dimensions in Appendix A11.1.) In an assembly operation, steel sheet A is glued onto steel sheet B to create a double-sheet thickness. Assume that the glue has no discernable thickness and that the unit-to-unit variation in thickness for both types of steel sheets is stable over time. The resulting thickness of the combined steel sheets is the quality characteristic of interest. The following process statistics have been collected concerning both types of steel sheets:

Steel Sheet A	Steel Sheet B
Mean = 2.50 inches	Mean = 4.75 inches
Std. dev. = 0.25 inches	Std. dev. = 0.50 inches

a. Compute the mean of the double-sheet thickness.

b. Compute the standard deviation of the double-sheet thickness.

11.4. (See Created Dimensions in Appendix A11.1) Rectangular sheets of material are produced in an assembly operation. Their dimensions are 9.0 inches in width by 14.0 inches in length. Assume that unit-to-unit variations among the widths and lengths of the rectangular sheets are stable over time. The area of the sheets is the quality characteristic of interest. The following process statistics have been collected for the widths and lengths of the rectangular sheets:

Width	Length
Mean = 9.0 inches	Mean = 14.0 inches
Std. dev. = 0.10 inches	Std. dev. = 0.40 inches

a. Compute the mean area of the rectangular sheets.

b. Compute the standard deviation of the area of the rectangular sheets.

11.5. The ABC Company produces steel tubes. The steel tube process is a stable cut-to-length operation that generates tubes that have a mean of 12.00 inches and standard deviation of 0.10 inches. The XYZ Company wishes to buy tubes from the ABC Company. The XYZ Company requires steel tubes between 11.77 inches and 12.23 inches in length.

a. Compute C_p.

b. Compute CPU.

c. Compute CPL.

d. Compute C_{pk}.

e. Compute Z_{LSL}.

f. Compute Z_{USL}.

    g. Compare and contrast the preceding capability indices with respect to their ability to explain the capability of the ABC Company's steel tube process.

    h. Discuss the managerial implications of the capability indices you computed in parts a through f.

11.6. The LMN Company wishes to buy tubes from the ABC Company of Exercise 11.5. The LMN Company requires steel tubes 11.95 inches long with a tolerance of 0.30 inches.

    a. Compute C_p.

    b. Compute CPU.

    c. Compute CPL.

    d. Compute C_{pk}.

    e. Compute Z_{LSL}.

    f. Compute Z_{USL}.

    g. Compare and contrast the preceding capability indices with respect to their ability to explain the capability of the ABC Company's steel tube process.

    h. Discuss the managerial implications of the capability indices you computed in parts a through f.

11.7. The Arco Company produces plastic containers. The plastic container process is a stable operation that generates containers with a mean volume of 12,500.00 cubic inches and standard deviation of 10.00 cubic inches. The Beta Company wishes to buy plastic containers from the Arco Company. The Beta Company requires plastic containers with a volume between 12,495.00 cubic inches and 12,545.00 cubic inches.

    a. Compute C_p.

    b. Compute CPU.

    c. Compute CPL.

    d. Compute C_{pk}.

    e. Compute Z_{LSL}.

    f. Compute Z_{USL}.

    g. Compare and contrast the preceding capability indices with respect to their ability to explain the capability of the Arco Company plastic container process's ability to meet the Beta Company's specifications.

    h. Discuss the managerial implications of the capability indices you computed in parts a through f.

11.8. Refer to Exercise 11.7. The Largo Corporation wishes to buy plastic containers from the Arco Company. The Largo Corporation requires plastic containers with a volume of 12,495.00 cubic inches and a tolerance of 20.00 cubic inches.

    a. Compute C_p.

    b. Compute CPU.

    c. Compute CPL.

    d. Compute C_{pk}.

    e. Compute Z_{LSL}.

f. Compute Z_{USL}.

g. Compare and contrast the preceding capability indices with respect to their ability to explain the capability of the Beta Company's plastic container process.

h. Discuss the managerial implications of the capability indices you computed in parts a through f.

11.9. How do you determine a process's capability, given that the only information available comes from an attribute process capability study?

11.10. Answer the following questions concerning QI stories:

a. Discuss the purpose of a QI story.

b. List the seven steps in a QI story.

c. Explain the relationship between the seven steps in a QI story and the four stages of the PDSA cycle.

11.11. Define capability of a process in statistical terms. Consider the Empirical Rule in your definition.

11.12. Answer the following questions concerning the data requirements for process capability studies:

a. Discuss the data requirements to conduct an attribute process capability study. Consider the number of time periods and the number of subgroups per time period.

b. Discuss the data requirements to conduct a variables process capability study. Consider the number of time periods and the number of subgroups per time period.

References

1. AT&T (1956), *Statistical Quality Control Handbook,* 10th printing, May 1984 (Indianapolis: AT&T).

2. A. Camp, "Methods for the Improvement of Quality and Productivity," Class Project, University of Miami School of Business Administration, 1986.

3. Ford Motor Company, modified from Operations Support Staffs, "Statistical Process Control Case Study," *Introduction to Ford's Operating Philosophy and Principles and Statistical Management Methods—Participant Notebook* (Ford Motor Company), September 1983.

4. H. Gitlow and S. Gitlow (1987), *The Deming Guide to Quality and Competitive Position* (Englewood Cliffs, NJ: Prentice Hall).

5. H. Gitlow and P. Hertz, "Product Defects and Productivity," *Harvard Business Review,* September–October 1983, pp. 131–141.

6. V. Kane, "Process Capability Indices," *Journal of Quality Technology,* 18, January 1986, pp. 41–52.

7. D. Wheeler and D. Chambers (1986), *Understanding Statistical Process Control* (Knoxville, TN: SPC Press).

8. D. Wheeler and D. Chambers (1992), *Understanding Statistical Process Control,* 2nd ed. (Knoxville, TN: SPC Press).

Appendix **A11.1**

Created Dimensions

When parts are assembled, new dimensions are created; these new dimensions have statistical distributions [see Reference 1, pp. 119–127]. For example, if two boards are glued together to form a double-thick board, the distribution of the thickness of the double-thick boards is a newly created dimension. Management must be able to control and reduce the variation of these created dimensions so the final assemblies will perform as the customer desires over the product's life cycle. Understanding and controlling these created dimensions requires working knowledge of the statistical rules of created dimensions. If management does not pay attention to their statistical characteristics, these dimensions will fail to be within specification limits and will cause problems in production or service, will increase costs, and will lead to customer dissatisfaction. The discussion of specifications earlier in this chapter applies to created dimensions as well.

Law of the Addition of Component Dimension Averages

If component parts are assembled so that the individual component dimensions are added to one another, the average dimension of the assembly will equal the sum of the individual component average dimensions. Figure A11.1 illustrates this concept. If three component parts are glued together (assuming the glue takes no measurable dimensions), the average width of the assembled part equals the sum of the average individual part widths:

$$\overline{x}_{assembly} = \overline{x}_1 + \overline{x}_2 + \overline{x}_3 \qquad \textbf{(A11.1)}$$

where

$\overline{x}_{assembly}$ = average width of the assembly

$\overline{x}_1$ = average width of part 1

$\overline{x}_2$ = average width of part 2

$\overline{x}_3$ = average width of part 3

Part 1 has an average thickness of 10 mm, part 2 has an average thickness of 20 mm, and part 3 has an average thickness of 30 mm. Consequently, the average thickness of the final assembly is the sum of all three averages, 60 mm (10 mm + 20 mm + 30 mm):

$$\begin{aligned}
\overline{x}_{assembly} &= \overline{x}_1 + \overline{x}_2 + \overline{x}_3 \\
&= 10 \text{ mm} + 20 \text{ mm} + 30 \text{ mm} \\
&= 60 \text{ mm}
\end{aligned}$$

The preceding law holds only if the processes generating the components are in statistical control.

Law of the Differences of Component Dimension Averages

If component parts are assembled so that the individual component dimensions are subtracted from one another, the average dimension of the assembly will then equal the difference between the individual component average dimensions. Figure A11.2 illustrates

**FIGURE
A11.1
Addition of
Averages**

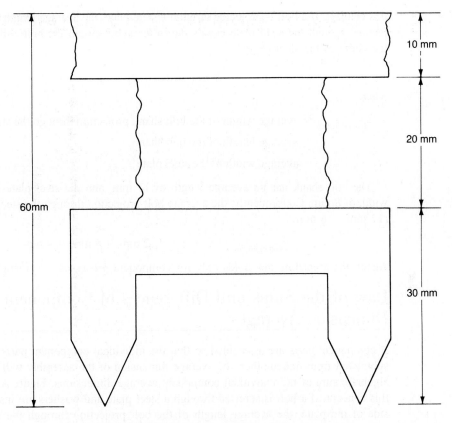

Width of assembly = 10 mm + 20 mm + 30 mm
= 60 mm

**FIGURE
A11.2
Differences of
Averages**

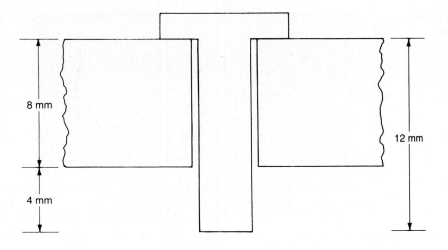

Bolt projection = 12 mm − 8 mm = 4 mm

this concept. If a bolt is projected through a steel plate, the average length of the bolt projection through the steel plate equals the difference between the bolt's shank length and the width of the steel plate:

$$\overline{x}_{\text{bolt projection}} = \overline{x}_s - \overline{x}_p \qquad \text{(A11.2)}$$

where

$\overline{x}_{\text{bolt projection}}$ = average length of the bolt shank projection through the steel plate

$\overline{x}_s$ = average length of the bolt shank

$\overline{x}_p$ = average width of the steel plate

The bolt shank has an average length of 12 mm, and the steel plate has an average width of 8 mm. Consequently, the average bolt projection through the steel plate is 4 mm (12 mm − 8 mm):

$$\overline{x}_{\text{bolt projection}} = \overline{x}_s - \overline{x}_p = 12 \text{ mm} - 8 \text{ mm} = 4 \text{ mm}$$

Again, the preceding law holds only for component processes in statistical control.

Law of the Sums and Differences of Component Dimension Averages

If component parts are assembled so that the individual component parts are added and subtracted from one another, the average dimension of the assembly will then equal the algebraic sum of the individual component average dimensions. Figure A11.3 illustrates this concept. If a bolt is screwed through a steel plate and washers are inserted on either side of the plate, the average length of the bolt projection through the steel plate and

FIGURE A11.3
Sums and Differences of Averages

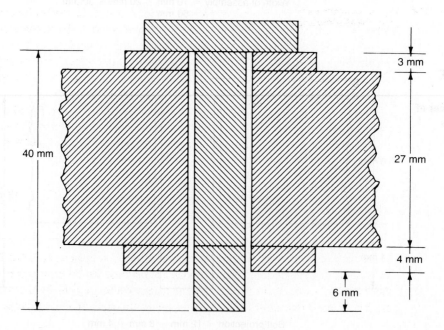

washers then equals the difference between the sum of the widths of the two washers and the steel plate, and the length of the bolt shank:

$$\overline{x}_{\text{bolt projection}} = \overline{x}_s - (\overline{x}_{w1} + \overline{x}_p + \overline{x}_{w2}) \qquad \textbf{(A11.3)}$$

where

$\overline{x}_{\text{bolt projection}}$ = average length of the bolt shank projection through both washers and the steel plate

$\overline{x}_s$ = average length of the bolt shank

$\overline{x}_{w1}$ = average width of the top washer

$\overline{x}_{w2}$ = average width of the bottom washer

$\overline{x}_p$ = average width of the steel plate.

The bolt shank has an average length of 40 mm, the steel plate has an average thickness of 27 mm, the top washer has an average thickness of 3 mm, and the bottom washer has an average thickness of 4 mm. Hence, the average bolt projection through the steel plate and both washers is 6 mm $[40\text{ mm} - (3\text{ mm} + 27\text{ mm} + 4\text{ mm})]$:

$$\overline{x}_{\text{bolt projection}} = \overline{x}_s - (\overline{x}_{w1} + \overline{x}_p + \overline{x}_{w2})$$
$$= 40\text{ mm} - (3\text{ mm} + 27\text{ mm} + 4\text{ mm})$$
$$= 6\text{ mm}$$

Again, the preceding law holds only for component processes in statistical control.

Law of the Addition of Component Dimension Standard Deviations

If component parts are assembled at random (for example, so that each component part is drawn randomly from its own bin with no selection criteria), the standard deviation of the assembly will be the square root of the sum of the component variances, regardless of whether the components are added or subtracted from each other. This law applies to assemblies in which the component parts combine linearly and are statistically independent.

For example, consider again the bolt projection in Figure A11.2.

Recall that $\overline{x}_s = 12$ mm and $\overline{x}_p = 8$ mm; consequently, we found from Equation (A11.2) that $\overline{x}_{\text{bolt projection}} = 4$ mm. Further, assume that the standard deviation of the bolt shank length, σ_s, is 0.010 mm and the standard deviation of the steel plate width, σ_p, is 0.008 mm. The standard deviation of the bolt projection is thus:

$$\sigma_{\text{bolt projection}} = \sqrt{\sigma_s^{\,2} + \sigma_p^{\,2}} \qquad \textbf{(A11.4)}$$
$$= \sqrt{(0.010)^2 + (0.008)^2}$$
$$= 0.0128\text{ mm}$$

We must realize that the standard deviation of the bolt projection is not 0.018 mm, the sum of the individual component standard deviations, but the square root of the sum of the individual component variances. This means that the assembly-to-assembly variation among random assemblies is not the same as the sum of the individual components' unit-to-unit variations. Again, the preceding law holds only for component processes in statistical control.

Law of the Average for Created Areas and Volumes

If areas and volumes are created by the assembly of component parts, then the average area or volume of the assembly will equal the product of the individual component average dimensions if the component processes are stable and independent. Figure A11.4 illustrates this concept. If a boxlike container is constructed with two short sides, two long sides, and two top/bottom sides, then the average internal volume of the boxlike container equals the product of the average length of the short side, the average length of the long side, and the average width of the sides:

$$\bar{x}_v = (\bar{x}_s)(\bar{x}_l)(\bar{x}_w) \qquad \text{(A11.5)}$$

where

$\bar{x}_v$ = average internal volume of the constructed container

$\bar{x}_s$ = average length of short side

$\bar{x}_l$ = average length of long side

$\bar{x}_w$ = average width of the sides

The average length of the short side is 3.0 mm, the average length of the long side is 8.0 mm, and the average width of the sides is 2.0 mm. Consequently, the average internal volume of the constructed container is 48 mm³ (3 mm × 8 mm × 2 mm).

$$\bar{x}_v = (\bar{x}_s)(\bar{x}_l)(\bar{x}_w) = (3 \text{ mm})(8 \text{ mm})(2 \text{ mm}) = 48 \text{ mm}^3$$

Again, the preceding law holds only for component processes in statistical control.

Law of the Standard Deviation for Created Areas and Volumes

If areas and volumes are created by the assembly of component parts, we can calculate the standard deviation of the created areas or volumes:

$$\sigma_{area} = \sqrt{\bar{x}_s^2\sigma_l^2 + \bar{x}_l^2\sigma_s^2 + \sigma_l^2\sigma_s^2} \qquad \text{(A11.6)}$$

FIGURE A11.4
Created Volume of a Container

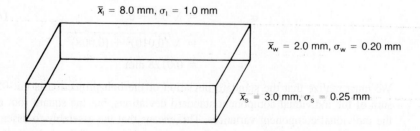

$\bar{x}_l = 8.0 \text{ mm}, \sigma_l = 1.0 \text{ mm}$

$\bar{x}_w = 2.0 \text{ mm}, \sigma_w = 0.20 \text{ mm}$

$\bar{x}_s = 3.0 \text{ mm}, \sigma_s = 0.25 \text{ mm}$

where

$\quad \bar{x}_s$ = average length of the short side

$\quad \bar{x}_l$ = average length of the long side

$\quad \sigma_s$ = standard deviation of length of the short side

$\quad \sigma_l$ = standard deviation of length of the long side

$\quad \sigma_{area}$ = standard deviation of the created internal area

Hence

$$\sigma_{volume} = [\bar{x}_s^2\bar{x}_w^2\sigma_l^2 + \bar{x}_l^2\bar{x}_w^2\sigma_s^2 + \bar{x}_s^2\bar{x}_l^2\sigma_w^2 + \bar{x}_s^2\sigma_l^2\sigma_s^2 \\ + \bar{x}_l^2\sigma_s^2\sigma_w^2 + \bar{x}_w^2\sigma_s^2\sigma_l^2 + \sigma_l^2\sigma_s^2\sigma_w^2]^{1/2} \tag{A11.7}$$

where

$\quad \bar{x}_w$ = average width

$\quad \sigma_w$ = standard deviation of the width

All equations assume that the component processes are stable and independent. Figure A11.4 illustrates this concept. If the means and standard deviations for the boxlike container's dimensions are as shown in Figure A11.4, then the standard deviation of the internal volume for the assembled container is:

$$\begin{aligned}
\sigma_{volume} &= [\bar{x}_s^2\bar{x}_w^2\sigma_l^2 + \bar{x}_l^2\bar{x}_w^2\sigma_s^2 + \bar{x}_s^2\bar{x}_l^2\sigma_w^2 + \bar{x}_s^2\sigma_l^2\sigma_s^2 + \bar{x}_l^2\sigma_s^2\sigma_w^2 \\
&\quad + \bar{x}_w^2\sigma_s^2\sigma_l^2 + \sigma_l^2\sigma_s^2\sigma_w^2]^{1/2} \\
&= [3^22^21^2 + 8^22^2(.25)^2 + 3^28^2(.20)^2 + 3^21^2(.20)^2 \\
&\quad + 8^2(.25)^2(.20)^2 + 2^2(.25)^2(1^2) + (1^2)(.25)^2(.20)^2]^{1/2} \\
&= \sqrt{36 + 16 + 23.04 + .36 + .16 + .25 + .0025} \\
&= \sqrt{75.8125} \\
&= 8.71 \text{ mm}^3
\end{aligned}$$

Again, the preceding law holds only for component processes in statistical control.

Process capabilities can be computed for created dimensions as follows. For example, suppose that the process capability studies for the thickness of the sheet, pin, and both washer subcomponents of the assembly in Figure A11.3 on page 464 were based on subgroups of five subcomponents and yielded:

$$\bar{x}_s = 40 \text{ mm} \quad \text{and} \quad \sigma_s = 0.0050$$
$$\bar{x}_{w1} = 3 \text{ mm} \quad \text{and} \quad \sigma_{w1} = 0.0007$$
$$\bar{x}_{w2} = 4 \text{ mm} \quad \text{and} \quad \sigma_{w2} = 0.0008$$
$$\bar{x}_p = 27 \text{ mm} \quad \text{and} \quad \sigma_p = 0.0030$$

Further, assume that all component processes are independent of each other and stable. The average bolt projection is:

$$\bar{x}_{bolt\ projection} = 40 \text{ mm} - 3 \text{ mm} - 27 \text{ mm} - 4 \text{ mm} = 6 \text{ mm}$$

The standard deviation of the bolt projection is:

$$\sigma_{\text{bolt projection}} = [(0.0050)^2 + (0.0007)^2 + (0.0008)^2 + (0.0030)^2]^{1/2}$$
$$= 0.00593 \approx 0.006$$

The process capability of the created bolt projection dimension is computed using Equations (11.1) and (11.2):

$$\text{UNL} = 6 \text{ mm} + 3(0.006) = 6 \text{ mm} + 0.018 \text{ mm} = 6.018 \text{ mm}$$
$$\text{LNL} = 6 \text{ mm} - 3(0.006) = 6 \text{ mm} - 0.018 \text{ mm} = 5.982 \text{ mm}$$

From the normal distribution, 99.73 percent of the bolt projections will be between 5.982 mm and 6.018 mm. Alternatively, using the Empirical Rule, virtually all of the bolt projections will be between 5.982 mm and 6.018 mm.

Bolt projection specifications are set at 5.99 ± 0.02 mm, or USL = 6.01 mm and LSL = 5.97 mm. Consequently,

$$Z_{\text{USL}} = \frac{(\text{USL} - \overline{\text{X}})}{\sigma}$$

$$Z_{\text{USL}} = \frac{(6.01 - 6.00)}{(0.006)} = \frac{0.01}{0.006} = 1.67$$

The process average is only 1.67 standard deviations below the upper specification limit, indicating that some output will be nonconforming. The fraction of output that was nonconforming in the period under study can be determined by examining the histogram of the output, as in our camshaft example.

$$Z_{\text{LSL}} = \frac{(\overline{\text{X}} - \text{LSL})}{\sigma}$$

$$Z_{\text{LSL}} = \frac{(6.00 - 5.97)}{0.006} = \frac{0.03}{0.006} = 5.00$$

The process average is 5.00 standard deviations above the lower specification limit, indicating the likely production of only conforming output.

Finally, created dimensions should be control charted because a created dimension can be out of control while component dimensions are in control. Never-ending improvement cannot progress without reducing unit-to-unit variations and moving the process toward nominal for created dimensions.

Chapter 12

Design of Experiments

Sections

Chapter Objectives

- To present the basic concepts of experimental design
- To present and illustrate certain flawed designs
- To describe how to evaluate a one-factor design and its limitations
- To describe factorial designs, discuss the concept of interaction, and illustrate with two, three, and five factors
- To describe and illustrate the fractional factorial design and discuss its advantages and assumptions

Introduction

Design of experiments (DoE) is a collection of statistical methods for studying the relationships between independent variables, the x's (also called factors, input variables, or process variables), and their interactions on a dependent variable, y (also called the outcome or response variable). Additionally, design of experiments can be used to minimize the effects of background variables on an understanding of the relationships between the x's and y. A background variable (also called a noise variable or lurking variable) is a variable that can potentially affect the dependent variable (y) in an experiment, but is not of interest as an independent variable (x).

The concepts of experimental design discussed in this chapter represent an active intervention into a process by employees; that is, process changes are planned and tested by employees, and the data resulting from those changes are studied to determine the effect of the process change. This kind of experiment does more than passively collect data from a functioning process; rather, it actively intervenes in the function of the process to collect data.

The ideas involved in the design of experiments are not new. They were originally developed by R. A. Fisher in England early in the twentieth century [see Reference 1, pp. 547–562 and Reference 2, pp. 1–10], whose original work focused on improving agricultural experimentation. Fisher's contributions to experimental design were based on several fundamental principles. First, he developed an experimental strategy that purposely designed experiments to simultaneously study several factors of interest. This approach was considered novel, since it contrasted with the scientific method as practiced in the nineteenth century (and still practiced today) of varying only one factor at a time. Second, he developed the concept of randomization that allows for the control and measurement of variation resulting from factors not considered in the experiment. Fisher realized that in conducting an agricultural experiment in the field, not all factors could be foreseen; such unforeseen factors are called background variables. Thus, he determined the particular treatment levels received by each plot of land (his individual observations) by a method of random assignment. Any differences between different plots that received the same treatment could be considered to be due to random variation or experimental error.

Designs Based on Level of Process Knowledge

Experimental designs are used to study processes, products, or services. The purpose of an experimental design depends on the level of knowledge available concerning the process, product or service being studied. **Screening designs** are used when there is a low level of knowledge about the x's that are critical to optimizing y. Researchers use these experiments to identify the key x's to optimizing y, using very few trials. **Full factorial designs** are used when researchers have a low level of knowledge of the interactions between the key x's necessary to optimizing y. **Fractional factorial designs** are used when there is a moderate level of knowledge about the interactions between the key x's needed to optimize y, using an economical number of trials. **Response surface methodology designs** are used when there is a high level of knowledge about the key x's, and their interactions, needed to optimize y. These are some of the more common types of experimental designs. In this chapter, after introducing several one-factor designs and noting their shortcomings, full factorial designs and selected fractional factorial designs will be discussed.

Some Flawed Experimental Designs

There are three classic **flawed designs.** They are the **one-factor-at-a-time strategy,** the **stick-with-a-winner strategy,** and the **change-many-factors-at-once strategy.** In order to understand the principles of design of experiments, it is useful to understand why these strategies are flawed.

One-Factor-at-a-Time Experiments

In one-factor-at-a-time experiments, the researcher simply changes one x at a time to determine its effect on the y. They are simple to design and analyze, but they have shortcomings. First, they provide no information on interactions between factors. Second, experimenters may run out of time and/or money before they have enough information to make an informed decision. Table 12.1 shows 8 trials in an experiment. Each column in Table 12.1 (except the first and last columns) represents one of the **independent variables**, also called **factors**, or **input variables**, or **process variables**, or x's, that are manipulated to optimize the **dependent variable** (last column), also called a **response variable** or **outcome** or y. Each row in Table 12.1 (except the first row) represents one possible combination of settings for the x's. Each cell contains either a "+" or a "−." The "−" represents the low or current setting for an independent variable (x). The "+" represents the high setting for an independent variable. For example, suppose x_2 = machine speed. If x_2 = −, the machine is set at the low speed. If x_2 = +, the machine is set at the high speed. The standard trial or trial 1 (second row in Table 12.1) sets all of the independent variables at the low level. Trial 2 (third row in Table 12.1) sets x_1 at the high level, but x_2 through x_7 are set at the low levels, and so on.

An example of a one-factor-at-a-time experiment would be trying one vitamin (x) at a time to decrease cholesterol (y). For example, suppose your total cholesterol level is 270. In a one-factor-at-a-time experiment, you would first take No-Flush niacin for one month and measure your cholesterol at the end of the one month time period. Suppose it is 220. Next, stop taking the niacin and begin taking red yeast for one month and measure your cholesterol again. Suppose it is 240. Third, stop taking red yeast and begin taking garlic for one month and measure your cholesterol. Suppose it is 260. What would you conclude from this experiment? No-Flush niacin lowers your cholesterol? Red yeast lowers or raises your cholesterol? Garlic lowers or raises your cholesterol? Do you know anything about the interactions between niacin and red yeast, niacin and garlic, red yeast and garlic? This experiment assumes that the vitamins have no residual effects; that is, they lose potency as soon as you stop taking them. Is this true? Does the experiment provide any information about residual effects of the vitamins?

> No-flush niacin lowers your cholesterol, red yeast maybe lowers it, but what about the effect of taking niacin first? Garlic maybe lowers it, but what about the effect of taking niacin and red yeast first? In addition, do you know anything about the interactions between niacin and red yeast, niacin and garlic, red yeast and garlic? Does the experiment provide any information about residual effects of the vitamins?

TABLE 12.1
One-Factor-at-a-Time Experiments

Description	x_1	x_2	x_3	x_4	x_5	x_6	x_7	y
Standard	−	−	−	−	−	−	−	
Trial 2	+	−	−	−	−	−	−	
Trial 3	−	+	−	−	−	−	−	
Trial 4	−	−	+	−	−	−	−	
Trial 5	−	−	−	+	−	−	−	
Trial 6	−	−	−	−	+	−	−	
Trial 7	−	−	−	−	−	+	−	
Trial 8	−	−	−	−	−	−	+	

Since all of these questions are still undetermined after the experiment has been undertaken, this one-factor-at-a-time approach is not a very useful design.

Stick-with-a-Winner Experiments

Stick-with-a-winner experiments suffer some of the same shortcomings as one-factor-at-a-time experiments. First, they provide limited, and possibly misleading, information on interactions between factors. Second, experimenters may run out of time and/or money before they have enough information to make an informed decision. Third, although they seem to be scientific, they are not. Table 12.2 shows a stick-with-a-winner design. The first trial sets all of the x's at their low (or current) levels, yielding y = 1.2. The second trial sets x_1 = + and x_2 through x_7 = −, yielding y = 1.8. Since 1.8 > 1.2, the third trial sets x_1 = x_2 = +, and x_3 through x_7 = −, yielding y = 1.6. Since 1.6 < 1.8, the fourth trial sets x_1 = +, reverses x_2 back to the low (−) setting, sets x_3 = +, and x_4 through x_7 = −, yielding y = 1.7. This process of sticking with a winner continues through all of the trials.

This stick-with-a-winner design, like the previous one-factor-at-a-time design, is a very flawed experimental design, since it leaves many questions unanswered.

Change-Many-Factors-at-Once Design

A change-many-factors-at-once design suffers all of the shortcomings of the one-factor-at-a-time experiment, plus an additional shortcoming: you cannot even determine the effects of the individual x's. Table 12.3 shows a change-many-factors-at-once design.

Returning to the cholesterol example, the change-many-factors-at-once design would go from measuring cholesterol after taking no vitamins for one month, to measuring cholesterol after taking niacin, red yeast, and garlic for one month. This is an all or nothing experiment. It is a common and flawed form of experimentation, offering no information about the effects of the individual x's or their interactions.

TABLE 12.2
Stick-with-a-Winner Design

Description	x_1	x_2	x_3	x_4	x_5	x_6	x_7	y
Standard	−	−	−	−	−	−	−	1.2
Trial 2	+	−	−	−	−	−	−	1.8
Trial 3	+	+	−	−	−	−	−	1.6
Trial 4	+	−	+	−	−	−	−	1.7
Trial 5	+	−	−	+	−	−	−	2.0
Trial 6	+	−	−	+	+	−	−	2.2
Trial 7	+	−	−	+	+	+	−	2.1
Trial 8	+	−	−	+	+	−	+	2.5

TABLE 12.3
Change-Many-Factors-at-Once Design

Description	x_1	x_2	x_3	x_4	x_5	x_6	x_7	y
Standard	−	−	−	−	−	−	−	1.2
Trial 2	+	+	+	+	+	+	+	1.8

One-Factor Designs

All too often, experiments on a dependent variable y are done that consider only one independent variable x. To illustrate a **one-factor design** in which there is only a single factor to be investigated, consider the manufacture of integrated circuits. Integrated circuits are produced on silicon wafers that are ground to target thickness during an early stage of the production process. The wafers are positioned in various locations on a grinder and kept in place throughout a vacuum decompression process. The goal of this particular experiment is to study the thickness of a wafer at different positions on the wafer. To accomplish this, a sample of 30 wafers is selected and the thickness of each wafer at five different positions (positions 1, 2, 18, 19, and 28) is measured. The results are presented in Table 12.4 (see 🟤 CIRCUITS).

A visual descriptive analysis of the data that ignores their time ordering can be done by using two graphical methods, the **dotplot**, and the **box-and-whisker plot**.

TABLE 12.4
Thickness of Wafers in an Integrated Circuit Manufacturing Process

Source: K. C. B. Roes and R. J. M. M. Does, "Shewhart-Type Charts in Nonstandard Situations," *Technometrics,* 37, 1995, pp. 15–24.

Position 1	Position 2	Position 18	Position 19	Position 28
240	243	250	253	248
238	242	245	251	247
239	242	246	250	248
235	237	246	249	246
240	241	246	247	249
240	243	244	248	245
240	243	244	249	246
245	250	250	247	248
238	240	245	248	246
240	242	246	249	248
240	243	246	250	248
241	245	243	247	245
247	245	255	250	249
237	239	243	247	246
242	244	245	248	245
237	239	242	247	245
242	244	246	251	248
243	245	247	252	249
243	245	248	251	250
244	246	246	250	246
241	239	244	250	246
242	245	248	251	249
242	245	248	243	246
241	244	245	249	247
236	239	241	246	242
243	246	247	252	247
241	243	245	248	246
239	240	242	243	244
239	240	250	252	250
241	243	249	255	253

FIGURE 12.1
Minitab
Dotplot of
the Wafer
Thickness for
the Five
Positions

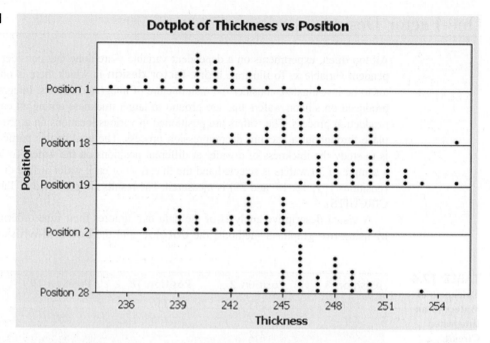

The dotplot provides a two-dimensional graph with the variable of interest on the x axis and the number of dots plotted vertically on the y axis. Figure 12.1 presents a dotplot obtained from Minitab of the wafer thickness for the five positions.

Observe from Figure 12.1 that there appear to be substantial differences in the distribution of thicknesses for the five positions. Position 1 has a thickness that appears centered between 239 and 243. Position 2 has a thickness centered around 242 and 243. Position 18 has a thickness centered at 245 and 246. Position 19 has a thickness centered between 249 and 250. Position 28 has a thickness centered at 246 and 247. All positions are approximately normally distributed with a range of 12 or 13 thickness units.

A second graph for comparing the groups, the box-and-whisker plot, is a graphical representation of the five-number summary that consists of the minimum value, the **first quartile** (Q_1 or 25th percentile), the **median,** the **third quartile** (Q_3 or 75th percentile), and the maximum value. The vertical line drawn within the box represents the location of the median value in the data. The vertical line at the left side of the box represents the location of Q_1 and the vertical line at the right side of the box represents the location of Q_3. Thus, the box contains the middle 50 percent of the observations in the distribution. The lower 25 percent of the data are represented by a dashed line (i.e., a *whisker*) connecting the left side of the box to the location of the smallest value, $x_{smallest}$. Similarly, the upper 25 percent of the data are represented by a dashed line connecting the right side of the box to $x_{largest}$. Figure 12.2 demonstrates the relationship between the box-and-whisker plot and the frequency polygon. Four different types of distributions are depicted with their box-and-whisker plots and corresponding polygons.

FIGURE 12.2
Box-and-Whisker Plots and Corresponding Polygons

Area under each polygon is split into quartiles corresponding to the five-number summary for the respective box-and-whisker plot.

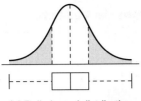

(a) Bell-shaped distribution

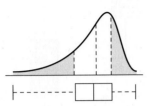

(b) Left-skewed distribution

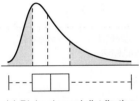

(c) Right-skewed distribution

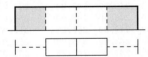

(d) Rectangular distribution

When a data set is perfectly symmetrical, as is the case in Figure 12.2a and d, the mean and median are the same, as we saw in Chapter 5. In addition, the length of the left whisker will equal the length of the right whisker, and the median line will divide the box in half.

When the data set is left skewed, as in Figure 12.2b, the few small observations distort the mean toward the left tail. For this hypothetical left-skewed distribution, 75 percent of all data values are found between the left edge of the box (Q_1) and the end of the right whisker ($x_{largest}$). Therefore, the long left whisker contains the distribution of only the smallest 25 percent of the observations, demonstrating the distortion from symmetry in this data set.

For the right-skewed data set in Figure 12.2c, the concentration of data points will be on the low end of the scale (i.e., the left side of the box-and-whisker plot). Here, 75 percent of all data values are found between the beginning of the left whisker ($x_{smallest}$) and the right edge of the box (Q_3), and the remaining 25 percent of the observations are dispersed along the long right whisker at the upper end of the scale.

Figure 12.3 represents the box-and-whisker plot obtained from Minitab of the wafer thickness for the five positions.

From Figure 12.3, it appears that the thickness for position 19 is greater than for the other positions. The thicknesses for positions 1 and 2 appear lower than the other positions. Note that the asterisks represent outlier values. Additionally, all positions are relatively symmetric and equally variable.

A numeric descriptive analysis of the data that ignores their time ordering is shown in Figure 12.4.

A visual analysis of the raw wafer thickness data that considers their time ordering is shown in the **run chart** in Figure 12.5. It shows that position 19 has the highest average thickness.

Figure 12.6 shows an **individuals and moving range chart** of the wafer thickness data by position over time, showing that position 19 is the thickest position, but all positions have approximately the same average range.

The one-factor design is useful in examining differences due to a single factor of interest. However, it does not provide the ability to measure how two or more factors interact in their effect on a response variable of interest.

Two-Factor Factorial Designs

A **two-factor factorial design,** also called a **two-factor design,** is an experimental design that simultaneously evaluates the effects of two factors (x's) on a dependent variable (y). Factors can have any number of **levels.** However, this text will consider only factors with two levels, or **treatments,** such as high and low, or on and off.

FIGURE 12.3
Minitab Box-and-Whisker Plot of the Wafer Thickness for the Five Positions

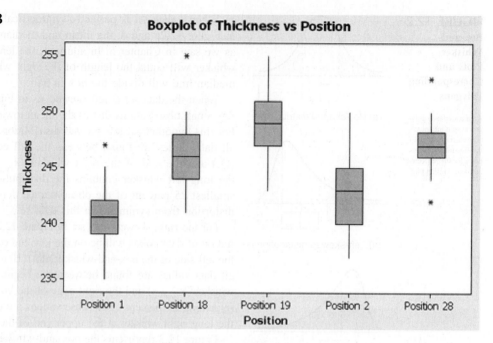

FIGURE 12.4 Descriptive Statistics of Wafer Thickness by Position

Variable	Position	N	N*	Mean	StDev	Minimum	Q1	Median	Q3	Maximum	Range	IQR
Thickness	Position 1	30	0	240.53	2.62	235.00	239.00	240.50	242.00	247.00	12.00	3.00
	Position 18	30	0	246.07	2.90	241.00	244.00	246.00	248.00	255.00	14.00	4.00
	Position 19	30	0	249.10	2.66	243.00	247.00	249.00	251.00	255.00	12.00	4.00
	Position 2	30	0	242.73	2.79	237.00	240.00	243.00	245.00	250.00	13.00	5.00
	Position 28	30	0	247.07	2.15	242.00	246.00	247.00	248.25	253.00	11.00	2.25

FIGURE 12.5
Minitab Run Chart of Thickness of Wafer Data

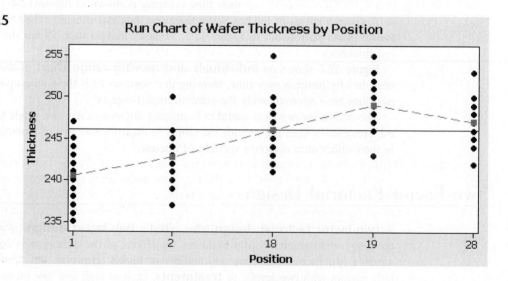

FIGURE 12.6 **Minitab Individuals and Moving Range Chart of Wafer Thickness Data**

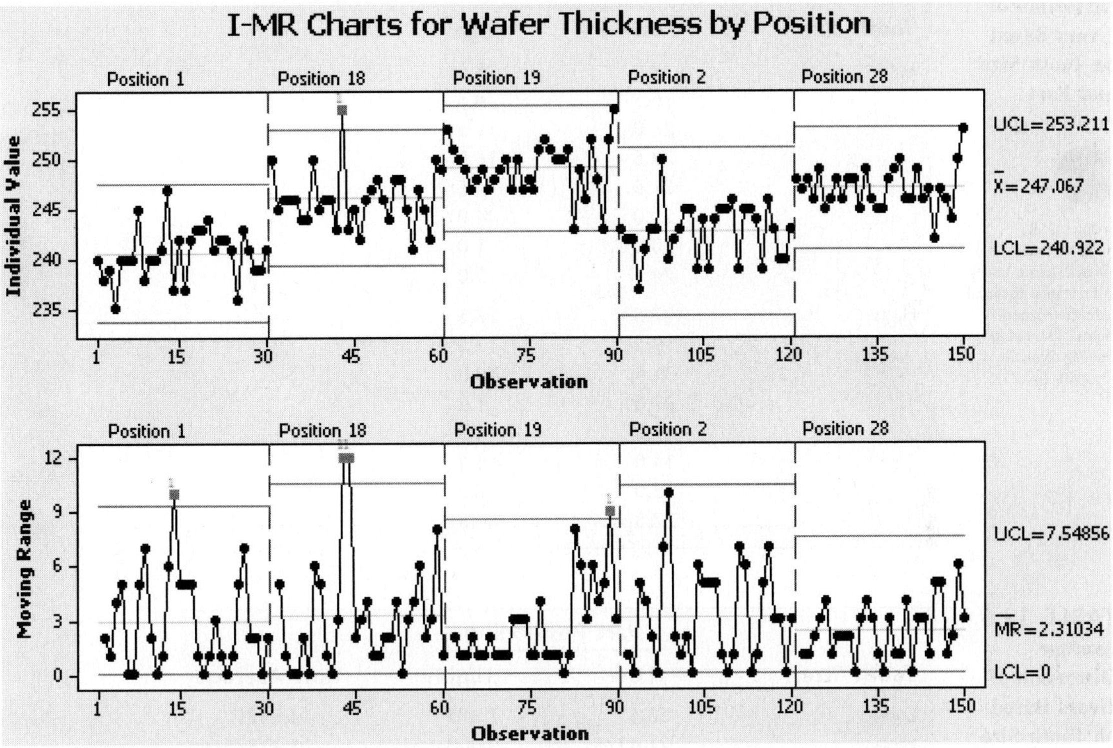

I-MR Charts for Wafer Thickness by Position

An example concerning the distortion of drive gears in automobiles will be used to illustrate a two-factor design. The factors studied were the tooth size of the gear and the part positioning. A study of eight gears for each tooth size and part positioning combination is displayed in Table 12.5 (see ☞ GEAR).

The particular design in this example is called a 2×2 design. The first number refers to the number of levels for the first factor and the second number refers to the number of levels for the second factor. This design is also referred to as a 2^2 design where the exponent refers to the fact that there are two factors and the base refers to the fact that each has two levels, or treatments.

From Table 12.5, the averages for each combination of tooth size and part positioning can be obtained. These are presented in Table 12.6.

From Table 12.6, several conclusions can be reached. In terms of the individual factors, called the **main effects,** there is very little difference in the average distortion between the low and high levels of tooth size (14.9375 versus 15.2188). The size of the effect for tooth size is $15.2188 - 14.9375 = 0.2813$. However, there is a substantial difference in the average distortion between the low and high levels of part positioning. The low level of part positioning has an average distortion of 21.9688, while the high level of part positioning has an average distortion of 8.1875. Thus, the effect due to part

TABLE 12.5
Distortion of Gears Based on Tooth Size and Part Positioning

Source: D. R. Bingham and R. R. Sitter, "Design Issues in Fractional Factorial Split-Plot Experiments," *Journal of Quality Technology,* 33, 2001, pp. 2–15.

Tooth Size	Part Positioning	
	Low	High
Low	18.0	13.5
	16.5	8.5
	26.0	11.5
	22.5	16.0
	21.5	−4.5
	21.0	4.0
	30.0	1.0
	24.5	9.0
High	27.5	17.5
	19.5	11.5
	31.0	10.0
	27.0	1.0
	17.0	14.5
	14.0	3.5
	18.0	7.5
	17.5	6.5

TABLE 12.6
Average Distortion of Gears Based on Tooth Size and Part Positioning

Tooth Size	Part Positioning		
	Low	High	Row Average
Low	22.5	7.375	14.9375
High	21.4375	9.000	15.21875
Column Average	21.9688	8.1875	15.0800

positioning is $21.9688 - 8.1875 = 13.7813$. These two main effects are illustrated in the main effects plot obtained from Minitab in Figure 12.7.

Now that the main effects of tooth size and parts positioning have been studied, the question remains as to what exactly is meant by the term **interaction.** This concept can first be examined by considering what would be meant by the absence of interaction.

If there is no interaction between two factors A and B, then any difference in the dependent or response variable between the two levels of factor A would be the same at each level of factor B.

In terms of the factors in this example, if there was no interaction between tooth size and part positioning, any difference in distortion between low tooth size and high tooth size would be the same under conditions of low part positioning as under conditions of high part positioning. From Table 12.6, observe that for a low level of tooth size, the difference in distortion between low and high levels of part positioning is 15.125, while for a high level of tooth size, the difference in distortion between low and high levels of part positioning is 12.4375.

The interaction between two factors can be presented in an **interaction plot.** If there is no interaction between the factors, the lines for the two levels will be parallel. Figure 12.8 contains an interaction plot obtained from Minitab for the gear example.

FIGURE 12.7
Minitab Main
Effects Plot
of Tooth Size
and Part
Positioning

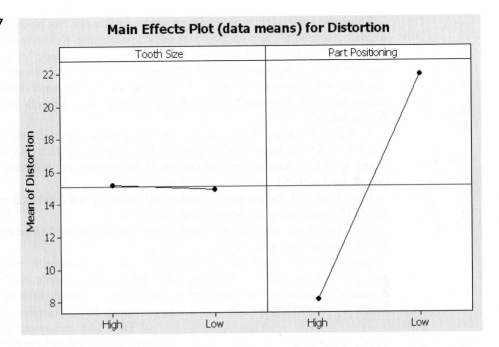

FIGURE 12.8
Minitab
Interaction
Plot for the
Gear Example

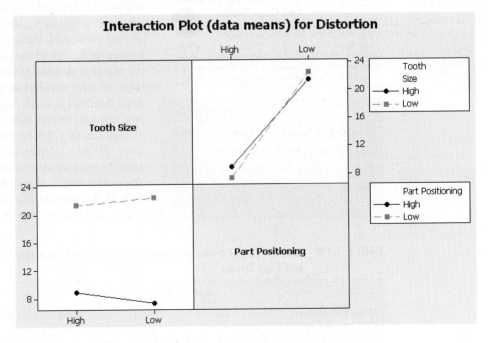

Either the bottom left or the top right panels of this plot can be used, depending on whether you want to focus on tooth size or part positioning. Referring to the upper right panel, the levels on the horizontal axis represent the part positioning levels for each tooth size. Referring to the lower left panel, the levels on the horizontal axis represent the tooth size levels for each part positioning. An examination of either panel shows that the lines are roughly parallel, indicating very little interaction between the tooth size and part positioning factors.

To study an example that has a clear interaction present, consider the manufacture of roller bearings. The factors studied were outer ring osculation (factor A) and cage design (factor B). The results in terms of the life of the bearings are presented in Table 12.7 (see ● BEARINGS).

From Table 12.7, the averages for each combination of ring osculation and cage design can be obtained. These are presented in Table 12.8.

The main effects plot for these data is displayed in Figure 12.9 and the interaction plot is presented in Figure 12.10.

From Table 12.8, and Figure 12.9, the life of the roller bearings is much higher at the high level of ring osculation than at the low level of ring osculation (64.75 versus 19.5). In addition, the life of the roller bearings is slightly higher at the high level of cage design than at the low level of cage design (46 versus 38.25). However, a further study of Table 12.8 and an examination of Figure 12.10 reveal that there is an interaction effect between ring osculation and cage design. This is clearly apparent in the lower left panel of Figure 12.10. At the low level of ring osculation, there is very little difference in the life of the roller bearing for the two cage designs. However, at the high level of ring osculation, the life of the roller bearings is much higher at the high level of cage design than at the low level of cage design (74.5 versus 55). The existence of this interaction effect complicates the interpretation of the main effects. You cannot conclude that there is a difference in the average life of low and high ring osculation because the difference is

TABLE 12.7 **Life of Roller Bearings Based on Ring Osculation and Cage Design**

Source: G. E. P. Box, "Do Interactions Matter?" *Quality Engineering*, 2, 1990, pp. 365–369, and C. Hellestrand, "The Necessity of Modern Quality Improvement and Some Experience with Its Implementation in the Manufacture of Roller Bearings," *Philosophical Transactions of the Royal Society*, London, A327, 1989, pp. 529–537.

	Cage Design	
Ring Osculation	**Low**	**High**
Low	17	19
	26	16
High	25	21
	85	128

TABLE 12.8 **Average Life of Roller Bearings Based on Ring Osculation and Cage Design**

	Cage Design		
Ring Osculation	**Low**	**High**	**Row Average**
Low	21.5	17.5	19.50
High	55.0	74.5	64.75
Column Average	38.25	46.0	42.125

FIGURE 12.9
Minitab Main
Effects Plot
for the Life
of Roller
Bearings

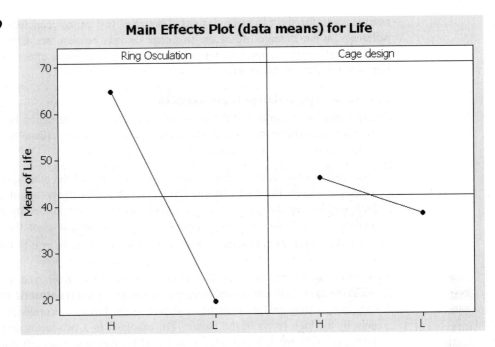

FIGURE
12.10
Minitab
Interaction
Plot for the
Life of Roller
Bearings

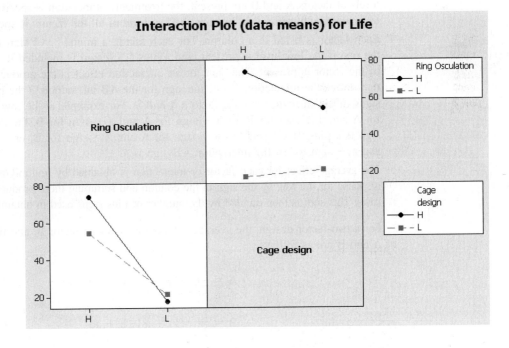

not the same for the two cage designs. Likewise, you cannot conclude that there is a difference in the average life of the two cage designs because the difference is not the same for both types of ring oscillations. In sum, the interaction effect takes precedence over any involved main effects.

Notation for Interaction Effects

Determining the magnitude of the effect of each factor and interaction becomes complex when many factors are involved. A special notation is used to facilitate the computations. The steps involved are as follows.

1. One level of each factor is designated as the low level and the other level is designated as the high level. The high and low levels are defined by the nature of the factor (e.g., high speed versus low speed). In cases where levels are not defined by the factor being studied, it is common practice to set the current operating level as the low level.

2. A shorthand notation assigns a lowercase letter such as a, b, or c to the high level of each factor.

3. A table is developed in which the columns represent the factors and their interactions, while the rows represent the different combinations, called **treatment combinations,** created by setting the factors at their different levels. Treatment combinations are defined only by the high levels of the factors. For example, in a two-factor design, if only the high level of factor A is present, the treatment combination is specified as a. If only the high level of factor B is present, the treatment combination is specified as b. If the high levels of factors A and B are present, the treatment combination is specified as ab. The treatment combination that contains the low level of all the factors is specified as (1).

4. Each factor is listed in a column. For each factor, a minus (−) sign is included in the row if the low level is present, and a plus (+) sign is included if the high level of the factor is present. The sign for an interaction effect is the product of the signs that define the interaction. Thus, the sign for the AB interaction is the product of the signs in the particular row for factors A and B. For example, if the row has a + sign for A and a + sign for B, or a − sign for A and a − sign for B, the interaction AB sign is a plus. If the row has a + sign for A and a − sign for B, or a − sign for A and a + sign for B, the interaction AB sign is a −.

5. The average effect for each factor or interaction is obtained by multiplying the average response for the row by the sign in the column and summing these products over all the rows. This sum is then divided by the number of plus signs used in obtaining the effect.

For a two-factor design, the average effects for factor A, factor B, and the interaction of A and B are as follows.

$$A = \frac{1}{2}[-(1) + a - b + ab] \qquad (12.1a)$$

$$B = \frac{1}{2}[-(1) - a + b + ab] \qquad (12.1b)$$

$$AB = \frac{1}{2}[(1) - a - b + ab] \qquad (12.1c)$$

TABLE 12.9 **Obtaining Average Effects for Factors A, B, and AB in the 2^2 Design for the Drive Gears Data**

Treatment Combination	Notation	Average Response	Tooth Size A	Part Positioning B	AB
Low tooth size, low part positioning	(1)	22.5000	−	−	+
High tooth size, low part positioning	a	21.4375	+	−	−
Low tooth size, high part positioning	b	7.3750	−	+	−
High tooth size, high part positioning	ab	9.0000	+	+	+

To apply Equations (12.1a) through (12.1c), return to the example concerning drive gears in automobiles, the results of which are summarized in Table 12.6 on page 478. The treatment combinations using the special notation are displayed in Table 12.9.

From Equations (12.1a) through (12.1c) and Table 12.9,

$$A = \frac{1}{2}(-22.500 + 21.4375 - 7.3750 + 9.0000)$$

$$= \frac{0.5625}{2}$$

$$= 0.28125$$

Thus, the average for the high tooth size is 0.28125 greater than the average for the low tooth size, a conclusion previously stated on page 477.

$$B = \frac{1}{2}(-22.50000 - 21.4375 + 7.3750 + 9.0000)$$

$$= -\frac{27.5625}{2}$$

$$= -13.78125$$

Thus, the average for the high part positioning is 13.78125 lower than for low part positioning.

$$AB = \frac{1}{2}(22.50000 - 21.4375 - 7.3750 + 9.0000)$$

$$= \frac{2.6875}{2}$$

$$= 1.34375$$

The interaction means that the average effect of combining the high level of tooth size and part positioning is 1.34375 greater than the average difference between the gears at the two tooth sizes. This is obtained from the fact that the average distortion for high tooth size and high part positioning is 1.625 greater than the average distortion for low tooth size and high part positioning (9.0 as compared to 7.375), while the difference in the average distortion for high tooth size as compared to low tooth size is 0.28125 (15.21875 − 14.9375). The difference between 1.625 and 0.28125 is the interaction effect of 1.34375.

Factorial Designs Involving Three or More Factors

The two-factor factorial design is the most elementary of all factorial designs. In this section, the concepts developed for the two-factor 2^2 design in the preceding section are extended to the more general factorial design with three or more factors. In this design, there are 2^k treatment combinations, where k = the number of factors, each with two levels.

A Three-Factor Factorial Design

In a three-factor design, we have $2^3 = 2 \times 2 \times 2 = 8$ treatment combinations. Table 12.10 extends the format of Table 12.9 to the 2^3 design in **standard order.** Standard order is an arrangement for listing trials in which the first factor alternates between $-$ and $+$, the second factor alternates between $-,-$ and $+,+$, the third factor alternates between $-,-,-,-$ and $+,+,+,+$, and so on, as shown in Table 12.10.

The magnitude of the main effects and interactions can be measured by using the shorthand notation presented in Table 12.10. For each of the main effects, the average effect consists of the average at the high level of the factor minus the average at the low level of the factor, or, using step 5 in "Notation for Interaction Effects" on page 482:

$$A = \frac{1}{4}[-(1) + a - b + ab - c + ac - bc + abc] \quad \textbf{(12.2a)}$$

$$B = \frac{1}{4}[-(1) - a + b + ab - c - ac + bc + abc] \quad \textbf{(12.2b)}$$

$$C = \frac{1}{4}[-(1) - a - b - ab + c + ac + bc + abc] \quad \textbf{(12.2c)}$$

The two-way interactions are measured as one-half the difference in the average of one effect at the two levels of the other effect. Thus for the interactions AB, AC, and BC, we have

$$AB = \frac{1}{4}[(1) - a - b + ab + c - ac - bc + abc] \quad \textbf{(12.3a)}$$

$$AC = \frac{1}{4}[(1) - a + b - ab - c + ac - bc + abc] \quad \textbf{(12.3b)}$$

$$BC = \frac{1}{4}[(1) + a - b - ab - c - ac + bc + abc] \quad \textbf{(12.3c)}$$

TABLE 12.10
Obtaining Effects for Factors A, B, C and Interactions AB, AC, BC, and ABC in the 2^3 Design in Standard Order

Notation	Contrast						
	A	B	C	AB	AC	BC	ABC
(1)	−	−	−	+	+	+	−
a	+	−	−	−	−	+	+
b	−	+	−	−	+	−	+
ab	+	+	−	+	−	−	−
c	−	−	+	+	−	−	+
ac	+	−	+	−	+	−	−
bc	−	+	+	−	−	+	−
abc	+	+	+	+	+	+	+

The ABC interaction is defined as the average difference in the AB interaction for the two levels of factor C. Thus,

$$\text{ABC} = \frac{1}{4}[-(1) + a + b - ab + c - ac - bc + abc] \quad \textbf{(12.4)}$$

To illustrate the 2^3 design, suppose that in the roller bearing example discussed in Table 12.7 on page 480, in addition to ring osculation and cage design, there is a third factor, the heat treatment used. The results from this experiment are presented in Table 12.11 (see 🔘 BEARINGS).

The eight treatment combinations and their responses are presented geometrically in Figure 12.11.

TABLE 12.11   **Results for a 2^3 Design Involving the Life of Roller Bearings Based on Ring Osculation, Cage Design, and Heat Treatment**

Source: G. E. P. Box, "Do Interactions Matter?" *Quality Engineering,* 2, 1990, pp. 365–369, and C. Hellestrand, "The Necessity of Modern Quality Improvement and Some Experience with Its Implementation in the Manufacture of Roller Bearings," *Philosophical Transactions of the Royal Society,* London, A327, 1989, pp. 529–537.

Treatment Combinations				
Ring Osculation	Cage Design	Heat Treatment	Notation	Life
Low	Low	Low	(1)	17
High	Low	Low	a	25
Low	High	Low	b	19
High	High	Low	ab	21
Low	Low	High	c	26
High	Low	High	ac	85
Low	High	High	bc	16
High	High	High	abc	128

FIGURE 12.11
Geometric Representation of the 2^3 Design

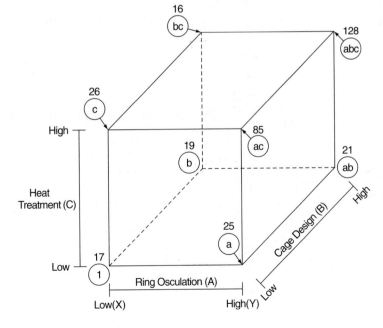

TABLE 12.12
Obtaining
Effects for
Factors A, B,
C and
Interactions
AB, AC, BC,
and ABC in
the 2^3 Design

Notation	Life	Contrast						
		A	B	C	AB	AC	BC	ABC
(1)	17	−	−	−	+	+	+	−
a	25	+	−	−	−	−	+	+
b	19	−	+	−	−	+	−	+
ab	21	+	+	−	+	−	−	−
c	26	−	−	+	+	−	−	+
ac	85	+	−	+	−	+	−	−
bc	16	−	+	+	−	−	+	−
abc	128	+	+	+	+	+	+	+

Table 12.12 represents the format needed to obtain the effects for the roller bearing example.

From Table 12.12 and Equations (12.2a)–(12.2c), (12.3a)–(12.3c), and (12.4),

$$A = \frac{-17 + 25 - 19 + 21 - 26 + 85 - 16 + 128}{4}$$

$$= \frac{181}{4}$$

$$= 45.25$$

$$B = \frac{-17 - 25 + 19 + 21 - 26 - 85 + 16 + 128}{4}$$

$$= \frac{31}{4}$$

$$= 7.75$$

$$C = \frac{-17 - 25 - 19 - 21 + 26 + 85 + 16 + 128}{4}$$

$$= \frac{173}{4}$$

$$= 43.25$$

$$AB = \frac{+17 - 25 - 19 + 21 + 26 - 85 - 16 + 128}{4}$$

$$= \frac{47}{4}$$

$$= 11.75$$

$$AC = \frac{+17 - 25 + 19 - 21 - 26 + 85 - 16 + 128}{4}$$

$$= \frac{161}{4}$$

$$= 40.25$$

$$BC = \frac{+17 + 25 - 19 - 21 - 26 - 85 + 16 + 128}{4}$$

$$= \frac{35}{4}$$

$$= 8.75$$

$$ABC = \frac{-17 + 25 + 19 - 21 + 26 - 85 - 16 + 128}{4}$$

$$= \frac{59}{4}$$

$$= 14.75$$

The main effects plot for these data is displayed in Figure 12.12 and the interaction plot is presented in Figure 12.13.

From the effects computed using Equations (12.2a)–(12.2c), (12.3a)–(12.3c), and (12.4), the main effects plot illustrated in Figure 12.12, and the interaction plot in Figure 12.13, we may conclude that:

1. The average life is 45.25 greater for high ring osculation than for low ring osculation.
2. The average life is 7.75 greater for high cage design than for low cage design.
3. The average life is 43.25 greater for high heat treatment than for low heat treatment.

FIGURE 12.12
Minitab Main Effects Plot for the Life of Roller Bearings in the 2^3 Experiment

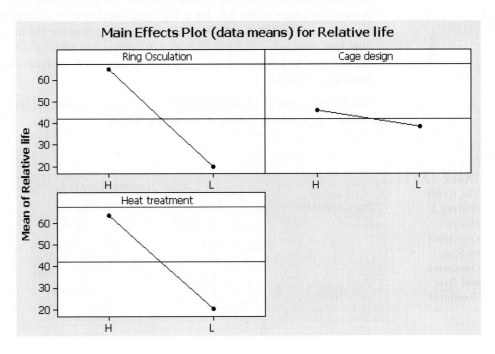

FIGURE 12.13

Minitab Interaction Plot for the Life of Roller Bearings in the 2^3 Experiment

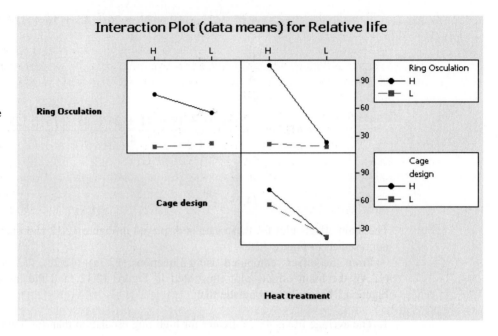

Interaction Plot (data means) for Relative life

4. The interactions range from 8.75 for BC to 40.25 for AC. The effects of A and C are interacting because of the large effect caused by the presence of the high level of ring osculation and the high level of heat treatment. This interacting effect means that the average difference in the life for a high ring osculation as compared to a low ring osculation is 40.25 higher for a high heat treatment than for the average of low and high heat treatments. There is also an ABC interaction effect since the effect on the life becomes higher when high levels of ring osculation, cage design, and heat treatment are combined.

   The AC interaction effect can be studied further by reorganizing the results of Table 12.11 into Table 12.13, which focuses on these two factors.

TABLE 12.13

The Roller Bearing 2^3 Design Organized by Ring Osculation and Heat Treatment

Ring Osculation	Heat Treatment	
	Low	High
Low	17	26
	19	16
	Cell mean = 18	Cell mean = 21
High	25	85
	21	128
	Cell mean = 23	Cell mean = 106.5

From Table 12.13, observe that the average life is 5 greater for high ring osculation than low ring osculation when low heat treatment is used, but is 85.5 greater for high ring osculation than low ring osculation when high heat treatment is used. The difference of $85.5 - 5 = 80.5$, divided by two to account for the two levels of factor C, represents the interaction effect of 40.25 for factors A (ring osculation) and C (heat treatment).

As additional factors are included in a factorial design, it becomes more difficult to determine which factors and interactions are important and which are unimportant. An approach that relies on the **analysis of variance** method of statistical inference may be used [see References 4, 6, and 7]. However, here we use a graphical approach involving the **half-normal plot** [see Reference 4, pp. 311–41] is used. This is a type of normal probability plot in which the estimated effects in rank order are plotted on normal probability paper. For a factorial design with k factors, the cumulative proportion for an effect is obtained as follows:

$$p_i = \frac{R_i - 0.5}{2^k - 1} \qquad \textbf{(12.5)}$$

where:

R_i = ordered rank of effect i

p_i = cumulative proportion for ordered effect i

k = number of factors

Using Equation (12.5), the cumulative effect for the smallest effect ($i = 1$) is

$$p_1 = \frac{1 - 0.5}{2^3 - 1}$$

$$= \frac{0.5}{7}$$

$$= 0.071$$

The estimated effects and their corresponding cumulative proportions for the roller bearing design are summarized in Table 12.14.

TABLE 12.14	Effect	Average Effect	R_i	p_i
Estimated	B	7.75	1	0.071
Effects,	BC	8.75	2	0.214
Ranks, and	AB	11.75	3	0.357
Cumulative	ABC	14.75	4	0.500
Proportions	AC	40.25	5	0.643
for the Roller	C	43.25	6	0.786
Bearing 2^3	A	45.25	7	0.929
Design				

**FIGURE
12.14**
**Minitab
Normal
Probability
Plot for the 2^3
Design for the
Roller Bearing
Example**

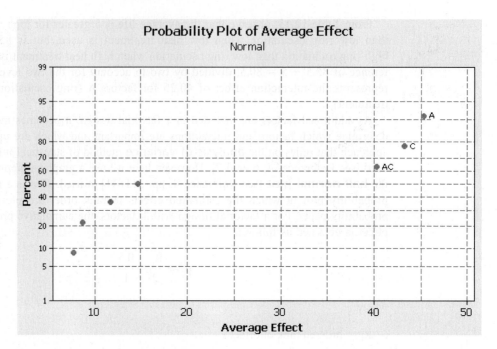

These estimated effects and their associated cumulative proportions are plotted in the normal probability plot of Figure 12.14, using Minitab.

The normal probability plot is used to determine which factors and interaction effects are not important (and thus, not different from zero). Any factors or interactions whose observed effects are due to chance are expected to be randomly distributed around zero, with some being slightly below zero and others being slightly above zero. These effects will tend to fall along a straight line. The effects that may be important have average values different from zero and are located a significant distance away from the hypothetical vertical line that represents no effect.

From Figure 12.14, observe that although all effects seem different from zero, the most important effects are A, C, and AC. These results are consistent with those seen in the main effects plot and the interaction plot of Figures 12.12 and 12.13.

A Five-Factor Factorial Design Example

To study a factorial design that has more than three factors, consider an experiment involving a cake mix. Each year millions of cake mixes are sold by food processing companies, consisting of a packet containing flour, shortening, and egg powder that will (hopefully) provide a good-tasting cake. A determination of the amount of each of these ingredients to maximize the tastiness of the cake must consider the fact that consumers may not follow precisely the recommended oven temperature and baking time. An experiment is conducted in which each factor is tested at a higher level than called for in the instructions and at a lower level than called for in the instructions. The goal of the experiment is to determine which factors have an effect on the taste

TABLE 12.15
Taste Rating for Cake Mix Combinations

Source: G. E. P. Box, S. Bisgaard, and C. Fung, "An Explanation and Critique of Taguchi's Contributions to Quality Engineering," *Quality and Reliability Engineering International*, 4, 1988, pp. 123–131.

Treatment Combination	Oven Temp (A)	Baking Time (B)	Flour (C)	Shortening (D)	Egg Powder (E)	Rating Score (Y)
(1)	–	–	–	–	–	1.1
a	+	–	–	–	–	3.8
b	–	+	–	–	–	3.7
ab	+	+	–	–	–	4.5
c	–	–	+	–	–	4.2
ac	+	–	+	–	–	5.2
bc	–	+	+	–	–	3.1
abc	+	+	+	–	–	3.9
d	–	–	–	+	–	5.7
ad	+	–	–	+	–	4.9
bd	–	+	–	+	–	5.1
abd	+	+	–	+	–	6.4
cd	–	–	+	+	–	6.8
acd	+	–	+	+	–	6.0
bcd	–	+	+	+	–	6.3
abcd	+	+	+	+	–	5.5
e	–	–	–	–	+	6.4
ae	+	–	–	–	+	4.3
be	–	+	–	–	+	6.7
abe	+	+	–	–	+	5.8
ce	–	–	+	–	+	6.5
ace	+	–	+	–	+	5.9
bce	–	+	+	–	+	6.4
abce	+	+	+	–	+	5.0
de	–	–	–	+	+	1.3
ade	+	–	–	+	+	2.1
bde	–	+	–	+	+	2.9
abde	+	+	–	+	+	5.2
cde	–	–	+	+	+	3.5
acde	+	–	+	+	+	5.7
bcde	–	+	+	+	+	3.0
abcde	+	+	+	+	+	5.4

rating of the cake, and the levels of those factors that will result in a cake with the highest taste rating. Five factors are to be considered: flour, shortening, egg powder, oven temperature, and baking time. Only one observation for each of the $2^5 = 32$ treatment combinations is obtained. The taste rating for each treatment combination is presented in Table 12.15 (see 💿 CAKE).

The estimated effects can be obtained by extending Equations (12.2a)–(12.2c), (12.3a)–(12.3c), and (12.4) to the 2^5 factorial design. Figure 12.15 presents the estimated effects obtained from Minitab for the cake mix design.

FIGURE 12.15

Minitab Estimated Effects for the Cake Mix Example

```
Estimated Effects and Coefficients for Rating (coded units)

Term                                           Effect     Coef
Constant                                                  4.759
Flour                                           0.431    0.216
Shortening                                      0.344    0.172
Egg Powder                                      0.781    0.391
ovenTemp                                       -0.044   -0.022
BakeTime                                       -0.006   -0.003
Flour*Shortening                                0.131    0.066
Flour*Egg Powder                               -0.081   -0.041
Flour*ovenTemp                                  0.394    0.197
Flour*BakeTime                                 -0.094   -0.047
Shortening*Egg Powder                          -0.994   -0.497
Shortening*ovenTemp                             0.131    0.066
Shortening*BakeTime                             0.244    0.122
Egg Powder*ovenTemp                             0.294    0.147
Egg Powder*BakeTime                             0.056    0.028
ovenTemp*BakeTime                              -2.194   -1.097
Flour*Shortening*Egg Powder                    -0.231   -0.116
Flour*Shortening*ovenTemp                       0.344    0.172
Flour*Egg Powder*ovenTemp                       0.006    0.003
Flour*Shortening*BakeTime                       0.131    0.066
Flour*Egg Powder*BakeTime                       0.394    0.197
Flour*ovenTemp*BakeTime                         1.194    0.597
Shortening*Egg Powder*ovenTemp                  0.069    0.034
Shortening*Egg Powder*BakeTime                 -0.044   -0.022
Shortening*ovenTemp*BakeTime                    0.256    0.128
Egg Powder*ovenTemp*BakeTime                    0.394    0.197
Flour*Shortening*Egg Powder*ovenTemp           -0.194   -0.097
Flour*Shortening*Egg Powder*BakeTime           -0.181   -0.091
Flour*Shortening*ovenTemp*BakeTime             -0.181   -0.091
Flour*Egg Powder*ovenTemp*BakeTime              0.056    0.028
Shortening*Egg Powder*ovenTemp*             -0.406   -0.203
  BakeTime
Flour*Shortening*Egg Powder*                 0.281    0.141
  ovenTemp*BakeTime
```

Using Figure 12.15, the values for the entire set of effects are:

One Effect	Two Effects	Three Effects	Four Effects	Five Effects
A = 0.431	AB = 0.131	ABC = −0.231	ABCD = −0.194	ABCDE = 0.281
B = 0.344	AC = −0.08	ABD = 0.344	ABCE = −0.181	
C = 0.781	AD = 0.394	ACD = 0.006	ABDE = −0.181	
D = 0.044	AE = −0.094	ABE = 0.131	ACDE = 0.056	
E = −0.006	BC = −0.994	ACE = 0.394	BCDE = −0.406	
	BD = 0.131	ADE = 1.194		
	BE = 0.244	BCD = 0.069		
	CD = 0.294	BCE = −0.044		
	CE = 0.056	BDE = 0.256		
	DE = −2.194	CDE = 0.394		

**FIGURE
12.16**

Minitab
Normal
Probability
Plot of the
Estimated
Effects for the
Cake Mix
Design

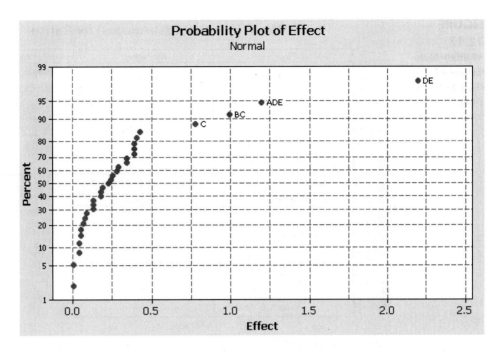

Figure 12.16 is a normal probability plot obtained from Minitab of the estimated effects for the cake mix design.

Figure 12.17 presents a main effects plot, and Figure 12.18 consists of an interaction plot for the cake mix design.

From Figure 12.16, factor C (egg powder), the BC (shortening–egg powder) interaction, the DE (oven temperature–baking time) interaction, and the ADE (flour–oven temperature–baking time) interaction are far from a hypothetical vertical line at zero. Note that these terms are statistically significant according to criteria developed by Lenth [see Reference 6, pp. 469–473]. The importance of these interactions complicates any interpretation of the main effects. Although egg powder affects taste rating (with high amount providing a better rating than low amount), the importance of the shortening–egg powder interaction means that the difference in egg powder is not the same for the two levels of shortening. Since neither effect D nor E was important, the DE (oven temperature–baking time) interaction indicates a crossing effect in which the rating is greater for high oven temperature combined with low baking time or low oven temperature combined with high baking time. The importance of the ADE (flour–oven temperature–baking time) interaction means that the interaction of oven temperature and baking time is not the same for low and high amounts of flour.

To further our understanding of these results, the interaction plots in Figure 12.18 can be examined along with Tables 12.16, 12.17, 12.18, and 12.19, which provide the average values for combinations of shortening and egg powder, oven temperature and baking temperature, and oven temperature and baking time for each level of flour.

From Figure 12.18 and Table 12.16, observe that for low levels of shortening, the rating is much better for the high level of egg powder (5.475) than for the low level of egg

**FIGURE
12.17**
**Minitab Main
Effects Plot for
the Cake Mix
Design**

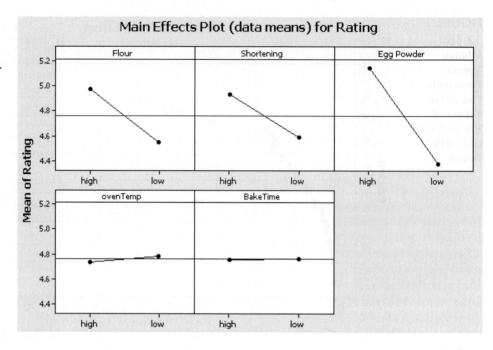

**FIGURE
12.17**
**Minitab Main
Effects Plot for
the Cake Mix
Design**

**FIGURE
12.18**
**Minitab
Interaction
Plot for the
Cake Mix
Design**

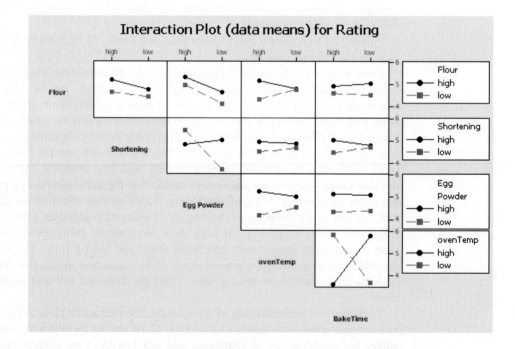

TABLE 12.16 Average Rating for Each Level of Shortening and Egg Powder

	Egg Powder	
Shortening	Low	High
Low	3.7000	5.475
High	5.0375	4.825

TABLE 12.17 Average Rating for Each Level of Oven Temperature and Baking Time

Oven Temperature	Baking Time	
	Low	High
Low	3.6875	5.875
High	5.8375	3.6375

TABLE 12.18 Average Rating for Each Level of Oven Temperature and Baking Time for the Low Level of Flour

Oven Temperature	Baking Time	
	Low	High
Low	3.025	6.50
High	5.975	2.675

TABLE 12.19 Average Rating for Each Level of Oven Temperature and Baking Time for the High Level of Flour

Oven Temperature	Baking Time	
	Low	High
Low	4.35	5.25
High	5.70	4.60

powder (3.70). For a high level of shortening, the results are quite different. The rating is slightly better for low egg powder (5.0375) than for high egg powder (4.825).

Turning to the interaction of oven temperature and baking time, from Figure 12.18 and Table 12.17, observe that the average rating is best for low oven temperature and high baking time (5.875) or high oven temperature and low baking time (5.8375). The rating is worse when there is both low oven temperature and low baking time (3.6875) or high oven temperature and high baking time (3.6375). However, the interaction of oven temperature and baking time is different for each of the two levels of flour. From Tables 12.18 and 12.19 the interaction seen in Table 12.17 is much more pronounced for the low level of flour than for the high level of flour.

Thus, how do we choose the levels of flour, shortening, and egg powder that will result in the highest rating? Based on these results, we would choose high flour, low shortening, and high egg powder. The rationale for this is as follows:

- According to Tables 12.18 and 12.19, using a high level of flour will improve the rating and reduce the effect of oven temperature and baking time.
- According to Table 12.16, using a low level of shortening and a high level of egg powder provides the best rating.
- In addition, the consumer should be warned not to use oven temperature and baking time that are both too low or both too high.

Fractional Factorial Designs

When four or more factors are to be considered, it often becomes costly or impossible to simultaneously run all possible treatment combinations. For example, four factors, each with two levels, involve 16 treatment combinations; five factors, each with two levels, involve 32 treatment combinations, as we saw in the last example; and seven factors, each with two levels, involve 128 treatment combinations. Thus, as the number of factors in our experiment increases, there needs to be a rational way of choosing a subset of the treatment combinations so that an experiment with meaningful results can be undertaken. One way to do this is through the use of a fractional factorial design.

In a fractional factorial design, only a subset of all possible treatment combinations is used. One approach is to choose the treatment combinations so that each main effect can be independently estimated without being confused or **confounded** with any estimate of the two factor interactions. When a main effect or an interaction is confounded, its effect cannot be isolated from the main effect of some other factor or interaction. Designs in which main effects are confounded with two-way interactions (such as A being confounded with BC) are called **resolution III designs.** In other words, confounding main effects (1 factor) with two-way interactions (2 factors) yields resolution III designs (1 factor + 2-way interaction = resolution 3 design). Designs in which main effects are not confounded with two-way interactions are called **resolution IV designs.** In resolution IV designs, a two-way interaction such as AB is confounded with another two-way interaction such as CD. In other words, confounding main effects (1 factor) with three-way interactions (3 factors) yields resolution IV designs (1 factor + 3-way interaction = resolution 4 design). Similarly, confounding two-way interactions (2 factors) with other two-way interactions (2 factors) yields resolution IV designs (2-way interaction + 2-way interaction = resolution 4 design). Designs in which each main effect and each two-factor interaction can be independently estimated without being confounded with any other main effects or interactions are called **resolution V designs.** In these designs, main effects and two-way interactions are confounded with three-way or higher order interactions (such as ABC or ABCD). In other words, confounding main effects (1 factor) with four-way interactions (4 factors) yields resolution V designs (1 factor + 4-way interaction = resolution 5 design). Similarly, confounding two-way interactions (2 factors) with three-way interactions (3 factors) yields resolution V designs (2-way interaction + 3-way interaction = resolution 5 design).

Choosing the Treatment Combinations

In order to choose a subset of the treatment combinations, we begin by referring to the 2^4 design. Table 12.20 presents all the possible treatment combinations for this full factorial design, along with the pattern of pluses and minuses for the main effects (the columns headed by A, B, C, and D) and the ABCD interaction.

In a fractional factorial design in which half the treatment combinations are chosen, only eight treatment combinations are available from the possible 16 combinations of a 2^4 design. Of course, with only eight treatment combinations, we cannot obtain as much information as we do from the full factorial 2^4 design in which there are 16 combinations. If we are willing to assume that the four-way interaction, ABCD, is not significant, the fraction or subset of eight treatment combinations, called a **half-replicate,** out of the possible 16 could be selected so that either:

- The eight treatment combinations all have a plus sign in the column headed by ABCD, or

- The eight treatment combinations all have a minus sign in the column headed by ABCD.

TABLE 12.20
Treatment
Combinations
for the 2^4
Design in
Standard
Order

Notation	A	B	C	D	ABCD
(1)	−	−	−	−	+
a	+	−	−	−	−
b	−	+	−	−	−
ab	+	+	−	−	+
c	−	−	+	−	−
ac	+	−	+	−	+
bc	−	+	+	−	+
abc	+	+	+	−	−
d	−	−	−	+	−
ad	+	−	−	+	+
bd	−	+	−	+	+
abd	+	+	−	+	−
cd	−	−	+	+	+
acd	+	−	+	+	−
bcd	−	+	+	+	−
abcd	+	+	+	+	+

If such a design is used, the ABCD interaction would be considered the **defining contrast,** from which the factors and interactions that are confounded with each other could be determined.

The determination of the treatment combinations to be selected begins by focusing first on factor A. With ABCD as the defining contrast, factor A is confounded with interaction BCD since A and ABCD differ only by BCD. BCD is also called an **alias** of A, since the effects of BCD and A cannot be separated in this fractional factorial design. In essence, the A main effect is equivalent to the BCD interaction. If we are willing to assume that the BCD interaction is negligible, when we evaluate the average main effect of A, we state that this is the effect of factor A (even though it could have been the effect of the BCD interaction). (If the half-replicate chosen has a plus sign in column ABCD, then A is confounded with BCD. If the half-replicate chosen has a minus sign in column ABCD, then A is confounded with −BCD.) In a similar manner, B is confounded with ACD; C is confounded with ABD; D is confounded with ABC; AB is confounded with CD; AC is confounded with BD; and AD is confounded with BC.

From this pattern of confounded effects, observe that in this design, called a 2^{4-1} fractional factorial design, the two-factor or two-way interaction terms are confounded with each other. Thus, we cannot separate AB and CD, AC and BD, and AD and BC. If any of these interaction terms are found to be important, we will not be able to know whether the effect is due to one term or the other.

As a first example of a fractional factorial design, we will examine a 2^{4-1} design in which eight treatments are chosen from the total of 16 possible combinations and the defining contrast is ABCD. In addition to the experimental design shown in Table 12.12, Box [see Reference 3, pp. 619–627] reported another experiment in which four factors are used to study the average life of bearings produced. The four factors are the manufacturing process for the balls (standard or modified), the cage design (standard or modified), the type of grease (standard or modified), and the amount of grease (normal or large). A half-replicate of a full factorial design is used. The full factorial design is shown in Table 12.21.

TABLE 12.21
Sixteen
Treatment
Combinations
in a 2^4
Experiment in
Standard
Order

Notation	Average Life (Y)	A	B	C	D	Defining Contrast ABCD
(1)		−	−	−	−	+
a		+	−	−	−	−
b		−	+	−	−	−
ab		+	+	−	−	+
c		−	−	+	−	−
ac		+	−	+	−	+
bc		−	+	+	−	+
abc		+	+	+	−	−
d		−	−	−	+	−
ad		+	−	−	+	+
bd		−	+	−	+	+
abd		+	+	−	+	−
cd		−	−	+	+	+
acd		+	−	+	+	−
bcd		−	+	+	+	−
abcd		+	+	+	+	+

TABLE 12.22   **Average Life for Eight Treatment Combinations in the 2^{4-1} Experiment in Standard Order**

Source: Reprinted from G. E. P. Box, "What Can You Find Out From Eight Experimental Runs," *Quality Engineering*, 4, 1992, pp. 619–627.

Notation	Average Life	A	B	C	D	AB + CD	AC + BD	AD + BC
(1)	0.31	−	−	−	−	+	+	+
ab	2.17	+	+	−	−	+	−	−
ac	1.37	+	−	+	−	−	+	−
bc	0.92	−	+	+	−	−	−	+
ad	1.38	+	−	−	+	−	−	+
bd	0.73	−	+	−	+	−	+	−
cd	0.95	−	−	+	+	+	−	−
abcd	2.57	+	+	+	+	+	+	+

The half-replicate (using only the + signs from the ABCD column) from the defining contrast (ABCD) is shown in Table 12.22 (see ☀ BEARINGS2).

We see that the two-way interactions are confounded with each other, specifically AB with CD, AC with BD, and AD with BC. This is a resolution IV design.

Using the results presented in Table 12.22, for this 2^{4-1} design there are $2^{4-1} - 1 = 7$ effects that can be evaluated (A, B, C, D, AB, AC, and AD) as long as we realize that A is confounded with BCD, B is confounded with ACD, C is confounded with ABD, D is confounded with ABC, AB is confounded with CD, AC is confounded with BD, and AD is confounded with BC. Using an expanded version of Equations (12.2a)–(12.2c), (12.3a)–(12.3c), and (12.4), the average effects for these factors obtained from Minitab are presented in Figure 12.19.

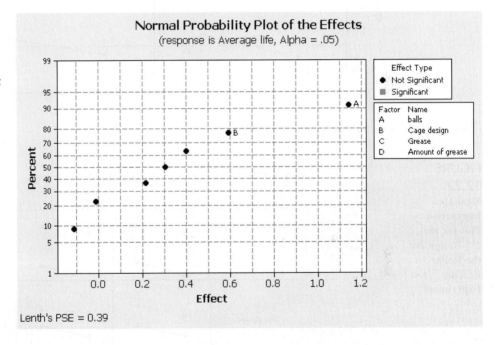

FIGURE 12.19	Factorial Fit: Average life versus balls, Cage design, ...
Minitab Estimated Effects for the Roller Bearing Fractional Factorial Design	Estimated Effects and Coefficients for Average life (coded units)

Term	Effect	Coef
Constant		1.30000
balls	1.14500	0.57250
Cage design	0.59500	0.29750
Grease	0.30500	0.15250
Amount of grease	0.21500	0.10750
balls*Cage design	0.40000	0.20000
balls*Grease	-0.11000	-0.05500
balls*Amount of grease	-0.01000	-0.00500

FIGURE 12.20

Minitab Normal Probability Plot for the 2^{4-1} Design for the Roller Bearing Experiment

These average effects are depicted in Figure 12.20 in a normal probability plot of the effects. Figure 12.21 is a main effects plot and Figure 12.22 is an interaction plot.

From Figure 12.20, observe that factor A and possibly factor B appear to plot away from this line. From Figure 12.21, it appears that average life is higher for modified ball bearings than for standard ball bearings and that average life may be higher for a modified cage design than a standard cage design. From Figure 12.22, none of the interactions appears to be important.

Now that fractional factorial designs have been introduced with the 2^{4-1} design, a second example involving a 2^{5-1} design will be considered. This experiment, reported by Kilgo [see Reference 5, pp. 45–54], studies the process of using carbon dioxide to extract oil from peanuts in a production process. The response variable is the amount of oil that can dissolve in the carbon dioxide, or the solubility. Five factors are to be studied. They

FIGURE 12.21
Minitab Main Effects Plot for the 2⁴⁻¹ Design for the Roller Bearing Experiment

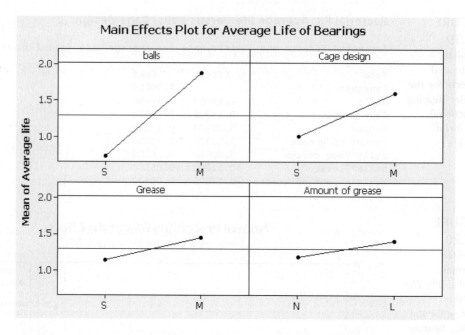

FIGURE 12.22
Minitab Interaction Plot for the 2⁴⁻¹ Design for the Roller Bearing Experiment

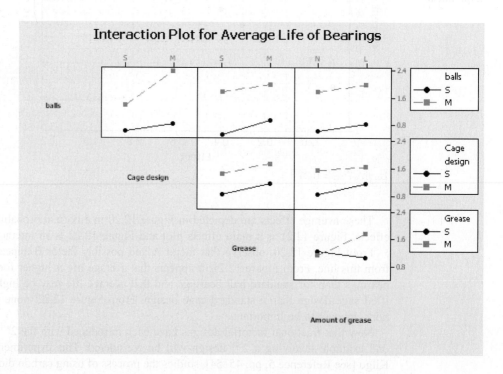

are labeled as follows: A = carbon dioxide pressure, B = carbon dioxide temperature, C = peanut moisture, D = carbon dioxide flow rate, E = peanut particle size. Two levels of each factor (a low and a high) are chosen. A half-replicate of a 2^5 design is selected due to budgetary constraints. The standard order matrix for a full factorial 2^5 design is shown in Table 12.23.

The results of the half-replicate experiment (using the − signs in the ABCDE column) are presented in Table 12.24 (see ☞ PEANUT).

The subset or fraction of 16 treatment combinations used in Table 12.24 is based on the five-factor interaction ABCDE as the defining contrast. This produces a resolution V design in which all main effects and two-factor interactions can be estimated independently of each other. Each main effect is confounded with a four-factor interaction,

TABLE 12.23
Standard Order Design Matrix for a Full Factorial 2^5 Experiment

Notation	Response Variable (Y)	A	B	C	D	E	ABCDE
(1)		−	−	−	−	−	−
a		+	−	−	−	−	+
b		−	+	−	−	−	+
ab		+	+	−	−	−	−
c		−	−	+	−	−	+
ac		+	−	+	−	−	−
bc		−	+	+	−	−	−
abc		+	+	+	−	−	+
d		−	−	−	+	−	+
ad		+	−	−	+	−	−
bd		−	+	−	+	−	−
abd		+	+	−	+	−	+
cd		−	−	+	+	−	−
acd		+	−	+	+	−	+
bde		−	+	+	+	−	+
abcd		+	+	+	+	−	−
e		−	−	−	−	+	+
ae		+	−	−	−	+	−
be		−	+	−	−	+	−
abe		+	+	−	−	+	+
ce		−	−	+	−	+	−
ace		+	−	+	−	+	+
bce		−	+	+	−	+	+
abce		+	+	+	−	+	−
de		−	−	−	+	+	−
ade		+	−	−	+	+	+
bde		−	+	−	+	+	+
abde		+	+	−	+	+	−
cde		−	−	+	+	+	+
acde		+	−	+	+	+	−
bcde		−	+	+	+	+	−
abcde		+	+	+	+	+	+

TABLE 12.24
Data for the
Peanut
Experiment

Source: Reprinted from M. Kilgo, "An Application of Fractional Factorial Experimental Designs," *Quality Engineering,* 1, 1989, pp. 45–54.

Treatment		Treatment	
Combination	Response	Combination	Response
(1)	29.2	de	22.4
ae	23.0	ad	37.2
be	37.0	bd	31.3
ab	139.7	abde	148.6
ce	23.3	cd	22.9
ac	38.3	acde	36.2
bc	42.6	bcde	33.6
abce	141.4	abcd	172.6

TABLE 12.25
Confounded
Effects for the
2^{5-1} **Design**
with ABCDE
as the Defining
Contrast

Main Effects	Confounded with Four-Way Effects	Two-Way Effects	Confounded with Three-Way Effects
A	BCDE	AB	CDE
B	ACDE	AC	BDE
C	ABDE	AD	BCE
D	ABCE	AE	BCD
E	ABCD	BC	ADE
		BD	ACE
		BE	ACD
		CD	ABE
		CE	ABD
		DE	ABC

while each two-factor interaction is confounded with a three-factor interaction. For this design, the set of confounded effects is summarized in Table 12.25.

Using an expanded version of Equations (12.2a)–(12.2c), (12.3a)–(12.3c), and (12.4), the average effects for these factors obtained from Minitab are presented in Figure 12.23.

These average effects are depicted in Figure 12.24 in a normal probability plot. Figure 12.25 is a main effects plot, and Figure 12.26 is an interaction plot.

If we can assume that all three-way and higher order interactions are negligible, we observe, from Figure 12.23, that factors A and B and the AB interaction plot are far away from a hypothetical vertical line at zero. Note that Minitab indicates that these terms are statistically significant according to criteria developed by Lenth [see Reference 6, pp. 469–473]. From Figure 12.25, note that the average amount dissolved is higher for high carbon dioxide pressure than for low carbon dioxide pressure and is higher for high carbon dioxide temperature than for low carbon dioxide temperature. However, the interaction plot displayed in Figure 12.26 indicates a clear interaction of carbon dioxide pressure and temperature. High carbon dioxide pressure combined with high carbon dioxide temperature greatly increases the average amount of oil dissolved.

FIGURE 12.23
Minitab Estimated Effects for the Peanut Oil Fractional Factorial Design

```
Estimated Effects and Coefficients for Amount dissolved (coded units)

Term                                      Effect     Coef
Constant                                             61.206
CO2 pressure                              61.837     30.919
CO2 temperature                           64.287     32.144
peanut moisture                            5.312      2.656
CO2 flow rate                              3.788      1.894
Peanut particle size                      -6.038     -3.019
CO2 pressure*CO2 temperature              52.613     26.306
CO2 pressure*peanut moisture               4.688      2.344
CO2 pressure*CO2 flow rate                 9.263      4.631
CO2 pressure*Peanut particle size         -3.613     -1.806
CO2 temperature*peanut moisture            3.088      1.544
CO2 temperature*CO2 flow rate              2.563      1.281
CO2 temperature*Peanut particle size      -0.363     -0.181
peanut moisture*CO2 flow rate              1.137      0.569
peanut moisture*Peanut particle size      -4.437     -2.219
CO2 flow rate*Peanut particle size         0.237      0.119
```

FIGURE 12.24
Minitab Normal Probability Plot for the Peanut Oil Experiment

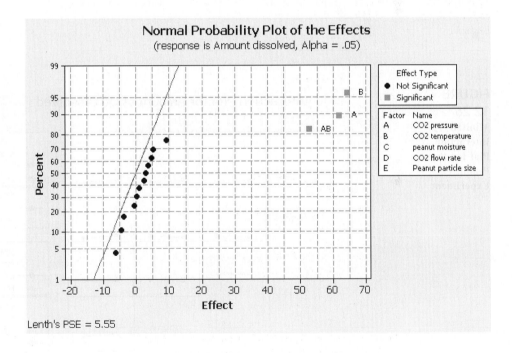

In this section, we have discussed two examples of fractional factorial designs that are used when it is not feasible to evaluate all possible treatment combinations. These two designs are only a small subset of the variety of fractional factorial designs that may be selected. The 2^{4-1} and 2^{5-1} designs are examples of designs that involve the selection of a half-replicate (8 out of 16, or 16 out of 32 treatment combinations) of a full factorial

FIGURE
12.25
Minitab Main
Effects Plot for
the Peanut Oil
Experiment

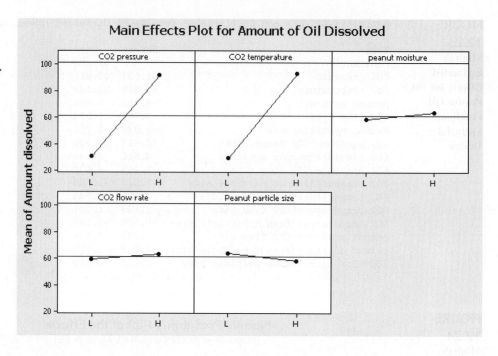

FIGURE
12.26
Minitab
Interaction
Plot for the
Peanut Oil
Experiment

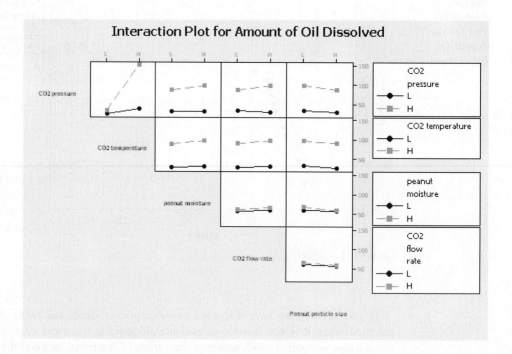

design. Other designs can use a **quarter-replicate** (such as a 2^{5-2} and 2^{6-2} design) or even smaller portions of a factorial design in which only main effects can be estimated (for instance, a 2^{15-11} design). It is also possible to study designs in which there are more than two levels for a factor. Discussion of such designs is beyond the scope of this text [see References 4, 6, 7, 8, and 9].

Summary

In this chapter we have discussed and illustrated the basic aspects of design of experiments. We have described certain flawed designs and why they should not be used, one-factor designs, factorial designs, and fractional factorial designs.

The factorial design, by allowing for the measurement of the size of interaction effects, offers a substantial benefit as compared to the one-factor design approach. The fractional factorial design allows us to determine effects when the number of trials required by a full factorial design is not feasible.

Although a number of designs were discussed and illustrated, it is important to realize that the topics covered have barely scratched the surface of the subject of the design of experiments. Other designs and the analysis of variance approach are covered in more advanced texts.

Key Terms

alias, *497*
analysis of variance, *489*
box-and-whisker plot, *473*
change-many-factors-at-once strategy, *470*
confounded, *496*
defining contrast, *497*
dependent variable, *471*
dotplot, *473*
experimental design, *470*
factor, *471*
first quartile Q_1, *474*
flawed design, *470*
fractional factorial design, *470*
full factorial design, *470*
half-normal plot, *489*

half-replicate, *496*
independent variable, *471*
individuals and moving range chart, *475*
input variable, *471*
interaction, *478*
interaction plot, *478*
level, *475*
main effect, *477*
median, *474*
one-factor-at-a-time strategy, *470*
one-factor design, *473*
outcome, *471*
process variable, *471*
quarter-replicate, *505*
resolution III design, *496*

resolution IV design, *496*
resolution V design, *496*
response surface methodology design, *470*
response variable, *471*
run chart, *475*
screening design, *470*
standard order, *484*
stick-with-a-winner strategy, *470*
third quartile Q_3, *474*
treatment, *475*
treatment combination, *482*
two-factor design, *475*
two-factor factorial design, *475*

Exercises

12.1. A sporting goods manufacturing company wants to compare the distance traveled by golf balls produced by each of four different design molds. Ten balls are manufactured with each design and are brought to the local golf course for testing by the club professional. The order in which the balls are hit from the first tee with a driver is randomized so that the pro does not know which design is being hit. All 40 balls are hit in a short period of time in which the environmental conditions are essentially the same. The results (distance traveled in yards) for the four designs are as follows (see 🔎 GOLFBALL):

	Designs		
1	**2**	**3**	**4**
206.32	203.81	217.08	213.90
226.77	223.85	230.55	231.10
207.94	206.75	221.43	221.28
224.79	223.97	227.95	221.53
206.19	205.68	218.04	229.43
229.75	234.30	231.84	235.45
204.45	204.49	224.13	213.54
228.51	219.50	224.87	228.35
209.65	210.86	211.82	214.51
221.44	233.00	229.49	225.09

a. Obtain a dotplot for the four designs.
b. Obtain a box-and-whisker plot for the four designs.
c. On the basis of the results of parts a and b, what conclusions can you reach concerning the four designs?

12.2. The following data represent the lifetimes of six different alloys (see 🔎 ALLOY):

	Alloy				
1	**2**	**3**	**4**	**5**	**6**
999	1,022	1,026	974	1,002	1,008
1,010	973	1,008	1,015	967	996
995	1,023	1,005	1,009	995	996
998	1,023	1,007	1,011	990	1,001
1,001	996	981	995	998	1,011

Source: P. Wludyka, P. Nelson, and P. Silva, "Power Curves for the Analysis of Means for Variances," *Journal of Quality Technology,* 33, 2001, pp. 60–65.

a. Obtain a dotplot for the six alloys.
b. Obtain a box-and-whisker plot for the six alloys.
c. On the basis of the results of parts a and b, what conclusions can you reach concerning the six alloys?

12.3. The data in the ♣ CONCRETE2 file represent the compressive strength in thousands of pounds per square inch (psi) of 40 samples of concrete taken 2, 7, and 28 days after pouring.

Source: O. Carrillo-Gamboa and R. F. Gunst, "Measurement-Error-Model Collinearities," *Technometrics*, 34, 1992, pp. 454–464.

   a. Obtain a dotplot for the compressive strength after 2, 7, and 28 days.

   b. Obtain a box-and-whisker plot for the compressive strength after 2, 7, and 28 days.

   c. On the basis of the results of parts a and b, what conclusions can you reach concerning the compressive strength after 2, 7, and 28 days?

12.4. A cat food company is interested in exploring ways to expand its market share by offering new products. An experiment is conducted that compares two new food products, one with salmon and one with chicken liver, along with two existing products, one with kidney and one with shrimp. In addition, a supermarket brand of a beef-based product is included in the study. A local animal shelter agrees to participate in the study. A random sample of 50 cats from the population at the shelter is selected. Ten cats are randomly assigned to each of the five products tested. Each of the cats is presented with 3 ounces of the selected food in a dish at feeding time. The response variable of interest is operationally defined as the amount of food eaten during a 10-minute period that begins when the filled dish is presented to the cat (see ♣ CATFOOD).

Ounces Eaten for Five Cat-Food Products				
Kidney	**Shrimp**	**Chicken Liver**	**Salmon**	**Beef**
2.37	2.26	2.29	1.79	2.09
2.62	2.69	2.23	2.33	1.87
2.31	2.25	2.41	1.96	1.67
2.47	2.45	2.68	2.05	1.64
2.59	2.34	2.25	2.26	2.16
2.62	2.37	2.17	2.24	1.75
2.34	2.22	2.37	1.96	1.18
2.47	2.56	2.26	1.58	1.92
2.45	2.36	2.45	2.18	1.32
2.32	2.59	2.57	1.93	1.94

   a. Obtain a dotplot for the five cat foods.

   b. Obtain a box-and-whisker plot for the five cat foods.

   c. On the basis of the results of parts a and b, what conclusions can you reach concerning the five cat foods?

12.5. The following data represent the hardness of water obtained from five different wells (see ☞ WELLWATER):

A	B	C	D	E
908	692	1170	245	334
1180	706	1120	242	327
930	789	1110	252	326
833	742	885	256	306
960	780	1130	254	294
871	776	840	270	290
913	739	1320	256	291
1040	782	1130	268	268
918	736	1080	246	294

a. Obtain a dotplot for the five wells.

b. Obtain a box-and-whisker plot for the five wells.

c. On the basis of the results of parts a and b, what conclusions can you reach concerning the five wells?

12.6. The effects of developer strength (factor A) and development time (factor B) on the density of photographic plate film are being studied. Two strengths and two development times are used, and four replicates for each treatment combination are run. The results (larger is better) are as follows (see ☞ PHOTO):

Developer Strength	Development Time (minutes) 10	Development Time (minutes) 14	Developer Strength	Development Time (minutes) 10	Development Time (minutes) 14
1	0	1	2	4	6
	5	4		7	7
	2	3		6	8
	4	2		5	7

a. Determine the effects for factor A, factor B, and the interaction of A and B.

b. Obtain a main effects plot for factors A and B.

c. Obtain an interaction plot.

d. On the basis of the results of parts a–c, what conclusions can you reach concerning the importance of factor A, factor B, and the interaction of A and B on development time?

12.7. An experiment is designed to study the effect of two factors on the amplification of a stereo recording. The factors are type of receiver (two brands) and type of amplifier (two brands). For each combination of factor levels, three tests are performed in which decibel output is measured. A higher decibel output means a better result. The coded results are as follows (see AMPLIFY):

	Amplifier	
Receiver	A_1	A_2
	9	8
R_1	4	11
	12	16
	7	5
R_2	1	9
	4	6

a. Determine the effects for factor A, factor B, and the interaction of A and B.

b. Obtain a main effects plot for factors A and B.

c. Obtain an interaction plot.

d. On the basis of the results of parts a–c, what conclusion can you reach concerning the importance of factor A, factor B, and the interaction of A and B on amplification?

12.8. Integrated circuits are manufactured on silicon wafers through a process that involves a series of steps. An experiment is carried out to study the effect of the cleansing and etching steps on the yield (coded to maintain confidentiality). The results are as follows (see YIELD2):

	Etching Step	
Cleansing Step	New	Standard
New	38	34
	34	19
	38	28
Standard	31	29
	23	32
	38	30

Source: J. Ramirez and W. Taam, "An Autologistic Model for Integrated Circuit Manufacturing," *Journal of Quality Technology,* 32, 2000, pp. 254–262.

a. Determine the effects for factor A, factor B, and the interaction of A and B.

b. Obtain a main effects plot for factors A and B.

c. Obtain an interaction plot.

d. On the basis of the results of parts a–c, what conclusions can you reach concerning the importance of factor A, factor B, and the interaction of A and B on yield?

12.9. An experiment is designed to study the effect of two factors on the fire-retardant treatment of fabrics. Factor A is the type of fabric (cotton versus polyester) and factor B corresponds to two different fire-retardant treatments (X and Y). The results from four replications of each combination of the two factors (expressed in terms of the number of inches of a fabric burned after a flame test, with a smaller value indicating a better result) are as follows (see FIRE):

Fabric	Treatment		Fabric	Treatment	
	X	Y		X	Y
Cotton	39	28	Polyester	46	29
	36	31		50	25
	42	31		45	32
	45	30		48	35

a. Determine the effects for factor A, factor B, and the interaction of A and B.

b. Obtain a main effects plot for factors A and B.

c. Obtain an interaction plot.

d. On the basis of the results of parts a–c, what conclusions can you reach concerning the importance of factor A, factor B, and the interaction of A and B on the fabric burned?

12.10. Polyvinyl chloride (PVC) is a polymer that is used in numerous applications in industry. PVC is produced by polymerizing the vinyl chloride monomer (VCM) in a batch chemical reactor. The VCM, dispersants, and initiators are added to water and reacted at a controlled temperature to produce the desired molecular-weight resin. A study is conducted to measure the effect of operators and resin railcars on the particle size of the resin. Two resin samples are selected for each operator–resin railcar combination. The results are as follows (see PVC):

Operator	Resin Railcar	Samples	
1	1	36.2	36.3
1	2	35.3	35.0
2	1	35.8	35.0
2	2	35.6	35.1

Source: R. A. Morris, and E. F. Watson, "A Comparison of the Techniques Used to Evaluate the Measurement Process," *Quality Engineering*, 11, 1998, pp. 213–219.

a. Determine the effects for factor A, factor B, and the interaction of A and B.

b. Obtain a main effects plot for factors A and B.

c. Obtain an interaction plot.

d. On the basis of the results of parts a–c, what conclusion can you reach concerning the importance of factor A, factor B, and the interaction of A and B on the particle size?

12.11. A soft drink bottler is interested in obtaining more uniform fill heights in the bottles filled in the bottling process. Theoretically, the filling machine fills each bottle to the correct level, but in practice, there is variation around this target. Three variables can be controlled in the filling process: the percent carbonation (at 10 and 12 percent), the pressure (at 25 and 30 psi), and two levels for line speed (200 and 300 bottles per minute). The bottler decides to run five trials for each of the 8 combinations of levels of these factors. The results in terms of deviation from target are as follows (see 💿 SFTDRINK):

Percent Carbonation	Operating Pressure	Line Speed	Deviation from Target (mm)				
10	25 psi	200	−4.8	−3.7	−1.9	−0.8	−4.8
12	25 psi	200	0.2	2.1	2.6	0.4	1.7
10	30 psi	200	−3.0	−0.7	2.3	−1.5	−1.1
10	25 psi	300	−2.5	−0.9	−1.1	1.6	−0.1
12	30 psi	200	3.3	1.6	4.0	2.7	3.4
12	25 psi	300	3.0	1.7	5.3	4.0	1.5
10	30 psi	300	1.3	1.2	1.5	1.0	1.5
12	30 psi	300	6.8	5.4	4.3	7.2	7.3

a. Compute the average effect for each main effect (factor) and interaction.

b. Obtain a plot of the main effects.

c. Obtain a plot of the interactions.

d. On the basis of the results of part a, set up a half-normal probability plot of the main effects and interactions.

e. What conclusions can you draw from the results of part d?

f. What levels of percent carbonation, operating pressure, and line speed should be used to reduce the deviation from the target? Explain your reasons for selecting these levels.

12.12. It is widely believed, among one-tenth-scale electric remote-control model car racing enthusiasts, that spending more money on high-quality batteries, using gold-plated connectors, and storing batteries at low temperatures will improve battery-life performance. An experiment is conducted that uses these three factors to determine the battery life as measured by the time to discharge (in minutes). The results are as follows (see 💿 MODELCAR):

Battery	Connector Design	Temperature	Time
Low	Standard	Ambient	93
High	Standard	Ambient	489
Low	Gold-plated	Ambient	94
High	Gold-plated	Ambient	493
Low	Standard	Cold	72
High	Standard	Cold	612
Low	Gold-plated	Cold	75
High	Gold-plated	Cold	490

Source: E. Wasiloff and C. Hargitt, "Using DOE to Determine AA Battery Life," *Quality Progress*, March 1999, pp. 67–71.

a. Compute the average effect for each main effect (factor) and interaction.

b. Obtain a plot of the main effects.

c. Obtain a plot of the interactions.

d. On the basis of the results of part a, set up a normal probability plot of the main effects and interactions.

e. What conclusions can you draw from the results of parts b–d?

 12.13. Considerable effort has been made to develop and utilize polycrystalline diamond compact (PDC) cutters in oil and mining applications. An experiment is conducted to evaluate the effect of rake angle (in degrees), thrust (in pounds), and speed (in rpm). Two performance variables, the penetration rate (inches/minute) and torque (inch-pounds) are considered. A high penetration rate and a low torque are considered desirable performance attributes. Two samples are obtained for each combination of rake angle, thrust, and speed. The results are as follows (see 🔧 PDCBIT):

Rake Angle	Thrust	Speed	Penetration Rate		Torque	
7	100	500	4.00	1.09	13	12
7	100	750	12.54	5.00	20	3
7	200	500	6.75	8.18	62	45
7	200	750	6.25	20.00	25	65
15	100	500	5.25	5.57	7	20
15	100	750	9.27	7.03	13	10
15	200	500	13.50	16.92	75	55
15	200	750	24.60	20.57	45	37

We wish to know, for each of the performance variables of penetration rate and torque, whether there is a significant effect due to rake angle.

a. Compute the average effect for each main effect (factor) and interaction.

b. Obtain a plot of the main effects.

c. Obtain a plot of the interactions.

d. On the basis of the results of part a, set up a half-normal probability plot of the main effects and interactions.

e. What conclusions can you draw from the results of parts b–d?

f. What levels of rake angle, thrust, and speed should be used to improve performance? Explain your reasons for selecting these levels.

12.14. In an experiment concerning the tensile strength of yarn spun for textile usage, four factors are considered in measuring the tenacity or breaking strength in the filling yarn: side-to-side aspects of the fabric (nozzle versus opposite); yarn type (air spun versus ring spun); pick density, or the number of yarns across a fabric (35 versus 50); and air-jet pressure (30 psi versus 45 psi). The results are summarized in the following table (see ☞ YARN2):

Side to Side	Yarn Type	Pick Density	Air Pressure	Tenacity
Nozzle	Air spun	35	30	24.50
Opposite	Air spun	35	30	23.55
Nozzle	Ring spun	35	30	25.98
Nozzle	Air spun	50	30	24.63
Nozzle	Air spun	35	45	23.73
Opposite	Ring spun	35	30	25.00
Opposite	Air spun	50	30	24.51
Opposite	Air spun	35	45	22.05
Nozzle	Ring spun	50	30	24.68
Nozzle	Ring spun	35	45	24.52
Nozzle	Air spun	50	45	25.68
Opposite	Ring spun	50	30	23.93
Opposite	Ring spun	35	45	23.64
Opposite	Air spun	50	45	25.78
Nozzle	Ring spun	50	45	24.10
Opposite	Ring spun	50	45	24.23

Source: Reprinted from R. Johnson, T. Clapp, and N. Baqai, "Understanding the Effect of Confounding in Design of Experiments: A Case Study in High Speed Weaving," *Quality Engineering.* 1, 1989, pp. 501–508.

a. Compute the average effect for each main effect (factor) and interaction.

b. Obtain a plot of the main effects.

c. Obtain a plot of the interactions.

d. On the basis of the results of part a, set up a half-normal probability plot of the main effects and interactions.

e. What conclusions can you draw from the results of part d?

12.15. An experiment is conducted to study the time (in minutes) it takes to cook rice in a cooker that has an inner water area and an outer water area. Four factors are considered: amount of rice (1 cup versus 2 cups); amount of inner water (2 cups versus 3 cups); amount of outer water (0.5 cup versus 1 cup); and type of rice (short grain versus long grain). A half-replicate of a full factorial design is used. The results follow (see ☛ RICE):

Rice (cups)	Inner Water (cups)	Outer Water (cup)	Type	Cooking Time of Rice (minutes)
1	2	0.5	short	26.4
2	3	0.5	short	28.9
2	2	1.0	short	28.4
2	2	0.5	long	27.1
1	3	1.0	short	30.1
1	3	0.5	long	28.6
1	2	1.0	long	27.9
2	3	1.0	long	31.5

a. Compute the average effect for each main effect (factor) and interaction.

b. Obtain a plot of the main effects.

c. Obtain a plot of the interactions.

d. On the basis of the results of part a, set up a half-normal probability plot of the main effects and interactions.

e. What conclusions can you reach concerning the importance of each of the main effects and interactions on the average cooking time of rice?

12.16. An experiment is conducted to study the effect of four factors on scores in the game of American darts. The four factors are: amount of room lighting (75 watts versus 100 watts); practice prior to playing (none versus 5 minutes); consumption of beer (none versus two cans); and whether a radio is playing in the background (no versus yes). A half-replicate of a full factorial design is used. The scores of an experienced dart player in the experiment follow (see ☛ DARTS):

Lighting (watts)	Practice	Beer (cans)	Radio	Score
75	None	0	No	89
100	5 minutes	0	No	87
100	None	2	No	71
100	None	0	Yes	76
75	5 minutes	2	No	68
75	5 minutes	0	Yes	76
75	None	2	Yes	68
100	5 minutes	2	Yes	67

a. Compute the average effect for each of the four main effects and the interaction effects.

b. Set up a normal probability plot of the average effects.

c. On the basis of the results of part b, which effects appear to be important?

d. Set up a main effects plot.

e. Set up interaction plots.

f. What conclusions can you reach concerning the importance of each of the main effects and interactions on score?

12.17. Referring to the experiment discussed on page 502 concerning peanut oil, in addition to a response measure of solubility, the total yield of oil per batch of peanuts is obtained. The results follow (see 🔎 PEANUT2):

Treatment Combination	Response	Treatment Combination	Response
(1)	63	DE	23
AE	21	AD	74
BE	36	BD	80
AB	99	ABDE	33
CE	24	CD	63
AC	66	ACDE	21
BC	71	BCDE	44
ABCE	54	ABCD	96

Source: Reprinted from M. Kilgo, "An Application of Fractional Factorial Experimental Designs," *Quality Engineering,* 1, 1989, pp. 45–54.

a. Compute the average effect for each of the five main effects and the interaction effects.

b. Set up a normal probability plot of the average effects.

c. On the basis of the results of part b, which effects appear to be important?

d. Set up a main effects plot.

e. Set up an interaction plot.

f. What conclusions can you reach concerning the importance of each of the main effects and interactions on the yield?

12.18. (Individual or class project.) Suppose that we wish to study the factors that affect the time it takes to boil 1 quart of water on a stove. Among the factors that may be studied are:

A, type of water (e.g., tap, bottled, or distilled)

B, use of a cover for the pot (no or yes)

C, size of pot (small or large)

D, salt added to water (no or yes)

E, type of pot (aluminum or stainless steel)

a. Provide an operational definition for the time it takes to boil 1 quart of water on a stove.

b. Compare the operational definitions of others that may have performed the same experiment. Are there any differences between them? Explain.

Once the factors have been chosen, use a fractional factorial design or a full factorial design to obtain the boiling time for each treatment combination. With the results obtained:

c. Completely analyze the data to determine the factors and interactions that affect the boiling time.

d. Which treatment combinations will result in the lowest boiling time? Explain.

12.19. (Individual or class project.) Suppose that we wish to study the factors that affect the time and distance that a paper airplane is able to fly. Among the factors that may be studied are:

A, type of paper (construction versus bond)

B, weight of the plane, that is, paper clips on bottom of the plane (no versus yes)

C, front width

D, front diameter

E, rear width

F, rear diameter

a. Provide an operational definition for flying time and distance.

b. Compare the operational definitions of others that may have performed the same experiment. Are there any differences between them? Explain.

Once the factors have been chosen, use a fractional factorial design or a full factorial design to obtain the flying time and distance traveled for each treatment combination. With the results obtained:

c. Completely analyze the data to determine the factors and interactions that affect the flying time and distance.

d. Which treatment combinations will result in the highest flying time and longest distance? Explain.

12.20. (Individual or class project.) In an experiment involving the construction of a paper helicopter, the objective is to design a paper helicopter that has maximum flying time when dropped from a particular height, such as 12 feet. Among the factors are:

A, paper type (regular versus bond)

B, wing length (3.00 in. versus 4.75 in.)

C, body length (3.00 in. versus 4.75 in.)

D, body width (1.25 in. versus 2.00 in.)

E, paper clip (no versus yes)

F, fold (no versus yes)

G, taped body (no versus yes)

H, taped wing (no versus yes)

Source: Reprinted from G. E. P. Box, "Teaching Engineers Experimental Design with a Paper Helicopter," *Quality Engineering*, 4, 1992, pp. 453–459.

a. Provide an operational definition for flying time.

b. Compare the operational definitions of others who may have performed the same experiment. Are there any differences between them? Explain.

Once the factors have been chosen, use a fractional factorial design or a full factorial design to obtain the flying time for each treatment combination. With the results obtained:

c. Completely analyze the data to determine the factors and interactions that affect the flying time.

d. Which treatment combinations will result in the highest flying time? Explain.

References

1. S. Bisgaard, "Industrial Use of Statistically Designed Experiments: Case Study References and Some Historical Anecdotes," *Quality Engineering,* 4, 1992, pp. 547–562.

2. G. E. P. Box, "Fisher and the Design of Experiments," *American Statistician,* 34, 1980, pp. 1–10.

3. G. E. P. Box, "What Can You Find Out From Eight Experimental Runs," *Quality Engineering,* 4, 1992, pp. 619–627.

4. C. Daniel, "Use of Half-Normal Plots in Interpreting Factorial Two-Level Experiments," *Technometrics,* 1, 1959, pp. 311–341.

5. M. Kilgo, "An Application of Fractional Factorial Experimental Designs," *Quality Engineering,* 1, 1989, pp. 45–54.

6. R. V. Lenth, "Quick and Easy Analysis of Unreplicated Factorials," *Technometrics,* 31, 1989, pp. 469–473.

7. *Minitab for Windows Version 14* (2003) (State College, PA: Minitab, Inc.).

8. D. C. Montgomery (2001), *Design and Analysis of Experiments,* 5th ed. (New York: John Wiley & Sons).

9. J. Neter, M. H. Kutner, C. Nachtsheim, and W. Wasserman (1996), *Applied Linear Statistical Models,* 4th ed. (Homewood, IL: Richard D. Irwin).

Appendix **A12.1**

Using Minitab for the Design of Experiments[1]

Using Minitab to Obtain a Dotplot

To obtain a Dotplot using Minitab, open the ☻ **CIRCUITS.MTW** worksheet. Select **Graph | Dotplot,** and then:

1. In the Dotplots dialog box, shown in Figure A12.1, select the **One Y With Groups** choice. Click the **OK** button.

2. In the Dotplot—Data Source dialog box, shown in Figure A12.2, in the Graph variables: edit box enter **C7** or **Thickness.** In the Categorical variables for grouping edit box, enter **C8** or **Position.**

---

[1] The instructions and dialog boxes are based on the beta version of Minitab 14. Subsequent versions of Minitab may differ slightly from what is presented in this appendix.

**FIGURE
A12.1**
**Minitab
Dotplots
Dialog Box**

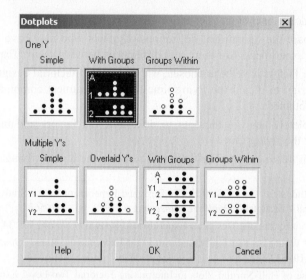

**FIGURE
A12.2**
**Minitab
Dotplot—Data
Source Dialog
Box**

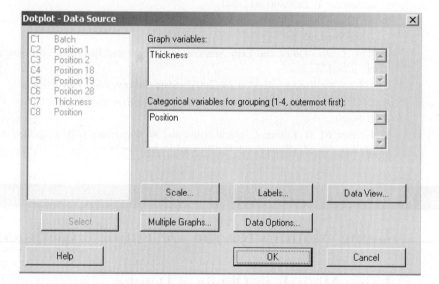

3. Click the **OK** button.

The output obtained will be similar to Figure 12.1 on page 474.

Using Minitab to Obtain a Box-and-Whisker Plot

To obtain a box-and-whisker plot using Minitab, open the 🕿 **CIRCUITS.MTW** work-sheet. Select **Graph | Boxplot,** and then:

1. In the Boxplots dialog box, shown in Figure A12.3, select the **One Y With Groups** choice. Click the **OK** button.

**FIGURE
A12.3**
**Minitab
Boxplots
Dialog Box**

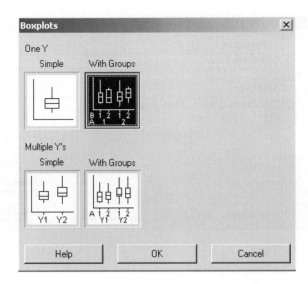

**FIGURE
A12.4**
**Minitab
Boxplot—Data
Source Dialog
Box**

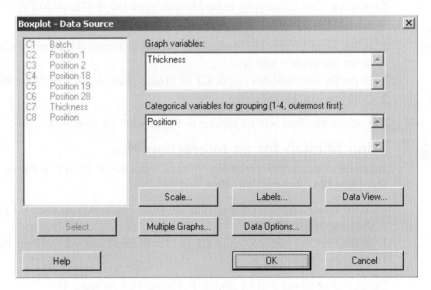

2. In the Boxplot—Data Source dialog box, shown in Figure A12.4, in the Graph variables: edit box enter **C7** or **Thickness.** In the Categorical variables for grouping edit box, enter **C8** or **Position.**

3. Click the **OK** button.

The output obtained will be similar to Figure 12.3 on page 476.

FIGURE A12.5
Minitab Main
Effects Plot
Dialog Box

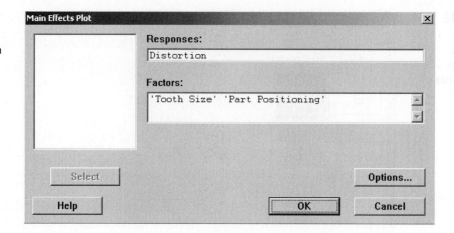

Using Minitab for a Main Effects Plot

To obtain a Main Effects plot using Minitab, open the ✿ **GEAR.MTW** worksheet. Select **Stat | ANOVA | Main Effects Plot,** and then:

1. In the Main Effects Plot dialog box, shown in Figure A12.5, enter **C3** or **Distortion** in the Responses: edit box.
2. In the Factors: edit box, enter **C1** or **'Tooth Size'** and **C2** or **'Part Positioning'**.
3. Click the **OK** button.

The output obtained will be similar to Figure 12.7 on page 479.

Using Minitab for an Interaction Plot

To obtain an Interaction plot using Minitab, open the ✿ **GEAR.MTW** worksheet. Select **Stat | ANOVA | Interactions Plot,** and then:

1. In the Interactions Plot dialog box, shown in Figure A12.6, enter **C3** or **Distortion** in the Responses: edit box.
2. In the Factors: edit box, enter **C1** or **'Tooth Size'** and **C2** or **'Part Positioning'**.
3. Click the **OK** button.

The output obtained will be similar to Figure 12.8 on page 479.

Using Minitab to Obtain Estimated Effects and a Normal Probability Plot in a Factorial Design

To obtain the estimated effects in a factorial design along with a normal probability plot using Minitab, open the ✿ **CAKE.MTW** worksheet. Select **Stat | DOE | Factorial | Analyze Factorial Design,** and then:

1. Select Yes in the Minitab dialog box, shown in Figure A12.7, that appears because Minitab has not yet created a design.

**FIGURE
A12.6**
**Minitab
Interactions
Plot Dialog
Box**

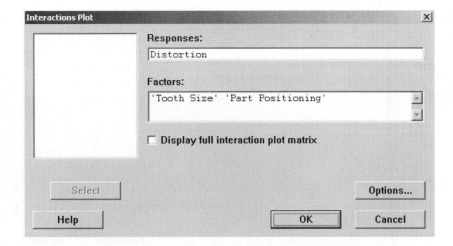

**FIGURE
A12.7**
**Minitab Dialog
Box to Create
a Design**

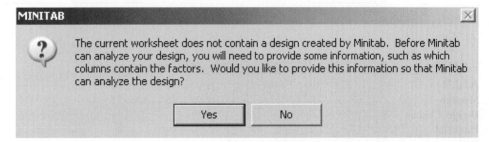

2. In the Design Custom Factorial Design dialog box, shown in Figure A12.8, enter **C1** or **Flour, C2** or **Shortening, C3** or **Egg Powder, C4** or **OvenTemp, C5** or **Bake-Time** in the Factors: edit box.

3. Click the **Low/High** button.

4. Enter the low and high values for each factor in the Design Custom Factorial Design-Low/High dialog box, as shown in Figure A12.9.

5. Click the **OK** button.

6. In the Analyze Factorial Design dialog box, shown in Figure A12.10, enter **C6** or **Rating** in the Responses: edit box.

7. Select the **Terms** button. In the Analyze Factorial Design dialog box, shown in Figure A12.11, note that since this is a full factorial design, the Include terms in the model up through order: drop-down list box is **5.**

8. Click the **OK** button.

9. Select the **Graphs** button. In the Analyze Factorial Design-Graphs dialog box, shown in Figure A12.12, under Effects Plots, select the **Normal** check box to obtain a normal probability plot for the effects.

**FIGURE
A12.8**
Minitab
Design Custom
Factorial
Design Dialog
Box

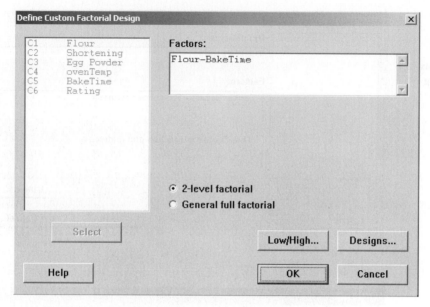

**FIGURE
A12.9**
Minitab
Design Custom
Factorial
Design—
Low/High
Dialog Box

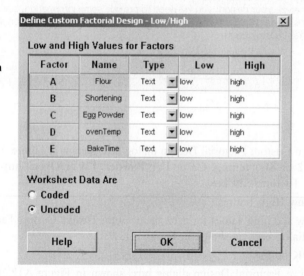

10. Click the **OK** button.
11. In the Analyze Factorial Design dialog box, shown in Figure A12.10, click the **OK** button.
12. To remove the plotted lines from the normal probability plot, move the cursor to one of the lines and right click. Select **Delete** from the Menu.

The output obtained will be similar to Figures 12.15 and 12.16 on pages 492 and 493.

FIGURE A12.10
Minitab Analyze Factorial Design Dialog Box

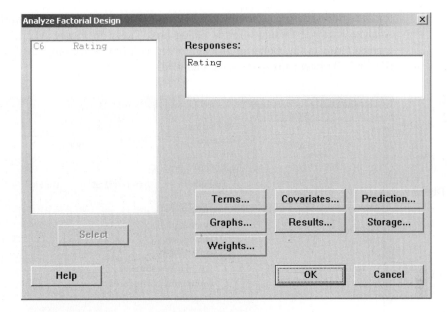

FIGURE A12.11
Minitab Analyze Factorial Design—Terms Dialog Box

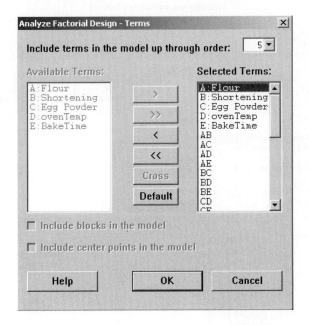

Using Minitab to Obtain Estimated Effects and a Normal Probability Plot in a Fractional Factorial Design

Follow the steps shown for the factorial design, except for step 5. In the Analyze Factorial Design—Terms dialog box, enter the value in the edit box that indicates the highest inter-actions included in the model. For example, in the 2^{4-1} fractional factorial design used for the roller bearing example, open the 🐞 **BEARINGS2.MTW** worksheet. In the Analyze Factorial Design—Terms dialog box, shown in Figure A12.13, enter **2** in the Include terms in the model up through order: edit box, since only the AB, AC, AD, BC, BD, and CD interactions are to be included.

FIGURE A12.12
Minitab Analyze Factorial Design— Graphs Dialog Box

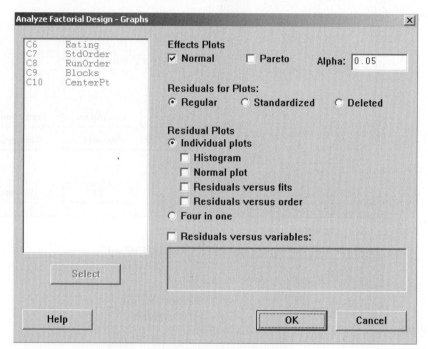

FIGURE A12.13
Minitab Analyze Factorial Design—Terms Dialog Box

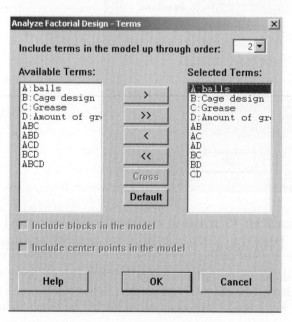

Chapter 13

Inspection Policy

Sections

Introduction

Inspecting Goods and Services

Acceptance Sampling

A Theoretical Invalidation of Acceptance Sampling

The kp Rule for Stable Processes

Inspection Policies for Chaotic Processes

Summary

Key Terms

Exercises

References

Appendix A13.1: Proof that the Number of Defectives in a Sample Is Independent of the Number of Defectives in the Remainder for Lots Drawn from a Stable Process

Appendix A13.2: Derivation of the kp Rule for Stable Processes

Chapter Objectives

- To introduce three alternative inspection policies: no inspection; 100 percent inspection; and sampling inspection, or acceptance sampling
- To discuss three classes of acceptance sampling plans: lot-by-lot acceptance sampling; continuous flow acceptance sampling; and special sampling plans
- To discuss the disadvantages of using acceptance sampling
- To demonstrate the lack of validity of acceptance sampling plans for stable processes
- To discuss and illustrate the kp rule, an optimal inspection policy for stable processes
- To discuss exceptions to the kp rule, when testing is destructive or the product tested is a homogeneous mixture
- To discuss inspection policies for unstable processes, for the cases of mild chaos and severe chaos
- To discuss exceptions to the rules for inspecting unstable processes

Introduction

This chapter introduces policies and procedures for inspection of incoming, intermediate, and final goods and services. Three options exist for inspection of goods and services: (1) no inspection, (2) 100 percent inspection, and (3) sampling inspection. The first part of the chapter focuses on sampling inspection, commonly called acceptance sampling, as a method to determine whether to accept, reject, or screen goods and services. Three types of acceptance sampling plans are discussed: lot-by-lot plans, continuous flow plans, and special sampling plans. The second part of the chapter presents a theoretical argument against using acceptance sampling plans, followed by a discussion of the kp rule, an alternative inspection procedure that minimizes the total cost of inspection for incoming, intermediate, and final goods and services. The chapter ends with two mathematical proofs of the arguments made.

Inspecting Goods and Services

Goods or services enter an organization from a vendor or are passed on internally from one part of the organization to another, such as department to department, or operation to operation within a department. These goods or services move inter- or intraorganizationally either in discrete lots or in continuous flows, and have certain customer-specified quality characteristics.

Organizations or their subcomponents require some method for minimizing the total cost of inspecting incoming and intermediate goods or services plus the cost to repair and test these goods and services in process; or of inspecting final goods or services that fail to meet specifications because of a defective good or service used in production. The three alternatives for inspection of goods or services are:

1. No inspection (send items straight into use with no screening)
2. 100 percent inspection (screen all goods or services to weed out defectives)
3. **Sampling inspection,** also known as **acceptance sampling** (screen a sample of goods or services to determine if the remainder should be accepted, rejected, or screened)

Historically, acceptance sampling has been considered useful if the inspection process is destructive (100 percent inspection will destroy all goods or services), the cost of 100 percent inspection is high, or too many units have to be inspected.

Acceptance Sampling

The purpose of acceptance sampling is to determine the disposition of goods or services: accept, reject, or screen. We wish to select the disposition that minimizes the cost of inspection in order to achieve a desired level of quality (called the **acceptable quality level** or **AQL,** as discussed in Chapter 11). Figure 13.1 shows several types of acceptance sampling plans [see Reference 3, pp. 161–414].

FIGURE 13.1
Acceptance
Sampling
Plans

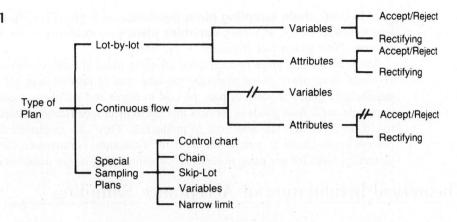

Lot-by-Lot Acceptance Sampling

Lot-by-lot acceptance sampling plans are used to inspect goods or services whenever the goods or services can conveniently be grouped into lots. All lot-by-lot acceptance plans are based on accepting, rejecting, or screening the remainder of the lot based on the number of defects found in the sample. **Lot-by-lot plans** can be designed for both attribute data and variables data. Such plans can also be broken down into **acceptance/ rejection plans** (plans in which a sample of items is drawn from the lot and the remainder of the lot is accepted or rejected based on an analysis of the sample) or **rectifying plans** (plans that call for either total or partial screening of the remainder). The most common acceptance/rejection lot-by-lot acceptance sampling plan for variables used in American industry today is **Military Standard 414** [see Reference 3, pp. 291–305]. This plan is used to control the fraction of incoming material that does not conform to specifications for variables data. The most common acceptance/rejection lot-by-lot acceptance sampling plan for attributes is **Military Standard 105D** [see Reference 3, pp. 217–248]. This plan is used to constrain suppliers so that they will deliver at least an acceptable quality level of goods or services for attribute data.

Continuous Flow Acceptance Sampling

Continuous flow plans are used to inspect goods or services whenever the goods or services cannot be grouped into lots—for example, goods on conveyor belts or goods on a continuous moving line. Only rectifying attribute sampling plans exist for continuous flow processes. The most common acceptance sampling plan in this category used today is **Military Standard 1235B** [see Reference 3, pp. 406–413]. All continuous flow acceptance plans are based on a **clearance number,** the number of conforming units observed between the occurrence of two defective units. If the number of units between two defective units is greater than the number of units specified in the clearing sample, the units will be accepted and shipped; otherwise, they will be 100 percent inspected.

Special Sampling Plans

Other types of acceptance sampling plans have been developed that are of the lot-by-lot type, but are applied to a series of lots considered as a group. They are called **special sampling plans.** These plans include **control chart plans** [see Reference 3, pp. 536–540], **chain sampling plans** [see Reference 3, pp. 177–179], **skip-lot plans** [see Reference 3, pp. 252–253], **variables plans** [see Reference 3, pp. 340–365], and **narrow limit plans** [see Reference 3, pp. 271–272].

Much attention is given to acceptance sampling plans in many textbooks and courses. However, these plans do not minimize the total cost of inspection of (1) incoming and intermediary goods or services plus the cost to repair and test these goods and services in process or (2) final goods or services that fail to meet specifications because of a defective good or service that was used in production. They also emphasize inspection, not process improvement to remove the need for inspection. Furthermore, there is a strong theoretical basis for not using acceptance sampling plans, as we demonstrate below.

A Theoretical Invalidation of Acceptance Sampling

A discussion of the lack of validity of acceptance sampling must consider the stability, or lack of stability, of the process's output which is to undergo inspection. Let us first consider the case of a stable process.

Stable Process

Suppose a lot of N independent items is drawn from a stable process that generates 100p percent defective output, and that x of the items are defective and $N - x$ are conforming. Here the number of defectives is binomially distributed with fraction defective p. This is extremely common in stable processes. Then

$$N = \text{total number of items in the lot}$$
$$x = \text{number of defective items in the lot}$$
$$N - x = \text{number of conforming items in the lot}$$
$$E(x/N) = p = \text{fraction defective items in the process}$$

Suppose a sample of n items is drawn from the lot of N items (without replacement, because of the finite nature of the lot), such that r of the items are defective and $n - r$ of the items are conforming. Then

$$n = \text{total number of items in the sample}$$
$$r = \text{number of defective items in the sample}$$
$$n - r = \text{number of conforming items in the sample}$$
$$E(r/n) = p = \text{estimated fraction defective items in the process}$$

The selection of the sample from the lot creates a new entity we will call the remainder, or the rest, of the lot. The remainder is composed of $N - n$ items, such that $x - r$ of the items are defective and $(N - n) - (x - r)$ are conforming. Then

$$N - n = \text{total number of items in the remainder}$$
$$x - r = \text{number of defective items in the remainder}$$
$$(N - n) - (x - r) = \text{number of conforming items in the remainder}$$
$$E[(x - r)/(N - n)] = p = \text{estimated fraction defective items in the process}$$

Figure 13.2 illustrates this sequence of item groupings.

FIGURE 13.2
**Selection of
Samples
Drawn from
Lots from a
Process**

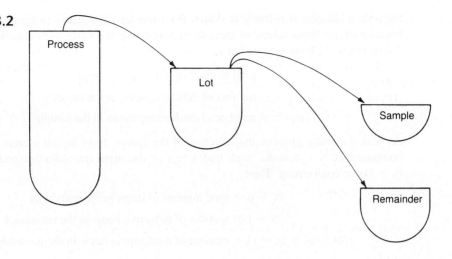

If it can be shown that the number of defectives in the sample is independent of, or not correlated with, the number of defectives in the remainder, then acceptance sampling plans that determine the disposition of a remainder (accept, reject, or screen) based on the number of defectives in a sample are invalid; this proof appears in Appendix A13.1.

In other words, the number of defectives in the sample and in the remainder are both binomially distributed with the same mean fraction, p, and are independent. For example, if a lot of 1,000 fair coins were tossed repeatedly and a sample of 50 of the 1,000 were drawn each time for inspection, the fraction of heads in the sample and in the remainder would both be distributed around p = 0.5, but the number of heads in the sample would be independent of the number of heads in the remainder. This means the distribution of heads in the remainder associated with samples yielding 0 heads would be the same as the distribution of heads in the remainder associated with samples yielding 50 heads. Hence, the results of the sample are not useful in predicting what would happen to the remainder; acceptance sampling plans that determine the disposition of the remainder based on samples are thus not valid for a stable process. This surprising result [see Reference 4, pp. 415–425 and Reference 1, p. 258] does not mean that **statistical inference** is invalid—that is, that a random sample from a population does not provide information about the frame. Rather, it says only that samples provide no information about remainders from stable processes. An alternative to acceptance sampling from stable processes must be found. W. Edwards Deming offered, as an alternative, the kp rule, to be discussed later in this chapter.

Chaotic Process

Suppose a lot of N items is drawn from a chaotic or unknown process. In the lot, x of the items are defective and N − x are conforming, and the process fraction defective p varies from lot to lot (or day to day) and is not predictable. Then

$$N = \text{total number of items in the lot}$$

$$x = \text{number of defective items in the lot}$$

$$N - x = \text{number of conforming items in the lot}$$

Suppose a sample of n items is drawn from the lot of N items (without replacement, because of the finite nature of the lot) such that r of the items are defective and n − r of the items are conforming. Then

$$n = \text{total number of items in the sample}$$

$$r = \text{number of defective items in the sample}$$

$$n - r = \text{number of conforming items in the sample}$$

As with the stable process, the selection of the sample from the lot creates a remainder composed of N − n items, such that x − r of the items are defective and (N − n) − (x − r) are conforming. Then

$$N - n = \text{total number of items in the remainder}$$

$$x - r = \text{number of defective items in the remainder}$$

$$(N - n) - (x - r) = \text{number of conforming items in the remainder}$$

As before, Figure 13.2 represents the sequence of item groupings discussed in this section.

Here we can show that the number of defectives in the sample, r, is correlated with the number of defectives in the remainder, x − r. Thus, when p varies widely and unpredictably from lot to lot, the information from a sample provides insight into the remainder. Going back to the coin example, if lots of 1,000 biased coins were tossed repeatedly and samples of 50 of the 1,000 were drawn each time for inspection, the distribution of the fraction of heads in the samples and in the remainders would not be distributed around 0.5; rather, they would be related to the actual fraction of heads in the lot and would be correlated. Similarly, the number of defectives in the sample and remainder would be correlated. Hence, acceptance sampling plans that determine the disposition of a remainder (accept, reject, or screen) based on the number of defectives in a sample are valid for a chaotic process. Later in this chapter, we will discuss the larger question of whether it is the most cost-effective plan given the chaotic nature of the process.

Note that as processes are stabilized as a result of quality efforts, acceptance plans that are valid for chaotic processes—albeit at high cost—will no longer be effective on the stable process.

The kp Rule for Stable Processes

Given a stable process and the knowledge that acceptance sampling plans are not effective on stable processes, we are left with only two of the inspection alternatives discussed at the beginning of this chapter: no inspection or 100 percent inspection. We discuss here Deming's **kp rule,** which specifies when to do no inspection and when to do 100 percent inspection so as to minimize the total cost of incoming and intermediate materials, final products, and repairing and testing those products that fail. The rule is derived in Appendix A13.2.

The assumptions for the use of the kp rule are not restrictive and are applicable to many common situations [see Reference 2, pp. 237–311, Reference 5, and Reference 6, pp. 121–127].

1. All items are tested (inspected) before they move forward in the process. In other words, all nonconforming items are detected by a final inspection. When all items will not be subjected to a final inspection, the rule can be modified to reflect the possibility that a certain fraction of nonconforming parts, f, would be caught and the remaining fraction, 1 − f, would continue on into production or into the hands of customers [see Reference 1, p. 123].

2. Inspection is completely reliable. If an item is defective, it will fail inspection. As Deming wrote, "A **defective part** is one that by definition will cause the assembly to fail. If a part declared defective at the start will not cause trouble further down the line, or with the customer, then you have not yet defined what you mean by a defective part." [See Reference 1, p. 268.]

3. The item vendor will give the buyer an extra supply of items, S, to replace any defective items found. The supplier adds the cost of these items onto her bill, either directly or indirectly. This cost is an overhead cost and would be present regardless of the inspection plan used. Hence, it need not be included in the cost function to be minimized.

The following notation is necessary to determine when to do 100 percent inspection and when to do no inspection:

p = the average incoming fraction of defective items in incoming lots of items

Recall that the process under study is stable and has a meaningful average incoming fraction of defective items, p, in incoming lots of items.

k_1 = the cost to initially inspect one item

k_2 = the cost to dismantle, repair, reassemble, and test a good or service that fails because a defective item was used in its production

If a process is stable around the fraction p, the kp rule states

1. If k_1/k_2 is greater than p, then 0 percent inspection. That is, no inspection is the policy that minimizes the total cost. This occurs if the fraction of incoming defective items, p, is very low, the cost of inspecting an incoming item is high, and the cost of the defective item getting into production is low; therefore, no inspection is needed. The rationale is that there is little risk or penalty associated with incoming defective items.

2. If k_1/k_2 is less than p, then 100 percent inspection. That is, 100 percent inspection is the policy that minimizes the total cost. This occurs if the fraction of incoming defective items, p, is high, the cost of inspecting an incoming item is low, and the cost of the defective item getting into production is high; therefore 100 percent inspection is needed. The rationale here is that there is great risk and penalty attached to incoming defective items.

3. If k_1/k_2 equals p, then either 0 percent or 100 percent inspection. A decision must be made as to whether 0 percent or 100 percent inspection should be done in this case. In general, if p is not based on a substantial past history, 100 percent inspection is vital for safety's sake.

To summarize, the kp rule will minimize the total cost of incoming and intermediary materials and final product for a stable process by proper selection of a 0 percent or

100 percent inspection policy. If the process under study is stable, then whether item i is defective is independent of whether any other item is defective. Hence, item i should be inspected, or not inspected, according to whether k_1/k_2 is greater than or less than p. Recall that item i is a randomly selected item, and policy set for item i applies to any item. We can thus extend the policy for item i to all items in the lot. Consequently, either all or no items in the lot should be inspected, depending on whether the break-even point, k_1/k_2, is greater than or less than p.

It is important to note that 0 percent inspection does not mean zero information. Small samples should always be drawn from every lot—or on a skip-lot basis—for information about the process under study. This information should be recorded on control charts to facilitate process improvement [see Reference 1, p. 273]. The cost of these small samples is assumed to be a cost of doing business, and consequently is not considered in the cost function to be minimized.

The kp rule is appropriate between any two points in an organization's interdependent system of stakeholders, such as internally, in the vendor's processes, or between the firm and the vendor.

An Example of the kp Rule

A car manufacturer is deciding whether to purchase $25 million worth of equipment that would test engines purchased from vendors. The vendor's process is stable. The following has been determined:

- The inspection cost to screen out incoming defective engines is $50 per engine ($k_1 = \$50$).
- The cost for corrective action if a defective engine gets into production is $500 per defective engine ($k_2 = \$500$).
- On average, 1 in 150 incoming engines is defective ($p = 1/150 = 0.0067$).

Consequently, $k_1/k_2 = 50/500 = 0.1$. Note that 0.1 is greater than 0.0067. Therefore, k_1/k_2 is greater than p, and the correct course of action would be to do no initial inspection on incoming engines to achieve minimum total cost.

If no engines are inspected, the auto company would expect to incur the $500 cost in 1 out of 150 engines. This translates into an average corrective action cost of $3.33 per engine ($500 \times 1/150$). By eliminating initial inspection, the company would save $46.67 per engine ($50 - \$3.33$) on average. As the company purchases 4,000 engines per day, this translates into a daily savings of $186,680 ($4{,}000 \times \$46.67$), not including the savings of $25 million for testing equipment, interest on that money, and time freed up to work on improving quality! The next step in the pursuit of quality is for the auto company to work with its engine vendor to reduce the fraction of defective engines [see Reference 1, pp. 276–277].

Exceptions to the kp Rule

Destructive Testing

The kp rule does not apply to **destructive testing,** in which an item is destroyed in conducting the test. The only solution in destructive testing is to achieve statistical control such that $k_1/k_2 > p$ so that no inspection (other than routine small samples of the process) is the minimum cost policy. Note that achieving statistical control with $k_1/k_2 > p$ is always the best solution regardless of whether the test is destructive or nondestructive [see Reference 1, pp. 274–275].

Homogeneous Mixtures

The kp rule does not apply to **homogeneous mixtures**—for example, a gallon sampled from a tank of brine. It does not matter whether we draw off the gallon from the top of the tank, or middle, or bottom. In this case, the sample is identical in composition to the remainder; hence, we can make judgments about the remainder from the sample [see Reference 1, p. 285].

Component Costs of k_1 and k_2

Some costs to consider when calculating k_1 and k_2 are shown in Exhibit 13.1 [see Reference 6, p. 124]. The costs required to compute k_1 are usually known; a firm's financial personnel should be helpful in computing k_1. However, the costs required to compute k_2 are generally unknown and frequently difficult to estimate (for example, the cost of customer dissatisfaction from recalls or lawsuits). A reasonable policy is to estimate k_2 without the more subjective costs. If $k_1/k_2 < p$, there is no need to estimate the other components of k_2. On the other hand, if $k_1/k_2 > p$ without including the subjective costs, an estimate of these missing costs may then have to be made to determine more accurately the relationship between p and k_1/k_2.

EXHIBIT 13.1 *Component Costs of k_1 and k_2*	**Some Inspection Costs (k_1)**
	
	Capital equipment
	   Initial cost
	   Depreciation (also considers residual value)
	   Planned production volumes
	   Cost of capital
	Operating costs
	   Labor
	   Rent, utilities, maintenance
	   Piece cost (outside vendor quote)
	
	Possible Detrimental Costs (k_2)
	
	Added costs of processing the nonconforming item further
	Cost of sorting lots later to find a nonconforming item
	Cost of repairing batches of assemblies later
	Cost of lost production later if lots of parts or batches of assemblies must be guaranteed pending sorting and repair
	Warranty costs
	Cost of recalls
	Lawsuits ($k_2 \to \infty$ for safety items)
	Customer loyalty impinging upon future sales

Inspection Policies for Chaotic Processes

Given a chaotic process and the knowledge that acceptance sampling plans are appropriate for such processes, we have the three inspection alternatives discussed earlier: (1) no inspection, (2) 100 percent inspection, and (3) some form of acceptance sampling. Our choice between alternatives 1 and 3 to achieve savings over 100 percent inspection (alternative 2) depends on the nature of the chaos in the process.

Mild Chaos

If the fraction defective in the process under study wanders in an unpredictable manner so that the fractions for the worst lots are below k_1/k_2, as shown in Figure 13.3, then no inspection (except for routine sampling of the process) should be performed. Significant effort, however, should be directed toward stabilizing the process from the information in the routine samples.

If the fraction defective in the process under study wanders in an unpredictable manner so that the fractions for the best lots are above k_1/k_2, then 100 percent inspection should be performed, as shown in Figure 13.4. Again, significant effort should be directed toward stabilizing the process by using the information from 100 percent inspection.

FIGURE 13.3
Mild Chaos with Low Fraction Defective

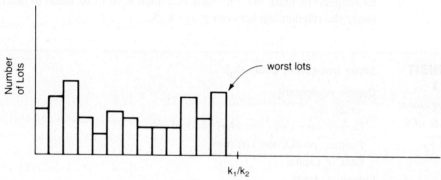

FIGURE 13.4
Mild Chaos with High Fraction Defective

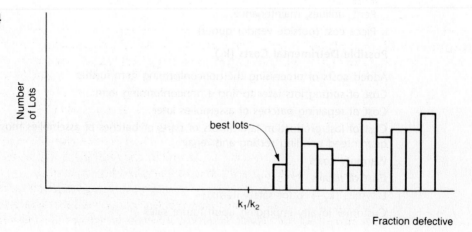

These two cases are considered mild chaos because the distribution of the fraction defective is chaotic within bounds. Of course, these bounds can disappear at any moment. These are not situations where we should be lulled into thinking that the chaos will always stay within bounds. Chaos is like a wild beast that can run anywhere at anytime, including beyond any earlier boundary.

Severe Chaos

If the fraction defective in the process under study wanders in an unpredictable manner within a narrow range around k_1/k_2, the most practical plan is 100 percent inspection of all lots. No effort at acceptance sampling can justify the cost of administering the plan [see Reference 1, p. 271].

If the fraction defective in the process under study wanders in an unpredictable manner within a wide range around k_1/k_2, J. Orsini has devised a rule that yields substantial savings over 100 percent inspection [see Reference 5]:

- If k_1/k_2 is less than 1/1,000, then inspect 100 percent of the incoming lots.
- If k_1/k_2 is between 1/1,000 and 1/100, then test a sample of 200. If there are no defectives, then accept the remainder. Inspect the entire remainder if at least one defective item is found in the sample.
- If k_1/k_2 is greater than 1/100, then do no inspection.

This rule is also helpful in working with a vendor to bring the vendor's process into control. A running record of the samples of 200 can be kept, and the number of defectives can be charted, sample by sample. Feedback to the vendor is extremely helpful in identifying problems.

Exceptions to Rules for Chaos

The rules for unstable processes are subject to the same exceptions as the kp rule for stable processes. Further, if items come into a firm from an unknown vendor, the optimal policy is to perform 100 percent inspection until enough information has been collected to construct a control chart(s) for the vendor's process/product; we can then select the best inspection plan. Since for safety items k_2 is infinite, 100 percent inspection should also be carried out for critical parts and safety items.

Summary

This chapter has discussed different types of acceptance sampling plans: lot-by-lot plans, continuous sampling plans, and special sampling plans. Lot-by-lot acceptance sampling plans are used to inspect goods or services whenever the goods or services can be conveniently grouped into lots. Continuous flow acceptance sampling plans are used to inspect goods or services whenever the goods or services cannot be grouped into lots—for example, goods on a conveyor belt. Special sampling plans are used for lots found in series. These acceptance sampling plans do not, however, minimize the average total cost of inspection of incoming, intermediate, and final goods and services. A theoretical argument invalidating acceptance sampling has been presented.

Plans for minimizing the average total cost of testing incoming materials and final product, called the kp rule, were analyzed. One plan is used for stable processes, and the other plan is used for chaotic processes, subject to exceptions when testing is destructive or we are dealing with homogeneous mixtures. Both plans require the collection and control charting of either inspection data or routine samples to achieve process stability and pursue continuous and never-ending improvement.

Key Terms

acceptable quality level, *526*	defective part, *531*	Military Standard 414, *527*
acceptance/rejection plans, *527*	destructive testing, *532*	narrow limit plans, *528*
acceptance sampling, *526*	homogeneous mixtures, *533*	rectifying plans, *527*
AQL, *526*	kp rule, *530*	sampling inspection, *526*
chain sampling plans, *528*	lot-by-lot plans, *527*	skip-lot plans, *528*
clearance number, *527*	Military Standard 105D, *527*	special sampling plans, *527*
continuous flow plans, *527*	Military Standard 1235B, *527*	statistical inference, *529*
control chart plans, *527*		variables plans, *528*

Exercises

13.1. Discuss the three possible alternatives for the inspection of goods or services.

13.2. a. Explain the purpose of acceptance sampling.

   b. Explain the purpose of lot-by-lot acceptance sampling plans. Describe the situations in which lot-by-lot acceptance sampling plans are used as a basis for action on a lot of goods.

   c. Explain the purpose of Military Standard 414.

   d. Explain the purpose of Military Standard 105D.

   e. Explain the purpose of continuous flow acceptance sampling plans.

   f. Briefly describe the operation of continuous flow acceptance sampling plans.

13.3. Explain why acceptance sampling plans are theoretically incorrect for stable processes and should not be used as a basis for action. Mathematically defend your explanation.

13.4. Explain why acceptance sampling is theoretically correct but not economical for chaotic processes and consequently should not be used as a basis for action.

13.5. a. Describe the kp rule for stable processes.

   b. Explain the assumptions required to use the kp rule.

   c. List several examples of k_1 inspection costs.

   d. List several examples of k_2 inspection costs.

13.6. Explain the term mild chaos and its significance to taking action on incoming or intermediary material or on final product.

13.7. A radio manufacturer has a policy of inspecting every incoming radio speaker to ensure it conforms to specifications. What information would you need to question the wisdom of this inspection policy?

13.8. The production manager of Exercise 13.7's radio company learned about the kp rule. He used past inspection data concerning the proportion of defective radio speakers purchased per day to construct a p chart with variable sample size. The p chart indicated that the incoming stream of radio speakers was stable with respect to the fraction of defective radio speakers purchased each day. The average fraction of defective radio speakers was found to be 0.002. Further study showed that it costs approximately $0.50 to inspect an incoming radio speaker and that it costs approximately $7.50 to repair a radio with a defective speaker before it leaves the factory.

    a. Use the kp rule to determine if 0 percent of 100 percent inspection should be used for incoming radio speakers.

    b. What should management do about the incoming radio speaker process, given your answer in part a?

13.9. Explain the term severe chaos. Describe an inspection rule that can be used when a process exhibits severe chaos.

References
1. W. E. Deming (1950), *Some Theory of Sampling* (New York: John Wiley & Sons).
2. W. E. Deming (1982), *Quality, Productivity and Competitive Position* (Cambridge, MA: Massachusetts Institute of Technology Center for Advanced Engineering Study).
3. A. Duncan (1986), *Quality Control and Industrial Statistics,* 5th ed. (Homewood, IL: Irwin).
4. A. Mood, "On the Dependence of Sampling Inspection Plans under Population Distributions," *Annals of Mathematical Statistics,* 14, 1943, pp. 415–425.
5. J. Orsini (1982), "Simple Rule to Reduce Total Cost of Inspection and Correction of Product in State of Chaos," doctoral dissertation, Graduate School of Business Administration, New York University.
6. G. P. Papadakis, "The Deming Inspection Criteria for Choosing Zero or 100 Percent Inspection," *Journal of Quality Technology,* 17, July 1985, pp. 121–127.

Appendix **A13.1**

Proof that the Number of Defectives in a Sample Is Independent of the Number of Defectives in the Remainder for Lots Drawn from a Stable Process

To prove: Given a stable process with 100p percent defective, the number of defectives in a sample of n items drawn from a lot of size N is independent of the number of defectives in the remaining $N - n$ items.

Proof:

$$n = \text{number of items in the sample}$$

$$N = \text{number of items in the lot}$$

$$r = \text{number of defective items in the sample}$$

$$x = \text{number of defective items in the lot}$$

$$x - r = \text{number of defective items in remaining } N - n \text{ items}$$

$$f(x) = \text{the probability of x defectives in a lot of N items drawn from a stable process with 100p percent defective}$$

$$f(r) = \text{the probability of r defectives in a sample of n items drawn from a stable process with 100p percent defective}$$

$f(r \mid x)$ = the conditional probability of r defectives in a sample of n items drawn from a lot of N items given that the lot contains x defectives

$f(r \text{ and } (x - r))$ = the joint probability that there are r defectives in the sample of n items and x − r defectives in the remaining N − n items

We must show that $f(r \text{ and } (x - r)) = f(r)f(x - r)$.

The joint probability of x defectives in the lot and r defectives in the sample is given by

$$f(x \text{ and } r) = f(x)f(r \mid x)$$

The number of defectives, x, in a lot of size N with fraction defective p, where $q = 1 - p$, is binomially distributed:

$$f(x) = \binom{N}{x} p^x q^{N-x}$$

Similarly, the number of defectives, r, in a sample of size n is binomially distributed:

$$f(r) = \binom{n}{r} p^r q^{n-r}$$

and the number of defectives, x − r, in the remaining N − n items is also binomially distributed:

$$f(x - r) = \binom{N - n}{x - r} p^{x-r} q^{(N-n)-(x-r)}$$

The number of defectives, r, in a sample of size n, given a total of x defectives in a lot of size N, has a hypergeometric distribution, given by

$$f(r \mid x) = \frac{\binom{n}{r}\binom{N - n}{x - r}}{\binom{N}{x}}$$

Then

$$f(x \text{ and } r) = \binom{N}{x} p^x q^{N-x} \frac{\binom{n}{r}\binom{N - n}{x - r}}{\binom{N}{x}}$$

This can be written as:

$$f(x \text{ and } r) = p^{x-r+r} q^{N-x-n+n-r+r} \binom{n}{r}\binom{N - n}{x - r}$$

or, rearranging,

$$f(x \text{ and } r) = \binom{N - n}{x - r} p^{x-r} q^{(N-n)-(x-r)} \binom{n}{r} p^r q^{n-r}$$

or

$$f(x \text{ and } r) = f(x - r)f(r)$$

This is the probability of x defectives in a lot of size N and r defectives in a sample of size n. But this is the same as the probability of x − r defectives in N − n items and r defectives in n items. So

$$f(x \text{ and } r) = f((x - r) \text{ and } r)$$

Then

$$f((x - r) \text{ and } r) = f(r)f(x - r)$$

If the joint probability of two events equals the product of their unconditional probabilities, the events must be independent. Thus, the number of defectives in a sample of n items is independent of the number of defectives in the remaining N − n items.

Appendix **A13.2**

Derivation of the kp Rule for Stable Processes

Let

p = the average fraction of defective items in incoming lots of items

k_1 = the cost to initially inspect one item

k_2 = the cost to dismantle, repair, reassemble, and test a good or service that fails because a defective item was used in its production

k = the average cost to test one or more items to find a conforming item from the supply, S, to replace a defective item found

   $= k_1/(1 - p)$

C_1 = the cost to initially inspect one item

C_2 = the cost to repair a failed good or service

Further, let

x_i = 1 if item i is defective, and

x_i = 0 if item i is conforming

Now, if one item, item i, is randomly drawn from a lot, then the probability that it is defective is p. The cost to initially inspect item i is

$$C_1 = k_1 + kx_i \qquad \text{if we test item i, and}$$
$$C_1 = 0 \qquad \text{if we do not test item i}$$

C_1 is composed of the cost to initially test one item plus the cost to replace the item if it is found to be defective. Hence,

$$C_1 = k_1 + k \qquad \text{if item i is tested and found to be defective}$$
$$C_1 = k_1 \qquad \text{if item i is tested and found to conform}$$
$$C_1 = 0 \qquad \text{if item i is not tested}$$

The cost to repair a failed good or service due to item i is

$$C_2 = (k_2 + k)x_i \qquad \text{if we do not initially test item i}$$

$$C_2 = 0 \qquad \text{if we do initially test item i}$$

C_2 is composed of the cost to repair a failed good or service if item i was not initially inspected. Hence

$$C_2 = k_2 + k \qquad \text{if item i was not initially inspected and item i is defective}$$

$$C_2 = 0 \qquad \text{if item i was not initially inspected and item i is conforming}$$

$$C_2 = 0 \qquad \text{if item i was initially inspected}$$

C_1 and C_2 are mutually exclusive as they cannot occur simultaneously for a given item; if one is positive, the other is zero. The total cost for item i is

$$C = C_1 + C_2$$

Table A13.1 summarizes the cost structure for inspection versus no inspection for item i [see Reference 1, p. 302].

Table A13.2 extends the cost structure for inspection versus no inspection to the average cost per item over the lot. In this case x_i is replaced by p because

$$p = \sum_{i=1}^{N} [x_i/N]$$

None of the other elements in Table A13.2 is affected because they are constants.

Now, the break-even point between inspection and no inspection can be determined by setting the total cost for inspection equal to the total cost for no inspection. That is, at the break-even point, Cost (inspect) = Cost (do not inspect):

$$k_1 + kp = k_2p + kp$$

$$k_1 = k_2p$$

$$p = k_1/k_2$$

TABLE A13.1
Cost Structure for Inspection Decision for Item i

Inspect the Item?	C_1	C_2	Total Cost $C = C_1 + C_2$
Yes	$k_1 + kx_i$	0	$k_1 + kx_i$
No	0	$(k_2 + k)x_i$	$(k_2 + k)x_i$

TABLE A13.2
Cost Structure for Inspection Decision for Average Item

Inspect the Item?	C_1	C_2	Total Cost $C = C_1 + C_2$
Yes	$k_1 + kp$	0	$k_1 + kp$
No	0	$(k_2 + k)p$	$k_2p + kp$

Part 3

Administrative Systems for Quality Management

Top management, including the board of directors, must initiate and lead quality management efforts. One of the first tasks for top management is to learn about the various theories, models, and techniques in the field. They then must formulate a quality management model suited to the nuances of the organization. Quality management models will differ from organization to organization.

Part 3 presents one possible model of quality management. This model is presented to stimulate the thinking of top managers. It represents an "ideal" for promoting quality management, which must be continuously pursued, and improved, by the leadership of an organization. The model presents a possible sequencing of activities that can be used to transform an organization.

Chapter 14 introduces the "detailed fork model": it is shaped like a fork with a handle, a neck, and three prongs. The handle is "management's commitment to transformation." The neck is "management's education." The first prong is "daily management." The second prong is "cross-functional management," and the third prong is "policy management." The fork analogy is used because quality management is an implement of nourishment for an organization: it feeds an organization, so its people have the energy to transform and pursue their goal of never-ending improvement. The chapter also discusses the handle of the fork, or management's commitment to transform an organization; top management generates and directs the energy necessary to transform an organization.

Chapter 15 discusses the neck of the fork, or the education and self-improvement activities of top managers. Studying the System of Profound Knowledge, the 14 points, and a transformation model is necessary to understand the theoretical and practical underpinnings of the new management and to help cope with the upheaval that often results from the transformation.

Chapter 16 discusses Prong 1: daily management, or the development, standardization, control, improvement, and innovation of methods (processes) used by employees in their daily routine. This "housekeeping" is accomplished through the Standardize-Do-Study-Act (SDSA) cycle and the improvement and innovation of "best-practice" methods through the Plan-Do-Study-Act (PDSA) cycle.

Chapter 17 discusses Prong 2: cross-functional management, whose purpose is to develop, standardize, control, improve, and innovate organizational processes across divisions and departments. This is carried out to optimize quality, cost, delivery, service, quantity, and safety. As expertise is developed with cross-functional processes, they are moved into daily management processes, if appropriate.

Chapter 18 discusses Prong 3: policy management, performed by using the PDSA cycle to improve and innovate the methods responsible for the difference between corporate performance and customer needs and wants, or to change the direction of an organization.

Chapter 19 presents a discussion of the resource requirements for organizational transformation, including a template for evaluating the necessary requirements, the time frame for each stage of the transformation, associated levels of responsibility at each stage, and resource needs at each stage.

Chapter 14

The Fork Model for Quality Management: The Handle, or Transformation

Sections

Chapter Objectives

- To examine aids to promoting the transformation of an organization to quality management
- To examine barriers to the transformation of an organization to quality management
- To discuss the need for commitment by top management to quality management
- To illustrate how top management can respond to crises in two company cases, one Japanese and one American
- To illustrate how top management can create a crisis resulting in the transformation to quality management

- To illustrate how top management can create a vision to enable the transformation to quality management
- To discuss how top management can initiate and carry out a plan for the transformation to quality management

Introduction

Before any quality management efforts can be undertaken, the top management of an organization must make a commitment to transformation, or "the handle" of the fork model for quality management. In this chapter we explain what is required to sustain, coordinate, and promote that commitment.

Quality management is a never-ending journey. However, all journeys begin with one step. The moment the leadership of an organization takes that first step, the organization has started a quality management program. The time required to reap the benefits from quality management depend on the resources allocated to the process. The best time to begin quality management is now. Like a person who wants to lose weight and finds reasons not to start a diet, organizations manufacture excuses to put off the transformation. There is no specific time that is better than another to begin quality management.

Aids to Promoting Quality Management

Different needs and situations stimulate an organization to pursue quality management. Some examples of aids that promote the **transformation** of an organization to quality management include the desire to:

- Exceed customer requirements.
- Improve the organization's image.
- Increase market size.
- Increase market share.
- Improve employee morale.
- Create a common mission.
- Improve communication.
- Standardize processes.
- Create best practices.
- Improve the physical environment.
- Resolve problems before they become crises.
- Bridge responsibility gaps.
- Improve the documentation of processes, products, and services.
- Improve the design of processes, products, and services.
- Improve manufacturing and delivery of service.
- Produce uniform products, at low cost and suited to the market (improve quality).
- Increase profits.

Barriers to Quality Management

What stops an organization from pursuing quality? Examples of barriers that hinder the transformation of management of an organization include:

- Inability to change the mindset (paradigms) of top management.
- Inability to maintain momentum for the transformation.
- Lack of uniform management style.
- Lack of long-term corporate direction.
- Inability to change the culture of the organization.
- Lack of effective communication.
- Lack of discipline required to transform.
- Fear of scrutiny by supervisor.
- Fear of process standardization.
- Fear of loss of individualism.
- Fear of rigidity.
- Lack of financial and human resources.
- Lack of training and education.
- Lack of management commitment.

Top Management's Reluctance to Commit

Lack of management commitment will stop a quality management effort before it begins. If transformation promises improvement in all areas of the organization, why is it not embraced by all top managers? One reason may be that many managers are unwilling to acknowledge companywide success stories based on quality management theory.

Top managers may not be pro–quality management because it is not their own creation. Alternatively, they may fear failure to meet short-term goals or to manage effectively. Leaders are reluctant to change because they have been personally successful; the organization beneath them may be falling apart, but as long as they continue to get raises and positive performance appraisals, they can deny the rampant problems.

Leaders who verbally promote quality management but impede quality management by their actions create a situation called "the slow death." The slow death is similar to a plant whose leaves (workers), branches (supervisors), and trunk (middle management) have a natural inclination to grow, but a gardener (top management) who neglects to provide water. Over time, the plant will die, as will quality management, without the necessary nourishment of top management.

Responding to a Crisis

Top management must create and direct the energy necessary to transform an organization. As suggested by Noriaki Kano [see Reference 4, pp. 14–15], there are only two sources for this energy, a **crisis** or a **vision,** as shown in steps 1 and 2 of the detailed fork model in Figure 14.1.

Many companies begin a program of quality management as a reaction to crises discovered by top management. This section describes the crises in two companies, one Japanese and one American, which led to their embarking on a quality management transformation. They each successfully resolved their crises using quality management.

JUKI Corporation

JUKI Corporation is a Japanese manufacturer of products ranging from sewing machines to industrial robots. In 1973, JUKI management uncovered external and internal crises, which led them to exert the energy leading to quality improvement. The external crises included:

1. An inability to be competitive due to low quality and productivity.
2. Union problems.

The internal crises included:

1. Using the "genius approach" to research and development. JUKI management relied on the creative abilities of employees to generate new products. This process did not allow management to predict, with any degree of accuracy and dependability, new improvements and innovations in products and services.

FIGURE 14.1   **Detailed View of the Fork Model**

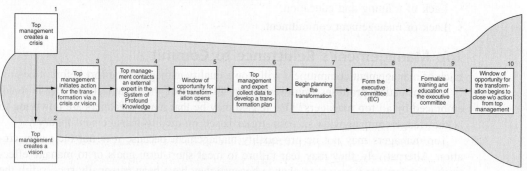

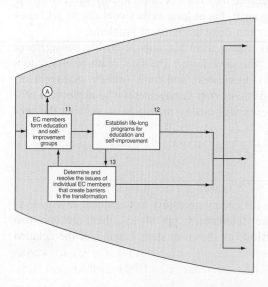

FIGURE 14.1   (concluded)

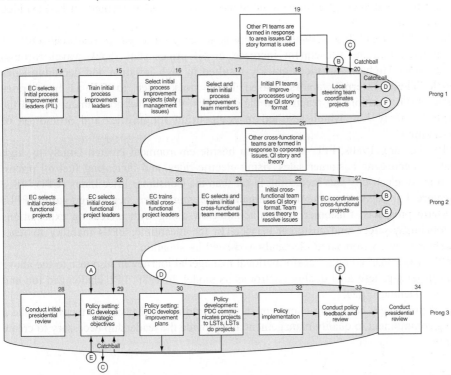

2. Behaving with a "market-out" point of view. JUKI management created an organization in which products were produced and sold without determining the needs of customers.

3. Depending on the skill of individual workers to get the job done. JUKI management relied on the nonreplenishable uniqueness of each individual to get jobs done, as opposed to standardizing work methods through training so that all relevant employees could do a particular job.

4. Acting as firefighters. JUKI employees reacted to crises; they did not proactively improve processes to prevent crises from occurring in the future.

JUKI Corporation embarked on a transformational managerial journey in response to the above crises using Japanese total quality control as its model. In 1976, JUKI challenged for, and won, the **Deming Prize.** The Deming Prize is the quality management equivalent of a black belt in karate. It is awarded by the Japanese Union of Scientists and Engineers (J.U.S.E.).

Florida Power and Light Company

Florida Power and Light Company (FPL) is the largest utility furnishing the generation, transmission, distribution, and sale of electricity in the state of Florida. It experienced steady growth throughout its history. However, the pace of this growth increased dramatically in 1946, making it difficult for FPL's leaders to plan, finance, construct, and operate the utility. As FPL grew, so did its managerial processes, becoming ever more cumbersome and unresponsive to customer needs. Nevertheless, because FPL had been able to maintain stable prices for its customers, it had avoided any potential crises.

In 1974, FPL's ability to control costs was severely curtailed. In that year, OPEC's oil embargo and the subsequent increase in oil prices sent shock waves through the economy. Higher fuel prices quickly resulted in high inflation and declining sales growth. These external factors caused FPL's stock price to fall as bond rates increased. Furthermore, in reaction to the oil crisis, the federal government passed the National Energy Act, which resulted in competition for utilities and promotion of conservation.

"By the early 1980s, FPL was facing a hostile environment created largely by high inflation, decreasing customer sales, rising electric rates, and increasing fuel oil prices. The price of electricity was increasing faster than the Consumer Price Index (CPI)." [See Reference 3, p. 8.] At the same time, competitive pressures were beginning to affect FPL's long-term prospects. Customer dissatisfaction grew along with increasing expectations for reliability, safety, and customer service. In the meantime, FPL's inability to react quickly to new environmental demands worsened its situation.

FPL also embarked on a transformational managerial journey in response to the above crises using Japanese total quality control as its model. In 1989, FPL challenged for, and won, the Deming Prize.

In both of these cases, top management uncovered crises that caused them to make a strong commitment to quality management and provide the leadership necessary to create quality.

Creating a Crisis

Top management can uncover and bring to the forefront the real or potential crises that face an organization, as shown in step 1 of Figure 14.1. One method top management can use to create a crisis is asking a probing question, such as one which Kano has proposed: "What are the quality requirements of our major product/service demanded by our major customers?" Frequently, top management is unable to answer this question, creating a crisis when they realize that they are out of touch with their customers' needs.

Another method by which top management can create a crisis is by conducting a **brainstorming** session on the crises that face the organization and analyzing the results with an **affinity diagram,** two tools that were discussed in Chapter 10. Exhibit 10.1 shows an application of brainstorming to identify the crises facing a university. Exhibit 10.2 shows an application of an affinity diagram to organize and clarify the crises facing a university.

Creating a Vision

Top management can also initiate action for the transformation via a vision, as shown in step 2 of Figure 14.1. A vision can stimulate top management to expend the energy needed to transform an organization. This idea is critical for organizations not facing a crisis: a vision can replace a crisis as a rallying point for the creation of quality.

An example of a vision that drove top management to transform an organization is a situation that occurred in a social service agency. The agency, a group home program for troubled teenagers, was achieving its mission, adequately providing temporary shelter and basic care for adolescents separated from their families. However, the top management of the agency knew, through surveys of clients and referral agents, what the program needed to change to provide other services. These services included individual, group and family therapy, academic counseling, and an overall plan coordinated by the clients, along with social workers, psychologists, house parents, teachers, and other involved staff members.

Top management had a vision of transforming the agency to one in which the needs of the clients were met in a more professional manner, utilizing a team to carry out an integrated plan. There was no crisis that stimulated this transformation. Top management saw a need to change the organization to exceed the clients' needs, which were not being addressed by the program in its current state.

One technique that can be used to create a vision is to imagine the following scenario, in which the developer(s) of the vision personify the organization; that is, pretend the organization is a person.

> Imagine it is 100 years in the future and your organization has just died. All the stakeholders of the organization are standing around the coffin and the clergyman reads the eulogy. The eulogy ends with these words: Here lies *insert the name of your organization,* it was known and loved for *insert the reason here.*

The reason inserted above is the vision of your organization. A vision should be a noble statement of long-term purpose. It should inspire people to take action to transform their organization.

Once top management has established a vision for an organization and its interdependent system of stakeholders, it can utilize brainstorming and the affinity diagram to identify issues that will prohibit realization of the vision. The topic of the brainstorming session can be: "What are the barriers that discourage realization of our vision."

Initiating Action for the Transformation

Top management initiates action for the transformation via a crisis and/or a vision, as shown in step 3 of Figure 14.1. They synthesize, study, and digest the crises facing the organization, as well as formulate and articulate the vision of the organization. If they feel it is warranted, they communicate the information about the crises and/or vision to relevant stakeholders. This process promotes commitment to the transformation among both top management and stakeholders.

Retaining Outside Counsel

After management has communicated the crises and the vision, they may wish to retain outside counsel, as shown in step 4 of Figure 14.1, for two reasons. First, expertise in the **System of Profound Knowledge,** discussed in Chapter 2, is not likely to be found within an organization. Second, organizations frequently cannot recognize their own deficiencies; that is, they do not know what they do not know.

Window of Opportunity Opens

Once outside counsel has been retained, a **window of opportunity** for the transformation opens, as shown in step 5 of Figure 14.1. The window of opportunity has an unspecified time limit, which varies from organization to organization. If signs of transformation do not become obvious to the stakeholders of an organization, they will not believe that top management is serious about transformation, and the window of opportunity for transformation will begin to close. This is a common reason for the failure of quality management efforts in organizations.

Collecting Data to Develop a Transformation Plan

An important role of outside counsel is to help top management assess the current status, and predict the future condition, of relevant stakeholders with respect to the transformation. They determine the barriers against and the aids for a fruitful transformation at all levels within an organization and throughout the organization's interdependent system of stakeholders, as shown in step 6 of Figure 14.1.

Individuals have different reasons for wanting to, or not wanting to, promote quality management. Individuals will have different interpretations of what is involved in quality management. A leader must know each of these reasons, and how the different reasons interact with each other and with the aim of quality management. Consequently, a leader must obtain input from the stakeholders of his or her organization.

A generic **Gantt chart,** discussed in Chapter 10, for a transformation plan is shown in Table 14.1. Top management appoints a team to complete the Gantt chart, asks outside counsel to complete the Gantt chart, or some combination of these two options. The start and stop times in the Gantt chart are a function of top management's urgency to transform to quality management.

Step 6 of Figure 14.1 involves the "Introductory Step," the "Plan the Study" step, and the "Collect Data" step of the Gantt chart in Table 14.1. An explanation of each step appears in the right-most column of the Gantt chart.

Planning the Transformation

Top management develops a transformation plan once the data have been collected in step 6, as shown in step 7 of Figure 14.1. Step 7 involves the "Analyze the Data" step and the "Act on the Analysis" step of the Gantt chart in Table 14.1. Again, an explanation of each step appears in the right-most column of the Gantt chart.

Forming the Executive Committee

Top management forms an **executive committee** (EC) that consists of all policy makers in the organization. The chairman of the EC is the president or chief executive officer of the organization, as shown in step 8 of Figure 14.1. The EC should not exceed five or six members, plus a facilitator. It is important to include only policy makers on the EC.

Training the Executive Committee and Beyond

The EC ensures that all of its members are appropriately trained, as shown in step 9 of Figure 14.1. This training includes: (1) quality management theory—for example, Six Sigma management, discussed in Chapter 20; (2) the psychology of the individual and

TABLE 14.1 Gantt Chart for Conducting "Barriers against" and "Aids for" Analysis

Steps	Month												Comments
	1	2	3	4	5	6	7	8	9	10	11	12	
Introductory Step													
Develop a Gantt chart for the analysis													
Plan the Study													
Identify real and potential crises													See step 1 of the fork model.
Synthesize information about crises													Top management studies and summarizes the real and/or potential crises facing the organization.
Write out real and potential crises													Top management prepares a document that clearly describes the real or potential crises facing the organization.
Prepare a memorandum													Top management prepares a memorandum explaining that a survey will be mailed to all employees which will study "barriers against" and "aids for" quality management. The memorandum contains the following informational items: (1) explanation that the output from the survey will be a series of action plans to deal with employees' concerns about quality management, (2) explanation of the crises facing the organization, (3) information on why quality management can help address the crises, and (4) guarantees concerning the anonymity of respondents.
Design the survey													Team members design a survey that contains an informational section and a questionnaire section. The informational section includes information from the memorandum and instructions on how to complete and submit the survey. The questionnaire section contains the following questions: (1) In your opinion, what barriers will prevent quality management from working in your organization? (2) In your opinion, what aids will promote quality management in your organization?
Prepare a reminder message for nonrespondents													Team members prepare a reminder message for the nonrespondents to the first distribution of the survey. The message should say: If you have already responded to this survey, please disregard this message.

(continued)

TABLE 14.1 (continued)

Steps	Month												Comments
	1	2	3	4	5	6	7	8	9	10	11	12	
Design the data collection plan													Team members design a two-wave mail survey. The reminder message is mailed to the entire mailing list between the first and second waves to encourage nonrespondents to respond to the survey.
Distribute the memorandum													See "Prepare a memorandum" above.
Collect the Data													
Distribute the survey													Team members distribute the survey to all employees. See "Design the survey" above.
Collect the completed surveys													Team members collect the completed surveys and determine the number of nonrespondents.
Plan for nonrespondents													Team members recognize that nonresponse bias exists in a survey if nonrespondents differ from respondents.
Send reminder message													Team members send the reminder message to all persons who received the survey. See "Prepare a reminder message for nonrespondents."
Determine the severity of nonresponse bias													Team members determine if the responses to the second wave of the questionnaire are different from the first wave of the questionnaire. If they are similar, then it is assumed that nonresponse bias is not a severe problem, and first- and second-wave responses are combined and analyzed together. If they are different, then it is assumed that nonresponse bias is a problem and expert counsel should be asked for advice on how to rectify the situation.
Analyze the Data													
Separate the questionnaire data													Team members separate the data from question 1 and question 2. Question 1 yields "barriers against" data and question 2 yields "aids for" data.
Create a code book from the "barriers against" data													Team members create a code book from the "barriers against" data. A code book is used to develop classification categories for verbal statements and to generate a frequency distribution of the number of verbal statements in each category.

TABLE 14.1 (concluded)

Steps					Mon	th							Comments
	1	2	3	4	5	6	7	8	9	10	11	12	
Create a code book from the "aids for" data													Team members create a code book for the "aids for" data.
Identify the root cause code book "barriers against" classification(s)													Team members consider the frequency counts for each classification *and* the effect a particular classification has on all other classifications when selecting the root cause classification(s) for which it is critical to develop action plans.
Identify the root cause code book "aids for" classification(s)													Repeat the above for "aids for" classifications and frequency counts.
Act on the Analysis													
Identify action items for each "barriers against" and "aids for" root cause													Team members determine the detailed action items necessary to resolve root cause "barriers against" quality management and to promote root cause "aids for" quality management.
Assign action items													Team members, with the support of top management, assign action items to individuals or areas using a matrix diagram. The rows of the matrix are action items and the columns of the matrix are people or areas. Team members study the matrix to create logical workloads.
Develop plans for each action item													Responsible individuals or areas develop action plans to resolve "barriers against" quality management and/or to promote "aids for" quality management.
Approve action plans													Top management approves all action plans or calls for their revision.
Initiate action plans													Top management puts each action plan into play in the organization.
Check on the progress of action plans													Team members periodically study the effect of the action plans in resolving "barriers against" quality management and in promoting "aids for" quality management.
Promote the action plans													Top management promotes the action plans to create an environment favorable to quality management.

team [see Reference 6]; (3) basic statistical tools, such as those discussed in Chapters 3 and 5; and (4) administrative systems for quality, including developing competence in daily management, cross-functional management, and policy management, as discussed in Chapters 16, 17, and 18, respectively.

Window of Opportunity Begins to Close

Once the above phase of education and training is complete, the window of opportunity for the transformation begins to close unless the members of the EC take two actions, as shown in step 10 of Figure 14.1. First, they promote the plan to transform the organization, as shown in the last line in the Gantt chart in Table 14.1, from its current management paradigm to a quality management paradigm. Again, the steps to develop and execute the plan are discussed in the right-most column of the Gantt chart in Table 14.1. Second, they diffuse quality management theory and practice within the organization and outside the organization to relevant stakeholders, such as the board of directors, stockholders, suppliers, customers, regulators, and the community.

Diffusion of Quality Management

The **diffusion** step of the model explains how to disseminate quality management among the different areas within an organization and from one organization to another, such as suppliers, subcontractors, and regulators.

It is not always obvious how to achieve this. For example, creating a newsletter or having a meeting for all interested persons is not necessarily the way to reliably diffuse innovations. Other methods are needed. This section discusses such methods for both inter (between) and intra (within) firm diffusion [see Reference 1, pp. 543–559, and Reference 5].

Potential adopters of quality management fall into one of five categories: **innovator, early adopter, early majority, late majority,** and **laggard.** [See Reference 5, pp. 263–265.]

Innovators are venturesome, cosmopolitan, and friendly with a clique of innovators. They possess substantial financial resources and understand complex technical knowledge. However, they may not be respected by the members of their organization. They are considered to be unreliable by their near peers because of their attraction to new things. Innovators are frequently the gatekeepers of new ideas into their organization.

Early adopters are well respected by their peers, opinion leaders, and role models for other members of their organization. They are the embodiment of successful, discrete use of ideas. Early adopters are the key to diffusing ideas such as quality management.

Early majority deliberate for some time before adopting new ideas and interact frequently with their peers. They are not opinion leaders.

Late majority require peer pressure to adopt an innovation. They have limited economic resources that require the removal of uncertainty surrounding an innovation.

Laggards are very isolated in their organization. They are suspicious of innovation and their reference point is in the past.

The successful diffusion of quality management must consider several factors. First, it must involve opinion leaders. The EC identifies opinion leaders by asking: "Who would we go to for advice about quality management within our organization?" They prepare a **motivational plan** to induce opinion leaders to undertake quality management. The motivational plan must have the commitment of the executive committee and should consider a balance of extrinsic and intrinsic motivators. Second, it must provide a quality management process that is adequately developed and not too costly for potential adopters at all levels within the organization. Third, it must develop the learning capacity of potential adopters of quality management. Fourth, it must systematically improve management's understanding of the factors that affect the success and/or failure of quality management and improve their ability to communicate these factors to potential adopters. Finally, it must increase intimacy between potential adopters and the diffusers of quality management.

If the above activities do not occur, or do not occur effectively, then the window of opportunity for the transformation to quality management begins to close. The next step in promoting quality management is for the EC, with the assistance of outside counsel, to focus attention on top management's intellectual and emotional commitment to quality management. This occurs as the members of the EC enter the "neck" of the fork model.

Decision Point

The end of the **handle** is the first critical decision point in the **fork model for quality management.** If the members of the EC discover that the energy to do quality management is not present in the organization, then a "no go" decision is made and all efforts toward quality management stop. On the other hand, if the members of the EC discover that the energy to do quality management is present in the organization, then a "go" decision is made and the quality management effort proceeds to the neck stage of the fork model.

Summary

This chapter presented a discussion of the handle of the fork model for quality management that is presented in this book. The handle is management's commitment to transformation, without which there can be no transformation. Aids to promoting quality management and barriers to it are presented. Lack of management commitment is a barrier that is addressed in this chapter.

Top management's reluctance to commit to quality management arises from managers who are unwilling to acknowledge success stories of quality management, who are not pro-quality because it is not their own creation, who are scared of failure to meet short-term goals or to manage effectively, or who are reluctant to change because they have been personally successful.

There are two sources for the energy needed by top management to transform an organization: a crisis or a vision. Two cases are presented that show how companies responding to crises were stimulated to begin a process of quality management: JUKI (a Japanese manufacturer) and Florida Power and Light Company (an electric utility). If a company is not currently faced with an obvious crisis, top management can uncover and bring to the forefront any hidden crises that exist.

Alternatively, top management can begin the transformation by creating its own vision as a rallying point for the introduction of quality. This is critical for organizations that are not facing a crisis.

After top management makes the commitment to transformation, the first action may be retaining outside counsel, because an expert in the System of Profound Knowledge will not likely be in-house, and the organization frequently cannot recognize its own deficiencies. Outside counsel may help top management determine the "barriers against" and "aids for" transformation, and works with top management to develop a plan for the transformation.

Next, top management forms an executive committee (EC), which consists of all policy makers in the organization. The EC carries out the plan for transformation. Unless the members of the EC exhibit signs of transformation to relevant stakeholders, the window of opportunity for the transformation begins to close.

Questions for self-examination are presented to stimulate thought and discussion in an organization that is contemplating transformation to quality management.

Key Terms

affinity diagram, *548*
brainstorming, *548*
crisis, *545*
Deming Prize, *547*
diffusion, *554*
early adopter, *554*
early majority, *554*

executive committee, *550*
fork model for quality management, *555*
Gantt chart, *550*
handle, *555*
innovator, *554*
laggard, *554*

late majority, *554*
motivational plan, *554*
System of Profound Knowledge, *549*
transformation, *544*
vision, *545*
window of opportunity, *550*

Exercises

14.1. Can quality management succeed without the commitment of top management? Explain why or why not.

14.2. Is it necessary to accept all of the paradigms of quality management to start quality management? What are they?

14.3. Can an organization ease into quality management?

14.4. What are some barriers that hinder the transformation of an organization to quality management?

14.5. What are some aids that promote the transformation of an organization to quality management?

14.6. Does quality management apply to the service aspects of an organization?

14.7. How much training is needed for quality management, by level?

14.8. How much will quality management cost? Is it possible to compute this figure?

14.9. How long will it take to achieve quality management in an organization?

14.10. What is the best time to begin quality management?

14.11. Can one organization's quality management process become the blueprint for another organization's quality management process?

14.12. Is it helpful to visit organizations with successful quality management processes? If yes, why? If no, why?

14.13. How is quality management spread in an organization?

References

1. Karen Cool, Igemar Dierickx, and Gabriel Szulanski, "Diffusion of Innovations Within Organizations: Electronic Switching in the Bell System, 1971–1982," *Organization Science,* 8, No. 5, September/October 1997, pp. 543–559.

2. W. E. Deming (1994), *The New Economics: For Industry, Government, Education,* 2d ed. (Cambridge, MA: M.I.T. Center for Advanced Engineering Studies).

3. FPL corporate document, "Description of Quality Improvement Program QIP-Corporate," December 1988.

4. Noriaki Kano, "A Perspective on Quality Activities in American Firms," *California Management Review,* Spring 1993, pp. 14–15.

5. Everett Rogers (1995), *Diffusion of Innovations,* 4th ed. (New York: The Free Press).

6. P. Scholtes (1988), *The Team Handbook: How to Use Teams to Improve Quality* (Madison, WI: Joiner Associates).

Chapter 15

The Fork Model for Quality Management: The Neck, or Management's Education

Sections

Chapter Objectives

- To examine management concerns about the process of education and self-improvement
- To discuss the role of education, training, and self-improvement groups to identify and resolve barriers to organizational transformation
- To discuss and illustrate how the System of Profound Knowledge impacts transformation
- To illustrate how the quality management expert guides group meetings
- To present several case studies illustrating how top management uses the System of Profound Knowledge to transform their decision-making processes
- To illustrate how workshops can promote understanding of the System of Profound Knowledge

- To examine personal barriers to transformation and illustrate the use of a questionnaire to identify problem areas
- To discuss the attributes of a quality management leader
- To discuss how to make a go or no-go decision

Introduction

Once the top management of an organization commits to transformation, its members enter a period of education and self-improvement, or "the neck" of the detailed fork model for quality management. In this chapter, we explain what top management needs to do to promote and coordinate its education and self-improvement with respect to the organizational transformation.

Management's Fears Concerning Education and Self-Improvement

Education and self-improvement are both exciting and frightening processes. Top managers who have decided to become involved in these processes look forward to and fear them. They are anxious to learn about themselves and the improvement process, but they also have concerns. Some questions they may be pondering are:

- What actually happens in meetings about quality management?
- Will I lose power?
- Will I be embarrassed?
- Will I look stupid?
- Will I "get it"?
- Will I be able to do it?
- Will I have to change my personality?
- Will I be exposed as incompetent?
- Will I have to justify myself to the others?

These fears and questions are a natural reaction to the task that lies ahead for top management. As quality guru Philip Crosby has often noted, "The only one who welcomes change is a wet baby." Education and self-improvement are difficult, soul-searching activities that have a profound effect on the individual and the organization. It takes courage and strength of character to involve oneself in these processes. The guidance of an outside expert and the support of colleagues who share the same concerns will be very valuable during this arduous process.

Education and Self-Improvement Groups

One of the first tasks of the **executive committee,** or EC, described in Chapter 14, is forming one or more **education, training, and self-improvement groups,** as shown in step 11 of the **detailed fork model** in Figure 14.1. The aim of each group is to expand and deepen its understanding of Deming's theory of management.

A group contains between three and six members, and meets frequently (weekly, for example). The areas of concentration are studying the **System of Profound Knowledge,** introduced in Chapter 2, and identifying and resolving personal barriers to transformation. The purpose of these areas of concentration is to transform an individual's or organization's decision-making process from producing "lose-lose" or "win-lose" decisions to generating "win-win" decisions.

Studying the System of Profound Knowledge

The System of Profound Knowledge is discussed by the group, under the tutelage of an expert who creates an environment in which group members deepen their understanding of how the System of Profound Knowledge might affect organizational and personal decision-making. The expert may use group meetings, role-playing, case studies, or workshops to generate the individualized feedback necessary for each top manager so that she can transform personally, and consequently, promote the transformation of the organization.

The purpose of this type of session is not to "mess with" anybody's personal beliefs and values, but rather to make them aware of an alternative system of beliefs, the System of Profound Knowledge, and its potential impact on them and their decision-making processes.

Group Meeting Example

An example of a group meeting in which the concepts of the System of Profound Knowledge are being discussed is presented below. The group consists of the **QM (quality management) expert;** the CEO of the company, Bob; the VP of Sales, Carol; the VP of Production, Ted; and the VP of Quality, Alice.

QM expert:	Last time we were in the middle of a heated debate about **intrinsic** versus **extrinsic motivation.** I'd like to continue that discussion. Carol, you were having a hard time figuring out how you were going to motivate your people without sales incentives.
Carol:	I still am. I've been thinking about it a lot. Some of my people will do a good job, even without the awards, but there are others who need that carrot to get them going.
Ted:	I know what you mean. I feel the same way, except it's worse in Production. If I don't reward them for output, they'll just slack off.
QM expert:	Alice, what are your feelings?
Alice:	I agree with Deming's theory of management, but I'm at a loss as to what can replace our incentives. I understand Carol and Ted's concerns.
QM expert:	Bob, what do you think about what you're hearing?
Bob:	I feel pretty much the same way, but I guess we have to try and look at it differently. We need to address everyone's concerns, and at the same time, we have to be looking for ways to change our system to be more in line with the direction we're going in.
QM expert:	I feel that we're making some progress. Everyone seems open to some more information about alternative action. Last time you weren't as receptive. Let's get into how we can create joy in work at

	your company, without relying on extrinsic rewards. We'll start with each of you telling us what motivates you to do your job. Bob, let's hear from you first.
Bob:	Well, I have to tell you that I enjoy getting my paycheck. (Everyone laughs.) But that's an extrinsic motivator.
QM expert:	I appreciate your honesty, Bob. Nobody expects you to work for no pay. But I'm sure there are other things that make you get up and come to work.
Bob:	Sure—I love what I do. It's a challenge running this company. I have to be on my toes, always thinking, planning, and learning. It's exciting watching my ideas get played out, especially when they work. I like mentoring people, watching them grow and develop. Do you want me to keep going?
QM expert:	Actually, that's enough for now. You've given us a lot to work with. All the motivators that Bob mentioned, aside from his paycheck, of course, were intrinsic. Our task now is to transform the organization so that each and every employee in it can experience the same positive feelings about work that Bob has expressed. What I'd like to do now is some role-playing. Ted, I want you to pretend that you're one of the line workers in your department, Sam, reporting for his shift. Alice, I want you to be Ted.
Ted (as Sam):	Good morning, Mr. Lawrence.
Alice (as Ted):	Hi Sam. No time for chit-chat this morning. We've got to get to work to fill the Dynamic order that just came in.
Ted (as Sam):	That might be a problem. The sorter was giving us a problem yesterday. Unless the night shift took care of it, it's going to have to be down for awhile.
Alice (as Ted):	Why didn't you tell Jim yesterday?
Ted (as Sam):	I tried to see Jim, but he was in a meeting with you the whole afternoon.
QM expert:	Let's stop right there. Ted, what were you experiencing?
Ted:	I was feeling bad and getting angry. First, the guy barely says good morning to me. Then he starts blaming me for something that's not my fault.
Carol:	I think we all do that to the line workers. When we're under pressure, we take everything out on them.
Bob:	When you think about it, why would they want to come to work? No wonder we have such a high absentee rate.
QM expert:	I think we're really onto something here. If we can make working here a more positive experience for all employees, we can begin to create intrinsic motivation for everyone, not just Bob.

The above example demonstrates the role of the QM expert and the desired atmosphere of the group setting. The QM expert is supportive and provides continuity from one meeting to the next. She creates a nonjudgmental atmosphere in which group members are comfortable about expressing themselves. The QM expert includes everyone in the group in discussions and helps the leader become a role model for the others. The expert praises the group for growth and gently pushes the members when they are at an impasse. She then summarizes where the group is going next and identifies the task in relation to the transformation.

Case Studies

Some case studies in which top managers use the System of Profound Knowledge to change their decision-making process are presented below. The QM expert works through selected case studies with each group, depending upon the particular issues and concerns about quality management raised by group members. It will take time and patience for top management to change their paradigms from the traditional set to the set proposed by Deming.

Business Example: The Alcoholic Employee

My name is Chuck. As the manager of a department in my company, I supervise 27 employees. Carl, one of my subordinates, repeatedly comes into work drunk. His behavior causes productivity, safety, and morale problems among his coworkers. Additionally, his behavior affects the customers and suppliers of our department, the Human Resources department, his family and friends, and stockholders.

As part of my job, I try to understand the situation from the perspective of each stakeholder in my department. Whenever possible and appropriate, I talk to each stakeholder about the situation and identify his perspective.

> Situation from Carl's perspective: I'm in a lot of emotional pain. I don't know how to handle my situation. Everybody is on my back.
>
> Situation from coworkers' perspective: We're sorry that Carl developed a drinking problem, but why does the boss let him get away with it? He makes my job more dangerous. He could get me seriously hurt.
>
> Situation from customer's perspective: Carl's output isn't up to standard. He creates a lot of problems for me and for the people further down the line.
>
> Situation from supplier's perspective: My customers are starting to blame me for some of Carl's problems. I wish somebody would deal with Carl.
>
> Situation from HR department's perspective: We recently discovered Carl developed a drinking problem that affects his performance on the job.
>
> Situation from Carl's family's and friends' perspective: We are worried about Carl. He is getting more emotionally distant and physically abusive every day. He needs help. We don't know what to do. We are worried that he will lose his job—then what will happen to us?
>
> Situation from the stockholders' perspective: We want maximum profitability from the company, hopefully in the short term, but definitely in the long term.

Upon careful review of the situation from the perspective of each stakeholder, I conclude that there is no win-win solution, only win-lose or lose-lose solutions. Consequently, I think about the new paradigms presented in Chapters 1 and 2 to create options for resolving the situation such that all stakeholders can "win."

I study the new paradigms and decide that the paradigm "improve the process that creates results, don't just demand results" is an excellent new way to think. In other words, change the company's policies and procedures concerning inappropriate behavior and dealing with the drunk employee. Given this shift in thinking, I develop the following potential win-win solution:

1. Organizational policies and procedures should be continuously studied and improved to decrease the frequency of employees who experience drinking problems. This is accomplished by improving hiring, training, and supervisory practices. This is a long-term solution.

2. The company must work with each employee who has a drinking problem. If he or she cannot resolve the drinking problem in an Employee Assistance Program, the company will help to identify a community program, such as Alcoholics Anonymous. While in the community program, the company will provide benefits, but no compensation. The company will stick by the employee as long as the community program says the employee is working toward a positive resolution of the problem. The employee understands that if he stops making progress in the community program, the company will terminate his employment. This is a short-term solution for the company and the alcoholic employee, and a long-term solution for the company and all other employees who see the company's treatment of its sick employees.

Finally, I check to see if the solution using the new paradigm creates a win-win from the perspective of each stakeholder.

Chuck:	I believe that the solution is a win-win. The company gets a more productive and joyful workforce in the long run, and treats employees with problems in a humane way in the short run. All employees see and understand both the short- and long-run behavior. The company realizes that it will have a superior workforce in the long run and a more secure workforce in the short run.
Carl:	I get help with my drinking problem. I believe that the solution is a win-win. If I can't resolve my drinking problem in an Employee Assistance Program, the company will help me find a community program like Alcoholics Anonymous, which can help me. I understand that if I stop making progress in the eyes of the community program, the company will terminate my employment.
Carl's coworkers:	We believe that the solution is a win-win. We like the policy that the company has adopted for dealing with alcoholic employees. It is great that the company recognizes both their responsibilities and the worker's responsibilities in the policy.
Carl's customers and suppliers:	We believe that the solution is a win-win. We like the policy that the company has adopted for dealing

with alcoholic employees. It is great that the company recognizes both its responsibilities and the worker's responsibilities in the policy.

HR department: We believe that our policy creates a win-win for all stakeholders of the conflict.

Carl's family and friends: We believe that the solution is a win-win. Carl is getting help. The company is doing more that its fair share.

Stockholders: We believe that the solution is a win-win. An environment of employee well-being and concern is created that will yield the maximum return on our assets.

A true win-win solution has been created through adopting a new paradigm of management.

Company policies that deal with an alcoholic employee by providing time-limited substance abuse counseling create a possible wake-up call and consequent "win" for the employee and his or her family and friends. Chuck does not believe counseling creates a "lose" for the employee with the drinking problem. Rather, it creates a needed wake-up call. Moreover, over time the need for posttermination substance abuse counseling will decrease as a result of improved hiring, training, and supervisory processes.

Daily Life Example: The Misbehaving Child

My name is Alice and I am a new mother. Recently, I brought my two-year-old daughter, Lisa, to a restaurant for a nice lunch. I gave Lisa a plastic toy. She briefly chewed the toy and then threw it on the floor with great delight. I picked up the toy, scolded her not to throw it again, and gave her the toy. This scenario repeated itself 12 times over the course of lunch. Both my daughter and I got increasingly frustrated and upset playing this game.

As the decision-maker, I identified the perspective of each stakeholder, as best I could, given the situation.

Alice's perspective: My child is misbehaving. It is embarrassing and I can't enjoy my lunch. Other patrons of the restaurant are looking at me.

Lisa's perspective: I like throwing my toy on the floor, but I don't like mommy yelling at me.

Patrons' perspective: We wish that mother would keep her child quiet.

I realized that a win-win solution did not exist given my current situation. Consequently, I considered the new paradigms for some possible insights. I realized that my method of inspecting my child's behavior was the relevant process in this situation. And yelling at her was just demanding results that she couldn't deliver. So, I decided to change the process that makes results. My solution was to attach the toy with a string to my daughter's blouse. This way, she can throw the toy, but I don't have to pick it up. This process improvement clearly created a win-win for all stakeholders of the situation. I win because I can enjoy lunch. My daughter wins because she can throw her toy. The patrons win because they can enjoy a nice, quiet lunch.

Business Example: The Lean Organization

My name is Jan. I am a midlevel manager in my organization. The employees in my department are exhibiting signs of low morale. One of my responsibilities is to keep morale high to promote a productive workforce. I am frustrated because there are few promotion slots and little money for pay raises that I can use to motivate my people. I don't know what to do other than to offer a kind word whenever possible.

I identified the other stakeholders of the situation. They are: my boss, my employees, suppliers to my department, and customers of my department. I spoke with each stakeholder to identify their perspectives on the situation at hand.

My boss's perspective: One of the MBOs I set for my staff managers was to keep morale high in their departments. I said I would measure morale by comparing the average number of sick days per employee this year over last year. If the ratio is greater than 1.0 for one of my staff members, there may be a problem.

My employees' perspective: Our manager is always pushing us for more productivity, but he never gives us more pay or bonuses. He always wants something for nothing. He never shares the company's wealth with us.

My suppliers' perspective: Our customer (*my department*) is always trying to blame us for their quality problems. Why don't they clean up their act before they start blaming everyone else?

My customers' perspective: The subcomponents we receive from our supplier (*my department*) have an unacceptably high proportion of defective parts. Also, the subcomponents frequently do not arrive on time.

Clearly, a win-win solution does not exist in the current situation. Consequently, I considered the new paradigms. I believe that promoting a balance of extrinsic and intrinsic motivation, as opposed to only extrinsic motivation, can be used to develop a win-win solution for all stakeholders. I decide that through **empowerment** (the **SDSA** and **PDSA cycles**), I will create an environment that will promote a workplace in which employees can release their intrinsic motivation. I understand that each worker is simultaneously stimulated by intrinsic and extrinsic motivation. I recognize the constraints placed on my ability to manage as a result of limited extrinsic rewards. However, I am aware that I can create for my subordinates a work environment conducive to the release of their intrinsic motivation. I actively promote the empowerment process in my department.

Finally, I check with all stakeholders to determine if a win-win solution has been developed from their perspective.

Jan:	I win because I am doing a great job; my employees' morale is high.
Jan's boss:	My employees win because they experience joy in work and pride in the outcome.
My employees:	We win because we enjoy our work.
My suppliers and customers:	We win because we are working with a great partner.

A win-win situation has been created among the stakeholders of the original situation. As corporate conditions improve, top management should review its package of extrinsic motivators and consider options such as profit-sharing.

Daily Life Example: The Competitive Husband

My name is Martin. I have always enjoyed sports and am a very competitive person. I apply my competitive nature to all aspects of my life. My marriage is in trouble. My wife and I wife fight all the time. I don't like to lose arguments with my wife, or anybody else for that matter.

I tried to identify the problems in our marriage from my wife's perspective. She also thinks that our marriage is not doing well. She thinks I am too stubborn.

Clearly, my wife and I are deeply involved in a lose-lose situation. We can't think of anything to do to save our marriage. Consequently, we consider the new paradigms. We decide that we must start cooperating, instead of competing.

We agree to cooperate to find solutions to frequently occurring problems that create a win for both. Now, we keep a diary of arguments with each other and make a **bar chart** of the frequency of each type of argument. We select the most frequently occurring argument and **brainstorm** ways to eliminate it from our lives to create a win-win solution for both of us. Our marriage has been getting better over time. We both look forward to an improved relationship and future.

Business Example: The Profit Center

My name is Michael. I am the chief operating officer of my organization. My company has five mills. I want to maximize the profitability of each mill. Nobody talks about it, but it seems that mill managers sometimes sabotage each other's profitability by demanding resources that could better be used elsewhere. An analysis shows considerable variation in mill manager rankings based on mill profitability. It seems to rotate, year to year.

The situation from the perspective of my mill managers seems to be that each one wants to be the number one mill in profitability, to get the largest bonus. Unfortunately, they will not share improved methods with each other. I cannot figure out how to get them to cooperate to maximize overall profitability for the company. Consequently, I consider the new paradigms.

I decide that the problem may be that I am promoting optimization of the component parts of the system, not optimization of the entire system, through my compensation plan. I work with the mill managers to develop a compensation plan that is connected to the overall profitability of the organization, via profit-sharing, as opposed to mill profitability.

Over time, my mill managers become a unified team. It is in each mill manager's best interests to help his fellow mill managers improve their operations. If a "star" mill manager is unhappy with the new paradigm, then the organization helps him find employment in a traditional organization where his specific talents will be appreciated and rewarded. The entire top management team agrees that the new compensation creates a win-win for all stakeholders of the organization.

Workshops

Two examples of workshops that promote understanding of the System of Profound Knowledge are presented below. The first involves each member of the executive committee individually preparing an executive summary explaining the System of Profound Knowledge. The second involves the entire membership of the executive committee jointly developing a matrix explaining the relationships between the components of the

System of Profound Knowledge and the **14 points for management,** discussed in Chapter 2.

Recall from Chapter 2 that the assumptions underlying the System of Profound Knowledge are:

- Manage to improve the process that creates results
- Manage using a balance of intrinsic and extrinsic motivation
- Manage to promote cooperative efforts
- Manage to optimize the entire organization

Also recall some of the salient points of the components of the System of Profound Knowledge:

- **Systems theory** involves defining a system, understanding who is responsible for stating the aim of the system, understanding the interdependence among the components of the system, and appreciating the need to optimize the entire system.
- The **theory of variation** involves understanding special and common causes of variation and knowing who is responsible for the resolution of each type of variation, understanding the meaning of stability and capability with respect to a process, and knowing when you can predict a process's future output.
- The **theory of knowledge** involves understanding how to acquire process knowledge, understanding that management is prediction, knowing how to develop operational definitions, and knowing why copying success can lead to disaster.
- **Psychology** involves understanding: (1) people and the interaction between people and circumstances; (2) that people learn in different ways, and at different speeds; and (3) intrinsic and extrinsic motivation.

Workshop 1

In the first workshop, the members of the executive committee individually prepare an executive summary for the QM expert explaining the System of Profound Knowledge in lay terms. The QM expert critiques each executive summary and returns it to its author. This process is repeated as many times as is necessary for each member of the EC to exhibit understanding of the System of Profound Knowledge, in the opinion of the QM expert.

The executive summary should contain: (1) an introduction; (2) an explanation of the purpose of the System of Profound Knowledge; (3) a description of each of the underlying assumptions of the System of Profound Knowledge, with an example of each assumption; and (4) an explanation of each component of the System of Profound Knowledge, with examples of each relevant point.

Workshop 2

The second workshop requires that the entire executive committee prepare a matrix explaining the interrelationships between the four components of the System of Profound Knowledge and the 14 points for management. The rows of the matrix are the 14 points and the columns of the matrix are the four components of the System of Profound Knowledge. Each cell explains how a particular point (of the 14 points) emanates from a particular component of Profound Knowledge. For example, part of the interrelationship between systems theory and Point 1 (Create constancy of purpose toward improvement of product and service, with the aim to become competitive and to stay in business and to provide jobs) is that: "An organization must have an aim stated by its management." Another example of an interrelationship is between the theory of variation and Point 1: "Management must work to reduce person-to-person variation of the understanding of the organizational aim."

In this workshop, the entire executive committee prepares a matrix for the QM expert. The QM expert critiques the matrix and returns it to the members of the executive committee. This process is repeated as many times as is necessary for the members of the executive committee to attain understanding of the System of Profound Knowledge, in the opinion of the QM expert.

Establishing Life-Long Programs for Education and Self-Improvement

The period of education and self-improvement should be extended indefinitely into the future, as shown in step 12 in Figure 14.1. An outside consultant may be instrumental in developing an individualized plan of study for each member of the executive committee.

Identifying and Resolving Personal Barriers to Transformation

Each member of the EC should identify and resolve any issues that create barriers to the transformation, as shown in step 13 of Figure 14.1. Examples of individual barriers to the transformation are the following beliefs:

- Extrinsic motivators bring out the best in people.
- Focusing on results yields improvement of results.
- Firefighting will improve an organization in the long term.
- Effective decisions can be made using guesswork and opinion.
- Rational decision-making can be performed using only visible figures.
- Quantity is inversely related to quality.
- Your most important customer is your superior.
- Management's function is to construct, execute, and control plans.
- Competition is superior to cooperation, and winners and losers are necessary in any interaction.

Each member of the EC examines his or her own opinions on the above beliefs or others that would impede the transformation. The QM expert can use the following questionnaire to pinpoint problem areas that individuals may be experiencing. [See Reference 4.]

Directions:

1. On pages 569 and 570 is a list of managerial traits (labeled A through J) that have been placed on a 0–10 scale.
2. Place an X on each scale to indicate the degree to which you exhibit a particular trait in your daily management style.
3. Remember, there are no right or wrong answers.

A. With respect to employees, I believe in:

1	2	3	4	5	6	7	8	9	10

Fostering motivation through rewards and punishment

Neutral

Fostering motivation through pride and satisfaction in work

B. With respect to employees, I believe in:

1	2	3	4	5	6	7	8	9	10

Managing for the short term using daily production reports and/or quarterly measures of profit

Neutral

Managing for the long term by expanding the market for all

C. In making any organizational decision, I believe in:

1	2	3	4	5	6	7	8	9	10

Focusing on the result of a process with an emphasis on numerical goals and quotas

Neutral

Focusing on the process to get results with an emphasis on improvement and innovation

D. I believe in:

1	2	3	4	5	6	7	8	9	10

Managing with a traditional hierarchical organizational chart

Neutral

Managing with an emphasis on customer-supplier relationships

E. For the success of my organization, I believe that:

1	2	3	4	5	6	7	8	9	10

Optimizing my own situation or competition is most important

Neutral

Optimizing the system of interdependent components or cooperation is most important

F. With respect to employees, I believe in:

1	2	3	4	5	6	7	8	9	10

Managing by formal appraisal process

Neutral

Managing through informal feedback and coaching

G. I believe in:

1	2	3	4	5	6	7	8	9	10

Basing decisions on visible figures such as ROI calculations

Neutral

Basing decisions on operational definitions, visible figures, and considering the effect of invisible figures

H. I believe that:

1	2	3	4	5	6	7	8	9	10

Management cannot be responsible for all components of an organization

Neutral

Management is responsible for all components of an organization

I. I believe that:

1	2	3	4	5	6	7	8	9	10

Management's job is planning, organizing, directing, and evaluating	Neutral	Management's job is prediction through understanding the capability of processes and people as well as the interaction between them

J. I believe that:

1	2	3	4	5	6	7	8	9	10

Managers should not necessarily be leaders	Neutral	Managers should be leaders

A leader who manages in accordance with Deming's theory of management will have a score of 10 on each of the above questions and a total score of 100 points. The closer a manager's score is to 1 for a given question, the less the manager leads in accordance with the System of Profound Knowledge. A QM expert can use a manager's scores on these questions to pinpoint the elements of the System of Profound Knowledge that a manager is having difficulty internalizing.

After identifying the specific areas in need of attention, the expert and individual manager meet to discuss why holding a particular belief is detrimental to transformation. In-depth, private sessions may be necessary to understand the "whys" and "ramifications" of and "alternatives" to the above beliefs. The behaviors that these beliefs promote are also discussed, and ways of changing both attitudes and behaviors are suggested.

Identifying and resolving personal barriers is one of the most important areas in the transformation of an organization because it addresses the root cause of the most common reason for failure: lack of commitment on the part of top management. The following section presents an example of a private session between the QM expert and Bob, the CEO of The Universal Company.

QM expert: I wanted to meet with you individually because I sensed an area that you're not entirely comfortable with.

Bob: Let's get something out in the open. What is it?

QM expert: Promoting cooperation instead of competition.

Bob: (Thinks for a moment.) You're pretty sharp.

QM expert: That's what you pay me for. Anyway, it's an area that a lot of top guys have trouble with. After all, you got where you are by being the best you can and beating out other people. It follows that you want to keep competing, and encourage your people to do the same.

Bob: I guess.

QM expert: When you were in high school did you play a sport?

Bob: Yeah, football.

QM expert:	Did you play varsity?
Bob:	No, and I was miserable about it. I really wanted that letter, but the coach wouldn't put me on the team.
QM expert:	So you remember how it felt?
Bob:	Like it was yesterday. I hated it.
QM expert:	What did you hate?
Bob:	I was trying as hard as the guys who made the team. And I'm not so sure the guys on the team were better than I was.
QM expert:	Exactly—that's Deming's point. Competition doesn't help anybody improve. It just creates winners and losers. Do you think you're creating this kind of situation anywhere for our people?
Bob:	I guess I am. We have an "Employee of the Month" contest. Only one person wins. I'm sure there are others who deserve to win, too. Their morale probably hits the floor when they don't win.
QM expert:	I'm sure you're right. Now that you understand the downside of competition at a gut level, I know we'll be able to work on improvement in this area.
Bob:	Thanks for the feedback. I don't think I would have come to this by myself.
QM expert:	That's what I'm here for. I'm glad I could help.

The Quality Management Leader

Top management's education and self-improvement include group and individual study of the System of Profound Knowledge and the identification and resolution of personal barriers to transformation. Guided by an expert, the quality management leader will develop a management style to incorporate the attributes necessary to lead the organization. [See Reference 2, pp. 125–128.] The quality management leader should possess the following characteristics:

1. A leader sees the organization as a system of interrelated components, each with an aim, but all focused collectively to support the aim of the system of interdependent stakeholders. This type of focus may require suboptimization of some components of the system.

2. A leader tries to create for everybody interest and challenge, joy in work, and pride in the outcome. She tries to optimize the education, skills, and abilities of everyone, and helps everyone to improve. Improvement and innovation are the aim. [See Reference 2, p. 125.]

3. A leader coaches and trains, and does not judge and punish. [See Reference 2, p. 126.] She creates security, trust, freedom, and innovation. A leader is aware that creation of trust requires that she take a risk. [See Reference 1.] A leader is an active listener and does not pass judgement on those to whom she listens.

4. A leader has formal power, power from knowledge, and power from personality. A leader develops and utilizes the power from knowledge and personality when

operating in an existing paradigm of management. However, a leader may have to resort to the use of formal power when shifting from one paradigm of management to another.

5. A leader uses plots of points and statistical calculation with knowledge of variation to try to understand both the leader's performance and that of her people. A leader is someone who knows when people are experiencing problems that make their performance fall outside of the system and treats the problems as special causes of variation. These problems could be common-cause to the individual (long-term alcoholic) but special-cause to the system (alcoholic works differently from his peers).

6. A leader understands the benefits of cooperation and the losses from competition. [See Reference 2, p. 128, and Reference 3.]

7. A leader does not expect perfection.

8. A leader understands that experience without theory does not facilitate prediction of future events. For example, a leader cannot predict how a person will do in a new job solely on the basis of experience in the old job. A leader has a theory to predict how an individual will perform in a new job.

9. A leader is able to predict the future to plan the actions necessary to pursue the organization's aim. Rational prediction of future events requires that the leader continuously work to create stable processes with low variation.

A manager who does not possess the above attributes will have problems with the transformation. Again, it may be necessary to arrange for private sessions between some members of the EC and an expert in Deming's theory of management to discuss in depth, and confidentially, the "whys" and "ramifications" of the above attributes. As with beliefs, this step may be critical to a successful transformation because it goes to the root cause of the most common reason for failing to transform an organization: lack of commitment on the part of top management.

The Decision Point

Once the **neck** phase is well under way, the members of the EC face their last critical decision point in the fork model. If the members of the EC discover that they cannot overcome their difficulties with Deming-based quality management, then a no-go decision is made and all efforts toward Deming-style quality management stop. On the other hand, if the members of the EC discover that they have overcome their difficulties with Deming-based quality management, then a go decision is made and the quality management effort proceeds to the prongs of the fork model. These prongs begin with:

1. Selecting initial process improvement leaders in the departments, as shown in step 14 of Figure 14.1.

2. Selecting initial cross-functional process improvement projects to address issues concerning transformation that span departments within the organization, as shown in step 21 of Figure 14.1.

3. Conducting an initial presidential review of the policy of the organization, as shown in step 28 of Figure 14.1.

Summary

This chapter presented a discussion of the neck of the fork model, management's education and self-improvement. After top management of an organization commits to transformation, its members enter a period of education and self-improvement. These are difficult, soul-searching activities that have a profound effect on the individual and the organization.

One of the first tasks of the executive committee (EC) is forming one or more education, training, and self-improvement groups that concentrate on studying the System of Profound Knowledge and identifying and resolving personal barriers to transformation.

The System of Profound Knowledge is often discussed by the executive committee under the guidance of a quality management expert. The expert creates an environment in which group members deepen their understanding of how the System of Profound Knowledge might affect organizational and personal decision-making. The chapter provided an example of a group session, in dialogue form, to illustrate the role of the QM expert and the desired atmosphere of the group setting. Several case studies and workshops were presented that can be used by group members to deepen their understanding of the System of Profound Knowledge.

Another area that is important in management's education and self-improvement is identifying and resolving personal barriers to transformation. Each member of the EC examines her opinions to determine if she holds any beliefs that would be detrimental to the transformation. The QM expert can use a questionnaire to help pinpoint problem areas that individuals may be experiencing. Identifying and resolving personal barriers is one of the most important areas in the transformation because it addresses the root cause of the most common reason for failure: lack of commitment on the part of top management. In-depth, private sessions, as illustrated, may be necessary between the QM expert and an individual manager.

Characteristics of the quality management leaders were discussed. These attributes are necessary if the leader hopes to transform an organization. Guided by an expert, the leader will develop these traits through the use of the methods presented in this chapter.

Key Terms

14 points for management, *567*

bar chart, *566*

brainstorm, *566*

detailed fork model, *559*

education, training, and self-improvement groups, *559*

empowerment, *565*

executive committee, *559*

extrinsic motivation, *560*

intrinsic motivation, *560*

neck, *572*

PDSA cycle, *565*

psychology, *567*

QM (quality management) expert, *560*

SDSA cycle, *565*

System of Profound Knowledge, *560*

systems theory, *567*

theory of knowledge, *567*

theory of variation, *567*

Exercises

15.1. Discuss management's fears and concerns over an organizational transformation from the current management paradigm to a quality management paradigm. Which of the concerns do you think are the most problematic? Why?

15.2. Give an example of a win-lose or lose-lose situation that is converted into a win-win situation. What are the benefits of achieving this?

15.3. Personally answer the questionnaire in "Identifying and Resolving Personal Barriers to Transformation." What is your total score? In which areas do you differ from a Deming-type manager? Discuss the significance of your findings.

References

1. Carlisle and Parker (1989), *Beyond Negotiation* (New York: John Wiley & Sons).

2. W. E. Deming (1994), *The New Economics: For Industry, Government, Education,* 2nd ed. (Cambridge, MA: M.I.T. Center for Advanced Engineering Studies).

3. Alfie Kohn (1986), *No Contest* (New York: Houghton Mifflin).

4. L. McNary (May 1993), *The Deming Management Theory: A Managerial Leadership Profile for the New Economic Age,* doctoral dissertation (Albuquerque, NM: University of New Mexico). On microfilm with the University of Michigan, Ann Arbor.

16

The Fork Model for Quality Management: Prong 1, or Daily Management

Sections

Chapter Objectives

- To describe the selection of process improvement leaders (PILs), initial projects, and initial project teams
- To define daily management, or the methods for managing daily work
- To describe and discuss function deployment and the development of an integrated flowchart to determine the existence of non-value-added steps, if any, in a function
- To discuss the development of results-oriented and process-oriented key indicators to monitor a best-practice method
- To discuss the improvement and innovation of an existing process by the use of data-based decision-making tools, the use of change concepts, and the use of benchmarking
- To illustrate daily management by means of personal and business case studies
- To describe the process of management review of daily management projects
- To discuss the role of empowerment in successful daily management
- To discuss the development of local steering teams to coordinate daily management projects at the departmental level

Introduction

In this chapter, we explain what is required to develop, standardize, deploy, maintain, improve, and innovate the methods required for daily work in all areas of an organization. Daily work is managed through "daily management," Prong 1 of the model presented in this section of the book.

When top management is ready to begin the organizational transformation, it needs concrete ways of translating theory into practice. Daily management is one of the vehicles used to accomplish this task.

Selecting Initial Project Teams

The members of the **executive committee (EC)** select initial **process improvement leaders (PILs)** in departments of the organization, as shown in step 14 of the detailed fork model in Figure 14.1. PILs can be assigned full-time or part-time. The decision to have only full-time PILs, only part-time PILs, or both types of PILs depends on the needs of project teams.

Early in a transformation, an organization may need a greater proportion of full-time PILs; as the transformation proceeds, a smaller proportion of full-time PILs may suffice. The change in the need for full-time PILs is generally due to an increase in the general level of quality knowledge in the organization and, consequently, a decrease in the need for the aid provided to project teams by full-time PILs.

PILs receive training in basic quality control tools as covered in previous chapters, and in the psychology of the individual and the team [see Reference 8], as shown in step 15 of the detailed fork model in Figure 14.1.

Next, the members of the EC select the initial projects to be addressed by project teams, as shown in step 16 of Figure 14.1. Once the PILs and the projects have been determined, the members of the EC, in consultation with the PILs, select the members of each initial project team, as shown in step 17 of Figure 14.1. Project teams are formed with a specific purpose, consist of people from the same area or small unit, and exist in perpetuity. All project team members receive training in basic quality control tools and the psychology of the individual and the team, as shown in step 17 of Figure 14.1.

Performing Daily Management

After training, each initial project team works on one or more methods through **daily management,** as shown in step 18 of Figure 14.1. Daily management, or **Prong 1** of the detailed fork model, is developing, standardizing, deploying, maintaining, improving, and innovating the methods required for daily work. The development, standardization, and deployment of methods for **daily work** is called **housekeeping** [see Reference 3, pp. 158–159] because "it is a procedure which sets things in order."[1] The maintenance, improvement, and innovation of methods for daily work are called daily management.

---

[1] Quotation from Louis Schultz, Process Management International, Minneapolis, MN, 1990.

Note that daily management is used in two different contexts in this section: first, it describes developing, standardizing, deploying, maintaining, improving, and innovating the methods required for daily work, and second, it describes only the maintenance, improvement, and innovation of methods for daily work.

Housekeeping

The housekeeping functions of daily management are developed through a procedure called **function deployment** [see Reference 6, pp. 55–61], which requires that relevant employees determine what functions are required to perform each method needed in their daily work. Each function is subject to the scrutiny of the following questions:

1. *Why* is this function required?
2. *What* is this function intended to achieve? *What* is the aim of this function?
3. *What* resources are necessary for this function?
4. *What* target must be set to allocate appropriate resources to this function to optimize the aim of the organization?
5. *Where* in the process should this function take place?
6. *When* should this function be implemented?
7. *Who* is responsible for this function?
8. *How* does this function contribute to the optimization of the system of interdependent stakeholders for the organization?
9. *What* measurements are used to monitor this function?
10. *How* will this function be carried out?
11. *Does* this function contain non-value-added steps?

Housekeeping is practiced through the **SDSA cycle** and its four stages. The Standardize stage involves teaching employees how to study and understand the causal factors that affect each critical method they work with, using flowcharts. The employees developing the **best-practice method** use the flowchart to highlight non-value-added steps, and work toward eliminating them. Employees can also use other tools to understand the causal systems that affect their methods, such as **cause-and-effect diagrams, interrelationship diagrams,** and **simulations.** All the employees who use a particular method compare notes on causal factors and develop one best-practice method, as seen through a **best-practice flowchart.**

At this stage, question 11 can be addressed by using an **integrated flowchart.** This type of flowchart adds at least one dimension to a typical flowchart. An example of an integrated flowchart with an extra dimension to highlight non-value-added steps in a process is shown in Figure 16.1. The non-value-added steps are shaded in gray.

An integral part of preparing a best-practice method is developing **key indicators** to monitor the best-practice method. Key indicators can yield data that are measurable or nonmeasurable. Nonmeasurable data, also called unknown and unknowable data [see Reference 1, pp. 121–122], frequently include the most important business figures, such as the cost of an unhappy customer or the benefits of a proud employee. It is not accurate to assume that if a process cannot be measured, it cannot be managed. Nonmeasurable data, like interactions with other people, are managed on an ongoing basis.

FIGURE 16.1 **Integrated Flowchart Showing Value-Added and Non-Valued-Added Steps**

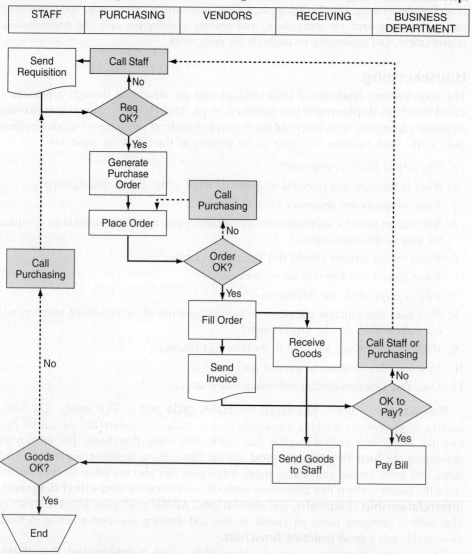

Legend: Non-value-added steps are shown in gray.
Adapted from: PQ Systems, *Total Quality Transformation* (Miamisburg, OH).

The Do stage entails a project team conducting a **planned experiment** to collect measurements on key indicators for determining the optimal configuration of the best-practice method on a trial basis. The Study stage consists of project team members studying the measurements on the key indicators for determining the effectiveness of the best-practice method. The Act stage involves the establishment of a standardized best-practice method, using a best-practice flowchart. This is then formalized by training all relevant employees in the best-practice method and by updating **training manuals.**

A best-practice method can be quite complex, taking into account a great number of contingencies. For example, if a customer has complaint A, follow method A; however, if a customer has complaint B; follow method B; and so on. Or, if a customer has complaint A and claims it is urgent, follow method A1; however, if a customer has complaint A and places no urgency on the matter, follow method A2.

Measurements on Key Indicators

Best-practice methods are monitored through measurements taken on key indicators. Key indicators possess two important characteristics that make them useful in a system of quality management: first, they are **operationally defined,** which promotes communication between people, as discussed in Chapter 4; and second, they monitor results and the processes that generate results.

Key indicators are either results-oriented or process-oriented. **Results-oriented key indicators,** called **R criteria,** are used to evaluate the results of a method. They are called **control points** or **check points. Process-oriented key indicators,** called **P criteria,** are used to evaluate a method that creates results. They are called **control items** or **check items.** As Imai points out, "P criteria call for a long-term outlook, since they are directed at people's efforts and often require behavioral change. On the other hand, R criteria are more direct and short term." [See Reference 3, p. 18]. Figure 16.2 depicts the relationship between P criteria and R criteria.

The relationship between control points and control items is shown in the following example. Safety is a control item (P criteria), while the number of injuries per 100 employees per month is a control point (R criteria).

The relationship between manager and subordinate can be defined in terms of control items and control points. A control item for a manager (e.g., safety) is measured or evaluated at a control point by a subordinate (e.g., number of injuries per 100 employees per month). In this way, an interlocking set of R and P key indicators are developed throughout an organization.

Daily Management

After a best-practice method has been developed and deployed by a project team, housekeeping activities give way to daily management activities. Daily management is used to determine the actions necessary for a project team to maintain, improve, or

FIGURE 16.2
Relationship Between P and R Criteria

Modified from Masaaki Imai (1986), *Kaizen: The Key to Japan's Competitive Success* (New York: Random House), p. 18.

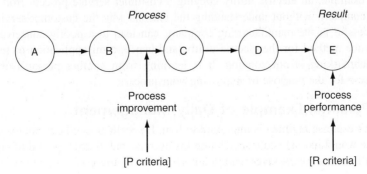

innovate methods. Daily management is performed to decrease the difference between process (actual) performance and customer requirements. A process with a large variance not centered on a desired customer requirement creates a problematic difference between process performance and customer needs. Daily management is needed to reduce process variation and center the process on **nominal,** or the desired customer requirement.

Daily management is accomplished by using the **PDSA cycle** and its four stages. In the Plan stage, a plan is developed to improve or innovate a standardized best-practice method. The plan can take the form of a modified best-practice flowchart.

Ideas for improvement or innovation of a process come from study of the causal factors that affect it. There are many tools that can be used to help employees understand causal factors, falling into three categories. The first category includes data-based decision-making tools such as **check sheets, Pareto diagrams, histograms, run charts, control charts,** and **scatter diagrams.** The second category includes proven change concepts [see Reference 5, pp. 295–359], such as incorporating technology into the process, shifting demand patterns to off-peak times in a process, reducing controls in a process, performing tasks in parallel in a process, conducting training in a process and outsourcing steps of a process. The third category is **benchmarking.** All three categories assist an individual or team doing daily management to modify the existing best-practice flowchart to a revised best-practice flowchart.

The plan is monitored by taking measurements on key indicators on a small-scale or trial basis, and tested through a planned experiment by project team members in the Do stage. In the Study stage, the effects of the plan are studied by examining measurements on key indicators, and in the Act stage, appropriate corrective actions are taken. These corrective actions can lead to a new or modified plan, or are formalized through training all relevant employees and updating training manuals. The PDSA cycle continues indefinitely in an uphill progression of never-ending improvement.

With respect to benchmarking, it is important to note that the success of another person or organization is not a rational basis for turning the PDSA cycle. For example, isolating one component of System A and expecting it to work within the context of System B is not necessarily valid; the reasons for the success in System A may not be present in System B. Therefore, imitating without a true understanding of the conditions or causal factors surrounding the imitated system can lead to misapplication of the PDSA cycle. For example, an electric utility copying a customer service process from a manufacturing company, without understanding the reasons why the customer service process was successful in the manufacturing company, can lead to a poorly conceived revised best-practice method for the electric utility, and hence, a misapplication of the PDSA cycle. Benchmarking is not copying. It is learning from another person's or organization's process for the purpose of improving your process.

A Personal Example of Daily Management

Bart's exercise regimen is important to him. He realizes that he is not exercising as much as he would like. He collects data on his exercise habits for a period of eight weeks. The data from his initial investigation are shown in Figure 16.3.

FIGURE 16.3
Initial Analysis of Exercise Habits

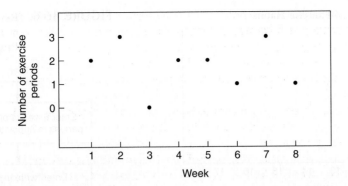

Analysis of the data leads Bart to question his method for "making exercise happen." He realizes that he has no method, so he develops the flowchart shown in Figure 16.4.

Bart discusses his exercise method with his physician during week 9 of his exercise process. His physician states, on the basis of medical facts, that Bart should exercise for 40 minutes at least three times per week. Thus, he establishes a target of three exercise periods per week. The measurement for this method is the number of 40-minute exercise periods per week. Bart records the number of 40-minute exercise periods per week, shown in Figure 16.5.

FIGURE 16.4
Flowchart of Exercise Program

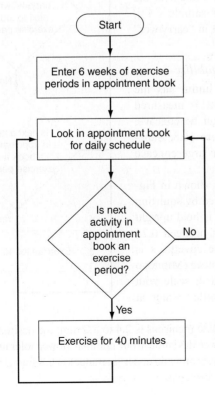

The record shows that the target of three exercise periods per week is achieved for weeks 10 through 15, but not in weeks 16 and 17. This leads Bart to go back and examine his method. In so doing, he discovers that the reason he failed to exercise three times in weeks 16 and 17 was that he simply forgot during those weeks. He realizes that his exercise method has to be changed to prevent this from happening in the future. He revises his method to add in a notation to "write in more exercise periods" after his last noted exercise period. This revision is shown in Figure 16.6.

Bart collected more data and consistently met his target for weeks 18 through 28, as shown in Figure 16.7.

A Business Example of Daily Management

In the following business example [see Reference 4, pp. 603–614], we see how daily management and the PDSA cycle work in a business setting.

Cold gas plasma treatment consists of exciting gas molecules to strip and recombine the electrons in the surface of a polymer. By varying the conditions of cold gas plasma treatment, it is possible

FIGURE 16.5 **Analysis of Exercise Habits**

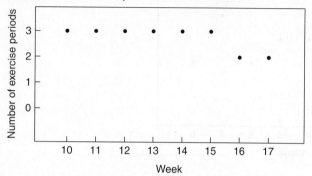

FIGURE 16.6 **Revised Flowchart of Exercise Program**

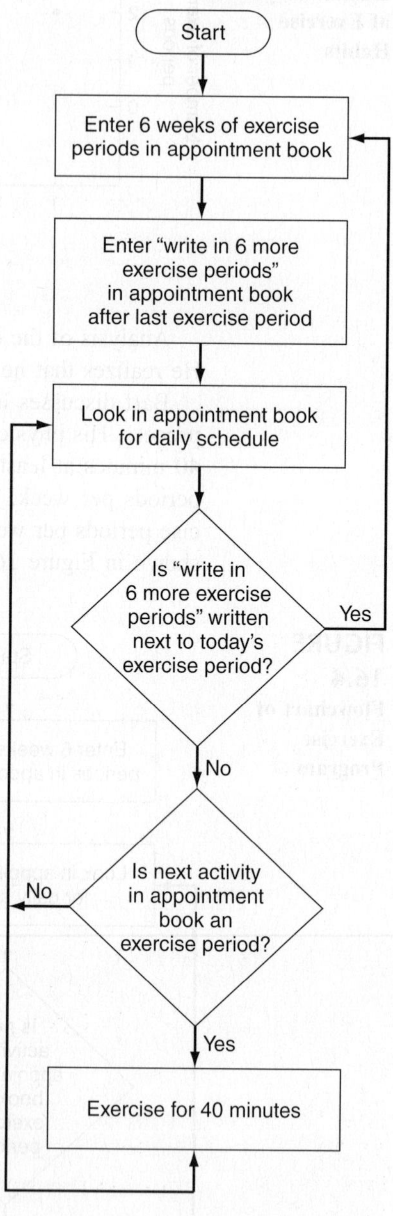

to obtain a particular effect on the surface of a polymer, such as superior bonding, printing, potting, or wetting.

Cuvettes are molded plastic containers used to hold a sample for analysis. In this study, cold gas plasma treatment is used to improve the wettability of the surface of cuvettes, allowing for accurate analysis of the sample. Poor wettability causes material from sample i to remain in the cuvette after the introduction of sample i + j, where j = 1 to m. This can result in "carryover" error.

Operational Definition of Wettability

A surface is wettable when a liquid has the ability to spread on it. Wettability is measured by meniscus size; a meniscus can be concave, convex, or flat, as shown in Figure 16.8. Superior wettability is exhibited by a large concave meniscus.

Measurement of a meniscus is shown in Figure 16.9. The distance x is obtained by squirting distilled water into a cuvette that is held upright at eye level such that point A is between 0.25 and 0.50 in from the base of the cuvette. x is measured by using an optical eyepiece (Mitutoyo 183 or equivalent) with a millimeter scale with gradations of 0.10 mm and distilled water at room temperature (72 ± 10°F).

The specification for an acceptable meniscus is 2.4 to 3.2 mm; the desired level, or nominal, is 2.4 mm, the acceptable lower deviation from nominal (lower tolerance) is 0.0 mm, and acceptable upper deviation from nominal (upper tolerance) is 0.8 mm. That is, a meniscus below 2.4 or over 3.2 is not acceptable.

FIGURE
16.7
**Continuing
Record of
Exercise**

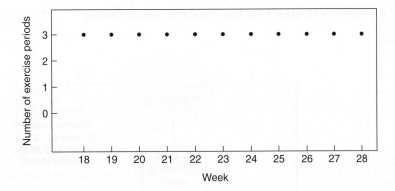

FIGURE
16.7
**Continuing
Record of
Exercise**

FIGURE
16.8
**Illustration of
Meniscus**

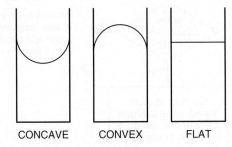

CONCAVE   CONVEX   FLAT

FIGURE
16.9
**Measurement
of Meniscus**

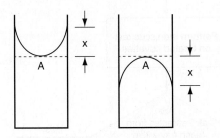

Background Information

The cold gas plasma treatment method has been employed in the process under study for over 5 years. Discussions with the process engineer, area supervisor, and operators reveal that the cold gas plasma treatment process produces output that meets specifications most of the time. If the meniscus size is below the lower specification limit or above the upper specification limit, the cuvette is not accepted. Operators measure, but do not record, meniscus measurements.

Operators collect data for a control chart analysis of the cold gas plasma treatment process. The operators fill in a process control data sheet, as shown in Figure 16.10, and record meniscus measurements directly onto a control chart.

Process Flowchart

A flowchart of the cold gas plasma treatment process prior to control chart analysis is shown in Figure 16.11. In most cases, a cuvette will be reprocessed if its meniscus

FIGURE
16.10
**Process
Control Data
Sheet**

Date: _____   Time in: _____   Time out: _____

Part Number: 6603624   Lot Number: _____

Lid number: _____   Bottom number: _____

(In) Vacuum: _____   (Out) Vacuum: _____

Quantity: 70   Quantity inspected: 5   Inspected by: _____

FIGURE 16.11   Flowchart of Original Cold Gas Plasma Treatment Process

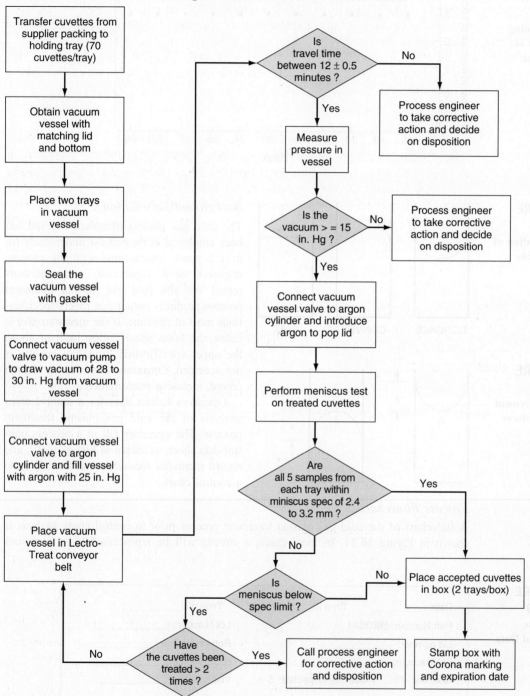

specification is below the lower specification limit. This is reflected by the loop in the flowchart. Usually, the lower specification limit will be met with two or three loops through the process. If the equipment is malfunctioning, the process engineer is called to take corrective action.

The PDSA cycle is turned twice in this case study. The first turn stabilizes the cold gas plasma treatment process. The second cycle improves the capability of the cold gas plasma treatment process.

PDSA Cycle 1

In the first cycle, the Plan stage consists of understanding and analyzing the present situation by constructing the flowchart of the current process, as shown in Figure 16.11, and collecting meniscus measurements from 20 subgroups of cold gas plasma treated cuvettes for an $\bar{x}$ and R chart, as shown in Figure 16.12 (see ☻ COLDGASPLASMA1). Each subgroup consists of a random sample of 5 cuvettes from a tray of 70 cuvettes. Each production run consists of 20 trays. The cuvettes within a tray are assumed to be homogeneous by the process engineer.

FIGURE 16.12 **Minitab Control Chart for Meniscus Measurements**

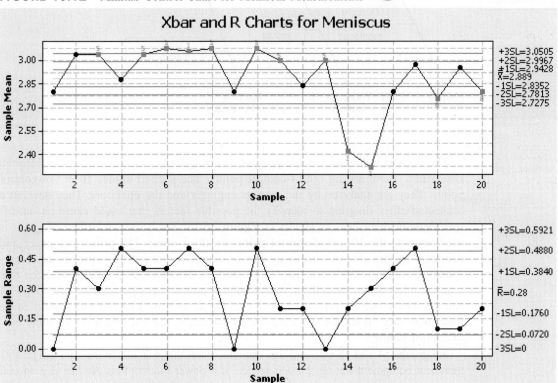

FIGURE 16.13 **Cause-and-Effect Diagram: Reasons for Meniscus to Fall Out of Specification Limits**

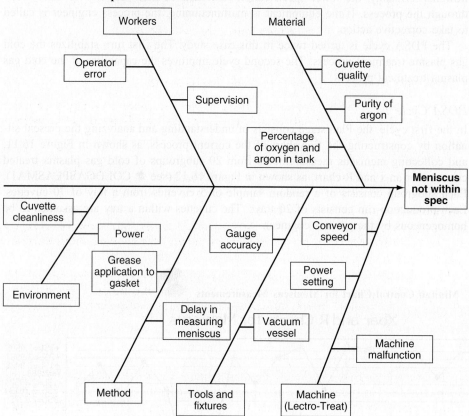

The R chart indicates a stable process with respect to variation, using the Minitab zone rules. There are no out-of-control points. The x̄ chart shows 10 out-of-control points. They are analyzed by the process engineer and the operators. They develop a cause-and-effect diagram to identify the possible factors that could cause an out-of-specification meniscus, as shown in Figure 16.13. The cause-and-effect diagram is used to study the 10 out-of-control points on the x̄ chart. The process engineer and operators are not able to assign any special causes to the out-of-control points corresponding to subgroups 6–10, 14–16, 18, and 20. However, it is quickly realized that a power interruption caused the out-of-control points corresponding to subgroups 14 and 15. These two points cause the UCL, the x̄̄, and the LCL on the x̄ chart to be lower than they should be. This creates a false out-of-control signal for all other out-of-control points.

Subgroups 14 and 15 are from one vacuum vessel that was inside the cold gas plasma treatment equipment during the occurrence of a power interruption. As this is a special cause, a new policy is instituted concerning electrical failure of the cold gas plasma treatment equipment, as shown in Exhibit 16.1.

EXHIBIT 16.1

Excerpts from Procedures Manual Reflecting Policy Change for Electrical Failure

Corona Treatment of Cuvettes

7.16 Close cuvette vessel valve.

7.17 Disconnect argon/oxygen vacuum from cuvette vessel valve.

    7.17.1 Record "In Vacuum" on the *Process Control Data Sheet,* Figure 3.

    7.17.2 Record "In Vacuum" on *Cuvette Vessel Usage Log,* Figure 2.

7.18 Immediately place vessel on Lectro-Treat conveyor belt.

    Note: Vessels must be placed onto the center of the conveyor in single file one behind the other, and with the valve end of the vessel facing the conveyor entrance. Spacing is not a concern.

    Note: Vessels *must not* be placed side by side.

    7.18.1 Log treatment time in and time out on *Process Control Data Sheet.*

7.19 Travel time for a vessel must be 12 ± 0.05 min.

7.20 Remove vessel from Lectro-Treat.

    7.20.1 In the event of electrical failure during the vessel treatment process, the cuvettes must be removed and scrapped, MRR disposition is to be performed on a weekly basis.

7.21 *Immediately* attach the 30-in. Hg vacuum gauge to vessel.

    7.21.1 Open vessel valve and note reading. If vacuum is equal or greater than 15 in. Hg, then record "Vacuum Out" on *Process Control Data Sheet.*

The operator is asked why the two trays indicated by the out-of-control points for subgroups 14 and 15 are not identified in the comments section of the log as having occurred during a power interruption. The operator says that because of her limited English-speaking abilities, she did not know what to write in the log. A new policy that log sheet comments could be written in English or Spanish was established by the area supervisor.

The Do stage in the first cycle consists of testing the two new policy guidelines during full-scale operation of the cold gas plasma treatment process.

The Study stage in the first cycle consists of determining if all the operators know what to do in case of a power interruption and if all the operators write their process comments on the log sheet in English or Spanish. The effectiveness of the power interruption policy cannot be verified because there are no further power failures during the course of this study.

The Act stage in the first cycle consists of updating the procedures manual to ensure that the new policies are followed by operators, as shown in Exhibit 16.1.

PDSA Cycle 2

In the second cycle, the Plan stage consists of monitoring the process by plotting 20 new subgroups (see ☻ COLDGASPLASMA2) on the $\bar{x}$ and R charts, as shown in Figure 16.14. Again, the R chart indicates a stable process. However, a cyclical pattern is observed on the $\bar{x}$ chart, indicated by every fifth and sixth subgroup being near or below the lower control limit. In the past, the operators would not have noticed anything abnormal because the individual meniscus measurements are within specification limits.

FIGURE 16.14 **Minitab Control Chart on 20 New Meniscus Measurements**

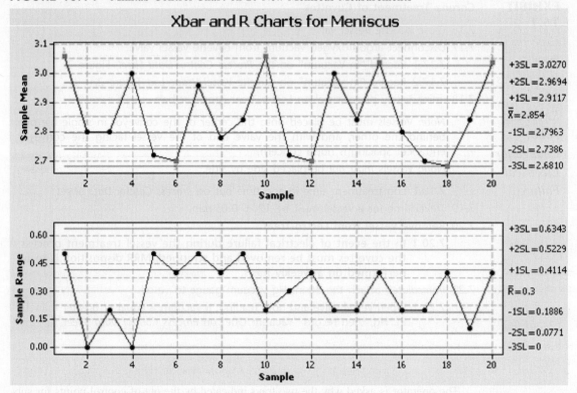

An analysis is done by the process engineer using the previously developed cause-and-effect diagram, as shown in Figure 16.13. In the process engineer's opinion, the cyclical pattern on the $\bar{x}$ chart indicates that the meniscus problem is related to one of the vacuum vessels used in the cold gas plasma treatment process. Consequently, the process engineer expands the subcauses for "vacuum vessel" on a new cause-and-effect diagram, as shown in Figure 16.15.

Vacuum vessel 021 is identified from the log sheets as the troublesome one. The process engineer concludes that the cause of the problem is a leak either in the gasket area or in the valve area of vacuum vessel 021.

The Do stage in the second cycle consists of testing vacuum vessel 021 for leaks in the gasket and valve areas. It is determined that the leak is in the gasket seating area of the vessel. Vacuum vessel 021 is scrapped in conformance with company procedure and a new vessel is installed in its place.

The Study stage in the second cycle consists of sampling 24 additional subgroups (see ✿ COLDGASPLASMA3) to determine the stability of the cold gas plasma treatment process. New $\bar{x}$ and R charts indicate that it is stable, as shown in Figure 16.16.

The Act stage of the second cycle consists of changing the procedures manual for the cold gas plasma treatment process to ensure that there is a standardized method for

FIGURE 16.15
Cause-and-Effect Diagram: Reasons for Meniscus Problems Due to Vacuum Vessel

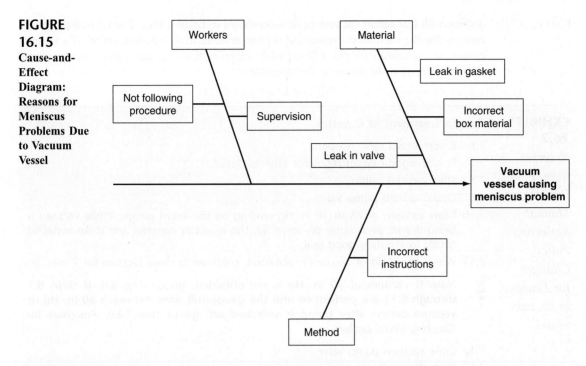

FIGURE 16.16   **Minitab Control Chart on 24 Additional Meniscus Measurements**

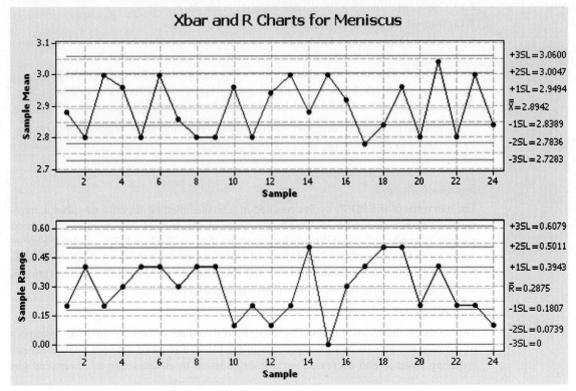

dealing with leakage in vacuum vessels, as shown in Exhibit 16.2. The revised procedure ensures that the vacuum is maintained for two minutes in the vacuum vessel. If a vacuum cannot be maintained for two full minutes, the procedures manual states the appropriate course of action to be taken by the operator.

EXHIBIT 16.2 *Excerpts from Procedures Manual Reflecting Policy Changes for Leakage in Vacuum Vessel*	**Corona Treatment of Cuvettes**

7.6   Ensure vessel valve is open.

7.7   Ensure argon-oxygen regulator valve is closed.

7.8   Start vacuum pump.

7.9   Open vacuum pump valve.

7.10 Draw vacuum of 28 to 30 in. Hg reading on the vessel gauge. While vacuum is being drawn, *press firmly* on vessel lid. Use a rubber hammer and strike vessel lid gently to ensure a good seal.

7.11 When 30 in. Hg of vacuum is obtained, continue to draw vacuum for 2 min.

Note: If vacuum of 30 in. Hg is *not* obtained, go to step 8.0. If steps 8.1 through 8.11 are performed and the gauge still does *not* reach 30 in. Hg or vacuum decays after pump is switched off, go to step 12.0, *Procedure for Checking Vessel Leakers.*

7.12 Close vacuum pump valve.

7.13 Shut off vacuum pump.

7.14 Open argon/oxygen valve until vacuum reads 25 in. Hg.

7.15 Shut off argon/oxygen regulator.

   7.15.1 Hold vacuum for 1 min. If vacuum does not drop below 22 in. Hg, then proceed to step 7.16.

   7.15.2 If vacuum decays below 22 in. Hg, repeat steps 7.4 through 7.15.1.

      7.15.2.1 If leak continues to occur, replace the Teflon valve and tube. See step 13.0, *Valve and Tube Replacement.*

Note: If the vessel continues to leak after valve and tube replacement, go to step 12.0, *Procedure for Checking Vessel Leakers.*

Improved Process

The two turns of the PDSA cycles resulted in a revised method for cold gas plasma treatment, as shown in Figure 16.17. On the basis of the last 24 data points, the revised method is stable; its capability is indicated by $Z_{USL} = 2.47$ and $Z_{LSL} = 4.02$, and its upper natural limit (UNL) is 3.264 mm and lower natural limit (LNL) is 2.526 mm, compared to the specification values of 3.2 and 2.4, respectively. Further improvements can now address reducing the UNL to within the specification limits.

Conclusion

This study produced several benefits. First, it produced benefits to the internal customers of the cold gas plasma treatment process in the form of reduced network costs from not recycling cuvettes and decreased surface degradation to cuvettes due to fewer cold gas

FIGURE 16.17 Flowchart for Revised Cold Gas Plasma Treatment Process

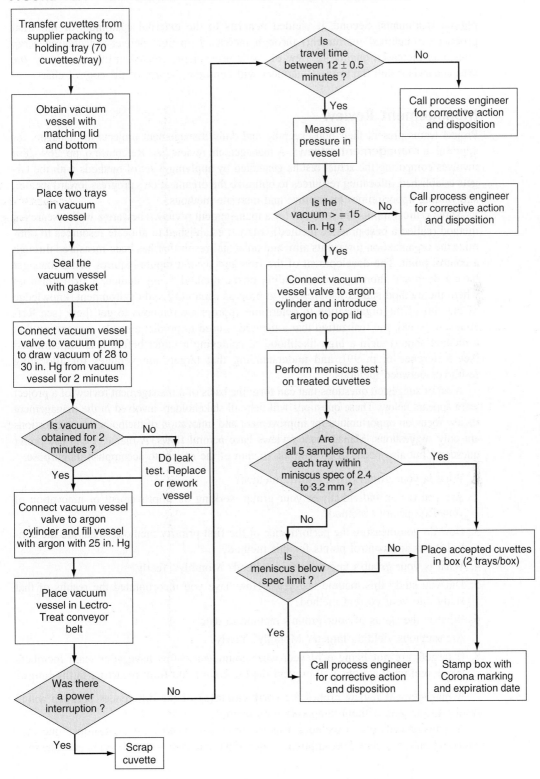

plasma treatments. Second, it yielded benefits to the external customers of the final product (a chemical instrument) through increased on-time delivery, decreased scrap rates, and increased quality. In view of the improvements created in this case study, the area supervisor and the process engineer will continue the use of the control chart.

Management Review

Project teams present their housekeeping and daily management projects to managers for approval in **management reviews.** A management review [see Reference 6, pp. 269–280] involves comparing the actual results generated by applying a set of methods with the targets established, allocating resources to optimize the organization's progress toward its aim, and finding opportunities to improve and innovate methods.

Three critical inputs are required for a management review. They are a well-researched method (called a best-practice method), a target established to allocate resources to optimize the organization toward its aim, and an actual result that has been measured through a control point. The development of the first and second inputs requires that a manager have a deep and thorough understanding of the method being studied, a firm grasp on where the method stands with respect to process capability and environment, knowledge of the aim of the organization to determine appropriate methods to get there [see Reference 6, p. 98], the realization that a method is used to predict a result, recognition that a method should yield a high likelihood of achieving a target before it is implemented [see Reference 6, p. 99], and understanding that targets are vehicles for allocating resources between methods.

A set of suggested questions that can form the basis of a management review of a project team appears below. These questions will help all stakeholders involved in the management review focus on opportunities for improvement and innovation of methods. These questions are only suggestions. Management reviews have natural flows. A manager can use preset questions, but also needs to go with the rhythm of the review to accomplish its purpose.

1. What is your group's first priority method?
2. Are you (as an individual) or your group working on improvement or innovation of your first priority method?
3. How do you measure the performance of the first priority method? What are the control items and control points for this method?
4. What is your group's target for this method? Monthly? Yearly?
5. Did you study this method last year? How have you incorporated the results of that study into your current method?
6. What is the status of your group's method to date?
7. Are methods yielding targets? Monthly? Yearly?
8. If targets are not being achieved, what countermeasures have your team members taken, and what actions will prevent the same situation from recurring in the future?

A management review probes the **root cause(s)** of the differences between actual results and targets without tampering with methods.

A management review includes a questioning process that asks questions "one inch wide and one mile deep," as opposed to questions that are "one mile wide and one inch deep." This means that the management review probes root causes to a high level of detail. A technique that helps people probe for root causes in the above manner is the **5W1H process** [see Reference 3, p. 235]. The 5W1H process is used to ask "why" a problem occurs five times and then "how" the problem can be resolved, as opposed to just asking "how" the problem can be resolved. Historically, a person asks a question like, "Why didn't the lawn get mowed this week?" and gets an answer like, "The mower broke." This usually leads to the person responsible for mowing the lawn being blamed and no improvement in the lawn-mowing process. What the 5W1H process is suggesting is something like the following:

Sample 5W1H Process

Question 1:   *Why* didn't the lawn get mowed this week?

 Answer 1:   The mower broke.

Question 2:   *Why* did the mower break?

 Answer 2:   The bearing burned out.

Question 3:   *Why* did the bearing burn out?

 Answer 3:   The bearing burned out because it wasn't oiled properly.

Question 4:   *Why* wasn't the bearing oiled properly?

 Answer 4:   The bearing wasn't oiled properly because the oil line was clogged.

Question 5:   *Why* was the oil line clogged?

 Answer 5:   The oil line was clogged because there is no routine and proactive maintenance program to examine the oil line.

Question 6:   *How* can we resolve this problem so it doesn't happen again?

 Answer 6:   Develop and follow a policy of routine and proactive maintenance for the oil line.

As you can see, questions 1 through 5 focus on the root cause (why) of the problem, while the last question focuses on how to improve a process; the procedure promotes asking questions that are "one inch wide and one mile deep."

Variance Analysis

Management reviews should be conducted in accordance with Deming's theory of management. Not all sources of variation are due to special causes. A manager following Deming's theory of management does not tamper with processes under her control. Instead, causes of variation are separated into common and special sources by statistical methods. Then, employees work to resolve special sources of variation, and management works to remove common sources of variation by modifying methods.

The management review focuses on whether the actual method used by an employee follows the best-practice method. Figure 16.18 shows the relationship between following methods and achieving targets.

FIGURE 16.18
Relationship between Following Methods and Achieving Targets

Source: Noriaki Kano, Science University of Tokyo, presented April 1, 1990, Atlanta.

	Achieved targets?	
Followed method?	Yes	No
Yes	1	3
No	2	4

Cell 1 shows the outcome of an employee following a best-practice method as the attainment of a target.

Cell 4 shows the outcome of an employee not following a best-practice method as the failure to attain a target. To reverse this failure, the employee follows the best-practice method. In this case, the management review determines answers to the following questions:

1. What best-practice method was not followed?
2. Who failed to follow the best-practice method? Note: The focus is on system problems, not on the individual. This will help promote joy in work and pride in the outcome.
3. Why did the employee not follow the best-practice method? Was it due to ignorance, misunderstanding, lack of training, negligence, problems with a machine, or problems with raw materials?
4. Should the best-practice method be changed to resolve problems due to ignorance, misunderstanding, lack of training, negligence, problems with a machine, or problems with raw materials?

Cell 2 shows the outcome of an employee not following a best-practice method as the attainment of a target. In this case, depending on prevailing pressures, the employee may adopt a slower pace when determining why the method used yielded the target.

Cell 3 shows the outcome of an employee following the best-practice method as the failure to attain a target. In this case, the best-practice method is improved or innovated, and/or a change is made in the target; the employee is not blamed. This change is accomplished by asking the following questions proposed by Kano:

1. What best-practice method missed its target?
2. How can the best-practice method be changed to attain its target?
3. Must the best-practice method be changed to resolve problems due to ignorance, misunderstanding, lack of training, problems with a machine, or problems with raw materials?
4. What target was missed?
5. How much was the target missed over time? Is the process under study stable? Will adjustment of the target result in tampering with the best-practice method?
6. Why was the target missed? Was the target set incorrectly because of ignorance, lack of training, problems with a machine, problems with raw materials, management or by guesswork?

Once these questions are answered, the necessary information may be available for improvement or innovation of the best-practice method or change of the target. These questions focus on improvement and innovation of the best-practice method, not on blaming the individual.

Frequently, it is not possible to investigate the negative scenarios presented in cells 2, 3, or 4 on a daily basis. One day may not provide enough time to perform all four stages of the PDSA cycle to achieve the desired improvement and/or innovation.

Empowerment

Steps 18 and 19 of Figure 14.1 include empowering employees through daily management [see Reference 7, pp. 50–57]. **Empowerment** is a term commonly used by managers in today's organizational environment. However, it has not been operationally defined, and its definition varies from application to application. Currently, the popular definition of empowerment relies loosely on the notion of dropping decision-making down to the lowest appropriate level in an organization. The basic premise of empowerment is that if people are given the authority to make decisions, they will take pride in their work, be willing to take risks, and work harder to make things happen. Frequently, the reality of empowerment is that employees are empowered until they make a mistake; then the hatchet falls. Most employees know this and treat the popular concept of empowerment with the lack of respect it merits; empowerment in such a form is destructive to quality management.

Empowerment in a quality management sense has a dramatically different aim and definition. Its aim in quality management is to increase pride in work and joy in the outcome for all employees.

The definition of empowerment that translates this aim into a realistic objective is as follows: empowerment is a process that provides an individual or group of employees the opportunity to:

1. Define and document methods.
2. Learn about methods through training and development.
3. Improve and innovate best-practice methods that make up systems.
4. Utilize latitude in their own judgment to make decisions within the context of best-practice methods.
5. Trust superiors to react positively to the latitude taken by employees making decisions within the context of best-practice methods.

Empowerment starts with leadership, but requires the commitment of all employees. Leaders provide employees with all five opportunities stated above. Employees accept responsibility for:

1. Increasing their training and knowledge of methods and the systems of which they are a part.
2. Participating in the development, standardization, improvement, and innovation of best-practice methods.
3. Increasing their latitude in decision-making within the context of best-practice methods.

Latitude to make decisions within the context of a best-practice method refers to the options an employee has in resolving a problem within the confines of a best-practice method, not to modification of the best-practice method. Differentiating between the need to change the best-practice method and latitude within the context of the best-practice method takes place at the operational level.

Empowerment can exist only in an environment of trust that supports planned experimentation concerning ideas to improve and innovate best-practice methods. These ideas can come from individuals or from the team, but tests of the worthiness of those ideas are conducted through planned experiments under the auspices of the team (the Do stage of the PDSA cycle). Anything else will result in chaos.

Individual employees are taught to understand that increased variability in output will result if each employee follows his or her own method. This increased variability will create additional cost and unpredictable customer service. Employees must be educated about the need to reach consensus on one best-practice method.

The best-practice method will consist of **generalized procedures** and **individualized procedures.** Generalized procedures are standardized procedures that all employees follow. Individualized procedures are procedures that afford workers the opportunity to utilize their individual differences by creating their own standardized procedures. However, the outputs of individualized procedures are standardized across employees. Individualized procedures can be improved through personal efforts. In the beginning of a quality improvement effort, employees and management may not have the knowledge to allow for individualized procedures.

A professor following an approved departmental syllabus for a certain course is an example of an employee using a generalized procedure. When that professor injects her own examples, experiences, and jokes, she is using individualized procedures.

Empowerment is operationalized at two levels. First, employees are empowered to develop and document best-practice methods using the SDSA cycle. Second, employees are empowered to improve or innovate best-practice methods through application of the PDSA cycle.

Continuing the PDSA Cycle

As managers see the results from improved processes, they will want to expand the number of daily management project teams. This should be discouraged in the beginning of a quality management effort.

Instead, managers should be asked to direct their existing project teams to continually subject the processes already under study to more iterations of the PDSA cycle. The benefit of this action is ensuring that managers learn how to continuously improve and innovate processes, not how to make one improvement in a process and jump to another process. Management reviews are an excellent vehicle to promote this type of training experience. Reviewers can ask the following question: "Can I see your improvement action memoranda for this process?" Those reviewed should be able to show multiple improvement action memoranda, including changes to training programs, for the process they are studying with their project team.

Coordinating Project Teams

As the initial process improvement teams begin to show positive results, other process improvement teams will be formed by area or department managers in response to localized issues, as shown in step 19 of Figure 14.1.

The initial and other process improvement teams require resources, such as PILs, members to work on projects, training, financial resources, physical space in which to meet, and the direction and guidance of a higher level of management.

As the number of teams increases, a structure to coordinate and manage the teams at the department level is necessary. The structure is called a **local steering team (LST)**, as shown in step 20 of Figure 14.1. Each department's LST has the responsibility to coordinate daily management projects, as shown in steps 18 and 19 of Figure 14.1.

Summary	This chapter presented a discussion of Prong 1 of the fork model, daily management. Daily management is used to develop, standardize, deploy, maintain, improve, and innovate the methods required for daily work.

The first phase of implementing daily management involves selecting initial project teams. Process improvement leaders (PILs) are chosen by the executive committee and trained in basic quality control tools and the psychology of the individual and the team. Then the initial projects are determined, and project teams are formed.

After training, each initial project team works on one or more methods using daily management. Daily management includes housekeeping, which is the development, standardization, and deployment of methods required for daily work, and, in its second sense, daily management is the maintenance, improvement, and innovation of methods for daily work.

Housekeeping functions are developed through a procedure called function deployment. This is the way employees determine what functions are required to perform each method they use in their daily work. Housekeeping is accomplished by employing the SDSA cycle. The objective is to determine the best-practice method for each function. Best-practice methods are monitored through key indicators that are operationally defined and measure the results and the processes that generate results.

After a best-practice method has been developed and deployed by a project team, housekeeping activities give way to daily management activities. Daily management is used to reduce process variation and to center the process on the customer's requirements. The PDSA cycle is used in daily management in a continuous progression of never-ending improvement.

Project teams present their housekeeping and daily management projects to managers for approval in management reviews. This is the process that involves comparing actual results with established targets. It is critical that management reviews take into account common and special causes of variation. If a management review is done properly, there is no place for tampering with the process or blaming employees for problems out of their control.

Empowering employees through daily management has as its aim, in a quality management sense, to increase joy in work. It is operationalized at two levels. First, employees are empowered to develop and document best-practice methods using the SDSA cycle. Second, they are empowered to improve and innovate best-practice methods through the continuous application of the PDSA cycle.

As the initial process improvement teams begin to show positive results, and more teams are formed by area or department managers, a structure coordinates the teams at the department level. This structure is called the local steering team.

Exercises

16.1. Reread the personal example of daily management in this chapter under "A Personal Example of Daily Management." Perform a similar analysis for yourself by selecting a problematic key process in your life, and do the following:

Plan

a. Flowchart the process.

b. Identify the key objective(s) of the process.

c. Identify the key indicator(s) for each key objective.

d. Develop a change concept using data analysis, benchmarking, or the list of change concepts in Chapter 10 to develop a revised and improved flowchart.

Do

e. Use the revised flowchart in a pilot study.

Study

f. Study the effect of the revised flowchart on the relevant key indicator(s).

Act

g. If the change is positive, formalize it by placing it in your daily routine; if the change is negative, go back to the Plan stage of the PDSA cycle and identify another change concept.

16.2. Reread the business example of daily management in this chapter under "A Business Example of Daily Management." Perform a similar analysis for your organization by selecting a problematic key process, and do the following:

Plan

a. Flowchart the process.

b. Identify the key objective(s) of the process.

c. Identify the key indicator(s) for each key objective.

d. Develop a change concept using data analysis, benchmarking, or the list of change concepts in Chapter 10 to develop a revised and improved flowchart.

Do

e. Use the revised flowchart in a pilot study,

Study

f. Study the effect of the revised flowchart on the relevant key indicator(s),

Act

g. If the change is positive, formalize it by training all relevant employees in the revised process and putting it in your training manuals; if the change is negative, go back to the Plan stage of the PDSA cycle and identify another change concept.

References

1. W. E. Deming (1986), *Out of the Crisis* (Cambridge, MA: M.I.T. Center for Advanced Engineering Studies).

2. H. Gitlow, S. Gitlow, A. Oppenheim, and R. Oppenheim, "Telling the Quality Story," *Quality Progress,* September 1990, pp. 41–46.

3. Masaaki Imai (1986), *Kaizen: The Key to Japan's Competitive Success* (New York: Random House).

4. Kannan Krishnan, and Howard Gitlow, "Quality Improvement in the Treatment of Cold Gas Plasma: A Case Study," *Quality Engineering,* 9, No. 4, 1997, pp. 603–614.

5. G. Langley, L. Nolan, T. Nolan, C. Norman, and L. Provost (1996), *The Improvement Guide: A Practical Approach to Enhancing Organizational Performance* (San Francisco: Jossey-Bass).

6. Shigeru Mizuno (1988), *Company-Wide Quality Control* (4-14, Asasaka 8-chome, Minato-ku, Tokyo 107, Japan: Asian Productivity Organization).

7. David Pietenpol and Howard Gitlow, "Empowerment and the System of Profound Knowledge," *International Journal of Quality Science,* 1, No. 3, 1996, pp. 50–57.

8. P. Scholtes (1988), *The Team Handbook: How to Use Teams to Improve Quality* (Madison, WI: Joiner Associates).

Chapter

17

The Fork Model for Quality Management: Prong 2, or Cross-Functional Management

Chapter Objectives

- To describe the primary and auxiliary areas appropriate for the application of cross-functional management
- To discuss the selection and composition of cross-functional teams
- To describe and illustrate the steps in implementing cross-functional management
- To discuss how to structure cross-functional management teams in small and large organizations, and how to coordinate multiple teams

- To discuss and illustrate problems that can arise in implementing cross-functional management with respect to longevity, membership, focus, resources, and communication
- To illustrate the improvement in a cost-cutting process by using cross-functional management rather than traditional methods
- To illustrate the application of cross-functional management in new product development
- To illustrate the application of cross-functional management in creating a performance appraisal system

Introduction

In this chapter, we explain what is required to develop, standardize, deploy, maintain, improve, and innovate methods that cross areas in an organization. Cross-functional management is Prong 2 of the quality management model.

Cross-functional management [see Reference 2, pp. 33–36] is critical to the quality management model because it weaves together the vertical (line) functions of management with the horizontal (interdepartmental) functions of management. Kaoru Ishikawa states "in order to be called a fabric, both horizontal and vertical threads need to be woven together, and only when horizontal or cross-functional management threads are woven together with vertical threads can a company be considered similarly cohesive." [See Reference 1, pp. 4–5.] Cross-functional management is important because it promotes the reorganization of corporate management systems to improve interdepartmental communication and cooperation, and provides clear lines of responsibility for that reorganization.

The primary areas for the application of cross-functional management include quality management (quality control and quality improvement), cost management (profit management, expense management, and cost reduction), delivery management (production quantity management, delivery date management, and production system management), and personnel management (human development, education, and work morale enhancement). Quality and cost are usually the first areas to receive attention in cross-functional management.

The auxiliary areas for the application of cross-functional management include new product development (R&D, technology development, and production technology), sales management (marketing, sales activity management, and sales expansion), safety management (safety/hygiene control, labor safety control, and environmental control), and QC promotional support (QC circle standardization). Primary cross-functional areas are permanent. Auxiliary cross-functional areas change according to current and expected conditions.

Selecting Initial Cross-Functional Teams

The members of the **executive committee** (EC) form initial cross-functional teams, as shown in step 21 of the detailed fork model in Figure 14.1, usually in the areas of quality or **cost management.** The EC selects a leader for each team, as shown in step 22 of Figure 14.1, and allocates appropriate resources for the education and training of the leader, as shown in step 23 of Figure 14.1. Each cross-functional leader should be an executive with the title of senior vice president or vice president in charge of a function. The EC uses the recommendations of the team leader to select members for the initial cross-functional teams, as shown in step 24 of Figure 14.1. Team size is kept to a minimum, generally about five people. All team members are trained in appropriate theory and practice, as shown in step 24 of Figure 14.1. Team members should be executives with the rank of director or above. Team members do not all have to come from affected areas. A diversity of opinion and knowledge is helpful, but it is not necessary to have all affected areas represented on a cross-functional team. The team facilitator should be an executive in charge of a function, such as personnel. The support staff for a cross-functional team should be from the facilitator's home department because the facilitator needs to have the authority to make things happen for his or her cross-functional team [see Reference 2, p. 45].

Implementing Cross-Functional Management

Cross-functional management, or **Prong 2** of the detailed fork model, involves the following activities:

- Studying and applying Deming's theory of management to company-wide systems.
- Developing measurements for company-wide systems.
- Coordinating and optimizing company-wide systems within departmental methods.
- Allocating resources for cross-functional and departmental methods by establishing targets.
- Ensuring that each department performs its deployed methods in daily management.
- Monitoring company-wide systems with respect to targets from a corporate level (management review).
- If necessary, taking action utilizing the PDSA cycle to decrease the difference between actual results and targets (variance analysis).

The following steps are used to implement cross-functional management [see Reference 3, p. 108]:

1. Clarify the purpose or aim of the cross-functional management effort. Is it to deploy a cross-functional process into a division or department to achieve a rational divisional or departmental target? Quality improvement and cost reduction are examples of cross-functional processes deployed into divisional or departmental processes to attain a rational divisional or departmental target? Or, is the purpose of cross-functional management to improve a divisional or departmental process that affects areas across the organization to achieve a rational divisional or departmental target? R&D and human resources are examples of divisional or departmental processes that affect areas across an organization and must be improved to attain a rational target.

2. Prepare a list of the divisions or departments that will participate in the proposed cross-functional team.

3. Construct an **integrated flowchart** of the proposed process: a flowchart arranged in a matrix format with stakeholders, tools, and documents of the process as the

columns, and steps of the proposed process under study in the rows. The listing of each step in the proposed process should include the required activities and needed items, the individual or group responsible to perform the activity, and the persons responsible for the results of the activity. The cells of the matrix indicate the relationships between stakeholders, tools and documents, and the steps of the proposed process. An example of an integrated flowchart for a **personnel management** process appears in Figure 17.1.

4. Create measures to monitor the existing and proposed processes.
5. Identify and select priority projects using the proposed process and measures developed by team members. Application of the **System of Profound Knowledge** is the key to effective cross-functional management. With respect to quality, such a project might reduce the number of customer complaints. With respect to cost, such a project might decrease the cost to manufacture a product.

As expertise is developed with company-wide systems, it is deployed into daily management methods where appropriate, as shown in step 25 of Figure 14.1.

Structures for Cross-Functional Management

Several administrative structures can be used to promote cross-functional management. In small organizations, one cross-functional team comprising all relevant executives can be established to coordinate and optimize company-wide systems. In large organizations, one cross-functional team comprising appropriate executives can be established to coordinate and optimize each company-wide system. For example, there could be one team for **quality management,** one team for safety/hygiene management, and so on. Another alternative for large organizations is to allow a functional department to coordinate and optimize one company-wide system. For example, the Human Resources department could coordinate and optimize the company-wide systems dealing with the enhancement of employee morale.

Frequently, executives claim that they do not have time for cross-functional management because of the demands of their daily routine. It may be necessary for these executives to exercise daily management to remove non-value-added routines from their schedules in order to free up time for cross-functional management.

Cross-functional teams report directly to the members of the EC and have the highest level of decision-making authority. They perform the Plan and Study phases of the **PDSA cycle** for company-wide systems. Implementation of company-wide systems, the Do and Act phases of the PDSA cycle, is carried out by line departments in daily management.

Coordinating Cross-Functional Teams

As the initial cross-functional teams successfully improve company-wide systems, the EC will form new cross-functional teams, as shown in step 26 of Figure 14.1. The EC reviews, manages, and coordinates all cross-functional teams, as shown in step 27 of Figure 14.1.

A cross-functional management review of the line departments affected by cross-functional policy is conducted by a cross-functional team leader, one or more times per year, in order to study departmental management from a company-wide perspective, and

FIGURE 17.1 Integrated Flowchart of the Personnel Management Process

Stakeholders of the Personnel Management Process

Personnel Management Process		Labor Pool	Candidates	Hires	Employees	Supervisors	Top Management	HR Dept.	Regulations	Unions	Measures
HUMAN RESOURCES PLANNING	Forecast employment requirements						○	□	○	○	
	Determine available external resources within relevant labor pools							□			
	Determine when, why, and in what numbers employees will be needed					□	○	□	○		
	Develop work schedules			○	○	□					
	Identify replacement needs			○	○	□	○	○	○		
	Identify training needs			○	○	□		○	○		
RECRUITMENT	Develop job descriptions					○		□	○		
	Locate qualified job candidates	○				○		□	○	○	

A

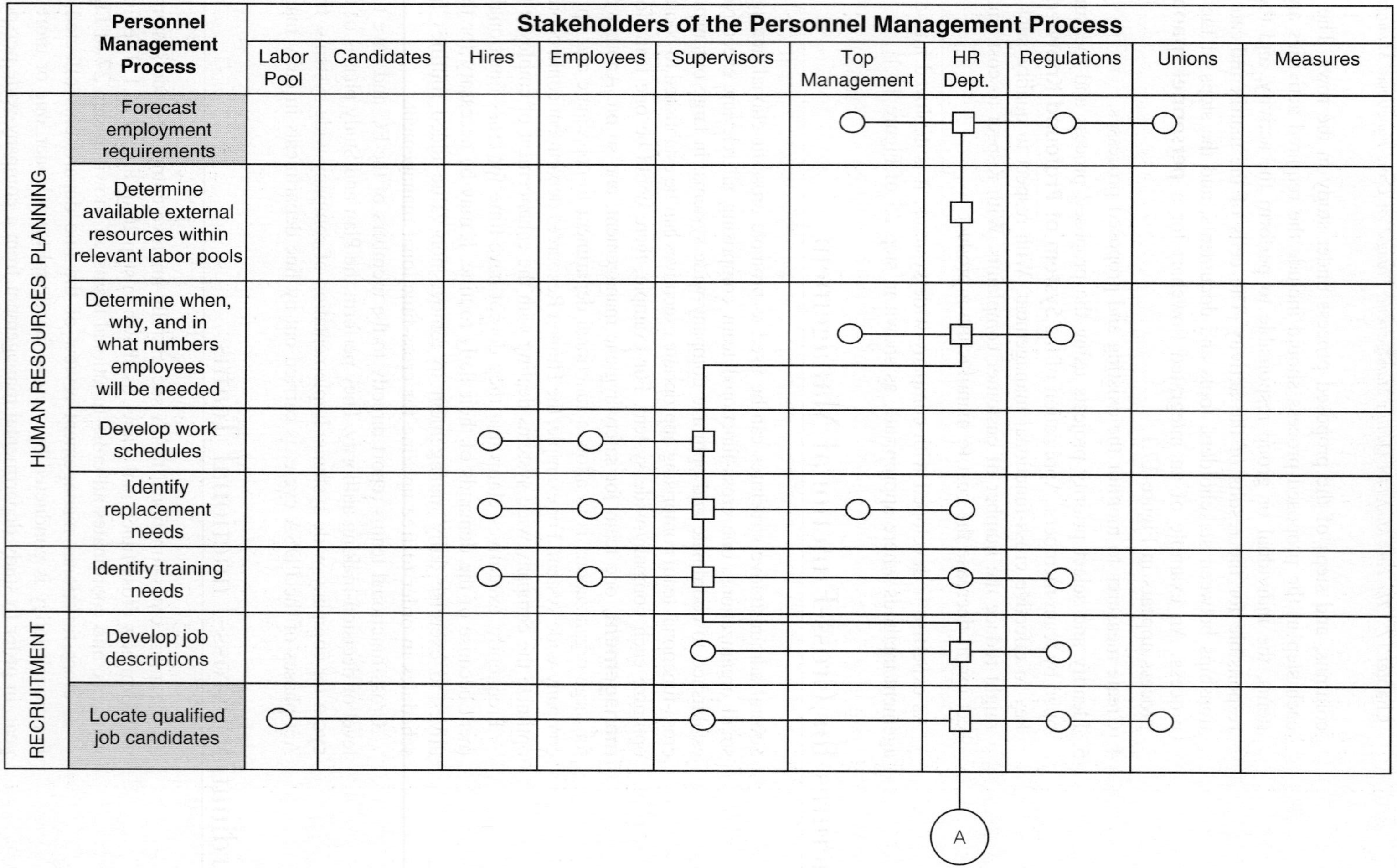

FIGURE 17.1   (continued)

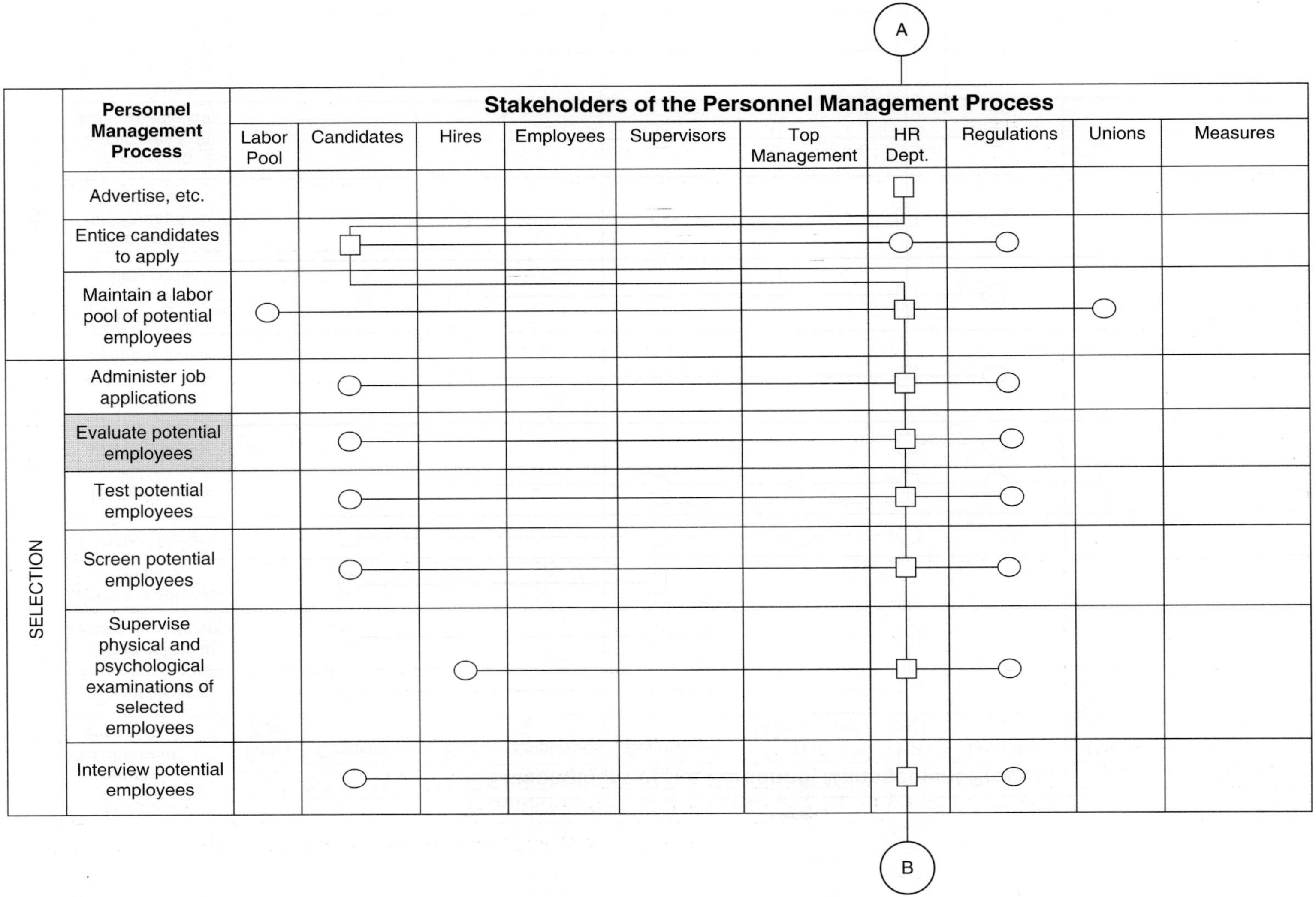

Stakeholders of the Personnel Management Process

Personnel Management Process	Labor Pool	Candidates	Hires	Employees	Supervisors	Top Management	HR Dept.	Regulations	Unions	Measures
Advertise, etc.							□			
Entice candidates to apply		□					○	○		
Maintain a labor pool of potential employees	○						□		○	
Administer job applications		○					□	○		
Evaluate potential employees		○					□	○		
Test potential employees		○					□	○		
Screen potential employees		○					□	○		
Supervise physical and psychological examinations of selected employees			○				□	○		
Interview potential employees		○					□	○		

SELECTION

FIGURE 17.1 (continued)

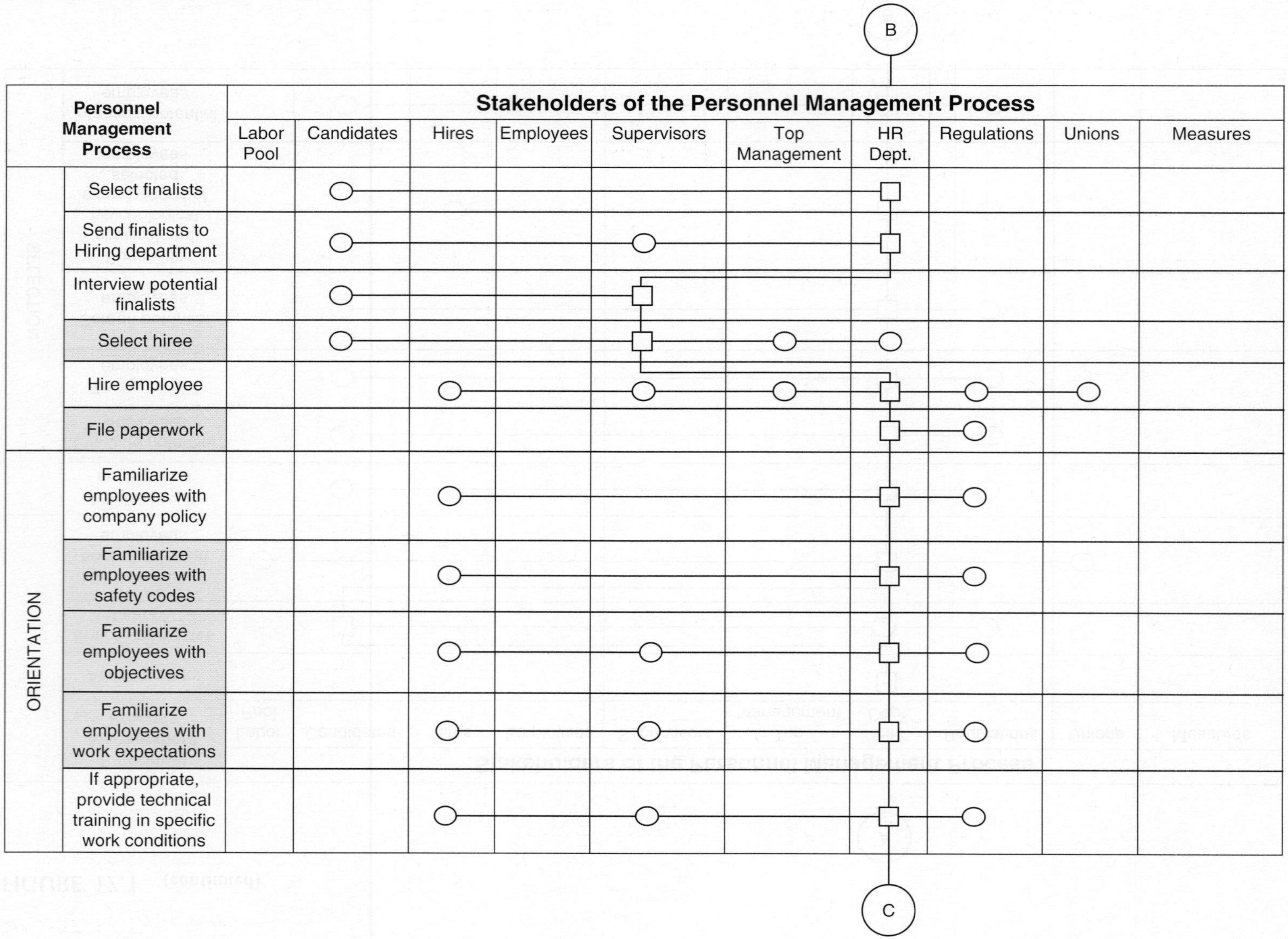

Stakeholders of the Personnel Management Process

Personnel Management Process	Labor Pool	Candidates	Hires	Employees	Supervisors	Top Management	HR Dept.	Regulations	Unions	Measures
Select finalists		○					□			
Send finalists to Hiring department		○			○		□			
Interview potential finalists		○			□					
Select hiree		○			□	○	○			
Hire employee			○		○	○	□	○	○	
File paperwork							□	○		
ORIENTATION — Familiarize employees with company policy			○				□	○		
Familiarize employees with safety codes			○				□	○		
Familiarize employees with objectives			○		○		□	○		
Familiarize employees with work expectations			○		○		□	○		
If appropriate, provide technical training in specific work conditions			○		○		□	○		

B

C

FIGURE 17.1 (continued)

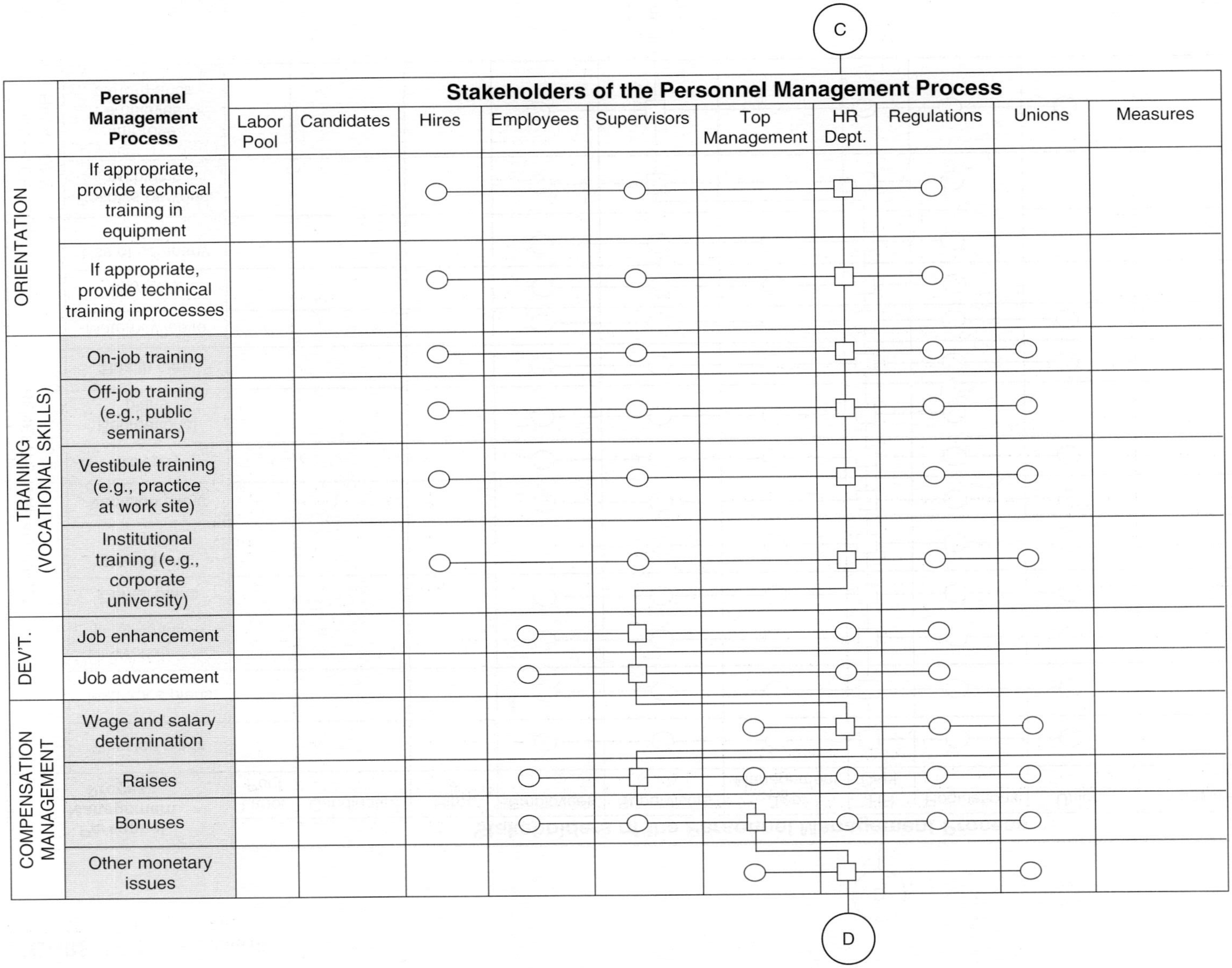

Stakeholders of the Personnel Management Process

Personnel Management Process		Labor Pool	Candidates	Hires	Employees	Supervisors	Top Management	HR Dept.	Regulations	Unions	Measures
ORIENTATION	If appropriate, provide technical training in equipment			○		○		□	○		
	If appropriate, provide technical training in processes			○		○		□	○		
TRAINING (VOCATIONAL SKILLS)	On-job training			○		○		□	○	○	
	Off-job training (e.g., public seminars)					○		□	○	○	
	Vestibule training (e.g., practice at work site)			○		○		□	○	○	
	Institutional training (e.g., corporate university)			○		○		□	○	○	
DEV'T.	Job enhancement				○	□		○	○		
	Job advancement				○	□		○	○		
COMPENSATION MANAGEMENT	Wage and salary determination					□	○	□	○	○	
	Raises				○		○	○	○	○	
	Bonuses				○	□	□	○	○	○	
	Other monetary issues						○	□	○	○	

FIGURE 17.1 (continued)

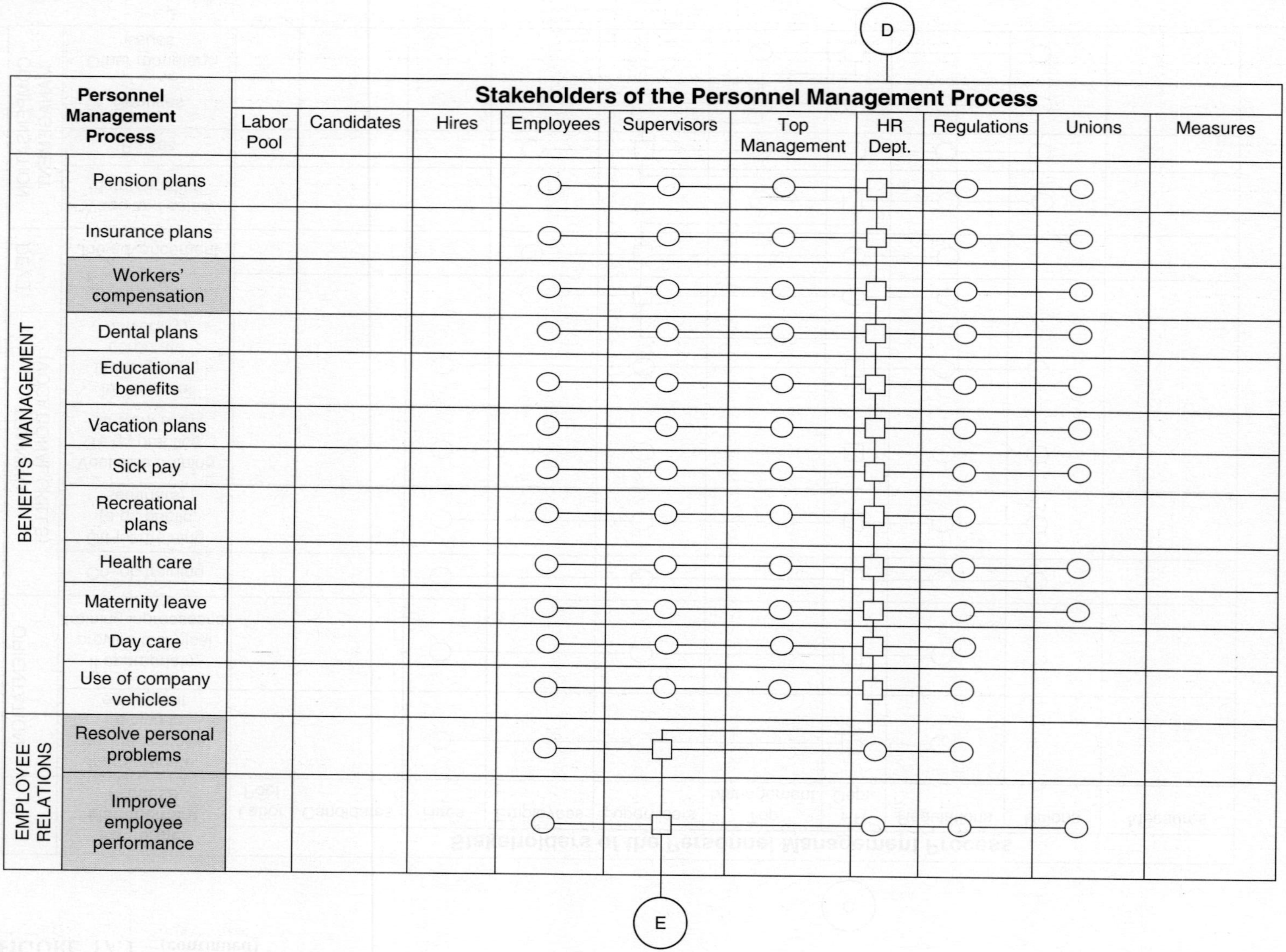

Stakeholders of the Personnel Management Process

Personnel Management Process		Labor Pool	Candidates	Hires	Employees	Supervisors	Top Management	HR Dept.	Regulations	Unions	Measures
BENEFITS MANAGEMENT	Pension plans				○	○	○	□	○	○	
	Insurance plans				○	○	○	□	○	○	
	Workers' compensation				○	○	○	□	○	○	
	Dental plans				○	○	○	□	○	○	
	Educational benefits				○	○	○	□	○	○	
	Vacation plans				○	○	○	□	○	○	
	Sick pay				○	○	○	□	○	○	
	Recreational plans				○	○	○	□	○		
	Health care				○	○	○	□	○	○	
	Maternity leave				○	○	○	□	○	○	
	Day care				○	○	○	□	○		
	Use of company vehicles				○	○	○	□	○		
EMPLOYEE RELATIONS	Resolve personal problems				○	□		○	○		
	Improve employee performance				○	□		○	○	○	

D

E

FIGURE 17.1 (concluded)

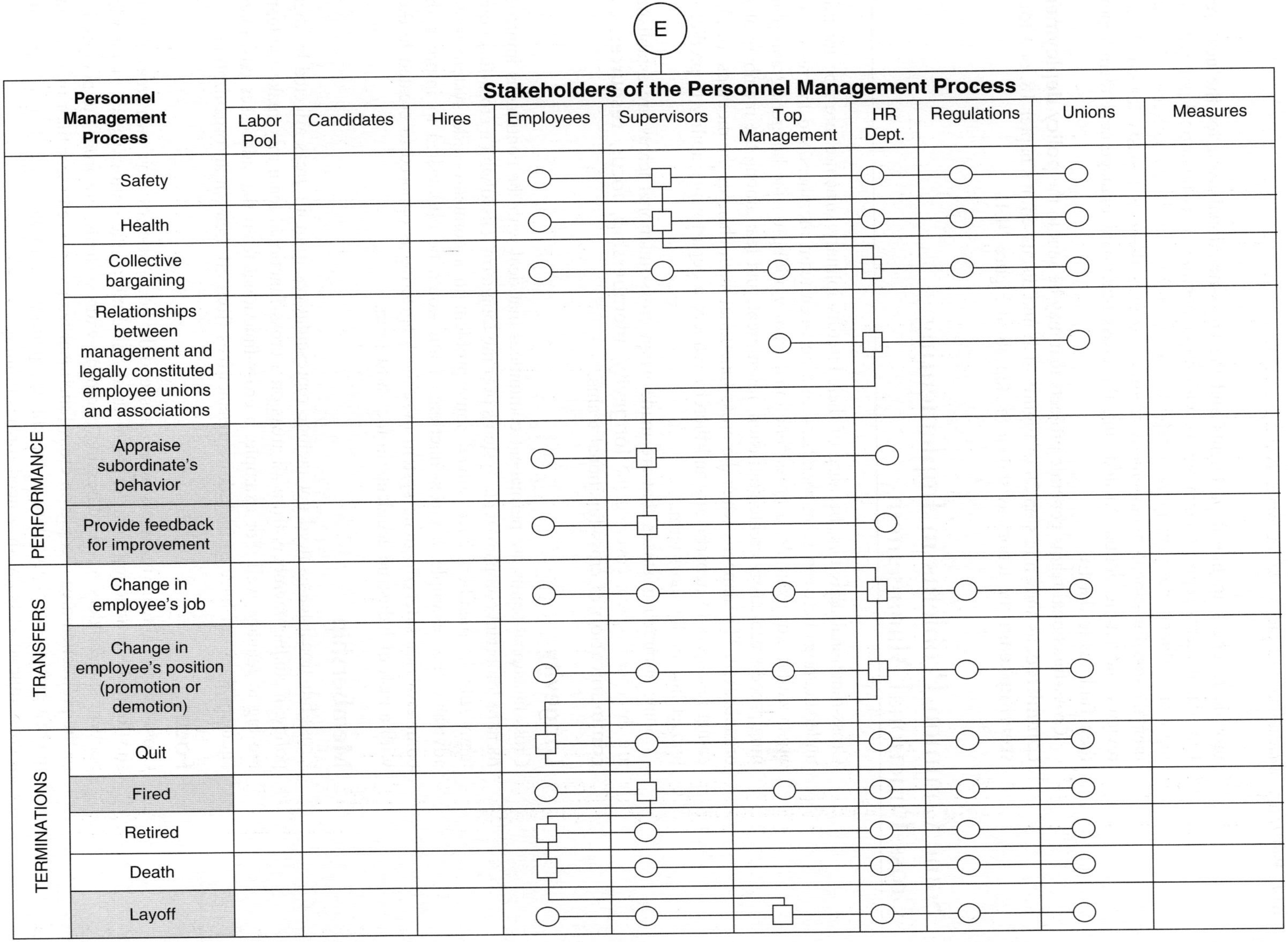

Ⓔ

Stakeholders of the Personnel Management Process

Personnel Management Process		Labor Pool	Candidates	Hires	Employees	Supervisors	Top Management	HR Dept.	Regulations	Unions	Measures
	Safety				○	□		○	○	○	
	Health				○	□		○	○	○	
	Collective bargaining				○	○	○	□	○	○	
	Relationships between management and legally constituted employee unions and associations						○	□	○	○	
PERFORMANCE	Appraise subordinate's behavior				○	□		○			
	Provide feedback for improvement				○	□		○			
TRANSFERS	Change in employee's job				○	○	○	□	○	○	
	Change in employee's position (promotion or demotion)				○	○	○	□	○	○	
TERMINATIONS	Quit				□	○	○	○	○	○	
	Fired				○	□	○	○	○	○	
	Retired				□	○		○	○	○	
	Death				□	○		○	○	○	
	Layoff				○	○	□	○	○	○	

provide feedback to line departments and the cross-functional team for the next year. Line departments report their progress with implementing cross-functional policy by filing a cross-functional management report. The cross-functional team collects all departmental cross-functional management reports and uses them as a basis for conducting reviews and taking action. In addition, the cross-functional management team reports their findings to the EC.

Cross-functional teams generate projects that may be sent to the **policy deployment committee,** as shown in step 29 of Figure 14.1, and discussed in Chapter 18, or a **local steering team** for action, as shown in step 30 of Figure 14.1.

Some Common Problems in Implementing Cross-Functional Management

Cross-functional activities, because of their interdisciplinary structure, are ripe for misunderstandings between team members, and between team members and the rest of the organization. For example, a cross-functional team working on the budgeting and planning process can easily create confusion, resentment, and fear among the members of an organization. This happens when the cross-functional team changes the methods for allocating resources to departments and thereby reduces a department's ability to predict its budget line in the short term.

Some common mistakes that are made when cross-functional teams are established are discussed below, covering the **longevity, membership, focus, resources,** and **communication** of cross-functional teams.

Longevity

Cross-functional teams are permanent committees that deal with the continuous improvement of important company-wide systems over the long term. Dissolving a cross-functional team after its members have solved some problem in a company-wide system is not advisable. For example, a cross-functional team would be established to improve the company-wide safety/hygiene system over the long term, as opposed to created to deal with a rash of industrial accidents in the short term.

Membership

Cross-functional teams need not include representatives from all areas affected by their policy; including members from all areas on a cross-functional team may make the team too big to manage well. For example, a cross-functional team that addresses cost management does not have to include representatives from all areas in an organization.

Focus

Cross-functional team members must transcend the boundaries of their own areas. A person from the production area learns to think in terms of the entire system of interdependent stakeholders when addressing company-wide systems, not from the perspective of the production area. People on cross-functional teams who represent their own special interest groups, not the welfare of the entire organization, are not ready to participate on a cross-functional team; they need further training.

Communication

It is extremely important that cross-functional policy be communicated to all relevant members of an organization's interdependent system of stakeholders. Only through communication can people understand and buy into the company-wide changes that can emanate from a cross-functional team. Recall from step 10 of Figure 14.1, the diffusion of a new idea, in this case a cross-functional policy, requires a specific plan of action that is based on the appropriate theories of communication.

A Generic Example of Cross-Functional Management: Standardization of a Corporate-Wide Method for Cutting Cost

This section demonstrates how cross-functional management utilizes the System of Profound Knowledge to create new processes to resolve existing problems in corporate-wide processes. The corporate-wide process examined in this section is the cost-cutting process.

Traditional Cost-Cutting Process

A common process for cutting costs x percent or y dollars consists of three steps. First, managers build up a layer of inefficiency over time. For example, if a job becomes obsolete because of computerization, the person holding the job is transferred to other work or let go, but the job is not deleted from the payroll. If the manager is asked to cut cost by x percent or y dollars, she puts forth the hidden resources from the obsolete job. Second, managers identify nonessential expense items. For example, in some departments training dollars or gifts/awards dollars or travel dollars are nonessential to the functioning of the department. If the manager cannot cut her costs x percent or y dollars using the method in the first step, she will cut nonessential expense items in the budget, in part or in whole. Third, managers prioritize essential expense items for budget cuts. For example, managers may rank their personnel from most meritorious to the least meritorious, or from most senior to most junior. If the manager cannot cut her costs x percent of y dollars using the methods in the first and second step, she will begin to cut essential expense items until the required x percent or y dollars cost cut is achieved in her area.

The above process for cutting costs causes managers to hide resources from top management. Frequently, these hidden resources are desperately needed elsewhere in the organization. This results in suboptimization of the organization as a whole.

Cross-Functional Management Cost-Cutting Process

A cross-functional management cost-cutting process is used by a manager to attain a rational x percent or y dollars decrease in costs using process improvement in her area. The following steps explain how the manager applies a cross-functional management process in her daily management.

1. Clarify the purpose or aim of the proposed daily management process in terms of a x percent or y dollars cut in costs. The x percent or y dollars cut in costs should not be an arbitrary numerical goal, but rather, it should be based on actual information, such as break-even analysis.

2. Prepare a list of the divisions or departments that are affected by the proposed daily management process.

3. Construct an integrated flowchart of the proposed daily management process that reflects the x percent or y dollars cut in costs.

4. Identify measures to monitor the existing and proposed daily management process. Show actual documentation on costs and revenues for the existing and proposed daily management process.

5. Implement the proposed process and measures. Show documentation on costs and revenues for the proposed process.

If the proposed daily management process achieves the x percent or y dollars cost cut, team members continue to improve the process. If the proposed daily management process does not achieve the cost-cutting goal, team members continue to try with the help of higher management. If this is successful, team members continue to improve the process.

If the proposed daily management process does not achieve the x percent or y dollars cost cut with the help of higher management, then top management makes decisions about the reallocation of organizational resources. If this is successful, it is a temporary measure and team members continue to try to cut costs, with the assistance of top management or outside expertise, if needed.

Application of the CFM Cost-Cutting Process in Human Resources

In this section we apply the above cross-functional management cost-cutting process to the Selection subsystem of the Personnel Management process in Figure 17.1. The aim of the application is to cut costs in the Human Resources department by $100,000. The $100,000 cost cut is not an arbitrary numerical goal. It is based on analyses of industry practices and the cost structure of all departments in the organization. Top management has determined that the Human Resources department needs to cut costs by $100,000 to optimize the entire organization. Other departments' cost cuts range between $0 and $1,500,000.

A list of the stakeholders of the Selection subprocess of the Personnel Management process includes new hires, employees, supervisors, top managers, and the employees of the Human Resources department. The director of the Human Resources department will chair this team.

An integrated flowchart of the existing Selection subprocess can be seen in the *Selection* section of Figure 17.1. The key measure used to monitor the effect of change on the Selection subprocess is the number of screening examinations (scholastic verification, crime check, and drug test) per month. Baseline data will be collected for the measure before any process change is put into practice. Data will also be collected for the measure after any process change is put into practice. The relevant costs for the existing cost-cutting process include scholastic verification costs ($15.50 per candidate), crime check costs ($24.50 per candidate), and drug test costs ($84.00 per candidate). If there are n candidates who are screened in a month, then the monthly screening cost is $124n.

An improvement to the existing Selection subprocess shown in Figure 17.1 is to move the *Supervise physical and psychological examinations of selected employees* step from its current position in the Selection process after *Screen potential employees* and before *Interview potential employees* to a position after the *Select hiree* step and before the *Hire employee* step. The logic of this change is that a very low percentage of candidates fail the screening examinations; hence, screening examinations do not effectively reduce the candidate pool. Screening examinations should be done only on the finalist candidate for a given job, to minimize costs.

The relevant costs for the improved Selection subprocess are one set of screening examinations for each finalist, for each job. If a finalist passes the screening examinations, then the total screening cost for any given job is $124.

The Human Resources department used to conduct about 83 or 84 screening examinations per month, or 1,000 per year, at a yearly cost of $124,000. Now, the Human Resources department conducts screening examinations only on finalists. For the same period of time, there were 100 finalists. The screening costs in the new process are $12,400, assuming all finalists pass their screening examinations. This represents a savings of $111,600 ($124,000 − $12,400), which surpasses the needed cost cut of $100,000.

A Manufacturing Application: Toyota Forklift

In this section, we present the cross-functional management **quality assurance process** for **new product development** used in all six divisions of the Toyota Motor Corporation [see Reference 2, pp. 85–97]. The process was developed using the five-step cross-functional management model presented in "Implementing Cross-Functional Management" on page 602. Additionally, this section includes an application of the model in the development of the Toyota X300 forklift.

Each division of Toyota is responsible for the development of new products. The process begins with input from the long-range business plan and annual policy statement of a division. The departments in each division responsible for new product development assume development tasks based on Toyota's cross-functional quality assurance process, as shown in Figure 17.2. These responsibilities span product planning through production preparation.

Management reviews are conducted by managers to check and follow up new product development at predetermined intervals. **Design reviews** are conducted at appropriate places in the quality assurance system to determine whether it is appropriate to advance to the next phase of new product development.

Quality Assurance Activity in the Development of the X300 Forklift

The Toyota design review system was used in the development of the X300 forklift at Toyota Forklift. This system integrated six design reviews into the development of the X300 forklift.

The basic idea behind the development of the X300 forklift was to provide an excellent product through farsighted prediction of market trends and customer needs, and to win customer satisfaction and trust.

FIGURE 17.2   Toyota's Cross-Functional Quality Assurance Process

Reprinted from *Cross-Functional Management: Principles and Practical Applications,* Kenji Kurogane, editor-in-chief. Copyright © 1993 by Asian Productivity Organization. Reprinted by permission of the Asian Productivity Organization. Distributed in the U.S., Canada, and Western Europe by Quality Resources, White Plains, NY 10601.

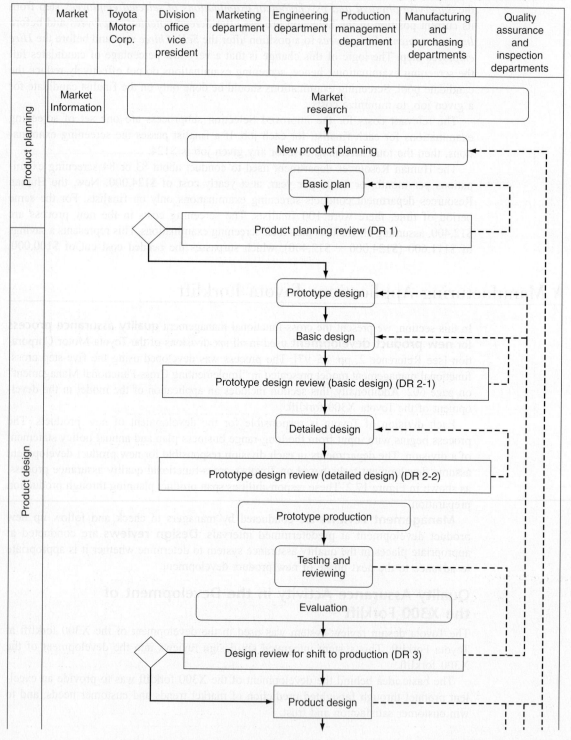

FIGURE 17.2 (concluded)

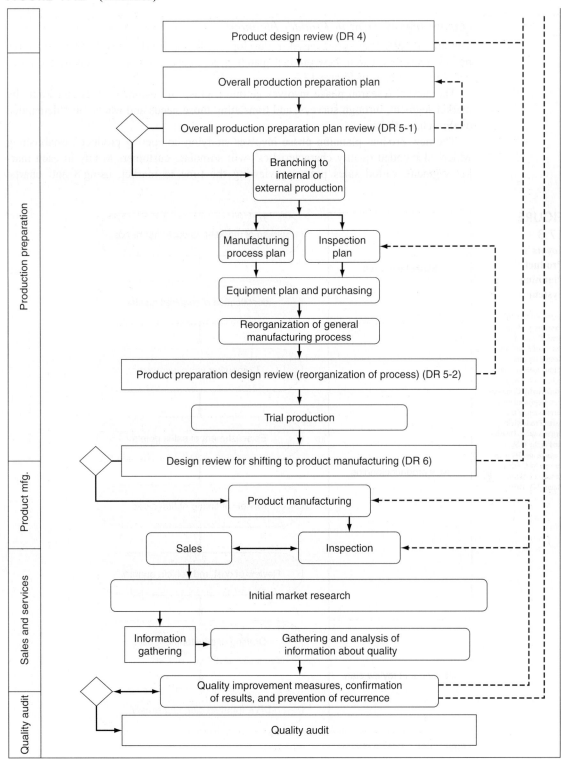

Legend: DR = design review

Quality Improvement in Product Planning

The product planning system used to develop the Toyota forklift X300 consists of three phases: market research, new product planning, and developing and reviewing the product plan, as shown in Figure 17.3.

The market research phase involves getting a grasp of customer needs and wants by market segment, through surveys, and translating those needs and wants into "demanded quality characteristics."

The new product planning phase involves studying competing products; establishing which "demanded quality characteristics" will stimulate customers to buy in each market segment, called sales points; reviewing the time to market, using Gantt charts,

FIGURE 17.3

Toyota's Product Planning System

Reprinted from *Cross-Functional Management: Principles and Practical Applications,* Kenji Kurogane, editor-in-chief. Copyright © 1993 by Asian Productivity Organization. Reprinted by permission of the Asian Productivity Organization. Distributed in the U.S., Canada, and Western Europe by Quality Resources, White Plains, NY 10601.

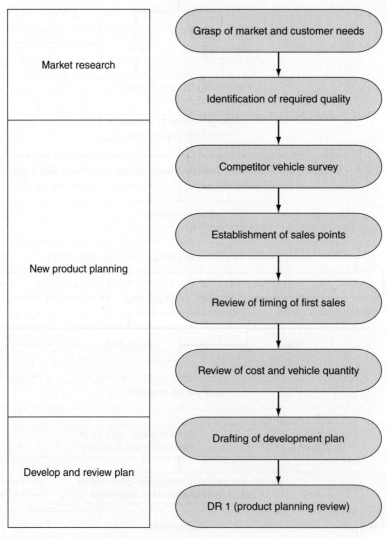

Legend: DR = design review

PERT/CPM, or other scheduling methods; reviewing the production costs of the product; and forecasting the demand for the product in each market segment.

The develop and review plan phase involves drafting a development plan for the X300 forklift and conducting a product planning review.

Quality Improvement in Product Design

The product design system used to develop the X300 forklift consists of six phases: prototype design, prototype production, test and review, evaluation, shift to production, and product design, as shown in Figure 17.4.

The prototype design phase involves conducting an engineering policy review for the new product functions. This includes developing a detailed list of relevant processes, parts, mechanisms, and functions with specifications, preparing a critical functions evaluation report, and performing bottleneck engineering of relevant processes.

The prototype production phase involves a detailed design review of the X300 forklift.

The test and review and evaluation phases involve establishing test conditions and evaluation criteria through surveys of actual usage conditions and an accelerated endurance bench test. Life expectancy is estimated on the basis of test results and survey data. The above activities increase the degree of comfort at Toyota Forklift in predicting that the design of the X300 is going according to plan and will require few modifications later in its life cycle.

The shift to production phase involves a pass or fail review to shift to trial production.

The product design phase involves the finalization of detailed product drawings and a product design review to determine conformance of design quality to overall quality specifications.

Quality Improvement in Production Preparation

The production preparation system used to develop the X300 forklift consists of eight phases: developing a general production plan, developing a manufacturing process plan, developing an equipment plan, purchasing equipment, reorganizing individual processes to ensure machine capability, reorganizing the entire production process to ensure system capability, trial production, and shifting to product manufacturing, as shown in Figure 17.5 on page 619.

The general production plan involves obtaining confirmation of existing product and process problems, conducting a review to determine if those problems have been resolved, and identifying the characteristics of machines and equipment that were deployed in the product design phase.

The manufacturing process plan involves conducting failure modes and effect analysis (FMEA) on the characteristics of machines and equipment, and discovering any bottleneck problems resulting from equipment and production methods.

The equipment plan phase involves determining the specifications of the equipment required to manufacture the X300 forklift for cost estimation purposes.

The equipment purchasing phase involves confirming the capability of machines and equipment after specifications have been costed out, generating purchase orders for machinery and equipment, and conducting a design review for the completed machines and equipment processes.

FIGURE 17.4 Toyota's Product Design System

Reprinted from *Cross-Functional Management: Principles and Practical Applications*, Kenji Kurogane, editor-in-chief. Copyright © 1993 by Asian Productivity Organization. Reprinted by permission of the Asian Productivity Organization. Distributed in the U.S., Canada, and Western Europe by Quality Resources, White Plains, NY 10601.

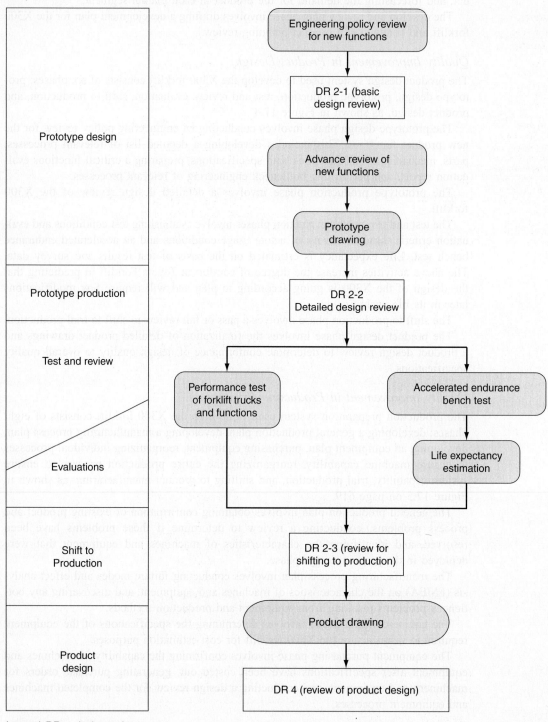

Legend: DR = design review

**FIGURE
17.5**

**Toyota's
Production
Preparation
System**

Reprinted from *Cross-Functional Management: Principles and Practical Applications*, Kenji Kurogane, editor-in- chief. Copyright © 1993 by Asian Productivity Organization. Reprinted by permission of the Asian Productivity Organization. Distributed in the U.S., Canada, and Western Europe by Quality Resources, White Plains, NY 10601.

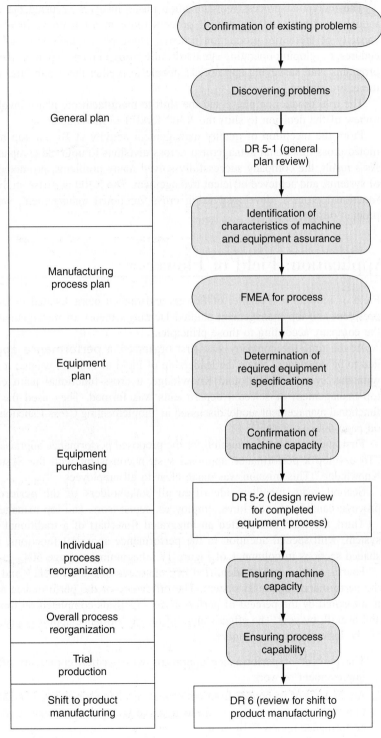

Legend: DR = design review

The individual process reorganization phase involves ensuring the capacity of individual machines, and the overall process reorganization phase involves ensuring the capacity of the entire production process. These phases include establishing work procedures, developing operating standards, allocating human resources, developing training programs, and surveying appropriate people to predict the capabilities of machines and the entire system.

The trial production phase and the shift to manufacturing phase involve a pass or fail review of the decision to shift the X300 forklift to manufacturing.

From the inception of quality management activity at Toyota, top management promoted cross-functional management across divisions to upgrade company-wide systems. As a result, the company successfully solved many problems, promoted standardization of systems, and achieved efficient management. The X300 is a case study in how a cross-functional process, developed using cross-functional management, was used for new product design.

A Service Application: Field of Flowers

Field of Flowers is a retailer of flowers and related items located in Davie, Florida. Its president and top management studied Deming's theory of management and structured the company according to those principles.

At the time the company was first organized, a **performance appraisal system** had to be developed. Since the leadership of Field of Flowers wanted it to be in keeping with the System of Profound Knowledge, a cross-functional team composed of the top management of selected departments was formed. They used the five-step cross-functional management model discussed in "Implementing Cross-Functional Management" on page 602.

First, the team stated a mission for the proposed performance appraisal system. It was: "To develop a performance appraisal system consistent with the System of Profound Knowledge." This mission was made clear to all employees.

Second, team members identified all stakeholders of the performance appraisal process: candidates, new hires, employees, supervisors, and top management.

Third, the team constructed an integrated flowchart of a traditional human resource system, with special attention to the performance appraisal functions, as shown in the shaded sections in column 1 of Figure 17.1 beginning on page 604.

Fourth, team members identified key measures of the efficiency and effectiveness of the performance appraisal system. The efficiency of the performance appraisal process is measured by the percent of performance appraisals completed on time, by supervisor and overall, by year. The effectiveness of the performance appraisal process is measured by the following key indicators:

1. The percent of performance appraisals with written comments offering ideas for improvement of work.

2. An analysis of responses from employees receiving a negative evaluation to the question "Did you know what to do to improve your job performance upon leaving your performance review?" by year.

Fifth, team members developed modifications to the integrated flowchart shown in Figure 17.1 based on the System of Profound Knowledge. The ideas for the modifications came from the work of Peter Scholtes [see Reference 4]. Scholtes identified the following functions as the components of a performance appraisal system:

- Provide feedback to employees on their work.
- Provide a basis for salary increases and bonuses.
- Identify candidates for promotion.
- Provide periodic direction of an employee's work.
- Provide an opportunity to give recognition, direction, and feedback regarding special projects.
- Identify needs for training, education, and skill or career development.
- Provide an equitable, objective, defensible system that satisfies the requirements of the 1964 Civil Rights Act and the Equal Opportunity Commission guidelines of 1966 and 1970.
- Provide a channel for communication.

The Revised System

The *Provide feedback for improvement* step in the *Performance* section of Figure 17.1 is redefined to be providing an employee with feedback on his work. Feedback can be provided by: identifying the major processes in which the employee is involved, identifying the major work group or groups to which the employee belongs, developing a list of major feedback resources for the employee (e.g., key customers and suppliers), and developing an agenda and method for obtaining feedback from each feedback resource.

The *Wage and salary determination, Raises, Bonuses,* and *Other monetary issues* steps in the *Compensation Management* section and the *Workers' compensation* step in the *Benefits Management* section of Figure 17.1 are redefined to be providing a basis for salary increases and bonuses based on market rate (what it would cost to replace someone on the open market); accumulation of skills (flexibility due to acquired abilities); accumulation of responsibility (depth of contribution to a greater number of processes and influence over a larger number of employees); seniority within an organization and within a job classification; and prosperity (profit-sharing of the entire organization, not one segment of the organization).

The *Change in employee's position (promotion or demotion)* step in the *Transfers* section of Figure 17.1 is redefined to be identifying candidates for promotion by providing special assignments that contain elements of the promotion job; utilizing an assessment center to observe candidates exercising the skills needed in the promotion job under realistic conditions (if available); determining the needs and wants of the stakeholders of the promotion job with respect to the characteristics of the person who will assume the promotion job; and developing an organizational culture in which promotion is not the only vehicle for people to exercise leadership and influence, to get rewards and recognition, or to stretch and challenge themselves in their jobs and careers.

The *Familiarize employees with objectives* and *Familiarize employees with work expectations* steps of the *Orientation* section of Figure 17.1 are redefined to be providing periodic direction of employees by communicating the organization's strategic and business plans to help each employee define his work, and spending time with each employee to develop methods to promote the organization's strategic and business plans.

The *Job enhancement* step of the *Development* section and the *Appraise subordinate's behavior* step of the *Performance* section of Figure 17.1 are redefined to be providing an opportunity to give recognition, direction, and feedback to an employee regarding his work on special projects.

All of the training steps in the *Training (Vocational Skills)* section of Figure 17.1 are redefined to be identifying each employee's needs for training through the empowerment process; that is, each employee receives the training required to turn the SDSA and PDSA cycles for process improvement.

The *Forecast employment requirements* step of the *Human Resources Planning* section, the *Locate qualified job candidates* step of the *Recruitment* section, the *Select hiree* step of the *Selection* section, and the *Fired* and *Layoff* steps of the *Terminations* section of Figure 17.1 are redefined to be providing an equitable, objective, defensible system that satisfies the requirements of the 1964 Civil Rights Act and the Equal Opportunity Commission guidelines of 1966 and 1970. This is accomplished by committing to the values and spirit inscribed in the law, not just by conforming to the law.

The *Resolve personal problems* and *Improve employee performance* steps of the *Employee Relations* section of Figure 17.1 are redefined to be providing a channel for communication that otherwise would probably not occur. This can be accomplished by all employees in an organization asking and answering the following questions: With whom is it important to maintain communication? For what purpose? With what frequency? In what kind of setting, format, or agenda? Answers to the above questions should promote the flow of information and knowledge into channels of communication between people in organizations.

It is important to realize that all of the above processes form an interdependent system of processes. It does not make sense to adopt a new process for providing employees with a basis for salary and bonuses and not provide a process for identifying needs for training, education, and skill or career development. To do so may create a monster worse than the existing system of performance appraisal. For example, guaranteeing salary based on seniority without any process to improve the employee or organizational processes could be a formula for disaster.

Given the integrated flowchart in Figure 17.1 and redefinition of the above steps in the flowchart, the Field of Flowers cross-functional team reconceptualized the performance appraisal process. The results are presented in the following excerpts, paraphrases, and unwritten understandings from the Field of Flowers Employees Handbook.

Excerpts are shown in regular type. Unwritten understandings are in italics. Comments by the authors of this text are noted in bold italics.

Issue 1: Provide Employees Feedback on Their Work

All associates have the following rights: . . . the right to have access to all useful, pertinent information about the enterprise and about one's particular job . . . This includes the right to participate in the process or decision-making related to one's work area.

If you have questions or concerns about anything related to your employment, talk with your team leader. That person will assist you in every way possible.

Issue 2: Provide a Basis for Salary Increases and Bonuses

All employees begin their careers with Field of Flowers at the same hourly salary. This applies to everyone: floral arrangers, delivery personnel, sales associates, and so on. The orientation period for every potential associate is based on the needs of that particular individual. Thus, the length of orientation varies from person to person. After orientation is complete, employees become level two associates and their hourly salary is automatically raised to a standard level. After two years, level two associates become tenured associates and maintain their hourly salary plus profit-sharing. Associates who have achieved tenured status will be beneficiaries of profit-sharing for any year in which profit-sharing is appropriate (according to the established corporate guidelines). Percentage of profit-sharing will be based upon earned income. Part-time and full-time associates will participate in profit-sharing. *All employees know daily sales figures and are provided complete financial disclosure once each year so that they understand the distribution of profit-sharing.*

Issue 3: Identify Candidates for Promotion

Promotion. We believe in the benefits of advancing people from within the organization whenever possible. We recognize that this requires that numerous very able people be hired into entry level positions and be offered the opportunity to expand their knowledge.

Termination. *The following sections of the Employees Handbook deal with termination. We have decided to place these sections under issue 3 because they deal with termination (a form of demotion).*

All tenured associates have the right to employment security. In keeping with its philosophy of long-term commitment to its associates, Field of Flowers will consider layoffs of tenured associates only after all other remedies—including reduced profit expectations—have been exhausted. If workforce reductions become necessary for the survival of the company, then a council of tenured associates will be formed to advise management as to the best manner in which to make those reductions. In the case of severe disciplinary action or dismissal for cause, tenured associates will have the right to demand peer review of such action. An elected Associates' Council will review such cases; they will have the authority to overturn or revise the action taken.

During the Orientation process, especially during the first 90 days of employment, associates are expected to be attentive and interested in learning the procedures we follow. After the Trial Period ends and the associate is raised to Associate II, he or she is expected to follow the guidelines and procedures that were a part of the Orientation/Training. Any associate who deliberately and knowingly refuses to adhere to established procedures can be dismissed without following the usual measures that preclude termination without counseling and documentation.

Issue 4: Provide Periodic Direction to Employee's Work

Field of Flowers' leadership provides feedback to employees by stating and constantly pursuing their mission, taking responsibility for processes, and working with employees to develop plans for the methods needed to achieve the Field of Flowers mission.

Field of Flowers has a statement of mission and values. This statement creates a culture in which leadership provides direction to employees. The statement appears below:

> **In management, the first concern of the company is the happiness of the people who are connected with it. If the people do not feel happy and cannot be made happy, that company does not deserve to exist.**
> **–Ishikawa**

The primary mission of Field of Flowers is to provide stable, safe, fulfilling employment for our family of associates. We realize that the way to accomplish this is to be recognized by the community as the company, in our chosen field of endeavor, which provides the highest quality products and services to its customers.

We believe in the importance of constancy of purpose toward never-ending improvement of the processes which produce our products and services. We further believe that the leadership of the company must take responsibility for these processes. Associates must not be held accountable for improving results if they do not have the authority or the resources to change the processes which produce those results.

We must always be alert to the harm that can result from setting arbitrary numerical goals and standards without providing the methods for achieving them.

Issue 5: Provide an Opportunity to Give Recognition, Direction, and Feedback to an Employee Regarding Her Work on Special Projects

All associates are given opportunities to grow and develop in ways that are mutually beneficial to themselves and the company. Such growth and development can include special projects. It is the responsibility of management to set into motion and nurture the improvements and innovations developed by associates. This type of leadership will stimulate the intrinsic motivation of associates.

Issue 6: Identify an Employee's Needs for Training, Education, and Skill or Career Development

The Management Team (top management of Field of Flowers) accepts complete responsibility for accurately and adequately training all associates. By empowering associates with knowledge and skill, stress is reduced and their employment experience can be pleasant and rewarding.

We believe in vigorous programs for training and education so that our associates are able to grow as workers as well as in other aspects of their lives.

. . . training and a supportive attitude on the part of leadership, will empower front line associates to make decisions on their own.

Tuition reimbursement is available to associates with at least one year of service. Company approval is required prior to enrollment and will be determined on a case by case basis.

Issue 7: Provide an Equitable, Objective, Defensible System That Satisfies the Requirements of the 1964 Civil Rights Act and the Equal Opportunity Commission Guidelines of 1966 and 1970

We are committed to selecting the most qualified person for each position in our company. Our success is dependent upon our maintaining high standards and emphasizing teamwork! All personnel selections are in accordance with Equal Employment Opportunity guidelines.

Each employee contributes to Field of Flowers' success; each will be treated fairly.

Issue 8: Provide a Channel for Communication

The company culture of Field of Flowers promotes open, multi-way communication within and between all levels of employees. The performance appraisal process at Field of Flowers is a daily ongoing process of communication that constantly seeks to increase employees' ability to take pride in their work and joy in the outcome, and to optimize its interdependent system of stakeholders.

The development of the performance appraisal system was the first step (Standardize) of the SDSA cycle. The team progressed through the Do, Study, and Act stages and now continuously works on improvement of the performance appraisal system through application of the PDSA cycle.

In addition to the above eight issues, the management team at Field of Flowers works continuously to improve their human resource planning, recruitment, selection, and orientation processes. They believe that the need for the remedial aspects of performance appraisal is inversely related to the quality of the people that enter their organization. Conversely, they believe that the need for the constructive aspects of performance appraisal is always present in an organization.

Summary

Chapter 17 discussed cross-functional management, Prong 2 of the quality management model presented in this book. Cross-functional management is important because it weaves together the vertical (line) functions of management with the horizontal (interdepartmental) functions of management. Primary applications of cross-functional management include quality management, cost management, delivery management, and personnel management. Other applications are new product development, sales management, and safety management.

The members of the executive committee initially form cross-functional teams and select their leaders. The leader, who should be an executive in charge of a function, recommends the members for the team—preferably no more than five people. It is not necessary for all team members to come from affected areas. All team members are trained in appropriate theory and practice.

In small organizations, one cross-functional team comprising all relevant executives can be established to coordinate and optimize all company-wide systems. In large organizations, one cross-functional team can be set up for each company-wide system, such as quality management, safety management, or personnel management. The EC reviews, manages, and coordinates all cross-functional teams. Cross-functional management reviews are conducted at least yearly by the cross-functional team leader.

Implementing cross-functional management is difficult because of its interdisciplinary nature. To ensure the success of a cross-functional team, it is created with the expectation that it will be permanent and will deal with continuous improvement of a company-wide system over the long term. Cross-functional team members learn to think in terms of the whole system, not just their areas. Communicating the results of the cross-functional team's work is extremely important.

We examined a generic cross-functional management system for cutting costs in a standardized fashion across the different areas in an organization; a cross-functional management system for new product development used in a manufacturing company, Toyota Forklift; and how a service company, Field of Flowers, used a cross-functional team to create its performance appraisal system.

Key Terms

communication, *610*
cost management, *601*
cross-functional management, *602*
design reviews, *613*
executive committee, *601*
focus, *610*
integrated flowchart, *602*
local steering team, *610*

longevity, *610*
management reviews, *613*
membership, *610*
new product development, *613*
PDSA cycle, *603*
performance appraisal systems, *620*
personnel management, *603*

policy deployment committee, *610*
Prong 2, *602*
quality assurance process, *613*
quality management, *603*
resources, *610*
System of Profound Knowledge, *603*

References

1. K. Ishikawa, "Management in Vertical-Threaded Society," *Quality Control,* 32, No. 1, 1981, pp. 4–5.

2. K. Kurogane (1993), *Cross-Functional Management: Principles and Practical Applications* (Tokyo: Asian Productivity Organization).

3. S. Mizuno (1988), *Company-Wide Total Quality Control* (Tokyo: Asian Productivity Organization).

4. P. Scholtes (1987), *An Elaboration on Deming's Teachings on Performance Appraisal* (Madison, WI: Joiner Associates).

Chapter 18

The Fork Model for Quality Management: Prong 3, or Policy Management

Sections

Chapter Objectives

- To describe the committees required to accomplish policy management
- To describe the steps necessary to conduct an initial presidential review
- To discuss the role of the executive committee in the development of a strategic plan, with objectives based on the organization's vision and mission statements, values and beliefs, organizational and environmental factors, crises, key processes, and technology

- To discuss the role of the policy deployment committee in developing a set of integrated improvement plans
- To discuss the use of a dashboard in deploying the mission statement and the strategic and business presidential objectives
- To discuss the role of the executive committee and the local steering teams in policy implementation
- To discuss the role of the executive committee, policy deployment committee, and local steering teams in conducting periodic reviews and obtaining necessary feedback for promoting process improvement efforts
- To discuss the relationship between policy management and daily management
- To present detailed examples of policy management

Introduction

In this chapter we explain what is required to set policy, deploy policy, implement policy, study policy, provide feedback to employees on policy, and conduct a presidential review of policy in an organization. Policy management is Prong 3 of the quality management model presented in this book.

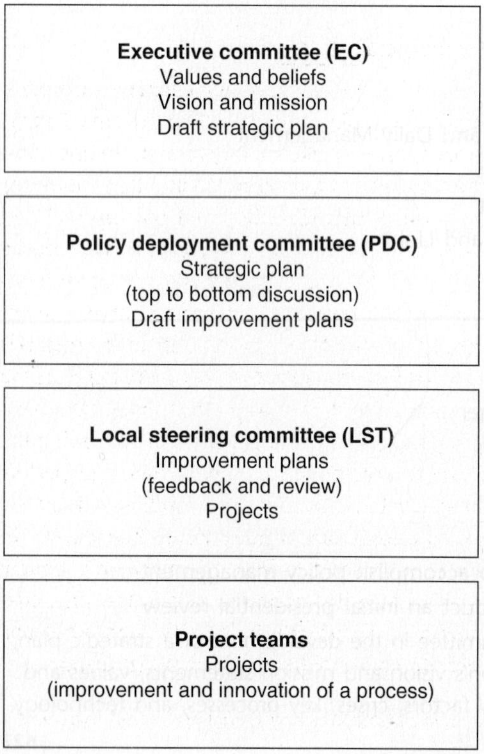

Policy management is performed by turning the PDSA cycle to improve and innovate the methods responsible for minimizing the difference between corporate results and corporate targets, or to change the direction of an organization. [See Reference 2; Reference 7, pp. 59–71; Reference 10; Reference 12.] Corporate targets are set to allocate resources between corporate methods. Policy management assumes that daily management and cross-functional management are at work in the organization.

Policy management is accomplished through an interlocking system of committees, as shown in Figure 18.1.

The executive committee (EC) is responsible for setting the strategic plan for the entire organization. This includes establishing values and beliefs, developing statements of vision and mission, and preparing a draft set of strategic objectives. The policy deployment committee (PDC) is responsible for deploying the strategic objectives in the entire organization. This includes developing an improvement plan (set of short-term tactics) for each department. A local steering team (LST) is responsible for implementing policy (short-term tactics) within a department by coordinating and managing project teams. Project teams implement policy through improvement and innovation of the processes highlighted for attention.

The local steering teams conduct meetings with project teams, called feedback and review sessions, to learn about team activity, promote quality theory and tools, and

FIGURE 18.1   **Committee Structure for Policy Management**

Executive committee (EC)
Values and beliefs
Vision and mission
Draft strategic plan

Policy deployment committee (PDC)
Strategic plan
(top to bottom discussion)
Draft improvement plans

Local steering committee (LST)
Improvement plans
(feedback and review)
Projects

Project teams
Projects
(improvement and innovation of a process)

manage and coordinate team activities to pursue company policy. The policy deployment committee conducts meetings with local steering committees, called mini-sitcons, to learn about team activity, promote quality theory and tools, coordinate and manage project teams to optimize company policy, and, if necessary, to reallocate resources between project teams (according to revised targets). Finally, the president meets with the leader of each department to understand the state of quality in the organization and to determine if policy (strategic objectives) is being implemented throughout the organization.

Initial Presidential Review

The president conducts an initial **presidential review,** as shown in step 28 of Figure 14.1, to determine the state of the organization and to develop a plan of action for the promotion of corporate policy. Presidential reviews are high-level studies of an organization's departments by the president or chief executive officer.[1]

During presidential reviews, the leaders of the departments explain to the president their mission and the status of projects emanating from the strategic and improvement plans. Normally, this information is conveyed through presentations. Much attention is devoted to the linkage between corporate and department strategies and the progress toward the achievement of these strategies. Problems in planning and executing these strategies are discussed, and attempts are made to identify the causes of these problems. Through the presidential review, the president is able to evaluate the state of quality and management in the organization.

Reasons for Conducting the Presidential Review

Presidential reviews are conducted, first, to determine the extent of achievement of organizational policy. Reviews are conducted to verify the implementation of improvement plans and to assess and improve the management process used to achieve the mission. In one company, the president found that one of his policies had been misinterpreted and that the troops were marching in the opposite direction. The mistake was identified and quickly rectified to avert much wasted effort. This is not a rare occurrence in large organizations, because information is filtered by each layer of management. Second, presidential reviews are conducted to determine the cost to the organization of achieving its strategic and improvement plans. Third, presidential reviews are conducted to prevent deterioration in those methods which have not been highlighted for attention in **policy management,** or **Prong 3** of the detailed fork model, as a result of the reallocation of resources to methods that have been highlighted for attention. Finally, presidential reviews identify the major problems facing the organization. The president tries to discover those problems that affect functional performance but cannot be solved at the functional level. Generally, these problems must be addressed at the company level since the causes cross many organizational boundaries. In this way, no single function has the authority to promote solutions. Most major company problems are cross-functional and thus difficult to identify; because of its cross-functional nature, the presidential review provides a significant opportunity to identify such problems. Once identified, these problems are turned over to appropriate cross-functional teams.

---

[1] This section of the chapter was rewritten from material prepared by Francisco "Tony" Avello of Florida Power and Light Company, Miami, FL, 1992.

Benefits of Presidential Reviews

One benefit of presidential reviews is that they create a dialogue between the president and midlevel management, encouraging an atmosphere of trust that helps bring out information about problems. The information provides an opportunity for the president to promote joy in work and pride in the outcome for all employees.

Another benefit is the insight they give to the president about the operations and culture of the organization. Frequently, this information is not available through normal channels of communication. Examples of information that can be gleaned by the president include the skill level of the managers and supervisors, the attitudes of employees toward improvement of methods, and employee morale. This information is necessary to promote the strategic and improvement plans.

The president will have a good understanding of the major problems facing the organization after a full round of presidential reviews. So, to a certain extent, she should have a good idea about the possible causes of problems. The president knows the areas that should be involved in the improvement activities, and should also know the attitudes and skills of employees in carrying out the strategic and improvement plans. Finally, she knows the level of training that will be needed throughout the organization to work on the strategic and improvement plans.

Barriers to the Presidential Review

Initially, the president may resist conducting a presidential review because of demands on her time. All too often, there is a desire to obtain information from an **executive summary;** however, the executive summary does not provide sufficient information to establish or change the direction of the company. One company president tells the story of how he went from opposing presidential reviews to so thoroughly embracing them that he began to conduct half-day reviews on a quarterly basis with each of his departments.

Selecting the Departments and Topics to Review

Departments and topics are selected for presidential review by examining the policies and projects that were not successful in previous years, or failures of the management system. These problems identify the departments that are candidates for presidential review. It is important that the president does not assign fault for problems. Blame-fixing makes people defensive and unwilling to identify problems. It creates fear in the workplace. The president must take responsibility for problems in the system.

Another way of selecting departments and/or topics for presidential review is to review all departments. This has the advantage of not singling out any department's past failures, thus avoiding a threatening situation. One drawback to this approach is that a greater number of departments must be reviewed. Ultimately, the culture of the company and the existing organizational climate will dictate which alternative is best. The issue of not creating a threatening situation is an important one and should be weighed carefully before deciding which approach to take.

Informing the Departments to be Reviewed

Once the topics and functions have been identified, the next step is to announce the reviews. This is done through a meeting of senior managers, where the purpose of the reviews is explained, the names of the departments that will participate in the reviews are announced, and the format of the reviews is discussed. If necessary, the president should offer staff members help in further clarifying the objectives, guidelines, and manner of the reviews. This is also a good time to define the ground rules to follow during the reviews.

Ground Rules for the Presidential Review

Probably the most important ground rule for presidential review is that the presenter submits his department's report at least one week prior to the review. This rule is usually resisted, since most presenters will make changes to their presentation until the last minute. However, as will become apparent in the next section, it is important to enforce this rule. Another important ground rule is using data to support the points of the presentation. Since the reviewer will be using the presentation as a vehicle to acquire information for establishing company policies, the presentation must rely on facts.

The presenting department may bring and use as many presenters as needed to fully explain the principal issues or to answer questions. The president usually invites managers from related departments to the review, not only to make them aware of the important issues of that department, but also for them to get a glimpse of the review procedures and thus help them prepare for their own reviews. The atmosphere of the review should be informal but serious.

Preparing for the Review

Proper preparation for a presidential review is important. Many reviews fail before they begin because of poor preparation by the president. Good reviews are the result of careful prior study of the presenter's report, allowing the president to establish a focus for the review, identify issues needing clarification, and formulate questions.

It is critical to have a staff department help the president prepare for the reviews. Usually, this task is assigned to the Quality Department, but it may be any department knowledgeable about the presidential review process and quality management in general. The assigned department assists the president in fully understanding the present situation of the presenting department and in developing a list of topics or broad questions to ask the presenters. More specific questions will normally follow from the answers given by the presenters. The president conducts the review and should become knowledgeable enough to conduct future reviews without extensive help; therefore, a key task of the staff department assisting the president is to instruct and coach the president so that he or she can become a competent reviewer.

Conducting the Review

Usually, the review begins with a presentation by the management of a department, rather than by the team members who performed the work in the department. This structure is critical because it places management "in the line of fire" for quality improvement efforts. Management must be involved with, and learn about, quality management in order to effectively perform its responsibilities in a presidential review. The presentation is followed by a question and answer period that is led by the president. It is customary to allow the presenter to finish the presentation without interruption, except for clarifying questions.

When the presenter has concluded, the president begins the question and answer period. It is her opportunity to probe deeply into issues to determine the possible causes of problems. Often, the president will be persistent and ask the same question several times to get the appropriate answer. For critical issues or when the answers are not provided, **action items** with due dates are established. The presenters demonstrate the results of the action items at a later date.

The following questions are examples of the type of questions the president might ask a presenter.

1. What is the mission of your department?
2. Does your department's mission support the company's mission?
3. How do you know if you are pursuing company policy?
4. What procedures do you follow when you discover that you are not pursuing company policy?
5. Can you show me an example of a corrective action you have taken when your department was not pursuing company policy?
6. How did you analyze the failure to pursue company policy?
7. How did you know if the corrective action was effective?
8. What are the major problems/opportunities of your department?
9. How do these problems/opportunities manifest themselves?
10. Can you give me an example?
11. What effects do these problems/opportunities have on your department and/or on your customers?
12. Who are your customers?
13. What are your customers' needs and wants?
14. How, and how often, do you assess your customers' needs and wants?
15. Can you show me how you are ensuring the satisfaction of your customers' needs and wants?

The attitude of the president during the review is critical. Often, the president has to be persistent to obtain the answers she needs to make decisions. In some cases, the president pushes the presenters to obtain a desired performance level or behavior; this may be seen as judgmental or harsh by the presenters. The president's job is to establish an atmosphere of teamwork, providing constructive criticism, examples of ideas for improvement, and/or guidance on where to go for help.

The staff department members and consultant helping the president during the review should assume a low profile. They should ask questions only at the request of the president, after the president has finished her own questions.

After the reviews, the staff department and/or the consultant meet with the president to identify her successful and unsuccessful actions and behaviors during the review. The purpose of this meeting is to instruct and coach the president in improving her skills as a reviewer.

Keys to Successful Reviews

The most important determinant in a successful presidential review is whether the president can gain the trust of management. It is critical that presenters feel they will not be punished in any way if they disclose problems in their departments.

Another key to a successful review is the quality of the preparation by the president and his staff. If they learn all they can about the topic being reviewed, research and analyze the past accomplishments and failures of the department being reviewed, and focus on problem areas that offer good opportunities for improvement, they are more likely to create a positive review process.

Another important factor in a successful review is the assignment of action items to presenters when data are not provided as requested. Failure to assign action items when needed may communicate to the organization that mediocrity is acceptable.

It is important to concentrate on process and results, rather than only results, in presidential reviews. The president can help the presenter see how poor results are most likely due to a deficiency in a management process. Also, the president should set an example by identifying and working to improve deficiencies in the presidential review process.

Presidential Reviews and Daily Management

The early phases of **daily management** should include the initial presidential review process, as shown in step 28 of the detailed fork model in Figure 14.1. This is important to ensure the active involvement of all levels of management in the quality management system.

Policy Setting

Once the initial presidential review is complete, the president has information critical to setting policy. Policy management involves:

1. Establishing statements of vision and mission.
2. Developing organizational values and beliefs.
3. Identifying organizational and environmental factors that affect policy.
4. Identifying crises facing the organization.
5. Determining key organizational processes that affect stakeholders.
6. Identifying technological issues facing the organization.
7. Establishing strategic objectives, as shown in step 29 of Figure 14.1.
8. Developing a set of integrated improvement plans for the departments, as shown in step 30 of Figure 14.1.

Executive Committee (EC)

The members of the **executive committee** (EC) work to understand the pros and cons for transformation of the organization from the perspective of each stakeholder group. The top management of an organization asks the question "Does my organization have the motivation and energy necessary to make quality happen?" The data from this question is collected, summarized, and analyzed through a **force field analysis,** a technique that lists the "forces for" and "forces against" a particular action or issue, as shown in Table 18.1.

The comparative weight of the "forces for" transformation versus the "forces against" transformation is a subjective decision on the part of top management. After analysis, if the members of the EC determine that the "forces for" transformation outweigh the "forces against" transformation, they develop a strategic plan to accomplish this.

The Strategic Plan

A **strategic plan** lists the long-term strategic objectives of an organization. **Strategic objectives** are based on a thorough analysis of statements of vision and mission; values

TABLE 18.1
Generic Lists for a Force Field Analysis

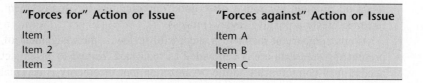

"Forces for" Action or Issue	"Forces against" Action or Issue
Item 1	Item A
Item 2	Item B
Item 3	Item C

FIGURE 18.2
Development of Strategic Objectives

and beliefs; organizational and environmental factors; crises, if any; key processes that affect stakeholders; and technology. Figure 18.2 depicts the relationship between these six items and the strategic objectives.

Statements of Vision and Mission

Deming's theory of management addresses the need to establish constancy of purpose toward improvement of product and service with a plan to become competitive, stay in business, and provide jobs, as articulated in Point 1 of Deming's 14 points, discussed in Chapter 2. Statements of vision and mission are starting points for constancy of purpose.

A **vision statement** is developed by the top management of an organization. It defines the organization's future state. It is a dream that comes from the "hearts" of top management; it should evoke emotion, be easily remembered, state a noble purpose, and create a rallying point for all concerned with the organization.

The **mission statement**, developed by top management, reveals the current reason for the existence of an organization, providing a rallying point for all stakeholders; it should be short and easily remembered by all stakeholders of the organization.

Values and Beliefs

A statement of the **values and beliefs** that govern an organization's culture is necessary to provide predictable uniformity and dependability to the decision-making process. This statement forms the foundation for the decision-making process. Values and beliefs are theories about life and organizations that have been modified and improved by cultural, educational, familial, organizational, and personal experiences. Through the adoption of Deming's theory of management, an organization can develop a set of values and beliefs that form its foundation, and focus on creating a "win-win" environment for all stakeholders of an organization. These are discussed below.

- *Manage to optimize the entire system, not just your component of the system.* Local optimization creates suboptimization of the entire system. For example, maximizing profit in one division of a company may decrease profit for the entire company.

- *Manage to create a balance of* **intrinsic** *and* **extrinsic motivation;** *do not just motivate people using extrinsic motivation.* Intrinsic motivation is the individual's desire to do something for its own value, as opposed to extrinsic motivation that relies on rewards or punishments for the individual. For example, empower people to promote joy in work, as well as using well-thought-out pay plans.

- *Manage with a long-term process and results orientation, not with a short-term results-only orientation.* Process and results management promotes improvement and innovation of organizational processes. Highly capable processes facilitate prediction of the future and, consequently, a higher likelihood of achieving the organizational mission. For example, study a process, collect data, and develop ideas for improving the process to permanently remove problems, as opposed to simply demanding fewer problems.

- *Manage to promote cooperation, not competition.* In a competitive environment, most people lose. The costs resulting from competition are unknown and unknowable, but huge. Competition causes individuals, or departments, to optimize their own efforts at the expense of other stakeholders. This form of optimization seriously erodes the performance of the system of interdependent stakeholders. For example, get departments and divisions to work together for the common good, as opposed to working against each other for their individual good.

Organizational and Environmental Factors

A **SWOT** (organizational **s**trengths and **w**eaknesses and environmental **o**pportunities and **t**hreats) **analysis** is used to assist the members of the EC in selecting the strategic objectives that ensure the best fit between the internal strengths and weaknesses of an organization and the external opportunities and threats that face an organization. The members of the EC identify strengths and opportunities that bypass weaknesses and threats. This information is then used as input in developing the strategic objectives of the organization.

An excellent method for performing a SWOT analysis is for the members of the EC to appoint a team of appropriate people to conduct four **brainstorming** sessions and to create four **affinity diagrams.** One brainstorming session is conducted on the organization's strengths and an affinity diagram is developed to bring out the underlying structure of the strengths. A similar analysis is conducted for weaknesses, opportunities, and threats.

Portions of an affinity diagram from a SWOT analysis of a university are shown in Table 18.2. The items on the left side provide the structure of the strengths, weaknesses, opportunities, and threats, while the bracketed items on the right side provide the brainstormed ideas underlying the structure of the strengths, weaknesses, opportunities and threats.

Crises

The members of the EC determine if any **crises** currently face the organization. If so, the members of the EC communicate this information to all stakeholders to create the energy necessary to improve quality. Management uses the output from the brainstorming session and affinity diagram in step 1 of Figure 14.1 to highlight existing crises. Highlighting crises in this fashion is an important job of top management. Again, it is necessary for leadership to isolate a crisis to generate the energy necessary to improve quality.

Key Processes That Affect Stakeholders

Data are collected to determine the requirements important to the customers served by an organization, called the **voice of the customer,** discussed in Appendix A18.1, and

TABLE 18.2
SWOT
Analysis for a
University

Strengths	
Academic	Faculty, research, library, . . .
Financial	Management system, . . .
Diversity	Multicultural, . . .
Business	Continuous improvement process, ability to plan, training
Life Style	Encourages holistic health, total fitness centers, . . .
Weaknesses	
Communication	Ineffective, . . .
Infrastructure	Space, parking, funding, . . .
Financial	Tuition, budget, . . .
Reputation	Local versus international, sports, . . .
Technology	Insufficient use, . . .
. . .	
Opportunities	
Student base	Local, international, retrain downsizers, . . .
Resources	Donations, local economy, alliances, media, . . .
International	Sister universities worldwide, globalization
Technology	Easy access to potential students, . . .
. . .	
Threats	
Increased costs	Technology, salaries, tax changes, insurance, . . .
Corporate support	Employee tuition reimbursement, downsizing, . . .
Litigation	Litigious society, . . .
. . .	

the requirements important to all levels of employees in the organization, called the **voice of the business,** discussed in Appendix A18.2. Determination of these will help the members of the EC identify the **key processes** or methods, whose level of performance will affect the selection of strategic objectives.

Voice of the customer and voice of the business data are summarized into a single prioritized list of the organizational processes to be highlighted for attention through the strategic objectives, called the **table of tables,** discussed in Appendix A18.3. There are many possible structures and scoring schemes for a table of tables; a generic table of tables is shown in Figure A18.5 in Appendix A18.3.

Table 18.3 shows sections of a table of tables for a university. The university table of tables has stakeholder groups and their needs/wants in the rows and university processes in columns 2 through 16. Column 1 shows the average total weight of each stakeholder need/want from a survey conducted in each stakeholder segment. Total weight is a measure of importance and severity to stakeholders. It ranges from 1 to 25, where 1 is not important and not severe and 25 is important and severe. The numbers in the cells indicate the strength of the relationship between a stakeholder need/want and a university process. Relationship values are measured on a 0 (blank) to 9 scale, where 0 (blank) indicates no relationship and 9 indicates a strong relationship. For each cell in a given row, the average total weight for the row is multiplied by the cell relationship value to yield a cell value. Finally, the cell values are summed up for each column. This assumes that

TABLE 18.3   Portions of the Table of Tables for a University

Stakeholder Groups	University Processes															
	1	2	3	4	5	6	7	8	9	10	11	12	13	14	15	16
	Total Weight	Employee Hiring & Training	Communication Systems	Strategic Planning	Facilities Administration	Building & Expansion	Student Training	⋮	⋮	⋮	⋮	⋮	⋮	Grant Administration	Food Services	⋮
Students																
Value of education	18	9	9	9	1	3	9							0	0	
Quality of academic major	18	9	6	3	0	3	9							0	0	
Quality of instruction	16	9	6	3	3	3	9							0	0	
Availability of courses	14	3	3	1	0	1	0							0	0	
Accuracy of financial awards	16	1	1	3	0	9	0							0	0	
Career preparation	14	9	9	3	0	1	9							0	0	
Attitude of faculty	16	9	3	3	0	0	3							0	0	
Academic reputation	16	9	9	9	3	1	9							0	0	
Quality of academic advising	14	9	3	3	0	3	1							0	0	
Challenge offered by program of study	16	9	9	3	0	0	2							0	0	
Relationship with other students	9	3	3	3	3	0	2							0	0	
Class size	9	1	3	3	1	1	1							0	0	

(continued)

TABLE 18.3 (concluded)

		5244	4066	3827	2704	2578	2244							865.5	386.5	
Buildings and Grounds																
. . .																
Design new facilities to minimize life cycle needs	20	1	6	9	9	9	9							0	0	
Consolidate authority for buildings	9	0	3	1	9	3	0							0	0	
Schedule classrooms to minimize costs	8	1	0	1	9	9	1							0	0	
. . .																
Granting Agencies																
. . .																
Employers																
. . .																
Administration																
. . .																
Staff																
. . .																
Faculty																
. . .																
Board of Directors																
. . .																
Donors																
. . .																
State Government																
. . .																
Federal Government																
. . .																
Etc.																
. . .																
Process Weights		5244	4066	3827	2704	2578	2244							865.5	386.5	

all stakeholder groups are equally important in developing strategic objectives. The column totals provide a weighted value for each university process in satisfying important and severe stakeholder needs/wants. In this example, "Employee Hiring & Training" (weight = 5244) and "Communication Systems" (weight = 4066) are the university processes that are most critical to satisfying stakeholder needs and wants. These are the inputs from the table of tables to establishing strategic objectives for the university.

Technology

The members of the EC collect data on technological advances of products and services in the industry, substitute products and services, future products and services, and management technology. All forms of technology are considered when establishing policy via strategic objectives. The same procedure is used to analyze technology data as is used to analyze crisis and SWOT data.

Develop Strategic Objectives and a Budget

The members of the EC utilize the information gathered in the above six areas to create a short list of three to five strategic objectives on which the organization will focus extra effort in the next three to five years, through policy management. Next, the members of the EC establish an initial budget to allocate resources between strategic objectives. It is important that strategic plans identify all available resources, such as financial, human, and plant and equipment. Resources are allocated to methods by setting **targets.** Targets may be reset at a later date to optimize the interdependent system of stakeholders of an organization. Strategic objectives must be accomplished in addition to the regular functioning of the organization.

Policy Deployment Committee (PDC)

The members of the EC communicate to the members of the **policy deployment committee** (PDC) the pros and cons for transformation, vision and mission statements, values and beliefs, and strategic objectives.

The members of the PDC develop a set of **integrated improvement plans,** as shown in step 30 of Figure 14.1, to promote the strategic objectives. Improvement plans, or **tactics,** prioritize processes, or methods, for attention through policy management. Resources are allocated between methods by setting targets. An improvement plan usually follows a one- to two-year time horizon. The members of the PDC utilize the following steps to construct a set of integrated improvement plans.

Step 1a

Develop the **corporate improvement plans** needed to promote the corporate strategic objectives. **Gap analysis** is used to study the root cause(s) of the difference between customer and employee requirements, and organizational performance for each strategic objective. The members of the PDC assign a group of staff personnel to study the gap for a particular strategic objective. For example, the group might study the gap over time and determine that it is stable and contains only common variation. Next, they construct a **Pareto diagram** of the common causes of the gap, isolate the most significant common cause, and develop a **cause-and-effect diagram,** as discussed in Chapter 10. The staff personnel then study the relationship between the suspected root (common) cause and the size of the gap. If they determine the relationship to be significant, they recommend to the members of the PDC a tactic for consideration as part of the organization's improvement plan.

FIGURE 18.3 Relationship between Corporate Strategic Objectives and Corporate Improvement Plans

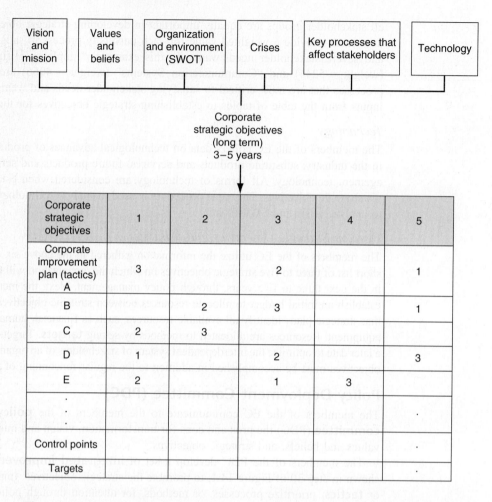

The relationship between corporate strategic objectives and corporate improvement plans or tactics can be seen in Figure 18.3. Relationships are measured on the following scale: 3 = strong relationship, 2 = moderate relationship, 1 = weak relationship, and blank = no relationship.

Every strategic objective should be adequately serviced by one or more tactics. If a strategic objective is not being serviced by any tactic, or not adequately serviced, one or more new tactics are developed to service the strategic objective. All columns of the matrix in Figure 18.3 should contain at least one score of two or three.

Step 1b

Develop the **departmental improvement plans** or tactics needed to promote the departmental strategic objectives.

Organizations need a mechanism for setting policy and allocating responsibility and resources in departments and divisions to promote corporate policy. Such a mechanism can be seen in Figure 18.4.

Section A of Figure 18.4 provides departmental management with an opportunity to create departmental vision and mission statements that promote the corporate vision and

**FIGURE
18.4
Setting Policy
and Allocating
Responsibility
and Resources**

Source: Abstracted
from *Florida Power
and Light Company,
Description of Quality
Improvement Program,
Southern Division,*
1988, p. 16.

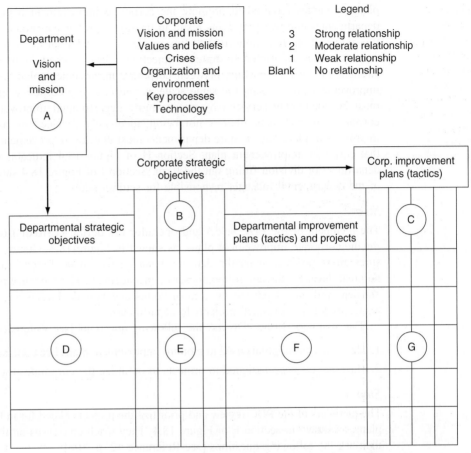

Objective of form: To show the relationship between corporate strategic objectives and improvement plans, and departmental strategic objectives and improvement plans.

mission statements. Section B of Figure 18.4 lists the corporate strategic objectives (the columns of Figure 18.3). Section C of Figure 18.4 lists the corporate improvement plans or tactics (the rows of Figure 18.3). Section D of Figure 18.4 lists the departmental strategic objectives. Departmental management considers all the information utilized in developing the corporate strategic objectives when developing the departmental strategic objectives. Section E of Figure 18.4 shows the strength of relationships between corporate strategic objectives and departmental strategic objectives. Relationships are measured on the following scale: 3 =strong relationship, 2 = moderate relationship, 1 = weak relationship, and blank = no relationship. Every corporate strategic objective must be adequately serviced by one or more departmental strategic objectives; if a corporate strategic objective is not being adequately serviced by any departmental strategic objectives, then one or more departments must develop strategic objectives to service that corporate strategic objective. Section F of Figure 18.4 lists the departmental improvement plans or tactics required to promote the corporate improvement plans or tactics. The departmental improvement plans result in quality improvement projects. When entering this information, it is important to line up departmental improvement plans with their corresponding departmental strategic objectives. Section G of Figure 18.4 shows the strength of the relationships between corporate improvement plans and departmental improvement plans, using the same scale as above. Every corporate improvement plan must be adequately serviced by one or more departmental improvement plans; if a corporate improvement plan is not being adequately serviced by any departmental improvement plan, one or more departments must develop improvement plans to service that corporate improvement plan. Section H of Figure 18.4 indicates the name of the department or division filling out the form. Section I of Figure 18.4 shows the signature of the departmental manager responsible for setting policy.

Step 2

The members of the PDC select and operationally define **control points** and targets for the corporate improvement plans, as shown in Figure 18.3. Control points are measures about policies or results that are managed with data. Targets are the desired, or nominal, level for the control points set by management. These control points and targets are deployed into departmental control points and targets. Targets are used to allocate resources for improvement projects to departments.

The members of the PDC ask the following questions [see Reference 12, p. 106]:

1. Have the control points used to monitor improvement plans been operationally defined?
2. Have targets been assigned to projects to optimize the corporate strategic objectives?

Step 3

The members of the PDC review and prioritize the projects called for in the improvement plans, as shown in section F of Figure 18.4. They reach consensus on the priorities, and then ask the following questions [see Reference 12, p. 106]:

1. Are priority projects well defined?
2. Will taking care of these priority projects help achieve the strategic objectives?
3. Are there better ways to achieve the strategic objectives?
4. Have the costs associated with pursuing the strategic objectives been studied?
5. Have the most appropriate projects been highlighted for study in the improvement plans?
6. Are projects defined with enough specificity so that everyone understands them?
7. Were projects discussed with relevant people and groups?
8. Were constraints on methods considered by the PDC?
9. Has the effectiveness of the projects been studied?
10. Are sufficient resources available for the projects?

Step 4

The members of the PDC communicate the projects that emanate from corporate and and departmental improvement plans to the **local steering teams** (LSTs), including the allocation of resources. The members of the PDC and an LST come to consensus on projects, targets, and resources in meetings called **catchball** sessions.

Local Steering Teams (LSTs)

The members of the LSTs are responsible for coordinating and carrying out the projects set out in the corporate and departmental improvement plans. The members of the PDC and LSTs should reach consensus on the priorities assigned to methods via targets that allocate resources. The members of LSTs ask the following questions [see Reference 12, p. 106]:

1. Are priority projects well defined?
2. Will taking care of these priority projects help achieve the improvement plans and strategic objectives?
3. Are there better ways to achieve the strategic objectives?

Policy Deployment

The mission statement and presidential objectives (both strategic and business) are deployed or cascaded throughout an organization using a tool called a **dashboard.** A dashboard is used by management to clarify and assign accountability for the "critical few" key objectives, and their corresponding key indicators and projects/tasks, that are needed to steer an organization toward its mission.

A Simple Dashboard

An example of an organizational chart from a university is shown in Figure 18.5. It highlights the relationship between a third tier manager and a fourth tier manager at the university.

The dashboard between the third (vice president of business services) and fourth (chief of campus police) tier manager in Figure 18.5 is shown in Table 18.4.

FIGURE 18.5
Partial Organizational Chart of the University of Miami

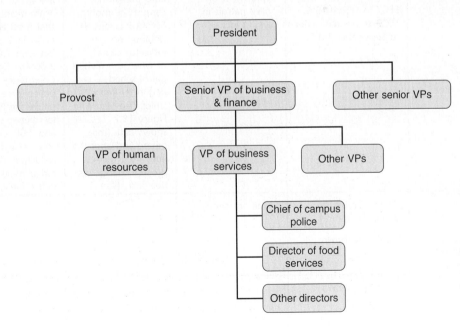

TABLE 18.4 Portion of a Dashboard from the Organizational Chart in Figure 18.5: Mission Statement for Business Services Department of the Business and Finance Division of the University of Miami: "Optimum SAS." Note: SAS = Security, Assets, and Services

Vice President of Business Services		Chief of Campus Police		
Key Objectives	Key Indicators	Key Objectives	Key Indicators	Tasks or Projects
Improve security on campus	SEC1: Number of murders, by month	No murders. No objective other than to continue with current processes	SEC1: List of murders, by month	No murders. No task or project
	SEC2: Number of rapes, by month	Detail not shown		
	SEC3: Number of robberies, by month	Detail not shown		
	SEC4: Number of aggravated assaults, by month	Detail not shown		
	SEC5: Number of burglaries, by month	Reduce number of open doors on campus	SEC5A: Number of open doors, by department, by building, overall, by month	Chief of Police established a team to study SEC5. Team members determined that most burglaries occurred when doors were left open (SEC5A).
	SEC6: Number of larcenies, by month	Detail not shown		
	SEC7: Number of auto thefts by month. See SEC7 in Figure 18.6. SEC7 shows data prior to September 1999.	Optimize deployment of police patrols in parking lots	SEC7A: Number of auto thefts on campus by month. SEC7A includes a notation on the indicator chart of when the revised patrol schedule was begun by Police Chief. See SEC7A in Figure 18.7. SEC7A shows data from before and after the auto theft team's process change was put into effect.	Chief of Police established a team to study SEC7. Team members determined that most auto thefts occur in 2 parking lots between 7:00 A.M. and 7:00 P.M. Consequently, Chief redeployed the police force to heavily patrol the 2 problematic lots between 7:00 A.M. and 7:00 P.M. SEC7 showed a dramatic reduction after redeployment of the police force.
	SEC8: Number of arsons, by month	Detail not shown		
Protect university assets	Detail not shown			
Improve university services	Detail not shown			

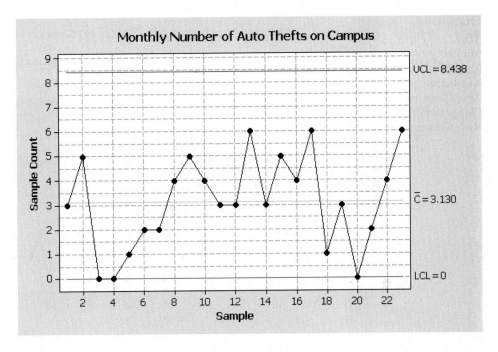

FIGURE 18.6
Minitab Monthly Number of Auto Thefts on Campus

The mission of the Business Services department is "optimum SAS" (security, assets, and services). The vice president of business services promotes the Business Services department mission through three **key objectives:** (1) improve security on campus, (2) protect university assets, and (3) improve university services. The first key objective is measured through eight **key indicators:** (1) number of murders by month (SEC1), (2) number of rapes by month (SEC2), (3) number of robberies by month (SEC3), (4) number of aggravated assaults by month (SEC4), (5) number of burglaries by month (SEC5), (6) number of larcenies by month (SEC6), (7) number of auto thefts by month (SEC7), and (8) number of arsons by month (SEC8). An example of a key indicator can be seen in Figure 18.6, showing a c chart of the number of auto thefts by month (SEC7) before a daily management team implemented a change to the process for responding to auto thefts.

The chief of campus police promotes the mission of the Business Services department by studying his superior's (the vice president of business services) key indicator data to identify his key objectives. For example, the police chief establishes a team to study the number of auto thefts by month (SEC7). The team members determine that most auto thefts occur in two campus parking lots between 7:00 A.M. and 7:00 P.M. The chief redeploys the police force to heavily patrol the two problematic lots between those hours. Subsequently, there is a drastic reduction in the number of auto thefts by month (SEC7), as shown in the c chart in Figure 18.7 (SEC7A).

Benefits of a Dashboard

A dashboard has both strategic and tactical benefits. The strategic benefits of a dashboard include deploying the mission statement throughout the levels of an organization, from top to bottom, through the development of a cascading and interlocking set

FIGURE 18.7
Minitab
Monthly
Number of
Auto Thefts on
Campus after
Redeployment

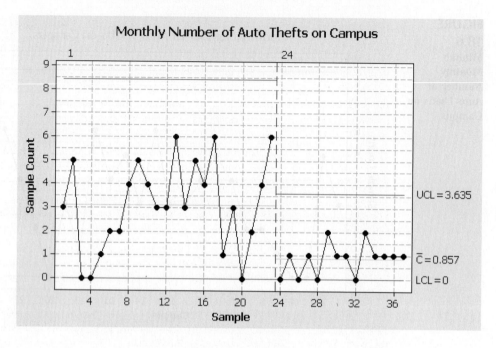

of key objectives and key indicators; monitoring deployment of the organizational mission statement, via key objectives, throughout the organization; pursuing the organizational mission and its derivative key objectives through improving and innovating processes as measured by key indicators; balancing management's attention between customer, process, employee, and financial key objectives as measured through key indicators; and increasing communication between, and within, the levels of an organization.

The tactical benefits of a dashboard include linking all processes or jobs to the organization's mission statement; improving each employee's comprehension of his job responsibilities and accountabilities so that each employee understands the effects of special causes of variation and common causes of variation on his job and on decision-making in the organization; eliminating tampering with a process, so that each employee understands the effects of special causes of variation and common causes of variation on his job and on decision-making in the organization; and developing and testing hypotheses about the effectiveness of potential improvements to a process.

Technical Terms

There are four major technical terms associated with dashboards: key objective, key indicator, task and project.

Key Objectives

There are two kinds of key objectives: **business objectives** and **strategic objectives.** Business objectives are the goals that must routinely be pursued within an organization if it is to function, such as producing paper in a paper mill, answering customer inquiries in a call center, preparing paychecks in an accounting department, or doing ROI calculations in a finance department.

Strategic objectives are the goals that must be accomplished to pursue the presidential strategy of an organization. For example, one of the strategic objectives of the University of Miami is to "gerontologize" the entire university. Any objective, at any level, within the university that promotes "gerontologizing" the university is a strategic objective. Any other objective (if it does not support another of the president's strategies) is not a strategic objective; it is a business objective. Another example of a strategic objective is the implementation of **Six Sigma** management as the method for conducting business at General Electric. Any GE objective, at any level, that promotes Six Sigma management is a strategic objective. Any other objective (if it does not support another of the president's strategies) is not a strategic objective; it is a business objective.

There are four basic categories of key objectives [see Reference 11, p. 69]: financial; process improvement; customer satisfaction; and employee growth and development. A key objective can encompass one or more of these categories. Examples of each key objective category are shown below.

Examples of **financial key objectives** include management's and stockholders' desire for more profit, market share, dominance and growth, and the desire for less waste, turnover, financial loss and customer defection.

Examples of **process improvement and innovation key objectives** include management's desire for consistency and uniformity of output, high productivity of employees, products that are easy to build and low cost to produce, products that meet technical specifications, products that do not incur warranty costs, and products that are easy to distribute throughout the channels of distribution.

There are four types of **customer satisfaction key objectives:** customers' desired outcomes, customers' undesired outcomes, customers' desired product and service attributes, and customers' desired process characteristics. Examples of customer satisfaction key objectives include customers' desired outcomes such as "joy, security, personal time, belonging, and health," and customers' undesired outcomes such as avoidance or elimination of "death, taxes, discomfort, wasted time, and frustration." Examples of customers' desired product and service attribute key objectives include "ease-of-use, accessibility, low cost of ownership, durability and appeal." Examples of customers' desired process characteristic key objectives include "timely arrival of product, no waiting time, and ease of acquisition."

Examples of **employee growth and development key objectives** include improving leadership skills, providing training opportunities, providing educational opportunities, and creating the opportunity to work on stimulating special assignments.

Key Indicators

A key indicator is a measurement that monitors the status of a key objective. There are five types of key indicators: attribute indicators, measurement indicators, binary indicators, list by time period indicators, and Gantt chart indicators.

Attribute indicators are used when a key objective is being monitored using attribute data (**classification** or **count data**) over time. Some examples of attribute-type classification indicators are percentage of defective products produced by week, percentage of customer base complaining per month, and percentage of accounts receivable over 90 days by quarter. Some examples of attribute-type count indicators are number of industrial accidents per week, number of customer complaints per month, and number of thefts per quarter.

Measurement indicators are used when a key indicator is being monitored using measurement-type data. Measurement data can be displayed over time in the following formats: run chart, average and range by time period, average and standard deviation by time period, or distribution by time period.

Binary indicators (yes/no by date) are used when a key indicator monitors whether an action has been accomplished by a given date. An example of a binary key indicator is "Computer system operational by July 12, 2004? (yes or no)."

List indicators are used when a key indicator monitors a group of people or items for compliance with some deadline or standard. Two examples of list key indicators are "List of employees not trained in the new safety standards by December 31, 2004" and "List of laboratories not up to federal code standards as of June 15, 2004."

Gantt chart indicators are used when a key indicator is a record-keeping device for following the progression in time of the tasks required to complete a project. A Gantt chart indicates which tasks are on or behind schedule; an example is shown in Figure 18.8.

Figure 18.8 shows that activity C cannot start before time 5 since activity B must be completed before activity C can begin. As each activity (or part thereof) is completed, the appropriate bar is shaded. At any point in time, then, it is clear which activities are on schedule and which are not. The Gantt chart in Figure 18.8 shows that as of week 13 activities D, E, and H are behind schedule, while G has actually been completed (because it is all shaded) and hence is ahead of schedule.

Flag Diagrams

A tool used to track the contributions of subordinate key objectives to the pursuit of a superior key objective is called a **flag diagram** [see Reference 8, p. 3 and p. 34, and Reference 1], as shown in Figure 18.9.

FIGURE 18.8
Generic Gantt Chart

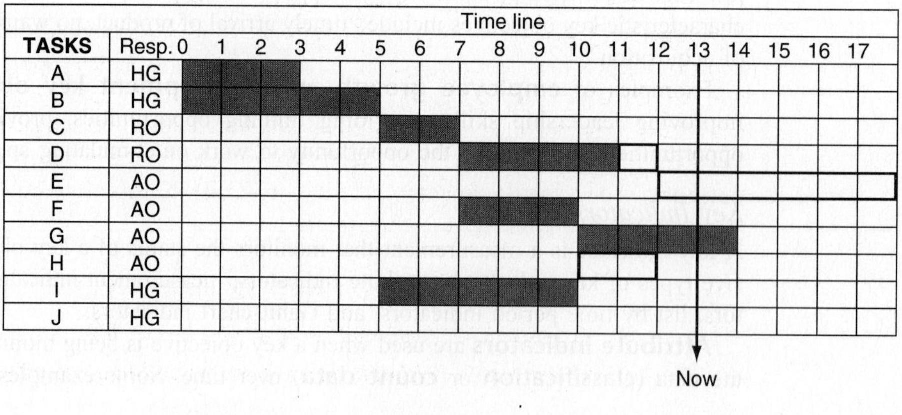

TASKS	Resp.	0	1	2	3	4	5	6	7	8	9	10	11	12	13	14	15	16	17
A	HG																		
B	HG																		
C	RO																		
D	RO																		
E	AO																		
F	AO																		
G	AO																		
H	AO																		
I	HG																		
J	HG																		

Time line

Now

FIGURE 18.9
Generic Flag
Diagram

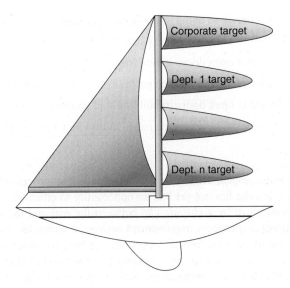

Corporate target

Dept. 1 target

Dept. n target

There are two types of flag diagrams, additive flag diagrams and nonadditive flag diagrams.

Corporate indicators are the summation of departmental indicators in some applications of flag diagrams. An example of an **additive** or **linear flag diagram** in which the corporate indicator (y) is a linear combination of the departmental indicators $(x_1 + x_2 + x_3 + x_4)$ can be seen in the case of burglaries on a university campus as a function of the buildings that the burglaries occurred in, where

$$y_i = \text{total burglaries on campus in month i}$$
$$x_{1i} = \text{burglaries in building 1 in month i}$$
$$x_{2i} = \text{burglaries in building 2 in month i}$$
$$x_{3i} = \text{burglaries in building 3 in month i}$$
$$x_{4i} = \text{burglaries in building 4 in month i}$$

In other applications of flag diagrams, corporate indicators are not the summation of departmental indicators. For such **nonadditive flag diagrams,** knowledge, experience, and statistical expertise are required to determine the relationships between corporate and departmental indicators. An example of a nonlinear flag diagram in which the corporate indicator (y) is not a linear combination of the departmental indicators $[y = f(x_{11}, x_{12}, x_{21}, x_{22}, x_{31}, x_{32}, x_{41}, x_{42})]$ can be seen in the number of burglaries on a university campus as a function of the number of doors left open (unlocked) in the building the burglaries occurred in, where

$$y_i = \text{total burglaries on campus in month i}$$
$$x_{11i} = \text{number open doors in building 1 in month i}$$
$$x_{12i} = \text{number of hours police patrol in building 1 in month i}$$

$$x_{21i} = \text{number open doors in building 2 in month i}$$

$$x_{22i} = \text{number of hours police patrol in building 2 in month i}$$

$$x_{31i} = \text{number open doors in building 3 in month i}$$

$$x_{32i} = \text{number of hours police patrol in building 3 in month i}$$

$$x_{41i} = \text{number open doors in building 4 in month i}$$

$$x_{42i} = \text{number of hours police patrol in building 4 in month i}$$

Tasks and Projects

A **task** is a process improvement activity in which the necessary process change is known by the process owner, but she has not yet had an opportunity to effectuate the change. The need for a task is determined by a chronic gap between the real and the ideal value of a key indicator. A **project** is a process improvement activity in which the necessary process change is unknown by the process owner. Generally, the process owner forms a process improvement team to identify and test the necessary process change. The need for a project is determined by a chronic gap between the real and the ideal value of a key indicator.

There are three categories of projects or tasks [see Reference 9]: zero projects or tasks, increase projects or tasks, and decrease projects or tasks. Each category is explained below with examples.

In a **zero project** or **task** the ideal value of a key indicator is zero or the optimal difference between the current value and the ideal value of a key indicator is zero. The purpose of a zero project or task is: (1) to get the current value of a key indicator to be zero (the ideal value of the key indicator) by a given date or (2) to reduce the gap to zero between the current value of a key indicator and the ideal value of a key indicator by a given date. Examples of zero tasks or projects are to reduce to zero the proportion defective units by day, or to reduce unit-to-unit variation of the mean and standard deviation of gold bar weights around nominal.

In an **increase project** or **task** the ideal value of the key indicator is x units or y percentage points higher than the current value of the key indicator. The purpose of an increase task or project is: (1) to get the real value of a key indicator to be x units or y percentage points higher by a given date, (2) to raise the ideal value of the key indicator by a given date, or (3) to establish or clarify the ideal value for a key indicator by a given date. Examples of increase projects or tasks are to increase revenue or to increase profit. Sometimes it is possible to redefine the first type of increase project or task as the second type of zero project or task.

In a **decrease project** or **task** the ideal value of the key indicator is x units or y percentage points lower than the current value of the key indicator. The purpose of a decrease task or project is: (1) to get the current value of a key indicator to be x units or y percentage points lower by a given date, (2) to lower the ideal value of the key indicator by a given date, or (3) to establish or clarify the ideal value for a key indicator by a given date. Zero is not a rational target for a decrease task or project; for example, most costs of doing business cannot be zero if the business is still operating. Examples of decrease tasks or projects are to reduce costs or to decrease cycle time. Sometimes it is possible to redefine the first type of decrease project or task as the second type of zero project or task.

Developing a Dashboard

Policy setting, discussed in the previous section of this chapter, is the method for identifying the presidential key objectives of an organization from its mission statement, its values and beliefs, a SWOT analysis, a list of crises, a list of technological issues, and an analysis of the key processes affecting stakeholders. Vice presidential objectives can be identified once presidential objectives and indicators have been listed in the first two columns of a dashboard. This is accomplished by each vice president studying the president's key indicators relating to his area of responsibility and identifying the actions required to improve the president's key indicator to achieve a desirable state for a presidential key objective. For example, Figure 18.6 on page 645 shows how the campus chief of police studied the vice president of business services' (his boss's) key indicator on the number of auto thefts by month (SEC7) and determined the parking lots and times of day that auto thefts occurred most frequently on campus. The police chief established his key objective of redeploying campus police patrols with this information. He established his key indicator to be the number of auto thefts on campus per 1000 students on campus by month, as shown in Figure 18.7 (SEC7A). The process of a subordinate studying his superior's key indicators to identify his key objectives is critical to the creation of effective dashboards.

Managing with a Dashboard

Top management uses a dashboard at monthly operations review meetings for several purposes. First, managers use dashboards to clarify mission statements and key objectives, and accountability for them, among all personnel and areas. Second, managers use dashboards to promote statistical thinking about reacting to fluctuations in key indicators. For example, is the sales volume for last month due to a special or common cause of variation in the selling process? Third, managers use dashboards to clarify and reduce the perception that most of the daily crises (called "helter skelter" items) requiring immediate and special attention are really special cases of known key objectives. A manager's ability to recognize helter skelter items as special cases of key objectives reduces the amount of tension involved in dealing with a multitude of crises *du jour*. Fourth, a manager uses dashboards to develop and test hypotheses concerning potential changes to processes. Hypothesis tests usually require a task or project to analyze a key indicator in order to identify a change concept to improve this or some other key indicator, as illustrated in Figure 18.7 for the auto theft example. Stacking key indicators at adjacent levels in a dashboard can be used to identify **correlations** between them. Correlations can assist personnel in the development of hypotheses leading to improvement of a process, and hence, achievement of a key objective. Nonadditive flag diagrams and **multiple regression analysis** can be used to develop and test hypotheses relating several lower level key indicators to a higher level key indicator. Fifth, a manager can use dashboards to ensure the routine and regular updating of key indicators.

Managers can use the following questions when conducting a monthly review meeting to get the most out of their dashboard. [See Reference 11, p. 70.]

- Are the key objectives and key indicators on the dashboard the "best" set of objectives and indicators to attain the organization's mission statement?
- Is the dashboard balanced with respect to customer, process, employee, and financial objectives? Do any areas have too much, or too little, representation on the dashboard?

- What products and/or services are most critical to the organization's achieving its mission statement? List the top 5 or 10 products and services.
- Are targets being met in a timely fashion for all key objectives? Remember, targets are set to allocate resources to projects.
- What process is used to manage, perform, and improve project work?
- Which key indicators on the dashboard are used to measure customer satisfaction and dissatisfaction? Are these measures operationally defined? Are these measures adequate?
- What process is used to reward/punish project work? Does the process consider the effects of special and common causes of variation on rewards and punishments?
- Does the organization have the ability to identify the return on investment from its dashboard? How is ROI measured?

Deployment of Key Objectives throughout an Organization

Key objectives are deployed by the members of the PDC through assignment of responsibility for action to people or groups of people in departments, as shown in step 31 of the detailed fork model in Figure 14.1. The assignment of responsibility is discussed by the members of the PDC and LST in meetings called **mini-sitcons,** which consider the costs to improve and/or innovate processes. After costs have been identified, it may be necessary to renegotiate project budgets. This process continues until all parties reach a consensual agreement on projects; recall from the section "Policy Deployment Committee (PDC)" that this is called catchball. Finally, the members of the PDC ensure that the agreed-upon projects incorporate the information determined in the table of tables.

The assignment of responsibility for a project to a manager creates an opportunity to conduct a project that will result in improved or innovated **best-practice** methods, the allocation of necessary resources, and an obligation to predict the contribution of projects to strategic objectives.

Deployment of a project or task is complete when a **project team** has been assigned responsibility to improve and/or innovate a method. Figure 18.10 shows the projects, channels of communication, type of coordination, and resources necessary to implement policy in a department. Column A of Figure 18.10 shows departmental key objectives, from section D of Figure 18.4 on page 641. Column B of Figure 18.10 shows the departmental improvement plans or tactics needed to promote the departmental key objectives, shown in section F of Figure 18.4. Column C of Figure 18.10 shows the project(s) necessary for each departmental key objective. Each manager assigned a project must sign the appropriate line of column C indicating his or her acceptance of the project. Column D of Figure 18.10 shows the channels of communication and types of coordination between departments needed to carry out the projects shown in column C. The manager of each department named as a necessary supporter of a project must sign the appropriate line of column D, indicating his or her willingness to assist in the conduct of the project. Column E of Figure 18.10 shows the additional financial and human resources needed to carry out the projects shown in column C.

FIGURE 18.10 Project Coordination Matrix

Departmental strategic objectives	Departmental improvement plan(tactics)	Project	Other depts. affected/ coordination needed	Resources ▪ Dollars ▪ People
A	B	C	D	E

The members of an LST ask the following questions of all project team members [see Reference 12, p. 106]:

1. Are information channels between all relevant people and groups open to promote the improvement plan?
2. Has a detailed schedule been set up for carrying out the improvement plan?

Policy Implementation

Policy is implemented in two ways, as shown in step 32 of the detailed fork model in Figure 14.1: first, when teams work on projects to improve and/or innovate processes, and second, when departments use the revised processes and measure their results with respect to improvement plans and strategic objectives.

The members of the EC assign responsibility for the promotion of each strategic objective to a high-level executive. The executive removes any impediments to progress for his strategic objective. Furthermore, the executive coordinates efforts with respect to the strategic objective throughout the organization. Finally, the members of the PDC, in conjunction with the members of various LSTs, may have to modify improvement plans as they proceed over time.

Policy Feedback and Review

Periodic **management reviews** are conducted at two levels, as shown in step 33 of Figure 14.1. First, the members of the EC review progress toward each strategic objective and its improvement plans monthly. Brief presentations for each strategic objective are made by the high-level executive responsible for that strategic objective. Twice a year, each strategic objective is selected for a detailed management review. The detailed review probes deeply into the issues surrounding a strategic objective. The members of the EC must insist that all process modifications are supported by sound analysis. This may require that action items be assigned to the high-level executive responsible for a strategic objective. The members of the EC must also follow up on the action items. Second, the members of the PDC and of appropriate LSTs review progress for each project. The purpose of these reviews is to provide feedback to project team members that promotes process improvement efforts. The members of the PDC must make sure that all process modifications are supported by sound analysis of data. This may require that action items be assigned to the members of a project team. The members of the PDC must also follow up on the action items.

In **feedback and review,** the members of the EC, PDC, or appropriate LSTs ask the following questions of project team members:

1. Does your organization have a vision statement and a mission statement?
2. Do you know what they are?
3. Do you understand how you can contribute to the vision and mission of your organization? How do you know?
4. Does your department have vision and mission statements?
5. Do you know what they are?
6. Do you understand how you can contribute to the vision and mission of your department? How do you know?
7. Do you understand the methods by which you will achieve the vision and mission of your department? Organization?
8. Do you know which methods are most critical to pursue the vision and mission of your department? Organization?
9. Do you know the aims of these methods?
10. Do the aims of these methods support the aims of your department? Organization?
11. Are these methods necessary?
12. What are the critical control points for these methods?
13. Have the critical control points been operationally defined?
14. Have you used the **SDSA cycle** to standardize methods?
15. Have you used the **PDSA cycle** to improve and innovate methods?
16. Do you understand who the customers of these methods are?
17. Do you understand the needs of those customers?
18. Do you know who the suppliers of these methods are?
19. Do you understand the needs of those suppliers?
20. Do you understand how these methods interact with other methods in your department? Organization? How do you know?
21. Have you been trained in team skills and basic quality improvement tools?
22. Have you received training in the methods critical to your job?
23. Is your training in job skills updated as your job changes over time?
24. Have training manuals been updated as jobs change over time?
25. Do you receive feedback on the performance of the methods with which you work on a continuous basis?
26. Do you feel ownership of the methods with which you work?
27. Do you take pride in your work?

28. Do you take joy in your work?

29. Are you an empowered employee? How do you know?

30. Does your supervisor lead you in the conduct of planned experiments aimed at improvement and innovation of methods?

31. Do you have the latitude to modify the methods you use on your job to take advantage of your unique skills and abilities?

32. Do you need the latitude you have with respect to a method?

33. Can all of your colleagues who perform a particular method produce equal outcomes?

34. Do you trust your supervisor to support the decisions you make within the latitude given to you in respect to a particular method?

35. Is your supervisor working toward eliminating fear in your department? Organization? How do you know?

36. Are you implementing the improvement plan and/or projects per schedule?

37. Are records being kept of quality improvement efforts?

38. Are you revising the improvement plan as necessary?

The members of the EC and PDC ask the following questions of themselves:

1. Are we effectively conducting management reviews?

2. Are we improving and innovating the management review process?

3. Are methods being standardized and revised as required by the improvement plan?

Presidential Review

Finally, the president conducts the presidential review, shown in step 34 of Figure 14.1, of the major areas within the organization. Department managers present their efforts using the **quality improvement story** format, discussed in Chapter 11. The purpose of the presidential review is to collect information used to establish the quality strategy and goals of the organization and to determine progress toward presidential policy. Presidential reviews provide input for setting policy for the following year, as shown in step 29 of Figure 14.1 and described in the earlier section "Initial Presidential Review." The management system is improved with each successive policy management cycle.

Flowchart of Policy Management

An **integrated flowchart** depicting the relationship between the PDSA cycle and the five steps of policy management, and corporate and department responsibility for policy management, is shown in Figure 18.11.

Relationship between Policy Management and Daily Management

The relationship between policy management and daily management can be understood by viewing an organization as a tree. The vision is the root system, the mission is the trunk, the strategic objectives yield the major branches, and the improvement plans are

FIGURE 18.11
Integrated Flowchart of the Relationship between the PDSA and Policy Management

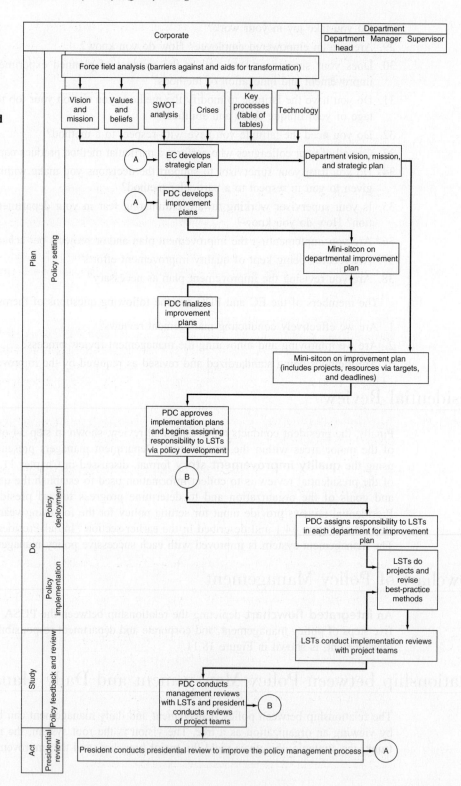

smaller branches emanating out of the strategic objective branches. As expertise is developed with policy management methods, they are moved into daily management methods.

Frequently, employees claim they do not have time for policy management because of the demands of their daily routine. However, recall that undertaking daily management and **cross-functional management** removes non-value-added daily routine to free up time for policy management.

A Personal Example of Policy Management

This section of the chapter presents the application of policy management to a person's life. All the steps of policy management are used in this example, which demonstrates how to implement the detailed procedure. Bart is a 40-year old manager in a large company. For the most part, his life has gone according to his plans. He is a respected manager, earns a comfortable salary, and is reasonably happy in his personal and family life. As he enters his forties, Bart begins to wonder whether he can improve his situation. Stimulated by what he is involved in at work, he decides to apply the principles of quality management to his life.

Policy Setting

Pros and Cons to Transformation

Bart performs a force field analysis and asks himself the following question: "Do I have the energy necessary to do quality management in my life?" From the force field analysis, he finds the "forces for change" to be more compelling than the "forces against change," as shown in Table 18.5. Bart decides to apply policy management in his life.

Values and Beliefs

Bart feels that the values and beliefs embodied in Deming's theory of management are completely consistent with his own, so he adopts these values and beliefs. They are: (1) manage to optimize the entire system, (2) manage to create a balance of intrinsic and extrinsic motivation, (3) manage with a process and results orientation, and (4) manage to promote cooperation.

Vision and Mission

Bart's personal vision and mission define his future desired state and his current reason for existence.

Personal Vision   To be at peace with my world and to generate positive energy into the universe.

Personal Mission   To continuously improve my mind, body, and relationships.

TABLE 18.5
Force Field Analysis

Force for Change	Forces against Change
Some dissatisfaction with my current life situation	No time to establish a policy management plan
Complaints from spouse, daughter, and brother	Family, friends, and colleagues will think I am a lunatic
Need to be more efficient and productive at work	

Organizational and Environmental Factors

Bart conducts a SWOT analysis of himself. An abbreviated listing of strengths, weaknesses, opportunities, and threats is shown below.

Strengths. Honest, forthright, mature, intelligent, excellent educational background, inquisitive, considerate, willing to help others with their problems, physically healthy, excellent communicator, strong support system of family and friends, well-established and ingrained values and beliefs, financially secure, professionally secure, able to stay focused, capable of retaining many facts until a strategy emerges, open to new ideas, resources available for self-improvement . . .

Weaknesses. High cholesterol, 25 pounds overweight, unilingual, resents working in nonproductive groups, not good at understanding other people's viewpoints, inability to change own behavior, poor short-term memory, low frustration tolerance . . .

Opportunities. Excellent business contacts, professional opportunities expanding, excellent system of personal mentors, increased ability to travel . . .

Threats. Increased demands to spend time working at the expense of personal life, parents passing away and not being prepared for the loss, the unknown and unknowable risks of life . . .

Synthesis. Bart studies his SWOTs and looks for strengths and opportunities that overcome his weaknesses and threats. He decides that his "available time for" and "ability to understand the benefits of" a healthy life style will help him overcome his physical and emotional condition.

Crises

The crisis known to Bart is diminution in quality of life due to moderate swings in mood (too much common variation in a stable system).

Key Processes

Voice of the customer and voice of the business analyses help prioritize processes for improvement attention. The purpose of these analyses is to provide customer and personal input into the determination of strategic objectives.

Voice of the Customer

Bart surveys each of his stakeholders and asks them to answer the following question: "From your perspective, what should I focus on to pursue my mission statement?" Data are collected from each individual. All issues that emerge from this analysis are quantified on a "dynamite" scale; the scale ranges from 1 stick of dynamite (unimportant or done well) to 5 sticks of dynamite (very important and not done well). The dynamite scale was developed to create data that can be averaged. The dynamite data are being used to impart a feel for which issues are priority issues in Bart's pursuit of his mission. The dynamite data were analyzed using Pareto-type analysis.

Spouse The spouse's survey indicates 17 separate items of concern, which are grouped into four subcategories: "child care responsibility," "home care responsibility," "finances," and "time allocation." All 17 items are rated on the dynamite scale, as shown in Table 18.6.

An analysis of the priority rankings shown in Table 18.7 indicates that 36.6 percent of the spouse's issues involve household chores: "shop at supermarket," "shop at drug

TABLE 18.6
Voice of
Customer for
Spouse

Category	Customer Ranking Survey Results (dynamite scale)
(a) Child care responsibility	
1. Drive child to/from school	1
2. Prepare child's dinner	2
3. Care for ill child	2
4. Help child with homework	1
(b) Home care responsibility	
1. Shop at supermarket	5
2. Shop at drug store	5
3. Go to dry cleaner	5
4. Sort clothes for wash	1
5. Make bank deposits	4
(c) Finances	
1. Prepare household accounts	1
2. Generate family income	1
3. Manage expense control	1
(d) Time allocation	
1. Decrease work time	4
2. Increase family time	2
3. Increase play time with child	2
4. Decrease business travel	2
5. Increase pleasure travel	2

TABLE 18.7
Analysis of
Spouse's Voice
of the
Customer Data

Category	Rank	%	Cum.	%
Shop at supermarket	5	12.2	12.2*	36.6% of
Shop at drug store	5	12.2	24.4*	spouse's issues
Go to dry cleaner	5	12.2	36.6*	involve household
Decrease work time	4	9.6	46.2	chores
Make bank deposits	4	9.6	55.8	
Increase family time	2	4.9	60.7	
Increase play time with child	2	4.9	65.6	
Decrease business travel	2	4.9	70.5	
Increase pleasure travel	2	4.9	75.4	
Prepare child's dinner	2	4.9	80.3	
Care for ill child	2	4.9	85.2	
Drive child to/from school	1	2.45	87.65	
Help child with homework	1	2.45	90.10	
Sort clothes for wash	1	2.45	92.55	
Prepare household accounts	1	2.45	95.00	
Generate family income	1	2.45	97.45	
Manage expense control	1	2.45	99.90	
TOTAL	41	99.90		

store," and "go to dry cleaner." Therefore, "home care responsibility" is the spouse's critical area of concern.

Child The child's survey indicates three items of concern, as shown in Table 18.8.

An analysis of the child's issues indicates that "increase play time" is the most critical area of concern; it accounted for 44 percent of the child's issues, as shown in see Table 18.9

Parents and Brother The parents' and brother's survey indicates several items of concern, as shown in Table 18.10.

An analysis of the parents' and brother's concerns shows that 45 percent of all issues directly involve the brother, as shown in Table 18.11. The brother's three issues are: "share private feelings and dreams," "increase private time together," and "support each other."

TABLE 18.8
Voice of the Customer for Child

Category	Customer Ranking Survey Results (dynamite scale)
Child	
(a) Increase play time	4
(b) Relax sleepover rules	2
(c) Decrease food restrictions	3

TABLE 18.9
Analysis of Child's Voice of the Customer Data

Category	Rank	%	Cum.	%
Increase play time	4	44	44*	44% of
Decrease food restrictions	3	33	77	child's issues
Relax sleepover rules	2	23	100	involve play
TOTAL	9	100		

TABLE 18.10
Voice of the Customer for Parents and Brother

Category	Customer Ranking Survey Results (dynamite scale)
(a) Father	
1. Increase private time together	3
2. Go to sporting events together	2
3. Work on car together	2
4. Work on garden together	2
(b) Mother	
1. Determine common interests	4
2. Increase private time together	3
(c) Brother	
1. Increase private time together	4
2. Share private feelings and dreams	5
3. Learn to support each other	4

TABLE 18.11
Analysis of Parents' and Brother's Voice of the Customer Data

Category	Rank	%	Cum.	%
Brother—Share private feelings and dreams	5	17	17*	45% of
Brother—Increase private time together	4	14	31*	issues
Brother—Learn to support each other	4	14	45*	involve
Mother—Determine common interests	4	14	59	commu-
Mother—Increase private time together	3	10	69	nication
Father—Increase private time together	3	10	79	with
Father—Go to sporting events together	2	7	86	brother
Father—Work on car together	2	7	93	
Father—Work on garden together	2	7	100	
TOTAL	29	100		

Voice of the Business

The voice of the business seeks to answer the following question: "What should I focus on to pursue my mission?" Bart compiles a list of 11 issues that are critical to the fulfillment of his mission, as shown in Table 18.12.

These 11 issues are rated with respect to severity, urgency, trend, and importance to customer, as shown in the prioritization matrix in Table 18.13. The ratings are then

TABLE 18.12
Voice of the Business

1. Increase pleasure travel with spouse
2. Increase private study time
3. Maintain study group time
4. Increase play time with child
5. Increase fun time with friends
6. Increase exercise time
7. Decrease body weight
8. Plan and shoot fireworks displays
9. Plan and execute special events
10. Increase private time with spouse
11. Improve financial security

TABLE 18.13
Prioritization of Matrix of the Voice of the Business

Category	Severity	Urgency	Trend	Import to Customer	TOTAL SCORE
1. Increase travel with spouse	1	1	2	3	6
2. Increase private study time	1	1	4	5	20
3. Maintain study group time	1	1	2	5	10
4. Increase play with child	3	3	4	4	144
5. Increase fun with friends	1	1	2	3	6
6. Increase exercise time	3	3	3	5	130
7. Decrease body weight	4	4	4	4	256
8. Fireworks displays	1	1	2	1	2
9. Special events	1	1	3	3	9
10. Increase time with spouse	2	2	4	5	80
11. Improve financial security	1	1	3	3	9

multiplied to obtain a total score for each issue. This method is used to demonstrate an alternative to the dynamite scale used in the voice of the customer analysis.

The items in the matrix are then arranged in descending order of priority, as shown in Table 18.14.

An analysis of the data in Table 18.14 is shown in Table 18.15.

Four of the 11 issues account for 90.7 percent of Bart's issues. These include "decrease body weight," "increase play time with child," "increase exercise time," and "increase time with spouse."

Table of Tables

The prioritized issues from the voice of the customer and voice of the business studies are combined into one prioritized list in the rows of Table 18.16. The processes that compose Bart's life are listed in its columns.

The *importance to customer or employee scale,* shown in column A in Table 18.16, is ranked from 1 (unimportant to customer or employee) to 5 (important to customer or employee). The rankings are developed by company personnel and are modifications of

TABLE 18.14
Ranking of Voice of the Business Data

Category	Severity	Urgency	Trend	Importance to Customer	TOTAL SCORE
7. Decrease body weight	4	4	4	4	256
4. Increase play with child	3	3	4	4	144
6. Increase exercise time	3	3	3	5	130
10. Increase time with spouse	2	2	4	5	80
2. Increase private study time	1	1	4	5	29
3. Maintain study group time	1	1	2	5	10
9. Special events	1	1	3	3	9
11. Improve financial security	1	1	3	3	9
1. Increase travel with spouse	1	1	2	3	6
5. Increase fun with friends	1	1	2	3	6
8. Fireworks displays	1	1	2	1	2

TABLE 18.15
Analysis of the Voice of the Business Data

Category	Total Score	%	Cum. %
7. Decrease body weight	256	38.1	38.1*
4. Increase play with child	144	21.4	59.5*
6. Increase exercise time	130	19.3	78.8*
10. Increase time with spouse	80	11.9	90.7*
2. Increase private study time	20	3.0	93.7
3. Maintain study group time	10	1.5	95.2
9. Special events	9	1.3	96.5
11. Improve financial security	9	1.3	97.8
1. Increase travel with spouse	6	0.9	98.7
5. Increase fun with friends	6	0.9	99.6
8. Fireworks displays	2	0.3	99.9
TOTAL	672	99.9	

TABLE 18.16   Table of Tables for Bart

Legend:
- ⊙ Strong relationship
- ○ Moderate relationship
- △ Weak relationship
- ▽ No Relationship

Score:
- 3
- 2
- 1
- 0

	Brother—increase communication—VOC (feelings, time, support)	Daughter—play time—VOB and VOC (increase play time with child)	Spouse—household chores—VOC (supermarket, drug store, dry cleaner)	Increase exercise time—VOB	Decrease body weight—VOB	Needs and Wants	Partial Listing of Methods That Are Important to Bart
135				⊙	⊙	Weight	Fitness
75				⊙		Diet (food intake)	
135				⊙	⊙	Exercise	
0						Joy in work	Occupation
0						Revenue	
0						Travel	Leisure
2.67		△				Entertainment	
25				△		Education	Learning
0						Training	
0							Spiritual
27.67		△		△		Self-esteem	Psychological
45				△	△	Well-being	
31.68	○	○		△		Joy	
8.68	○	⊙				Love	Relationships
10.02	⊙	○	⊙			Communication	
8.01		⊙				Fun	
80.34	○		⊙			Sharing responsibility	
	1	4	5	4	5	Importance to customer or employee (A)	
	3	3	1	1	1	Current level of performance to customer or employee (B)	
	2	2	5	5	5	Desired level of performance by management (C)	
	0.67	2.67	25	20	25	Total Weight = A(C/B)	

the rankings identified in the voice of the customer and voice of the business studies. The scale indicates that "decrease body weight" (5), "increase exercise time" (4), "household chores" (5), and "increase play time with child" (4) are important to customers and Bart.

The *current level of performance to customer or employee scale,* shown in column B in Table 18.16, is ranked from 1 (large gap between customer or employee desired requirements and actual performance) to 5 (small gap between customer or employee desired requirements and actual performance). The rankings are developed by company personnel. The gap analyses of "decrease body weight," shown in Figure 18.12, "increase exercise time," shown in Figure 18.13, and "household chores," shown in Figure 18.14, all indicate large gaps between desired and actual performance, in the opinion of the company personnel. Specifically, the gap analysis of "decrease body weight," in Figure 18.12, shows that Bart's average body weight has steadily increased to 172 pounds. According to Bart's physician, he should weigh 145 pounds. Additionally, the gap analysis of "increase exercise time," in Figure 18.13, shows that Bart has not been capable of maintaining the required three exercise periods per week. He achieved three exercise periods per week in only 25 percent of the weeks in the trial period. Finally, gap analysis of "household chores," in Figure 18.14, shows that Bart has not been capable of maintaining the necessary one trip per week to the supermarket, drug store, and dry cleaner most of the time during the trial period.

The *desired level of performance by management* scale, shown in column C in Table 18.16, is ranked from 1 (improvement is not urgent) to 5 (improvement is urgent). Again, the rankings are developed by company personnel based on management's view of the urgency to improve voice of the customer or voice of the business items. The scale indicates that "decrease body weight," "increase exercise time," and "household chores" are all deemed in need of urgent improvement attention by Bart.

The *total weight* scale, shown in column A(C/B) in Table 18.16, is computed by multiplying the *importance to customer or employee* scale by the *desired level of performance by management* scale to obtain a significance indicator (1 signifies extreme unimportance and 25 indicates extreme importance). This significance indicator is divided by the *current level of performance* scale. The resulting number is the *total weight* scale. A *total weight* of 0.2 $[(1 \times 1)/5]$ indicates a very unimportant voice of the customer or voice of the business item, while a *total weight* of 25 $[(5 \times 5)/1]$ indicates an extremely important voice of the customer or voice of the business item. The *total weight* scale shows the need to focus attention on "decrease body weight" (total weight = 25), "increase exercise time" (total weight = 20), and "household chores" (total weight = 25) in Bart's strategic objectives, as shown in Table 18.16.

The cells of Table 18.16 show the strength of the relationships between voice of the customer and voice of the business issues and the processes that compose Bart's life. A doughnut symbol indicates a strong relationship (value = 3), a circle indicates a moderate relationship (value = 2), a triangle indicates a weak relationship (value = 1), and a blank indicates no relationship (value = 0). The cell relationships are determined by company personnel familiar with the processes listed in the columns, and issues listed in the rows, of the table of tables. A numeric quantity is computed for each cell by multiplying the value for its symbol by the *total weight* of its row. For example, the value for the cell defined by the "fitness—weight" column and the "decrease body weight" row is 3. The *total weight* of its row is 25. Hence, the numeric quantity computed for

FIGURE 18.12   Gap Analysis of Bart's Daily Weight

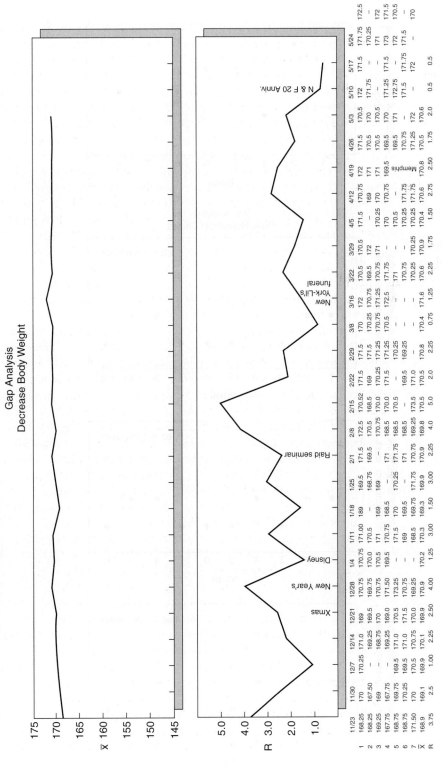

FIGURE 18.13
Gap Analysis Exercise Time

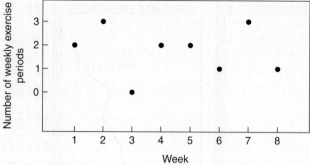

FIGURE 18.14
Gap Analysis Household Chores

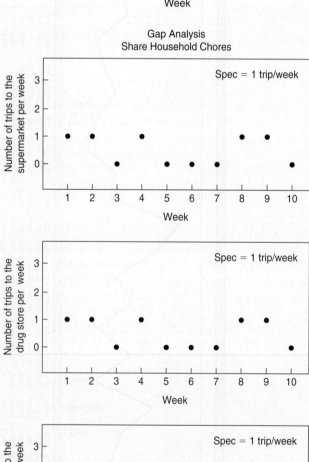

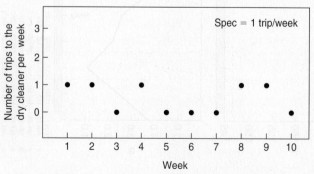

the cell is 75 (3 × 25). This operation is done for each cell in the table of tables. Finally, the numeric quantities are summed for each column.

The table of tables reveals that "weight" (priority = 135), "exercise" (priority = 135), and "shared responsibilities" (priority = 80.34) are the processes that must receive attention in Bart's strategic objective if he is to surpass the needs and wants of his customers and himself, as shown in the bottom row of Table 18.16.

Technology

Bart realizes that using a treadmill at home while watching television, as opposed to jogging outside, makes him want to exercise more.

Develop Strategic Objectives

Bart's strategic objectives are:

1. To become healthy.
2. To continually improve personal relationships.

They emerge from an analysis of Bart's vision and mission statements, his values and beliefs, a SWOT analysis of his life, the crises Bart faces, the key processes that have to be improved to delight Bart's stakeholders, and technological issues that might affect Bart's life. The best quality management method for generating strategic objectives is a thoughtful, yet subjective, analysis of all inputs by the members of the executive committee. It is critical that all stakeholders agree to support the strategic objectives.

Develop the Improvement Plans

Bart brainstorms a list of the barriers that prevent him from becoming healthier (*strategic objective 1*) as part of a gap analysis. The list includes the following potential causes: too much body weight, too little exercise, unbalanced diet, too much stress, and too little sleep. An analysis of the interrelationships between the potential causes indicates that "too little exercise" is the root cause that affects poor health in Bart's life, as shown in Figure 18.15.

The arrows between the items on the **interrelationship diagram** indicate the direction of "cause to effect" relationships, for example, "too much stress" partially causes "too little

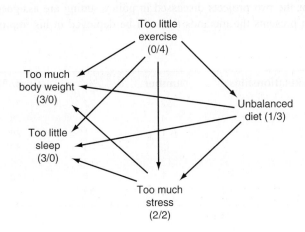

FIGURE 18.15
Interrelationship Diagraph Causes of Diminished Health

Too little exercise (0/4)

Too much body weight (3/0)

Unbalanced diet (1/3)

Too little sleep (3/0)

Too much stress (2/2)

sleep," while "too much stress" is partially caused by (the partial effect of) "too little exercise." The numbers in parentheses under each item on the interrelationship diagraph, such as (1/3) under "Unbalanced diet," indicate the number of arrows entering (affecting) an item and leaving (causing) another item, respectively. The item with the largest number of arrows entering it is called the "root effect" item because it is affected by so many other items. Root effect items are frequently viewed as the sources of problems, but since they are affected by so many other items, it is difficult to do anything about them. "Too much body weight" and "too little sleep" are the root effect items in this interrelationship diagraph. They make sense in that these are commonly the things people worry about with respect to health, but they are difficult to do anything about because they are affected by so many other things. On the other hand, "too little exercise" is the "root cause" item in this interrelationship diagraph; it affects (causes) the most other items. This is the improvement tactic Bart should focus on to pursue his first strategic objective.

Bart collects frequency data from his diary for a two-month period on the barriers that prevent him from improving his personal relationships, as part of a gap analysis. The barriers include the following potential causes: failure to share responsibilities (house care, child care, time allocation), moderate swings in mood, not good at understanding other people's viewpoints, poor short-term memory, low frustration tolerance, and increased demand to spend time at work. Table 18.17 shows the frequency of occurrence of each barrier, extracted from Bart's diary, and that failure to share house care responsibilities is the most significant cause that affects Bart's personal relationships.

The above gap analyses indicate that Bart needs to construct improvement plans to deal specifically with developing an exercise regimen (tactic for strategic objective 1) and sharing house care responsibilities (tactic for strategic objective 2), if he wants to achieve his strategic objectives.

Bart operationally defines control points and establishes targets for an exercise regimen and house care responsibilities: in particular, going to the supermarket, drug store, and dry cleaner. The purpose of the targets is to allocate the resources available to Bart between his improvement plan tactics. In this case, the targets are based on medical science and years of experience with the chores. Control points and targets are shown in Table 18.18.

Policy Deployment

Responsibility for the two projects discussed in policy setting are assigned to Bart. The following section presents the methods that will be deployed in his improvement plan.

TABLE 18.17
Pareto Analysis of Personal Relationships

Cause of Poor Relationships	Number	%	Cum. %
Responsibilities	52	72	72
Mood	4	6	78
Viewpoints	1	1	79
Memory	2	3	82
Frustration	12	17	99
Time	1	1	100
Total	72	100	

TABLE 18.18
Control Points and Targets

Strategic Objective	Improvement Plan (tactics)	Control Point	Target
To become healthy	develop an exercise regimen	# of exercise periods/week	3
To continually improve personal relationships	do supermarket shopping	# trips/week	1
	do drug store shopping	# trips/week	1
	go to dry cleaner	# trips/week	1

FIGURE 18.16
Method for Shopping at Supermarket

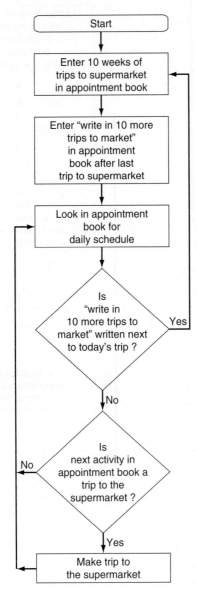

1. An Exercise Regimen

Bart's method for improving his exercise regimen was discussed under "A Personal Example of Daily Management" in "Daily Management," Chapter 16.

2. House Care Responsibilities

Plan (Developing a Plan)   An important process in Bart's life highlighted for attention is "sharing responsibility" with his spouse, especially household chores such as shopping at the supermarket, shopping at the drug store, and picking up and dropping off clothes at the dry cleaner.

Bart uses the data from the gap analysis in Figure 18.14 for all three activities. Analysis of this gap data leads him to the realization that he needs to develop methods for "sharing responsibilities." He develops the flowcharts (methods) shown in Figures 18.16, 18.17, and 18.18.

Do (Implementing the Plan)   Bart records the number of trips to each location for ten weeks after development of the methods. The data are shown in Figures 18.19, 18.20 and 18.21.

Study (Checking the Effectiveness of the Plan)   The records show that all three targets are being met using the above methods.

Act (Take Action)   Action to modify the current method is taken if a trend develops indicating failure of the methods to meet targets. Continuous monitoring and documentation of the causes for additional trips will help modify the current practices and assure achievement of targets.

Policy Implementation

All methods in the improvement plan are implemented and monitored on a weekly basis: exercise regimen, trips to the supermarket, trips to the drug

FIGURE 18.17 **Method for Shopping at Drug Store**

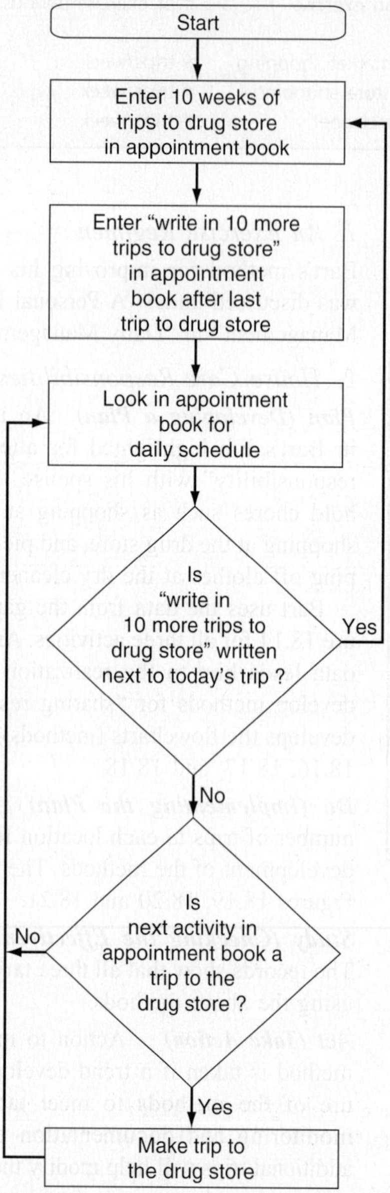

```
                    ┌──────────── Start ────────────┐
                              │
                    ┌─────────────────────┐
                    │ Enter 10 weeks of   │
                    │ trips to drug store │◄───────┐
                    │ in appointment book │        │
                    └─────────────────────┘        │
                              │                     │
                    ┌─────────────────────┐        │
                    │ Enter "write in 10  │        │
                    │ more trips to drug  │        │
                    │ store" in           │        │
                    │ appointment book    │        │
                    │ after last trip     │        │
                    │ to drug store       │        │
                    └─────────────────────┘        │
                              │                     │
                    ┌─────────────────────┐        │
                    │ Look in appointment │◄──┐     │
                    │ book for            │   │     │
                    │ daily schedule      │   │     │
                    └─────────────────────┘   │     │
                              │                │     │
                        ╱ Is "write in ╲       │     │
                       ╱ 10 more trips  ╲  Yes │     │
                      ╱ to drug store    ╲─────┘─────┘
                      ╲ written next to  ╱
                       ╲ today's trip ? ╱
                        ╲              ╱
                              │ No
                        ╱ Is next     ╲    No
                       ╱ activity in   ╲──────┐
                      ╱ appointment     ╲     │
                      ╲ book a trip to  ╱     │
                       ╲ the drug store?╱     │
                        ╲              ╱      │
                              │ Yes           │
                    ┌─────────────────────┐   │
                    │ Make trip to        │   │
                    │ the drug store      │───┘
                    └─────────────────────┘
```

FIGURE 18.18 **Method for Shopping at Dry Cleaner**

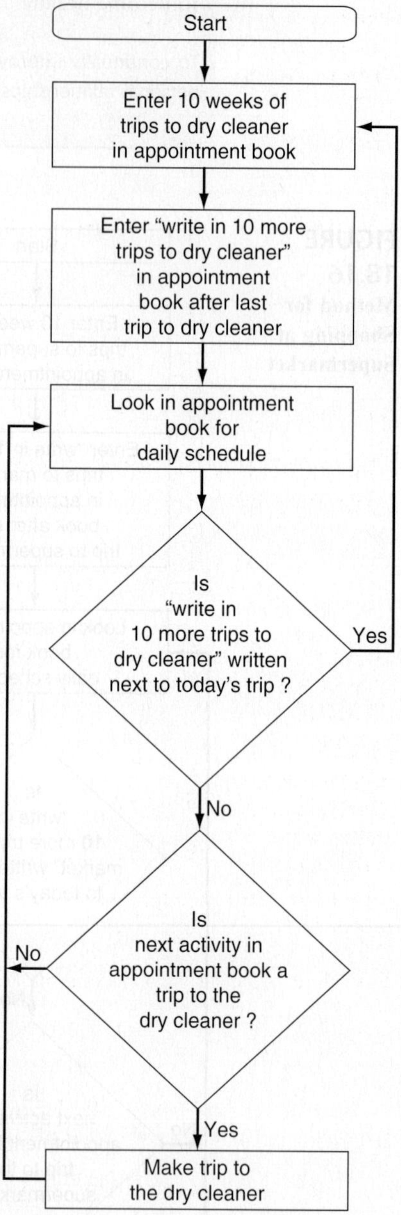

```
                    ┌──────────── Start ────────────┐
                              │
                    ┌──────────────────────┐
                    │ Enter 10 weeks of    │
                    │ trips to dry cleaner │◄──────┐
                    │ in appointment book  │       │
                    └──────────────────────┘       │
                              │                     │
                    ┌──────────────────────┐        │
                    │ Enter "write in 10   │        │
                    │ more trips to dry    │        │
                    │ cleaner" in          │        │
                    │ appointment book     │        │
                    │ after last trip      │        │
                    │ to dry cleaner       │        │
                    └──────────────────────┘        │
                              │                     │
                    ┌──────────────────────┐        │
                    │ Look in appointment  │◄──┐     │
                    │ book for             │   │     │
                    │ daily schedule       │   │     │
                    └──────────────────────┘   │     │
                              │                │     │
                        ╱ Is "write in ╲       │     │
                       ╱ 10 more trips  ╲  Yes │     │
                      ╱ to dry cleaner   ╲─────┘─────┘
                      ╲ written next to  ╱
                       ╲ today's trip ? ╱
                              │ No
                        ╱ Is next     ╲    No
                       ╱ activity in   ╲──────┐
                      ╱ appointment     ╲     │
                      ╲ book a trip to  ╱     │
                       ╲ the dry cleaner?╱    │
                              │ Yes           │
                    ┌──────────────────────┐  │
                    │ Make trip to         │  │
                    │ the dry cleaner      │──┘
                    └──────────────────────┘
```

FIGURE 18.19
Continuation of Run Charts— Number of Trips per Week to the Supermarket

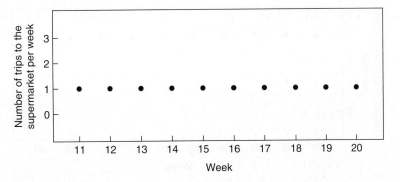

FIGURE 18.20
Continuation of Run Charts— Number of Trips per Week to the Drug Store

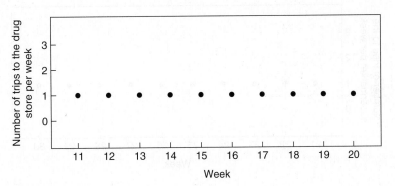

FIGURE 18.21
Continuation of Run Charts— Number of Trips per Week to the Dry Cleaner

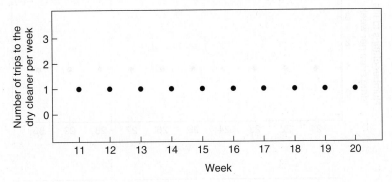

store, and trips to the dry cleaner. All methods are yielding predicted results for a 10-week period, as shown in Figures 18.22, 18.23, 18.24, and 18.25.

Policy Study and Feedback

All methods implemented in the improvement plan are subject to monthly management reviews by Bart. He finds that the methods are yielding predicted results. A year-end management review will be conducted at the appropriate time to determine if the methods remain effective with respect to optimization of Bart's interdependent system of stakeholders.

FIGURE 18.22 Continuation of Run Charts— Number of Exercise Periods per Week

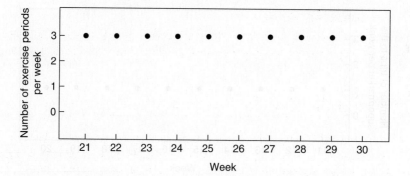

FIGURE 18.23 Continuation of Run Charts— Number of Trips per Week to the Supermarket

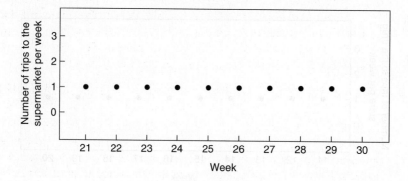

FIGURE 18.24 Continuation of Run Charts— Number of Trips per Week to the Drug Store

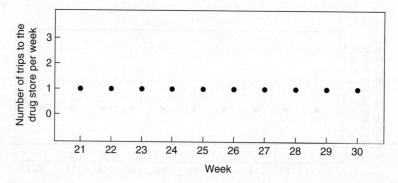

FIGURE 18.25 Continuation of Run Charts— Number of Trips per Week to the Dry Cleaner

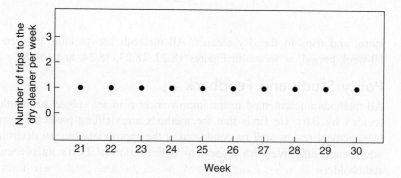

Presidential Review

Presidential review in the case study of personal policy management is equivalent to the yearly management reviews conducted by Bart himself of his strategic and improvement plans.

A Business Example of Policy Management

Florida Power and Light Company (FPL) is the largest utility furnishing the generation, transmission, distribution, and sale of electricity in the state of Florida. From its inception in 1925, FPL has experienced steady growth. In November 1989, Florida Power and Light Company achieved international recognition when its employees challenged for, and won, the prestigious **Deming Prize** for quality. The Deming Prize is awarded annually by the Japanese Union of Scientists and Engineers (JUSE) to companies that excel in the practice of the Japanese method of quality management. FPL was the first non-Japanese company to win the Deming Prize. [See Reference 5, pp. 123–158.]

Reasons for the Quality Improvement Program (QIP)

By the early 1980s, FPL was facing a hostile environment created largely by high inflation, decreasing customer sales, rising electric rates, and increasing fuel oil prices. The price of electricity was increasing faster than the Consumer Price Index (CPI). At the same time, competitive market pressures were beginning to affect FPL's long-term prospects. Customer dissatisfaction grew as FPL failed to meet increasing expectations for reliability, safety, and customer service. In the meantime, FPL's inability to react quickly to new environmental demands added to its plight.

Objectives of the Quality Improvement Program

It was clear to FPL's leadership that their existing managerial structures were not keeping pace with FPL's rapidly changing internal and external environments. Above all, they recognized that FPL was facing four significant crises that warranted a complete restructuring of their managerial systems.

Crisis 1:   Internal and external environments changing faster than FPL could adapt

Crisis 2:   Declining customer confidence and satisfaction

Crisis 3:   Uncertainty of the future of nuclear power supply

Crisis 4:   Price of electricity increasing faster than the Consumer Price Index

As described by FPL's top executives, crisis 1 was an internal issue that involved changing FPL's corporate culture. FPL had to change its mode of thinking from a supply-oriented mindset to a customer-oriented mindset, from a power generation company to a customer service company. To accomplish this, FPL's managers needed a process that would allow them to identify and address the key issues surrounding customer satisfaction.

Crises 2, 3, and 4 were related to external issues. FPL's leadership realized that these issues required systematic and resourceful management, guided by a vision, a mission, and strong strategic and business plans.

The first step toward resolving these crises was the installation of a new management system. Prior to 1985, **management by objectives** (MBO) had been FPL's principal policy for setting and achieving corporate goals. However, company top management had concluded that MBO was not capable of resolving the issues at the core of the four crises with which the company was to grapple. In particular, MBO's focus on the company's point of view rather than on the customers' needs conflicted with the establishment of a new corporate culture and consequently, with the resolution of crisis 1. Also, MBO did not provide a systematic method for measuring and achieving corporate objectives. A system was needed that would be responsive to changes in FPL's operating environment, as well as to the needs of the customers. To this end, FPL established its quality improvement program (QIP).

Reacting to the Crises

Determining Customer Needs

To a great extent, the success of FPL's new management process, QIP, would depend on the development and application of a tool that could systematically identify and prioritize the needs of FPL's customers. FPL's diverse customer base is composed of direct customers (residential, commercial, and industrial users) and indirect customers (regulatory and governmental agencies, such as the Nuclear Regulatory Commission, the Florida Public Service Commission, environmental and regulatory agencies, state and local governments, and the Federal Energy Regulatory Commission).

The tool FPL developed to understand the voice of the customer for each of its market segments is the table of tables, shown in Figure 18.26. It is used to build customer needs into FPL processes. The table of tables shows the prioritized concerns of FPL's diverse customer segments with regard to "sales and service quality," "delivery," "safety," "cost," and "corporate responsibility." By applying the table of tables, FPL was able to develop strategies to resolve its four crises.

- Crises 2 and 4 were partially resolved by improving sales and service processes, which lowered costs and allowed FPL management to decrease the price of electricity.
- Crises 1 and 3 were partially resolved by increasing the level and value of communications between FPL and its operating environment.

The development of the table of tables was the key to identifying and prioritizing customer needs and wants. In turn, this information was used to resolve internal and external crises by establishing corporate responsibility (for example, for process improvement action), which was disseminated throughout the organization via policy management.

Establishing Divisional Objectives

Prior to FPL's quality improvement program, each division pursued its own vision and key objectives based on its unique set of characteristics, as shown by the differences between divisions in Figure 18.27b. More often than not, divisional objectives were optimized before corporate objectives. This made it difficult to coordinate divisional objectives within the context of corporate policy and led to interdivisional rivalries and suboptimization of the corporate whole.

To counter this situation, FPL management modified their quality improvement program (QIP) to include policy management. Policy management coordinated all divisional visions, missions, strategic plans, and business plans with each other, and with FPL's corporate vision, mission, strategic plan, and business plan. For example, the

FIGURE 18.26
FPL's Table of Tables

Source: Florida Power and Light Company, *Description of Quality Improvement Program,* Corporate Unit, 1988, p. 11.

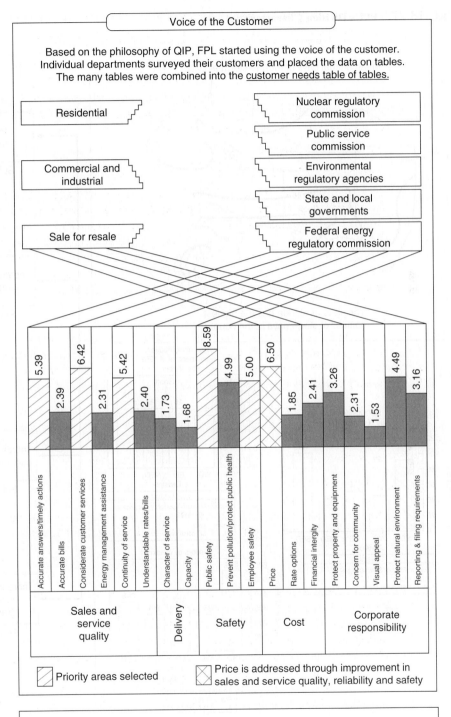

FIGURE 18.27 **FPL's Division Characteristics**

Source: Florida Power and Light Company, *Description of Quality Improvement Program,* Southern Division, 1988, p. 2, and Corporate Unit, 1988, p. 11.

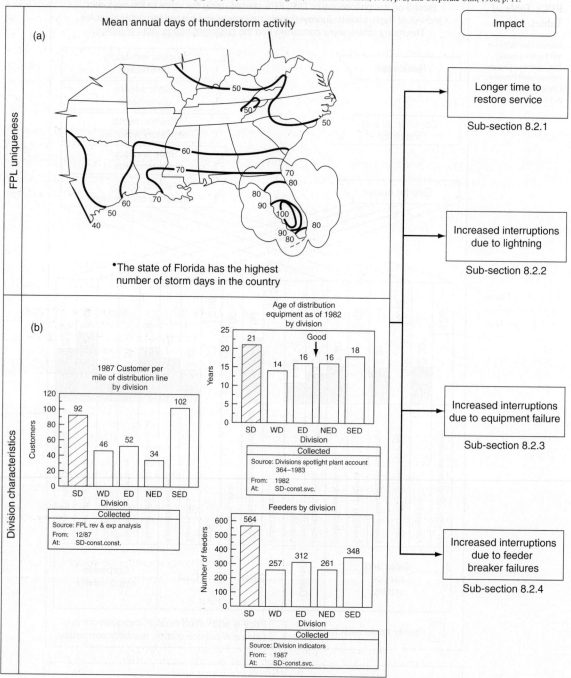

Southern Division's vision is as follows: *We will improve all aspects of operations to increase customer satisfaction and be recognized as the best managed division.* Note that this vision seems to stimulate competition between divisions and would violate Deming's concept of globally optimizing the system of interdependent stakeholders. However, at the time FPL was following Japanese total quality control, not Deming's theory of management. The Southern Division's vision is supported by two key objectives. They are: (1) improve continuity of service as measured by "service unavailability" through the use of the QIP components and (2) improve customer satisfaction through the use of the QIP components as measured by "complaints to the Florida Public Service Commission" and "customer satisfaction survey indicators."

The Southern Division's objectives were derived from an examination of "priority problems at the time FPL management introduced QIP" and the Southern Division's vision, shown in Figure 18.28. The "priority problems at the time FPL management introduced QIP" resulted from the four crises which shaped FPL's corporate vision, mission, strategic plan, and each division's vision. Likewise all other divisions' vision and key objectives reflect corporate policy.

**FIGURE
18.28**
**FPL Southern
Division Vision
and Objectives**

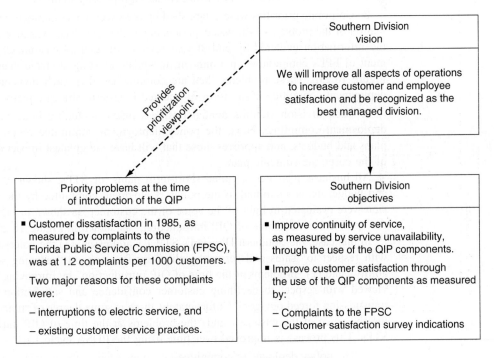

Southern Division
vision

We will improve all aspects of operations to increase customer and employee satisfaction and be recognized as the best managed division.

Provides prioritization viewpoint

Priority problems at the time
of introduction of the QIP

- Customer dissatisfaction in 1985, as measured by complaints to the Florida Public Service Commission (FPSC), was at 1.2 complaints per 1000 customers.

  Two major reasons for these complaints were:

  – interruptions to electric service, and

  – existing customer service practices.

Southern Division
objectives

- Improve continuity of service, as measured by service unavailability, through the use of the QIP components.

- Improve customer satisfaction through the use of the QIP components as measured by:

  – Complaints to the FPSC

  – Customer satisfaction survey indications

Other objectives of Southern Division
– Continue employee safety program
– Continue cost control activities

Note: In 1991, FP&L switched from being organized by division to being organized by function. This switch was based on a scan of FP&L's environment. The scan indicated the need to streamline FP&L to make it more competitive in the 1990s.

Corporate policies are established by the executive committee with the help of the table of tables and an examination of FPL's business environment. Once set, policies are communicated to each division in the form of strategic, or long-term plans. In response, each division submits an annual business, or short-term plan detailing its predicted contribution toward the realization of the corporate strategic plan.

For example, the table of tables representing the voice of the customer and "problems at the time of QIP Introduction" were used to guide the development and approval of short-term business plans as follows:

1. The table of tables, shown in Figure 18.29a, prioritized the concerns of FPL's diverse customer base and helped FPL's executive committee define the areas that were of greatest importance to customers. As an example, the table of tables has a category titled "sales and service quality," under which fall the following related items: accurate answers/timely actions, accurate bills, considerate customer service, energy management, continuity of service, and understanding rates/bills.

All these items were important to FPL's customers. However, of these items, only "accurate answers/timely actions," "considerate customer services," and "continuity of service" were identified by the customers as high-priority items.

2. Corporate priorities were established by the executive committee through an examination of the problems FPL was experiencing at the time. The executive committee uses the information gathered by end-of-year reviews of internal customers, and an assessment of FPL's competitive environment, to update existing strategic plans, as shown in Figure 18.29b. These problems then are communicated to each division by the policy deployment committee in the form of updated long-term strategic plans.

3. Each division submits annual business plans, including budgets, to the policy deployment committee. Next, the policy deployment committee reviews the business plans and budgets, and approves those that will have the greatest impact on achievement of the corporate strategic plan.

All business plan items, called short-term plans, or STPs, shown in Figure 18.29c, and budget items submitted to the policy deployment committee by the Southern Division were evaluated in light of the voice of the customer, as shown in Figure 18.29a and the "problems at the time of QIP introduction," as shown in Figure 18.29b.

In this case, the Southern Division's STP 1.1 addresses: (1) the voice of the customer with respect to "sales and service quality" by focusing on "reducing service unavailability," and (2) "problems at the time of QIP introduction" by improving "reliability" as viewed with respect to declining customer confidence and satisfaction and "reducing transmission forced outages." Unfortunately, there is some degree of subjectivity in aligning the voice of the customer and "the problems at the time of QIP introduction" with STPs. This process is improved over time using the PDSA cycle.

4. The policy deployment committee examines each of the division's STPs in light of their contribution to the corporate strategic plan, as shown in Figure 18.29c for the Southern Division's contribution to the corporate strategic plan. For example, STP 1.1 was highly correlated (⊙) with FPL's company goal to "improve customer satisfaction with sales and service quality," was moderately correlated (○) with "improve utilization of resources to stabilize costs," and was weakly correlated (△) with "strengthen effectiveness in nuclear plant operation and regulatory performance."

FIGURE 18.29 Business Plan Items

Source: Florida Power and Light Company, *Description of Quality Improvement Program*, Corporate Unit, 1988, p. 11.

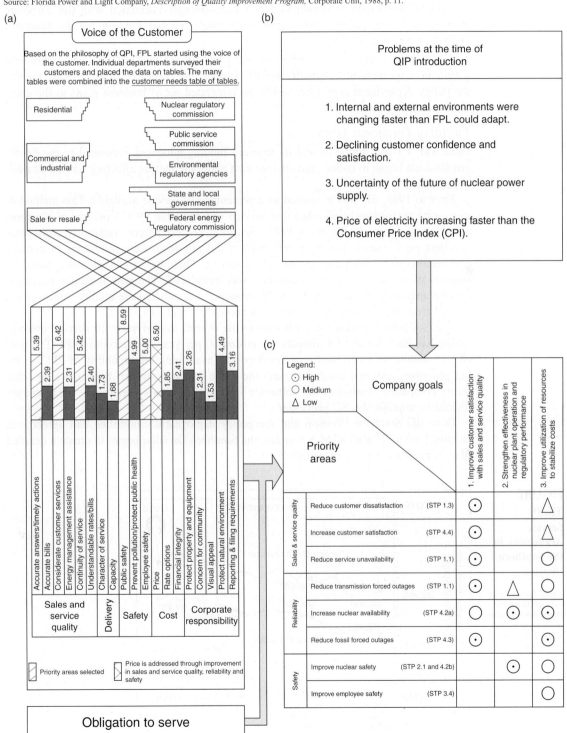

Because the Southern Division's STPs were strongly correlated with the corporate strategic plan, the policy deployment committee approved funding for the Southern Division's business plan.

5. The policy deployment committee integrates all the divisions' business plans into a system of business plans which mutually support the corporate strategic plan. Finally, the policy deployment committee sends the integrated set of business plans to the executive committee.

Fulfilling Divisional Objectives

Once STP 1.1 was approved and its required funding allocated, personnel in the Southern Division began to collect and analyze data about the factors affecting service unavailability (SU).

Prior to 1986, SU was measured as a percentage of service available. This method of measuring performance indicated that service was available 99.991 percent of the time, as shown in Figure 18.30. From FPL's viewpoint, 99.991 percent reliability constituted excellent performance. However, this number did not adequately reflect the customer's true requirement, which was uninterrupted service. Therefore, a new measure, based on minutes of service outage per customer, was introduced. The new indicator portrayed service unavailability as a number to be reduced; it quantified the quality improvement needed from the customer's viewpoint, as shown in Figure 18.31.

The Southern Division's contribution to the overall improvement of service unavailability had been set at 54.8 minutes per customer, per year, by year-end 1988. The goal of 54.8 minutes is a designed goal developed by examining the capability of FPL's existing processes, external conditions, and the voice of the customer, benchmarking other utility companies, analyzing the corporate strategic plan, and determining the resources needed to improve the SU processes.

Once the Southern Division and the policy deployment committee had agreed, via catchball, on a SU goal of 54.8 minutes, the Southern Division began to create a detailed plan to decrease service unavailability.

FIGURE 18.30
Service Availability in the Southern Division

Source: Florida Power and Light Company, *Description of Quality Improvement Program*, Southern Division, 1988, p. 46.

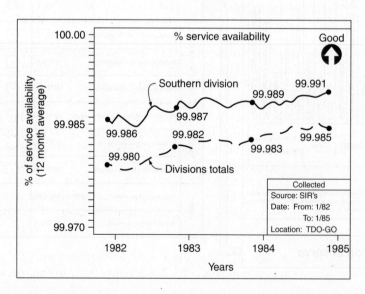

FIGURE 18.31   **Southern Division Service Unavailability**

Source: Florida Power and Light Company, *Description of Quality Improvement Program,* Southern Division, 1988, p. 46, Corporate Unit, 1988, p. 11.

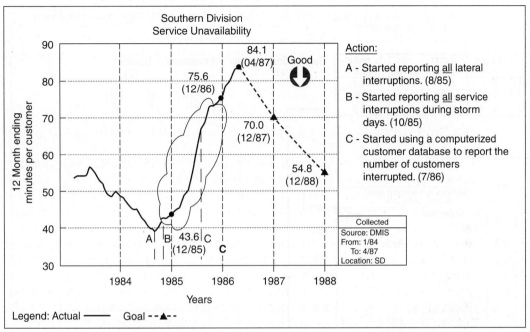

Creating a Plan

Service unavailability is measured in terms of the "frequency" and the "duration" of power outages; service unavailability = frequency × duration. We assume that SU is a stable process. Consequently, Southern Division personnel broke down the 54.8 minutes of SU per customer per year into 1.52 minutes of SU per customer per year due to frequency and 36.1 minutes per customer per year due to duration. (The goals of 36.1 and 1.52 were designed goals, as shown in Figure 18.32a.)

The Southern Division has certain unique characteristics that directly affect the level of service unavailability. For example, the division has a greater number of feeders, its distribution equipment is older, and it is second only to the South-Eastern Division in the number of customers per mile of distribution line, as shown in Figure 18.27b. (Feeders are major electric lines that carry electricity from the generating plants to a major service area or subarea. When a power outage is reported and the cause is not immediately known, work crews are dispatched to check the lines feeding the affected area.) These factors, along with Florida's propensity for thunderstorms and lightning strikes, as shown in Figure 18.27a, increased the frequency and duration of power outages in the area. The Southern Division's quality improvement (QI) team collected and analyzed data on the factors contributing to outages to better understand the causes of service unavailability.

Frequency

The Pareto chart in Figure 18.32b breaks down SU due to frequency, as measured by customer minutes interrupted (CMI) by major categories. Fifty-six percent of all CMI

FIGURE 18.32 Assignment Responsibility for Reducing Customer Minutes Interrupted

Planning for 1988 target

(a)

- The Division vice president's objective was to reduce service unavailability to 54.8 minutes per customer by year end 1988. Policy deployment was used to address this objective.

- In view of our characteristics (see Section 1.3) we will work on duration and four frequency major categories.

	Target 1987	Target 1988	Δ '87-'88	% reduction
SU	70.0	54.8	15.2	21.7
F	1.65	1.52	0.13	7.8
D	42.4	36.1	6.3	14.9

Service unavailability = Frequency × Duration
(SU)   (F)   (D)

$$\frac{\Delta SU}{SU} \approx \frac{\Delta F}{F} + \frac{\Delta D}{D}$$

(b)

Customer minutes interrupted by major categories

N = 54,887,000

(Pareto chart values: 12.5 (23%), 9.3 (40%), 9.2 (56%), 8.9 (73%), 6.2 (84%), 5.5 (94%), 3.3 (100%))

Major categories: Natural, OH equipment, UG equipment, Accidents, Protect device, Unknown, Others

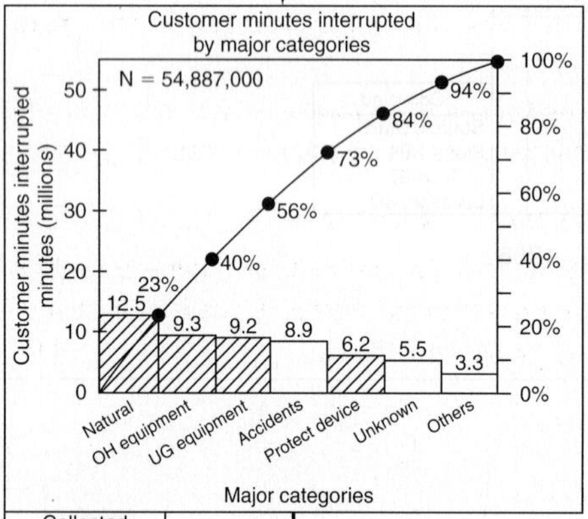

Collected
Source: DMIS
Form: 1/86
To: 12/86
Location: SD

	% reduction in duration	CMI target reduction	Section
Feeder duration	11.4	5,945,000	8.2.1
Other	3.5	1,806,000	-----
	14.9		

Frequency projects assignment matrix

(c)

Major category \ Districts	South Dade (DS)	Hialeah (HL)	Dade North (DS)	Miami (ME)	Miami Beach (MB)	Remarks	% reduction in frequency	CMI target reduction	Section
Natural	4.6	(1.6)	1.6	4.3	0.3	HL already working in this area (major $ investment)	1.4	714,000	8.2.2
Overhead equipment	3.3	2.2	1.4	(2.5)	0.4	Oldest overhead system	1.0	536,000	8.2.3
Underground equipment	(4.6)	2.2	1.4	0.6	0.4	Large underground area in South Dade	1.6	840,000	–
Protective device	1.7	0.9	(1.1)	1.7	0.7		0.7	370,000	8.2.4
						Other	3.1	1,624,000	–
							7.8		

(Header for district table: Customer minutes interrupted (millions))

Legend:

( ) = Responsible District General Manager

- Each District General Manager was made responsible for reducing CMIs (in their assigned major category) throughout the entire Southern Division.

- Members from the Division Engineering Department were assigned to participate in order to provide technical support.

are due to the top three categories: "natural," "overhead equipment," and "underground equipment."

The fourth category, "accidents," refers in part to outages caused by automobile accidents. Because many of the causes for this factor are not within FPL's control this category was skipped in favor of the fifth category, "protective device." Data pertaining to the top three categories and the "protective device" category were stratified by district, as shown in the frequency projects assignment matrix of Figure 18.32c.

The information incorporated into this matrix was used by the QI team to assign responsibility for reducing customer minutes interrupted (CMI) among the five districts within the Southern Division. For example, although the Hialeah district was not a leader in CMIs due to "natural" causes, the district was already working on outages due to "natural" causes and had made a major monetary investment, so they were assigned responsibility to reduce CMI due to "natural" causes. On the other hand, when responsibility was assigned for reductions in CMI due to "underground equipment," the South Dade district's large CMI due to "underground service" made it the obvious choice.

Once assigned responsibility to eliminate a major category of CMI, each district in the Southern Division organized QI teams to improve relevant standardized methods.

Hialeah District Creating a Plan: "Natural" Causes

The biggest cause of CMI was attributable to "natural" causes, as shown in Figure 18.32b. Consequently, the Hialeah district's QI team stratified "natural" causes to gain a better understanding of its root causes, as shown in Figure 18.33a.

FIGURE 18.33   **Hialeah District Creating a Plan**

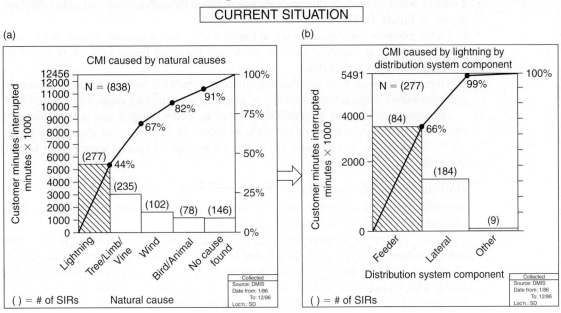

FIGURE 18.34   **Analysis of Feeder Interruptions in the Hialeah District**

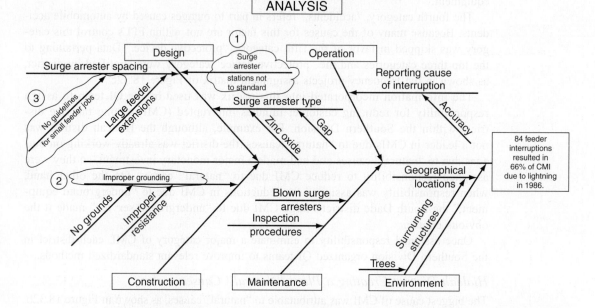

The Hialeah QI team identified lightning as the most significant factor affecting CMI due to "natural" causes. Additional CMI data concerning the effects of lightning strikes on the components of the electrical distribution system, such as feeder and lateral, were gathered and displayed on a Pareto chart, shown in Figure 18.33b. From this, it is clear that lightning damage to feeders accounted for 66 percent of CMI due to "natural" causes. Further analysis of this problem was initiated through a cause-and-effect diagram, shown in Figure 18.34.

Of the possible root causes shown in Figure 18.34, "surge arrester stations not to standard," "improper grounding," and "no guidelines for small feeder jobs" were identified by the team for further analysis.

From this analysis, team members identified a correlation between feeder interruptions and substandard surge arrester stations, as shown in potential root cause 1 in Figure 18.35.

Improper grounding as a contributing factor to feeder outages was not verified as a root cause based on analysis of the data, as shown in potential root cause 2 in Figure 18.35. Nevertheless, the QI team found that 68 percent of feeders were not up to FPL standards.

Hialeah District Deploying the Plan

Immediate action was taken to bring all surge arrester stations not to standard, on feeders with one or more interruptions, up to standard.

Further preventive measures were taken to check small jobs for surge arrester protection because of the correlation between the size of the feeder job and the percentage of jobs not up to standard, as shown in second stage analysis/countermeasure in Figure 18.35. This included using daily management as a vehicle for implementing a revised best-practice method to ensure proper surge protector design for small jobs.

FIGURE 18.35 Analysis and Countermeasures in Hialeah District

Source: Florida Power and Light Company, *Description of Quality Improvement Program,* Southern Division, 1988, p. 53.

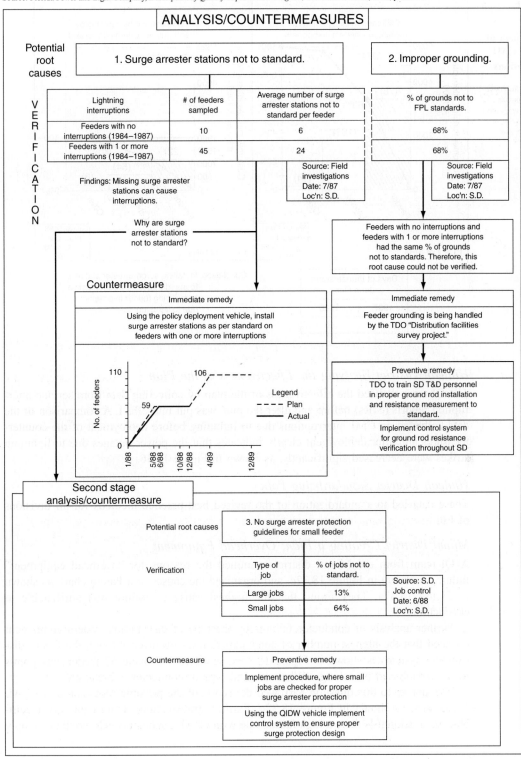

**FIGURE
18.36**

**Comparison of
Data on CMI
Interruptions**

Source: Florida Power
and Light Company,
*Description of Quality
Improvement Program,*
Southern Division,
1988, p. 54.

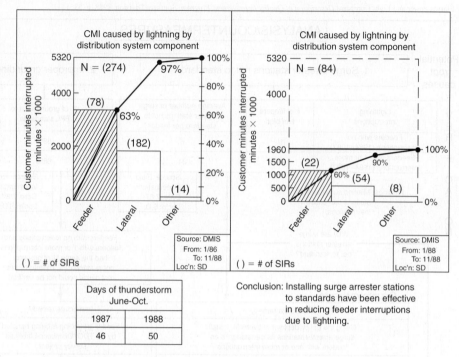

Hialeah District Verifying the Effectiveness of the Plan

The QI team verified the effectiveness of the plan by collecting data from service interruption reports (SIRs) before and after the plan was put into effect. A comparison of the data collected on CMI interruptions due to lightning before deployment of the countermeasures and after deployment clearly indicates that the power outages due to lightning strikes were decreased significantly, as shown in Figure 18.36.

Hialeah District Standardizing Policy

These data led to standardization of the revised best-practice methods for all divisions of FPL.

Miami District Creating a Plan: Overhead Equipment

A QI team from the Miami district examined the reasons for "overhead equipment" failure, as shown in Figure 18.32c, and organized the causes in a Pareto chart, as shown in Figure 18.37a. They found that the highest cause of failure was attributable to conductors.

Further analysis of conductor failures by the type of distribution system component revealed that the highest number of conductor failures occurred through the feeder distribution system, as shown in Figure 18.37b. Stratification of the 62 feeder data points was accomplished by asking: "What size and type of conductor is breaking?"

The answer to this question narrowed the scope of the possible root causes to #2 AL conductors, as shown in Figure 18.37c. Further stratification of the data was accomplished by asking: Is there a high failure rate with #2 AL conductors? Or, are there simply

FIGURE 18.37   Miami District Creating a Plan

Source: Florida Power and Light Company, *Description of Quality Improvement Program,* Southern Division, 1988, p. 55.

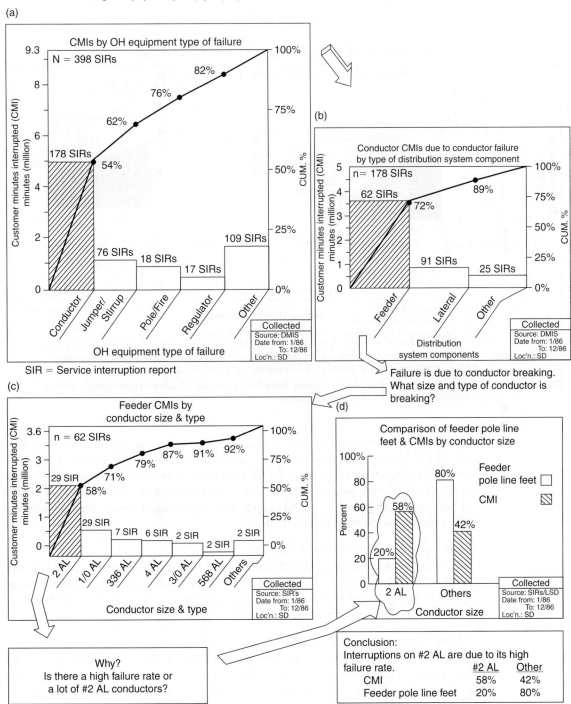

FIGURE 18.38 **Miami District Analyzing the Situation**

Source: Florida Power and Light Company, *Description of Quality Improvement Program,* Southern Division, 1988, p. 58.

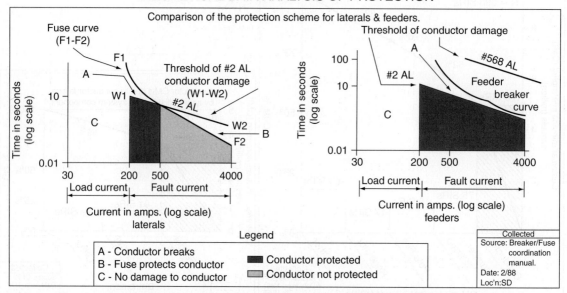

ANALYSIS

THEORETICAL DATA ANALYSIS OF PROTECTION

Comparison of the protection scheme for laterals & feeders.

FINDINGS:
- #2 AL conductors on the feeders are not properly protected by the breaker above 200 amps.
- #2 AL conductors on the laterals are adequately protected for 500 amps or more.

CONCLUSION:
- #2 AL feeder branches are not properly protected by breaker. This theoretical analysis verifies that improper protection is the root cause.

a lot of #2 AL conductors? The answers to these questions are illustrated in Figure 18.37d, clearly showing that #2 AL conductors make up 20 percent of the total number of conductors and account for 58 percent of all conductor failures. An analysis of #2 AL conductors indicated that they were protected against power surges in excess of 500 amperes. However, #2 AL conductors failed when power surges exceeded 200 amperes, as shown in Figure 18.38.

Miami District Deploying the Plan

As a result of their findings, the QI team revised best-practice methods to include the installation of fuse switches on all #2 AL feeder branches to protect them against power surges in excess of 200 amperes. The revised best-practice methods were implemented in June 1988 and were completed by December 1988.

Miami District Verifying the Effectiveness of the Plan

The QI team observed there was an initial drop in CMI due to #2 AL failures by tracking the number of CMIs and their duration after the implementation of the plan. However, as illustrated in Figure 18.39, the number of interruptions continued to increase.

**FIGURE
18.39
Miami District
Verifying the
Effectiveness
of the Plan**

Source: Florida Power
and Light Company,
*Description of Quality
Improvement Program,*
Southern Division,
1988, p. 57.

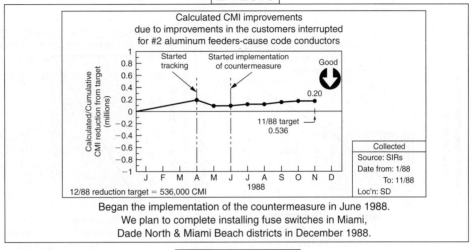

| COUNTERMEASURE |
| INSTALL FUSE SWITCHES ON #2 AL FEEDER BRANCHES |

| EFFECTS |

Calculated CMI improvements
due to improvements in the customers interrupted
for #2 aluminum feeders-cause code conductors

Began the implementation of the countermeasure in June 1988.
We plan to complete installing fuse switches in Miami,
Dade North & Miami Beach districts in December 1988.

| STANDARDIZATION |

• A policy statement was issued to standardize the installation of fuses on feeder branches in Southern Division.

| FUTURE PLANS |

• Install fuse switches on #2 AL feeder branches in Hialeah, and South Dade districts. This will complete the installation of fuse switches.
• Continue to investigate #2 AL conductor failures on feeders and laterals.

Miami District Standardizing the Plan

A policy statement was issued to standardize the installation of fuses on feeder branches in the Southern Division. Further, installation of fuse switches on #2 AL feeders was planned for the Hialeah and South Dade districts. The QI team had uncovered one part of the problem, but as evidenced by the data, the problem of #2 AL failures was not completely resolved. Continued study of the #2 AL conductor failure problem was indicated to assure all possible causes and solutions had been exhausted.

Dade North District Creating the Plan: Protective Devices

A QI team from the Dade North district was established to study the causes of CMI due to "protective devices," as shown in Figure 18.32c. The team members discovered that the predominant cause of CMIs attributable to "protective devices" was the failure of breakers, as shown in Figure 18.40, left panel. Further, of the breakers that failed, the ones that could not be closed, or returned to operative mode, either manually or remotely accounted for the highest CMIs, as shown in Figure 18.40, right panel.

FIGURE 18.40 **Dade North District Creating the Plan**

Source: Florida Power and Light Company, *Description of Quality Improvement Program,* Southern Division, 1988, p. 58.

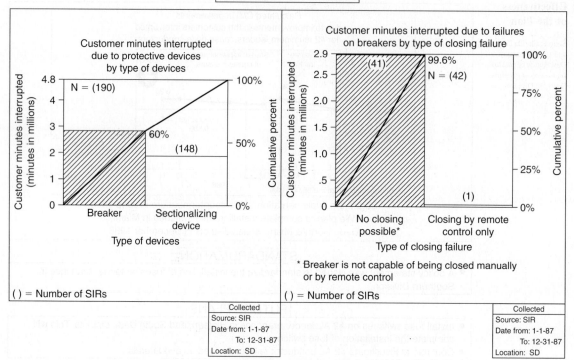

Stratification of the data on breakers that failed and could not be closed (41 cases) indicated that "binding linkage" was the most significant cause of failures (binding linkages accounted for 62.46 percent of CMI), as shown in Figure 18.41. Continued examination of the 22 failures due to binding linkage revealed that ITE-VBK linkages and GE ML-10 linkages were the two linkage types most likely to fail and were the two linkage types with the greatest contribution to CMI, as shown in Figure 18.42, top panel. An examination of the number of ITE-VBK linkages and GE ML-10 linkages in use made it clear that ITE-VBK linkages were a more significant contributor to CMI than GE ML-10 linkages, as shown in Figure 18.42. The QI team found that ITE-VBK linkages were failing at a higher frequency than other linkages because they were not within tolerances, as shown in Figure 18.42, bottom.

The team's proposed revised best-practice methods provided for more specific maintenance procedures for ITE-VBK breakers and additional training with respect to maintenance procedures.

FIGURE 18.41

Analysis of Protective Devices In Dade North District

Source: Florida Power and Light Company, *Description of Quality Improvement Program,* Southern Division, 1988, p. 57.

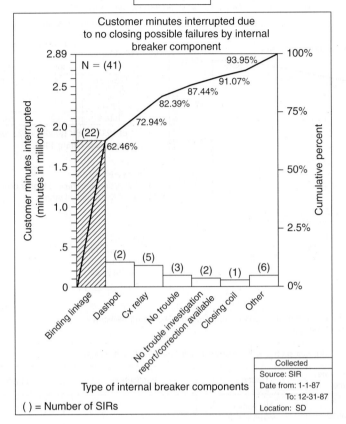

Dade North District Standardizing the Plan

The revised best-practice method was very successful in reducing the ITE-VBK linkage problem, as shown in Figure 18.43 on page 693. As a result, revised best-practice methods were instituted in the Dade North district, along with Industrial and Perrine Service Centers, to standardize the maintenance procedures in place prior to February 1989.

Duration

Duration represents the average number of minutes each customer is without electrical service. It is computed by taking the total number of customer minutes interrupted (CMI) and dividing by the total number of customers interrupted. A QI team in the Southern Division stratified CMI duration data for a six-month period from July to December 1986 by type of distribution system component and determined that feeders were the major cause of CMI due to duration, as shown in Figure 18.44. The duration of actual and predicted service outages due to feeders in the Southern Division was plotted over time to gain a better understanding of how feeder failures affected total CMI, as shown in Figure 18.45 on page 694.

FIGURE 18.42   Examination of Linkages in the Dade North District

Source: Florida Power and Light Company, *Description of Quality Improvement Program,* Southern Division, 1988, p. 59.

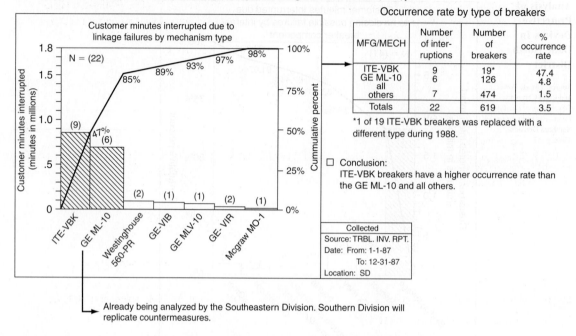

Occurrence rate by type of breakers

MFG/MECH	Number of interruptions	Number of breakers	% occurrence rate
ITE-VBK	9	19*	47.4
GE ML-10	6	126	4.8
all others	7	474	1.5
Totals	22	619	3.5

*1 of 19 ITE-VBK breakers was replaced with a different type during 1988.

☐ Conclusion:
ITE-VBK breakers have a higher occurrence rate than the GE ML-10 and all others.

Collected
Source: TRBL. INV. RPT.
Date: From: 1-1-87
To: 12-31-87
Location: SD

Already being analyzed by the Southeastern Division. Southern Division will replicate countermeasures.

But why such a high occurrence of failures in ITE-VBK breakers?

Symptoms	Occurrence rate	Cause	Verification	Countermeasures
Incorrect latch check switch adjustment	15 of 18	Not within tolerance of .018"-.025"	ITE representative reviewed specifications, inspected breakers and conducted maintenance. Findings: Procedures not sufficiently specific.	1. More specific maintenance procedures required.
Excessive play in the impact trip coil rods	8 of 18	Did not meet clearance requirements of .0625"		
Mechanisms out of adjustment	4 of 18	Out of pre-set factory adjustment as marked on mechanism.		2. Additional maintenance training required.

Examining the Feeder Problem

Next, the QI team compared the Southern Division's CMI due to duration against the records of all other divisions. The finding was that the Southern Division had the worst record and the Western Division laid claim to the best record; the difference was 13.1 minutes, as shown in Figure 18.44. Consequently, the Western Division was used as the benchmark for the development of a "new feeder restoration" best-practice method.

FIGURE 18.43 Standardizing the Plan in the Dade North District

Source: Florida Power and Light Company, *Description of Quality Improvement Program,* Southern Division, 1988, p. 60.

EFFECTS

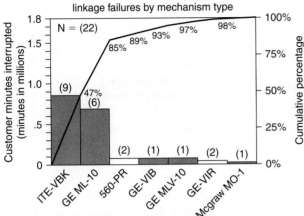

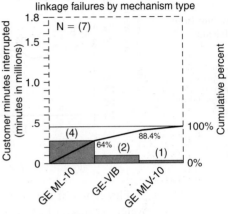

( ) = Number of SIRs

■ = Notes failures 1/1/87 thru 11/31/87

□ = Notes failures 11/1/87 thru 12/31/87

■ = Notes failures 1/1/88 thru 11/30/88

FIGURE 18.44

Causes of CMI Due to Duration in the Southern Division and the Western Division

Source: Florida Power and Light Company, *Description of Quality Improvement Program,* Southern Division, 1988, p. 48.

The team stratified the factor of duration (CMI) by type of distribution system component

$$CMI = Duration \times \sum_{i=1}^{n} C_i$$

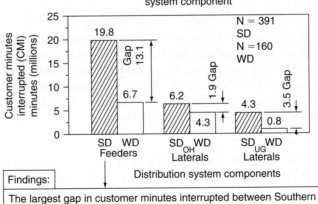

SD vs WD by distribution system component

Findings:

The largest gap in customer minutes interrupted between Southern and Western Division was the feeder distribution component

$$Duration = \frac{CMI}{CI} = \frac{\sum_{i=1}^{D} (restoration\ time)[(number\ of\ customers\ interrupted)]}{\sum number\ of\ customers\ interrupted} = \frac{\sum_{i=1}^{n} L_i C_i}{\sum_{i=1}^{n} C_i}$$

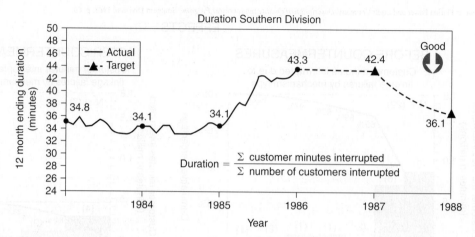

Source: Florida Power
and Light Company,
*Description of Quality
Improvement Program,*
Southern Division,
1988, p. 59.

**FIGURE
18.45**
**Service
Outages Due
to Feeders in
the Southern
Division**

Flowcharts of the feeder restoration process for the Southern and Western Divisions were prepared to further isolate the differences between the two divisions, as shown in Figure 18.46.

The comparisons of the flowcharts revealed two key differences:

1. Sending the troubleman to designated disconnect switches called the pickup point (PUP) (Western Division method), instead of the substation (Southern Division method), when the damaged location is not known, emphasizes restoration of electric service to customers first.

2. Using a binary search procedure to identify downed feeders speeds up the process of isolating the damaged location (Western Division method).

In the Southern Division, when service interruptions were reported, the service dispatcher would guide the troubleman to the area where, based on the incoming calls, the damaged feeder section was most likely to be found. The troubleman would literally follow the line flow from electric pole to electric pole looking for the downed feeder. By contrast, the Western Division had established midpoints between feeders and substations. When a power outage was reported, the troubleman was dispatched to a midpoint. That point would be checked to determine if the problem was in the line feeding that midpoint or exiting that midpoint. Power was then restored to the operational feeder by redirecting the current. The Western Division's method restored power to the greatest number of people in the shortest possible time.

Deploying the Plan

After identifying the major differences in the feeder restoration best-practice methods between the Southern and Western Divisions, the following changes were made to the Southern Division's feeder restoration best-practice method:

1. A feeder restoration process was developed that adopted the philosophy of the Western Division's binary search practice.

2. Predetermined pickup points were designated for all 617 feeders in the Southern Division.

FIGURE 18.46   Flowcharts of the Feeder Restoration Process for the Southern and Western Divisions

Source: Florida Power and Light Company, *Description of Quality Improvement Program,* Southern Division, 1988, p. 49.

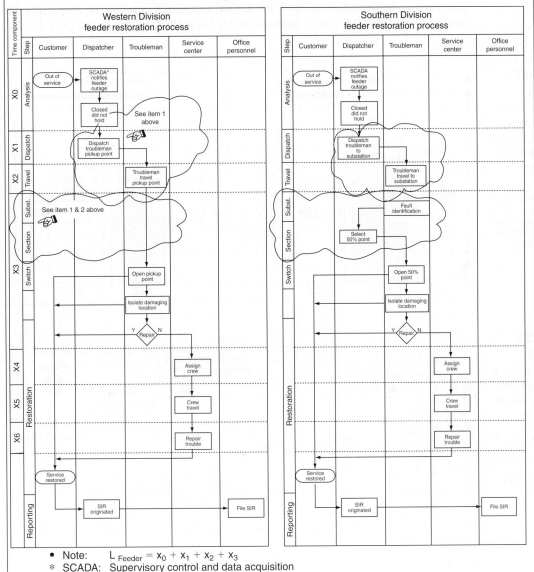

ANALYSIS

The team developed the feeder restoration processes for the Western Division (best division) and Southern Division (worst division) and compared them.

The comparison of processes flows revealed two differences (shown in clouds below).

1. Sending the troubleman to designated disconnect switches called the pickup point (PUP), instead of the substation (SD method), when the damaged location is not known, emphasizes restoration of electric service to customers first.

2. Western Division predetermines all open points for feeders, which eliminates the time required to select 50% point.

- Note: $L_{Feeder} = x_0 + x_1 + x_2 + x_3$
- * SCADA: Supervisory control and data acquisition

These measures isolated the damaged feeder line section quickly and emphasized restoration of service by rerouting power to as many customers as possible. When a service outage report is received, the midpoint between the service outage and the substation is calculated and a troubleman is dispatched. Upon location of the problem area, service is rerouted through other feeders, or through another substation.

Verifying the Effectiveness of the Plan

The effects of the Southern Division's new feeder restoration best-practice method resulted in a $5.7\,(31.7 - 26.0)$ minute decrease in feeder restoration time, as shown in Figure 18.47.

Standardizing Policy

The revised best-practice method for feeder restoration resulted in surpassing the designed goals for CMI due to duration in 1987 and 1988, as shown in Figure 18.48.

FIGURE 18.47
Verifying the Effectiveness of the Plan in the Southern Division

Source: Florida Power and Light Company, *Description of Quality Improvement Program*, Southern Division, 1988, p. 50.

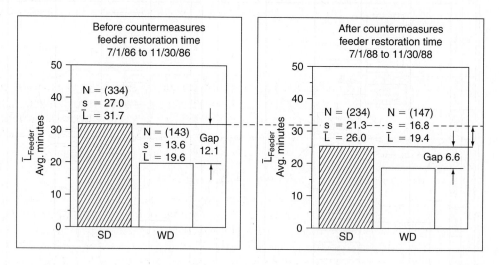

FIGURE 18.48
Standardizing the Policy in the Southern Division

Source: Florida Power and Light Company, *Description of Quality Improvement Program*, Southern Division, 1988, p. 49.

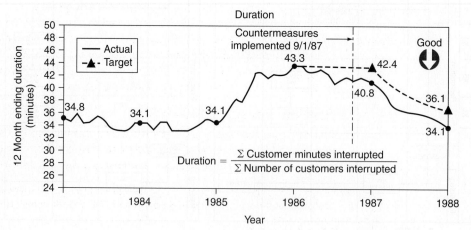

Review of FPL Case Study

FPL's QIP is driven by the voice of the customer. The organization conducts extensive customer surveys to identify the needs of its diverse customer segments, and then prioritizes the needs of its customers through the development and use of the table of tables.

Next, the executive committee develops a strategic plan that reflect the needs of the customers, as well as the realities of FPL's competitive environment.

The voice of the customer, as reflected in the strategic plan, is disseminated throughout the organization by the policy deployment committee. Next, each division submits a business plan to the policy deployment committee. The business plans are approved and funded by the policy deployment committee. FPL's QIP involves everyone in the organization in setting and meeting business plans through daily management. Daily management provides a system for translating corporate policy into daily best-practice methods that can be standardized and improved via the SDSA and PDSA cycles.

Employees of FPL were able to resolve their four crises through their QIP. The accomplishments of FPL employees culminated in 1989 when John J. Hudiburg, then CEO of FPL, accepted the coveted Deming Prize from the Japanese Union of Scientists and Engineers.

The Evolution of Quality at Florida Power and Light[2]

The quality process at Florida Power and Light Company has evolved and matured through multiple phases, including those leading up to the Deming Prize in 1989 and, equally important, those that evolved or advanced the process to respond to market changes. The four phases defining the evolution of quality are the preliminary phase, intensification phase, mature phase, and high-performance phase.

Preliminary Phase (1981–1985)

The first formal quality efforts began in 1981 with the introduction of quality improvement teams. Top management was encouraged to learn more about the TQM process as a means to address current challenges of the company. Operating costs were rising higher than inflation and customer dissatisfaction was increasing. Despite FPL's being a natural monopoly, management believed there was a better way to run the business. After reviewing several models, FPL selected the Japanese model and engaged the services of the Union of Japanese Scientists and Engineers (JUSE) and established a relationship with the Kansai Electric Power Company in Osaka, a 1984 Deming Prize winner. With the assistance of its Japanese friends and counselors, the quality improvement program (QIP) was developed and implemented company-wide in 1985. The employees during this phase were introduced to the seven basic quality improvement (QI) tools and team management techniques.

Intensification Phase (1986–1989)

The initial phase was succeeded by the intensification phase that brought a stronger alignment to company performance and further developed the capabilities of FPL's employees. To inculcate the skills into the culture, employees were required to use a rigorous

---

[2] This section was prepared by J. Michael Adams, Director of Quality, FPL Company/FPL Group, Inc., May 2000. The authors thank J. Michael Adams and FPL for their generous support in the preparation of this case study.

seven-step problem-solving process, called the "QI Story," when attempting to solve problems. Employees were reviewed for their abilities in demonstrating their use of seven basic QI tools. In this phase, two new elements were added to evolve into a TQM system: policy deployment and quality in daily work. Policy deployment enabled employees to focus on a few company-wide high-priority issues rather than dilute their impact by working on local matters of lesser impact. Quality in daily work provided the beginning of statistical process control and strengthened the understanding and relationship of internal customers to external customers. Two percent of the employees were trained as "application experts" (AEs) in more sophisticated tools and techniques. They learned and applied tools and techniques such as Weibull analysis, failure modes and effects analysis, regression analysis, design of experiments, and general reliability tools and techniques.

The three elements of teams, policy deployment, and quality in daily work constituted a TQM quality system supported with an employee education and development foundation. Two structures were launched to reinforce the new culture: application of tools and techniques; and sharing solutions. The EXPO structure was a convention-like atmosphere with booths, exhibits or storyboards displaying various improvements. In 1987, the President's Cup Team Competition began as a mechanism to judge the "quality of quality" throughout the organization and role-model various tools and techniques reflective of the development strategy.

Around the same time, hundreds of visitors to FPL were gaining further insight into the quality movement. Although FPL had adopted the Japanese quality approach, it played a leadership role in the founding of the Malcolm Baldrige National Quality Award, testifying to the U.S. Congress as to its benefits for the American economy, crafting the criteria, and assisting with endowing the award.

In the summer of 1988, a decision was reached that FPL would challenge for the Deming Prize. The challenge that lasted for almost an entire year required employees to accelerate the pace of improvements and to put in many extra hours for further development or preparation for the exam itself. Commensurate with this effort, building TQM capabilities also provided operational benefits including substantial reduction in unplanned power plant outages and dramatic reductions in customer complaints, service reliability, and personnel injuries. In November 1989, after an intensive two-week on-site examination, FPL became the first non-Japanese company to win the Deming Prize.

After the Deming Prize (the 1990s)

The Deming Prize is presented to an organization that demonstrates the potential to systematically improve its performance. A quality system therefore must endure and accommodate change to be successful in its performance objectives.

The early 1990s posed a series of changes internally and externally to FPL, including a new CEO, a changing marketplace, and the catastrophic Hurricane Andrew in 1992, all of which had impact on the approach, deployment, and reinforcement of the tenets of quality.

Mature Phase (1990–1997)

The new CEO, James L. Broadhead, recognized the changing marketplace as well as the potential of the organization. He altered the course of FPL to compete in a deregulated marketplace. A key success factor in a competitive marketplace is to be a low-cost provider. In 1989, however, FPL was the highest-cost major electric utility in its region.

While winning the Deming Prize was an honor of which all employees were proud, there was a widespread feeling among employees that FPL's quality program had become very mechanical and inflexible. The paper-oriented bureaucracy that served the organization in its development was actually now creating barriers to continuous improvement. At this point in the quality journey, the employees were a well-developed, homogenous group with thorough process and tools knowledge. At the same time, the rate of change toward deregulation was underestimated and the transition from monopoly to competition would be realized sooner, thus requiring a more flexible and faster organization. The mature phase is one that fully integrates the TQM components into the general business structure.

An employee team was assembled to review and provide recommendations to advance the quality program. Some of the recommendations included easing up on the mandatory structures that prohibited the benefits of the workforce's knowledge from being applied toward performance rather than process. Some primary changes to the system included no longer requiring the seven-step QI story for all problem solving, ultimately dispersing the rather large quality staff to positions within the operating organization, and maintaining a small corporate quality office as part of a company-wide reorganization. This office would interface with contemporary marketplace practices like **benchmarking** and **reengineering** to keep the organization current. Quality was positioned as part of the way FPL does business. Quality plans and business plans were no longer separate and management would take on the role of facilitator and coach to improvement as a part of their job.

The reorganization was the outcome of eight employee teams researching various disciplines including human resources, the marketplace, regulatory issues, and technological advancements. With it came a new vision: "to be the preferred provider of safe, reliable, cost-effective electricity-related products and services for all customer segments."

Supporting the vision included four areas of focus: strong customer orientation, commitment to quality, cost-effective operations, and speed and flexibility. These were maintained throughout the 1990s, with safety added in 1999. The division and district geographic areas and layers of management were eliminated, reducing the layers from twelve to five. In light of the changing marketplace, and the new vision and areas of focus, the performance measures were also changed, commensurate with a competitive market. With the new direction, the capabilities could be exercised to perform with alignment and contribution to the areas of focus.

In 1994, FPL underwent a post–Deming Prize review at the request of the chairman. Overseas winners of the Deming Prize can volunteer for the review, while in Japan it is mandatory. It is usually conducted three years after the award. FPL's original request was deferred, however, to allow for the restoration and recovery from Hurricane Andrew in August 1992. Dr. Kume and Dr. Akao conducted the review. Both were Deming Prize examiners in 1989 and requested to review those sites they had previously visited and knew thoroughly.

They reviewed power plants and a customer care center and conducted sessions with most operating and staff groups, concluding with the executive team. They appraised the organization's realization of its potential for business performance citing best practices in benchmarking, empowerment, creative use of technology, and quality promotion. As with any review, they also provided guidance to further improve the system. Jim Broadhead was asked to present FPL's evolution and results of the review at the International Conference on Quality in Yokohama in 1996.

High-Performance Phase (1997–Present)

In 1997, the quality system evolved to further advance the organization commensurate with the competitive marketplace, while assessing the new fledgling business initiatives at FPL and the skills of a growing, new workforce. Using a customized version of the Baldrige criteria, a team of internal experienced assessors regularly performs assessments on business units and gauges the organization relative to the four phases. Sample characteristics describing a high-performance organization include work systems for enterprise profitability, leveraged use of technology, backward and forward integration, customization, upper decile performance, and leveraged learning. In 1999, following nine business unit assessments, a core team of examiners analyzed its findings and drafted recommendations for organizational continuous improvement to the senior executives.

FPL concluded the decade and millennium with high levels of performance as well as continued contribution and leadership to the quality movement. The EXPO continues as a sharing opportunity for all employees of FPL Group, Inc., while the President's Cup Team Competition enters its fourteenth year. The 1990s proved successful with dramatic improvements. Decade-end performance was at all-time highs with segmented customer satisfaction levels at targeted levels, and fossil plant availability reached 93 percent (up from 77 percent in 1990), while nuclear availability reached 94 percent (up from 77 percent in 1990). The power plants performed at upper decile performance levels and have provided that capability to FPL Energy, a new power generation subsidiary of FPL Group, Inc. Other performance achievements include operation and maintenance (O&M) cost reduction of 36 percent since 1990 at residential electricity prices 16 percent below those of 1985 (8.34 cents/kWh compared to 6.97 cents/kWh). Considering inflation, that equates to over a 60 percent difference. Service reliability had some variation in the early decade, but since 1997 alone there has been a 45 percent improvement in reliability at levels significantly better than the national average. Improvement occurred in reducing the average length of interruption as well as the frequency.

Jim Broadhead was 1999–2000 president of the Foundation for the Malcolm Baldrige National Quality Award, while other employees serve as judges and examiners for various quality awards in the nation.

The quality system continues to evolve, driven by market conditions and practices and certainly with lessons learned throughout.

Summary

Chapter 18 discussed policy management, Prong 3 of the quality management model presented in this book. Policy management is performed by using the PDSA cycle to improve and innovate the methods responsible for the difference between corporate results and corporate targets, or to change the direction of an organization. Policy management includes setting policy, deploying policy, studying policy, providing feedback to employees on policy, and conducting presidential reviews of policy. Policy management is accomplished through the workings of an interlocking system of committees, including the executive committee (EC), the policy deployment committee (PDC), local steering teams (LSTs), and project teams.

The president conducts an initial presidential review to determine the state of the organization and to develop a plan of action for the promotion of corporate policy. This promotes a dialogue between the president and midlevel management and brings out information about problems. After a few rounds of presidential reviews, the president will have a good understanding of the major problems facing the organization and their possible causes.

The executive committee (EC) is responsible for setting the strategic plan for the entire organization, which includes establishing values and beliefs, developing statements of vision and mission, and preparing a draft set of strategic objectives. Techniques such as an affinity diagram, SWOT analysis, and the table of tables are used to gather information and develop strategic objectives.

Members of the policy deployment committee (PDC) develop a set of integrated improvement plans to promote the strategic objectives. The members of the PDC use tools such as gap analysis, Pareto diagrams, and cause-and-effect diagrams to develop the departmental and corporate improvement plans needed to promote departmental and corporate strategic objectives. The members of the local steering teams (LSTs) are responsible for coordinating and carrying out the projects set up in the corporate and departmental improvement plans.

Strategic objectives and improvement plans are deployed by the PDC through assignment of responsibility for action to people or groups of people in departments. Techniques used in policy deployment include catchball and flag diagrams.

Policy is implemented when teams work on projects to improve and/or innovate processes. It is also implemented when departments use the revised processes and measure their results with respect to improvement plans and strategic objectives.

Periodic management reviews are conducted at two levels. First, the members of the EC review progress toward each strategic objective and its improvement plans monthly. Second, the members of the PDC and appropriate LSTs review progress for each project. The purpose of these reviews is to provide feedback to project team members that promotes process improvement efforts.

Applications of policy management to a person's life and to the Florida Power and Light Company were presented in this chapter. These examples demonstrate the steps of policy management and how they are implemented.

Key Terms

action item, *632*

additive flag diagram, *649*

affinity diagram, *635*

attribute indicators, *647*

benchmarking, *699*

best practice, *652*

binary indicators, *648*

brainstorming, *635*

business objectives, *646*

catchball, *642*

cause-and-effect diagram, *639*

classification data, *647*

control point, *642*

corporate improvement plan, *639*

correlation, *651*

count data, *647*

crises, *635*

cross-functional management, *657*

customer satisfaction key objectives, *647*

daily management, *633*

dashboard, *643*

decrease project, *650*

decrease task, *650*
Deming Prize, *673*
departmental improvement plan, *640*
employee growth and development key objectives, *647*
executive committee, *633*
executive summary, *630*
extrinsic motivation, *635*
feedback and review, *654*
financial key objectives, *647*
flag diagram, *648*
force field analysis, *633*
Gantt chart indicators, *648*
gap analysis, *639*
increase project, *650*
increase task, *650*
integrated flowchart, *655*
integrated improvement plan, *639*
interrelationship diagraph, *667*

intrinsic motivation, *635*
key indicators, *645*
key objectives, *645*
key process, *636*
linear flag diagram, *649*
list indicators, *648*
local steering team, *642*
management by objectives, *673*
management review, *653*
measurement indicators, *648*
mini-sitcon, *652*
mission statement, *634*
multiple regression analysis, *651*
nonadditive flag diagram, *649*
Pareto diagram, *639*
PDSA cycle, *654*
policy deployment committee, *639*
policy management, *629*
presidential review, *629*

process improvement and innovation key objectives, *647*
project, *650*
project team, *652*
Prong 3, *629*
quality improvement story, *655*
reengineering, *699*
SDSA cycle, *654*
Six Sigma, *647*
SWOT analysis, *635*
strategic objectives, *633, 646*
strategic plan, *633*
table of tables, *636*
tactic, *639*
target, *639*
task, *650*
values and beliefs, *634*
vision statement, *634*
voice of the business, *636*
voice of the customer, *635*
zero project, *650*
zero task, *650*

Exercises

18.1. Prepare a personal mission statement.

18.2. List your values and beliefs. Do they form an entire system of behavior?

18.3. List your strengths, weaknesses, opportunities, and threats. Develop a list of your strengths and opportunities that bypass your weaknesses and threats.

18.5. List the technological issues relevant to your life.

18.6. Construct a table of tables for your life using all of your relevant stakeholders, for example, spouse or significant other, parents, friends, colleagues, etc. What are the critical processes in your life?

18.7. Develop a list of key objectives for your life.

18.8. Develop a list of key indicators for each of your key objectives.

18.9. Construct a dashboard for your life.

18.10. Identify your high-priority projects or tasks.

18.11. Conduct an SDSA/PDSA cycle on one of your high-priority projects.

References

1. Leo Aldecocea (May 4, 1990), *A Flag System Application for Monitoring Timeliness of Installation for a Daily Process* (Coral Gables, FL: University of Miami).

2. Wayne Brunetti (1993), *Achieving Total Quality: Integrating Business Strategy and Customer Needs* (White Plains, NY: Quality Resources).

3. *FPL's Total Quality Management—Participant Handbook,* 1st ed., copyright 1990 by the University of Miami Institute for the Study of Quality in Manufacturing and Service and QUALTEC, Inc. (an FPL subsidiary).

4. Florida Power and Light Company, Research, Economics, and Forecasting Department, *Supplement to the Customer Needs Table of Tables,* Version 5, 1990.

5. H. Gitlow and E. Loredo, "Total Quality Management at Florida Power & Light Company: A Case Study," *Quality Engineering,* 5, No. 1, 1992–1993, pp. 123–158.

6. H. Gitlow and PMI (1990), *Planning for Quality, Productivity and Competitive Position* (Homewood, IL: Dow Jones–Irwin).

7. Kaoru Ishikawa (1985), *What is Total Quality Control? The Japanese Way* (Englewood Cliffs, NJ: Prentice Hall), pp. 59–71.

8. Noriaki Kano (October 1, 1986), *Second Report on TQC at Florida Power & Light Company* (Miami, FL).

9. N. Kano, M. Yamaura, M. Toyoshima, and K. Nishinomiya, "Study on the Methods for Solving Increase, Reduction, and Zero Problems Encountered in the Promotion of TQC: Parts I and II," unpublished paper.

10. Bob King (1989), *Hoshin Planning: The Developmental Approach* (Metheun, MA: GOAL/QPC).

11. Robin Lawton, "Balance Your Balanced Scorecard," *Quality Engineering,* March 2002, p. 69.

12. Shigeru Mizuno (1988), *Management for Quality Improvement: The 7 New QC Tools* (Cambridge, MA: Productivity Press).

Appendix **A18.1**

The Voice of the Customer

The term "customer" includes both external customers and indirect customers [see Reference 3, Unit 12, p. 4]. External customers are the organizations or individuals who buy or use an organization's goods or services. Indirect customers are organizations that guard the welfare of external customers, such as regulatory commissions and governmental agencies. The term "indirect customer" was introduced by Florida Power and Light Company.

The voice of the customer [see Reference 3, Unit 12, p. 4 and pp. 10–22] is a tool used to: (1) define the ever-changing market segments for customers, (2) determine and prioritize the customer requirements of each market segment, (3) identify the processes or methods used to respond to the customer requirements of each market segment, (4) construct a matrix that explains the relationships between "the customer requirements of each market segment" and "the processes or methods used to respond to the customer requirements," and (5) prioritize the processes or methods used to respond to customer requirements. Data collected from a voice of the customer analysis is used to formulate the strategic objectives of an organization. The steps for conducting a voice of the customer study are shown below.

1. *Define the ever-changing market segments for customers.* The term "market segment" explains the dynamic and changing homogeneous groupings of customers with respect to the demographic, psychographic, and purchasing behavior variables that affect their decision to purchase and/or use a good or service. Focus groups and surveys, as well

as other tools, are used to identify customer requirements for each market segment. Special care is taken to identify and define the customer requirements of noncustomers and future market segments.

2. *Determine and prioritize the customer requirements of each market segment.* Management collects and analyzes observational, survey, and experimental data to understand the voice of the customer by market segment. The question asked of a sample of customers from each market segment is "From your perspective, what requirements must the organization surpass to pursue the mission statement?"

   For example, Figure A18.1 shows a prioritized list of customer requirements that were collected by randomly sampling Florida Power and Light residential customers. For each market segment, each customer requirement is scored on three scales: first, an "importance to the customer" scale; second, a "current level of performance in the eyes of the customer" scale; and third, a "desired level of performance by management to optimize the interdependent system of stakeholders" scale. The "total weight" is computed for each customer requirement in each market segment. Total weight is a measure of the need to take action on a customer requirement, a prioritization procedure adapted from the quality function deployment methods of Akao, as shown on the right side of Figure A18.1.

   The "importance to the customer" scale quantifies the importance of customer requirements for each market segment; it does not quantify how well the organization is currently handling customer requirements or how much improvement is required with respect to customer requirements. The scale is a 1 to 5 scale, where 1 = very unimportant and 5 = very important. "Importance to the customer" scores are obtained by computing the average ratings for each customer requirement for each market segment from survey and/or focus group data.

**FIGURE
A18.1
Prioritized List
of Customer
Requirements**

Source: *FPL's Total
Quality Manage-
ment—Participant
Handbook,* 1st ed.,
copyright 1990 by the
University of Miami
Institute for the Study
of Quality in Manu-
facturing and Service
and QUALTEC, Inc.
(an FPL subsidiary),
Unit 12, p. 13.

Direct Quality Requirements
(what customers want)

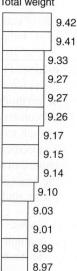

Direct Quality Requirements (what customers want)	Total weight
1. Quality repair work	9.42
2. Accurate electric bills	9.41
3. Honest trustworthy management	9.33
4. Safely maintained company equipment	9.27
5. Fair treatment of all customers	9.27
6. Friendly and courteous employees	9.26
7. No damage to customers' or public property	9.17
8. Accurate answers to questions	9.15
9. Quickly restored power	9.14
10. Safe nuclear plants	9.10
11. Low environmental pollution	9.03
12. Electricity—good value for the money	9.01
13. Timely actions on customers' complaints	8.99
14. Concern for customers' problems	8.97

The "current level of performance" scale quantifies the gap between customer requirements and organizational performance. This scale is a 1 to 5 scale, where 1 = very large gap and 5 = very small gap. The measure of current performance scale is obtained by computing the average ratings from survey or focus group data for each customer requirement for each market segment from the following question: "How is the organization doing with respect to exceeding customer requirement x?"

Customer requirements that show a significant gap are targeted for further study via gap analysis. For each customer requirement and market segment, gap analysis requires a measure of customer requirements, given by the "importance to the customer" scale, and a measure of current organizational performance, given by the "current level of importance" scale, to highlight the customer requirements that should be studied further with gap analysis.

Gap analysis is a procedure for studying the root cause(s) of the difference between customer requirements and organizational performance. It is based on the analysis of relevant data. Many different tools are helpful in gap analysis, such as flowcharting, the seven basic QC tools, and benchmarking. For example, the members of the EC might assign a group of staff personnel to study the root causes of the gap for a particular market segment. The group might study the gap over time and determine that it is stable and contains only common variation. Next, they could construct a Pareto diagram of the common causes of the gap, isolate the most significant common cause, and develop a cause-and-effect diagram. Next, the staff personnel would study the correlation between the suspected root cause and the most significant cause of the gap. If the staff personnel found the correlation to be significant, they would recommend to the members of the EC a plan of action for improving the current level of performance for that customer requirement.

The "desired level of performance" scale quantifies the desired level of performance for each customer requirement, for each market segment. The scale is a 1 to 5 scale, where 1 = small improvement in the organization's ability to exceed a customer requirement, and 5 = large improvement in the organization's ability to exceed a customer requirement. "Desired level of performance" scores are developed by staff personnel assigned by the EC. They conduct analyses of the levels of performance required for each customer requirement, for each market segment, to stay ahead of other organizations in the industry (using benchmarking) and future customer requirements.

The "total weight" score is a measure of the importance of the gap for each customer requirement, in each market segment. Total weight scores are computed as follows:

$$\text{Total weight} = (I \times D)/C$$

where:

I = importance to the customer

D = desired level of performance

C = current level of performance

3. *Identify the processes (methods) used to respond to the needs and wants of each market segment and indirect customer.* It is critical that the needs and wants of each appropriate market segment or indirect customer be serviced by identifiable methods.

FIGURE A18.2

Translating Customer Requirements into Methods

Translating Customers' Requirements into Methods

Customer Requirements
(what customers need and want)

Methods
(how organization responds)

Translating customer requirements into methods

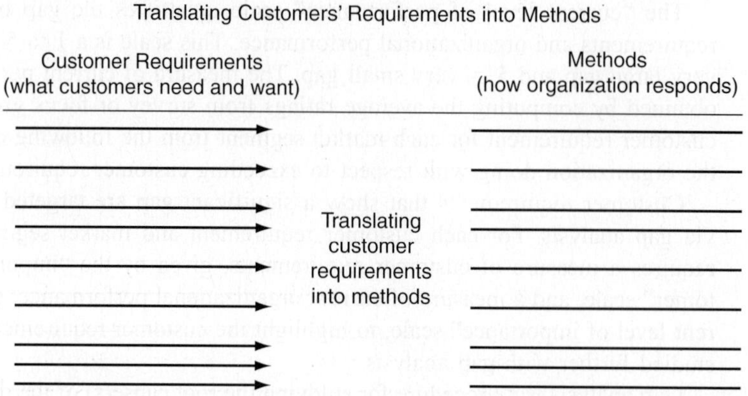

Source: *FPL's Total Quality Management— Participant Handbook,* 1st ed., copyright 1990 by the University of Miami Institute for the Study of Quality in Manufacturing and Service and QUAL-TEC, Inc. (an FPL subsidiary), Unit 12, p. 15.

Customer needs and wants are translated into improved and innovated methods by asking what methods are necessary to respond to each customer need or want. Figure A18.2 may be helpful.

4. *Construct a matrix that explains the relationships (cells of the matrix) between "customer requirements" (rows) and "the processes (methods) used to respond to customer requirements" (columns), for each market segment and each indirect customer.* The matrices for all market segments should have the same columns, or given market segment.

The relationships shown in the cells of each matrix are determined by a group of staff personnel assigned this responsibility by the EC. The staff uses its knowledge of the organization and customers, along with that of other knowledgeable people, to determine the relationships. The staff members assigned to determine the relationships between the rows and columns keep a record of their logic for each symbol placed in the matrix, so they will not be second-guessed at a later date. Relationships are measured on the following scale, where 3 = strong relationship, 2 = moderate relationship, 1 = weak relationship, and blank = no relationship. Sometimes, a doughnut symbol is used for a 3, a circle symbol is used for a 2, and a triangle symbol is used for a 1. These numbers or symbols are used whether the relationships are positive or negative. A matrix showing the needs and wants of a particular market segment and the methods needed to respond to the needs and wants of the customers in the market segment can be seen in Figure A18.3.

Every customer requirement must be adequately serviced by one or more methods. If a customer requirement is not being serviced by any method (or not adequately serviced), one or more methods are developed to service the customer requirement. If a method is not servicing (directly or indirectly) at least one customer requirement, the method is dropped or receives decreased attention by stakeholders.

5. *Prioritize the processes (methods) used to respond to customer requirements for attention in the strategic objectives of the organization.*

a. Compute the unnormalized weights, as shown in Figure A18.4, for each process, for a given market segment or indirect customer. For a given process, or column in Figure A18.3, multiply the "total weight" score for each customer requirement

FIGURE A18.3 Voice of the Customer Matrix for Residential Customers of Florida Power and Light Company

Source: Florida Power and Light Company, *Customer Needs Table of Tables*, Research, Economics and Forecasting Department, 1990.

Voice of the Customer Matrix
Residential Customers of Florida Power & Light Company

Processes which satisfy customer requirements

Relationship
⊙ Strong = 3
○ Moderate = 2
△ Weak = 1

Total weight

Processes (column headers):
Reporting and fitting requirements
Project natural environment
Concern for community
Protect customers'/public property
Prevent pollution/protect public health
Price management
Employee safety
Public safety
Visual appeal of facilities
Characteristics of electric power
Continuity of electric power
Understandable rates/bills
Customer programs and services
Considerate customer service
Accurate bills
Timely actions
Accurate answers

Customer requirements:

#	Customer requirements	Total weight
1.	Quality repair work	9.42
2.	Accurate electric bills	9.41
3.	Honest trustworthy management	9.33
4.	Safely maintained company equipment	9.27
5.	Fair treatment of all customers	9.27
6.	Friendly and courteous employees	9.26
7.	No damage to customers' or public property	9.17
8.	Accurate answers to questions	9.15
9.	Quickly restored power	9.14
10.	Safe nuclear plants	9.10
11.	Low environmental pollution	9.03
12.	Electricity–good value for the money	9.01
13.	Timely actions on customers' complaints/concerns/requests	8.99
14.	Concern for customers' problems	8.97
15.	Easy-to-read bills	8.94
16.	Keep rates down	8.86
17.	Minimize the number of power outages	8.79
18.	Minimize power fluctuations & surges	8.59
19.	Put equipments where it is not unsightly	8.45
20.	Programs to manage electric usage	8.21
21.	Flexible billing & payment arrangements	8.15
22.	Information about FPL services	8.14
23.	Outdoor lighting around home	7.82
24.	Involved in community activities	7.52
25.	Attracting new industry	7.14

FIGURE A18.4 Computation of Unnormalized and Normalized Weights

Source: Modified from Florida Power and Light Company, *Customer Needs Table of Tables*, Research, Economics and Forecasting Department, 1990.

Processes which satisfy customer requirements

Relationship
⊙ Strong = 3
○ Moderate = 2
△ Weak = 1

Customer requirements (with Total weight):

#	Customer requirements	Total weight
1.	Quality repair work	9.42
2.	Accurate electric bills	9.41
3.	Honest trustworthy management	9.33
4.	Safely maintained company equipment	9.27
5.	Fair treatment of all customers	9.27
6.	Friendly and courteous employees	9.26
7.	No damage to customers' or public property	9.17
8.	Accurate answers to questions	9.15
9.	Quickly restored power	9.14
10.	Safe nuclear plants	9.10
11.	Low environmental pollution	9.03
12.	Electricity—good value for the money	9.01
13.	Timely actions on customers' complaints/concerns/requests	8.99
14.	Concern for customers' problems	8.97
15.	Easy-to-read bills	8.94
16.	Keep rates down	8.86
17.	Minimize the number of power outages	8.79
18.	Minimize power fluctuations & surges	8.59
19.	Put equipment where it is not unsightly	8.45
20.	Programs to manage electric usage	8.21
21.	Flexible billing & payment arrangements	8.15
22.	Information about FPL services	8.14
23.	Outdoor lighting around home	7.82
24.	Involved in community activities	7.52
25.	Attracting new industry	7.14

Processes with Unnormalized weights ($\Sigma = 832.72$) and Normalized weights:

Process	Unnormalized weight	Normalized weight
Reporting and fitting requirements	0	.000
Project natural environment	36.42	.044
Concern for community	63.13	.076
Protect customers'/public property	36.84	.044
Prevent pollution/protect public health	36.42	.044
Price management	113.30	.136
Employee safety	0	.000
Public safety	36.62	.044
Visual appeal of facilities	25.35	.030
Characteristics of electric power	34.56	.042
Continuity of electric power	58.26	.070
Understandable rates/bills	45.24	.054
Customer programs and services	154.12	.185
Considerate customer service	74.25	.069
Accurate bills	28.23	.034
Timely actions	54.39	.065
Accurate answers	35.59	.043

by the relationship score between that process and each customer requirement, and add all products in a column. For example, the unnormalized weights for the process's "accurate answers" and "timely actions" are computed as follows, as shown in Figure A18.4:

Accurate answers:

$$35.59 = \left[9.15(3) + 8.14\,(1)\right]$$

where

9.15 = the total weight for "accurate answers to questions"

8.14 = the total weight for "information about FPL services"

    3 = the relationship between "accurate answers" and "accurate answers to question"

    1 = the relationship between "accurate answers" and "information about FPL services"

Timely actions:

$$54.39 = \left[9.14(3) + 8.99\,(3)\right]$$

as shown in Figure A18.4.

  b. Normalize the weighted values by dividing the individual weighted values by the sum of all weighted values, as shown in Figure A18.4.

  c. Prioritize the normalized weighted values over all methods to provide input into the selection of strategic objectives for the organization. For example, the above analysis indicates that "timely actions" would receive a higher priority for attention than "accurate answers."

Appendix **A18.2**

The Voice of the Business

The voice of the business is a tool for collecting and analyzing data about employee requirements, such as concerns and fears, with respect to the mission of an organization. Voice of the business studies require that all groups of employees answer the following question: "What requirements (e.g., concerns and fears) do you have with respect to the organization pursuing its mission?" Data from the answer to this question help to formulate the strategic objectives of an organization. The procedure for conducting a voice of the business study is described below.

1. *Collect and analyze the answers to the question posed above for each employee group, for example, top management, middle management, first-line supervisors, and hourly employees.* Brainstorming sessions, focus groups, surveys, and management reviews are examples of tools that are useful in collecting information about the above question. Affinity diagrams, interrelationship diagraphs, and cause-and-effect diagrams are

examples of tools that can be used to analyze the answers to the above question. These tools are discussed in Chapter 10 and in Reference 4.

2. *See step 2 in Voice of the Customer.* Determine and prioritize the employee requirements of each employee segment. Employee requirements are determined for each employee group, just as customer requirements are determined for each market segment and indirect customer.

3. *Identify the processes (methods) used to surpass the employee requirements for each employee group.* These processes are the same as or additions to the processes used to address the customer requirements in a voice of the customer study, as discussed in Appendix A18.1. Employee requirements are used in developing strategic objectives for the organization.

4. *Construct a matrix that explains the relationships (cells of the matrix) between "employee requirements" (rows) and "the processes (methods) used to respond to employee requirements" (columns), for each employee segment.* All voice of the customer and voice of the business matrices should have the same columns; see step 4 in Appendix A18.1.

5. *Prioritize the processes (methods) used to respond to employee requirements for attention in the strategic objectives of the organization.* See step 5 in Appendix A18.1.

Appendix **A18.3**

Table of Tables

The original concept of the table of tables was developed by the members of the Research, Economics, and Forecasting department of Florida Power and Light Company. The table of tables presented here is a variant of that. It considers customer requirements and employee requirements, and creates one prioritized list of processes (methods) to be highlighted for attention in the strategic objectives of the organization. [See Reference 4, p. 3.]

Building a Table of Tables

A graphic mock-up of a table of tables can be seen in Figure A18.5. [See Reference 4, p. 3.]

Note that the three voice of the customer subtables shown on the left side of the table of tables and the five voice of the business subtables shown on the right side of the table of tables share a common set of processes (methods) in their columns. The voice of the customer and voice of the business studies all result in prioritized lists of the common set of processes. The table of tables globally prioritizes the common processes from each subtable.

The group of staff employees selected by the EC establishes a weight for the process priorities from each direct and indirect customer group, or subtable, in the voice of the customer analysis and a similar weight for each employee group in the voice of the business analysis. As an illustration, each of the three customer groups on the left side of Figure A18.5 could receive equal weights of 0.333, 0.333, and 0.333, while the five

**FIGURE
A18.5
Generic Table
of Tables**

Source: Florida Power
and Light Company,
*Customer Needs Table
of Tables,* Research,
Economics and Fore-
casting Department,
1990.

Generic Table of Tables

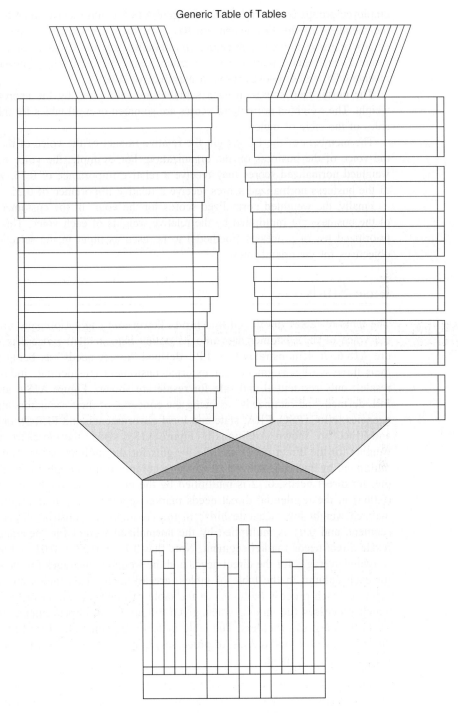

employee groups on the right side of Figure A18.5 could receive weights determined by the members of the EC, which are based on their assessment of the impact of each employee group on the organization. Thus, employee group 1 may receive 0.10, employee group 2 may receive 0.50, employee group 3 may receive 0.05, employee group 4 may receive 0.05, and employee group 5 may receive 0.30.

The normalized scores in each subtable are multiplied by the appropriate subtable weight. The weighted normalized scores are summed over all tables for the left and right sides of the table of tables.

The members of the EC weight the relative impact of the voice of the customer and the voice of the business on the organization. For example, the voice of the customer weighted normalized scores may receive a relative importance of 0.75, while the voice of the business normalized scores receive a relative importance of 0.25.

Finally, the weighted normalized scores for the voice of the customer and the voice of the business are multiplied by the relative weights of each voice. This results in one prioritized list of processes (methods) to be used as input in the selection of strategic objectives for the organization.

Case Study

The table of tables developed by Florida Power and Light Company in 1988 to input the voice of the customer data into its policy management process is shown in Figure A18.6. It demonstrates how FPL defined "direct needs" as being the desires of their three market segments for external customers (residential, industrial, sale for resale); only residential and sale for resale are shown. Figure A18.6 also shows how FPL defined "indirect needs" as being the concerns of their regulators and government agencies (NRC, PSC, ERA, state and local governments, and FERC); only NRC, PSC, and FERC are shown. Additionally, Figure A18.6 shows the pie charts containing the weights for the direct needs and the weights for the indirect needs. These weights are multiplied by each normalized weight in a column from the table of tables. For example, for direct needs, 0.72 is multiplied by the normalized weight for "accurate bills" (0.065) in the residential direct needs market segment, 0.27 is multiplied by the normalized weight for "accurate bills" in the commercial/industrial direct needs market segment, and 0.01 is multiplied by the normalized weight for "accurate bills" in the resale direct needs market segment. Note that $0.72 + 0.27 + 0.01 = 1.00$. Finally, the weighted averages for the direct needs and the weighted averages for the indirect needs, for each column in the table of tables, are averaged. This yields an overall priority value for each process (column) in the table of tables. These priority values indicate which processes (columns), when given attention for improvement, will maximally affect the most stakeholders. The table of tables demonstrates how FPL prioritized its quality elements (what it does, or processes) to better satisfy customer needs and wants via policy management.

FIGURE A18.6
Customer Needs Table of Tables

Source: Florida Power and Light Company, *Customer Needs Table of Tables,* Research, Economics and Forecasting Department, 1990.

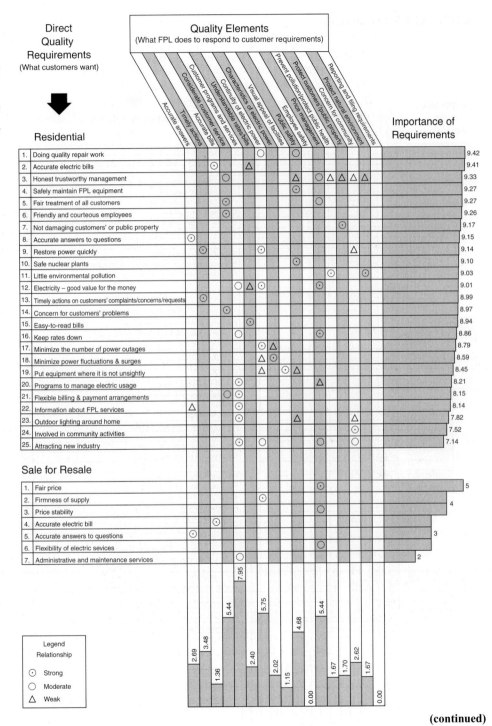

(continued)

FIGURE A18.6 (continued)

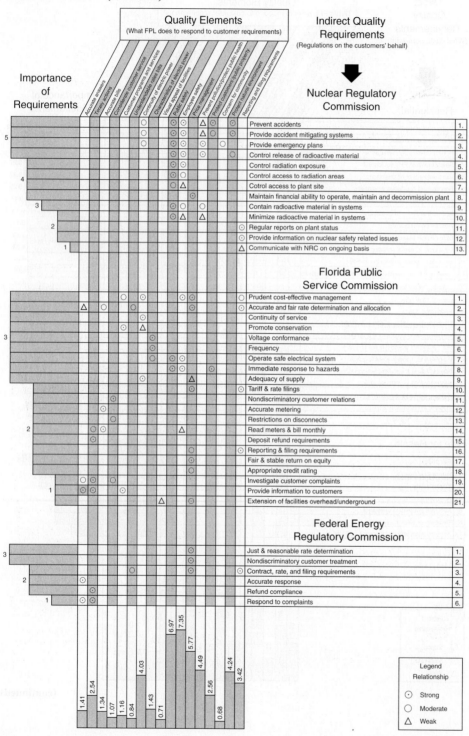

**FIGURE
A18.6
(concluded)**

Weighting of
Direct Needs

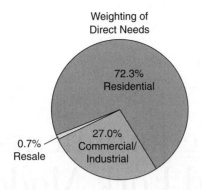

72.3%
Residential

27.0%
Commercial/
Industrial

0.7%
Resale

Weighting of
Indirect Needs

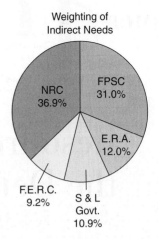

NRC
36.9%

FPSC
31.0%

E.R.A.
12.0%

F.E.R.C.
9.2%

S & L
Govt.
10.9%

NOTES
Importance of Requirements

1. Residential and Commercial/Industrial:
Mean rating (scale of 1–10) of customers
responding to Importance Survey.

2. Resale: 1–5 rating based on
analysis by functional staff.

3. NRC, ERA: 1–5 scale based on
consequence of noncompliance.

4. FPSC, Gov't, and FERC: 1–3
scale based on consequence of
noncompliance.

The Table of Tables represents
FPL's customers' needs and their
importance ratings of these needs.
It does not represent the Company's
ranking of functional areas.

*Employee Safety is one of management's
highest priorities; its importance is in
no way diminished by its ranking from
the customer needs perspective.

FPL

©Copyright 1990 Florida Power & Light Company
Research, Economics and Forecasting Department

Overall Ranking of
Corporate Quality
Elements

Category	Quality Element	Value	Rank
Sales and Service Quality	Accurate answers	4.10	11
Sales and Service Quality	Timely actions	6.02	8
Sales and Service Quality	Accurate bills	2.70	16
Sales and Service Quality	Considerate customer service	6.51	6
Sales and Service Quality	Customer programs and services	9.11	4
Sales and Service Quality	Understandable rates/bills	3.24	15
Delivery	Continuity of electric power	9.78	3
Delivery	Characteristics of electric power	3.45	12
Delivery	Visual appeal of facilities	1.86	17
Safety	Public safety	11.65	1
Safety	Employee safety*	7.35	5
Price	Price management	11.21	2
Corporate Responsibility	Prevent pollution/protect public health	6.16	7
Corporate Responsibility	Protect customers'/public property	4.26	10
Corporate Responsibility	Concern for community	3.30	14
Corporate Responsibility	Protect natural environment	5.91	9
Corporate Responsibility	Reporting and filing requirements	3.42	13

Chapter 19

Resource Requirements of the Detailed Fork Model

Sections

Introduction

The Template

Summary

Key Terms

Chapter Objectives

- To present a template for evaluating the resources requirements necessary for organizational transformation
- To present the time frame for each step in the transformation
- To specify levels of responsibility for each step in the transformation
- To describe the outcomes of each step in the transformation
- To summarize the resource needs at each stage of the transformation

Introduction

At this point in the study of the detailed fork model introduced in Chapter 14, some important questions arise: How long will it take the organization to "live" the fork model? How much will it cost? What resources will be needed from the organization? What resources will be needed from the consulting firm? In this chapter we present a template for answering some of these questions and estimating the resources necessary for the transformation of the organization. This chapter is only a sample template, which will have to be modified for a particular organization; there will be significant variation between organizations in the answers to these questions.

The Template

Generally, the fork model is implemented sequentially; that is, first the handle, then the neck, then Prong 1, then Prong 2, and finally Prong 3. Consider each part of the fork model as a phase of the quality management implementation process. Different implementation strategies may be used based on the characteristics and needs of the organization.

The following abbreviations are used throughout the **template:**

P	President
EC	Executive committee
LC	Lead consultant
PDC	Policy deployment committee
PIL	Process improvement leader
PITM	Process improvement team member
LST	Local steering team
CFPL	Cross-functional project leader
CFTM	Cross-functional team member

Phase 1: The Handle—Management's Commitment to Transformation

Step	Time Frame	Responsibility	Outcomes
Step 1: P creates a **crisis** to generate the energy for transformation	Early month 1	P	List of crises
Step 2: P creates a **vision** to generate the energy for transformation	Early month 1	P	Vision statement
Step 3: P initiates transformation using a crisis or a vision	Mid month 1	P	Publication of crisis and/or vision
Step 4: P contacts an **external expert** in the **System of Profound Knowledge** (LC)	Mid month 1	P	Retain LC
Step 5: **Window of opportunity** for transformation opens	Mid Month 1	P	Communication with all stakeholders about QM
Step 6: P and LC collect data for transformation plan	Months 1–2	P LC	Results of "barriers against" and "aids for" study
Step 7: P and LC begin planning transformation	Month 3	P (support and review) LC	Transformation plan
Step 8: P forms the EC	Month 3	P LC EC	EC is formed

(continued)

Step	Time Frame	Responsibility	Outcomes
Step 9: LC trains and educates EC and future QM experts	Months 4–6	LC EC members QM experts	Completion of training program with mastery by EC
Optional: EC selects individuals to become QM experts by pursuing an MS degree in QM. These people study for 1.5 to 2 years and come online after the first review by the P (see step 34 of the detailed fork model in Figure 14.1). One QM expert per 500 employees.	Months 5–24	EC members LC QM experts University program	Completion of MS in QM by QM experts LC assists EC in selecting a university program
Step 10: Window of opportunity for transformation begins to close without action from EC	Month 7 and beyond	EC members LC	Communication with all stakeholders about QM process

Phase 2: The Neck—Management's Education

Step	Time Frame	Responsibility	Outcomes
Step 11: EC forms **education and self-improvement** groups	Month 8 and beyond	LC EC	1. EC prepares executive summaries 2. EC role-plays 3. EC uses new paradigms to create win-win scenarios
Step 12: EC establishes a life-long process for education and self-improvement	Month 11 and beyond	LC EC	LC develops a learning and self-improvement plan for each EC member
Step 13: EC working with LC to resolve individual issues which create barriers to transformation	Month 11 and beyond	LC EC	EC resolves concerns with QM via "inventory" tool used by LC

Phase 3: Prong 1—Daily Management

Step	Time Frame	Responsibility	Outcomes
Step 14: EC selects initial PILs	Month 8	LC EC PILs	Selection of initial team leaders
Step 15: LC trains initial PILs	Month 8	LC Initial PILs	Train initial PILs in Tools and Methods for QI and Team Methods for QI
Step 16: Members of the EC evaluate the initial **process improvement projects** (daily management issues)	Month 8	LC EC Initial PILs	Initial projects selected

(continued)

Step	Time Frame	Responsibility	Outcomes
Step 17: EC members, in consultation with the team leader, select the initial process improvement team members.	Month 8	LC EC members Initial PILs	Teams are selected for each project
Experts train team members.		Initial PITMs	Team members are trained
Step 18: Initial process improvement teams conduct daily management using the QI story format.	Months 8 and beyond	Initial PILs Initial PITMs	QI story
Step 19: Over time, other process improvement teams are formed to improve daily management.	Month 11 and beyond	EC members New PILs New PITMs	QI stories
Experts train new team leaders and members together.		LC New PILs New PITMs	New team leaders and members are trained
Step 20: LSTs coordinate daily management projects	Month 8 and beyond	LST members PILs	QI stories

Phase 4: Prong 2—Cross-Functional Management

Step	Time Frame	Personnel	Outcomes
Step 21: Members of the EC evaluate initial **cross-functional projects**	Month 12 and beyond	EC members LC	Selection of cross-functional projects
Step 22: Members of the EC evaluate the initial cross-functional project leaders	Month 12 and beyond	EC members LC Initial CFPLs	Selection of cross-functional team leaders
Step 23: Experts train initial cross-functional project leaders	Month 13 and beyond	LC Initial CFPLs	Initial cross-functional team leaders are trained in (1) QM theory, (2) tools and methods of QI, and (3) team methods for QI.
Step 24: EC members, in consultation with the team leader, select the initial cross-functional team members.	Month 13 and beyond	EC LC Initial CFPLs Initial CFTMs	Initial cross-functional team members are trained in (1) QM theory, (2) tools and methods of QI, and (3) team methods for QI.
Experts train team members		LC Initial CFTMs	*(continued)*

Step	Time Frame	Personnel	Outcomes
Step 25: Initial cross-functional teams improve cross-functional issues using the System of Profound Knowledge	Months 14 and beyond	Initial CFPLs Initial CFTMs	QI stories
Step 26: Over time, other cross-functional teams may be formed to improve cross-functional issues	Month 17 and beyond	EC LC	New cross-functional teams are formed
Other cross-functional team leaders and members are trained by LC		LC New CFPLs New CFTMs	Cross-functional leaders and members are trained in (1) QM theory, (2) tools and methods of QI, and (3) team methods for QI.
Step 27: EC coordinates cross-functional projects	Month 14 and beyond	EC CFPLs	QI stories

Phase 5: Prong 3—Policy Management

Step	Time Frame	Personnel	Outcomes
Step 28: Conduct initial **presidential review**	Months 8 and beyond	P EC LC Selected PILs and PITMs CFPLs and CFTMs	Constructive critique of selected process improvement teams by P
Step 29: **Policy setting:** EC develops initial strategic objectives	Months 11 and beyond	EC LC	Strategic objectives
Step 30: Policy setting: Policy deployment committee develops improvement plans	Months 13 and beyond	PDC LC	Improvement plans for all areas
Step 31: **Policy deployment:** PDC communicates projects to LSTs. Local teams conduct projects.	Months 15 and beyond	PDC LSTs PILs and PITMs CFPLs and CFTMs LC	LSTs receive and work on QI stories
Step 32: **Policy implementation**	Months 15 and beyond	PDC LST PILs and PITMs CFPLs and CFTMs	Findings of QI stories are implemented

(continued)

Step	Time Frame	Personnel	Outcomes
Step 33: **Quality feedback and review**	Months 19 and beyond	PDC LST LC	All QI stories are reviewed by LSTs. Selected QI stories are reviewed by PDC and EC members.
Step 34: Presidential review	Months 22 through 24	P EC LC Selected PILs and PITMs	Selected QI stories are reviewed by P
QM experts come on line in the QM process	Month 25 and beyond	QM experts	QM experts facilitate system-wide promotion of QM activities

Overall Time Requirements

The template shown above is a tool that can help top management answer some of their questions about quality management and the resources necessary for its implementation. The template provides rough estimates for the time required to initially promote quality management in an organization in which top management is seriously committed to this goal. The model shows a minimum of 8 months to determine management's commitment to transformation; a minimum of 4 months to affect management's values and beliefs about business through education; a minimum of 4 months to produce results from daily management; a minimum of 6 months to begin cross-functional management; and a minimum of 17 months to begin policy management. The model shows a minimum of 2 years is required to pass through all phases of the fork model at least once.

Management's commitment to transformation has been demonstrated by passing through one cycle of the fork model. Future iterations of the fork model are on a one-year cycle. Hence, the handle of the fork model is utilized only on an as-needed basis. Management's education with respect to quality management continues indefinitely into the future. There is no fixed schedule for it; it happens when it is deemed necessary by a manager in need of training, the manager's supervisor, the EC, or the PDC. Likewise, daily management, cross-functional management, and the initial presidential review portion of policy management (step 28) continue indefinitely into the future. However, steps 29 through 34 of policy management take on a yearly cycle. For example, step 29 (policy setting—strategic objectives) takes approximately 1 month, step 30 (policy setting—improvement plans) takes approximately 1 month, step 31 (policy deployment) takes approximately 1 month, step 32 (policy implementation) takes approximately 6 months, step 33 (quality feedback and review) takes about 2 months, and step 34 (presidential review) takes about 1 month.

Summary

This chapter presented a template for answering questions about the resources required to promote the organizational transformation by applying the detailed fork model. Each application of the template requires the user to modify it for his or her organization. The time and cost structure is largely a function of the effort the organization devotes to the quality management process versus the effort it requires the consulting organization to devote to the quality management process.

Key Terms

crisis, *717*
cross-functional
projects, *719*
education and self-
improvement, *718*
external expert, *717*
policy deployment, *720*

policy implementation, *720*
policy setting, *720*
presidential review, *720*
process improvement
projects, *718*
quality feedback and
review, *721*

System of Profound
Knowledge, *717*
template, *717*
vision, *717*
window of opportunity, *717*

Part 4 introduces Six Sigma management, developed at Motorola Corporation in the 1980s and popularized in large part by General Electric Corporation in the 1990s.

In Chapter 20, Six Sigma management is defined and discussed. It is the relentless and rigorous pursuit of the reduction of variation in all critical processes to achieve continuous and breakthrough improvements that impact the bottom line of the organization and increase customer satisfaction. To state the definition of Six Sigma management in another way: it is an organizational initiative designed to create manufacturing, service, and administrative processes that produce approximately 3.4 defects per million opportunities. The DMAIC (Define-Measure-Analyze-Improve-Control) model to improve processes is presented as a template for achieving the goals of Six Sigma management.

Chapter 20

Six Sigma Management

Sections

Chapter Objectives

- To define Six Sigma management
- To discuss the relationship between the voice of the customer and the voice of the process
- To discuss and illustrate the conditions for a 3-sigma process and the percent output between its lower and upper specification limits
- To discuss and illustrate the conditions for a 6-sigma process and illustrate the improvement in percent output between its lower and upper specification limits
- To introduce the DMAIC (Define-Measure-Analyze-Improve-Control) model for improving a process through Six Sigma management
- To discuss the costs and benefits of Six Sigma management
- To discuss the roles and responsibilities of the individuals and bodies involved in Six Sigma management: the senior executive, the executive committee, the black belt, the green belt, the master black belt, the champion, and the process owner
- To introduce the technical terminology used in Six Sigma management
- To present a detailed case study of a green belt project

Introduction

"Six Sigma"® Management[1] is the relentless and rigorous pursuit of the reduction of variation in all critical processes to achieve continuous and breakthrough improvements that impact the bottom line of the organization and increase customer satisfaction. It is an organizational initiative designed to create manufacturing, service, and administrative processes that produce approximately 3.4 defects per million opportunities (DPMO). Current organizational strategies produce a maximum of approximately 6,210 defects per million opportunities. Some comparative examples [see Reference 9, p. 2.11] are shown in Table 20.1.

The difference between 6,210 defects per million opportunities (0.00621) and 3.4 defects per million opportunities (0.0000034) can be illustrated by a service with 20 component steps. If each of the 20 component steps has a quality level of 6,210 defects per million opportunities, the likelihood of a defect at each step is 0.00621 (6,210/1,000,000). By subtraction, the likelihood of a defect-free step is 0.99379 (1.0 − 0.00621). Consequently, the likelihood of delivering a defect-free final service is 88.286 percent, computed by multiplying 0.99379 by itself 20 times ($[1.0 - 0.00621]^{20} = 0.88286 = 88.286$ percent). However, if each of the 20 component parts has a quality level of only 3.4 defects per million opportunities (0.0000034), then the likelihood of delivering a defect-free final service is 99.99932 percent ($[1.0 - 0.0000034]^{20} = 0.9999966^{20} = 0.9999932 = 99.99932$ percent).

Another way to define Six Sigma management is that it is an organizational initiative designed to create manufacturing, service, and administrative processes that produce approximately 10 times fewer defects with a 50 percent reduction in cycle time every 2 years.

Relationship between the Voice of the Customer and the Voice of the Process

Six Sigma management promotes the idea that the distribution of output for a process (the **voice of the process**, discussed in Chapter 11) should take up no more than half of the tolerance allowed by the specification limits (the **voice of the customer**, also discussed in Chapters 11 and 18), assuming measurement data from a stable and normal

TABLE 20.1
Comparison between Current Results and Six Sigma Results

Current Standard Results (99% good)	Six Sigma Results
20,000 lost articles of mail per hour	7 lost articles of mail per hour
15 minutes of unsafe drinking water per day	15 minutes of unsafe drinking water every 8.75 years
5,000 incorrect surgical operations per week	1.7 incorrect surgical operations per week
2 short or long landings at most major airports per day	2 short or long landings at most major airports every 10 years

[1] "Six Sigma"® is a registered trademark of the Motorola Corporation.

FIGURE 20.1

Comparison of Voice of the Customer and Voice of the Process for a 3-Sigma Process with No Shift in Mean

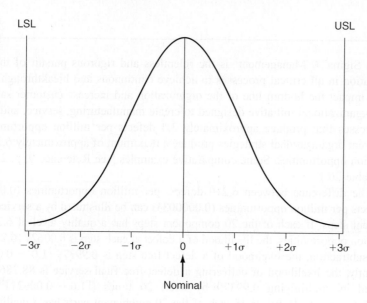

distribution of output whose mean can shift by as much as 1.5 standard deviations over time. A shift of 1.5 standard deviations in a process's mean over time has been suggested, by organizations such as Motorola, General Electric, and Allied Signal, as a common phenomenon early in an organization's Six Sigma process. Statisticians may argue about the correctness of the assumption of a 1.5-sigma shift in mean, but for the purposes of this text, we accept this common industrial assumption.

Figure 20.1 shows the voice of the customer as spoken in the language of a nominal value, m, and lower and upper specification limits, LSL and USL, for a quality characteristic. It also shows the voice of the process as spoken in the language of a distribution of process output for a quality characteristic. Figure 20.1 assumes that the distribution of process output (the voice of the process) is measurement data, is stable, and is normal; that the average process output is equal to nominal; and that the distance between nominal and either specification limit is 3 times the standard deviation of the process output. If these five conditions are met, then we can call the process presented in Figure 20.1 a **3-sigma process** with no shift in its mean. A 3-sigma process with no shift in mean is a process that will generate 2,700 defects per million opportunities; that is, 99.73 percent of its output will be between the lower specification limit (LSL) and the upper specification limit (USL), at least in the near future.

Figure 20.2 shows the distribution of the number of days to complete a monthly accounting report. The distribution is stable and normally distributed, with an average of 7 days and a standard deviation of 1 day. Figure 20.2 also shows a nominal value of 7 days, a lower specification limit of 4 days, and an upper specification limit of 10 days. The accounting reporting process is referred to as a 3-sigma process without a shift in mean because the process mean plus or minus 3 standard deviations is equal to the specification limits: in other words, USL = m + 3 sigma and LSL = m − 3 sigma. As stated earlier, this scenario will yield 2,700 defects per million opportunities, or one early or late monthly report in 30.86 years $[(1/0.0027)/12]$.

FIGURE 20.2
3-Sigma
Accounting
Reporting
Process with
No Shift in Its
Mean

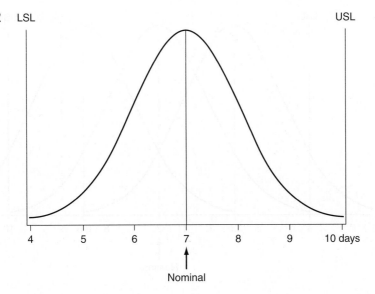

Figure 20.3 shows the voice of the customer and the voice of the process for a quality characteristic that is represented by measurement data; is stable; is normally distributed; has an average process output that can shift by as much as 1.5 standard deviations on either side of nominal; and has a distance between nominal and either specification limit of 3 standard deviations of process output. When these five conditions are met, we call the process a 3-sigma process with a 1.5-sigma shift in the mean. Such a process will generate 66,811 defects per million opportunities, or 93.33189 percent of its output between the lower specification limit (LSL) and the upper specification limit (USL), at least in the near future.

FIGURE 20.3
Comparison of
Voice of the
Customer and
Voice of the
Process for a
3-Sigma
Process with a
1.5-Sigma Shift
in the Mean

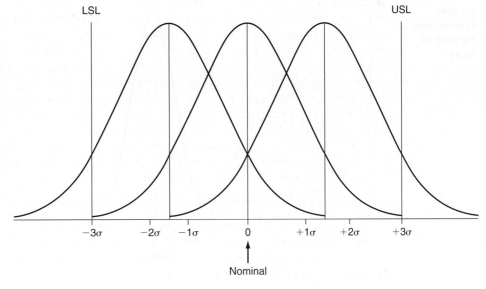

FIGURE 20.4
3-Sigma
Accounting
Reporting
Process with a
1.5-Sigma
Shift in the
Mean

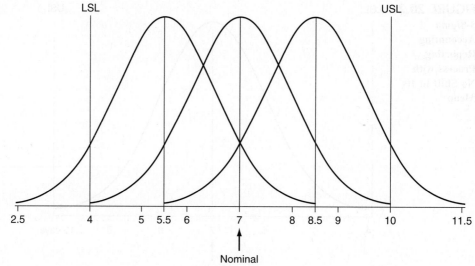

Figure 20.4 shows the accounting scenario of Figure 20.2, but the process average shifts by 1.5 standard deviations (the process average is shifted down or up by 1.5 standard deviations, or 1.5 days, from 7.0 days to either 5.5 days or 8.5 days) over time. The 1.5 standard deviation shift in the mean results in 66,811 defects per million opportunities, or one early or late monthly report in 1.25 years $[(1/.066807)/12]$.

In Figure 20.5 we have the scenario of Figure 20.1 except the voice of the process takes up only half the distance between the specification limits. The process mean remains the same as in Figure 20.1, but the process standard deviation has been

FIGURE 20.5
6-Sigma
Process with
No Shift in
Mean

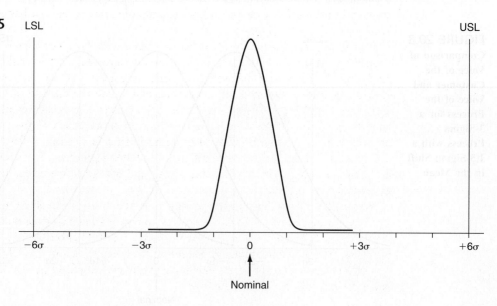

FIGURE 20.6

6-Sigma
Accounting
Process with
No Shift in
Mean

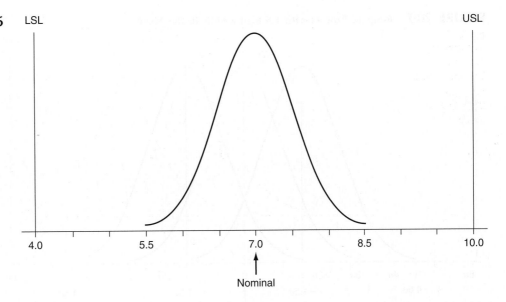

reduced to one-half day through application of process improvement tools and methods. In this case, the resulting output will exhibit 2 defects per billion opportunities, or 99.9999998 percent of its output will be between the lower and upper specification limits, at least in the near future. This is called a **6-sigma process** with no shift in its mean.

Figure 20.6 shows the output of the monthly accounting process in Figure 20.2, except its standard deviation has been reduced to one-half day through process improvement activities. This accounting process is now a 6-sigma process with no shift in mean. Its output will exhibit 2 defects per billion opportunities, or one early or late monthly report in 41,666.667 years $[(1/.000000002)/12]$.

Figure 20.7 shows the voice of the customer and the voice of the process for a quality characteristic that is represented by measurement data, is stable, and is normally distributed; where the average process output can shift by as much as 1.5 standard deviations on either side of nominal; and where the distance between nominal and either specification limit is 6 standard deviations of process output. If these five conditions are met, then we can call the process presented in Figure 20.7 a 6-sigma process with a 1.5-sigma shift in the mean. This is a process that will generate 3.4 defects per million opportunities, or 99.99966 percent of its output will be between the lower specification limit (LSL) and the upper specification limit (USL), at least in the near future.

Figure 20.8 shows the same scenario for the accounting process: the process average shifts by 1.5 standard deviations (the process average is shifted down or up by 1.5 standard deviations, or 0.75 days = 1.5 × 0.5 days, from 7.0 days to either 6.25 days or 7.75 days) over time. The 1.5 standard deviation shift in the mean results in 3.4 defects per million opportunities, or one early or late monthly report in 24,510 years $[(1/.0000034)/12]$. This is the definition of Six Sigma quality.

FIGURE 20.7 **6-Sigma Process with 1.5-Sigma Shift in the Mean**

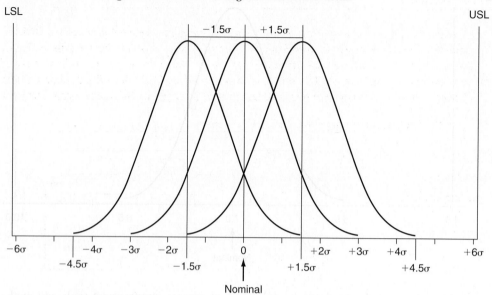

FIGURE 20.8 **6-Sigma Accounting Process with 1.5-Sigma Shift in the Mean**

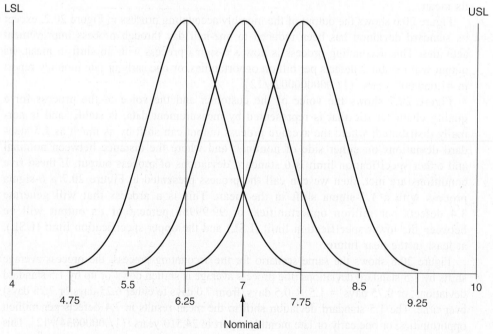

The DMAIC Model

The model that is used to improve a process in Six Sigma management is called the **DMAIC model:** Define-Measure-Analyze-Improve-Control. The relationship between the voice of the customer (nominal and specifications limits), the voice of the process (distribution of process output), and the DMAIC model is shown in Figure 20.9. The left side shows an old **flowchart** with its 3-sigma output distribution with a 1.5-sigma shift in the mean. The right

FIGURE 20.9 The DMAIC Model for Improvement of a Process

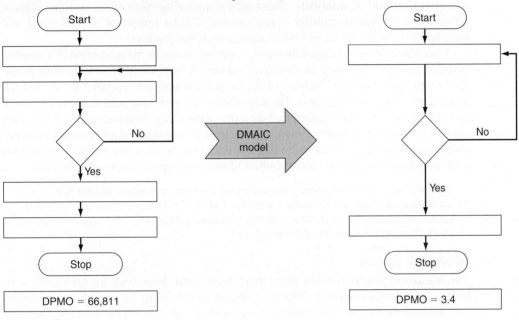

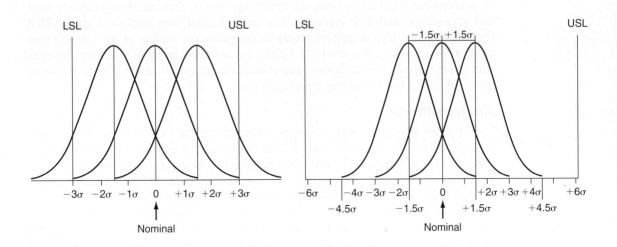

side shows a new flowchart with its 6-sigma output distribution with a 1.5-sigma shift in the mean. The method utilized in Six Sigma management to move from the old flowchart to the new flowchart through improvement of the process is called the DMAIC model.

We use the monthly accounting report example to demonstrate how to use the DMAIC model.

Define Phase

The **define phase** involves preparing a business charter (rationale for the project), understanding the relationships between suppliers, inputs, process, outputs, and customers (called **SIPOC analysis**); gathering and analyzing voice of the customer data to identify the **critical-to-quality** characteristics (CTQs) important to customers; and developing a project charter (problem statement of the project).

A Six Sigma team is assigned by top management to review the production of a monthly accounting report. This involves identifying the need for the project (relative to other potential projects), the costs and benefits of the project, the resources required for the project, and the time frame of the project. The team determines that management wants a monthly accounting report to be completed in 7 days (the normal time to complete is 7 days). They also determine that the report cannot be completed in less than 4 days (the relevant information is not available before then) and not later than 10 days (the report is needed for decision-making purposes). Team members identify the project charter as follows:

> Reduce (*direction*) the variability in the cycle time (*measure*) to produce an error-free accounting report (*process*) from the current level of 66,811 DPMO (a 3-sigma process with a 1.5-sigma shift in the mean) to 3.4 DPMO (a 6-sigma process with a 1.5-sigma shift in the mean) (*target*) by January 10, 2005 (*deadline*).

Measure Phase

The **measure phase** involves developing operational definitions for each critical-to-quality (CTQ) characteristic, performing studies to determine the validity (repeatability and reproducibility) of the measurement procedure for each CTQ, collecting baseline capabilities for each CTQ, and determining the process capability for each CTQ.

First, the members of the Six Sigma team define "variability in cycle time" such that all relevant personnel agree upon the definition; that is, they clearly identify the start and stop points needed to compute cycle time. Second, they perform a **gage R&R** (repeatability and reproducibility) **study** to determine the validity of the measurement process for variability in cycle time. Finally, the members of the team collect baseline data about variability in cycle time and statistically analyze it to get a clear picture of the capability of the accounting reporting process.

Analyze Phase

The **analyze phase** involves identifying upstream variables (x's) for each CTQ; operationally defining each x; collecting baseline data for each x; performing studies to determine the validity (repeatability and reproducibility) of the measurement process for each x; establishing baseline capabilities for each x; and understanding the effect of each x on each CTQ (variability in cycle time to produce an error-free accounting report).

First, team members identify all input and process variables that affect variability in cycle time, or the x variables. This activity has been referred to as **process mapping** or flowcharting, and was discussed in Chapter 4. In this project, team members identify the relevant x's as:

x_1 = number of days from request to receipt for line item A data

x_2 = number of days from request to receipt for line item B data

x_3 = number of days from request to receipt for line item C data

x_4 = number of days from request to receipt for line item D data

x_5 = number of days to reformat the line item data to prepare the report

x_6 = number of days to prepare the report

x_7 = accounting clerk preparing the report (Mary or Joe)

x_8 = number of errors in the report

x_9 = number of days to correct the report

x_{10} = accounting supervisor performing the corrections to the report (Harry or Sue)

x_{11} = number of signatures required before the report is released

Second, team members operationally define the above variables.

Third, team members perform gage R&R (repeatability and reproducibility) studies to determine the validity of their measurement systems.

Fourth, team members collect baseline data to determine the capability of each variable.

Finally, team members study the data and develop hypotheses about the relationships between the x's and the CTQ. In this case, x_1 (number of days from request to receipt for line item A data), x_3 (number of days from request to receipt for line item C data), x_7 (accounting clerk preparing the report), and x_{10} (accounting supervisor performing the corrections to the report) were found to be critical to the reduction in the variability of the cycle time to produce the accounting report. All the other x's did not substantially affect the CTQ.

Improve Phase

The **improve phase** involves designing experiments to understand the relationship between the CTQs and the x's; determining the optimal levels of critical x's that optimize the spread, shape, and center of the CTQs; developing action plans to implement the optimal level of the x's into the process under study; and conducting a pilot test of the revised process.

Team members conduct an experiment to specify the levels of the critical x's identified in the analyze phase, in order to optimize the spread, shape, and center of the time to produce the accounting report. The experiment reveals that team members have to work with the personnel responsible for line items A and C to decrease the average and standard deviation of days to forward the line items to the department preparing the report. Further, the experiment reveals that there is an interaction between the clerk preparing the report and the supervisor correcting the report. The analysis shows that if Mary prepares the report, it is best for Sue to correct the report, or if Joe prepares the report, it is best for Harry to correct the report. A pilot run of the revised process to produce the accounting report shows it could generate a predictable, or stable, normal distribution of days to produce the report with a mean of 7 days and a standard deviation of ½ day.

Control Phase

The **control phase** involves avoiding potential problems with the revised settings of the x's through risk abatement planning and mistake-proofing, standardizing successful process revisions in training manuals, controlling the revised settings of the critical x's, and turning the revised process over to the process owner for continuous improvement using the PDSA cycle.

Team members identify and avoid potential problems with x_1, x_3, x_7, and x_{10} using **risk management** and **mistake-proofing** techniques. For example, they establish procedures to ensure the coupling of clerks and supervisors, and data collection methods to identify and resolve future problems in the reporting process. The new process is standardized and fully documented. At this point, team members turn the revised process over to the process owner and celebrate their success. The process owner continues to work toward improvement of the revised process beyond its current level of output, which is an improved, stable, normal distribution of days to produce the report with an average of 7 days and a standard deviation of ½ day. This translates to a report being early or late about once every 24,500 years! The team chooses not to wait around for an error to occur.

Benefits and Costs of Six Sigma Management

A successful Six Sigma program will yield the following benefits to the management of an organization: improved process flows, improved communication through Six Sigma terminology (for example, DPMO and process sigma), reduced cycle times, enhanced knowledge and enhanced ability to manage that knowledge, higher levels of customer satisfaction, higher levels of employee satisfaction, increased productivity, reduced total defects, decreased work-in-progress (WIP), decreased inventory, improved capacity and output, increased quality and reliability, decreased unit costs, increased price flexibility, decreased time to market, faster delivery time, and increased liquid capital. Six Sigma projects generate an average of $250,000 in reduced costs or increased revenues. Additionally, these organizational benefits lead to the following stakeholder benefits: stockholders receive more profit because of decreased costs and increased revenues, customers are delighted with products and services, employees experience higher morale and more satisfaction from their joyful work, and suppliers provide higher-quality inputs.

On the other side of the profit equation, Six Sigma management requires the following resources: training time costs, material costs, training manual development costs, administrative and operating costs for DMAIC projects, infrastructure costs such as the costs of constructing and using organizational metric tracking systems, and monitoring DMAIC project costs. Anecdotal evidence strongly indicates that the benefits of a Six Sigma process far outweigh the costs, if the top management of an organization is firmly committed to Six Sigma management for the long term. As an example, see General Electric's recent and current Annual Reports.

Six Sigma Roles and Responsibilities

Senior Executive

The **senior executive** provides the impetus, the direction, and the alignment necessary for the ultimate success of Six Sigma management. The roles and responsibilities of a senior executive, with respect to Six Sigma management, are multifaceted. First, the senior executive leads the executive committee (EC) in linking organizational strategies to Six Sigma projects. Second, the senior executive participates on high-level policy management and cross-functional project teams. Third, she monitors and balances all Six

Sigma activities to avoid local optimization and organizational suboptimization. Fourth, the senior executive maintains a long-term view of the organization and acts as a liaison to Wall Street, explaining the long-term advantages of Six Sigma to investors. Fifth, the senior executive constantly and publicly champions Six Sigma management. Finally, the senior executive conducts presidential reviews of Six Sigma daily management and cross-functional management projects using Six Sigma theory and methods.

Six Sigma management can be a successful organizational strategy if top management is totally committed to the process. Total commitment means that the chief executive officer obligates substantial resources to Six Sigma management, including 25 percent or more of his or her time. The CEO must use policy management to create and manage a strategic view of the enterprise. She must be willing to engage all levels of the organization through organizational metric tracking systems and daily management and cross-functional Six Sigma DMAIC projects. The CEO must be willing to study and internalize the theory, tools and methods of Six Sigma management. Finally, the CEO must have a "burning desire" to create revolutionary change (cycle time, quality, cost, value) in her enterprise.

The most successful and highly publicized Six Sigma processes, such as those of General Electric, Motorola, Allied Signal, and Dupont, have had one thing in common: unwavering, clear and committed leadership from the top. There is no doubt in anyone's mind that Six Sigma management is "the way they do business. " Although it may be possible to initiate Six Sigma concepts and processes at lower levels, dramatic success will not be possible until the senior executive becomes engaged and takes a leadership role.

Executive Committee (EC)

The members of the **executive committee** (EC) compose a highly effective team that operates at the same level of commitment as the senior executive. The roles and responsibilities of the executive committee are multifaceted. First, the EC creates an organizational metric tracking system that cascades, or deploys, key objectives, that is, Six Sigma management and key indicators throughout the organization via policy management. Second, the EC empowers the **policy deployment committee** (PDC) to deploy key objectives throughout the organization via policy management. Third, the EC manages the organizational Six Sigma project portfolio toward optimization of the entire organization's bottom line. Fourth, the EC utilizes **catchball,** discussed in Chapter 18, to establish a reasonable and equitable project portfolio for each division/department within the organization. Fifth, the EC improves the Six Sigma process through constant iteration of the PDSA cycle. Sixth, the EC removes any and all high-level barriers to Six Sigma management. Finally, the EC provides the resources necessary for Six Sigma management.

Black Belt

The role and responsibilities of a **black belt** are multifaceted. First, a black belt is a full-time change agent. Second, a black belt is not a master of the process under study, but a master of the change process. Third, a black belt supervises the green belts working on a Six Sigma project, as discussed in the following section. Fourth, a black belt prepares a draft project charter for the Six Sigma projects under his supervision. Fifth, a black belt works closely with a project team to keep it functioning and progressing toward a speedy and effective conclusion to the Six Sigma project. Sixth, a black belt communicates with the individual responsible for the financial and political well-being of the team (called a champion, and discussed below). Seventh, the black belt serves as the team leader for Six Sigma projects because of his expertise in Six Sigma theory, tools, and methods. Eighth, the black belt helps team members analyze data and design experiments. Ninth, the black belt provides training in Six Sigma theory, tools, and methods. Tenth, the black belt helps team members prepare for management reviews and presidential reviews. Eleventh, the black belt recommends Six Sigma teams for Six Sigma projects. Finally, the black belt leads and coaches green belts leading simpler Six Sigma projects.

A black belt is the fastest path to the executive suite. Jack Welch, former chief executive officer of General Electric, is a black belt and devoted about 25 percent of his time to Six Sigma management. Chris Galvin, former chief executive officer of Motorola Corporation, is a black belt and devoted up to 50 percent of his time in the early years to Six Sigma activities and issues [see Reference 1, p. 8]. Black belts dedicate 100 percent of their time to one or more Six Sigma projects.

A black belt must pass a certification examination and lead at least two successful Six Sigma projects.

Green Belt

Most **green belts** serve as team members on Six Sigma projects. However, if a green belt acts as a team leader for simpler projects, then she has the following responsibilities. First, the green belt prepares a draft charter for the Six Sigma project. Second, she selects the team members. Third, the green belt communicates with the champion, black belt, and process owner concerning the status of the project. Fourth, the green belt facilitates the Six Sigma project team members. Finally, the green belt provides training in basic Six Sigma tools and methods.

A green belt spends one-quarter of her work time as a team member on one or more Six Sigma projects. Green belts are the "workhorses" of Six Sigma projects. Most managers in a Six Sigma organization have green belts.

A green belt must pass a certification examination and participate in at least one successful Six Sigma project.

Master Black Belt

The roles and responsibilities of a **master black belt** are multifaceted. First, a master black belt is a proven team leader and technical expert. Second, a master black belt is a teacher and mentor of black belts and green belts. Third, a master black belt simultaneously supervises several black belts and green belts. Fourth, the master black belt (in conjunction with the senior executive, members of the executive committee, and champions) is an ambassador of Six Sigma management. Finally, the master black belt continuously works to improve and innovate the Six Sigma management process.

A master black belt must complete a certification examination and successfully supervise at least two black belts in their completion of two successful Six Sigma projects each.

Champion

A **champion** is a member of the executive committee, or at least an individual who is trusted to report directly to a member of the executive committee. A champion takes a very active leadership and sponsorship role in implementing Six Sigma management. He works closely with the executive committee, the black belts, and the master black belts to carry out the following responsibilities: first, a champion translates the key objectives and key indicators from his section of the organizational metric tracking system into Six Sigma projects as part of policy management. Second, a champion prepares an initial draft of a project charter for each Six Sigma project under his auspices. Third, he assigns green belts and black belts to the Six Sigma projects under his auspices. Fourth, the champion removes obstacles to the effective and efficient functioning of the Six Sigma project teams under his auspices. Fifth, a champion provides a direct line of communication between a Six Sigma project team and the executive committee. Sixth, a champion obtains and manages the resources necessary for a Six Sigma project team to meet its project charter. Seventh, a champion conducts management reviews of each Six Sigma project team operating under his auspices. Finally, a champion keeps each Six Sigma project team under his auspices focused, by providing direction and guidance, on the attainment of its project charter.

A champion must pass a certification examination.

Process Owner

A **process owner** is the individual who has the ultimate authority to change a process. The process owner should be identified for every project or task that is entered onto an organizational metric tracking system. The roles and responsibilities of a process owner are multifaceted. First, a process owner monitors the performance of her process through key indicators. Second, a process owner empowers the people who work in her process (recall the quality management definition of empowerment in Chapter 2). Third, a process owner works with all Six Sigma project teams in her area to enable them to successfully complete their projects. Fourth, a process owner manages the process after completion of the Six Sigma project to sustain the gains made by the Six Sigma project team. Fifth, a process owner continues to improve and/or innovate her process through application of the PDSA cycle.

A process owner should pass the champion certification examination: effective Six Sigma projects require Six Sigma knowledge on the part of the process owner. For example, a process owner must understand the PDSA cycle to accept a project from the control phase of the DMAIC model.

Distinction between Black Belt and Green Belt Six Sigma Projects

Several criteria distinguish black belt and green belt Six Sigma projects. Green belt projects tend to be less involved (e.g., they have one CTQ and few x's), do not deal with political issues, do not require many organizational resources, do not require significant capital investment to realize the gains identified during the project, and utilize only basic statistical methods. On the other hand, black belt projects tend to deal with more complex situations that may involve two or more CTQs and many x's, may involve substantial political issues or be cross-functional in nature, require substantial organizational resources, may need substantial capital investment to realize the gains made during the project, and utilize sophisticated statistical methods.

Six Sigma Industrial Training Programs

It is common practice to teach Six Sigma black belt training in four sessions of five days each, separated by three weeks. The first week's session covers the define and measure phases of the DMAIC model. The second week's session covers the analyze phase of the DMAIC model. The third week's session covers more of the analyze phase and the improve phase of the DMAIC model. The fourth week's session covers the control phase of the DMAIC model and future steps. Green belt training is covered in two sessions of five days each, separated by three weeks.

Six Sigma Terminology

Six Sigma management is replete with technical jargon that must be understood and mastered by the senior executive of an organization, the members of the executive committee of an organization, the process owners in an organization, and the champions in an organization. Green belts, black belts, and master black belts are the professors of Six Sigma technical terminology.

unit A unit is the item (e.g., product or component, service or service step, or time period) to be studied with a Six Sigma project.

defective A nonconforming unit is a defective.

defect A defect is a nonconformance on one of many possible quality characteristics of a unit that causes customer dissatisfaction. For each unit, each quality characteristic is defined by translating customer desires into engineering specifications. It is important to operationally define each defect for a unit; for example, if a word in a document is misspelled, that word may be considered a defect.

defect opportunity A defect opportunity is the most fundamental area for a defect. There may be many opportunities for defects within a defined unit. For instance, a service may have four component parts. If each component part has three opportunities for a defect, then the service has 12 defect opportunities. The number of defect opportunities is generally related to the complexity of the unit under study; that is, the more complex the unit under study, the greater the number of opportunities for a defect.

defects per unit (DPU) Defects per unit refers to the average of all the defects for a given number of units, that is, the total number of defects for n units divided by n. In the production of a 50-page document, the unit is a page; if there are 150 spelling errors, DPU would be 150/50 or 3.0. In ten 50-page documents, the unit is a 50-page document, the defect is a misspelled word, and if there are 75 spelling errors in all 10 documents, DPU is 75/10 or 7.5.

defects per opportunity (DPO) Defects per opportunity refers to the number of defects divided by the number of defect opportunities. In the service example above, there are 12 defect opportunities per unit (service). If there are 20 errors in 100 services, DPU would be 0.20. However, there are 12 opportunities per unit, and therefore 1200 opportunities in 100 units, so DPO would be 20/1200 or 0.0167. This DPO may also be calculated by dividing DPU by the total number of opportunities.

defects per million opportunities (DPMO) DPMO equals DPO multiplied by one million. Hence, for the above example, the DPMO is $(0.0167) \times (1,000,000)$, or 16,700 defects per million opportunities.

observed yield Observed yield is the proportion of units within specification divided by the total number of units; that is, if 25 units are produced and 20 are good, then the observed yield is 0.80 (20/25).

rolled throughput yield (RTY) RTY is the product of the observed yields from each step in a process. It is the probability of a unit passing through all steps of a process and incurring no defects. RTY = $1.0 - $ DPO. For example, if a process has three steps and the yield from the first step is 99.7 percent, the yield from the second

TABLE 20.2
DPMO and Process Sigma for a Process with a 1.5-Sigma Shift in the Mean

Source: BlueFire Partners, Minneapolis, MN.

Process Sigma	DPMO Shift = 1.5	Process Sigma	DPMO Shift = 1.5
6.0	3.40	3.0	66,810.60
5.9	5.40	2.9	80,762.10
5.8	8.50	2.8	96,809.20
5.7	13.40	2.7	115,083.10
5.6	20.70	2.6	135,686.80
5.5	31.70	2.5	158,686.90
5.4	48.10	2.4	184,108.20
5.3	72.40	2.3	211,927.70
5.2	107.80	2.2	242,071.40
5.1	159.10	2.1	274,412.20
5.0	232.70	2.0	308,770.20
4.9	337.00	1.9	344,915.30
4.8	483.50	1.8	382,572.10
4.7	687.20	1.7	421,427.50
4.6	967.70	1.6	461,139.80
4.5	1,350.00	1.5	501,350.00
4.4	1,865.90	1.4	541,693.80
4.3	2,555.20	1.3	581,814.90
4.2	3,467.00	1.2	621,378.40
4.1	4,661.20	1.1	660,082.90
4.0	6,209.70	1.0	697,672.10
3.9	8,197.60	0.9	733,944.50
3.8	10,724.10	0.8	768,760.50
3.7	13,903.50	0.7	802,048.10
3.6	17,864.50	0.6	833,804.30
3.5	22,750.30	0.5	864,094.80
3.4	28,717.00	0.4	893,050.40
3.3	35,931.10	0.3	920,860.50
3.2	44,566.70	0.2	947,764.90
3.1	54,801.40	0.1	974,042.60

step is 99.5 percent and the yield from the third step is 89.7 percent, then the rolled throughput yield is 0.997 × 0.995 × 0.897 or 88.98 percent.

process sigma Process sigma is a measure of the process performance determined by using DPMO and a normal distribution table. Process sigma is a metric that allows for process performance comparisons across processes, departments, divisions, companies, and countries. In Six Sigma terminology, the sigma value of a process is a metric used to indicate the number of defects per million opportunities, or how well the process is performing with respect to customer needs and wants.

Table 20.2 shows the relationship between DPMO and process sigma for a process with a 1.5-sigma shift in the mean.

A Six Sigma Case Study

The purpose of the following case study [see References 11 and 12] is to present a detailed view of the anatomy of a Six Sigma green belt project. The case study illustrates a green belt project from a fictitious company, Paper Organizers International.

TABLE 20.3 POI's Business Objectives and Indicators with Potential Six Sigma Projects

President		Director of Paper Shuffling Department		
Business Objectives	Business Indicators	Area Objectives	Area Indicators	Potential Six Sigma Projects
Increase the number of orders	Number of orders/ month (c chart)	Increase the number of orders in PSD	Number of orders in PSD/month (c chart)	New customer promotions project
Increase the number of POI services (filing, organizing, etc.) utilized by each customer	1. Average number of services utilized per customer/ quarter 2. Standard deviation of number of services utilized per customer/ quarter ($\bar{x}$ and s charts)	Increase the number of services utilized by each customer in PSD	1. Average number of services utilized per PSD customer/ quarter 2. Standard deviation of number of services utilized per PSD customer/ quarter ($\bar{x}$ and s charts)	Existing customer promotions project
Minimize production costs	Production costs/ month (I-MR chart)	Minimize production costs in PSD	Production costs in PSD/month (Figure 20.10: I-MR chart)	MSD quality project
Eliminate employee complaints	Number of employee complaints/month (c chart)	Eliminate employee complaints from PSD	Number of employee complaints from PSD/month (c chart)	Employee morale project

The Company

Paper Organizers International (POI) offers a full range of filing, organizing, and paper shuffling services. To accomplish these tasks, POI purchases metallic securing devices[2] (MSDs), staplers, hole punchers, folders, three-ring binders, and a full range of related products to serve its customers' paper handling needs. The employees, or internal customers, of Paper Organizers International use MSDs to organize piles of paper pending placement into folders or binders.

The Purchasing department of POI has noticed an increase in complaints from employees in the Paper Shuffling department (PSD) about MSDs breaking and failing to keep papers together. This creates opportunities for client papers to be mixed together. The Purchasing department would like to improve the process for purchasing MSDs to eliminate complaints from employees in the Paper Shuffling department.

Origin of the MSD Six Sigma Project

POI's mission statement is "Put the right information in the right place." To accomplish this mission, POI has established a cascading set of business objectives and business indicators, which ultimately result in potential Six Sigma projects, as shown in Table 20.3.

The monthly production costs in the Paper Shuffling department are shown on the individuals and moving range chart in Figure 20.10, as indicated in the next-to-last row in the fourth column in Table 20.3.

---

[2] The idea for a Six Sigma case study focusing on metallic securing devices (MSDs) was adapted from Cordis Corporation's (a division of Johnson & Johnson) Six Sigma training manuals which were developed by Oriel Inc. (Madison, WI). Metallic securing devices (MSDs) are paper clips.

FIGURE 20.10   **Individuals and Moving Range Chart of Monthly Production Costs in the Paper Shuffling Department**

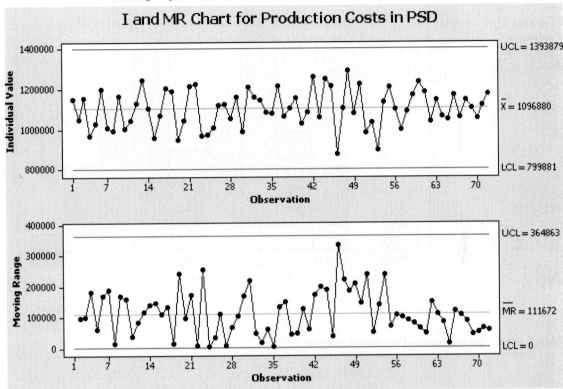

Figure 20.10 indicates that production costs are stable (with no special causes such as beyond a control limit or too many runs up and down) in the PSD with an average monthly cost of $1,096,880.00 and a standard deviation of $116,672 ($\overline{R}/d_2 = \$111,672/1.128$). Additionally, production costs are approximately normally distributed, as shown in Figure 20.11. Team members discover that PSD management considers monthly production costs to be very high given the volume of work being processed by the department.

The four potential Six Sigma projects shown in the last column of Table 20.3 are prioritized in Table 20.4, a matrix that weights the importance of each potential Six Sigma project to each of POI's business objectives.

The cell values are assigned by top management and are defined as follows: 0 = no relationship, 1 = weak relationship, 3 = moderate relationship, and 9 = strong relationship.

The Finance department develops the importance weights for each business objective to maximize the impact of Six Sigma projects on the bottom line of the organization. Consequently, the most critical project with respect to the business objectives is the MSD quality project, since the weighted average of 4.95 is higher than that of the other potential Six Sigma projects. The champion and the process owner of the MSD process prepare

FIGURE 20.11

Histogram of Monthly Production Costs in the PSD

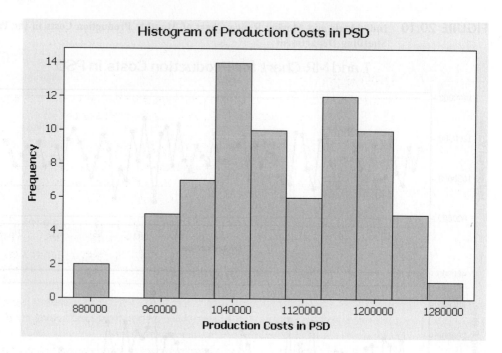

TABLE 20.4   **Prioritization of Six Sigma Projects**

Business Objective	Weight	New Customer Promotions Project	Existing Customer Promotions Project	MSD Quality Project	Employee Morale Project
		Potential Six Sigma Projects			
Increase the number of orders	0.35	3	3	0	0
Increase the number of POI services utilized by each customer	0.10	1	3	0	0
Minimize production costs	0.40	0	0	9	3
Eliminate employee complaints	0.15	0	0	9	9
Weighted average of potential Six Sigma projects		1.15	1.35	4.95	2.55

an initial project charter. It presents the business case for the MSD quality project to the members of the MSD quality project team.

Define Phase

The define phase has three components: prepare a business case with a project charter, do a SIPOC analysis, and conduct a voice of the customer analysis.

Prepare a Business Case with a Project Charter

Preparing a business case with a project charter requires team members to answer the following partially redundant questions; the redundancy in the questions helps team members distill the critical elements of the business case.

1. *What is the name of the process?* Answer: MSD purchasing process. The first step in the supply chain for the MSD process is the process for purchasing MSDs; hence, the first operation to be investigated by MSD quality project team members is the process for purchasing MSDs. Team members may study other factors that affect the quality of MSDs, such as method of use or shelf life, at a later time.

2. *What is the aim of the process?* Answer: The aim of the purchasing process as it relates to this project is to purchase MSDs that improve the productivity and morale of the employees in the Paper Shuffling department (PSD).

3. *What is the business case (economic rationale) for the project?* Question 3 is answered by addressing the following subquestions.

   a. *Why do the MSD project at all?* Answer: On the basis of a judgment sample of three employees and two managers from the PSD, team members determine that MSDs that cannot withstand four or more bends are unacceptable because they are unlikely to remain intact throughout the paper shuffling processes and will not hold papers tightly; this is called durability. Defective MSDs create costs for POI; for example, papers from different clients may get mixed together if not properly bound, requiring additional processing time; employees may have to use multiple MSDs for one project, creating additional material costs; and employees get frustrated and do not perform their jobs efficiently and productively, increasing labor costs. Additionally, team members discover that a large proportion of the boxes containing MSDs arrive to the PSD with five or more broken MSDs; this is called functionality. This creates additional processing costs for POI: for example, increased unit costs and frustrated and nonproductive employees and managers. Team members use the same judgment sample as above and determine that approximately 60 percent of individual MSDs do not meet durability criteria and 60 percent of MSD boxes do not meet functionality criteria, as shown in the survey questionnaire in Table 20.5 and the data matrix in Table 20.6.

   b. *Why do the MSD project now?* Answer: The Paper Shuffling department is experiencing very high monthly production costs, as shown in Figures 20.10 and 20.11. Also, internal customers, including managers and hourly employees, are submitting an increased number of complaints: 14 in the first quarter, 18 in the second quarter, and 32 in the third quarter, as recorded in the Purchasing department's complaint log for the fiscal year 2002. There are 100 hourly workers in the Paper Shuffling department.

TABLE 20.5
Survey
Questionnaire

Survey
Name: _____
1. Please estimate the percentage of MSDs that cannot withstand four or more bends. ____
2. Please estimate the percentage of MSD boxes that contain greater than five broken MSDs. ____

TABLE 20.6
Survey Data

Survey Number	Response Q1	Response Q2
1	55	70
2	50	55
3	60	65
4	65	60
5	70	50
Average	60	60

    c. What business objectives are supported by the MSD quality project? Answer: The MSD project is most strongly related to the "minimize production costs" and "eliminate employee complaints" business objectives, as shown in Table 20.4.

    d. What are the consequences of not doing the project? Answer: The consequences of not doing the project are decreased profit margins due to higher production costs and increased employee complaints due to frustration with materials.

    e. What projects have higher or equal priority? Answer: At this time, the MSD quality project has the highest priority, as shown in Table 20.4.

4. *What is the problem statement? What is the pain?* Answer: Low-quality MSDs create additional production costs and employee frustration.

5. *What is the goal, or desired state, for this project?* Answer: The champion and process owner of the MSD process initially determine that a 100-fold improvement in MSD quality (durability and functionality) should be the goal for the Six Sigma project. Note that a 100-fold improvement for this project is an arbitrary numerical goal and conflicts with Deming's 14 points for management, as discussed in Chapter 2 [see References 2, 3, and 4]. They derive the concept of a 100-fold improvement from Motorola's 1986 stated improvement rate of 10-fold every 2 years, or 100-fold every 4 years during the kickoff of the Six Sigma effort. Since a 100-fold improvement means the DPMO would decrease from 600,000 to 6,000, and a DPMO of 6210 represents a 4-sigma process, team members decide to use 4-sigma as the goal for the MSD project.

6. *What is the project scope?* Question 6 is answered by answering the following subquestions.

    a. What are the process boundaries? Answer: The starting point for the project is when the Purchasing department receives purchase orders from the PSD. The stopping point for the project is when the PSD places MSDs into inventory.

    b. What, if anything, is out-of-bounds? Answer: The project team cannot change the way employees handle or use MSDs.

    c. What resources are available for the project? Answer: The budget for the MSD project is $30,000.00. This includes estimated hourly salaries of project participants. The two team members are the only project participants who will incur additional

TABLE 20.7
Estimated
Labor Costs
for the Project

Position	Estimated Salary/Hour	Expected Number of Hours per Week	Expected Opportunity Costs for 21 Weeks	Expected Hard Costs for 21 Weeks (Direct Labor Costs)
Champion	$100	2	$4,200	
Process owner	$50	2	$2,100	
Black belt	$50	5	$5,250	
Team member	$25	10	$0	$5,250
Team member	$25	10	$0	$5,250
Finance representative	$45	2	$1,890	
IT representative	$50	2	$2,100	
Total			$15,540	$10,500

job responsibilities as a result of the project, as shown in Table 20.7, specifying both **opportunity costs** and **hard costs.** The estimated hard costs ($10,500) and total costs ($26,040) are less than the budget of $30,000.

d. *Who can approve expenditures?* Answer: Only the process owner can approve expenditures.

e. *How much can the team spend beyond $30,000.00 without seeking additional authority?* Answer: Nothing.

f. *What are the obstacles and constraints of the project?* Answer: The team must work within a $30,000 budget and a 21-week time constraint.

g. *What time commitment is expected of the team members?* Answer: Team members are expected to be present at weekly Friday morning meetings from 8:00 A.M. until 9:00 A.M. Team members are also expected to provide progress of project tasks at each meeting. Completion of project tasks may require additional hours of work per week.

h. *What will happen to each team member's regular job while he is working on the project?* Answer: Overtime hours, if any, will be compensated for team members and support staff. Note that the estimated rate for overtime labor is 1.5 times normal labor, and overtime labor is not included in the budget in Table 20.7.

i. *Is there a Gantt chart for the project?* Answer: A Gantt chart is shown in Table 20.8.

7. *What are the benefits of the project?* Answer: The soft benefits of the project include eliminating complaints from the Paper Shuffling department and increasing employee morale. The hard (financial) benefits of the project are minimizing labor costs and

TABLE 20.8   **Gantt Chart for the MSD Project**

Steps	Responsibility	1	2	3	4	5	6	7	8	9	10	11	12	13	14	15	16	17	18	19	20	21
Define	Black Belt	X	X	X	X	X	X															
Measure	Black Belt							X	X													
Analyze	Black Belt									X	X	X										
Improve	Black Belt												X	X	X	X	X	X				
Control	Black Belt																		X	X	X	X

TABLE 20.9
Labor Costs

100 employees in the Paper Shuffling department
× 40 hours/week/paper shuffling employee
× 10% of time devoted to clipping
@ 400 hours/week devoted to clipping in PSD
× $25/hour/paper shuffling employee
$10,000/week devoted to clipping
× 50 weeks/year
$500,000/year devoted to clipping
× 0.60 defective clips **(judgment sample estimate of durability of the current system).** Broken clips are not selected for use on jobs. This makes 0.6 a conservative estimate of the percentage of defective clips in the current system. Note: This conservative estimate does not include problems arising from defective clips not detected until after they have been used and have caused failure on the job.
$300,000/year on defective clipping for current system
× 0.0062 defective clips **(durability of the proposed system).** Again, broken clips are not selected for use on jobs.
$3,100/year on defective clipping for proposed system

material costs, estimated as follows:

The labor costs of the current and proposed systems are presented in Table 20.9.

Hence, the annual savings on labor costs from improving the MSD purchasing process is $296,900 ($300,000 − $3,100). The PSD incurs a 10 percent annual employee turnover. To capitalize on savings in labor costs, the department will now hire four new employees instead of ten new employees, for a savings of six full-time employees ($296,900/$25 = 11,876 hours; 11,876/40 hours per week/50 weeks per year = 5.938 ≈ 6 employees saved). Note that, alternatively, the PSD could now serve more customers with its current employee base.

The material costs of the current and proposed systems are shown in Table 20.10.

Hence, the annual savings on material costs from improving the MSD purchasing process is $44,820 ($75,000 − $30,180). This yields an annual total hard benefit savings of $341,720.00.

TABLE 20.10
Material Costs

100 employees in the Paper Shuffling department
× 60 projects/week/paper shuffling employee
× 50 weeks/year
@ 300,000 projects/year requiring 3,000,000 MSDs (10 clips per project on average)
× 0.60 defective clips (judgment sample estimate of current system).
7,500,000* clips must be used to complete 300,000 projects
× 0.01/clip
@ **$75,000/year on clips in current system**
× 0.0062 defective clips **(proposed system)**
3,018,000† clips must be used to complete 300,000 projects
× 0.01/clip
@ **$30,180/year on clips in proposed system**

*$1/(1 − 0.6) = 2.5$ clips needed to get a good clip. So, $3,000,000 × 2.5 = 7,500,000$.
†$1/(1 − 0.0062) = 1.006$ clips needed to get a good clip. So, $3,000,000 × 1.006 = 3,018,000$.

TABLE 20.11
Roles and
Responsibilities

Project Name: MSD Purchasing Process				
		Stakeholder		Supervisor's
Role	Responsibility	Signature	Date	Signature
Champion	Champion			
Process owner	Process owner			
Team leader	Black belt			
Team member 1	Team member 1			
Team member 2	Team member 2			
Finance representative	Finance representative			
IT representative	IT representative			

8. *What are the roles and responsibilities of team members?* Answer: The roles and responsibilities of team members are shown in Table 20.11.

Do a SIPOC Analysis

The second part of the define phase requires that team members perform a SIPOC analysis. Recall from the section "Define Phase" on page 743 that a SIPOC analysis is a simple tool for identifying the Suppliers and their Inputs into a Process, the high-level steps of a process, the Outputs of the process, and the Customer segments interested in the outputs. A SIPOC analysis of POI's Purchasing department is shown in Figure 20.12.

Conduct a Voice of the Customer Analysis

The third part of the define phase involves team members collecting and analyzing voice of the customer data, verbal or written information collected from a sample of users, in a selected market segment. The questionnaire used to collect data from users of MSDs in the PSD is shown in Table 20.12.

Team members analyze the voice of the customer data by market segment, as shown in column 1 of Table 20.13. Next, they use all the raw voice of the customer data points, shown in column 2 of Table 20.13, to create **affinity diagram** themes, discussed in Chapter 10, called **focus points,** shown as boldface numbers linking columns 2 and 3 in column 3 of Table 20.13. Next, team members identify the engineering issues underlying each focus point, called **cognitive issues,** shown in column 4 of Table 20.13. Team members then convert each cognitive issue into one or more quantitative engineering variables, called critical-to-quality (CTQ) variables, as shown in column 5 of Table 20.13. Finally, team members develop technical specifications for each CTQ, as shown in column 6 of Table 20.13.

Returning to the first part of the define phase, team members can now define the project's objectives.

Project Objective 1: Decrease (*direction*) the percentage of MSDs that cannot withstand four or more bends without breaking (*measure*) bought by the Purchasing department (*process*) to 00.62 percent (*goal*) by January 1, 2005 (*deadline*). Go for 4-sigma!

Project Objective 2: Decrease (*direction*) the percentage of boxes of MSDs with more than five broken clips (*measure*) bought by the Purchasing department (*process*) to 00.62 percent (*goal*) by January 1, 2005 (*deadline*). Go for 4-sigma!

FIGURE 20.12
SIPOC Analysis

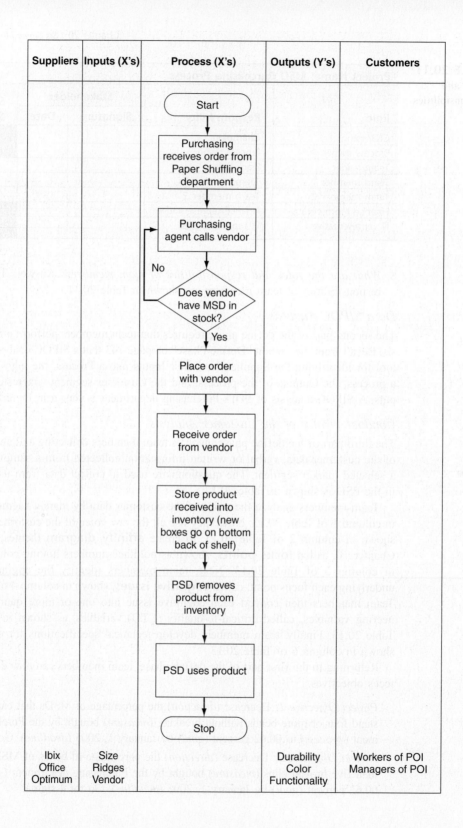

Suppliers	Inputs (X's)	Process (X's)	Outputs (Y's)	Customers
		Start		
		Purchasing receives order from Paper Shuffling department		
		Purchasing agent calls vendor		
		Does vendor have MSD in stock?		
		Place order with vendor		
		Receive order from vendor		
		Store product received into inventory (new boxes go on bottom back of shelf)		
		PSD removes product from inventory		
		PSD uses product		
		Stop		
Ibix Office Optimum	Size Ridges Vendor		Durability Color Functionality	Workers of POI Managers of POI

TABLE 20.12
Voice of the
Customer
Questionnaire

Questions
What emotions come to mind when you think about MSDs?
What needs and wants come to mind when you think about MSDs?
What complaints or problems would you like to mention about MSDs?

Note: These questions do not consider the opinions, feelings, and attitudes of the upstream, downstream, and external customers of the PSD.

TABLE 20.13   Analysis Table for Voice of the Customer Data

1	2	3	4	5	6
Selected Market Segment	Raw "Voice of the Customer" Data	Affinity Diagram Theme (Focus Point)	Engineering Issue (Cognitive Issue)	CTQ	Tech Specs
Paper organizing managers		Variation in durability 1	Durability	Ability to withstand bending	≥ 4 bends without breaking
	"My employees are frustrated about the MSDs. They complain that they break too fast." **1 & 2**	Variation in color 2	Color	The number of different MSD colors	= 1 color of MSDs
	"My employees are complaining that the MSDs are not holding up during the organizing process." **1**	Variation in functionality 3	Functionality	The number of broken MSDs in a box	≤ 5 broken MSDs in a box
	"The employees are also complaining that the color of the MSDs changes from one day to the next. It seems to be confusing them." **2**				
	"My employees are very unhappy with the purple and blue MSDs. They would prefer only one color of MSDs be used consistently." **2**				
	"My employees say that more than 5 MSDs per box arrive broken." **3**				
	"I've heard from numerous employees that the MSDs coming straight from inventory are already broken." **3**				
	. . .				
Hourly employees					
	"The MSDs are falling apart before we are ready to file the papers into binders. An MSD should be able to take at least 4 bends." **1**				
	"The MSDs aren't helping us to do our work efficiently." **1 & 2**				

(continued)

TABLE 20.13   (concluded)

1	2	3	4	5	6
	"I would prefer if we only used one color of MSDs." **2**				
	"I don't understand why we use different colors of MSDs." **2**				
	"The MSDs just break when trying to bend them over the paper stacks. They should take at least 4 bends" **1**				
	"It is very frustrating when you open a brand new box of MSDs and find that more than 5 of the clips are already broken." **3**				
	"It is very time consuming to sift out the broken MSDs from a brand new box coming straight from inventory." **3**				

A correlation exists between the project objectives. A broken MSD cannot withstand four or more bends because it is already broken. Improving the percentage of functional MSDs per box will increase the percentage of MSDs that can withstand four or more bends.

Measure Phase

The measure phase has three steps: operationally define the CTQs, perform a gage R&R study on each CTQ, and develop a baseline for each CTQ.

Operationally Define the CTQs

Team members operationally define durability and functionality by establishing criteria for durability and functionality, developing a test for each set of criteria, and formulating a decision rule for each criteria.

Operational definition for CTQ1: Durability.   *Criteria* for a selected MSD can be seen in Figure 20.13.

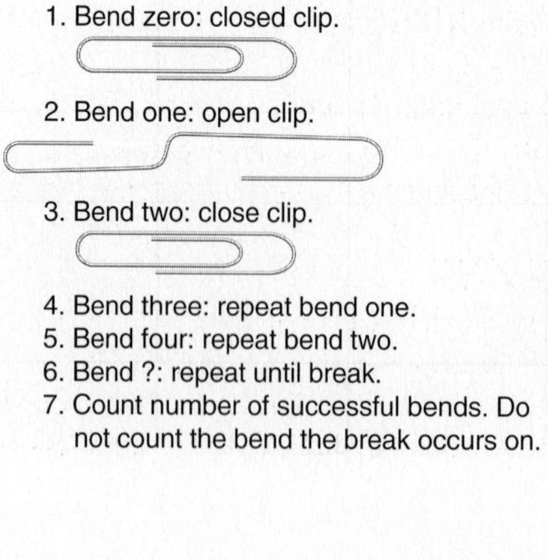

Test for a selected MSD:

1. Select the "top-front" box of MSDs on the shelf in the inventory room.
2. Close your eyes, then open the box of MSDs, then randomly select one intact MSD. No switching is allowed.
3. Utilize the criteria for the selected MSD.
4. Count the number of bends until breaking.

FIGURE 20.13
Criteria for Number of Bends of an MSD

1. Bend zero: closed clip.
2. Bend one: open clip.
3. Bend two: close clip.
4. Bend three: repeat bend one.
5. Bend four: repeat bend two.
6. Bend ?: repeat until break.
7. Count number of successful bends. Do not count the bend the break occurs on.

Decision for a selected MSD:

If the number of bends is ≥ 4, then MSD is conforming.

If the number of bends is < 4, then MSD is defective.

Operational definition for CTQ2: Functionality.   *Criteria* for a box of MSDs: Count the number of "broken" clips. A clip is "broken" if it is in two pieces, regardless of the relative sizes of the pieces. Clips can be broken only into two pieces.

Test for a box of MSDs:

1. Select the "top-front" box of MSDs on the shelf in the inventory room.
2. Count the number of "broken" clips.

Decision for a box of MSDs:

If the number of MSDs that are broken ≤ 5, then the box of MSDs is conforming.

If the number of MSDs that are broken > 5, then the box of MSDs is defective.

The same box of MSDs is used for both operational definitions.

Perform a Gage R&R Study on Each CTQ

Team members conduct an attribute gage R&R (repeatability and reproducibility) study on the measurement system of each CTQ to determine if it is adequate for the needs of the project. The measurement of durability requires a destructive test; hence, a simple gage R&R study was not done for durability at this time. In the near future, an operational definition of the testing process for durability will be established and testing will be audited to assure consistency. The measurement system for functionality is studied using the following sampling plan:

1. A shelf in the storage area contains boxes of MSDs purchased throughout the week. There are different types of MSD boxes in the storage area (different vendors, sizes, etc.).
2. The gage R&R study required two inspectors to sample the same 10 boxes of MSDs twice.
3. The top 10 boxes on the front of the shelf were selected for the gage R&R study.
4. The study is repeated as is deemed necessary by PSD management.

Two PSD managers have the responsibility of inspecting the MSDs for functionality; they are called inspector 1 and inspector 2. Both inspectors count the number of defective MSDs, twice, in random order. The functionality data are shown in Table 20.14, but not in random order (see ✿ GAGER&R).

A **gage run chart** shows that there is no variation within inspectors or between inspectors, as shown in Figure 20.14. All the variation is between the 10 boxes of MSDs. Hence, the measurement system is acceptable to measure functionality.

Develop a Baseline for Each CTQ

Team members conduct a study, as part of routine business, to determine the baseline capability for each CTQ. At the beginning of each hour, one box of MSDs is selected from the storage area. The procedure for selecting a box of MSDs is simply to select the top- and front-most box on the shelf. The selection process is not altered

TABLE 20.14
Gage R&R
Data for
Functionality

Box	Inspector	Count	Functionality
1	1	1	10
1	1	2	10
1	2	1	10
1	2	2	10
2	1	1	9
2	1	2	9
2	2	1	9
2	2	2	9
3	1	1	5
3	1	2	5
3	2	1	5
3	2	2	5
4	1	1	4
4	1	2	4
4	2	1	4
4	2	2	4
5	1	1	5
5	1	2	5
5	2	1	5
5	2	2	5
6	1	1	9
6	1	2	9
6	2	1	9
6	2	2	9
7	1	1	6
7	1	2	6
7	2	1	6
7	2	2	6
8	1	1	6
8	1	2	6
8	2	1	6
8	2	2	6
9	1	1	9
9	1	2	9
9	2	1	9
9	2	2	9
10	1	1	11
10	1	2	11
10	2	1	11
10	2	2	11

during a sampling period of two 8-hour shifts. Baseline capability data are shown in Table 20.15.

The yields for durability and functionality are both 0.375, as determined by the number of tests out of 16 trials shown in Table 20.15 that met their respective CTQs (that is, at least four bends for durability and no more than five broken MSDs per box for functionality). This indicates very poor levels of durability and functionality for the

FIGURE 20.14 Gage Run Chart for Functionality (Number of Defective MSDs in a Box)

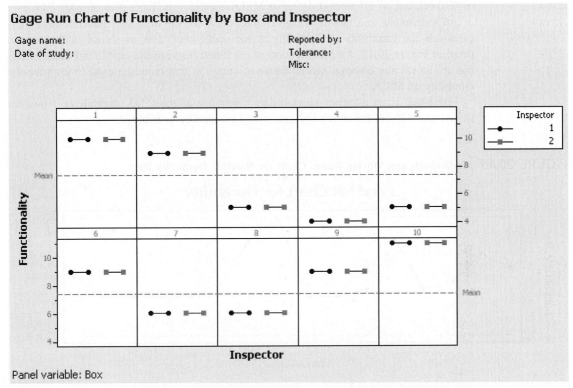

Panel variable: Box

TABLE 20.15
Baseline Capability Data

Hour	Durability	Functionality
Shift 1—Hour 1	5	12
Shift 1—Hour 2	7	4
Shift 1—Hour 3	3	8
Shift 1—Hour 4	2	6
Shift 1—Hour 5	9	1
Shift 1—Hour 6	2	5
Shift 1—Hour 7	1	11
Shift 1—Hour 8	1	9
Shift 2—Hour 1	12	6
Shift 2—Hour 2	9	6
Shift 2—Hour 3	3	9
Shift 2—Hour 4	1	5
Shift 2—Hour 5	1	4
Shift 2—Hour 6	1	5
Shift 2—Hour 7	1	9
Shift 2—Hour 8	4	10
Yield	6/16 = 0.375	6/16 = 0.375

MSDs received into the Paper Shuffling department and supports the initial yield estimates of 40.0 percent, or 60 percent defective MSDs, as shown in Table 20.6 on page 744.

An individuals and moving range (I-MR) chart for the durability baseline data indicates that the variability of durability is not stable over time, as shown in the bottom panel of Figure 20.15. An investigation of the range between the eighth and ninth MSDs did not reveal any obvious special cause of variation that could be used to improve the durability of MSDs.

The I-MR chart assumes approximate normality of the CTQ (durability). However, from Figure 20.16, the durability data are not normally distributed.

FIGURE 20.15 Individuals and Moving Range Chart for Baseline Durability Data

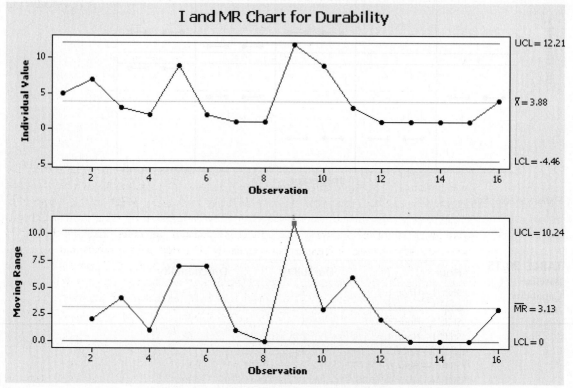

FIGURE 20.16
Dotplot of Baseline Durability Data

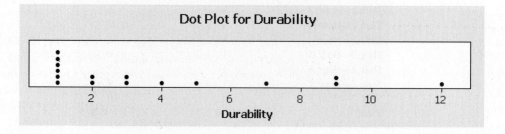

**FIGURE
20.17**
c Chart for
Durability

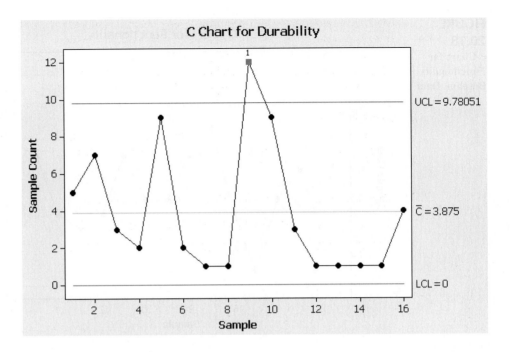

Hence, use of the durability I-MR chart is not advised at this time. However, the distribution of durability may approximate a Poisson distribution. Consequently, team members construct a c chart for the count of bends before each MSD breaks, as shown in Figure 20.17. This indicates a possible special cause during Shift 2—Hour 1 when 12 bends were observed for the durability test. Further investigation and notes related to the test do not reveal any obvious differences between the MSD tested and the others, although during the first hour the tester indicates that he may have bent the MSD more slowly than usual during the test, which may have caused less stress and consequently more bends.

A c chart for functionality, shown in Figure 20.18, indicates stability over time.

The functionality data appear to be approximately Poisson distributed as shown in Figure 20.19.

Hence, use of the functionality c chart is acceptable at this time. Finally, team members estimate the current process performance for each CTQ in Table 20.16.

Notice the desired 100-fold improvement shown in the DPMO columns (current = 625,000 and desired = 6,210). This is consistent with the goals stated in question 5 of the define phase of the DMAIC model.

Analyze Phase

The analyze phase has five steps: develop a more detailed process map (that is, more detailed than the process map developed in the SIPOC analysis of the define phase), construct operational definitions for each input or process variable (called x's), perform a gage R&R study on each x (test the adequacy of the measurement system), develop a baseline for each x, and develop hypotheses between the x's and y's. The y's are the output measures used to determine if the CTQs are met.

**FIGURE
20.18**
c Chart for
Functionality
Baseline Data

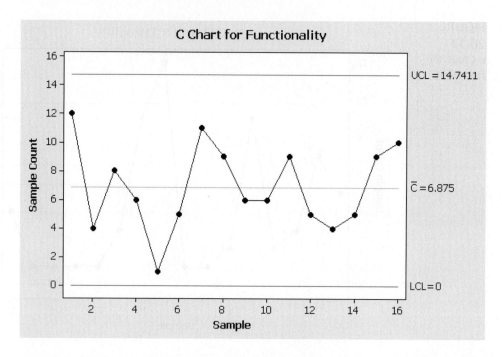

C Chart for Functionality

UCL = 14.7411
$\bar{C}$ = 6.875
LCL = 0

**FIGURE
20.19**
Dotplot for
Functionality
Baseline Data

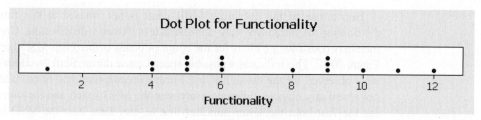

Dot Plot for Functionality

TABLE 20.16
Current
Process
Performance
for CTQs

CTQs	Yield		DPMO		Process Sigma	
	Current	Desired	Current	Desired	Current	Desired
Durability	37.50%	99.38%	625,000	6,210	~1.2	4.0
Functionality	37.50%	99.38%	625,000	6,210	~1.2	4.0

Develop a Detailed Process Map

Team members prepare a detailed process map identifying and linking the x's and y's, as shown in Figure 20.20.

Note that some Six Sigma project teams identify the x's in the measure phase of the DMAIC model. This is done when the x's have been defined and monitored prior to the start of the Six Sigma project through an organizational metrics tracking system. If the x's and CTQs were not defined and monitored prior to the start of the project, then the x's are monitored and analyzed in the analyze phase, as is the situation in this case study.

**FIGURE
20.20**
**Process Map
Linking CTQs
and x's for
the MSD
Purchasing
Process**

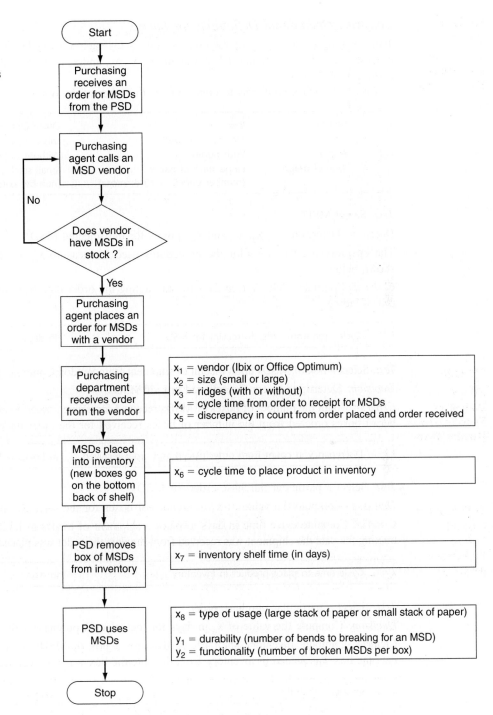

Construct Operational Definitions for Each x

Team members develop an operational definition for each x variable identified on the process map. The operational definitions for x_1, x_2, x_3, and x_8 relate to individual MSDs and are shown below.

Criteria: Each x conforms to either one or the other of the options.

x_1	Vendor	Ibix	Office Optimum
x_2	Size	Small (stock size)	Large (stock size)
x_3	Ridges	With ridges	Without ridges
x_8	Type of usage	Large stack of paper (number papers is 10 or more)	Small stack of paper (number papers is 9 or less)

Test: Select MSD.

Decision: Determine x_1, x_2, x_3, and x_8 options for the selected MSD.

The operational definitions for the procedures used to measure x_4, x_5, x_6, and x_7 are shown below.

Criteria: Compute cycle time in days by subtracting the order date from the date on the bill of lading.

x_4	Cycle time from order to receipt for MSDs	In days

Test: Select a box of MSDs upon receipt of shipment from vendor. Compute the cycle time.

Decision: Determine x_4 for the selected box of MSDs.

Criteria: Count the number of boxes of MSDs received for a given order. Subtract the number of boxes ordered from the number of boxes received for the order under study.

x_5	Discrepancy in count from order placed and order received	In boxes of MSDs by order

Test: Select a particular purchase order for MSDs.

Decision: Compute the value of x_5 in number of boxes for the selected purchase order.

Criteria: Compute cycle time in days to place a shipment of MSDs in inventory by subtracting the date the shipment was received from the date the order was placed in inventory.

x_6	Cycle time to place product in inventory	In days

Test: Select a particular purchase order.

Decision: Compute the value of x_6 in days for the selected purchase order.

Criteria: Compute inventory shelf life in days for a box of MSDs by subtracting the date the box was placed in inventory from the date the box was removed from inventory.

x_7	Inventory shelf life	In days

Test: Select a box of MSDs.

Decision: Compute the value of x_7 in days for the selected box of MSDs.

Perform a Gage R&R Study on Each x

Team members conduct gage R&R (reliability and reproducibility) studies for the x's. Recall that the purpose of a gage R&R study is to determine the adequacy of the measurement system for an x. In the MSD case, the gage R&R studies, not shown here, are satisfactory for all the x's.

Collect Baseline Data for Each x

Team members collect baseline data for each of the x's. Team members gather baseline data on durability (y_1) and functionality (y_2), and relevant x's using the following sampling plan: for a two-week period the first box of MSDs brought to the PSD each hour is selected as a sample; this yields a sample of 80 boxes of MSDs, as shown in Table 20.17 (see ❧ DATAMINING). For each sampled box, team members determine the durability (y_1) and functionality (y_2) measurements. Furthermore, they collect information concerning the vendor (x_1), size of the MSD (x_2), whether or not the MSD has ridges (x_3), and inventory shelf life (x_7). Note that the Purchasing department will separately study cycle time from order to receipt of order (x_4), discrepancy between ordered and received box counts (x_5), and cycle time from receipt of order to placement in inventory (x_6). These last factors may influence such concerns as choice of vendor, ordering procedures, and inventory control, but they do not impact durability and functionality. Furthermore, the MSDs are not tested after they are used so the type of usage (x_8) is not studied here. As indicated in the define phase, certain variables (e.g., x_4, x_5, x_6, and x_8) can be addressed in subsequent green belt projects.

The baseline data reveal that the yield for durability is 0.4625 (37/80) and the yield for functionality is 0.425 (34/80), as shown in Table 20.18. As before, this indicates very poor levels for the CTQs in the Paper Shuffling department. For comparison purposes, recall that the judgment sample carried out by the team during the define phase shows that the yield is approximately 40 percent (that is, the team assumed the failure rate was approximately 60 percent) for both durability and functionality. The slightly increased yields in this study can be due to natural variation in the process. The baseline data also show that 56.25 percent of all MSDs are from Office Optimum (x_1), 42.50 percent of MSDs are small (x_2), 50.00 percent of all MSDs are without ridges (x_3), and the average shelf time for boxes of MSDs (x_7) is 6.5 days, with a standard deviation of 2.5 days, as shown in Table 20.18.

Develop Hypotheses Relating the x's and y's (CTQs)

Team members develop hypotheses $(y = f(x))$ about the relationships between the x's and the y's in order to identify the x's that are critical to improving the center, spread, and shape of the y's with respect to customer specifications. This is accomplished through **data mining,** a method used to analyze passive data, that is, data that are collected as a consequence of running a process. In this case, the baseline data in Table 20.17 are the passive data set that will be subject to data mining procedures. Dotplots or boxplots of durability (y_1) and functionality (y_2) stratified by x_1, x_2, x_3, and x_7 can be used to generate some hypotheses about main effects (the individual effects of each x on y_1 and y_2). Interaction plots can be used to generate hypotheses about interaction effects (those effects on y_1 or y_2 for which the influence of one x variable depends on the level or value of another x variable) if all combinations of levels of x variables are studied. If all

TABLE 20.17 Baseline Data

Sample	Day	Hour	x_1	x_2	x_3	x_7	Durability	Function
1	Mon	1	1	0	0	7	2	5
2	Mon	2	0	1	0	7	2	9
3	Mon	3	0	0	1	7	10	7
4	Mon	4	0	1	0	7	1	4
5	Mon	5	0	0	0	7	7	3
6	Mon	6	0	1	1	7	2	5
7	Mon	7	0	1	1	7	1	9
8	Mon	8	0	0	0	7	7	5
9	Tue	1	0	1	0	8	2	8
10	Tue	2	0	1	0	8	1	7
11	Tue	3	0	1	0	8	1	13
12	Tue	4	1	1	1	8	9	5
13	Tue	5	1	1	0	8	9	9
14	Tue	6	1	1	1	8	10	11
15	Tue	7	1	1	1	8	10	11
16	Tue	8	0	0	1	8	8	9
17	Wed	1	1	1	1	9	8	11
18	Wed	2	1	0	0	9	1	11
19	Wed	3	1	1	1	9	10	11
20	Wed	4	0	0	0	9	7	11
21	Wed	5	1	1	1	9	9	9
22	Wed	6	0	0	1	9	9	5
23	Wed	7	1	0	1	9	2	11
24	Wed	8	1	0	0	9	1	10
25	Thu	1	1	0	1	10	1	14
26	Thu	2	0	1	1	10	1	10
27	Thu	3	1	1	1	10	8	13
28	Thu	4	0	0	1	10	10	12
29	Thu	5	0	0	0	10	7	14
30	Thu	6	0	1	1	10	3	13
31	Thu	7	0	0	0	10	9	13
32	Thu	8	1	1	1	10	8	11
33	Fri	1	0	1	0	1	2	0
34	Fri	2	0	1	0	1	2	1
35	Fri	3	0	1	0	1	1	6
36	Fri	4	0	1	0	1	3	3
37	Fri	5	0	1	0	1	2	2
38	Fri	6	1	1	0	1	10	6
39	Fri	7	0	0	1	1	10	0
40	Fri	8	0	1	0	1	2	0
41	Mon	1	0	1	1	4	3	4
42	Mon	2	0	1	0	4	3	7

TABLE 20.17   (concluded)

Sample	Day	Hour	x_1	x_2	x_3	x_7	Durability	Function
43	Mon	3	0	1	1	4	3	3
44	Mon	4	0	0	0	4	10	2
45	Mon	5	1	1	0	4	8	5
46	Mon	6	0	1	1	4	3	4
47	Mon	7	1	0	0	4	1	4
48	Mon	8	0	0	1	4	10	5
49	Tue	1	1	1	1	5	11	6
50	Tue	2	1	0	1	5	3	4
51	Tue	3	1	1	0	5	10	6
52	Tue	4	1	0	1	5	3	5
53	Tue	5	1	0	0	5	2	4
54	Tue	6	0	0	0	5	9	5
55	Tue	7	0	0	1	5	9	5
56	Tue	8	0	1	0	5	3	7
57	Wed	1	0	0	1	6	9	5
58	Wed	2	1	1	0	6	9	7
59	Wed	3	0	0	0	6	9	5
60	Wed	4	1	0	0	6	2	6
61	Wed	5	1	0	1	6	2	5
62	Wed	6	1	1	1	6	10	5
63	Wed	7	0	1	0	6	1	7
64	Wed	8	0	1	0	6	2	5
65	Thu	1	0	0	1	7	10	7
66	Thu	2	1	1	0	7	9	5
67	Thu	3	1	0	0	7	1	7
68	Thu	4	0	1	0	7	2	5
69	Thu	5	1	0	1	7	1	6
70	Thu	6	0	1	0	7	1	5
71	Thu	7	1	0	0	7	1	8
72	Thu	8	1	1	1	7	10	5
73	Fri	1	0	1	1	8	3	7
74	Fri	2	1	1	1	8	9	7
75	Fri	3	1	0	0	8	1	13
76	Fri	4	0	1	1	8	2	8
77	Fri	5	0	1	1	8	3	9
78	Fri	6	1	1	1	8	8	10
79	Fri	7	1	0	1	8	3	11
80	Fri	8	0	0	1	8	10	11

Legend:
x_1 = vendor (0 = Office Optimum and 1 = Ibix)
x_2 = size (0 = small and 1 = large)
x_3 = ridges (0 = without and 1 = with)
x_7 = inventory shelf time, in days

TABLE 20.18
Basic Statistics on Baseline Data

Variable		Proportion	Mean	Standard Deviation
y_1: Durability	4 or more bends/clip	0.4625	5.213	3.703
y_2: Functionality	5 or fewer broken/box	0.4250	7.025	3.438
x_1: Vendor	0 = Office Optimum	0.5625		
	1 = Ibix	0.4375		
x_2: Size	0 = small	0.4250		
	1 = large	0.5750		
x_3: Ridges	0 = without ridges	0.5000		
	1 = with ridges	0.5000		
x_7: Inventory shelf life	Shelf life in days		6.5000	2.5160

FIGURE 20.21
Dotplot for Durability by x_1 (Vendor)

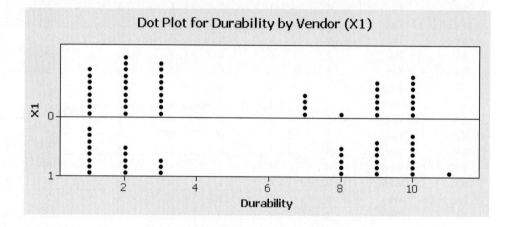

Dot Plot for Durability by Vendor (X1)

FIGURE 20.22
Dotplot for Durability by x_2 (Size)

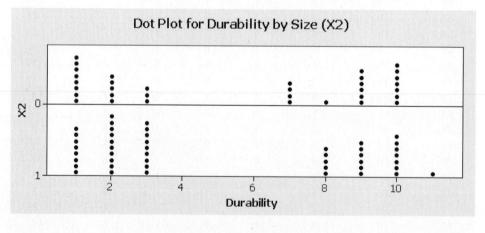

Dot Plot for Durability by Size (X2)

combinations of levels of x variables are not studied, then often interaction effects are not discovered. Frequently, screening designs are utilized to uncover interaction effects.

Team members construct dotplots from the baseline data in Table 20.17 to check if any of the x's, or main effects, impact durability (y_1) and functionality (y_2). The dotplots for durability are shown in Figures 20.21 through 20.24. The dotplots for functionality are shown in Figures 20.25 through 20.28.

**FIGURE
20.23**
**Dotplot for
Durability by
x_3 (Ridges)**

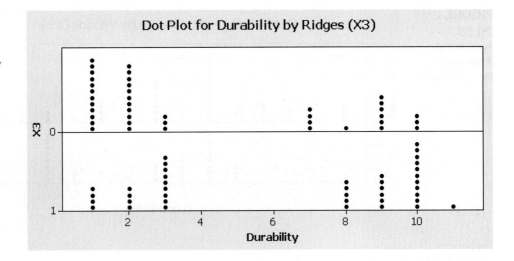

**FIGURE
20.24**
**Dotplot for
Durability by
x_7 (Shelf Life)**

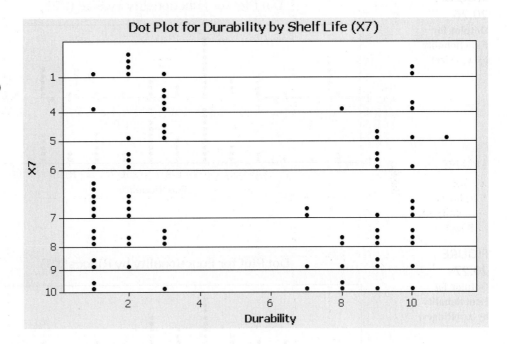

The dotplots for durability (y_1) indicate: (1) the values of durability tend to be low or high with a significant gap between 4 and 6 for x_1, x_2, x_3, and x_7, and (2) the variation in durability is about the same for all levels of x_1, x_2, x_3, and x_7. The dotplots for functionality (y_2) indicate: (1) the values of functionality tend to be lower when $x_1 = 0$ than when $x_1 = 1$, (2) the variation in functionality is about the same for all levels of x_2 and x_3, and (3) the values of functionality tend to be lower for low values of x_7.

**FIGURE
20.25**
Dotplot for
Functionality
by x_1 (Vendor)

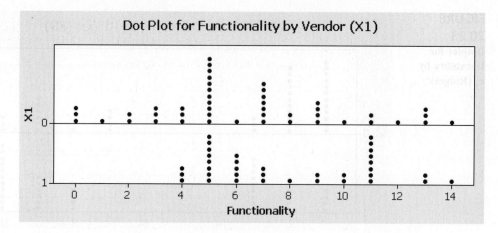

**FIGURE
20.26**
Dotplot for
Functionality
by x_2 (Size)

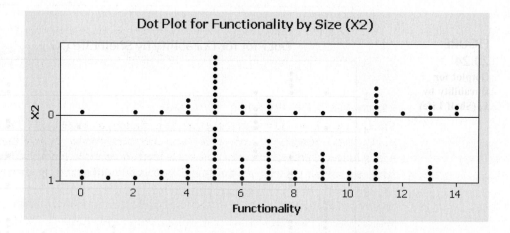

**FIGURE
20.27**
Dotplot for
Functionality
by x_3 (Ridges)

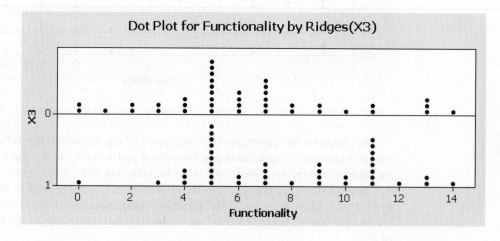

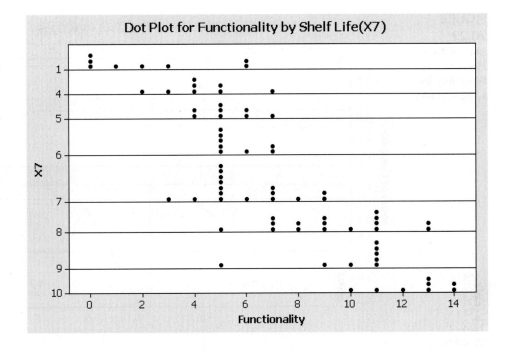

FIGURE 20.28
Dotplot for Functionality by x_7 (Shelf Life)

Discussion of the Analysis of Durability

Since there are no clear differences in the variation, or spread, of durability for each of the levels of x_1, x_2, x_3, and x_7, the team members wonder if there might be differences in the average, or center, for each level of the individual x's. Team members construct a main effects plot for durability to study differences in averages, as shown in Figure 20.29.

Figure 20.29 indicates that for the range of shelf lives observed there is no clear pattern for the relationship of shelf life (x_7) to the average durability. On the other hand, it appears that ridges $(x_3 = 1)$ has a positive relationship to the average durability. At first glance it would seem that the better results for the average durability are seen when the vendor Ibix is chosen using small MSDs $(x_1 = 1$ and $x_2 = 0)$, while using large MSDs from Office Optimum $(x_1 = 0$ and $x_2 = 1)$ yields worse results.

In the discussion of the dotplots and main effects plot, it was suggested that it is dangerous to come to any conclusions without knowing if there are interaction effects. As discussed in Chapter 12, an interaction effect is present when the amount of change introduced by changing one of the x's depends on the value of another x. In that case, it is misleading to choose the best value of the x's individually without first considering the interactions between the x's. Consequently, team members did an interactions plot for x_1, x_2, and x_3. x_7 was not included in the interactions plot because the main effects plot indicated no clear pattern or relationship with durability (y_1). All combinations of levels of the x variables must be present to draw an interactions plot. This is often not the case with passive data (that is, no plan was put in place to ensure that all combinations were observed in the data gathering phase). Fortunately, although not all combinations were observed equally, often they were all present. Figure 20.30 is the interaction plot for durability.

FIGURE 20.29
Main Effects Plot for Durability by x_1, x_2, x_3, and x_7

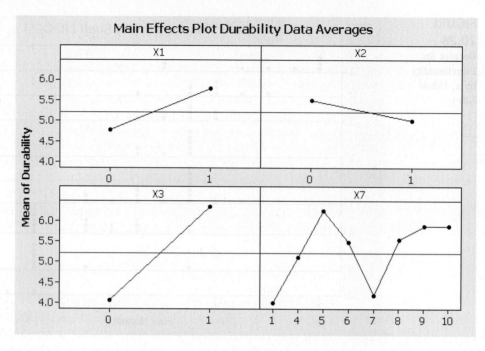

FIGURE 20.30
Interaction Effects Plot for Durability by x_1, x_2, and x_3

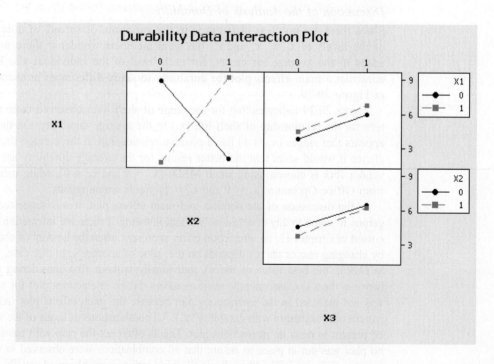

Interestingly, the interaction plot indicates that there is a possible interaction between x_1 (vendor) and x_2 (size). We know that when there is no interaction, the lines should be parallel to each other, indicating that the amount of change in average durability when moving from one level of each x variable to another level should be the same for all values of another x variable. This plot shows the lines on the graph of x_1 and x_2 are not parallel. The average durability is the highest when either large Ibix MSDs ($x_1 = 1$ and $x_2 = 1$) or small Office Optimum MSDs ($x_1 = 0$ and $x_2 = 0$) are used. This means the choice of vendor may depend on the size of MSD required. The main effects plot suggests that the best results for average durability would occur when small MSDs from Ibix are used, but the interactions plot suggests this combination would yield a bad average durability. In order to study all this further, the team decides that during the improve phase they will run a full factorial design to examine the relationship of x_1, x_2, and x_3 on durability (y_1) since the main effects plot indicates potential patterns. Again, there does not appear to be a relationship between durability (y_1) and x_7.

Discussion of the Analysis of Functionality

Figures 20.31 and 20.32 represent the main effects and interaction effects plots, respectively, for functionality (y_2).

The main effects plot indicates that higher values of shelf life (x_7) yield higher values for functionality (y_2). The team surmises that the longer a box of MSDs sits in inventory (that is, higher values of shelf life), the higher the count of broken MSDs (that is, functionality will be high). From a practical standpoint, the team feels comfortable with this conclusion. They decide the Purchasing department should put a Six Sigma project in place to investigate whether the potential benefit of either a "just in time" MSD ordering process or establishing better inventory handling procedures will solve the problem.

FIGURE 20.31
Main Effects Plot for Functionality by x_1, x_2, x_3, and x_7

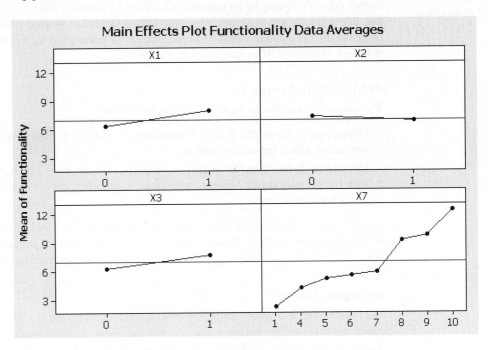

FIGURE 20.32

Interaction Effects Plot for Functionality by x_1, x_2, and x_3

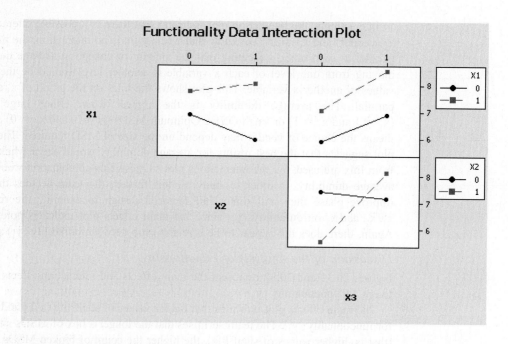

The interaction effects plot indicates a potential interaction between x_2 (size) and x_3 (ridges). The better results for functionality (that is, low values) are observed for large MSDs without ridges ($x_2 = 1$ and $x_3 = 0$). The reason for this will need to be studied further. Also, there may be an interaction between x_1 (vendor) and x_2 (size), but it appears that better results are observed whenever Office Optimum is used (that is, $x_1 = 0$). In other words, the average count of broken MSDs is lower (that is, functionality average is lower) whenever Office Optimum is the vendor.

Analyze Phase Summary

The analyze phase results in the following hypotheses:

Hypothesis 1: durability = $f(x_1 = \text{vendor}, x_2 = \text{size}, x_3 = \text{ridges})$ with a strong interaction effect between x_1 and x_2.

Hypothesis 2: functionality = $f(x_1 = \text{vendor}, x_2 = \text{size}, x_3 = \text{ridges}, x_7 = \text{shelf life})$ with the primary driver being x_7 with some main effect due to x_1 and an interaction effect between x_2 and x_3.

x_7 is the main driver of the distribution of functionality (y_2) and is under the control of the employees of POI. Hence, team members restructure hypothesis 2 as follows: functionality = $f(x_1 = \text{vendor}, x_2 = \text{size}, x_3 = \text{ridges})$ for each fixed level of x_7 (shelf life).

Improve Phase

The improve phase involves designing experiments, as discussed in Chapter 12, to understand the relationship between the y's and the vital x's and major noise variables, generating the actions needed to implement the levels of the vital few x's that optimize the shape, spread, and center of the distributions of the y's, developing action plans, and conducting pilot tests of the action plans.

Conduct Experiments

Team members conduct an experimental design to determine the effect of x_1 (vendor), x_2 (size), and x_3 (ridges), and their interactions, on the y's with $x_7 = 0$ (no shelf life—MSDs are tested immediately upon arrival to POI before they are placed in inventory). A 2^3 **full factorial design** with 2 replications (8 trials) is performed for durability and functionality. The factor conditions for vendor (x_1) are Office Optimum (-1) or Ibix (1); the factor conditions for size are "small" (-1) or "large" (1), and the factor conditions for ridges (x_3) are "without ridges" (-1) or "with ridges" (1). The experiment is set up in two blocks to increase experimental reliability, with the first 8 runs conducted in the morning and the second 8 runs conducted in the afternoon. The runs are randomized within each block. The purpose of the blocks and randomization is to help prevent lurking (background) variables that are related to time, such as time of day and order in which data are collected, from confusing the results. Additional information can be gathered since 16 trials were run, rather than the minimum of 8 trials, especially regarding potential interactions. The data from the 2^3 full factorial design, with 2 replications in run order with the first 8 runs constituting the first replicate, are shown in Table 20.19 (see ❂ FACTORIAL).

Pareto charts, discussed in Chapter 10, showing which of the vital few x's and the interactions between them have a statistically significant effect on durability (y_1) and functionality (y_2) at the 10 percent level of significance, can be seen in Figures 20.33 and 20.34, respectively.

The major effects (that is, those that have significance level less than 0.10, or confidence level over 90 percent) for durability are the interaction of vendor and size and the main effect due to ridges. There are no significant effects due to vendor, size, or ridges

TABLE 20.19   Durability and Functionality Data

Standard Order	Run Order	Vendor	Size	Ridges	Durability	Functionality
2	1	Ibix	Small	Without	1	8
4	2	Ibix	Large	Without	9	9
3	3	Office Optimum	Large	Without	1	8
8	4	Ibix	Large	With	11	8
5	5	Office Optimum	Small	With	10	0
6	6	Ibix	Small	With	4	2
7	7	Office Optimum	Large	With	4	3
1	8	Office Optimum	Small	Without	10	2
16	9	Ibix	Large	With	9	3
10	10	Ibix	Small	Without	3	0
12	11	Ibix	Large	Without	9	0
14	12	Ibix	Small	With	3	7
13	13	Office Optimum	Small	With	9	6
11	14	Office Optimum	Large	Without	2	4
9	15	Office Optimum	Small	Without	8	1
15	16	Office Optimum	Large	With	2	4

**FIGURE
20.33**
**Pareto Chart
of Effects for
Durability**

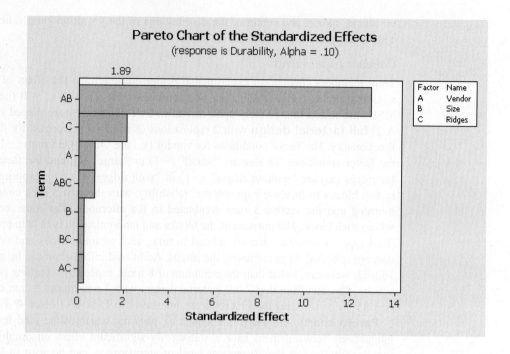

**FIGURE
20.34**
**Pareto Chart
of Effects for
Functionality**

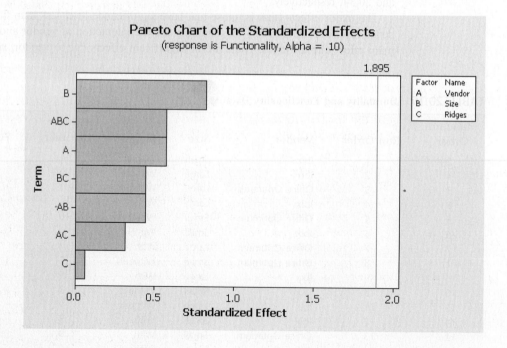

FIGURE 20.35
Interaction Effect Plot for Vendor and Size for Durability

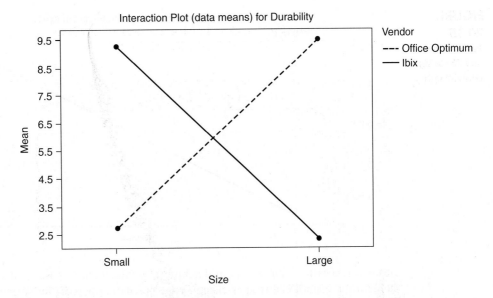

Interaction Plot (data means) for Durability

present for functionality. This indicates that since the effect of shelf life was held constant in this designed experiment, while it was shown to affect functionality in the data mining analysis, the team can restrict its attention to improving functionality by addressing shelf life first. As durability is the only outcome influenced by vendor, size, or ridges in this designed experiment, further consideration in this study will be restricted to durability. Another project can address shelf life and its effect on functionality.

Since interaction effects should be interpreted prior to studying main effects, the team decides to construct an interaction effect plot for vendor and size. Figure 20.35 is the interaction effect plot for vendor and size relative to durability.

The interaction effect plot between size and vendor shown in Figure 20.35 indicates that the best results for durability are obtained using small MSDs supplied by Office Optimum or large MSDs supplied by Ibix. The reasons for this interaction may be due to factors such as materials used for each size MSD, differences in supplier processes for each size MSD, or other supplier-dependent reasons. Team members can ask each vendor why its sizes show significant differences in average durability, if there is a preference to use only one vendor. Otherwise, the Purchasing department should buy small MSDs from Office Optimum or large MSDs from Ibix to optimize durability.

The only significant main effect not involved within a significant interaction effect is x_3 = ridges. The main effect for ridges on durability is shown in Figure 20.36.

The figure indicates that the average durability is about $6.5 - 5.4 = 1.1$ more when an MSD with ridges is used rather than an MSD without ridges. Therefore, since ridges is a main effect independent of any interaction effects, the right selection of MSDs is to use Office Optimum for small MSDs with ridges and Ibix for large MSDs with ridges. If the experimental results from Table 20.19 are used, then the average durability for Office Optimum's small MSDs with ridges is $(10 + 9)/2 = 9.5$ while the average durability for Ibix's large MSDs with ridges is $(11 + 9)/2 = 10.0$. Both averages are well above the required corresponding CTQ of at least 4. As long as the variation, or spread, of results is small enough so that no individual durability result is far from these averages, then the

FIGURE
20.36
Main Effects
Plot for Ridges
for Durability

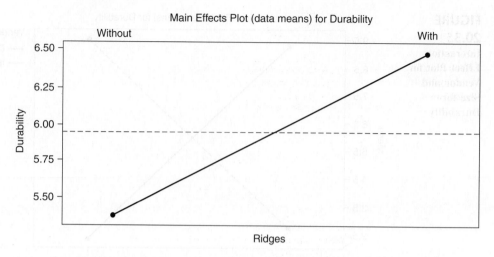

team is successful with respect to durability. The variation in these results can be monitored using control charts after changing the purchasing process for selecting MSDs.

Generate Actions to Implement the Optimized Levels of the x's

The team members decide to purchase all MSDs with ridges. In addition, the choice of vendor and size will be as follows: vendor = Office Optimum and size = small, or vendor = Ibix and size = large, to maximize average durability. In addition, the team decides to take on another project to reduce shelf life to less than 5 days to address functionality. The revised flowchart for the Purchasing department, incorporating the findings of the Six Sigma project, is shown in Figure 20.37.

Conduct a Pilot Test of the Revised System

The team members conduct a pilot test of the revised best-practice flowchart shown in Figure 20.37. Data for durability from the pilot test are shown in Table 20.20 (see ✿ PILOT).

Table 20.20 indicates that the RTY for durability is 100 percent. Functionality is also tested, but not shown here, using shelf life = 0 days; that is, the MSDs are tested immediately upon arrival to POI before they are placed in inventory. It results in an RTY of 75 percent better than the baseline RTY. The effect on functionality of shelf life and inventory control procedures will be investigated in subsequent projects if management decides these projects should be chartered.

Figure 20.38 shows that durability is in control with a higher mean number of bends for all MSDs in the pilot test. The test pilot data shown in Table 20.20 include results for both small MSDs from Office Optimum and large MSDs from Ibix.

Subsequently, team members realize that all other things being equal, large MSDs from Ibix should have a higher average durability then small MSDs from Office Optimum. Consequently, team members construct two control charts, one for small MSDs from Office Optimum (see ✿ PILOT-OFFICEOPTIMUM) and another for large MSDs from Ibix (see ✿ PILOT-IBIX) as shown in Figures 20.39 and 20.40, respectively.

Figures 20.38, 20.39 and 20.40 show that durability (y_1) is in control, but it is dangerous to compute any process capability statistics because of the small sample sizes. However, estimates for the mean and standard deviation of small MSDs from Office

**FIGURE
20.37**
**Revised
Flowchart for
the Purchasing
Department**

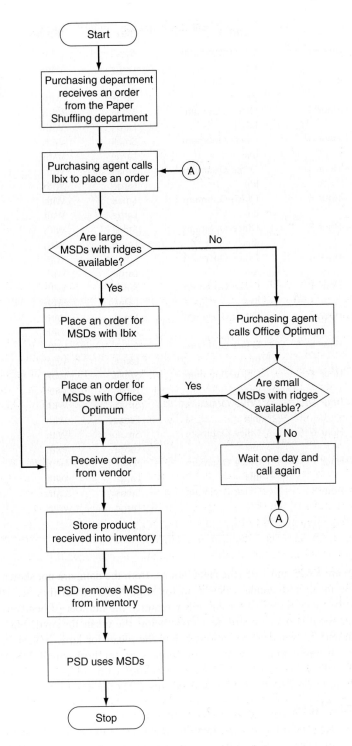

TABLE 20.20
Data from the Pilot Test

Hour	Vendor	Size	Ridges	Durability
Shift 1—Hour 1	Office Optimum	Small	With	10
	Ibix	Large	With	11
Shift 1—Hour 2	Office Optimum	Small	With	7
	Ibix	Large	With	11
Shift 1—Hour 3	Office Optimum	Small	With	10
	Ibix	Large	With	11
Shift 1—Hour 4	Office Optimum	Small	With	8
	Ibix	Large	With	11
Shift 1—Hour 5	Office Optimum	Small	With	9
	Ibix	Large	With	10
Shift 1—Hour 6	Office Optimum	Small	With	9
	Ibix	Large	With	9
Shift 1—Hour 7	Office Optimum	Small	With	8
	Ibix	Large	With	11
Shift 1—Hour 8	Office Optimum	Small	With	9
	Ibix	Large	With	10
Shift 2—Hour 1	Office Optimum	Small	With	9
	Ibix	Large	With	11
Shift 2—Hour 2	Office Optimum	Small	With	8
	Ibix	Large	With	10
Shift 2—Hour 3	Office Optimum	Small	With	10
	Ibix	Large	With	9
Shift 2—Hour 4	Office Optimum	Small	With	7
	Ibix	Large	With	9
Shift 2—Hour 5	Office Optimum	Small	With	7
	Ibix	Large	With	10
Shift 2—Hour 6	Office Optimum	Small	With	9
	Ibix	Large	With	11
Shift 2—Hour 7	Office Optimum	Small	With	10
	Ibix	Large	With	9
Shift 2—Hour 8	Office Optimum	Small	With	8
	Ibix	Large	With	11
RTY				32/32 = 1

Optimum are 8.625 and 1.05 (the calculations, from the data, are not shown here), respectively. The mean and standard deviation for large MSDs from Ibix are 10.25 and 0.83, respectively. Since the CTQ for durability requires the number of bends to be 4 or more, this requirement is 4.4 standard deviations below the mean for small MSDs from Office Optimum and 7.5 standard deviations below the mean for large MSDs from Ibix. Team members all agree that as long as the processes for both small MSDs from Office Optimum with ridges and large MSDs from Ibix with ridges remain in control, it is extremely unlikely that the MSDs will fail the CTQ for durability (y_1).

Control Phase

The control phase involves mistake-proofing the improvements and/or innovations discovered in the Six Sigma project; establishing a risk management plan to minimize

FIGURE 20.38   **Control Chart for Durability**

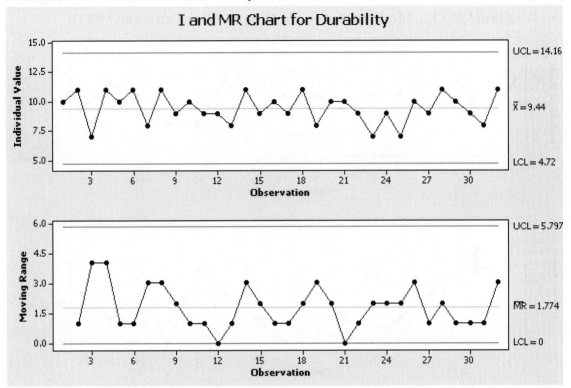

the risk of failure of product, service, or process; reporting the improvement and/or innovation in **ISO 9000** (discussed in Chapter 2) documentation; preparing a control plan for the process owners who will inherit the improved or innovated product, service, or process; and turning the improved process over to the process owner for continuous improvement using the PDSA cycle.

Mistake-Proof the Revised Process

Team members identify and prioritize two problems while mistake-proofing the process improvements discovered in the improve phase: (1) purchasing agents do not specify "with ridges" on a purchase order and (2) purchasing agents do not consider that the choice of vendor depends on the size of the MSDs being requested on the purchase order. Team members create solutions that make both errors impossible: (1) the purchase-order entry system does not process order unless "with ridges" is specified on the purchase order, and (2) the purchase-order entry system does not process an order unless Office Optimum is the selected vendor for small MSDs and Ibix is the selected vendor for large MSDs.

Develop a Risk Management Plan

Team members use risk management to identify two risk elements: (1) failing to train new purchasing agents in the revised purchasing process shown in Figure 20.37, and

FIGURE 20.39 **Control Chart for Durability for Small MSDs from Office Optimum**

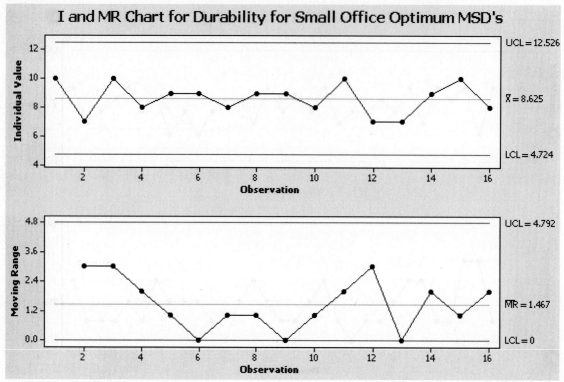

(2) Office Optimum and Ibix are out of MSDs with ridges. Team members assign risk ratings to both risk elements, as shown in Table 20.21.

Both risk elements must be dealt with in risk abatement plans. The risk abatement plan for "failing to train new purchasing agents" is to document the revised purchasing process in training manuals. The risk abatement plan for "vendor out of MSDs with ridges" is for POI to request that both Office Optimum and Ibix manufacture only MSDs with ridges because of their superior durability. This is a reasonable and acceptable suggestion to POI, Office Optimum, and Ibix because the cost structures for manufacturing MSDs with and without ridges are equal, and neither Office Optimum nor Ibix has other customers requesting MSDs without ridges. Office Optimum and Ibix agree to produce only MSDs with ridges after a six-month trial period in which they check incoming purchase orders for requests for MSDs without ridges. If the trial period reveals no requests for MSDs without ridges, then the POI Purchasing Department will revise Figure 20.37 and the appropriate ISO 9000 documentation to reflect the possibility of purchasing only MSDs with ridges. Additionally, Office Optimum and Ibix thank POI for pointing out to them that average durability is higher for MSDs with ridges than MSDs without ridges. Both vendors claim that they are going to experiment with possible different ridge patterns to further increase durability and decrease costs. Both vendors state that they anticipate decreased costs from producing only MSDs with ridges because of the lower amortized costs of having only one production line.

FIGURE 20.40   Control Chart for Durability for Large MSDs from Ibix

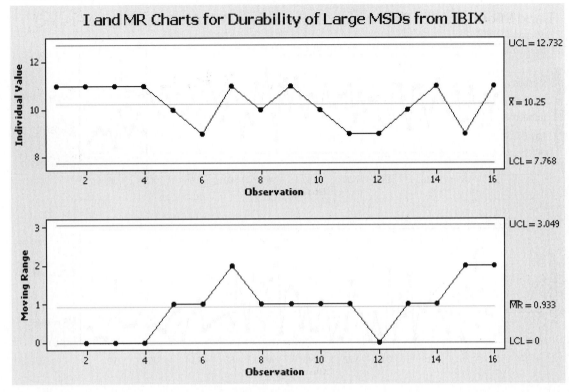

TABLE 20.21
Risk Elements
for Purchasing
Process

Risk Elements	Risk Category	Likelihood of Occurrence	Impact of Occurrence	Risk Element Score	
Failing to train new purchasing agents	Performance	5	5	25	High
Vendors out of MSDs with ridges	Materials	2	5	10	Medium

Scale: 1–5 with 5 being the highest.

Prepare ISO Documentation

Team members prepare ISO 9000 documentation for the revisions to the training manual for the purchasing process from Figure 20.37.

Develop a Control Plan

Team members develop a control plan for the Paper Shuffling department (PSD) that requires a monthly sampling of the boxes of MSDs in inventory. The purpose of the sampling plan is to check if the boxes of MSDs being purchased are either small Office Optimum

FIGURE 20.41 Control Chart for Production Costs in the PSD before and after the MSD Six Sigma Project

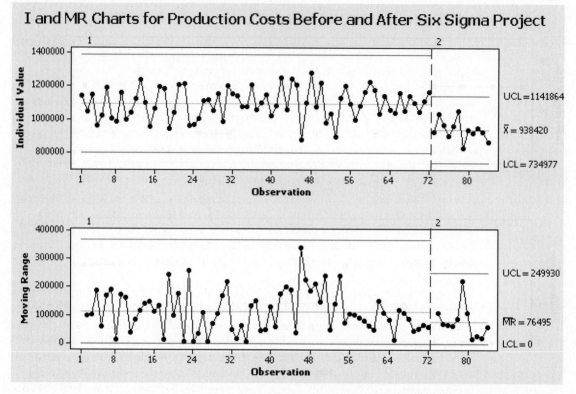

MSDs with ridges or large Ibix MSDs with ridges. The percentage nonconforming boxes of MSDs will be plotted on a p chart. PSD management will use the p chart to highlight violations of the new and improved purchasing process shown in Figure 20.37. The p chart will be the basis for continuously turning the PDSA cycle for the purchasing process.

Team members check the business indicator from the PSD metric tracking system, shown in Figures 20.10 and 20.11, and determine that production costs in the PSD decreased, probably as a result of the MSD Six Sigma project, as shown in Figure 20.41. The MSD project took effect in month 73 of Figure 20.41.

Turn Over the Process to the Process Owner

Team members turn over the improved process with a control plan to the process owner. The process owner accepts the process and continuously works to improve it using the PDSA cycle.

Summary

In this chapter, we defined Six Sigma management in terms of the number of defects per million opportunities, or a process that produces a maximum of approximately 3.4 defects per million opportunities (DPMO).

The relationship between the voice of the process, or the distribution of output, and the voice of the customer, or the specification limits, enables us to measure and describe the percent output in a given process. The conditions for a 3-sigma process with no shift in the mean are shown to result in 99.73 percent of output between the lower and upper specification limits, or 2,700 defects per million opportunities. The conditions for a 3-sigma process with a 1.5-sigma shift in the mean (a common industrial assumption early in the Six Sigma process) result in 93.33 percent of output between the lower and upper specification limits, or 66,811 defects per million opportunities.

On the other hand, when we examine a 6-sigma process with no shift in the mean, where the process standard deviation is half the distance between the specification limits, 99.9999998 percent of the resulting output will fall between the lower and upper specification limits. In terms of number of defects, this corresponds to 2 defects per billion opportunities. Similarly, the conditions for a 6-sigma process with a 1.5-sigma shift in the mean result in 99.99966 percent output between the specification limits, or 3.4 defects per million opportunities.

The DMAIC (Define-Measure-Analyze-Improve-Control) model is used in Six Sigma management to move a process from a 3-sigma output distribution with a 1.5-sigma shift in the mean to a 6-sigma output distribution with a 1.5-sigma shift in the mean. In the Define phase, SIPOC analysis is used to understand the relationships between suppliers, inputs, process, outputs, and customers in order to prepare a business charter, or the rationale for the project.

In the Measure phase, operational definitions are developed for each critical-to-quality characteristic (CTQ) and appropriate studies performed on each CTQ. In the Analyze phase, variables are operationally defined and their effects on each CTQ studied. In the Improve phase, designed experiments are used to determine the optimal levels of the variables identified in the Analyze phase. In the Control phase, potential problems with the revised values of the variables are studied through risk abatement planning and mistake-proofing.

The benefits and costs of Six Sigma management were discussed. Anecdotal evidence strongly indicates that the benefits of a Six Sigma process far outweigh the costs.

The roles and responsibilities of the individuals and bodies involved in Six Sigma management were presented. The senior executive provides the impetus, the direction, and the alignments necessary for the ultimate success of Six Sigma management. The members of the executive committee form a team to deploy key objectives and key indicators throughout the organization via policy management and provide the resources necessary for the success of Six Sigma management. The black belt functions as a full-time change agent and supervises the green belts, who serve as team members of Six Sigma projects and often act as team leaders. The master black belt is a teacher and mentor of black belts and green belts, and supervises both groups. A champion is a member of the executive committee or an individual who is trusted to report directly to the executive committee, providing a direct line of communication between each project team and the executive committee. The process owner has ultimate authority to change a process; he monitors the performance of the process through key indicators, empowers the people who work in the process, and manages the process after completion of the Six Sigma project.

Important technical terms were introduced, enabling clear communication between all individuals and groups involved in Six Sigma management.

A detailed case study of a Six Sigma Green Belt project illustrated all steps of Six Sigma management, from the development of business objectives and business indicators designed to accomplish the organization's mission, to the determination and implementation of optimal values of critical variables and a control plan.

Key Terms

3-sigma process, *726*
6-sigma process, *729*
affinity diagram, *747*
analyze phase, *732*
black belt, *735*
catchball, *735*
champion, *736*
cognitive issues, *747*
control phase, *733*
critical-to-quality (CTQ), *732*
data mining, *759*
defect, *738*
defect opportunity, *738*
defective, *738*
defects per million
opportunities (DPMO), *738*
defects per opportunity
(DPO), *738*

defects per unit (DPU), *738*
define phase, *732*
DMAIC model, *731*
executive committee, *735*
flowchart, *731*
focus points, *747*
full factorial design, *769*
gage R&R study, *732*
gage run chart, *751*
green belt, *736*
hard costs, *745*
improve phase, *733*
ISO 9000, *775*
master black belt, *736*
measure phase, *732*
mistake-proofing, *734*
observed yield, *738*
opportunity costs, *745*

Pareto chart, *769*
policy deployment
committee, *735*
process mapping, *732*
process owner, *737*
process sigma, *739*
risk management, *734*
rolled throughput yield
(RTY), *738*
senior executive, *734*
SIPOC analysis, *732*
Six Sigma
management, *725*
unit, *738*
voice of the customer, *725*
voice of the process, *725*

References

1. BlueFire Partners, *Executive Guide to Six Sigma,* Rev. 1, September 1999 (Minneapolis, MN).
2. W. E. Deming (1994), *The New Economics: For Industry, Government, Education,* 2nd ed. (Cambridge, MA: M.I.T. Center for Advanced Engineering Study).
3. W. E. Deming (1986), *Out of the Crisis* (Cambridge, MA: M.I.T. Center for Advanced Engineering Study).
4. H. Gitlow, "Innovation on Demand," *Quality Engineering,* 11, No. 1, 1998–1999, pp. 79–89.
5. H. Gitlow and S. Gitlow (1987), *The Deming Guide to Quality and Competitive Position* (Englewood Cliffs, NJ: Prentice Hall).
6. H. Gitlow and D. Levine (2005), *Six Sigma for Green Belts and Champions—A Step-by-Step User's Guide: Methods, Applications, and Implementation* (Upper Saddle River, NJ: Financial Times–Prentice Hall).
7. H. Gitlow and PMI (1990), *Planning for Quality, Productivity and Competitive Position* (Homewood, IL: Business One Irwin), pp. 83–89.
8. M. Harry and R. Schroeder (1999), *Six Sigma: The Breakthrough Management Strategy Revolutionizing the World's Top Corporations* (New York: Doubleday).
9. Mikel J. Harry (1997), *The Vision of Six Sigma: A Roadmap for Breakthrough,* 5th ed., Vol. 1 (Phoenix: Tri Star).
10. T. Pyzdek (1999), *The Complete Guide to Six Sigma* (Tucson: Quality).
11. D. Rasis, H. Gitlow, and E. Popovich, "Paper Organizers International: A Fictitious Six Sigma Green Belt Case Study—Part 1," *Quality Engineering,* 15, No. 1, 2002, pp. 127–145.
12. D. Rasis, H. Gitlow, and E. Popovich, "Paper Organizers International: A Fictitious Six Sigma Green Belt Case Study—Part 2," *Quality Engineering,* 15, No. 2, 2002, pp. 259–274.

Appendix A

Documentation of Minitab Data Files

The following is an alphabetical listing and description of all the Minitab files found on the CD that accompanies this text. The icons that appear throughout the text identify these files.

ACCIDENTMILL	Month and number of accidents (Chapter 7)
ACCIDENTS	Number of accidents per week for 52 weeks (Chapter 7)
ADMITTING	Day and amount of time (Chapter 8)
ALLOY	Lifetimes of 6 alloys (Chapter 12)
AMPLIFY	Receiver, amplifier, decibel output (Chapter 12)
ASSEMBLY	Assembly times (Chapter 5)
ATM	Day, total transactions, ATM transactions (Chapter 7)
BANK1	Waiting times for 15 customers (Chapter 5)
BANK2	Waiting times for 15 customers (Chapter 5)
BANKTIME	Waiting times of four bank customers per day for 20 days (Chapter 8)
BATTERIES	Lifetimes of 13 batteries (Chapter 5)
BEARINGS	Ring osculation, cage design, heat treatment, relative life, effect, average effect (Chapter 12)
BEARINGS2	Balls, cage design, grease, amount of grease, average life (Chapter 12)
BLACK	Day and blackness (Chapter 8)
BLOOD	Sample number, sample size, number missing (Chapter 7)
BOARD	Sample number, lengths of circuit boards (Chapter 8)
BOOK	Book number, errors, pages (Chapter 7)
BULBS	Manufacturer, lifetimes (Chapter 5)
BURR	Sample number, sample size, number with burrs (Chapter 7)
CAKE	Flour, shortening, egg powder, oven temperature, baking time, and rating score (Chapter 12)
CAMSHAFT	Day, date, depth (Chapter 11)
CAMSHAFT2	Day, date, depth (Chapter 11)

(continued)

CAMSHAFT3	Day, date, depth (Chapter 11)
CANISTER	Day and number of nonconforming film canisters (Chapter 6; Chapter 7)
CARTS	Weeks, number of data cartridges sent (Chapter 7)
CATFOOD	Type, ounces eaten (Chapter 12)
CHEMICAL	Viscosity for 120 batches (Chapter 5)
CHICKEN	Weight of chicken breasts (Chapter 5)
CHOCOLATE	Time, observation number, weight (Chapter 5)
CIRCUITS	Batch, position 1, position 2, position 18, position 19, position 28, thickness, position (Chapter 12)
CLOTH	Lot, square yards, defects (Chapter 7)
COATING	Time, head, thickness (Chapter 8)
COLDGASPLASMA1	Time, meniscus (Chapter 16)
COLDGASPLASMA2	Time, meniscus (Chapter 16)
COLDGASPLASMA3	Time, meniscus (Chapter 16)
CONCRETE2	Compressive strength 2, 7, and 28 days after pouring (Chapter 12)
COPPER	Coil, flaws (Chapter 7)
CORRECT	Orders, corrections (Chapter 7)
DARTS	Lighting, practice time, beer consumption, radio, score (Chapter 12)
DATAENTRY	Day, entries inspected, defective entries (Chapter 6; Chapter 11)
DATAENTRY2	Day, entries inspected, defective entries (Chapter 6)
DATAENTRY3	Day, entries inspected, defective entries (Chapter 6)
DATAMINING	Day, hour, vendor, size, ridges, inventory shelf life, durability, functionality (Chapter 20)
DELIVERY	Days from order to delivery (Chapter 5)
DENSITY	Day, batch density, for 30 days (Chapter 8)
DRINK	Amount of soft drink filled in a subgroup of 50 consecutive 2-liter bottles (Chapter 5; Chapter 8)
DRYCLEAN	Day and items returned for rework (Chapter 7)
ERWAIT	Record number, time (Chapter 8)
FACTORIAL	Standard order, run order, vendor, size, ridges, durability, functionality (Chapter 20)
FIRE	Fabric type, fire-retardant treatment, fabric removed (Chapter 12)
FUNDTRAN	Day, number of new investigations and number closed over a 30-day period (Chapter 7)
FURNITURE	Number of days between order and installation (Chapter 5)
GAGER&R	Box, inspector, count, functionality (Chapter 20)
GEAR	Tooth size, part positioning, distortion (Chapter 12)
GOLFBALL	Design, distance traveled (Chapter 12)
HOTEL	Day, time (Chapter 8)
INSULATOR	Day, number inspected, nonconforming (Chapter 7)
INSURANCE	Processing time (Chapter 5)
JEWELRY	Day and number of terminals with problems (Chapter 6)
KNOB	Time, sample number, sample 1, sample 2, sample 3, sample 4 (Chapter 8)
LABSLIP	Day, number of lab slips received, number of lab slips missing demographic information (Chapter 7)
LENGTH	Bin, number of items, defectives (Chapter 9)

(continued)

LEVER	Day, date, sample size, defectives (Chapter 9)
LEVER2	Day, date, sample size, defectives (Chapter 9)
LOGS	Day, log, length (Chapter 5)
MAILSPC	Day, total number of packages, late packages (Chapter 7)
MEDREC	Day, number of discharges, number of medical records not processed within five days (Chapter 7)
MODELCAR	Battery type, connector design, temperature, battery life (Chapter 12)
MOLDING	Day, sample size, defectives (Chapter 7)
MOWER	Day, mowers, number nonconforming (Chapter 7)
NATURAL	Day, date, group 1, group 2, group 3, group 4, group 5 (Chapter 9)
OPERATOR	Operator, defective lines (Chapter 11)
OPERATOR4	Cause, frequency (Chapter 10; Chapter 11)
OPERATOR4ERRORS	Day, errors (Chapter 11)
PACKAGING	Subgroup, weight (Chapter 11)
PAILS	Sample and number of defectives (Chapter 6)
PASTEINK	Sample and viscosity (Chapter 8)
PDCBIT	Rake angle, thrust, speed, penetration rate, torque (Chapter 12)
PEANUT	Carbon dioxide pressure, carbon dioxide temperature, peanut moisture, carbon dioxide flow rate, peanut particle size, amount of oil dissolved (Chapter 12)
PEANUT2	Carbon dioxide pressure, carbon dioxide temperature, peanut moisture, carbon dioxide flow rate, peanut particle size, yield (Chapter 12)
PH	Batch, pH (Chapter 8)
PHONE	Office, time to clear problems (Chapter 5)
PHONES	Order number, order size, number of phones returned (Chapter 7)
PHOTO	Strength, time, density (Chapter 12)
PILOT	Vendor, size, ridges, durability (Chapter 20)
PILOT-IBIX	Vendor, size, ridges, durability (Chapter 20)
PILOT-OFFICEOPTIMUM	Vendor, size, ridges, durability (Chapter 20)
PLASTIC	Lots, square feet, defects (Chapter 7)
PTFALLS	Month, patient falls (Chapter 7)
PVC	Operator, resin railcar, particle size (Chapter 12)
RADAR	Assembly and nonconformities (Chapter 7)
RADIO	Time, day (Chapter 8)
REEL	Reel, blemishes (Chapter 7)
REELS	Week, total reels, scrap reels (Chapter 7)
RICE	Amount of rice, amount of inner water, amount of outer water, type of rice, cooking time (Chapter 12)
RRLATE	Day, number of trains late (Chapter 6; Chapter 7)
SAFETY	Tour, number of unsafe acts (Chapter 7)
SCREWS	Subgroup, subgroup size, defectives (Chapter 5)
SERVICE	Day, calls, defectives (Chapter 6)
SFTDRINK	Percent carbonation, pressure, line speed, deviation from target (Chapter 12)
SORTED	Group, minute 1, minute 2, minute 3, minute 4, minute 5 (Chapter 8)
TELLER	Number of errors by tellers (Chapter 7)

(continued)

TELLERTIME	Hour and time (Chapter 8)
TILES	Day, sample size, number cracked (Chapter 6; Chapter 7)
TIRES	Tire lifetimes (Chapter 5)
TOLL	Day, sample size, number with exact change (Chapter 7)
TOLL2	Day, sample size, number with exact change (Chapter 7)
TRADE	Days, number of undesirable trades, number of total trades made over a 30-day period (Chapter 7)
TRANSMIT	Day, number of errors in transmission (Chapter 6; Chapter 7)
TRANSPORT	Days, patient transport times (in minutes) for samples of four patients per day over a 30-day period (Chapter 8)
VEHICLE	Day, vehicles, vehicles out of service (Chapter 7)
VIALS	Observation number, time, value 1, value 2, value 3, value 4, value 5, value 6 (Chapter 8)
WAGES	Employee, wages (Chapter 5)
WASHING	Machine, defects (Chapter 7)
WASHING2	Machine, defects (Chapter 7)
WATER	Type, pH, conductivity, TAMP, TOC (Chapter 8)
WELLWATER	Water hardness, well (Chapter 12)
WIP	Manufacture time, plant (Chapter 5)
YARN2	Side-to-side fabric aspects, yarn type, pick density, pressure, tenacity (Chapter 12)
YIELD	Date and yield (Chapter 8)
YIELD2	Cleansing step, etching step, yield (Chapter 12)

Appendix B

Tables

TABLE B.1 Control Chart Constants

Sources: A_2, A_3, B_3, B_4, c_4, d_2, d_3, D_3, D_4, E_2 from *ASTM Manual on the Presentation of Data and Control Chart Analysis* (Philadelphia, PA: ASTM, 1976), pp. 134–136. Copyright ASTM International. Reprinted with permission.

A_6, d_4, D_5, D_6 from D. J. Wheeler and D. S. Chambers, *Understanding Statistical Process Control*, 1st ed. (Knoxville, TN: Statistical Process Controls, 1986), pp. 307, 309, 312. Copyright 1986, SPC Press, Knoxville, TN. All rights reserved.

Number of Observations in Subgroup, n	A_2	A_3	A_6	B_3	B_4	c_4	d_2	d_3	d_4	D_3	D_4	D_5	D_6	E_2
2	1.880	2.659		0.000	3.267	0.7979	1.128	0.853	0.954	0.000	3.267	0.000	3.865	2.660
3	1.023	1.954	1.187	0.000	2.568	0.8862	1.693	0.888	1.588	0.000	2.574	0.000	2.745	1.772
4	0.729	1.628		0.000	2.266	0.9213	2.059	0.880	1.978	0.000	2.282	0.000	2.375	1.457
5	0.577	1.427	0.691	0.000	2.089	0.9400	2.326	0.864	2.257	0.000	2.114	0.000	2.179	1.290
6	0.483	1.287		0.030	1.970	0.9515	2.534	0.848	2.472	0.000	2.004	0.000	2.055	1.184
7	0.419	1.182	0.509	0.118	1.882	0.9594	2.704	0.833	2.645	0.076	1.924	0.078	1.967	1.109
8	0.373	1.099		0.185	1.815	0.9650	2.847	0.820	2.791	0.136	1.864	0.139	1.901	1.054
9	0.337	1.032	0.412	0.239	1.761	0.9693	2.970	0.808	2.915	0.184	1.816	0.187	1.850	1.010
10	0.308	0.975		0.284	1.716	0.9727	3.078	0.797	3.024	0.223	1.777	0.227	1.809	0.975
11	0.285	0.927	0.350	0.321	1.679	0.9754	3.173	0.787	3.121	0.256	1.744			
12	0.266	0.886		0.354	1.646	0.9776	3.258	0.778	3.207	0.283	1.717			
13	0.249	0.850		0.382	1.618	0.9794	3.336	0.770	3.285	0.307	1.693			
14	0.235	0.817		0.406	1.594	0.9810	3.407	0.762	3.356	0.328	1.672			
15	0.223	0.789		0.428	1.572	0.9823	3.472	0.755	3.422	0.347	1.653			
16	0.212	0.763		0.448	1.552	0.9835	3.532	0.749	3.482	0.363	1.637			
17	0.203	0.739		0.466	1.534	0.9845	3.588	0.743	3.538	0.378	1.622			
18	0.194	0.718		0.482	1.518	0.9854	3.640	0.738	3.591	0.391	1.608			
19	0.187	0.698		0.497	1.503	0.9862	3.689	0.733	3.640	0.403	1.597			
20	0.180	0.680		0.510	1.490	0.9869	3.735	0.729	3.686	0.415	1.585			
21	0.173	0.663		0.523	1.477	0.9876	3.778	0.724	3.730	0.425	1.575			
22	0.167	0.647		0.534	1.466	0.9882	3.819	0.720	3.771	0.434	1.566			
23	0.162	0.633		0.545	1.455	0.9887	3.858	0.716	3.811	0.443	1.557			
24	0.157	0.619		0.555	1.445	0.9892	3.895	0.712	3.847	0.451	1.548			
25	0.153	0.606		0.565	1.435	0.9896	3.931	0.709	3.883	0.459	1.541			
More than 25	$3/\sqrt{n}$			$1 - 3/\sqrt{2n}$	$1 + 3/\sqrt{2n}$									

TABLE B.2 2,500 Four-Digit Random Numbers

Source: Reprinted from *A Million Random Digits with 100,000 Normal Deviates* by the RAND Corporation (New York: The Free Press, 1955). Copyright 1955 and 1983 by The RAND Corporation.

5347	8111	9803	1221	5952	4023	4057	3935	4321	6925
9734	7032	5811	9196	2624	4464	8328	9739	9282	7757
6602	3827	7452	7111	8489	1395	9889	9231	6578	5964
9977	7572	0317	4311	8308	8198	1453	2616	2489	2055
3017	4897	9215	3841	4243	2663	8390	4472	6921	6911
8187	8333	1498	9993	1321	3017	4796	9379	8669	9885
1983	9063	7186	9505	5553	6090	8410	5534	4847	6379
0933	3343	5386	5276	1880	2582	9619	6651	7831	9701
3115	5829	4082	4133	2109	9388	4919	4487	4718	8142
6761	5251	0303	8169	1710	6498	6083	8531	4781	0807
6194	4879	1160	8304	2225	1183	0434	9554	2036	5593
0481	6489	9634	7906	2699	4396	6348	9357	8075	9658
0576	3960	5614	2551	8615	7865	0218	2971	0433	1567
7326	5687	4079	1394	9628	9018	4711	6680	6184	4468
5490	0997	7658	0264	3579	4453	6442	3544	2831	9900
4258	3633	6006	0404	2967	1634	4859	2554	6317	7522
2726	2740	9752	2333	3645	3369	2367	4588	4151	0475
4984	1144	6668	3605	3200	7860	3692	5996	6819	6258
2931	4046	2707	6923	5142	5851	4992	0390	2659	3306
3046	2785	6779	1683	7427	0579	0290	6349	0078	3509
2870	8408	6553	4425	3386	8253	9839	2638	0283	3683
1318	5065	9487	2825	7854	5528	3359	6196	5172	1421
6079	7663	3015	4029	9947	2833	1536	4248	6031	4277
1348	4691	6468	0741	7784	0190	4779	6579	4423	7723
3491	9450	3937	3418	5750	2251	0406	9451	4461	1048
2810	0481	8517	8649	3569	0348	5731	6317	7190	7118
5923	4502	0117	0884	8192	7149	9540	3404	0485	6591
8743	8275	7109	3683	5358	2598	4600	4284	8168	2145
2904	0130	5534	6573	7871	4364	4624	5320	9486	4871
6203	7188	9450	1526	6143	1036	4205	6825	1438	7943
3885	8004	5997	7336	5287	4767	4102	8229	2643	8737
4066	4332	8737	8641	9584	2559	5413	9418	4230	0736
4058	9008	3772	0866	3725	2031	5331	5098	3290	3209
7823	8655	5027	2043	0024	0230	7102	4993	2324	0086
9824	6747	7145	6954	0116	0332	6701	9254	9797	5272
6997	7855	6543	3262	2831	6181	1459	7972	5569	9134
3984	2307	4081	0371	2189	9635	9680	2459	2620	2600
6288	8727	9989	9996	3437	4255	1167	9960	9801	4886
5613	6492	2945	5296	8662	6242	3106	7618	9531	3926
9080	5602	4899	6456	6746	6018	1297	0384	6258	9385
0966	4467	7476	3335	6730	8054	9765	1134	7877	4501
3475	5040	7663	1276	3222	3454	1810	5351	1452	7212
1215	7332	7419	2666	7808	5363	5230	0000	0570	6353
6938	0773	9445	7642	1612	0930	6741	6858	8793	3884
9335	6456	4376	4504	4493	6997	1696	0827	6775	6029
3887	3554	9956	8540	0491	6254	7840	0101	8618	2207
5831	6029	7239	6966	1247	9305	0205	2980	6364	1279
8356	1022	9947	7472	2207	1023	2157	2032	2131	5712
2806	9115	4056	3370	6451	0706	6437	2633	7965	3114
0573	7555	9316	8092	5587	5410	3480	8315	0453	8136

TABLE B.2 (continued)

2668	7422	4354	4569	9446	8212	3737	2396	6892	3766
6067	7516	2451	1510	0201	1437	6518	1063	6442	6674
4541	9863	8312	9855	0995	6025	4207	4093	9799	9308
6987	4802	8975	2847	4413	5997	9106	2876	8596	7717
0376	8636	9953	4418	2388	8997	1196	5158	1803	5623
8468	5763	3232	1986	7134	4200	9699	8437	2799	2145
9151	4967	3255	8518	2802	8815	6289	9549	2942	3813
1073	4930	1830	2224	2246	1000	9315	6698	4491	3046
5487	1967	5836	2090	3832	0002	9844	3742	2289	3763
4896	4957	6536	7430	6208	3929	1030	2317	7421	3227
9143	7911	0368	0541	2302	5473	9155	0625	1870	1890
9256	2956	4747	6280	7342	0453	8639	1216	5964	9772
4173	1219	7744	9241	6354	4211	8497	1245	3313	4846
2525	7811	5417	7824	0922	8752	3537	9069	5417	0856
9165	1156	6603	2852	8370	0995	7661	8811	7835	5087
0014	8474	6322	5053	5015	6043	0482	4957	8904	1616
5325	7320	8406	5962	6100	3854	0575	0617	8019	2646
2558	1748	5671	4974	7073	3273	6036	1410	5257	3939
0117	1218	0688	2756	7545	5426	3856	8905	9691	8890
8353	1554	4083	2029	8857	4781	9654	7946	7866	2535
1990	9886	3280	6109	9158	3034	8490	6404	6775	8763
9651	7870	2555	3518	2906	4900	2984	6894	5050	4586
9941	5617	1984	2435	5184	0379	7212	5795	0836	4319
7769	5785	9321	2734	2890	3105	6581	2163	4938	7540
3224	8379	9952	0515	2724	4826	6215	6246	9704	1651
1287	7275	6646	1378	6433	0005	7332	0392	1319	1946
6389	4191	4548	5546	6651	8248	7469	0786	0972	7649
1625	4327	2654	4129	3509	3217	7062	6640	0105	4422
7555	3020	4181	7498	4022	9122	6423	7301	8310	9204
4177	1844	3468	1389	3884	6900	1036	8412	0881	6678
0927	0124	8176	0680	1056	1008	1748	0547	8227	0690
8505	1781	7155	3635	9751	5414	5113	8316	2737	6860
8022	8757	6275	1485	3635	2330	7045	2106	6381	2986
8390	8802	5674	2559	7934	4788	7791	5202	8430	0289
3630	5783	7762	0223	5328	7731	4010	3845	9221	5427
9154	6388	6053	9633	2080	7269	0894	0287	7489	2259
1441	3381	7823	8767	9647	4445	2509	2929	5067	0779
8246	0778	0993	6687	7212	9968	8432	1453	0841	4595
2730	3984	0563	9636	7202	0127	9283	4009	3177	4182
9196	8276	0233	0879	3385	2184	1739	5375	5807	4849
5928	9610	9161	0748	3794	9683	1544	1209	3669	5831
1042	9600	7122	2135	7868	5596	3551	9480	2342	0449
6552	4103	7957	0510	5958	0211	3344	5678	1840	3627
5968	4307	9327	3197	0876	8480	5066	1852	8323	5060
4445	1018	4356	4653	9302	0761	1291	6093	5340	1840
8727	8201	5980	7859	6055	1403	1209	9547	4273	0857
9415	9311	4996	2775	8509	7767	6930	6632	7781	2279
2648	7639	9128	0341	6875	8957	6646	9783	6668	0317
3707	3454	8829	6863	1297	5089	1002	2722	0578	7753
8383	8957	5595	9395	3036	4767	8300	3505	0710	6307

TABLE B.2   (continued)

5503	8121	9056	8194	1124	8451	1228	8986	0076	7615
2552	9953	4323	4878	4922	0696	3156	2145	8819	0631
8542	7274	9724	6638	0013	0566	9644	3738	5767	2791
6121	4839	4734	3041	3939	9136	5620	7920	0533	3119
2023	0314	5885	1165	2841	1282	5893	3050	6598	2667
9577	8320	5614	5595	8978	6442	0844	4570	8036	6026
0760	1734	0114	8330	9695	6502	3171	8901	7955	4975
0064	1745	7874	3900	3602	9880	7266	5448	6826	3882
6295	8316	6150	3155	8059	4789	7236	7272	0839	3367
7935	1027	8193	2634	0806	6781	0665	8791	7416	8551
4833	6983	5904	8217	9201	5844	6959	5620	9570	8621
0584	0843	7983	5095	3205	3291	1584	1391	4136	8011
2585	0220	0730	5994	7138	7615	1126	3878	6154	2260
2527	1615	8232	7071	9808	3863	9195	4990	7625	3397
7300	2905	1760	4929	4767	9044	6891	0567	2382	8489
8131	9443	2266	0658	3814	0014	1749	5111	6145	6579
1002	4471	5983	8072	6371	6788	2510	4534	5574	6761
8467	5280	8912	3769	2089	8233	2262	0614	0577	0354
2929	5816	2185	3373	9405	8880	5460	0038	6634	6923
5177	9407	7063	4128	9058	8768	1396	5562	2367	3510
4216	5625	6077	5167	3603	7727	8521	1481	9075	2267
7835	6704	2249	5152	3116	3045	2760	4442	9638	2677
0955	5134	3386	8901	7341	8153	7739	3044	9774	1815
1577	6312	3484	0566	0615	4897	5569	6181	9176	2082
1323	9905	9375	3673	4428	4432	1572	3750	4726	1333
5058	0357	3847	7323	6761	7278	7817	1871	9909	6411
9948	5733	1063	7490	9067	1964	6990	6095	1796	3721
5467	3952	7378	4886	6983	6279	6520	6918	0557	7474
9934	7154	1024	7603	3170	7686	8890	6957	2764	0033
3549	4023	3486	5535	1284	6809	5264	3273	6701	4678
9817	2538	0384	2392	4795	1035	7011	1117	6329	9990
0267	8615	5686	0259	0164	4220	7995	3776	8234	7195
3693	4287	8163	7995	0706	4162	9680	9238	8886	6858
5685	1277	2430	7366	8426	2466	1668	0223	6602	6413
0546	2889	1427	2377	8859	1708	3388	8878	3901	5711
1502	2023	6338	7112	0662	0741	9498	3232	7942	7038
9561	0803	8146	9106	8885	5658	0122	2809	1972	7146
0902	4037	0573	5512	7429	4919	3166	4260	3036	9642
8143	9995	5246	6766	9732	6980	2124	6592	1262	9289
2143	5933	5862	9482	6548	0964	4101	8510	1611	3207
9583	7614	1163	8028	1778	9793	1282	7389	6600	2752
9981	4463	4374	9979	8682	1211	3170	0502	2815	0420
7721	3114	5054	1160	5093	0249	0918	9587	8584	7195
1326	0260	7983	6605	8027	0853	2867	3753	7053	8235
4428	7173	2662	5469	1490	5213	8111	7454	7885	3199
7052	4595	7963	5737	0505	3196	3337	1323	8566	8661
8838	1122	2508	7146	0981	4600	1906	6898	1831	7417
8316	7399	1720	7944	6409	4979	1193	4486	8697	3453
5021	7172	3385	4514	0569	2993	1282	0159	0845	5282
9768	2934	6774	8064	1362	2394	4939	8368	3730	9535

TABLE B.2 (continued)

1236	2389	3150	9072	1871	8914	5859	9942	2284	0826
3889	3023	3423	2257	7442	2273	2693	4060	1078	8012
8078	5541	3977	9331	1827	2114	5208	7809	8563	8114
0239	7758	0885	2356	3354	4579	1097	4472	2478	0969
7372	7018	6911	7188	8014	7287	3898	2340	6395	4475
6138	1722	5523	1896	3900	9350	1827	4981	5280	6967
3916	4428	1497	9749	2597	3360	6014	3003	7767	4929
8090	7448	3988	1988	3731	0420	4967	3959	0105	4399
0905	6567	6366	3403	0657	8783	2812	4888	5048	5573
3342	2422	3204	6008	2041	8504	5357	3255	6409	5232
7265	6947	7364	7153	5545	1957	1555	2057	1212	5003
0414	3209	8358	6182	3548	3273	6340	9149	3719	0276
8522	1419	5221	6074	2441	5785	3188	5126	8229	7355
5488	0357	9167	5950	0861	3379	2901	8519	6226	2868
3325	5151	8203	4523	3935	3322	5946	6554	7680	1698
7597	1595	3240	8208	0221	5714	3352	4719	9452	7325
9063	7531	3538	3445	4924	1146	2510	7148	8988	9970
6506	1549	9334	3356	1942	6682	0304	9736	0815	4748
6442	0742	8223	9781	3957	0776	6584	2998	1553	9011
2717	1738	7696	7511	4558	9990	4716	5536	2566	2540
3221	3009	8727	5689	1562	3259	8066	0808	1942	8071
5420	5804	7235	8982	0270	1681	8998	3738	4403	5936
5928	6696	8484	7154	6755	3386	8301	6621	6937	2390
8387	5816	0122	9555	2219	6590	3878	0135	4748	2817
8331	5708	0336	8001	3960	4069	5643	6405	0249	5088
6454	2950	1335	7864	9262	1935	6047	5733	5213	0711
3926	0007	5548	0152	7656	2257	2032	8462	3018	4390
2976	0567	2819	6551	1195	7859	6390	2134	1921	9028
0631	0299	0146	2773	9028	1769	6451	3955	3469	0321
9754	4760	5765	5910	2185	4444	0797	5429	8467	7875
8296	8571	1161	9772	5351	5378	9894	3840	7093	1131
7687	3472	1252	9064	1692	1366	1742	8448	6830	8524
8739	7888	8723	9208	9563	6684	2290	6498	8695	5470
7404	1273	5961	3369	1259	4489	6798	7297	8979	1058
4789	4141	6643	7004	5079	4592	9656	6795	5636	4472
8777	7169	6414	5436	9211	3403	5906	6205	6204	3352
9697	6314	7221	8004	1199	4769	9562	7299	2904	8589
4382	1328	7781	8169	2993	7075	0202	3237	0055	8668
5720	8396	4009	3923	6595	5991	9141	5557	8842	4557
4906	7217	8093	0601	9032	6368	0793	9958	4901	2645
9425	8427	9579	1347	8013	2633	5516	7341	4076	4517
6814	8138	8238	1867	4045	9282	3004	3741	4342	4513
1220	9780	3361	2886	4164	1673	8886	3263	4198	8461
8831	8970	2611	1241	1943	6566	6098	5976	1141	1825
5672	8035	2961	6305	1525	4468	6468	4235	5102	7768
0713	1232	0107	1930	8704	5892	2845	8106	9397	6665
2118	6455	5561	3608	2433	8439	1602	1220	7755	7566
0215	1225	8873	4391	0365	2109	6080	6324	2684	3581
9095	8523	3277	0730	3618	4742	1968	3318	4138	0324
8010	9130	1285	4129	0032	1501	1957	9113	1272	9260

TABLE B.2 (concluded)

9263	7824	1926	9545	5349	2389	3770	7986	7647	6641
7944	7873	7154	4484	2610	6731	0070	3498	6675	9972
5965	7196	2738	5000	0535	9403	2928	1854	5242	0608
3152	4958	7661	3978	1353	4808	5948	6068	8467	5301
0634	7693	9037	5139	5588	7101	0920	7915	2444	3024
2870	5170	9445	4839	7378	0643	8664	6923	5766	8018
6810	8926	9473	9576	7502	4846	6554	9658	1891	1639
9993	9070	9362	6633	3339	9526	9534	5176	9161	3323
9154	7319	3444	6351	8383	9941	5882	4045	6926	4856
4210	0278	7392	5629	7267	1224	2527	3667	2131	7576
1713	2758	2529	2838	5135	6166	3789	0536	4414	4267
2829	1428	5452	2161	9532	3817	6057	0808	9499	7846
0933	5671	5133	0628	7534	0881	8271	5739	2525	3033
3129	0420	9371	5128	0575	7939	8739	5177	3307	9706
3614	1556	2759	4208	9928	5964	1522	9607	0996	0537
2955	1843	1363	0552	0279	8101	4902	7903	5091	0939
2350	2264	6308	0819	8942	6780	5513	5470	3294	6452
5788	8584	6796	0783	1131	0154	4853	1714	0855	6745
5533	7126	8847	0433	6391	3639	1119	9247	7054	2977
1008	1007	5598	6468	6823	2046	8938	9380	0079	9594
3410	8127	6609	8887	3781	7214	6714	5078	2138	1670
5336	4494	6043	2283	1413	9659	2329	5620	9267	1592
8297	6615	8473	1943	5579	6922	2866	1367	9931	7687
5482	8467	2289	0809	1432	8703	4289	2112	3071	4848
2546	5909	2743	8942	8075	8992	1909	6773	8036	0879
6760	6021	4147	8495	4013	0254	0957	4568	5016	1560
4492	7092	6129	5113	4759	8673	3556	7664	1821	6344
3317	3097	9813	9582	4978	1330	3608	8076	3398	6862
8468	8544	0620	1765	5133	0287	3501	6757	6157	2074
7188	5645	3656	0939	9695	3550	1755	3521	6910	0167
0047	0222	7472	1472	4021	2135	0859	4562	8398	6374
2599	3888	6836	5956	4127	6974	4070	3799	0343	1887
9288	5317	9919	9380	5698	5308	1530	5052	5590	4302
2513	2681	0709	1567	6068	0441	2450	3789	6718	6282
8463	7188	1299	8302	8248	9033	9195	7457	0353	9012
3400	9232	1279	6145	4812	7427	2836	6656	7522	3590
5377	4574	0573	8616	4276	7017	9731	7389	8860	1999
5931	9788	7280	5496	6085	1193	3526	7160	5557	6771
2047	6655	5070	2699	0985	5259	1406	3021	1989	1929
8618	8493	2545	2604	0222	5201	2182	5059	5167	6541
2145	6800	7271	4026	6128	1317	6381	4897	5173	5411
9806	6837	8008	2413	7235	9542	1180	2974	8164	8661
0178	6442	1443	9457	7515	9457	6139	9619	0322	3225
6246	0484	4327	6870	0127	0543	2295	1894	9905	4169
9432	3108	8415	9293	9998	8950	9158	0280	6947	6827
0579	4398	2157	0990	7022	1979	5157	3643	3349	7988
1039	1428	5218	0972	2578	3856	5479	0489	5901	8925
3517	5698	2554	5973	6471	5263	3110	6238	4948	1140
2563	8961	7588	9825	0212	7209	5718	5588	0932	7346
1646	4828	9425	4577	4515	6886	1138	1178	2269	4198

TABLE B.3   Normal Curve Probabilities

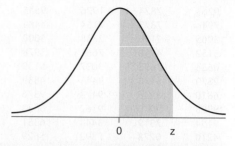

z	.00	.01	.02	.03	.04	.05	.06	.07	.08	.09
0.0	.0000	.0040	.0080	.0120	.0160	.0199	.0239	.0279	.0319	.0359
0.1	.0398	.0438	.0478	.0517	.0557	.0596	.0636	.0675	.0714	.0753
0.2	.0793	.0832	.0871	.0910	.0948	.0987	.1026	.1064	.1103	.1141
0.3	.1179	.1217	.1255	.1293	.1331	.1368	.1406	.1443	.1480	.1517
0.4	.1554	.1591	.1628	.1664	.1700	.1736	.1772	.1808	.1844	.1879
0.5	.1915	.1950	.1985	.2019	.2054	.2088	.2123	.2157	.2190	.2224
0.6	.2257	.2291	.2324	.2357	.2389	.2422	.2454	.2486	.2517	.2549
0.7	.2580	.2611	.2642	.2673	.2704	.2734	.2764	.2794	.2823	.2852
0.8	.2881	.2910	.2939	.2967	.2995	.3023	.3051	.3078	.3106	.3133
0.9	.3159	.3186	.3212	.3238	.3264	.3289	.3315	.3340	.3365	.3389
1.0	.3413	.3438	.3461	.3485	.3508	.3531	.3554	.3577	.3599	.3621
1.1	.3643	.3665	.3686	.3708	.3729	.3749	.3770	.3790	.3810	.3830
1.2	.3849	.3869	.3888	.3907	.3925	.3944	.3962	.3980	.3997	.4015
1.3	.4032	.4049	.4066	.4082	.4099	.4115	.4131	.4147	.4162	.4177
1.4	.4192	.4207	.4222	.4236	.4251	.4265	.4279	.4292	.4306	.4319
1.5	.4332	.4345	.4357	.4370	.4382	.4394	.4406	.4418	.4429	.4441
1.6	.4452	.4463	.4474	.4484	.4495	.4505	.4515	.4525	.4535	.4545
1.7	.4554	.4564	.4573	.4582	.4591	.4599	.4608	.4616	.4625	.4633
1.8	.4641	.4649	.4656	.4664	.4671	.4678	.4686	.4693	.4699	.4706
1.9	.4713	.4719	.4726	.4732	.4738	.4744	.4750	.4756	.4761	.4767
2.0	.4772	.4778	.4783	.4788	.4793	.4798	.4803	.4808	.4812	.4817
2.1	.4821	.4826	.4830	.4834	.4838	.4842	.4846	.4850	.4854	.4857
2.2	.4861	.4864	.4868	.4871	.4875	.4878	.4881	.4884	.4887	.4890
2.3	.4893	.4896	.4898	.4901	.4904	.4906	.4909	.4911	.4913	.4916
2.4	.4918	.4920	.4922	.4925	.4927	.4929	.4931	.4932	.4934	.4936
2.5	.4938	.4940	.4941	.4943	.4945	.4946	.4948	.4949	.4951	.4952
2.6	.4953	.4955	.4956	.4957	.4959	.4960	.4961	.4962	.4963	.4964
2.7	.4965	.4966	.4967	.4968	.4969	.4970	.4971	.4972	.4973	.4974
2.8	.4974	.4975	.4976	.4977	.4977	.4978	.4979	.4979	.4980	.4981
2.9	.4981	.4982	.4982	.4983	.4984	.4984	.4985	.4985	.4986	.4986
3.0	.4987	.4987	.4987	.4988	.4988	.4989	.4989	.4989	.4990	.4990

Index

LEARNING RESOURCES CENTRE